Behavior Therapy

TECHNIQUES AND EMPIRICAL FINDINGS

Behavior Therapy

TECHNIQUES AND EMPIRICAL FINDINGS

David C. Rimm
*Southern Illinois University
at Carbondale*

John C. Masters
University of Minnesota

ACADEMIC PRESS   New York and London
A Subsidiary of Harcourt Brace Jovanovich, Publishers

ACADEMIC PRESS, INC.
111 Fifth Avenue, New York, New York 10003

United Kingdom Edition published by
ACADEMIC PRESS, INC. (LONDON) LTD.
24/28 Oval Road, London NW1

Library of Congress Cataloging in Publication Data

Rimm, David C
    Behavior therapy: techniques and empirical findings.

    Bibliography: p.
    1.   Behavior therapy.   I.   Masters, John C., joint
author.   II.   Title.   [DNLM: 1.   Behavior therapy.
WM420 R577b 1974]
RC489.B4R55   616.8'914   73-22037
ISBN 0–12–588850–3

Contents

v

III. Assertive Training

IV. Modeling Procedures

V. Contingency Management Procedures

VI. Contingency Management in Institutional Settings

VII. Operant Methods in Self-Control

VIII. Extinction Procedures

IX. Aversive Control

X. Cognitive Methods

Preface

As noted by the title, two major thrusts are represented within the present text: the provision of detailed accounts of the variety of behavior therapy techniques and the description of those empirical findings which demonstrate the effectiveness of those techniques, thus validating their application in appropriate settings. There are, then, two fundamental questions to which this text is addressed: *How* does one design and execute a program of behavior therapy (how does one *do* behavior therapy) and why should a technique of *behavior therapy* be selected (what is the evidence demonstrating that behavior therapy is truly effective)?

From the outset, we must make one point clear: Behavior therapy is not merely a set of divergent techniques; it is a *discipline,* a unique orientation to the therapeutic treatment of behavior problems. If we were to attempt to describe the hallmark of this orientation in a single word, it would be *accountability:* There is a clear insistence that techniques designated as behavior therapy be derived from empirical research and, further, that they *remain* accountable as their therapeutic effectiveness is subjected to continued research. Inherent in this sort of accountability is the attitude that behavior therapy is an evolving dis-

cipline which is continually generating new techniques of ever
increased effectiveness and modifying current techniques in ways
which improve their effectiveness. There is an even more direct accountability to the client since he may raise questions regarding the
likely effectiveness of a technique which may be answered directly, with
references to empirical findings. This sort of accountability is sadly
lacking in most traditional psychotherapies. In our judgment it is much
more productive to answer such queries directly than interpret-
ing them away or passively reflecting upon them, which many traditional therapists may be inclined to do (or, indeed, which their mode of
therapy may require that they do). Thus a thorough and continuing
knowledge of empirical research is mandatory for the effective behavior therapist. In view of the burgeoning behavior therapy literature, it
becomes increasingly difficult for the responsible behavior therapist to
maintain contact with this literature. Review articles and contemporary
behavior therapy texts such as the present one provide a practical solution to this problem.

Our conceptualization of behavior therapy is quite broad. In addition
to the techniques more popularly identified with this label (desensitization, assertive training), we include operant procedures as well (although it is not uncommon to employ the term behavior *modification*
when referring to these techniques). Also included are certain cognitive
approaches, in particular the Rational-Emotive Therapy of Albert Ellis
and what we have termed the psychology of "reattribution." We believe
that the term *behavior therapy* need not imply the exclusion of these cognitive methods which share certain fundamental assumptions with the
"standard" behavior therapy techniques, assumptions that set them
apart from the traditional psychotherapies. These assumptions are discussed in detail in Chapter I.

In most chapters (that is, for those topics which lent themselves to
such a format), we have described the behavior therapy techniques
before discussing empirical findings. While this is intended in no way to
minimize the importance we attach to empirical research, it constitutes
a recognition that many readers will find research findings much more
meaningful and integral to the technique being discussed if they are
first provided with a concrete understanding of that technique.

The authors wish to express gratitude to Peter Nathan, Geoffrey
Thorpe, and Raymond Romanizyk, all of Rutgers University, for their
thorough reviews of the manuscript; they of course bear no responsibility for any of the book's shortcomings. We are grateful to Dr. Albert
Ellis, Professors Gordon Rader, Thomas Schill, Mary Jayne Capps, Ms.
Patricia Brown, and Mr. Jack Hunziker, for thoughtful comments on
selected chapters. Individually, we must express more personal grati-

tude to other individuals who have been instrumental in the completion of this text. David Rimm is especially indebted to his good friend and former colleague, Professor Gustav Levine, for his many helpful suggestions and continued encouragement. John Masters received constant support, both emotional and professional, from his colleague, friend, and wife, Dr. Mary Jayne Capps (-Masters). Finally, we wish to express appreciation for the skills (both cryptological and typographical) and patience of our manuscript secretaries, Mrs. Edith Marshall and Ms. Yvonne Wahler.

It is always a pleasure to coauthor a work with a friend and colleague. Thus the authors are pleased to acknowledge that the present volume was a totally collaborative venture in which each author participated equally. The order in which the authors are listed is arbitrary and does not in any way reflect differential contributions.

Figure Credits

Figure 4.1. From: Lovaas, O. I., Berberich, J. P., Perloff, B. F., and Schaeffer, B. Acquisition of Imitative Speech by Schizophrenic Children. *Science,* 11 February 1966, **151,** 706. Fig. 1. Copyright 1966 by the American Association for the Advancement of Science.

Figure 4.2. From: Lovaas, O. Ivar. "A Behavior Therapy Approach to the Treatment of Childhood Schizophrenia" from Minnesota Symposia on Child Psychology, Volume I, ed., John P. Hill. University of Minnesota Press, Minneapolis © 1967, University of Minnesota.

Figure 4.3. From: O'Connor, R. D. Modification of social withdrawal through symbolic modeling. *Journal of Applied Behavior Analysis,* 1969, **2,** 19. Fig. 1. Copyright 1969 by the Society for the Experimental Analysis of Behavior, Inc.

Figure 4.4. From: Chittenden, Gertrude E. An experimental study in measuring and modifying assertive behavior in children. *Monographs of the Society for Research in Child Development,* 1942, **7** (Whole No. 31). Copyright 1942 by the Society for Research in Child Development. Reprinted by permission.

Figure 4.5. From: Bandura, A., Grusec, J. E., and Menlove, F. L. Vicarious extinction of avoidance behavior. *Journal of Personality and Social Psychology,* 1967, **5,** 21. Fig. 1. Copyright 1967 by the American Psychological Association. Reprinted by permission.

Figures 4.6 and 4.7. From: Bandura, A. and Menlove, F. L. Factors determining vicarious extinction of avoidance behavior through symbolic modeling.

Journal of Personality and Social Psychology, 1968, **8,** 102, 103. Figs. 1 and 4. Copyright 1968 by the American Psychological Association. Reprinted by permission.

Figure 4.10. From: Ritter, B. The use of contact desensitization, demonstration-plus-participation, and demonstration alone in the treatment of acrophobia. *Behaviour Research and Therapy,* 1969, **7** (1), 160. Table 1.

Figure 5.3. From: Allen, K. E., Hart, B. M., Buell, J. S., Harris, F. R., and Wolf, M. M. Effects of social reinforcement on isolate behavior of a nursery school child. *Child Development,* 1964, **35,** 511–518. Copyright 1964 by the Society for Research in Child Development. Reprinted by permission.

Figure 5.5. From: Wahler, R. G. Setting generality: Some specific and general effects of child behavior therapy. *Journal of Applied Behavior Analysis,* 1969, **2,** 243. Copyright 1969 by the Society for Experimental Analysis of Behavior, Inc.

Figures 5.6 and 5.7. From: Ayllon, T. and Michael, J. The psychiatric nurse as a behavioral engineer. *Journal of the Experimental Analysis of Behavior,* 1959, **2,** 323–334. Figs. 1 and 4. Copyright 1959 by the Society for the Experimental Analysis of Behavior, Inc. Additional information and related research can be found in *The Token Economy: A Motivational System for Therapy and Rehabilitation* by T. Ayllon and N. H. Azrin published by Appleton-Century-Crofts, 1968.

Figure 5.8. From: Wahler, R. G., Winkel, G. H., Peterson, R. F., and Morrison, D. C. Mothers as behavior therapists for their own children. *Behaviour Research and Therapy,* 1965, **3,** 121. Fig. 5.

Figure 6.1. From: Ayllon, T. and Azrin, N. H. Reinforcer sampling: A technique for increasing the behavior of mental patients. *Journal of Applied Behavior Analysis,* 1968, **1,** 15–18. Figs. 2, 4, and 6. Copyright 1968 by the Society for the Experimental Analysis of Behavior, Inc. Additional information and related research can be found in *The Token Economy: A Motivational System for Therapy and Rehabilitation* by T. Ayllon and N. H. Azrin published by Appleton-Century-Crofts, 1968.

Figure 6.2. From: Ayllon, T. and Azrin, N. H. The measurement and reinforcement of behavior of psychotics. *Journal of the Experimental Analysis of Behavior,* 1965, **8,** 357–383. Figs. 4–7. Copyright 1965 by the Society for the Experimental Analysis of Behavior, Inc. Additional information and related research can be found in *The Token Economy: A Motivational System for Therapy and Rehabilitation* by T. Ayllon and N. H. Azrin published by Appleton-Century-Crofts, 1968.

Figures 6.3 and 6.4. Reprinted from George Fairweather *et al. Community Life for the Mentally Ill* (Chicago: Aldine Publishing Company, 1969); copyright © 1969 by Aldine Publishing Company. Reprinted by permission of the authors and Aldine Publishing Company. Figs. 12.1 and 12.2.

Figures 6.5, 6.6, and 6.7. From: Fairweather, G. W. *Social psychology in treating mental illness: An experimental approach.* New York: John Wiley & Sons, 1964.

Figure 6.8. From: Phillips, E. Achievement place: Token reinforcement procedures in a home-style rehabilitation setting for "predelinquent" boys. *Journal of Applied Behavior Analysis,* 1968, **1,** 217. Fig. 1. Copyright 1968 by the Society for the Experimental Analysis of Behavior, Inc.

Figure 6.9. From: Phillips, E. L., Phillips, E. A., Fixen, D. L., and Wolf, M. M.

Achievement place: Modification of the behaviors of pre-delinquent boys within a token economy. *Journal of Applied Behavior Analysis,* 1971, **4,** 45–59. Fig. 5. Copyright 1971 by the Society for the Experimental Analysis of Behavior, Inc.

Figures 6.10 and 6.11. From: Bailey, J. S., Wolf, M. M., and Phillips, E. L. Home-based reinforcement and the modification of pre-delinquents' classroom behavior. *Journal of Applied Behavior Analysis,* 1970, **3,** 227, 231. Figs. 1 and 6. Copyright 1970 by the Society for the Experimental Analysis of Behavior, Inc.

Figure 6.12. From: Bostow, D. E. and Bailey, J. S. Modification of severe disruptive and aggressive behavior using brief timeout and reinforcement procedures. *Journal of Applied Behavior Analysis,* 1969, **2,** 34, 36. Figs. 1 and 2. Copyright 1969 by the Society for Experimental Analysis of Behavior, Inc.

Figure 6.13. From: Staats, A. W. and Butterfield, W. H. Treatment of nonreading in a culturally deprived juvenile delinquent: An application of reinforcement principles. *Child Development,* 1965, **36,** 925–942. Fig. 4. Copyright 1965 by the Society for the Research in Child Development. Reprinted by permission.

Figure 6.14. From: Lovitt, T. C., Guppy, T. E., and Blattner, J. R. The use of a free-time contingency with fourth graders to increase spelling accuracy. *Behaviour Research and Therapy,* 1969, **7,** 153. Fig. 1.

Figure 6.15. From: Chadwick, B. A. and Day, R. C. Systematic reinforcement: Academic performance of underachieving students. *Journal of Applied Behavior Analysis,* 1971, **4,** 311–319. Fig. 1. Copyright 1971 by the Society for the Experimental Analysis of Behavior, Inc.

Figure 6.16. From: Packard, R. G. The control of "classroom attention": A group contingency for complex behavior. *Journal of Applied Behavior Analysis,* 1970, **3,** 20. Fig. 1. Copyright 1970 by the Society for the Experimental Analysis of Behavior, Inc.

Figure 6.17. From: O'Leary, K. D., Becker, W. C., Evans, M. B., and Saudargas, R. A. A token reinforcement program in a public school: A replication and systematic analysis. *Journal of Applied Behavior Analysis,* 1969, **2,** 9. Fig. 1. Copyright 1969 by the Society for the Experimental Analysis of Behavior, Inc.

Figure 8.1. From: Williams, C. The elimination of tantrum behavior by extinction procedures. *Journal of Abnormal and Social Psychology,* 1959, 59, 269. Fig. 1. Copyright 1959 by the American Psychological Association. Reprinted by permission.

Figure 8.2. From: Ayllon, T. and Haughton, E. Modification of symptomatic verbal behavior of mental patients. *Behaviour Research and Therapy,* 1964, **2,** 94. Fig. 3. Reproduced with the permission of Microform International Marketing Corporation exclusive copyright licensee of Pergamon Press Journal back files. Additional information and related research can be found in *The Token Economy: A Motivational System for Therapy and Rehabilitation* by T. Ayllon and N. H. Azrin published by Appleton-Century-Crofts, 1968.

Figure 8.3. From: Madsen, C. H. Jr., Becker, W. C., Thomas, D. R., Koser, L., and Plager, E. An analysis of the reinforcing function of "sit down" commands. In R. K. Parker (Ed.), *Readings in Educational Psychology.* Boston: Allyn and Bacon, 1968.

Figure 8.4. From: Ayllon, T. and Haughton, E. Modification of symptomatic verbal behavior of mental patients. *Behaviour Research and Therapy,* 1964, **2,** 87–97. Fig. 1. Additional information and related research can be found in *The Token Economy: A Motivational System for Therapy and Rehabilitation* by T. Ayllon and N. H. Azrin published by Appleton-Century-Crofts, 1968.

Figure 8.5. From: Poppen, R. L. Counterconditioning of conditioned suppression in rats. *Psychological Reports,* 1970, **27,** 659–671. Reproduced by permission.

Figure 8.6. From: Yates, A. J. The application of learning theory to the treatment of tics. *Journal of Abnormal and Social Psychology,* 1958, **56,** 179. Fig. 1. Copyright 1958 by the American Psychological Association. Reprinted by permission.

Figure 8.7. From: Ayllon, T. Intensive treatment of psychotic behavior by stimulus satiation and food reinforcement. *Behaviour Research and Therapy,* 1963, **1,** 57. Fig. 2. Additional information and related research can be found in *The Token Economy: A Motivational System for Therapy and Rehabilitation* by T. Ayllon and N. H. Azrin published by Appleton-Century-Crofts, 1968.

Figure 9.1. From: Feldman, M. P. and MacCulloch, M. J. *Homosexual behavior: Therapy and assessments.* Oxford: Pergamon Press, 1971. Reproduced with the permission of Microform International Marketing Corporation exclusive copyright licensee of Pergamon Press Journal back files.

Figure 9.2. From: Barlow, D. H., Leitenberg, H., and Agras, W. S. Experimental control of sexual deviation through the manipulation of the noxious scene in covert sensitization. *Journal of Abnormal Psychology,* 1969, **75** (5), 599. Fig. 1. Copyright 1969 by the American Psychological Association. Reprinted by permission.

Figure 9.3. From: Birk, L., Huddleston, W., Miller, E., and Cohler, B. Avoidance conditioning for homosexuality. *Archives of General Psychiatry,* 1971, **25,** 319. Figs. 1 and 2. Copyright 1971, American Medical Association.

Figures 9.4 and 9.5. From: Marks, I. M. and Gelder, M. G. Transvestism and fetishism: Clinical and psychological changes during faradic aversion. *British Journal of Psychiatry,* 1967, **113,** 714.

Figure 9.6. From: Voegtlin, W. L. and Broz, W. R. The conditional reflex of chronic alcoholism. X. An analysis of 3125 admissions over a period of ten and a half years. *Annals of Internal Medicine,* 1949, **30,** 582.

Behavior Therapy

TECHNIQUES AND EMPIRICAL FINDINGS

I

The Nature of Behavior Therapy

In this chapter we deal with the definition of behavior therapy, its origins, its basic assumptions, and its relationship to empirical and theoretical aspects of the scientific method. The chapter closes with a brief discussion of interviewing in behavior therapy.

What Is Behavior Therapy?

We include under the label *behavior therapy* any of a large number of specific techniques that employ psychological (especially learning) principles to deal with maladaptive human behavior. The term, "behavior," is interpreted broadly, encompassing covert responding (for example, emotions and implicit verbalizations), when such can be clearly specified, in addition to overt responding. Among the techniques included under

1

this label are systematic desensitization, assertive training, modeling, operant conditioning, extinction, and aversive conditioning, as well as certain techniques aimed at modifying patterns of thought.

Since the term, behavior therapy, was introduced in the late 1950s,[1] the field has undergone many significant developments—some of them quite recent. Not surprisingly, all behavior therapists are not yet in perfect agreement with respect to certain issues. One issue of contention is the very fundamental question of which techniques or approaches belong to behavior therapy and which do not. This is well illustrated by the conflicting points of view of Lazarus, who espouses a kind of eclecticism, and Wolpe, who favors what have become the more established behavior therapy techniques (see Franks, 1969, Chapter 1).

Disagreements of this nature are characteristic of any field that is still in a state of emergence and they are healthy because they motivate the kind of rethinking that often leads to more rigorous conceptualization. On the other hand, the reader should not be misled into concluding that behavior therapists typically define the boundaries of the discipline in some idiosyncratic manner. In fact there is far more agreement than disagreement in the field. This is witnessed by the great overlap in material covered in such prominent texts as Ullmann and Krasner (1969), Bandura (1969), Franks (1969), Kanfer and Phillips (1970), and Yates (1970). Much of this agreement arises from the several underlying assumptions (presented in a later section) common to the various behavior therapy techniques.

The reader has probably heard the term *behavior modification* and may wonder what its relationship is to behavior therapy. As Franzini and Tilker (1972) have pointed out, there is a certain lack of consistency in the use of these two labels. For example, Kanfer and Phillips (1969) and Bandura (1969) apparently equate the two terms, whereas Lazarus (1971) suggests that *behavior therapy* is usually associated with the treatment of anxiety using counterconditioning methods (for instance, systematic desensitization and assertive training), while *behavior modification* stresses operant procedures. In terms of popular usage, we are inclined to agree with Lazarus. Simply as a matter of convenience, however, in this volume, *behavior therapy* refers to the entire spectrum of techniques, including operant, as well as nonoperant, methods.

---

[1] According to Lazarus (1971), the label, "behavior therapy," was first used by Skinner, Solomon, Lindsley, and Richards in 1953, but apparently these authors did not use the term again. Lazarus, along with Eysenck, who independently used the term in 1959, are largely responsible for current usage.

The Origins of Behavior Therapy

Were it possible to review everything civilized man has written concerning improving his psychological condition, it is certain that one could find approximations to every technique practiced by modern behavior therapists. Franks (1969) described a variety of early applications, including Pliny the Elder's use of aversive conditioning in the treatment of alcoholism (Franks, 1963); the use of operant conditioning on the royal cavalry by the son of a Chinese emperor in order to effect the assassination of his father (Kreuger, 1961); and the application of procedures similar to reciprocal inhibition (see Chapter II) reported in Paris in 1845 (case described in Stewart, 1961). Wolpe (1969) recounted an interesting case reported by Leuret (Stewart, 1961) of a patient suffering from debilitating obsessions. Treatment involved having the patient engage in competing responses (reciting songs) with food contingent on such behavior.

As Franks (1969) intimated, while the above examples are of some historical interest, they should not be viewed as the major antecedents of modern behavior therapy. Vastly more influential were the writings of Pavlov (1927, 1928), whose experiments on what is now called classical, or respondent, conditioning are well known to students of introductory psychology; the work of Thorndike on reward learning (1898, 1911, 1913), a major precursor to what is now called instrumental, or operant, conditioning; and the writings and experiments of Watson and his associates (Jones, 1924; Watson, 1916; Watson & Rayner, 1920), which pointed to the application of Pavlovian principles to psychological disorders in human beings [an interest Pavlov himself later developed; see Franks (1969)].

Within the confines of academic psychology in the United States, a strong interest in the theoretical and empirical aspects of behaviorism has persisted from the early writings of Thorndike and Pavlov to the present day. That is, behaviorism defined in various ways has been an important part of experimental psychology for a good part of the twentieth century. With respect to the systematic *application* of behaviorism to human problems, only in the past 2 decades has an interest developed that in any way approximates its academic status. While relatively sporadic reports of attempts to apply behavior therapy to problems of a clinical nature can be found in the earlier literature, [Yates (1970) listed 28 appearing 1920–1939], their overall impact appears to have been minimal. It is true that developments in applied science tend to lag behind developments in pure science, but a delay of about 40 years requires explanation (Franks, 1969) in any event.

The failure of mental health practitioners to incorporate principles of scientific behaviorism is at least partially explained by the fact that throughout the first half of the century, therapy was restricted almost exclusively to psychiatrists. If their training was not entirely psychoanalytic in nature, it was certainly not in the principles of an experimentally based psychology. The logical professional person to stress such principles in his practice would, of course, have been the clinical psychologist. However, clinical psychology as a recognized profession only began to come into its own following World War II.

It is interesting that early theoretical efforts (that is, post-World War II) aimed at integrating clinical psychology and behaviorism often involved nothing more than translating Freudian concepts into behavioristic language (for example, Dollard & Miller, 1950). The usefulness of such translations is largely predicated on the assumption that psychoanalysis is an effective means of treatment. In general, however, therapists steeped in psychoanalysis and related dynamic schools of therapy have failed to provide hard data to support this crucial assumption. In a very influential paper, Eysenck (1952) presented data suggesting that neurotic individuals receiving psychotherapy might not fare any better than those who did not receive such treatment, with approximately two-thirds of each group showing improvement. It should be pointed out that Eysenck's data did not come from a controlled experiment but, instead, was derived from a survey of psychiatric outcome studies and insurance company and hospital records.

While some other investigations have tended to lead to similar conclusions (for example, Appel, Amper, & Scheffer, 1953; Levitt, 1963, dealing with a population of children), the many problems associated with such investigations have led certain writers (for example, Kiesler, 1966; Paul, 1967) to question seriously the validity of the "two-thirds improvement rate" dictum. For one thing, there is an obvious danger in lumping together all psychotherapists and patients in attempting to come up with an overall improvement rate. Bergin (1966), for example, in reviewing psychotherapy outcome studies (involving several forms of therapy), found that while average improvement for nontreated patients approximated that for patients receiving therapy, the treated patients showed more variability. In other words, treated individuals did tend to show greater change, but it was as likely to be in the undesirable, as in the desirable, direction.[2] But if one cannot make the generalization that

[2] With respect to the studies reviewed by Bergin, Bandura (1969, p. 55) has made the observation that when more "stringent and socially meaningful" improvement measures were employed, the effects of treatment were relatively less positive.

every psychotherapist should anticipate that every one of his clients would fare about as well were he not treated, the above findings (for instance, Eysenck, 1952) certainly have motivated thoughtful individuals to question seriously the overall value of the psychotherapeutic enterprise and to begin to seek out alternatives.

One such alternative was behavior therapy. Two books that were of paramount importance in establishing the foundations of this new discipline are Skinner's (1953) *Science and Human Behavior* and Wolpe's (1958) *Psychotherapy by Reciprocal Inhibition*. Skinner provided a basis for believing that much of human behavior can be understood in terms of the principles of operant conditioning; Wolpe offered a conceptualization of human neurosis in terms of Pavlovian and Hullinan learning principles (with a sizable dose of neurophysiology), and far more important, he outlined specific therapy techniques (for instance, systematic desensitization and assertive training) aimed at dealing with neurotic behavior. Wolpe also provided impressive case-history-outcome data to support the value of his so-called reciprocal-inhibition techniques (see Chapter II of this volume). Another significant contribution was Eysenck's (1960) *Behavior Therapy and the Neurosis*. And, in 1963, Eysenck founded the first behavior therapy journal, *Behavior Research and Therapy*. In 1968, a second behavior therapy journal appeared, which was devoted to operant approaches, the *Journal of Applied Behavior Analysis* (founded by Wolf). Then in 1970, Franks founded a third journal, *Behavior Therapy*, and in 1970, a fourth such journal, *Behavior Therapy and Experimental Psychiatry*, was started by Wolpe. Predictably, within the past decade a large number of behavior therapy texts also appeared; among them are: Eysenck (1964), Ullmann and Krasner (1965, 1969), Krasner and Ullmann (1965), Wolpe and Lazarus (1966), Wolpe (1969), Bandura (1969), Franks (1969), Kanfer and Phillips (1970), Yates (1970), and Lazarus (1971). Recent years have witnessed numerous behavior therapy conferences, and professional organizations such as the Association for the Advancement of Behavior Therapy and the Behavior Research and Therapy Society have come into being. Considering that scarcely a decade ago the term, behavior therapy, was not even part of the psychological vocabulary, the growth of the field has been nothing short of phenomenal.

This discussion of the origins of behavior therapy is not intended to provide anything other than an overview of the field's development. The reader wishing a more thorough historical analysis is referred to Ullmann and Krasner (1969). Valuable insights are also to be found in the introductory chapters of Franks (1969) and Yates (1970).

The Assumptions of Behavior Therapy

1. Relative to Psychotherapy, Behavior Therapy Tends to Concentrate on Maladaptive Behavior Itself, Rather than on Some Presumed Underlying Cause. Behavior therapy approaches differ considerably with respect to the emphasis placed on underlying processes in maladaptive behavior (Yates, 1970). Operant conditioners have the strongest philosophical commitment to remaining at a purely behavioral level. We have known operant conditioners who are unfriendly to methods such as systematic desensitization that, theoretically at least, are dependent on the existence and manipulation of events below the level of overt behavior (visual imagery anxiety). Opposition to what some label as "mentalism" is not without historical justification. (This issue is dealt with later in the chapter.)

The Wolpian methods emphasize alleviating maladaptive anxiety. Whereas the Skinnerian (that is, operant conditioner) might deal with the snake phobic simply by providing reinforcement for successively greater approach behaviors to a snake (since the problem *is* snake avoidance, for the Skinnerian), the Wolpian would conceptualize the problem in terms of an underlying cause, anxiety, and attempt to alleviate this internal state. It should be pointed out that while anxiety is by no means as "public" as overt avoidance behavior, for Wolpe it is a state of arousal having definite physiological referents, a state of arousal that can be detected (for instance, by the galvanic skin response). In other words, anxiety is an internal mediating response that is a good deal less obscure than underlying entities (for example, oedipal conflict and organ inferiority) typically postulated by schools of dynamic psychology.

Ellis's Rational-Emotive Therapy (Chapter X) is included in the present text because in our judgment it shares many of the assumptions common to the more traditional behavioral therapies. However, relatively speaking, Rational-Emotive Therapy is a depth approach. Thus, our snake phobic avoids snakes because he is anxious, but the anxiety is generated by irrational thoughts (self-verbalizations) that, themselves, follow from a faulty system of beliefs. It should be pointed out that in sharp contrast to the traditional depth approaches, the kinds of cognitive activity so essential to Ellis's theoretical position can be specified in a relatively concrete and unambiguous manner.

For the purposes of comparison, consider how a psychoanalyst might conceptualize a snake phobia. He would agree that the snake phobic does experience anxiety when confronted with a snake; but, below this anxiety might be the unconscious perception of phallic-like properties of the snake. At a more basic level, there might be repressed thoughts of castration, and at an even more fundamental level, a sexual love of mother, also repressed. Note that whereas for Wolpe the underlying anxiety can be detected by independent means, and for Ellis, cognitions conceived of as self-verbalization can readily become overt verbalizations, subject to public scrutiny, many of the underlying events postulated by psychoanalysis are, according to the theory, quite inaccessible.

Psychoanalytic and related dynamic approaches were created and have been perpetuated largely by individuals trained in the field of medicine (as the reader may know, psychiatrists are physicians who specialize in psychiatry). It is not surprising then that "models" of human maladaptive behavior associated with such approaches have tended to borrow rather heavily from concepts associated with physical illness. Hence, these dynamic conceptualizations have come to be identified with such labels as the "medical model," or the "disease model." In the medical model of psychological disorder, maladaptive behavior is assumed to be *symptomatic* of an underlying pathological state, or state of disease. It is also assumed that to cure the patient suffering from "mental illness," it is necessary to eliminate the inner state of pathology. That is, treating symptoms alone would be of no benefit and, in the long run, might be harmful, since the inner disease might be expected to intensify.[3] It is interesting that the psychodynamic adaptation of this model of illness is considerably more stringent on the matter of symptomatic treatment than the parent physical medicine model (witness the highly successful symptomatic treatment of cystic fibrosis, or the somewhat less successful, but very widespread, symptomatic treatment of the so-called common cold).

A corollary of assumption 1 is that behavior therapy tends *not* to follow the medical model. Again, this is a matter of degree. Were behavior therapy limited to operant conditioning, one could fairly say, "behavior therapy rejects the medical model, and in particular, the concept of the symptom." However, when one speaks of anxiety-mediated avoidance or self-verbalizations that give rise to maladaptive behavior, in a sense one is treating overt behavior as symptomatic of something else. This "something else," however, is not thought of as a disease state, related to overt behavior in some mysterious or poorly specified fashion. Instead, it refers to internal events *triggered by external stimuli* that serve to mediate observable responding. Another important difference that we have pointed out is that behavior therapy "internal" events are a good deal more accessible to the client, as well as to the therapist, than those of psychodynamic theory.

[3] It should be pointed out that emphasizing underlying causes of mental illness did not originate with Freud. As Ullmann and Krasner (1969) have noted, so-called "moral treatment" of the eighteenth and nineteenth centuries, which in certain respects is similar to behavior therapy, was criticized because it did not remove the underlying cause of the illness.

From the point of view of the welfare of the patient, whether or not the cause of his suffering can be attributed to events that are readily accessible is critical. To illustrate, Rimm served as therapist for a patient who had been hospitalized for most of his adult life. The patient, a 40-year-old male (his psychiatric diagnosis was anxiety neurosis), was well above average in intelligence and had completed some college. During the course of his lengthy hospitalization, he had been repeatedly exposed to therapists expounding the traditional medical model. He firmly believed that his problems emanated from his "mental sickness," and could not be convinced that the behavior of others, how tense he felt in certain situations, or what he said to himself in certain situations were especially relevant to his discomfort. That is, until "the doctors" cured him of his "disease," there was nothing to be done. To all who knew him well, the man appeared to be in genuine misery much of the time. In other words, whatever gains he accrued from failing to work actively on his problems were far exceeded by his evident distress.

The attitudes of individuals assigned to help patients obviously are equally critical in treatment. A psychiatrist, or psychiatric nurse, whose training has provided no alternatives to the disease model, will not be very inclined to view self-defeating behavior on the part of the patient as a consequence of stimulus events (especially contingencies of reinforcement). To illustrate, Rimm recalls a hospitalized patient who one day put his hand up the dress of an attractive ward nurse who happened to get in range. At a subsequent staff meeting, the decision was made to make no efforts at communicating to the patient the inappropriateness of such behavior, or to arrange contingencies such that future behaviors of this sort would be less likely to occur. After all, since the patient was mentally ill, what could one expect? From the patient's point of view, he engaged in a behavior that (taken by itself) most males would find reinforcing and presumably was reinforced. Unfortunately for the patient, the culture at large tends to deal harshly with males who publicly fondle unwilling females.

The examples just presented will be all too familiar to anyone who has spent any time on a traditional psychiatric ward. The point that many authors have made [see Bandura (1969); Szasz (1961); Ullmann & Krasner (1965, 1969)] is that adherence to the disease model has had the effect of diverting attention away from the events that account for maladaptive behavior and, indeed, encouraging such behavior.

As we have already made clear, behavior therapy does not uniformly reject every aspect of the medical model. However, behavior therapy does categorically reject the premise that maladaptive behavior is primarily a function of some relatively autonomous, highly inaccessible state of mental disease.

Symptom Substitution. As many writers [see Eysenck (1959); Yates (1958); Ullmann & Krasner (1965, 1969)] have noted, psychodynamic approaches (especially psychoanalytic theory) predict that removing a symptom while ignoring the underlying cause will result in either the reoccurrence of that symptom or the appearance of a substitute symptom. It is sometimes suggested that the hypothesis of symptom substitution follows from the medical model (Ullmann & Krasner, 1965), but this requires some qualification. If, by symptom substitution, we mean the appearance of new symptoms as a result of removal of old ones, this doctrine is *not* consistent with the medical model of physical illness, which *does* allow for symptomatic treatment and does not ordinarily anticipate untoward consequences of this. Thus, the physician in viewing fever as a symptom of an invasion of bacteria, nevertheless, does not expect aspirin therapy or alcohol rubs to somehow cause the appearance of a new ailment. Even certain psychiatric adaptations of the medical model allow for treatment that can best be described as symptomatic. Most psychiatrists who prescribe tranquilizers or electro-shock therapy would not argue that they are attempting to alleviate psychopathology at its most basic level, nor would they prescribe such treatment expecting new and terrible symptoms to appear.

In other words, the hypothesis of symptom substitution (we could use the term, "doctrine," because this is what it has become) does not follow from the medical model per se, but rather, from one specific psychiatric derivative of the medical model, namely, psychoanalytic theory. With respect to the psychoanalytic view of maladaptive behavior, the analogy is often made to a kind of closed hydraulic system. If something within the system gives rise to a build-up of pressure, this may cause a surface rupture, with fluid rushing out. However, since fluids are not compressible, dealing with rupture (analogous to treating symptoms) only increases the likelihood that a rupture will occur elsewhere. Given the appropriateness of this analogy to human psychological functioning, symptom substitution is a very plausible notion.

Naturally, the critical question from our point of view pertains to whether or not symptom substitution is likely to occur. As Bandura (1969) cogently pointed out, it is not really possible to disprove this doctrine once and for all, because therapists who apparently believe in symptom substitution have specified neither the nature of the substitute symptom nor the circumstances under which it should occur. On the other hand, it is possible for the behavior therapist to state *his own* version of the hypothesis (Cahoon, 1968) and test it on the chance that symptomatic treatment may indeed prove to be harmful. Generally, efforts in this direction (and there have been many) have involved employing behavior therapy to eliminate or weaken an undesirable behavior, waiting some reasonable period of time, and then querying the individual as to whether or not he has experienced some new symptom. Reviews of empirical findings (including case histories and controlled experiments) indicate that the evidence is overwhelmingly against symptom substitution (see Bandura, 1969; Lazarus, 1971; Paul, 1969b,c; Wolpe, 1969; Wolpe & Lazarus, 1966).

As other writers (for example, Bandura, 1969; Ullmann & Krasner, 1969) have noted, there are circumstances in which one maladaptive response may substitute for another. Bandura (1969, p. 51) cites the example of antisocial behavior that has been suppressed by punishment. If the individual is lacking in a socially acceptable response which could serve the same end, he is likely to engage in some other antisocial response. Wolpe (1969) notes that symptom substitution may occur when a particular overt act is eliminated but the underlying autonomic (emotional) response remains. For example, if so-called compulsive hand-washing is suppressed, the individual might conceivably learn another maladaptive anxiety-reducing response. Thus, there is no axiom of behaviorism which precludes the substitution of one maladaptive behavior for another. But from a practical point of view, it is a phenomenon only rarely observed.

2. *Behavior Therapy Assumes That Maladaptive Behaviors Are, to a Considerable Degree, Acquired Through Learning, the Same Way That Any Behavior Is Learned.* No currently popular theory of human behavior or personality would take issue with the view that human beings are, to a large extent, products of their environment. However, behavior therapy specifies rather precisely *how* the environment may influence people, in terms of established learning principles (for example, classical and operant conditioning, modeling).

It must be stressed that while maladaptive behavior differs from adaptive behavior in terms of its impact on the individual and those around him, "healthy" and "unhealthy" ways of responding are generally viewed as fundamentally alike in other respects. Both ways of responding directly reflect the individual's learning history and follow from the same general principles of learning (Ullmann & Krasner, 1969).

Clearly, no modern behaviorist would take the position that *all* maladaptive behavior is merely a consequence of an unfortunate learning history. One would be hard pressed to argue that the immediate behavioral deterioration following a traumatic central nervous system accident arises from the sudden acquisition of a large number of new habits (that is, learned responses). Similarly, few therapists would maintain that mental retardation (for example, associated with microcephaly, mongolism, cretinism, or hydrocephaly) arises exclusively, or even primarily, from unusual learning experiences.

3. Behavior Therapy Assumes That Psychological Principles, Especially Learning Principles, Can Be Extremely Effective in Modifying Maladaptive Behavior. It seems reasonable to assume some correspondence between the degree to which a particular response was learned (as opposed to having been genetically determined) and the ease with which it can be modified. On the other hand, as Davison (1968) has observed, the fact that a response can be modified through learning does not *prove* it was acquired through learning. For example, it is likely that certain components of human sexual arousal are innate. Yet everyday experience suggests that we can learn to be aroused (and later inhibit such arousal; see Chapter IX) in the presence of stimuli that initially were "neutral" (articles of clothing or pornographic literature).

The degree to which people in a position of social control are aware of the importance of relatively straightforward learning principles can be expected to have a major bearing on the welfare of their charges. Consider the case of a child who very early in life is diagnosed as severely mentally deficient (for instance, mongoloidism). This child has two serious strikes against him. First, assuming the diagnosis correct, there is something wrong with the way his brain functions, and it is unlikely that he will ever behave in a totally normal manner, no matter what kind of treatment he receives. Second, once he has been labeled severely mentally deficient, the child may automatically be assumed by a great many people (including some professionals) totally incapable of learning. As a result, rather than devoting the extra attention necessary to teach him things such as elementary speech, the child is treated in a custodial manner and fails to acquire many basic skills that he may be quite capable of acquiring. That certain rudimentary skills may be taught to such individuals has become abundantly clear in recent years (see Garcia, Baer, & Firestone, 1971; O'Brien, Azrin, & Bugle, 1972; O'Brien, Bugle, & Azrin, 1972).

Perhaps to a lesser extent, persons labeled as autistic, schizophrenic, or even epileptic are frequently victimized by "significant others" who severely underestimate the ability of these individuals to learn. When this happens, a major learning deficit may be expected, fulfilling the misguided prophecy.

4. Behavior Therapy Involves Setting Specific, Clearly Defined Treatment Goals. Behavior therapy does not conceptualize maladaptive responding as emanating from a "disturbed personality" (a term that would have little meaning for most behaviorists). Obviously, then, the goal of the therapist and client would not be to facilitate the reorganizing or re-structuring of the client's personality. Instead, the aim would be to help alleviate the specific problems that are interfering with the client's func-tioning, often by treating these problems in a relatively discrete manner. For this reason, certain writers (see Breger & McGaugh, 1965) have cri-ticized behavior therapy for ignoring states such as general unhappiness. The behavior therapist's preference is to determine the specific events that lead to broad statements such as "I'm unhappy all the time," or, "Life isn't worth living." The analogy may be made to physical medicine, wherein the patient who feels "generally poor" is asked to indicate spe-cific ailments that are often treated separately. The criticism that the physician is thereby ignoring his patient's "general health" would not seem to be justified.

The Importance of Stimulus Control.   The term *stimulus–response* (S–R) is often associated with behavioristic psychology. We prefer to avoid its usage, because for many it has a highly simplistic connotation that does not do modern behavior theory justice. On the other hand, a fundamen-tal precept is that behavior is under stimulus control and, when the be-havior therapist establishes his objectives, they are conceived of in terms of specific responses occurring lawfully in the presence of specific stim-uli. Thus, the therapist using systematic desensitization is not trying to free his client from "fearfulness," but rather from specific fears (for ex-ample, of high places or certain animals). And the operant conditioner would not attempt to increase the likelihood of all types of behavior in all circumstances, but, rather, specific responses to specific stimuli. Even Rational-Emotive Therapy (see Chapter X), which is not usually thought of as exemplifying S–R psychology, does postulate lawful stimulus–response relationships, with S and R bridged by the thoughts the patient has.

Behavior Therapy and Trait Psychology.   The position of most behavior therapists is that behavior is highly situation-specific. That is, by and large what people learn are specific ways of reacting to, or dealing with, specific situations. No one would argue that what we learn in one situa-tion does not carry over (that is, generalize or transfer) in some measure to other situations. However, the behaviorist would argue that this occurs far, far less than is suggested by traditional theorists (and by the layman, as well). The opposite point of view is that people acquire traits that give rise to similar responses in a wide variety of situations. For ex-ample, the individual who is labeled as aggressive is expected to be unusually aggressive in most situations; the liar is more likely to prevari-cate than a nonliar, no matter where he is; and the schizophrenic to emit more "crazy" behaviors than the "normal" person in any situation. Mischel (1968) has carefully examined the psychological research literature pertinent to traits. His general conclusion may be stated as follows: A person's behavior in one set of circumstances is generally a rather poor indicator of how he will respond in situations that are markedly different. In other words, different behavioral manifestations of the same "trait" do not intercorrelate very highly.[4] The behaviorists' position is that a far better predictor of future behavior in a given set of circumstances is past behavior in the same or similar circumstances.

5. *The Behavior Therapist Adapts His Method of Treatment to the Client's Problem.* Many forms of traditional psychotherapy provide essentially one method of treatment, regardless of the specific nature of the client's presenting complaint. While it is true that the psychodynamic therapist may occasionally opt to provide "support," rather than attempt to get at the deep-seated roots of the problem, this is usually seen as a stopgap procedure. If one assumes, as in the case of psychoanalytic and related approaches, that present difficulties usually stem from a lack of insight into critical childhood experiences, a single approach, aimed at achieving such insight, seems to be plausible. Similarly, if an individual's present problems are usually symptomatic of a need for "unconditional positive regard" (Rogers, 1961), client-centered therapists are quite justified in providing this as the principal mode of treatment.

In terms of the problems with which he is confronted, the behavior therapist is willing to assume a more varied etiology, although, obviously, learning is stressed. However, there is nothing in present learning formulations that suggests that maladaptive responses are acquired very early in life, or that they necessarily are mediated by the same pervasive mental state (for example, a low self-concept). As we shall see later in the chapter, behavior therapy does not require that the precise learning conditions giving rise to present difficulties be known. The point is that the behavior therapy conceptualization of how psychological disorders develop simply does not justify the use of what Bandura (1969, p. 89) has called an "all-purpose, single method" therapy. Instead, the therapist will employ different procedures, depending upon the nature of the problem. A person fearful of flying may be desensitized; a male who is timourous in the presence of attractive females may receive assertive training; the alcoholic may be offered aversive conditioning; the parent whose child frequently throws tantrums may be instructed in operant principles; the obese person may be taught principles of self-control; and so on.

[4] As Mischel (1968) has noted, traits associated with intellectual ability have somewhat more empirical support.

If a practitioner tends to view all psychological disorders as emanating from a common internal state or process, and especially if the state is said to be "unconscious," he will be most unlikely to interpret the client's "presenting" complaint as the client's *real* problem. The client, who is ruled by powerful, but unconscious, thoughts and impulses, is considered not competent to portray what is troubling him in anything but a superficial and distorted manner. In fact, the authors have known psychodynamically oriented therapists who universally assume that the client's true thoughts and feelings are, in fact, diametrically opposed to what he expresses during initial therapy sessions.

Behavior therapists, on the other hand, are considerably more likely to accept the client's presenting complaints as valid (if he did not suffer from these complaints, he would not have sought professional help). Naturally, one not need be an experienced professional practitioner to know that in any initial encounter, people are not always candid. The therapist, after all, is a stranger and, regardless of his formal credentials, time is required to establish an atmosphere of trust and confidence. Any experienced clinician will recall many cases involving clients who, after a few sessions, readily admitted to problems that were of far greater concern to them than problems initially presented. It is also very common to deal with clients' presenting initial complaints who report other unrelated problems during the course of therapy. Thus, the experienced behavior therapist does not assume that he has "a complete picture" of his client after 1 hour with him. At the same time, the client is generally viewed as an essentially competent source of pertinent information, whose basic problems may be specified without the necessity of hundreds of hours of some form of "uncovering" therapy.

The reader may wonder how a behavior therapist might deal with the more bizarre complaints of the hospitalized psychotic patient. In part, this would depend on the nature of the overall treatment program. In Chapter VI, ward programs based upon operant principles are described. Programs of this nature stress methodically ignoring bizarre, inappropriate behavior, on the expectation that it will extinguish, while, at the same time, reinforcing constructive, appropriate ways of behaving. The assumption is that if certain of the patient's complaints (for example, "I'm fearful because the Romans are going to crucify me.") are not very credible, this is at least partly a result of the attention he has received for such behavior. Individual treatment may readily be incorporated into operant programs. When this is done, the therapist's approach to the validity of presenting complaints would be qualitatively the same as that for outpatients in a consulting room office. Most individuals with a diagnosis of "psychosis" exhibit relatively normal behavior much of the time (especially if the ward program does not implicitly discourage this). The mere fact that a patient occasionally exhibits bizarre forms of behavior in no way implies that he possesses a "trait" of incompetence and that his complaints are in general not to be taken seriously.

6. *Behavior Therapy Concentrates on the Here and Now.* Individuals beginning therapy often have the expectation that they will be asked to delve into their early childhood experiences in minute detail. In fact, psychoanalytic and related approaches, which have predominated in the United States throughout most of this century, do strongly emphasize the importance of uncovering (that is, "working through") early events assumed to be critical.[5] The assumption is that the attainment of "insight" into these experiences (Fenichel, 1945) is of curative value. Associated with this assumption are two critical questions. First, how can we be sure that the content of such insights adequately describe actual childhood events? As has been frequently pointed out (see Bandura, 1969), insights presented to the therapist represent a particular class of verbal behaviors, subject to the same principles of learning that influence other behaviors. Verbal conditioning (Greenspoon, 1955, 1962), wherein an experimenter is able to increase certain types or classes of verbal response by selective reinforcement, has been repeatedly demonstrated in the laboratory; and given the presumably higher levels of motivation of most clients, influences of this nature might be expected to be even more potent in the therapeutic situation. A combination of selective reinforcement and verbal modeling could easily account for findings (see Heine, 1953) wherein clients tend to characterize their own behavior in terms of the orientation of their particular therapist. The situation is analogous to a student adopting the idiosyncratic language of a favorite professor or of an admired friend. Considerations of this nature have led Bandura to suggest that what has been labeled "insight" in the therapeutic interview might better be characterized as "social conversion."

But, even assuming the "validity" of insights obtained in psychotherapy, does it follow that they will necessarily lead to reduction in maladaptive responding? Consider the so-called "war neurotics" (Grinker & Spiegel, 1945), who in our experience are quite able to describe traumatic combat experiences that relate to their presenting complaints in a manner far too plausible to discount. Yet despite their apparent insights, their problems seem to remain. For example, Rimm treated a World War II veteran who had served as bombardier through

[5] Actually, among psychodynamic schools, thinking has tended to evolve in the direction of a greater emphasis on dealing more directly with present difficulties. This can be seen when one compares orthodox psychoanalysis (Freud, 1922, 1923) with the modified analytic approach of Alexander (Alexander, French, 1946), or the psychoanalytic ego psychology of Rappaport (Gill, 1967).

some 50 combat missions and who, some 20 years later, was still fearful of loud noises resembling the sounds of exploding flack or machine gun fire and of high places (prior to the war he had experienced neither fear). Whereas such insight appeared to be of little value, both fears were alleviated through systematic desensitization. We are not suggesting that every phobic person is able to recall precipitating traumatic events [Lazarus (1971) has presented data to the contrary [6]]. But persons who can, would, nevertheless, seem to remain phobic.

It should be obvious at this point that behavior therapy rejects the notion that the attaining of what might be labeled "historical insight" is curative. The necessity for detailed explorations of the client's childhood is also rejected, although a certain amount of biographical information is usually considered helpful. (This is dealt with when intake interviews are discussed later in this chapter.)

7. It Is Assumed That Any Techniques Subsumed under the Label Behavior Therapy Have Been Subjected to Empirical Test and Have Been Found to Be Relatively Effective.   As Kanfer and Phillips (1970) have noted, behavior therapy is very "self-conscious" when it comes to scientific validation of its techniques. As we see in the section to follow, empirical evidence may come in more than one form, with greater degrees of scientific control providing greater degrees of certainty. The behavior therapist does *not* assume that a technique is effective because it is derived from a widely held theory, or because an authority has labeled it effective in the absence of supporting evidence, or because common sense suggests its effectiveness. Naturally, our thinking is affected by factors of this nature that may serve as the source for hypotheses about human behavior. The essential point, however, is that these hypotheses must then be put to test.

It may seem quite obvious to the reader that any accepted mode of treatment ought to be based upon established scientific findings, rather than upon authority, convention, or suppositions bordering on folklore. It should be stressed, however, that this has not been the prevailing attitude throughout most of the history of psychotherapy. In the writings of

[6] Lazarus reports that of 100 patients whose presenting complaints included phobic reactions, only two could recall traumatic experiences that were clearly relevant. It is not clear from the report whether vicarious traumatic experiences were taken into account. The typical snake phobic has never experienced pain or injury in the presence of a snake, but has probably witnessed negative emotional responses on the part of others (especially in the movies, where snakes are almost always depicted as deadly). Similarly, the reader may know persons who, after witnessing the brutal bathtub murder sequence in Hitchcock's *Psycho,* were actually fearful of bathing. Recently, Rimm treated a male who was fearful of birds after seeing a rerun of Hitchcock's film, *The Birds,* on television. The reader is referred to Chapter IV for a discussion of vicarious conditioning.

orthodox analysis (for example, Fenichel, 1945) it is common practice to cite the edicts of Freud and other prominent analysts, much the way medieval scholastics cited Aristotelian proclamations as incontrovertible proof for their positions. Frequently, when cases are cited in the psychodynamic literature, no mention whatsoever is made of outcome, as if this were simply not an issue (see Astin, 1961).

Today clinical psychologists usually hold doctoral degrees awarded through academic departments of psychology. Most departments, ostensibly at least, adhere to the so-called "Boulder Model" of training (see Cook, 1966), wherein the clinical psychologist is assumed to possess critical scientific, as well as practical, skills. A fair portion of his training is devoted to statistics, learning theory, research design, etc., with his instructors repeatedly stressing the virtues of a "hard-nosed," rigorous approach in dealing with the subject matter of psychology. On the other hand, not infrequently in the same department (and often on internships), he finds himself exposed to other instructors or supervisors who may pay lip service to scientific rigor, but who clearly take a prescientific approach in dealing with clinical problems. Consider the student who questions his professor as to the value of clinical interpretations on the grounds that the interpretation is based upon a personality test that substantial research has shown to be of questionable validity. The professor's response might be that his own personal experience has provided him with a special "feel" for the test in question, or that one should approach such tests "intuitively." The student may receive the same sort of response when he poses questions concerning particular therapy tactics. What he is being told, implicitly, may be stated as follows: "While there may be a place for scientific psychology in the laboratory, when you get down to actual clinical cases, forget rigor. Instead, rely on the authority of experienced clinicians and, later, on personal experience, intuition, 'gut' reactions, etc."

Training of this nature is likely to produce a professional "dual personality," wherein the clinician pays due homage to the ethic of science, but, perhaps somewhat smugly, believes that in terms of clinical practice, doing one's "own thing" is the superior approach.

We are by no means advocating that the practitioner ignore his personal experience, or that of others. During any given therapy session, the clinician will be required to make many on-the-spot decisions pertaining to issues which have not been researched in a manner that would prove to be helpful. At such choice points, he can rely only on experience. On the other hand, the clinician who is confronted with a problem that has been well researched, but who pays such findings no heed, is clearly doing his client a disservice.

Behavior Therapy and the Scientific Method

The essence of science is prediction. That is, any scientific endeavor aims at establishing lawful relationships among observables, so that given one set of events, one can anticipate the occurrence of another set of events (Underwood, 1957; Paul, 1969a). In psychology, one such set of events might be the behavior leading to a high score on an IQ test. The second set might be behaviors leading to a high college grade-point average. If a relationship does exist between these two measures (and a positive relationship does exist), one is then able to predict, with some degree of accuracy, IQ from grade-point average, or vice versa. Naturally, the degree of predictability will be directly related to the strength of the relationship between the two measures. In this example, no effort is made to manipulate IQ or grade-point average. It is possible to determine the degree of relationship between them because they vary naturally. An investigation of this nature is empirical because it is based upon systematic observation. Such investigations are often referred to as *correlational studies.* The above is not an experiment, however, because, in an experiment, one set of events involves actual manipulations of some sort, with the effect of these manipulations constituting the second set of events. That is, the experimenter performs some activity and observes its measurable effects. If one were to provide subjects with a drug presumed to alter the level of intellectual functioning and then measure its effect on IQ (or grade-point average), one would be engaging in an experiment.

With respect to any mode of psychological therapy, the most fundamental question to be answered is: Does the treatment work (that is, is it beneficial, does it do what it is hypothesized to do)? To find this out, one must present the treatment and observe the consequences; in other words, conduct experiments. Therefore, throughout the remainder of this text, when the term, "empirical findings," is used, we are normally referring to experiments (whether they be at the primitive, case-history level, or are well-controlled investigations).

Levels of Experimentation and "Believability"

Assuming that we have adopted a scientific approach, what sort of evidence should we take to convince us that treatment X is an effective means for dealing with problem Y? To simplify the discussion, assume that alternative treatments are quite lacking in scientific support. The question then is, does treatment X "work"? Since no one would anticipate any one approach to human maladaptive behavior as always maximally effective, the question is best stated in a probabilistic manner. Given the nature of problem Y, what is the probability that treatment X will result in an appreciable improvement? Let us now consider sources of empirical information that should help answer this question.

Case Histories. Usually initial support for new treatment methods is to be found in published case histories. The client, viewed as patient rather than as an experimental subject, is treated by the practitioner, whose principal goal is to alleviate suffering. Following treatment, the degree of improvement is assessed (perhaps by comparing the client's pretreatment verbal report with that obtained following treatment). Sometimes follow-ups are performed perhaps after 1 month or 1 year) to determine whether reported improvement has been maintained.

The case history method may be viewed as a very crude experimental technique. While it is true that the therapist is actively *doing* something with his client and observing the results, controls are obviously lacking. First, assuming that objective evidence is provided that the client did indeed improve (maintained at some reasonable follow-up), we cannot specify with certainty the factors that led to the improvement. While it might have been specific aspects of the technique (in other words, any therapist would have obtained improvement with any such client), the therapist in a clinical setting is doing a great deal more than merely mechanically applying a technique. In some measure, he is probably providing his client with the expectation that he will get better, in which case improvement could be considered as a so-called placebo effect. He is probably also providing reassurance and support, which by themselves might be helpful to a given client. Even if the therapist were interacting with his client in what might be considered a mechanical manner, the therapist's personal characteristics (looks, manner of dress) might be expected to have some bearing on the outcome. Such factors might be expected to influence the credibility of the therapist, and credibility is known to have some bearing on how persons react to communications of a clinical nature (see Bergin, 1962).

Again, assuming that the client's improvement was real, the improvement might have been quite unrelated to therapy [witness the high rate of "spontaneous remission" reported by Eysenck (1952) and others]. When one considers that the client typically spends 1 hour per week in therapy, and 167 hours engaged in other activities, it can come as no surprise that the other activities may have a far greater impact than formal treatment.

Finally, truly objective assessments of improvement are rarely reported in the case history literature. Typically, the reader must rely on the therapist's impression of the client's self-report. Thus, we have two possible sources of bias and it is known that either can have a compromising effect on objectivity (Orne, 1962; Rosenthal, 1963).

Getting back to the hypothetical problem Y, suppose the only infor-

mation the therapist has is that treatment X was reportedly used successfully in a solitary case involving this problem. What then is the likelihood
that it will "work" in a present case? Obviously, there is no way to provide
a reasonable answer. If there seemed to be no danger in employing the
treatment, and especially if problem Y were of a particularly serious nature, results of the single case would probably be sufficient to motivate
most therapists to carry out the treatment, taking care to monitor its effects along the way.

Instead of just one case history, suppose there are, say, 20 such case
histories, all treated by the same clinician, and that 19 patients reportedly showed marked improvement. Naively, one might therefore conclude that the probability of success in the present case would be 19/20,
or .95. Considering the aforementioned difficulties inherent in the case
history method, one could not fairly make such a statement. On the
other hand, assuming that people who publish case histories have some
standards of objectivity and honesty, the finding may be taken as rather
suggestive.

Now, suppose that five therapists, each at a different clinic or hospital,
provided separate reports. Each report described roughly 20 clients who
suffered from problem Y and received treatment X. Suppose the improvement rate was approximately 95% for each of the five therapists.
While one therapist might be hopelessly prejudiced, or even fraudulent,
or have certain unique personal characteristics that actually account for
the improvement, the likelihood that all five reports would be so "con-
taminated" seems rather remote (Paul, 1969a). Indeed, these findings do
strongly suggest that when a therapist applies treatment X to problem Y,
it is very likely that improvement will occur.

Given this kind of information, any therapist would be far more comfortable employing the treatment than he would be, given the solitary
case history. On the other hand, it is still possible that treatment X, taken
by itself, is totally worthless, with improvement resulting entirely from
so-called nonspecific factors, or because the patients would have shown
the same rate of improvement without treatment. If nonspecific factors
were crucial, it might be argued that the treatment as a whole was still effective and should not be abandoned. A more economical alternative
would be to administer only the nonspecifics. With respect to spontaneous improvement, it could be argued that if in fact almost everyone
could be expected to recover in the absence of treatment, this would be
well known (that is, since such is not a matter of common knowledge, the
rate of spontaneous remission is probably far less than 95%). This
argument is not without some plausibility. If problem Y happened to be
a severe wrist fracture, and if treatment X resulted in complete healing
in 3 days, 95% of the time, few would argue that such results would have

been obtained without treatment. On the other side of the coin, few would be convinced of the curative powers of mentholated cigarettes on the basis of reliable findings that individuals who smoked them almost always recovered from colds within 3 weeks.

However, the above argument rests on the assumption that people are reasonably familiar with the natural course of the problem in question. In the case of psychological disorders, this is highly questionable. First, people seem a good deal more reticent to discuss their "psychological problems" than to discuss broken bones, bouts with the flu, etc. [considering societal attitudes toward individuals with a history of "mental illness," this is not surprising; see Farina and Ring (1965); Farina, Gliha, Boudreau, Allen, and Sherman (1971)]. In the main, it is the sharing of experiences that leads one to expect that relief from a cold should come within a week or two. If people generally do not share knowledge of their psychological difficulties, how is the layman to have any knowledge of rates of spontaneous remission for such disorders? Second, even if people *always* discussed such matters openly, the language the layman typically uses to characterize such disorders ("psycho"; "mental breakdowns") is vague in the extreme, and it is therefore unlikely that agreement could be reached as to rates of recovery. This same argument applies to many professionals, as well.

Let us return to our original question. To what extent can we "believe" in the efficacy of a treatment, given only case history data? From the above, it would seem that the more positive outcomes we have (especially when reported by practitioners working independently), the more reason there is to believe that the treatment is indeed effective. That is, case histories can provide legitimate evidence. However, because of the aforementioned limitations inherent in this approach, such evidence can never be taken as absolutely conclusive that the specifics of a particular treatment are beneficial.

Controlled Experiments.   Controls in an experiment refer to any of a sizable number of procedures employed to insure that the results can be interpreted in a relatively unambiguous, straightforward manner. Obviously, experimental control is not an "either–or" matter, but, instead, exists in degrees, dependent upon the rigor programmed into a particular investigation [this is well illustrated in Paul's careful analysis of research on systematic desensitization; see Paul (1969b, c); see also Paul (1969a)]. The greater the number of carefully instituted control procedures, the more conclusive the results.

Before proceeding further, it should be pointed out that psychological researchers typically employ one of two general strategies of control. The group strategy, the more common of the two, is illustrated in its

strategy

simplest form in the following experiment. We begin with a sizable number of individuals (subjects), let us say, 30. On a random basis, 15 are assigned to one group and 15 to the other. The first group receives some sort of treatment, and this group is designated the *experimental,* or *treatment,* group. The second group does not receive the treatment and is designated the *control* group. Usually, response measures are taken at the start and at the conclusion of the experiment, and the two groups are compared with respect to the average, or mean, degree of change. If the average degree of change did not differ at all between the two groups, the obvious conclusion is that the treatment had no effect. This is rare, however, since so-called "chance" factors (events over which the experimenter has no control) would probably account for some difference between the groups. So-called "inferential statistics" are used to help the experimenter decide whether the obtained group differences are large enough to be considered "real" (that is, very probably did not occur by chance and are, therefore, generalizable). In psychological research the following rule is generally followed: When the probability that an obtained mean difference between groups occurred by chance is less than .05, it is assumed that the difference, indeed, did not occur by chance. That is, the treatment had a "real" effect on the behaviors in question. When such is the case, the result is usually stated as follows: "Treatment X was found to have a significant effect on behavior Y." The reader unfamiliar with statistics may find this discussion confusing. The major point is that throughout this text whenever the term, "significant," is used within the context of an experimental finding, it means that the findings may be viewed as real or legitimate in the sense that they are very probably generalizable.[7] The reader should keep in mind that when we say a research finding is generalizable, it is generalizable only to a population of individuals who are similar to the subjects used in the experiment. This issue will be raised again when therapy analogue experiments are discussed later in this section.

The second general strategy involves working with a small number of subjects, with each subject serving as his own control. To illustrate, a particular behavior (behavior Y) is selected for investigation. For each subject, the frequency of occurrence of behavior Y is established during a base line (pretreatment) period. Then, treatment X is presented (perhaps the subject is reinforced for Y). Following this, treatment X is discontinued. Assuming that the treatment really did have an effect on

---

[7] The reader should be advised that when "significance" is used in this technical sense, it does not automatically imply that the particular experimental finding is of practical significance, although it may well be. Sometimes very weak treatment effects are significant in the statistical sense, but are of such small magnitude that the treatment in question may have little clinical value.

behavior Y, the frequency of this behavior should return to base line. Naturally, this is based upon the assumption that the treatment did not have an irreversible effect on behavior (for example, brain damage caused by ingestion of a toxic drug). The same procedure is followed for each subject, and to the extent that inspection of the data reveals marked similarities across subjects, one may generalize to the population from which the subjects came. This strategy, most often associated with operant conditioning studies, does not compare means or employ inferential statistics.

Whether a researcher opts for one or the other of the above strategies depends, in part, upon the nature of the problem investigated. For example, if one were interested in determining the effects of systematic desensitization on an airplane phobia, the subject-as-his-own-control strategy would hardly be adequate, since the subject would not be expected to revert to his pretreatment avoidance of flying following the administration of the treatment. On the other hand, working within an operant framework, when a behavior is related to reinforcing events in a simple, straightforward fashion, presenting and then withdrawing reinforcers would be expected to result in an increase in the reinforced response, followed by a return to base line. When appropriate, this strategy has the advantage of being economical (few subjects are required) and as Sidman (1960), one of the most vigorous opponents of the large-group statistical approach, has pointed out, it allows for examination of unusual individual patterns of responding that are lost when one focuses on group averages. On the other hand, Paul (1969a) has argued that in terms of establishing cause-and-effect relationships, the large-group strategy (in particular, the so-called "factoral" approach, which simultaneously examines the effects of many relevant factors) is the more powerful of the two. Paul would not maintain, however, that the subject-as-his-own-control strategy does not contribute to establishing the validity of a particular technique (especially, if different experimenters working in diverse settings report similar results). From the reader's point of view, both strategies may be considered useful in supporting the efficacy of therapy techniques. Since the large-group statistical methodology is the more popular of the two (most of the research reported in the present text employs this approach) the following discussion deals with certain issues related to this strategy.

The most elementary controlled group experiment, as we have suggested, involves only two groups of subjects: One group receives the treatment, the second does not. Suppose that the treatment group shows significantly greater improvement than the control group. What can we conclude? We can conclude that something in the interaction between the experimenter and his subjects accounted for a certain amount of improvement above and beyond what could be accounted for by the passage of time or by taking measures of the target behavior (since the control subjects experienced the same time lapse and underwent the same measuring operations). Is this tantamount to saying that treatment X really was effective in dealing with problem Y? It depends upon what is meant by "treatment." If treatment is defined as everything the therapist happened to do (it would probably be more correct to say the totality of interactions between the experimenter and subject), the answer would be "yes" (for the moment we shall ignore the issue of durability of improvement); but if by treatment we mean those aspects specific to the particular technique, excluding things not specific to the technique (for instance, placebo effects), no such affirmative conclusion can be reached, simply because nonspecifics have not been controlled. The reader who thinks nonspecifics are unimportant is referred to the psychological literature dealing with attempts to reduce cigarette smoking (see Keutzer, Lichtenstein, & Mees, 1968; and Bernstein, 1969). Some of this literature is discussed in Chapter VII, wherein placebo treatments are often found to be every bit as effective as the main treatment under investigation (in contrast to nontreated controls, who show significantly less improvement).

It is clear in light of our discussion that a second control group is needed, which exposes subjects to the same nonspecifics experienced by the treatment group, but does not include specific aspects of the treatment in question (Paul, 1969a). In medical research, for example, dealing with efficacy of a new drug, specifying such a treatment is not at all difficult. The "placebo" group receives a "pill" having all the apparent characteristics of the medication, and, naturally, receives the same instructions. In psychological research, especially involving therapy techniques, the task is far more difficult, because experimenter–subject interaction is a great deal more complex. In specifying the nonspecific control treatment, several features should be incorporated. There is evidence (see Oliveau, Agras, Leitenberg, Moore, & Wright, 1969) that improvement may be at least somewhat related to what the subject expects to get out of treatment.[8] Therefore, every effort should be made to provide the same degree of positive expectation found in the treatment group. This can be done with instructional sets, experimenter–subject interactions that can be interpreted by the subject as possibly therapeutic, or both. There is ample evidence (see Chapters V and VI) that attention can be a powerful reinforcer, in which case care should be taken to

---

[8] Certain proponents of the importance of expectancy in behavior therapy (Marcia, Rubin, & Efran, 1969; Wilkins, 1971) have gone rather overboard in the degree to which they have stressed the importance of this factor based upon existing research (see Rimm, 1970; Davison & Wilson, 1972).

insure that the nonspecific control subjects receive a degree of attention comparable to that given the treatment subjects. To control for experimenter characteristics, the same experimenter should be employed for both groups. Needless to say, these general comments are not intended to provide the reader with the skills necessary for carrying out therapy research. In specifying such an adequate control treatment, many factors specific to the particular investigation must be taken into account, and an appreciation for such factors probably requires extensive training and experience. On the other hand, it is hoped that the reader has been alerted to the crucial role of control groups of this nature (so often missing in published research) and is somewhat better able to evaluate the degree of experimental control when reading the psychological literature.

Placing subjects in control conditions raises an obvious ethical issue. After all, is not the experimenter denying treatment to individuals in need? It should be pointed out that most subjects in behavior therapy experiments are not individuals who deliberately seek out treatment in a clinic. Instead, they are generally persons functioning relatively well, but who have some specific difficulty and who volunteer for what they are told is an "experiment" that is to focus on that difficulty. Perhaps the most important point to be made is that the experimenter is not withholding a treatment that is *known* to be effective. Indeed, this is the whole point of the investigation. If it turns out that treatment subjects fare no better than controls, this is evidence the control subjects were not denied effective treatment. If treatment subjects do fare better, the experimenter is now in the excellent position of being able to offer the control subjects a treatment that now has scientific support. If there is a legitimate ethical issue, it is related to the fact that experimenters often do not provide control subjects with this option.

Thus far we have been assuming a single experimenter has conducted all treatments. As was true for the case history method, this severely limits generalizability. This problem may be dealt with by having several different experimenters conducting all treatments (Paul, 1969a), so that the experimenters are at least crudely representative of the population of individuals who would normally engage in such treatment.

In discussing the efficacy of a therapy technique, we are talking about changes in specific measures of human behavior. There are several different classes of responses that are examined in behavior therapy. Most behavior therapists would probably agree that the most important single measure involves an objective assessment of the target behavior itself. If the subject is fearful of snakes, the experimenter will carefully note the degree to which he will approach and interact with a harmless snake (see Lang & Lazovik, 1963; Davison, 1968). If he is fearful of public speaking, his apparent fearfulness will be rated by judges who observe him give a speech (see Paul, 1966). Self-report constitutes a second important class of measures. It is generally not assumed that merely because a person is now able to touch a snake, he no longer experiences distress. [There is evidence to the contrary; for example, Davison (1968).] Therefore, in addition to observing his behavior, the experimenter asks him to rate his subjective distress. A third class of response measures assesses the degree of physiological or emotional arousal. Frequently, theorists (among behavior therapists, most notably Wolpe, 1958, 1969) strongly identify anxiety with such arousal, and presumably if a person is no longer fearful in the presence of a given stimulus, this should be reflected in a reduction in emotionality, as determined by measures such as galvanic skin response, heart rate, respiration rate, etc. Another example of the use of physiological assessment is seen in the application of a device known as a plethesmograph in measuring penile erection in studies dealing with modification of sexual behavior (see Freund, 1963).

Additional measures sometimes used in such research include a variety of questionnaires (for example, The Taylor Manifest Anxiety Scale; see Taylor, 1953; The Fear Survey Schedule; see Wolpe & Lang, 1964) and scales measuring assertive behavior (for example, Wolpe & Lazarus, 1966; Lawrence, 1970), to mention but a few.

Experiments rarely employ all four types of the measures indicated. Naturally, when support can be obtained for the efficacy of a treatment from a variety of diverse measures, one cannot help but be more impressed than when one or two measures were employed. On the other hand, positive findings for an objective behavioral measure, along with similar results for self-report (in other words, the subject behaves in a more adaptive fashion and indicates that he feels more comfortable, effective, etc.), would argue rather strongly that treatment was indeed effective.

The positive effect of treatment, if the treatment is to have any practical value, must have some degree of durability. For this reason, it is important that therapy research include follow-up measures. Frequently, the follow-up measures are the same as those employed in the experiment proper, although sometimes novel, *in vivo* measures are used (see McFall & Marston, 1970). A major issue pertains to the amount of time that the experimenter should allow to elapse before taking his follow-up measures. Certainly, a period of but 2 or 3 days could not possibly allow for a convincing demonstration of the stability of treatment effects. On the other hand, certain writers (see Paul, 1969a) have pointed to problems inherent in attempting follow-ups on a truly long-term basis. For example, 1 year after treatment, a sizable number of subjects may not be available and, among those who are available, some may be unwilling to participate. Also, successful treatment would not ordinarily be expected to protect the subject from adverse learning experiences that might cause the reappearance of the same maladaptive behavior, and the longer the follow-up period, the more likely this is to occur. When such does occur, it is not reasonable to conclude, therefore, that the treatment was ineffective. These comments are especially applicable to certain investigations where treatment consists of removing the individual from an environment that regularly reinforces what society considers inappropriate behaviors, and placing him in an environment that reinforces appropriate behaviors. If, after successful treatment, he is returned to the original environment, the individual's failure to "relapse" could be taken as evidence that the assumptions of treatment were not valid (that is, if the maladaptive behavior really were under the control of these contingencies, it should return). But, assuming that there is nothing intrinsic to the subject's natural environment that will insure that the problem behavior will soon reappear, the question of a reasonable follow-up period remains.

One factor that should be taken into account is the frequency with which the individual is likely to be exposed to stimuli that, prior to treatment, typically gave rise to the maladaptive pattern of behavior. Consider the dog phobic who, following systematic desensitization, is able to interact with a dog and concludes that he is "cured." But, suppose that the improvement is a function of some nonspecific element of treatment (for example, the presence of the experimenter induced an atypical degree of confidence in the subject), and that during the course of a follow-up repeated exposures to real-life dogs convinced him that he was not cured. This would probably show up at the time of the follow-up assessment.[9] Here, it is likely that a follow-up of, let us say, 1 month, would be adequate to allow for such *in vivo* experiences. The majority of maladaptive behaviors dealt with in behavior therapy research might be expected to be under the control of external stimuli that occur with a relatively high frequency, suggesting that the follow-ups of 1 or 2 months, typically reported in the literature, are generally adequate. A large number of "analogue" experiments have employed snake-phobic subjects, and here it might be argued that the typical follow-up period is not sufficient to allow for real-life encounters with harmless snakes. In part, this would depend on where the subject lived (urban versus rural), but, even in the absence of exposure to actual snakes, the subject might be able to "test" out his response in situations where there exists some

[9] It might be argued that this is an issue of generalization of treatment, rather than stability of treatment. But a "pure" test of stability would necessitate placing the subject in something approximating a sensory-deprivation chamber during the entire follow-up period.

possibility that a snake may be lurking (under his house, in high grass), or, when presented with a snake depicted on television or in the movies.

Analogue Experiments. Controlled behavior therapy experiments are usually of the analogue variety. It is assumed that the experimenter's treatment of his subject is a somewhat simplified analogy of the practitioner's treatment of his patient. The subjects are volunteers taken from a nonclinical population (that is, they would be classified as "normal"). Ordinarily, in a given experiment, each subject evidences the same problem. Treatment, which is administered in a stereotypical fashion, deals only with the specified problem. As other researchers (see Kanfer & Phillips, 1969; Paul, 1969a) have noted, for reasons of ethics and experimental control the analogue approach is a desirable way of investigating the efficacy of treatment. However, from a practical point of view, the real purpose of carrying out analogue research is to provide practitioners with better methods for dealing with clinical problems (that is, problems of hospitalized patients or of clients who seek outpatient therapy). The critical question, then, is to what extent can one expect analogue results to generalize to clinical populations. Paul (1969a) has concluded that generalizability depends upon the "degree to which the variables studied in the laboratory share the essential characteristics of the variables in the clinical context [p. 54]." Some of these "essential characteristics" would include severity and duration of the target problem, the existence of other problems possibly correlated with the target problem (Zytowski, 1966), and levels of motivation.[10]

With respect to such essential characteristics, it seems fairly clear that generalization of analogue results to clinical settings can be expected to be a good deal less than perfect. As Paul (1969a) and Kanfer and Phillips (1969) have argued, the final test of whether a treatment method works in a clinical setting must be conducted in a clinical setting. Herein lies an

---

[10] Motivation is so frequently invoked as an explanation (often post hoc) for therapeutic success or failure that it has virtually become a cliché. This is unfortunate because, if by *motivation* we mean a set of external reasons (contingencies) for behavior change, then motivation is of paramount importance (witness the striking changes in ward behavior when token economy approaches are instituted, Chapter VI). It is likely that anyone who has ever worked with patients hospitalized in a Veterans' Administration hospital will testify to the frustration encountered in attempting to motivate patients to improve and thereby leave the hospital, when leaving the hospital often leads to a substantial loss of veterans' benefits. An honest dialogue between therapist and patient might be as follows:

> *Therapist:* "Let me help you behave in a normal manner and then you can be discharged."
> *Patient:* "What! Do you think I'm crazy?"

This is in no sense a criticism of the hospital, per se, but rather of a system that rewards maladaptive, dependent behavior.

important function of case history data. If we can conclude from analogue research (and certainly our conclusion should be based on more than one experiment) that the specifics of treatment X are effective in dealing with a class of problems Y, and if a sizable number of different therapists in different clinical settings report a high success rate (based on a large number of patients or clients) in dealing with a similar class of problems, this argues very strongly for the clinical or practical value of the treatment. Naturally, positive findings from controlled research conducted in a clinical setting will add to the strength of such a conclusion.

In summary, whether a particular technique X is of practical value in dealing with a given class of maladaptive behaviors, Y, is a matter of empirical findings. Controlled experiments, of the analogue variety, can provide convincing evidence that the technique is effective for certain populations. Nonspecific control groups, the use of different experimenters, the inclusion of several relevant response measures, and a reasonable follow-up all contribute to the believability of such findings. The degree to which one can generalize analogue findings to clinical settings is a function of communality of essential factors. Extensive case history findings and, when feasible, controlled research in the clinical setting, coupled with analogue findings, may provide conclusive evidence that the specific technique is of practical value.

Behavior Therapy and the Accumulation of Empirical Findings

In 1965, Rimm attended a seminar conducted by a prominent behavior therapist who expressed the view that since the principles for modifying human behavior were already well established, psychologists should concentrate their efforts on dealing with matters of ethics. In other words, the "data were in," and the question was how to use the data in an ethical and socially constructive fashion. When one witnesses the vast accumulation of empirical knowledge since then (much of which has appreciably altered the "behavior" of the practicing behavior therapist), it is clear that such a statement was quite premature. At that time, the empirical support for the effectiveness of systematic desensitization and assertive training was relatively weak, the "extinction" methods (for example, implosive therapy) of Chapter VIII were virtually unresearched, the important work of Bandura and his associates on modeling procedures and fear reduction had not yet appeared, behavioral approaches to self-control were largely in the conjectural stage, and the important role of cognitive factors in influencing behavior was not widely appreciated and, at that time, lacking in empirical support. Clearly, a wealth of clinically and theoretically relevant information has accumulated during this period of time. If, indeed, the data were by no means entirely "in" in 1965, would such a statement be correct today? Given existing trends, the answer is firmly in the negative, and from the point of view of the dedicated practitioner, this is crucial. A considerable portion of this text is devoted to "how to do it." If the practitioner incorporates some of these procedures in his practice, it is our fervent hope that he will not be oblivious to subsequent findings that indicate that the procedures, as described here, are in need of modification. To ignore such findings is to perform a disservice to one's clients. A fundamental defining characteristic of behavior therapy is its insistence that clinical practice be subject to continual modification as a function of the appearance of new factual data. To ignore this data is, in considerable measure, to fail to appreciate what behavior therapy is all about.

Behavior Therapy and Theory

The reader unfamiliar with developments in academic psychology may be surprised to learn that the role of theorizing has been a subject of considerable controversy. While the majority of psychologists are quite comfortable in dealing with issues on a theoretical level, certain others are decidedly not. Perhaps the most vigorous (and certainly the most publicized) opponent of psychological theorizing is Skinner (1950, 1953, 1971). Skinner's position is that, by and large, psychological theories have not contributed a great deal to the establishment of functional relationships (that is, lawful relationships between variables). Skinner is especially critical of theories that postulate hypothetical "inner causes" (sometimes referred to as hypothetical constructs) to account for observable behavior. Examples of such constructs are the id, ego, and superego of Freudian psychology, and constructs such as emotion and anxiety, as they are often used.

Constructs of this nature, as they are so often employed, provide what appears to be explanation of behavior. In fact, they are mentalistic pseudoexplanations that are circular, providing nothing more than a label for the behaviors they are postulated to explain. Consider the person who is observed to cry a great deal. An observer might say: "That's because he is an emotional person." But how does the observer know that the subject is emotional? Usually because he infers it from the crying behavior. What the observer is really saying is: "That person cries because he is emotional, which I infer from his crying." The circularity is obvious and it is equally obvious that nothing has been explained. In a similar vein, one might say that a person behaves impulsively because his ego strength is low, inferring this from the very behavior that one is attempting to explain. Psychological theories (especially theories of personality) have not infrequently postulated constructs of the above nature, and Skinner's criticisms are not without considerable foundation.

It is in the nature of hypothetical constructs that they have "surplus meaning" (Hilgard & Bower, 1966). That is, having been postulated, they assume a status not entirely dependent upon some specific instance of observable behavior. For example, a person whose crying is attributed to "emotionality" will be assumed to be emotional, even when he is not observed to be crying. Now, while it is true that in the above example accounting for crying in terms of emotionality was circular, it is still possible for the construct, "emotionality," to be of some scientific value. This will be the case if "emotionality" can be conceptualized in terms of certain specific properties that give rise to predictions about behaviors other than crying.

The major problem with hypothetical constructs, as they have so often been used in psychology, is that their defining characteristics have not been specified to the degree of precision necessary to allow for clear-cut predictions. Given a broad theory with a large number of such vaguely defined constructs, it is possible to "explain" virtually any observable behavior *after* it has been observed. For example, we have suggested earlier that the symptom substitution hypothesis would seem to follow from psychoanalytic theory, but that in recent years considerable evidence has been gathered that symptom substitution is very rare. It would seem only reasonable to take this as evidence against the theory (not that all of psychoanalytic theory is wrong, but that certain major assumptions may be invalid). However, at least one advocate of psychoanalytic theory (Weitzman, 1967) has recently provided a quotation from Freud (1936, p. 83) that, according to Weitzman, suggests that, indeed, one should not always expect symptom substitution, following symptomatic treatment. The passage in question is vague, failing to provide the reader with any clear notion of what antecedent conditions should or should not lead to the formation of substitute symptoms. Thus, while it is apparently possible to provide a psychoanalytic rationale, after the fact, for the failure of symptom substitution to occur, it seems highly questionable that in the case of a particular client there would be any clear theoretical basis for knowing this in advance. A theory, which by nature of its ambiguity has numerous built-in "loop holes" and "escape clauses," is almost impossible to disprove, but its scientific value is severely limited.

The essential problem with so many psychological constructs is not that the label *mentalistic* can be attached to them, but rather that they do not lead to clear-cut predictions. One area of psychology that has made considerable progress in the past decade is the study of cognition (in other words, the thinking process), in considerable measure because theorists have been careful to describe hypothesized underlying processes in relatively clear and concrete terms. Excellent examples of this include the work of Bower and his associates on conceptual organization in memory (see Bower, Clark, Lesgold, & Winzenz, 1969) and the experiments of Bower, and of Pavio and his collaborators on the role of visual imagery and recall (Bower, 1967; Paivio & Yuille, 1967; Yuille & Paivio, 1968). By making carefully thought-out assumptions concerning how people might most efficiently organize verbal material, Bower and his co-workers were able to effect remarkable increases in memory. Hypotheses regarding how visual images might serve as powerful encoding devices led to experimental findings wherein subjects showed dramatic increases in recall of verbal material. For other examples of the potency of "cognitive theorizing" see Kintsch (1970).

It is sometimes argued that theoretically based hypotheses of this nature are still irrelevant, inasmuch as the functional relationships with which they are associated would have been found even in the absence of any theorizing. This argument, technically, is impossible to refute, but at best suggests a grossly inefficient approach to research. Consider how likely it would be that a researcher who resolutely disregarded the construct, "visual imagery," would just happen to instruct his subjects to "memorize pairs of nouns by visualizing the objects which they represent interacting in a scene." Similar statements can be made regarding the likelihood of discovering systematic desensitization (Chapter II), while disdaining internal states such as anxiety, or happening upon certain of the cognitive methods of Chapter X, while denying the importance of mediational processes such as implicit verbalizations.

The argument that theory is irrelevant is somewhat more cogent when the theory in question makes predictions that everyday experiences render as obvious. For example, a "theory" of gravitation that merely makes the qualitative prediction that objects tend to fall to the ground is hardly in need of a test, nor would there be any need for empirical verification of a theoretically derived assertion that males tend to be sexually attracted to females. If theorizing were limited to predictions of such an obvious nature, it would clearly be a waste of time. The important point is that modern science is replete with examples of theorizing that have given rise to predictions not at all obvious or trivial. This is perhaps best seen in atomic physics where it has been necessary to postulate the existence of new, subatomic particles having very peculiar properties, with subsequent experimentation validating their existence. For example, the *neutrino,* assumed to have a negligible rest mass (but detectable energy and momentum), was postulated, in part, to satisfy the law of conservation of momentum. The neutrino hypothesis gave rise to experiments (see Semat, 1954), that indeed supported the existence of this very strange particle. Einstein's (1953) special theory of relativity gave rise to even more dramatic and unusual predictions (for example, that the mass of a body should vary with its velocity).[11] One can readily point to similar, although somewhat less dramatic, examples in psychology, including theoretical hypotheses leading to the aforementioned verbal-learning experiments, to numerous short-term memory studies (see Kintsch, 1970), to a large number of empirical investigations found in the mathematical psychology literature (the reader is referred to the *Journal of Mathematical Psychology;* also see Levine & Burke, 1972), as well as the theoretical considerations leading to the development of the cognitive therapy methods presented in Chapter X. Thus, it would seem clear that theory (in particular, the postulating of hypothetical constructs) does have an important role to play in science, including psychology, provided that such theory leads to testable predictions of a nontrivial nature.

The Importance of Simplifying Assumptions

It is a truism to say that human behavior is profoundly complex. One can postulate an almost endless number of plausible factors, both internal and external, to account for virtually any observable response made by an adult human being. Given this state of affairs, how is it possible to study or observe behavior in a manner that will allow for meaningful prediction (in this regard, it should be pointed out that the practitioner is every bit as concerned with prediction as the scientist)? An important part of the answer to this very fundamental question is that the observer *must be willing to make certain simplifying assumptions.* To illustrate what is meant by a simplifying assumption, any student of high school physics will be familiar with the formula for the distance traveled by free-falling bodies, $S = 16t^2$, where S is the distance fallen, and t is elapsed time. This formula is only an approximation, however, for it ignores air resistance, which itself is a complex function of atmospheric conditions, and the shape, texture, and velocity of the object. It also ignores the fact that the "constant" number (16) is not really constant, but varies with the distance from the object to the earth's center. Each time such a factor is deliberately ignored, we say a simplifying assumption is being made.

In the preceding example, it is essential to realize that even with the several simplifying assumptions, it is possible to use the formula,

---

[11] It is interesting that Skinner (1971, p. 184), the arch foe of psychological theorizing, advocates that psychology adopt the "strategy of physics," with its emphasis on environmental causation. In fact, much of the progress of modern physics can be attributed only to the physicists' willingness to deal with states or processes that initially could not be observed directly. Obviously, modern physics is not antienvironmental, but it is by no stretch of the imagination antitheoretical.

$S = 16t^2$, to make remarkably accurate predictions. However, if Isaac Newton had insisted on taking into account every conceivable factor in theorizing about freely falling bodies, it is quite likely that he would have given up in sheer frustration, thus depriving the world of an important formulation. A similar point is made by Skinner (1971): "If Gilbert or Faraday or Maxwell had had even a quick glimpse of what is now known about electricity, they would have had much more trouble in finding starting points and in formulating principles which did not seem 'oversimplified' [p. 159]."

Few would argue that the complexity of a falling rock in any way approximates the complexity of the human behaving organism. Imagine, then, the task of scientist or practitioner who attempts to take into account every conceivable causal factor in predicting what a person is going to do in any given situation. It would be an impossible task. As with the physicist, the student of human behavior has no choice but to make simplifying assumptions. This is exactly what the behavior therapist does. Suppose he is presented with a child who shows a high frequency of tantrum behavior. He will probably assume that such behavior is reinforced, perhaps by parental attention. This particular conception, or "model," of what is going on will enable him to gain whatever information is necessary to support or reject the assumptions on which it is based. If support is found, the therapist will be in a position to make concrete suggestions to the parents. If not, naturally, he will be forced to find an alternative approach. The point is that by making simplifying assumptions, the therapist (and theoretician, as well) will not be so overwhelmed by possibilities that he will be thrown into a virtual state of paralysis.

The sophisticated behavior therapist is well aware that he is making such simplifying assumptions. He would not take the position, for example that parental attention is the sole factor maintaining tantrum behavior or, on a more general level, that one can explain all of human behavior in terms of the principles underlying behavior therapy. Instead, he would argue that the behavioral "model," based upon such principles, is very *useful* in the prediction and modification of the way people behave. He does not claim to have a total understanding of human behavior, which, as Kanfer and Phillips (1970) have noted, is probably not even *necessary* for effective treatment.

The Initial Interview

The general guidelines we present here are similar to those presented by Wolpe (1969). In certain respects, the behaviorally oriented initial interview is similar to the interview that would be conducted by therapists of other orientations. The therapist's way of relating to his client, while not necessarily communicating "unconditional positive regard," nevertheless, should be marked by warmth and a concern for the client's welfare. Throughout this text, we present evidence for the efficacy of behavior therapy procedures, when efforts have been made to minimize such so-called nonspecific factors, and the reader may wonder why they are emphasized. First, no therapy can succeed if the client perceives his therapist as cold and indifferent and, therefore, drops out of treatment. Second, a major task of the therapist is to obtain a good deal of information from his client (some of which will be potentially embarrassing), and experience suggests that an atmosphere of warmth and acceptance will be facilitative of this goal. Third, it is reasonable to suppose that a therapist who is seen as understanding and caring can serve as a more potent source of social reinforcement for progress in treatment than one who is perceived as cold and uninterested.

For anyone who has observed the consulting-room manner of a behavior therapist, the above points may seem too obvious to mention. Unfortunately, among those who have not, it is very often assumed that the behaviorist interacts with his client in a cold, "objective" fashion, as Pavlov might have interacted to his dogs. From the above, this is clearly not the case (the reader in need of further convincing is referred to Lazarus, 1971). Any would-be practitioner who chooses to be a behavior therapist because he finds it difficult to put clients at ease, through using a more traditional approach, is advised to rethink his professional goals.

For the novice therapist, the first few moments of an initial interview may be very awkward indeed. Not infrequently the client says nothing, waiting for the therapist to make the first move. At such times the therapist might ask the client, "What's happening?", or simply smile and shrug his shoulders (communicating the same thing). Almost always this will be followed by the client verbalizing his "presenting complaint." The degree to which problems are clearly specified will vary considerably from client to client, but usually a considerable amount of questioning will be in order. As Lazarus (1971) has noted, the questions should pertain to delineating the problem behavior with respect to "*when*" it occurs, and "*what*" factors maintain it, rather than focusing on "*why*" the individual is behaving in such a maladaptive fashion. Consider the following examples:

Therapist: What seems to be the difficulty?
Client: I'm nervous a lot of the time. I'm afraid I'm gonna have a nervous breakdown.
Therapist: Can you tell me when you are most nervous? What sorts of situations or things make you the most nervous?
Client: Don't laugh. It's people. I'm really weird.

Therapist: Well, I wouldn't agree that that makes you weird, but it seems to be causing you a lot of discomfort. When you say "people," what exactly do you mean?

Client: O.K., when I say people, mostly it's crowds, like on the street, or in a supermarket. Strangers.

Therapist: Can you describe one or two situations where you really felt nervous?

Client: Like, last week, I was shopping in the Safeway supermarket. It was around 5:00, and it was very crowded. I started shaking and sweating, and got out of there as soon as I could.

Therapist: How did you feel after you left?

Client: Kind of stupid for having to leave. But, at least, I wasn't panicky. It's funny, because I was in there yesterday evening and felt O.K.

Therapist: Were there many people around, this time?

Client: No, the place was almost empty.

Therapist: How about another instance?

Client: I was walking down Market Street . . . the rush hour. . . . There were people all around, and I got that same really scared feeling.

Therapist: What did you do then?

Client: Almost ran to my car . . . I felt better once I was moving.

Therapist: What about being there when there aren't many people around?

Client: That wouldn't bother me . . . I'm sure it wouldn't.

Therapist: What about when you are with people you know . . . how do you feel then?

Client: It depends . . . sometimes O.K. and sometimes kind of up-tight . . . but nothing like when I'm in a crowd of strangers.

Therapist: Are there times when, say, you are in a crowded supermarket or on the street, and you don't feel so nervous.

Client: I think that if I had a good night's sleep the night before it doesn't seem quite as bad. But I'm never comfortable.

Therapist: How long have you had this problem?

Client: I've always been kind of nervous in crowds, but the last few years it's been getting worse. The first time it was really bad, was about 2 years ago. . . . I was in college then . . . it was exam week and I was uptight about that and had been up all night, studying. Next day I went shopping and, all of a sud-den, I got so nervous I thought I was gonna flip. Since then it's been a real problem. Look, am I crazy?

Therapist: I certainly wouldn't say so. You are a guy who has learned to be very uptight in certain situations, and our job is to teach you not to feel this way. There are techniques which are often very helpful in dealing with problems like yours. But, for the time being, I need some more information. What would you say the effect, or impact, of this problem is on your life?

Client: Well, whenever possible, I avoid crowds. I mean, not to the point of not going to work. I'm an accountant. When my wife can't shop, I go shopping, but I try to go when there aren't many people.

Therapist: Does your wife know about your problem?

Client: Not really . . . she thinks I get a little uptight in crowds, but she doesn't know how serious it is.

Therapist: Do you have other areas of difficulty . . . things you worry a lot about?

Note: The therapist has attempted to tie down the client's "phobia" to specific stimulus situations. He has also attempted to determine how the client responds to such episodes (he makes a hasty departure and experiences relief, although he castigates himself). Sometimes, phobic responses are maintained, in part by indirect consequences (for example, avoiding work, obtaining nurturance from a spouse). Certain of the therapist's questions were directed at this. Note that the client's concern with his overall mental condition was met with reassurance, but, more important, with an emphasis on dealing with the specific area of difficulty.

In the just cited example, the therapist's task was not especially difficult, since the client was readily able to describe his problem in behavioral terms. The client in the example below presents a considerably greater challenge.

Therapist: Well, what's happening with you?

Client: You know, I tried to kill myself last week.

Therapist: Yes. I read that on the referral. Can you tell me about it?

Client: Not much to tell . . . I feel rotten all the time . . . you know, depressed. Life's not worth living.

Therapist: Sounds like this isn't a very happy time in your life. How long has this been going on, I mean the bad feelings?

Client: Oh, God. Always.

Therapist: Have you ever attempted suicide before last week?

Client: Well, maybe not actual attempts, but I've thought about it before.

Therapist: I wonder if something happened fairly recently to make things worse.

Client: Sometimes I think it's just a waste of time talking about it. . . . I'm just a big nothing.

Therapist: Well, what's it like to be a nothing?

Client: I'm a failure . . . a big flop. I was a lousy student. I let my parents down because of that.

Therapist: How long have you been out of school?

Client: I graduated from high school 3 years ago.

Therapist: Did something happen in school to make you feel more depressed?

Client: My grades were no good. My parents wanted me to go to college. I didn't want to, and I probably couldn't have gotten into a decent school, anyway. My father was really disappointed. He said I'd amount to nothing.

Therapist: Tell me what your answer was when he said that.

Client: Nothing. What could I say? He was right.

Therapist: How have you gotten along with your parents since then?

Client: Mostly, I avoid them. They live in Chicago, so it's easy to do.

Therapist: I'd like to get back to your feelings about your parents later. Right now, I'd like to know more about what your life has been like recently, say in the last month or two. What's been happening to make you feel like a "nothing"?

Client: For one thing, I have a nothing job. I'm a secretary, and I don't even do that well. My typing is poor, and my shorthand is worse.

Therapist: How long have you had the job?

Client: About 2½ years.

Therapist: Is your boss dissatisfied?

Client: I don't know. He's never said so. I know I'm no good.

Therapist: Has anything happened recently at work to make you feel worse?

Client: Not really. Same old crap. You do what you're told and keep your mouth shut.

Therapist: Sounds like you resent that.

Client: Right now, I just don't care. Maybe, if I thought about it, I would.

Therapist: You haven't said anything about your social life. Do you have any close friends?

Client: No, not now. I did have this girl friend who I could talk to, but she got married and they moved to Chicago. Her husband is a policeman there.

Therapist: When was that?

Client: About 6 weeks ago.

Therapist: Did that depress you?

Client: Yes it did; very much.

Therapist: What about men?

Client: (Pause) I had a boy friend. We went together for about a year, but we broke up.

Therapist: When was that?

Client: A month ago. (Eyes begin to tear)

Therapist: Do you feel like talking about it?

Client: It's depressing, like everything else. Maybe I should. He just got tired of me. He even said so.

Therapist: Did he say why?

Client: (Long pause) I'm frigid. (Client begins to sob.) What's the use?

Therapist: I can see this is really getting you down. Can you tell me more about it? How does it show up?

Client: That's the reason Charles broke up with me. I wouldn't do it. I just couldn't. I've never done it with anyone.

Therapist: What happened with Charles?

Client: I made up my mind I was going to try. We were in his apartment. I had three drinks, which is a lot for me. I thought that would make me uninhibited. I even let him take all my clothes off. . . .

Therapist: (After a long silence) It's difficult for you to talk about, isn't it?

Client: Yes . . . I failed . . . I couldn't even do something that dumb animals do. . . . He tried to . . . you know, to make love. I panicked, and I think I screamed. Real cool, that's me!

Therapist: And then?

Client: He slapped me. He called me a cold-blooded, frigid bitch. Then he said he'd had it with me. That was the end of a whole year's relationship. (Loud sobbing, followed by silence)

Therapist: Do you remember how you felt at the time. Say, after he left?

Client: Horrible, just horrible. I should have been able to have sex with him. But I just couldn't.

Therapist: Do you think that had anything to do with your suicide attempt?

Client: I suppose so. After that, I started thinking about suicide seriously. The whole thing is so depressing.

Therapist: What are your feelings about having sex?

Client: It's stupid . . . I'm very uptight about it. That's why I've never done it.

Therapist: You know, I really think we are getting somewhere. Sounds like a couple of things have really gotten you down lately. Your best friend left the area. . . . You found yourself unable to perform sexually with Charles, and he ended a long relationship. That is quite a bit to have to handle. I think the thing

Client: about your job and your parents' expectations are important but, maybe, not nearly as important as these things that have been happening lately.

Client: (Long pause.) I think the most depressing thing of all is sex. I'm abnormal. I'll never be able to get married or have a family . . . it's so stupid! When I start feeling like this, then I just want to end it all.

Therapist: Have you considered any alternatives?

Client: Sure . . . I'll become a nun! I'm not even Catholic.

Therapist: Did you know there are psychological techniques that are very effective in dealing with problems like being uptight about sex?

Client: There are? You mean, talking about it for the next 5 years?

Therapist: Not at all. You learned to have negative feelings about sex and I'd like to help you unlearn them. A lot of people have been helped by the kind of therapy I have in mind. Sometimes, in a rather short period of time. Naturally, I'll need more information . . . mostly, I just want to get to know you better before we begin.

Note: In this example, the therapist's primary task was to pin down the depression to specific stimulus events, which he was able to do. The treatment referred to might be a combination of systematic desensitization and cognitive therapy for the sexual problem, possibly followed by some assertive training, since there is some indication that she may have difficulty standing up for her rights (for example, accepting unfair criticism).

In both of the examples presented, additional information is required before a specific behavior therapy procedure may be applied. In some degree the nature of this information will depend on the particular technique to be applied. Guidelines for gathering such information are presented in the methods section of each of the chapters to follow.

The Gathering of Background Information

Once the therapist has done a reasonable job of delineating the problem or problems that precipitated the client's plea for help, it is useful to delve somewhat into the client's background. Such information is often very helpful in supporting hypotheses about present behavior. For example, the client whose parents were particularly dominating might well benefit from assertive training, or the client who was reared in a conservative religious environment might be expected to experience anxiety in connection with sex; thus, desensitization or, perhaps, cognitive therapy might be of value. Such background information will also be useful in facilitating a constructive therapist–client relationship. To illustrate, consider the client who much admires his father, who apparently relates to his son in the manner of a benevolent despot. The therapist who presents the picture of an indecisive, "wishy-washy" individual might have far less leverage than one who is seen as confident. On the other hand, were the father seen as a cruel tyrant, an approach smacking of authoritarianism might only succeed in "turning the client off." Naturally, the therapist cannot be "all things to all people" [as Lazarus (1971) has noted, "a therapist cannot adapt his therapy or himself to every patient (p. 46)."]. However, adults are able, usually, to adjust their style of interaction somewhat as a function of who they are with, without appearing to be (or feeling) awkward or insincere, and most experienced therapists take advantage of this flexibility.

Wolpe (1969) suggests obtaining information in four general areas (assuming, of course, that this information has not already been gathered when the client's presenting complaints were explored). The first pertains to the client's familial experiences while he was growing up. This can most easily be accomplished by asking questions pertaining to each person thought to have had a significant impact on the client's development. This would include parents, siblings, and grandparents, if they exerted an appreciable influence, as well as close friends. Exploring the client's religious background is also useful. The second category of questions pertains to experiences in school (for example, relating to academic performance, teachers who had particular positive or negative impacts on the client, whether he participated in sports) and his employment history since leaving school. The third group of questions relates to sexual behavior. In this, as in other areas, questions should be posed in a tactful, sensitive manner. If the client shows unusual difficulty in discussing this, or any other topic, the therapist might be wise to defer the discussion until a more comfortable relationship has been established. In relation to sex, information pertaining to masturbation, dating behavior, circumstances surrounding the first experience with intercourse, and homosexual experiences may be of considerable value, along with information relating to sexual attitudes of the client's parents and those associated with his religious affiliation. Wolpe includes in this category questions pertaining to history and current status of the client's relationship with his spouse.

The final group of questions pertains to current social relationships. These questions focus on the extensiveness and intimacy of existing friendship relationships.

Clients, especially those who have been exposed to more traditional forms of psychotherapy, frequently have a set to engage in a seemingly

endless discussion of their past life (traditional approaches tend to reinforce such behavior). From the point of view of the behavior therapist,
this can be very counterproductive since it is antithetical to his "here-
and-now" orientation, which stresses problem-solving, rather than passive reflection. It is recommended that clients be gently dissuaded from
undue dwelling on such past experiences. At the same time, however,
care should be taken not to communicate to the client that he is forbidden to bring up relevant background material that, perhaps through
embarrassment, he avoided during the initial interview.

The Use of Relaxation Techniques

Sometimes the practitioner is confronted with a client who is so anxious, he is virtually incoherent. We have found that, in such instances, it
is sometimes very helpful to talk the client through some, or all, of the
deep-muscle-relaxation exercises presented in Chapter II before attempting to continue the interview. In this regard, doing nothing more
than presenting breathing exercises may have a striking effect.

II

Systematic Desensitization

Systematic desensitization, developed by Joseph Wolpe (1958, 1969), is aimed specifically at the alleviation of maladaptive anxiety. The technique, as it is most often employed, involves the pairing of deep muscle relaxation with imagined scenes depicting situations that the client has indicated cause him to feel anxious. The therapist usually operates on the assumption that if the client is taught to experience relaxation, rather than anxiety, while imagining such scenes, the real-life situation that the scene depicted will cause much less discomfort. Some of the considerable research and clinical literature supporting the efficacy of desensitization is reviewed in a later section of the chapter.

Background

Systematic desensitization is thought by Wolpe (1958, 1969) to follow the principle of _counterconditioning_. Counterconditioning simply means the use of learning procedures to substitute one type of response for another, and in desensitization, the attempt is made to substitute relaxation for anxiety. One of the first highly publicized examples of the use of counterconditioning-type procedures to overcome an anxiety response was reported by Mary Cover Jones (1924). She was successful in eliminating a fear of rabbits in a small boy by using a technique that involved, among other things, the pairing of eating (which presumably had the psychophysiological effect of inhibiting anxiety) with the presentation of the rabbit. However, it was not entirely clear what factors accounted for the fear reduction, and it remained for Wolpe (1958) some 3 decades later to offer a refined, systematic, and reasonably well-documented set of counterconditioning procedures, which were to have maximum impact on the fields of clinical psychology and psychiatry.

Wolpe's (1958) early experiments used cats as subjects. For one group of animals, each cat, while in its home cage, heard a buzzer that was followed by a painful electric shock. For a second group of animals, the buzzer was first paired with eating and later with shock; this procedure served to set up a conflict between two opposing drives, hunger and fear, both attached to the same stimulus, the sound of the buzzer. Prior research (see Masserman, 1943) had suggested that experimental "neurosis" resulted from a conflict situation, an idea originating in the writings of Freud. Wolpe reported finding that cats in the first group showed a fear response that was similar in intensity to that displayed by cats in the second (conflict) group, suggesting that conflict was not *necessary* for the establishment of neurotic reactions.

One of the principal consequences of the conditioning experience for animals in both groups was inhibition of eating. Wolpe then reasoned that if anxiety (conditioned by pairing the buzzer and shock) was able to inhibit the eating response, perhaps eating could inhibit the anxiety response. Wolpe (1958) used the term "reciprocal inhibition," after the physiologist Sherrington (1906). Since the animals showed the maximum anxiety in their home cages, and relatively less anxiety in cages physically different from their home cages, he began by presenting food pellets in very dissimilar cages. After the animals were observed to eat in those cages, they were transferred to cages more like their home cages and fed again. This process of gradually reintroducing the home-cage stimuli was continued until the animals showed no signs of anxiety in the home cage. By an analogous procedure, the buzzer was paired with food until it, too, elicited no apparent anxiety.

Following his research with cats, Wolpe (1958) began to search for responses in human beings that would inhibit anxiety and that could be used therapeutically. Interestingly enough, there appears to have been no systematic attempt on his part to employ the eating response, and the three principal classes of response that he came to use were relaxation, assertion, and sexual responses. In clinical practice today, relaxation is probably used most commonly to counter anxiety; with some sort of assertion, second; and sexual responding, a distant third.

The term *systematic desensitization* is used when the competing response is relaxation, although Wolpe assumes the same underlying reciprocal inhibition mechanism is operating when any of the three classes of competing responses is employed. The use of sexual arousal to inhibit anxiety is discussed later in this chapter. Because of its increasing importance, a discussion of assertive procedures is presented in a separate chapter (Chapter III).

The Applicability of Systematic Desensitization

An examination of the psychological and psychiatric literature reveals that a very broad spectrum of problems may be successfully dealt with using desensitization. A partial list of phobias that have been successfully treated includes fear of heights, driving, a variety of animals, insects, classroom examinations, flying, water, going to school, rejection by another, authority figures, injections, crowds, physical injury, and even fear of death. In addition, this technique has been employed with a variety of other disorders that are not obviously phobic in nature, including speech disorders (Walton & Mather, 1963); sexual deviations: 1) compulsive exposure (Bond & Hutchison, 1960); 2) homosexuality (Gold & Neufeld, 1965); 3) frigidity (Madsen & Ullmann, 1967); asthmatic attacks (Moore, 1965); insomnia (Geer & Katkin, 1966); alcoholism (Kraft & Al-Issa, 1967); and anger (Rimm, deGroot, Boord, Heiman, & Dillow, 1971), to mention just a few. Therapists using desensitization to treat such disorders usually assume that the disorders arise from fear attached to specifiable external events and as such are similar to phobic reactions. For instance, a particular alcoholic might drink excessively following any sort of failure experience that causes him to feel anxious; or a particular man might become anxious and be rendered impotent whenever his wife behaves in a manner indicative of even the slightest rejection, or a given individual suffering from obsessional thoughts might experience such thoughts only when confronted with an anxiety-provoking situation.

One of the more impressive facets of most of the behavior therapy techniques is the small number of sessions usually required to effect behavioral improvement, relative to the generally expected duration of more traditional therapy. Desensitization is no exception. The large-scale case history reports indicate a median number of sessions (involving actual desensitization) of 16–23, depending on the therapist (see Paul, 1969b), although as might be expected certain patients have required many more sessions.

Progressive Muscle Relaxation

Although progressive muscle relaxation is an important part of systematic desensitization, it may be used as a powerful therapeutic tool in its own right. Therapists frequently have employed progressive muscle relaxation by itself in treating a wide variety of disorders (including generalized anxiety, insomnia, headaches, neck and back pain, menstrual pain, writer's cramp, and even mild forms of agitated depression). In addition, there is nothing in the nature of this procedure that would preclude its use within the context of the more traditional psychotherapies or during the course of short-term counseling.

The most basic premise is that muscle tension is in some way related to anxiety, and that an individual will experience a very marked and comforting reduction in felt anxiety if tense muscles can be made to be loose and flaccid. A powerful and efficient method for effecting such a state of muscle relaxation involves the successive tensing and relaxing of voluntary muscles in an orderly sequence until all of the main muscle groups of the body are relaxed.

Behavior therapists differ somewhat in respect to the order in which muscles are to be relaxed, the duration of flexion and relaxation, and the extent to which hypnotic-like suggestions are to be employed (the reader is referred to Paul, 1969c, for a more detailed discussion of these differences). It should be stressed, however, that these differences tend to be rather minor. The method we use, presented below, is rather similar to that reported by Wolpe and Lazarus (1966).

Procedure.   The client is seated in a comfortable chair (reclining arm chairs are ideal). The therapist usually begins with an explanation of the rationale of deep muscle relaxation geared to the sophistication of the client. The therapist might say;

The tension [anxiety, agitation, discomfort] you normally experience [are currently experiencing] is more a physical state than a mental state. It comes from tense muscles, though you might not even be aware your muscles are tense . . . only that you feel uncomfortable. I am going to teach you to relax those tense muscles, systematically, so you will be calm instead of anxious. After you've learned the method, you will be able to do it on your own whenever you begin to feel tense [when you can't sleep at night; when your head begins to hurt]. The method requires tensing a particular muscle or set of muscles, then relaxing the same muscles . . . then tensing and relaxing the opposing set of muscles. [The therapist might demonstrate what he means by making a fist, relaxing his hand, extending his fingers, and relaxing once again, to illustrate what is meant by opposing sets of muscles.] After we have completed relaxing your hands, we will relax your arms, and then your shoulders, and so on until your entire body is relaxed.

Throughout this introduction and the remaining procedure, a calm, self-assured manner of speaking will probably facilitate relaxation.

At this point, as a precaution, the therapist should inquire as to whether the client has suffered any injuries (for instance, whiplash or injured back) or has any other physical disability that might result in pain or further injury were associated muscle groups tensed. Rarely is the response affirmative; but when it is, the therapist should take special care in dealing with these muscle groups, either by limiting the amount and suddenness of the tensing procedure, or by leaving them out of the relaxation induction entirely.

The client is now asked to get as comfortable as possible. Tight clothing (especially neckties) should be loosened, the client's legs should not be crossed, and all parts of his body should be supported by the chair. He is then asked to take a deep breath and slowly let it out. The first tension–relaxation cycle is then presented: "I want you to raise your arms and extend them out in front of you, and now make a fist with both your hands, really hard, really hard. Notice the uncomfortable tension in your hands and fingers. Do it really hard and notice the feeling of discomfort, of tension, which you are feeling in your hands." After approximately 10 seconds of tensing, the therapist says: "Now, when I say relax, I want your hands to fall on your lap as if they were made of lead . . . just let them fall . . . now, relax." More often than not the client's hands will *not* "fall" to his lap, but instead he will *place* them on his lap. If this occurs, the therapist may approach the client, saying: "Now, I'm going to raise your arm and then release it; and this time really let it fall to your lap." If the client's hand does fall, the therapist might say: "Good, you've got the idea." If the client persists in inhibiting the relaxation response, the therapist might model the appropriate behavior and following this, again raise the client's arm and release it. At this stage, even the most resistant, or difficult, subjects respond with the appropriate degree of flaccidity.

The client is then asked to go through the same exercise, with 10 seconds of tensing (again pointing out how tense and uncomfortable his hands feel) followed by "relax," followed by 10–15 seconds of relaxation, during which time the therapist might say (in a soothing, quiet tone): "Notice how the tension and discomfort are draining from your hands . . . being replaced by sensations of comfort, and warmth, and pleasure. Notice how your hands feel now in comparison to what they felt like when you were tensing. Notice the contrast. See how much better it feels to be relaxed." This completes the first tension–relaxation cycle.

Very often, naive subjects, when asked to tense one set of muscles, proceed to tense other groups automatically. For example, while making fists the client might be observed to catch his breath, grit his teeth, or squint. Obviously, this interferes with relaxation induction. Therefore, following the first exercise, it is well to suggest to the client that he is to tense *only* the muscle group he has been asked to tense, making a conscious effort *not* to tense other muscles. This is especially crucial after several groups of muscles have been relaxed, since the client may inadvertently tense muscles that have already undergone the tension–relaxation cycle. All of this should be pointed out, with an indication that while the habit of tensing muscles other than the target group is quite common, it is important that it be unlearned.

The client is then ready for the second tension–relaxation cycle. He is asked to extend his arms as before, but this time "do the opposite" of what was done on the previous exercise. The therapist might say: "Bend your fingers backward, the opposite of making a fist. Do it really hard . . . really hard. Notice the discomfort. Notice the tension." The client may still have a noticeable tendency to tense other muscles; and throughout this and subsequent tension periods when the therapist observes this, he should remind the client to tense only those muscles he is instructed to tense. Specific suggestions to relax those muscles inadvertently tensed are also helpful (for example, "breathe smoothly and evenly," or "relax your mouth . . . you are only to experience tension in your hands"). Following 10 seconds of tensing, the client is instructed to relax, and at this stage his hands will usually fall to his waist or to the arm rests. Again he is reminded of how tense he felt before, but how relaxed, calm, and comfortable his hands feel now. After 10–15 seconds of relaxation, he is asked to tense his bicep muscles ("imagine you're showing off your muscles at the beach," if that seems appropriate), with suggestions of tenseness and discomfort, as before. Often people will make fists and this should be immediately pointed out, with the suggestion that the client "shake" his hands loose (demonstrating) while the biceps are still tensed. After 10 seconds of tensing, he is instructed to relax; and during the 10–15 second relaxation period, appropriate relaxation suggestions are again provided.

Following this, the tricep muscles are tensed by extending the arms forward ("bending them the wrong way") with the usual commentary from the therapist designed to emphasize the uncomfortable sensations resulting from muscle tension. As before, this is immediately followed by 10–15 seconds of relaxation, again with the therapist pointing up the positive sensations associated with relaxation, stressing how these feelings contrast with what the client felt when tense. The same general procedure is followed for the remainder of the muscle groups. The entire sequence of exercises we employ is presented below.

1. *Hands.* The fists are tensed; relaxed. The fingers are extended; relaxed.

2. *Biceps and triceps.* The biceps are tensed; relaxed. The triceps are tensed; relaxed.

3. *Shoulders.* The shoulders are pulled back; relaxed. The shoulders are pushed forward; relaxed.

4. *Neck (lateral).* With shoulders straight, the head is turned slowly to the right, but to an extreme position; relaxed. With shoulders straight, the head is turned to left; relaxed.

5. *Neck (forward).* The head is brought forward until the chin digs into chest; relaxed. (Bringing the head back is *not* recommended.)

6. *Mouth.* The mouth is opened as wide as possible; relaxed. The lips are pursed as in exaggerated pout; relaxed.

7. *Tongue (extended and retracted).* With mouth open, the tongue is extended as far as possible; relaxed ("allow your tongue to come to a comfortable position in your mouth," during all relaxation phases involving the tongue). The tongue is "brought back" into the throat as far as possible; relaxed.

8. *Tongue (mouth roof and floor).* The tongue is "dug" into the roof of mouth, as hard as possible; relaxed. The tongue is "dug" into floor of mouth, as hard as possible; relaxed.

9. *Eyes.* The eyes are opened as wide as possible, until brow is visibly furrowed (this usually requires considerable encouragement, stressing tension in eyes and forehead); relaxed. (Getting the client to relax his eyes and brow following this exercise is often difficult. Gentle encouragement by the therapist to "relax the eyes and forehead just a little bit more" is recommended, especially when the therapist can discern tension about the eyes and forehead.) The eyes are closed as hard as possible until a definite squint is apparent; relaxed. (It is probably well to conclude the relaxation phase with instructions that the eyes be opened only slightly, but that concentration be such that the client does not "see" anything.)

10. *Breathing.* The client takes as deep a breath as is possible (encouragement to inhale "even more deeply" is desirable, since this is an extremely effortful response); relaxed ("resume normal, smooth, comfortable breathing"). The client exhales until "every drop of air leaves the lungs." (If instructions are followed, the client will be in considerable distress. Many individuals find it difficult to remain in this state for the full 10 seconds, and it is recommended that the tension phase be reduced to 5–7 seconds.) Relaxed ("resume normal, regular breathing").

11. *Back.* With the shoulders resting against the chair, the trunk of the body is pushed forward so as to arch the entire back; relaxed. For this exercise extreme care should be taken to prevent any injury to the back. The client should be advised to carry out the tensing phase rather slowly, and to relax immediately should he experience any pain.

12. *Midsection.* The midsection is raised slightly by tensing the buttock muscles; relaxed. The midsection is lowered slightly by digging the buttocks into the seat of the chair; relaxed.

13. *Thighs.* The legs are extended and raised approximately 6 inches above the floor (care should be taken that simultaneous tensing of the stomach muscles be minimal); relaxed ("allow the legs to fall to the floor"). Tensing the opposing set of muscles would normally involve bringing the forelegs back underneath the thighs. Since this would involve rather large-scale adjustments in body position that would tend to destroy rhythm and continuity, it would probably be well to omit this exericse. A reasonable alternative would be to have the client "dig" his heels or the backs of his feet into the floor.

14. *Stomach.* The stomach is pulled in as hard as possible "as if it were about to touch the backbone" (stomach exercises, like breathing exercises, are quite effortful and may require encouragement by the therapist); relaxed "until every muscle fiber in the stomach is relaxed"). The stomach is extended, "as if preparing for a punch in the abdomen"; relaxed ("until every muscle fiber is relaxed"). (For both stomach exercises, while it is possible to breath while tensing, it is difficult. For the stomach muscles *only,* if the client is observed to catch his breath, it may be best for the therapist to ignore this.)

15. *Calves and feet.* With legs supported, the feet are bent such that the toes are pointed toward the head; relaxed. With legs supported, feet are bent in opposite direction (cramping of the calf muscles may occur during tensing, at which point the therapist immediately says "relax," suggesting that the client "shake the muscles loose"); relaxed.

16. *Toes.* With legs supported and feet relaxed, the toes are "dug" in the bottom of shoes; relaxed. With the legs supported and feet relaxed, the toes are bent in the opposite direction touching the top of toe area of the shoes; relaxed.

Following completion of the last tension–relaxation cycle, the therapist may wish to bring about even deeper relaxation by an additional series of suggestions as illustrated by the following:

Now I want you to imagine, actually experience if you can, a wave of warm, comfortable, pleasant relaxation . . . a wave of relaxation that is going to permeate and engulf your entire body; so that when this wave of relaxation reaches a part of your body, this will be a signal to relax even further, totally relax that part of your body. Feel the wave of relaxation engulf your feet and now your calves and thighs so they are completely, totally, perfectly relaxed . . . and now your buttocks and midsection . . . warm relaxation making all the muscles loose and flaccid. Now your midsection and up your back and chest, and in your hands and arms, so that if any tension was there it is now draining away . . . draining away.

And this wonderful wave of relaxation is now reaching your shoulders and neck and covering your face so that your mouth is completely relaxed . . . totally relaxed . . . and now your tongue and facial muscles are becoming more and more relaxed . . . now your eyes are being permeated by this calm, wonderful wave of relaxation and your forehead . . . so relaxed, so relaxed, so pleasant . . . so heavy.

At this point the relaxation procedure is completed. The therapist will probably want to determine the degree to which it has been effective. He may ask the client to indicate on a 10-point scale how he feels, with 10 being as anxious as he has ever felt, and 1 indicating he is completely relaxed, as if he were about to slip into comfortable sleep. Most individuals receiving relaxation induction for the first time report relatively low levels of tension, usually 3 or lower on the 10-point scale. With increasing practice, the anxiety rating falls further, and after a few additional sessions, it is not uncommon for the client to report a rating of 1. Since the therapist's goal is to teach the client to relax himself, the client should be instructed to practice the technique on his own, perhaps each evening in bed. If the client reports difficulty instructing himself in relaxation, the therapist might tape a relaxation session that the client can listen to at his leisure. However, if the therapeutic goal is to teach the client to relax himself in situations in which listening to a tape would be inappropriate, the client should be encouraged to phase out the tape recorder once he feels he has mastered the technique.

Experimental evidence (Malmo, 1962) suggests that individuals tend to be highly idiosyncratic with respect to where they experience stress-induced muscular tension. Certain individuals may experience painful tension on a regular basis only in the shoulders, or forehead, or perhaps the back or neck. Therefore, in most cases, after the client has received the entire relaxation-induction procedure a few times, and in the process learned to identify where he usually feels the most tension, it is probably not necessary for him to go through all of the exercises to reach a very low level of tension. He may be able to attain a state of deep relaxation in a matter of only a few minutes by concentrating only on those muscle groups that normally become tense. This is important since the entire procedure may take as long as 40 minutes, and if the client believes that he must expend this much time and effort in order to achieve relaxation, it may tend to discourage him. In addition, if the relaxation is done in connection with desensitization, 40 minutes of relaxation each session would leave precious little time for desensitization.

Additional Comments.   Probably the most common error beginning therapists make is to rush the relaxation exercises. Even if the therapist proceeds at an appropriate speed, the client on his own initially is likely

to proceed too rapidly, especially if his initial level of tension is high. It should be pointed out that little in the way of relaxation will result from going through the exercises rapidly, in such calisthenic fashion. As we have suggested, practitioners differ somewhat with respect to the duration of the tension and relaxation phases, although most agree the tension phase should be at least 5 seconds, with a minimum of 10 seconds for relaxation. We have found tension periods of approximately 10 seconds coupled with 10–15 seconds of relaxation to be quite adequate in achieving deep levels of relaxation.

The vast majority of clients report a considerable decrease in felt discomfort following their first experience with deep muscle relaxation. Occasionally, however, one comes across an individual who has followed the instructions and who gives all visible signs of being relaxed (smooth breathing, heaviness of limbs, no signs of tension in forehead, mouth, or eyes, or in the voice), but who still verbalizes a feeling of "uneasiness." Naturally, appearances notwithstanding, this would be an indication of a high level of residual muscle tension. However, another interpretation is that the client has throughout much of his waking life experienced a high level of muscular tension; and when confronted with a bodily state grossly different from the accustomed one, the strangeness of the state of relaxation acts as a danger signal. The therapist may point this out, adding that the client may restore the accustomed bodily state at will, simply by tensing a few muscles; but that as he becomes more used to relaxation, the feeling of uneasiness will dissipate.

The Method of Systematic Desensitization

Systematic desensitization is an effective means for overcoming anxiety reactions conditioned to specific situations or events. Before describing the method, it is well to point out that the problems of individuals seeking help for such specific (as opposed to so-called "free-floating") anxiety reactions fall into one of two categories. Problems in the first category are those associated with irrational anxiety; for these, desensitization alone may be adequate for complete recovery. The anxiety is irrational provided that there is evidence that the client has sufficient *skills* for coping with whatever it is he fears; however, anxiety either causes habitual avoidance of the target situation, or if avoidance is impossible, anxiety depresses performance below the actual level of skill. For example, a skillful and experienced driver may avoid driving altogether following involvement in an accident (or may now drive with less apparent skill because his attention is impaired by a high level of anxiety).

For problems in the second category, the fear is in some measure rational, either because the individual is lacking in pertinent skills, or the target situation is inherently dangerous, or both. For such problems, desensitization alone will probably not be adequate, and in fact may be especially inappropriate. For example, a novice driver might be expected to avoid attempting to negotiate a treacherous ice-covered mountain road. Successful desensitization might have fatal consequences, and most therapists would opt instead to help the client increase his driving skill.

The therapist must decide which of his client's anxieties are irrationally based and which arise from rational considerations. If the decision is that a particular problem is primarily one of irrational anxiety, desensitization may well be an appropriate treatment, depending upon other factors to be discussed shortly. It is essential that the therapist consider very carefully whether the anxiety is in fact irrational, even when the client himself is convinced that what he "needs" is desensitization.

Rimm treated an individual who spent the greater part of his leisure hours in various of the more seedy bars in the San Francisco area. One of his stated therapeutic goals was to lose his fear of getting involved in barroom brawls so that he would be in a position to "beat the shit out of everybody in the place." He was not physically large and possessed no particular combative skills. This was pointed out, with the suggestion that were we to be successful in desensitizing him to this fear, and if he were then to engage in such behavior, he would not remain desensitized very long.

Clinicians frequently encounter individuals who desire heterosexual interaction but report intense anxiety when such situations arise. The beginning therapist will be tempted to employ desensitization immediately, on the assumption that his client has all the appropriate skills necessary to sustain such an interaction, but that he is inhibited by anxiety. Quite often such is not the case. The individual may be anxious because he knows he is lacking in necessary social skills (asking for a date, giving compliments, small talk, tipping the waiter, dancing, etc.), and instruction in these areas (perhaps assertive training: see Chapter III) might be more appropriate than desensitization. The therapist may determine whether his client's problem(s) results from a lack of skill by questioning him; or if his replies are vague, by asking him to role-play how he would handle certain situations. If it appears that the client's anxiety does not result from an objective lack of skills (or from an objectively dangerous situation), systematic desensitization may be an appropriate treatment.

The therapist's next task is to assess whether his client is a likely candidate for such treatment. Lang and Lazovik (1963) have shown a negative correlation between success in desensitization and the number of areas in which an individual experiences irrational anxiety. Thus, it would seem that an individual who reports only a few "phobias" might be expected to show more progress than the person who is phobic about a great many things.[1] To assess this dimension, a simple inquiry is usually sufficient, although some therapists have their clients fill out rating scales for a large number of the more common phobias; the Fear Survey Schedule (Wolpe & Lang, 1964) is used most commonly for this purpose. If the client's response is vague, the therapist might suggest a few common phobic areas, with "what about snakes, or spiders, or heights, or injections" to facilitate communication.

Once having established that the client's phobias are reasonably few in number, as is the case with most adults, the therapist should determine the degree to which he is able to imagine scenes by having him imagine some emotionally neutral, but familiar, scene (for example, the neighborhood post office) and indicating afterward the extent to which the image was clear or real. If the client reports that he was unable to create a reasonably clear image, which is somewhat unusual, the therapist may present a different scene, several times if necessary, to see whether practice facilitates imagining. If the client still reports being unable to experience a reasonably clear image, this probably should be taken as a counterindication for systematic desensitization, and the therapist should concern himself with some alternative strategy, such as in vivo desensitization.

If after one presentation, or several practice presentations, the client reports experiencing a clear image, the therapist should then present him with a scene that the client considers frightening; and again it should be determined whether the image is clear. Sometimes individuals can imagine neutral or pleasant scenes, but "block" on unpleasant scenes, and additional practice on imagining unpleasant scenes is necessary. If the client reports a clear image, it should be determined whether this causes him to feel anxious. *perceptual defense*

Research (Grossberg & Wilson, 1968; Rimm & Bottrell, 1969) suggests a positive relationship between rated clarity of a "frightening" image, and the degree to which physiological measures indicate anxiety. However, the correlation is by no means perfect; and as Wolpe (1958) has pointed out, some individuals can imagine quite clearly scenes that ought to be frightening to them without experiencing the expected emotional response. This is rather rare, occurring in only one individual in ten according to Wolpe (1969). With such individuals, desensitization would probably not be very effective (Wolpe, 1958).

---

[1] There is evidence that persons with a large number of phobias might benefit from cognitive methods such as Rational-Emotive Therapy (Meichenbaum, Gilmore, & Fedoravicius, 1971, see Chapter 10 of this volume).

The therapist's next task is to determine whether the client can relax with deep muscle relaxation. At this point, the therapist might ask the client to rate himself on the previously described 10-point anxiety scale for the purpose of comparison with the client's rating after the presentation of deep muscle relaxation. Following this, the client is taken through the complete relaxation procedure, and the anxiety rating is again taken. If the initial rating is moderately high (say, 5, or above), one can normally expect improvement of several scale points, suggesting the client is reasonably susceptible to the procedure. If no improvement is noted, the therapist should make certain he has adequately communicated the meaning of the anxiety-rating scale to the client. If following this step, there is still no evidence that relaxation has been effective, the therapist may make an additional attempt during a subsequent therapy session. If this also fails, the therapist must conclude that this method of relaxation induction is ineffective for the particular individual and may seek another means of relaxing the subject.

Certain researchers such as Brady (1966, 1967) report good results using quick-acting barbiturates to facilitate relaxation, while others (Slater & Leavy, 1966; Wolpe, 1969) report inducing relaxation by having the individual inhale a mixture of carbon dioxide and oxygen. However, these practices are not widespread; and most practioners would not have facilities or license to use them. Another, somewhat more feasible, strategy would be to find a response other than relaxation that successfully combats anxiety. Thoughts of sexual activity or eating, or any kind of pleasurable activity might be appropriate, although assertive responses are the most likely candidates.

In summary, then, before embarking upon desensitization the therapist should:

1. Determine that the client suffers from reasonably few phobias.
2. Determine that he can imagine negative scenes with appropriate emotion.
3. Determine that the deep-muscle-relaxation procedure can induce relaxation.

In view of the many "tests" that the client must pass before desensitization is begun, the reader might come to the conclusion that most individuals are poor candidates for this type of therapy. Such a conclusion is quite unfounded. Clinical and research findings strongly suggest that most individuals have relatively few phobias, can imagine fearsome scenes with the appropriate emotion, and are quite amenable to relaxation using the deep-muscle-relaxation procedure. The most compelling reason for employing systematic desensitization, of course, is that the method has met with such widespread success in the clinic, as well as in the laboratory. Clinical and experimental research supporting the efficacy of this method are reviewed later in the chapter.

The aforementioned screening procedures, as well as the first presentation of deep muscle relaxation, may on occasion be completed by the end of the first meeting; certainly in the majority of cases this can be accomplished by the end of the second or third session. Having decided to employ desensitization, the next task is to set up the hierarchy. The hierarchy is a graded series of situations or scenes that the client is later to imagine while in a state of relaxation. The scenes depict realistic, concrete situations relevant to the client's phobia. They may involve situations that the client has experienced or situations that he anticipates experiencing. It is important to point out that primary responsibility for thinking of items to be included in the hierarchy belongs to the client since only he has first-hand knowledge of what sorts of situations cause him anxiety. While some research (see Paul & Shannon, 1966) has suggested that progress may be achieved using a hierarchy not specifically tailored to a given client, individuals with the "same" phobia have had different learning histories and cannot be expected to respond in precisely the same manner given a particular scene. The therapist, of course, must present as much structure and aid as is necessary. He might begin by suggesting a "homework" assignment in which the client is to write down on index cards details describing a variety of scenes or situations pertinent to the phobia. Since the completed hierarchy is to be graduated with respect to the degree of anxiety elicited by the different scenes, the client is told that he is to select scenes that give rise to intense anxiety (9 and 10 on the anxiety scale), moderately strong anxiety (7 and 8), moderate anxiety (5 and 6), mild anxiety (2–4), and little or no anxiety (1 and 2).

At this point, it is probably well for the therapist to assist the client in setting up a few hierarchy items. A good way to accomplish this while providing additional structure is to set up anchor points for the hierarchy. This might consist of having the client think of an item that might be a 1 or a 2 on the anxiety scale. If the client were dog phobic, perhaps seeing a chained white toy poodle 100 yards away might qualify. The therapist should point out to the client that he must describe the scene in enough detail so that when the therapist presents the scene during desensitization, the client will indeed be imagining the correct scene. If the client presented the above poodle scene, the therapist might ask where the dog is located, what it is doing, to what it is chained, something about the neighborhood, and perhaps the time of day. Having provided an anchor for the low end of the hierarchy, the therapist then proceeds to establish the high anchor, by requesting a 9 or a 10. The client might suggest having an unchained German shepherd approach him. As before, the therapist must gather additional, detailed information. It should be pointed out to the client that the anchor points are not to be viewed as absolute, and that if he thinks of other items higher than the one just described or lower than the "low" anchor, he is simply to adjust the ratings of the old anchors accordingly.

The client should be instructed that in doing his homework, he should try to come up with scenes or situations that represent all 10 levels of anxiety so that the hierarchy is uniformly graduated. The total number of hierarchy items will, of course, depend upon the severity and breadth of the phobia, as Marquis and Morgan (1969) have pointed out. These authors suggest that in most cases, 10 items is sufficient, although for very severe anxiety reactions the gaps in a 10-item hierarchy may be too large to bridge. Also, for phobic reactions that have generalized to a variety of situations, 10 items may not be sufficient to cover all relevant situations. As a rule of thumb, the client might be instructed to develop a 10–15-item hierarchy, and if it appears that the severity or breadth of the phobia is such that this is inadequate, additional items may be introduced during the course of desensitization.

When the client returns with the completed hierarchy, the therapist should examine the scene descriptions with the client to insure that sufficient detail has been presented. Since the client has rated each item on the 10-point anxiety scale, it is now possible to present the hierarchy in graduated fashion. However, it is possible that the client has made scaling errors in setting up the hierarchy (for example, an item that he rated as "4" elicits more anxiety than another item rated "6"). While the consequences of such an error are not disastrous, errors of this nature will probably slow up therapy. As a safeguard against such errors, the therapist might ask the client to order the items in terms of the amount of anxiety elicited, independent of the previous anxiety ratings. If no inconsistencies appear between the prior ratings and the rankings, the hierarchy may be considered complete enough to begin therapy. If inconsistencies do appear, this can be pointed out, and the client can be asked to rerate the discrepant items.

The following are four hierarchies. The first two were obtained by Rimm; the third is taken from Wolpe (1969); and the fourth from Marquis and Morgan (1969). For Rimm's hierarchies, the first two items are presented here as they were presented to the clients, with the remainder presented in abbreviated form. The remaining two hierarchies are presented entirely in abbreviated form. The abbreviated items are presented to provide the reader with a general feel for hierarchy construction. Again, it must be stressed that items or scenes actually presented to the client would normally contain more detail.

The first hierarchy was used with a 40-year-old male who had developed a fear of heights shortly after his discharge from the Army Air Force during World War II. He was a navigator and had flown a large number of combat missions; he attributed his phobia to his wartime experiences. Items are in order of increasing anxiety.

1. You are beginning to climb the ladder leaning against the side of your house. You plan to work on the roof. Your hands are on the ladder, and your foot is on the first rung.

2. You are halfway up the ladder, and you happen to look down. You see the lawn below you and a walkway.

3. Driving with the family, road begins to climb.

4. Driving with family on California coastal highway, with dropoff to the right.

5. On California seashore cliff, approximately 30 feet from edge.

6. On California seashore cliff, approximately 6 feet from edge.

7. Driving with family, approaching mountain summit.

8. In commercial airliner, at the time of takeoff.

9. In commercial airliner, at an altitude of 30,000 feet.

10. In airliner, at an altitude of 30,000 with considerable turbulence.

11. On a California seaside cliff, approximately 2 feet (judged to be a safe distance) from the edge and looking down.

12. Climbing the town water tower to assist in painting, about 10 feet from ground.

13. Same as above, but about 20 feet from ground.

14. On the catwalk around the water tank, painting the tank.

Paul (1969b) has distinguished between *thematic* hierarchies, referring to hierarchies in which items are related to the same basic theme or label ("height" in the above example) and *spatial-temporal* hierarchies, in which the individual fears a rather specific situation or event, and where the items are graded with respect to how close they are in space (example: "distance from seaside cliff," or "height on water tower," in the above hierarchy) or time to the target situation. Paul would refer to the above as a *combined* hierarchy, since it is both thematic and spatial.

The second hierarchy was used with an insurance salesman in his early 40s. He experienced anxiety primarily when anticipating professional contacts with co-workers or clients, especially when there was some possibility of failure. It is a thematic hierarchy.

1. You are in your office with an agent, R.C., discussing a prospective interview. The client in question is stalling on his payments, and you must tell R.C. what to do.

2. It is Monday morning and you are at your office. In a few minutes you will attend the regularly scheduled sales meeting. You are prepared for the meeting.

3. Conducting an exploratory interview with a prospective client.
4. Sitting at home. The telephone rings.
5. Anticipating returning a call from the district director.
6. Anticipating returning a call from a stranger.
7. Entering the Monday sales meeting, unprepared.
8. Anticipating a visit from the regional director.
9. A fellow agent requests a joint visit with a client.
10. On a joint visit with a fellow agent.
11. Attempting to close a sale.
12. Thinking about attending an agents' and managers' meeting.
13. Thinking of contacting a client who should have been contacted earlier.
14. Thinking about calling a prospective client.
15. Thinking about the regional director's request for names of prospective agents.
16. Alone, driving to prospective client's home.
17. Calling a prospective client.

The next hierarchy, reported by Wolpe (1969, p. 117) was successfully employed with a 24-year-old female student. One of her problems was debilitating examination anxiety. Since the target situation seems rather specific, the hierarchy that follows is best described as spatial-temporal.

1. Four days before an examination.
2. Three days before an examination.
3. Two days before an examination.
4. One day before an examination.
5. The night before an examination.
6. The examination paper lies face down before her.
7. Awaiting the distribution of examination papers.
8. Before the unopened doors of the examination room.
9. In the process of answering an examination paper.
10. On the way to the university on the day of an examination.

Note that the first five items lie along a very natural temporal continuum. One might have expected, "On the way to the university . . . ," to be the next item, but instead this item is at the very top of the hierarchy. Similarly, "The examination paper . . ." item, contrary to what might have been expected, is not especially near the top of the hierarchy. This particular example is instructive in that it illustrates how idiosyncratic hierarchies really are and how important it is for the therapist to insure that the order of items is imposed by the client, rather than by the therapist on so-called logical or intuitive grounds.

The last hierarchy to be presented is reported in Marquis and Morgan (1969, p. 28). It was used with an individual who was extremely sensitive to criticism, especially in relation to the general subject of "mental health." It is a good example of a thematic hierarchy.

1. Friend on the street: "Hi, how are you?"
2. Friend on the street: "How are you feeling these days?"
3. Sister: "You've got to be careful so they don't put you in the hospital."
4. Wife: "You shouldn't drink beer while you are taking medicine."
5. Mother: "What's the matter, don't you feel good?"
6. Wife: "It's just you yourself, it's all in your head."
7. Service station attendant: "What are you shaking for?"
8. Neighbor borrows rake: "Is there something wrong with your leg? Your knees are shaking."
9. Friend on the job: "Is your blood pressure O.K.?"
10. Service station attendant: "You are pretty shaky, are you crazy or something?"

Before starting desensitization, the client should be asked to think of one or two scenes that he is able to imagine clearly and that give rise to pleasant, relaxing sensations. During desensitization, the client may be asked to imagine these scenes in order to facilitate relaxation between the presentation of hierarchy items. Scenes used by our clients have included the following: "Sitting on the front stoop of a mountain cabin drinking beer. It is a warm clear day and it is late in the afternoon." "On a massage table being massaged after a vigorous workout." "At home on a Sunday afternoon, listening to a favorite aria from Madame Butterfly." It is probably a good idea to encourage the client to practice imagining the scenes at home until he becomes adept at immediately bringing the appropriate images to mind when requested to do so.

The client and therapist are now ready to begin the actual desensitization procedure. The client by now probably has had several occasions to practice relaxation on his own and should experience little difficulty in inducing self-relaxation in a matter of several minutes. If, for some reason he cannot induce a state of relaxation in himself approximating "1" on the anxiety scale (certainly no higher than "2"), additional guided instruction is in order. However, the client should be encouraged to practice relaxation on his own until he can induce the desired state of relaxation in a relatively short period of time. When the client does indicate he is at or near "1," and there are no visible signs of anxiety, such as irregular breathing, movement in the extremities or around the mouth, the therapist may prepare him for the first scene.

The client is told he is going to be asked to imagine a scene, and he is to imagine it as clearly as possible. He is told that it is important to imagine only the scene presented to him. It is stressed that he imagine the scene as *he* would actually perceive it, in contrast to imagining an observor's view of him in the situation. He is advised that if the scene begins to change, he should "change it back" to its original form. Finally, he is told that if he experiences any anxiety at all, he should *immediately* signal this by raising his finger. Therapists differ somewhat with respect to how long a given scene should be imagined, although a fixed duration of 7–10 seconds from the time the scene has been presented is rather typical (Paul, 1969c) if no anxiety is signaled. Wolpe (1969) has suggested having the client *signal* when he has *gained* a clear image of the scene presented to him, and then having him continue imagining the scene for some specified interval, usually 5–7 seconds.[2]

The procedure of timing the duration of imagining from when the client signals having attained the image has two decided advantages over beginning the timing when the therapist has completed describing the scene. First, it allows for much better control over the amount of time the client is actually experiencing the image. This reduces the likelihood that the client will fail to signal anxiety, not because he has been desensitized to the scene, but because he did not have sufficient time to imagine it clearly. Second, the requirement that the client signal when experiencing a clear image acts as a built-in reminder to him that attaining clear, realistic images is an essential part of the treatment. Throughout the remainder of our discussion we will assume the following procedure (unless otherwise indicated) for presenting scenes: The client is given prior instructions to raise his finger when he is imagining the scene clearly. The therapist describes the scene to be imagined; and when the client signals a clear image, the therapist allows approximately 7 seconds to elapse (if no anxiety is signaled) before instructing the client to cease imagining the scene.

The first hierarchy scene is now presented. If no anxiety is signaled, when the 7 seconds have elapsed, the client should be instructed to stop imagining the scene. We are in agreement with Wolpe's (1969) suggestion that the client's level of anxiety be assessed, even after an item is successfully completed. This can be accomplished by quietly asking him where he "is" on the 10-point anxiety scale. It is not uncommon for subjects to indicate an elevation of 1 point or 2 on the scale, even though they failed to signal anxiety while imagining the scene. However, if no anxiety is signaled, and no increase in rated anxiety is reported (which usually means the client is still at "1"), and no signs of anxiety are apparent following an interval of 15–30 seconds, the client should be ready for the second presentation of the same scene.

The procedure is precisely the same for the second presentation as

---

[2] A somewhat similar procedure was suggested by Cautela (1966).

that for the first presentation. If anxiety is not signaled during the second presentation, and if there is no increase in rated or visible anxiety, the therapist should inquire whether the image was indeed clear before introducing the next hierarchy item. The therapist should make similar inquiries from time to time throughout the treatment procedure. Sometimes clients are able to avoid anxiety by surpressing or otherwise modifying the scenes so as to eliminate noxious elements. As an illustration, Rimm treated a client who was able to imagine without anxiety interpersonal scenes that in real life elicited considerable anxiety simply by blotting out the faces of the people involved. It was pointed out that this was self-defeating, and with a little additional practice, the client was able to include the missing faces.

Especially with beginning therapists, there is a strong tendency to "reinforce" the subject for not signaling anxiety. This may manifest itself in the therapist's saying (sometimes with a note of relief in his voice), "Good." While it might be argued that such a practice is therapeutic because it rewards and thereby strengthens the tendency to relax while imagining, there is the very real danger that what is being strengthened is the tendency *not to report anxiety*, independent of how the client feels. This is especially likely to be the case if, in addition to praising the client for not signaling anxiety, the therapist remains silent (or subtly conveys discomfort or displeasure) following the client's anxiety signals. To guard against this effect, we recommend that the therapist have some standard instruction whenever he wishes the client to cease imagining a scene, independent of whether anxiety was signaled: "Now I want you to stop imagining the scene" will probably suffice.

If the client signals anxiety while imagining any hierarchy scene, the therapist should immediately request that he stop imagining the scene, and steps should be taken to return the client to his former state of relaxation. For many a client, simply suggesting that he relax once again will result in deep relaxation in very short order. For others, several minutes may be required before the client indicates he is at or near "1" on the anxiety scale. In such cases, a more efficient procedure would be to have the client imagine the previously described pleasant scene. The positive feelings arising from imagining the pleasant scene are usually sufficient to overcome the remaining anxiety. If following about 1 minute of imagining the pleasant scene (with the client indicating a clear image), anxiety is *still* reported, the therapist might inquire which muscles still feel tense and then have the client perform the tension–relaxation exercises on those muscle groups. Regardless of the procedure used to induce relaxation following an anxiety signal, it is important that the therapist insure that a state of deep relaxation has been attained before desensitization is resumed. If there are no physical signs of anxiety, and if the client states himself at or near "1," it can be assumed that such a state has been reached.

The time elapsing between the anxiety signal and the resumption of desensitization is simply that period of time required to reinstate relaxation. If the anxiety signal occurred during the first presentation of a particular hierarchy scene, following relaxation induction, the same scene is presented again.

If during the second presentation, anxiety is still signaled, this may indicate that the client is not yet ready for this scene. If the scene in question is the first (lowest) of the hierarchy, the client and therapist must think of a new scene even less anxiety provoking than the present one. If the scene is not the first of the hierarchy, it may be that there is still some anxiety attached to the preceding scene. Therefore, following relaxation induction, the preceding scene is again presented. One or two presentations are usually enough to remove any residual anxiety associated with this scene, although this must be corroborated by the absence of an anxiety signal from the client. Following this step, the scene in question should be presented again.

A repeated signaling of anxiety at this point may indicate that the client is not sticking to the scene presented to him; instead he may be making modifications or additions so that the scene actually corresponds to a scene higher on the hierarchy. Such activity can be determined by asking the client to describe in detail what it was he experienced. This inquiry should deal not only with what the client visualized, but, in addition, what sorts of ruminative self-verbalizations he engaged in. Indeed, the client might visualize the scene as it was presented, but verbalize to himself some catastrophic circumstance not directly associated with the scene. For instance, we observed an individual being desensitized for a fear of flying. He was especially fearful when flying over open water. An inquiry revealed that when imagining such a scene, he would ruminate on the possibility of being eaten by sharks were the plane to crash into the sea. If the client has been changing the scene, or ruminating, in this manner, the therapist should remind him that it is essential to stay with the scene as presented to him. This is usually sufficient to enable the client to then imagine the scene without an increase in anxiety. If, in fact, the client indicates he *has* been imagining the scene as it was presented to him, and the hypothesis that the previous item was not completely desensitized has been ruled out, the therapist must now assume that the gap between the present and prior item is too great, and an additional hierarchy item must be constructed. As with all hierarchy items, the primary source must be the client, although the therapist might suggest that it be somewhat similar in content to the two adjacent hierarchy items and that it give rise to a degree of anxiety about midway between that elicited by the two adjacent items.

If the client does not signal anxiety during the first presentation of a given scene, but does during the second presentation, following relaxation induction the therapist should present the same scene again. If anxiety is not signaled, the item may be considered completed (although a cautious therapist may wish to present it one additional time). If the client *does* signal anxiety, the therapist should revert to the strategies just described.

This completes our discussion of the basic desensitization procedure, which is normally followed until the hierarchy has been successfully completed. However, before leaving the procedure section of this chapter, we must consider several additional important points relating to the mechanics of desensitization.

Transition from One Session to the Next

It is common practice (Marquis & Morgan, 1969) to begin a desensitization session with the last item successfully completed during the previous session. This provides a natural continuity between sessions and also serves as a check on whether any relapse has occurred.

It is also common practice to avoid ending a given session with an anxiety signal. As Lazarus and Rachman (1957) have pointed out, the client is likely to recall those events associated with the conclusion of the session. To insure that the session does end on a pleasant note, care should be taken *not* to present new hierarchy items during the last few minutes of the therapy hour. Instead, the time may be spent in other activities; for instance, in discussing the progress of therapy.

Length of the Desensitization Session

Wolpe (1969) reports that a typical desensitization session lasts 15–30 minutes. And Marquis and Morgan (1969) suggest that few individuals can tolerate much more than 20 minutes of continuous desensitization. While desensitization cannot be described as painful, it does require considerable effort and concentration on the part of the client; in most instances, 20 or 30 minutes might be thought of as a reasonable upper limit. In fact, in most instances, practical considerations limit the time that can be devoted to desensitization. Assuming the standard 50-minute therapeutic "hour," at least a portion of the time will be spent discussing the course of therapy and relevant life experiences. If the additional time required for the initial relaxation induction is added to this, it is unlikely that the remaining time will be in excess of 30 or 35 minutes.

On the other hand, if time is available, and if the client is able to maintain an adequate level of concentration and motivation, there is no theoretical reason for so limiting the duration of the session. In fact, Wolpin and Pearsall (1965) report successfully eliminating a phobic reaction in a single, continuous 90-minute session.

Desensitization for Multiple Phobias

Another question has to do with strategy to employ when the client wishes to work on more than one phobia, which is often the case (although Wolpe, 1969, reports that few clients evidence more than four phobias). Both Lazarus (1964) and Wolpe (1969) treat two or more phobias simultaneously, setting up separate hierarchies for each, and often drawing from each hierarchy during any given session. We consider this strategy more efficient than one treating the separate hierarchies sequentially.

Real-Life Contacts with the Phobic Stimuli

Frequently the therapist must make a decision regarding whether or not his client should be encouraged to place himself in situations depicted in the hierarchy *prior to* the completion of therapy. Both Bandura (1969) and Wolpe (1969) believe that such *in vivo* contacts may be beneficial, and Garfield, Darwin, Singer, and McBreaty (1967) report that such a procedure facilitated desensitization. However, a word of caution is in order. It would probably be most unwise to encourage the client to place himself in a situation corresponding to a hierarchy item not yet desensitized. While there might be some generalization of improvement from already completed hierarchy items to such a situation, the reverse could very easily take place. That is, the client might experience very intense anxiety in such a situation, which by the process of generalization might then cause previously desensitized scenes to give rise to anxiety. This, if it were to occur, would retard therapy, especially if the client viewed the experience as a failure indicating that the therapy was not really "working."

Even if the client's attempts at "testing himself" are in keeping with the progress already made in desensitization, inadvertently he may find himself suddenly confronted with a situation much higher on the hierarchy. For instance, a man being treated for sexual impotency arising from anxiety may have reached the stage where he can fondle his partner while maintaining an erection. If, however, his partner were to demand suddenly that they engage in coitus, the ensuing anxiety might result in loss of erection and feelings of failure combining to effect a serious setback to therapy. Unless one can insure that situations corresponding to a given hierarchy level are not likely to be transformed into more anxiety-provoking situations, it would probably be best to discourage such *in vivo* activity until the hierarchy is complete.

The Importance of Relaxation

Although some evidence (Davison, 1968) suggests that relaxation is necessary if desensitization is to be effective, Schubot (1966) found that this was true only for subjects who were initially *extremely* phobic. For moderately fearful subjects, the same degree of improvement occurred irrespective of whether relaxation was or was not paired with anxiety. It seems likely, however, that individuals seeking therapy for their phobias would be more like the extreme phobics than the moderate phobics in the Shubot study, suggesting the importance of relaxation in a clinical setting.

Nawas (see Nawas, Welsch, & Fishman, 1970; Miller & Nawas, 1970) and his co-workers have presented evidence suggesting that relaxation may not be necessary for successful desensitization, although their description of the snake-phobic subjects they used suggested that a good many of them may have been only moderately phobic. Interestingly enough, in one study in which relaxation was compared with other "competing responses" (muscle tension and neutral tasks), while the other competing responses when paired with phobic scenes were somewhat effective in causing fear reduction, relaxation was found to be significantly more effective.

Implosive therapy (discussed in detail in Chapter VIII), which bears a very superficial resemblance to desensitization, appears to hold some promise as an effective means for eliminating phobias. This procedure does not employ anything remotely akin to relaxation. However, the procedures and theoretical assumptions associated with implosive therapy differ so extensively from those for desensitization that results of research employing implosive therapy may have very little bearing on the role of relaxation in desensitization.

In conclusion, while evidence does suggest that muscle relaxation is not always necessary for fear alleviation (Rachman, 1968), there is considerable evidence that it facilitates systematic desensitization. Until research contraindicating the use of relaxation is forthcoming, the reader is encouraged to employ this procedure whenever desensitization is attempted.

The Importance of the Ascending Hierarchy

As has been indicated, the standard desensitization format requires that scenes be presented in graduated fashion. Items are ranked according to the amount of fear each elicits, and when presenting the scenes, the least fear-arousing ones are presented first. While available evidence suggests that this procedure is effective, one study (Krapfl, 1967) found that presenting the hierarchy in *descending* order was about as effective in reducing snake phobic behavior as the standard ascending-order procedure. By eliminating anxiety from the highest items of the hierarchy, by a process of generalization one would expect an automatic reduction of anxiety associated with the lower items. Thus, the procedure of presenting items in the descending order might seem to be more efficient. However, it should be pointed out that when items high on the hierarchy are presented first, the intense anxiety associated with them will probably necessitate a very large number of presentations before they are successfully desensitized. This is in contrast to the relatively few presentations required when the usual ascending order is employed. In other words, the descending-order procedure may not necessarily be more efficient. More important, as Bandura (1969) points out, the descending order procedure may cause the client considerable momentary distress (rarely encountered when the standard method is used), which may result in his prematurely terminating therapy.

Sexual Arousal and Anxiety

If, as Wolpe (1958, 1969) suggested, feelings of sexual arousal can inhibit anxiety, one ought to be able to effect desensitization by pairing such feelings with phobic stimuli. In actual practice, Wolpe (1958, 1969) has tended to limit the therapeutic use of sexual arousal to problems that are themselves sexual in content, including impotence and frigidity. Additionally, the practice has usually been to employ therapeutic sexual arousal in real-life (*in vivo*) situations, rather than when the client is simply imagining such situations. When a client has a readily available, and potentially understanding, sexual partner, the *in vivo* procedures might be expected to result in more rapid improvement than would be expected using systematic (symbolic) desensitization. In fact, Masters and Johnson (1970), who employ *in vivo* procedures somewhat similar to those prescribed by Wolpe, report phenomenal improvement rates following only 2 weeks of intensive treatment. Wolpe's general treatment approach will be presented here in summary form. For a more detailed description the reader is referred to Wolpe (1969) or to Masters and Johnson's (1970) excellent work, *Human Sexual Inadequacy*.

Treatment of sexual disorder should probably be preceded by a careful medical examination, to rule out physical or endrocrinological factors. In his approach to treatment, Wolpe (1969) places great emphasis on the availability of a cooperative sexual partner. The nature of the sexual disorder is explained to the partner, who is instructed to avoid making the client tense or anxious during sex-related activities. The psychological and physiological aspects of sexual functioning are discussed with both partners, to eliminate fears and misconceptions that either may have. The partners are dissuaded from viewing sexual malfunctioning as necessarily arising from some more deep-seated and generalized psychological disorder, or arising from some inherent lack of manliness or womanliness. The partners are informed that there is no urgency whatsoever for having immediate intercourse, thus removing the debilitating pressure to "perform." A series of self-paced, successive approximations to the desired sexual behavior is then begun. As with systematic desensitization hierarchies, the *in vivo* hierarchy is geared to the individual client's anxieties. If the partner is a relative stranger to the client (that is, Masters and Johnson's "surrogate partner," or as Wolpe recommends, if no one else is available, an understanding prostitute), it might be best to begin with a purely social encounter, such as having dinner together. More typically, if the partners are married, the hierarchy might begin with their lying in bed nude or partially nude, with no thought of physical contact of any kind. When this can be achieved with comfort, the next step might involve mutual touching, specifically avoiding genital or breast contact. This might be followed by a series of touches or caresses involving progressively more genital contact or perhaps by mutual hugging. *It is essential that at each stage the client feel that no additional demands will be made by his partner.* With this pressure removed, the client is much more likely to experience sexual arousal, which will further inhibit anxiety.

In treating impotence, when the male has reached the stage where he can lie on top of his partner without anxiety, the next step might involve having the penis contact the clitoris or other areas of the external genitalia, but without insertion. When this can be done with total comfort, a small amount of insertion might be followed by additional insertion and eventually movement. In the treatment of impotence, as well as other sexual disorders, it is well to discourage attempts at sexual activity when either of the partners is clearly fatigued or when situational factors (for example, momentary anger at one's partner) result in a temporary loss of desire. It is essential that the partners be candid with each other in communicating such feelings.

In treating premature ejaculation, Wolpe (1969) recommends a technique originally suggested by Semans (1956). The partner is encouraged to manipulate the penis, stopping just prior to ejaculation. This is repeatedly done, several times per session, over several sessions until the male can delay ejaculation for a half hour or more. Masters and Johnson (1970) describe a technique (the "squeeze technique") in which the partner manipulates the penis, but just prior to ejaculation applies pres-

× sec duration

sure to the head of the penis; this has the effect of inhibiting ejaculation. When in the vagina, just prior to ejaculation, the penis may be withdrawn, and the squeeze technique may be employed prior to reinsertion.

In describing the treatment of frigidity, Wolpe (1969) stresses systematic (imaginal), rather than *in vivo*, desensitization. While there is ample reason to believe systematic desensitization can be effective in eliminating this disorder, Masters and Johnson (1970) report extraordinarily high success rates (over 80%) using a short-term *in vivo* procedure coupled with a considerable amount of counseling. The procedure involves successive approximations, beginning with nongenital contact, proceeding to genital manipulation, and then to various coital positions. In the treatment of frigidity, as well as other sexual disorders, Masters and Johnson place great emphasis on the fostering of communication between partners, especially in relation to the sharing of sensations and feelings. Thus, in the *in vivo* treatment of the frigid woman, her partner's sexual interactions are guided in large measure by her own verbal and nonverbal cues. A cursory account of the Masters and Johnson treatment of frigidity would not do this well-reasoned and well-researched procedure justice, and the reader, therefore, is referred to their book.

Empirical Findings: Case Histories

As is often the case, systematic desensitization was adopted and employed by a number of therapists well in advance of the publication of the first reasonably well-controlled experiment supporting its efficacy (Lang & Lazovik, 1963). Probably the primary reason for this was the high "success rate" reported in the literature by practitioners, most especially Wolpe (1952, 1954, 1958, 1961). In Wolpe's (1958) most definitive work, *Psychotherapy by Reciprocal Inhibition*, he reported that of 210 clients treated, nearly 90% were either cured or much improved with a mean of only 31 interviews. It should be pointed out that many of these 210 individuals received procedures other than systematic desensitization (for instance, assertive training), although Paul (1969b) concluded after reviewing all of Wolpe's published data that Wolpe's success for desensitization alone was 92%. A "success" for Wolpe (1961) meant that the original problem (for example, phobia) had to be no greater than 20% of its original intensity, as measured by the client's rating.

Wolpe (1958) provided data indicating that for other forms of therapy, primarily psychoanalytic, the success rate did not exceed 60%. Comparisons of this nature are fraught with difficulties, since the groups (those treated by Wolpian methods versus those treated by traditional methods) may not be comparable with respect to intensity or nature of the presenting complaints, the duration of therapy, the criteria for assessing improvement, or the number of "dropouts." Also, the reader should be reminded that success in the clinic, even with such a large number of individuals, does not "prove" that a particular method really works (see Chapter I).

Lazarus (Paul, 1969b), who received his training from Wolpe, treated 220 individuals with systematic desensitization. Using improvement criteria similar to Wolpe's, Lazarus obtained a success rate of 85%, although many of the individuals in the sample received other forms of behavior therapy. Hain, Butcher, and Stevenson (1966), using systematic desensitization, but other procedures as well, reported improvement in 78% of the 27 patients they treated. Although the psychological and psychiatric literature contains a very large number of additional case histories with similarly positive results, in most instances, either the number of patients per report is small (usually only one), or the data for a variety of reasons are questionable.

Most behavior therapists in presenting case history data report not only the results at the time therapy was completed, but results from a later time. The follow-up period varies considerably from therapist to therapist and from patient to patient; and in many cases, the patient cannot be contacted for a follow-up interview. For patients for whom follow-up data are available, the period is usually no less than 1 month following termination of treatment and may be as long as several years. As we have suggested elsewhere (Chapter I), many traditional therapists would predict that following successful alleviation of a "symptom" using behavior therapy, that symptom would reappear, or a new symptom would replace the old one. Given the limitations of the case history method, it is still impressive that well-documented cases of symptomatic relapse or symptom substitution reportedly are very rare indeed (Wolpe, 1958, 1969).

In conclusion, while case history data cannot be used to establish the final validity of desensitization, a very large number of case histories clearly suggests that desensitization may be effective with a wide range of anxiety-related disorders and that improvement is enduring, with the appearance of substitute symptoms quite rare. For a thorough review of this literature, the reader is referred to Paul (1969b).

Empirical Findings: Experimental Evidence

Snake Phobia

Lang and Lazovik (1963) published the first controlled experiment testing systematic desensitization. This experiment and a considerable amount of the research to follow employed snake-phobic individuals as subjects. The impetus for choosing this phobia as the target behavior in a great deal of the behavior therapy research arose partly from the fact that fear of harmless snakes is relatively common in our culture. Additionally, however, the symbolic sexual significance of the snake in psychoanalytic writings (Fenichel, 1945) is well known, and it was felt that if any maladaptive behavior could be considered as symptomatic of an underlying psychosexual conflict, it should have been fear of harmless snakes. If the psychoanalytic point of view is generally correct, one would predict that snake avoidance would be very difficult to dislodge, and that alleviation of this fear, when it did occur, would almost certainly be followed by symptom substitution.

Lang and Lazovik (1963) found appreciably greater reduction in the behavioral measure of snake avoidance for subjects who had undergone desensitization than for nontreated control subjects, who showed almost no change. Similar, though somewhat weaker results were obtained when the measure of change was the subject's own rating of how he felt in the presence of the test snake. Six months later a follow-up was conducted, and interestingly enough, the difference between the desensitization group and the controls on both measures was somewhat greater than it was immediately following treatment. Care was taken to determine whether new symptoms (phobias) appeared, and the evidence for symptom substitution was negative.

By adhering to the rules of sound experimental logic, Lang and Lazovik were able to provide convincing evidence that the set of procedures labeled *systematic desensitization* does result in behavior change. It is quite possible, however, that such a behavior change has little to do with the specifics of desensitization, but instead results from the fact that the subjects *perceived* the procedures as therapeutic and expected them to work.

In order to check on the possibility of placebo effects, Lang, Lazovik, and Reynolds (1965) presented desensitization to one group of snake phobics and what they called pseudotherapy to a second group. The pseudotherapy, or placebo procedure, included some of the elements of the desensitization procedure, but excluded crucial elements that according to Wolpe (1958, 1969) would have been necessary for improvement. This procedure included as well a general discussion of different aspects of the subject's life. These experimenters found greater improvement in the desensitization subjects than in the pseudotherapy subjects, who behaved very similarly to subjects who had received no treatment of any kind in the previous study (Lang & Lazovik, 1963). Thus, it would appear that the success obtained by Lang and Lazovik in their original study could not have been the result of a simple placebo effect.

Davison (1968), also working with snake phobics, provided evidence suggesting that the *pairing* of imagined fearful stimuli and relaxation is critical in systematic desensitization. One group of subjects received standard desensitization (that is, relaxation plus the presentation of hierarchy items). A second group received relaxation paired with hierarchy items unrelated to the snake phobia (common childhood experiences). A third group was exposed to the snake hierarchy, but without relaxation; and a fourth group served as a no-treatment control. In terms of the subject's willingness to approach a harmless snake, the desensitization group showed significantly greater improvement than each of the other groups (they showed virtually no change from pretest to posttest). Among desensitization subjects, a high positive correlation was found between behavioral improvement and anxiety reduction as measured by self-report. No follow-up was reported.

The Davison study provides additional support for the efficacy of systematic desensitization. More important, it lends support to a counterconditioning interpretation (that is, the necessity of relaxation as a competing response). However, as we have indicated earlier in the chapter, the precise role of relaxation is still a matter of some controversy.

Anxiety in Public Speaking

Paul (1966) demonstrated the effectiveness of desensitization in the treatment of a widespread and frequently debilitating fear, the fear of public speaking and related interpersonal anxiety. In addition, he showed that desensitization was superior to traditional insight-oriented therapy when both forms of therapy were conducted for the same length of time (5 weeks, 1 hour per week). It might be argued that no one could expect progress in traditional therapy in only 5 weeks. However, the 5-week period was selected because the therapists conducting the insight therapy, each of whom was quite experienced, indicated that this period of time would be sufficient to effect a change in the target problem. The main measures of speech anxiety were self-report prior to having to give a speech before a strange audience, objective manifestations of fear while giving the speech, and physiological measures of emotion determined just prior to giving the speech. Although insight subjects showed somewhat greater improvement than nontreated controls, they did not differ in performance from an additional group receiving an attention placebo treatment; and again, the desensitization group was superior to all other groups on all three measures. Six weeks later, a follow-up revealed very similar results. At that time, a careful check on symptom substitution provided no evidence that such had occurred.

Woy and Efran (1972) reported a partial replication of Paul's study in which an additional variable, subject expectancy, was manipulated. One group of speech-anxious subjects was given a drug described as a fast-acting tranquilizer and told that this would augment treatment. A second group was told they would not receive the drug. Subjects in both groups received five 50-minute desensitization sessions. A third group served as nontreated controls. Consistent with Paul's findings, on most measures the desensitization subjects improved significantly more than did the controls. On only one measure, self-perception of improvement, did the positive-expectancy group show significantly greater change than the neutral-expectancy group. No follow-up was reported.[3]

Test Anxiety

Among members of any student population, test anxiety represents another problem area of considerable importance to the individual, since severe test anxiety can seriously impair academic performance and thus jeopardize an individual's prospective professional career. Several studies have provided evidence that test anxiety may be treated effectively using systematic desensitization. Among these are reports by Emery and Krumboltz (1967) and Suinn (1968). In both studies, test-anxious individuals receiving desensitization reported greater reduction in test anxiety than nontreated control subjects. A study by Johnson (1966), which included a placebo control group, provided additional support for desensitization as an effective means of dealing with test anxiety.

Summary

Although this review of the controlled experimentation is not meant to be exhaustive, it should be sufficient to convince the reader that there exists ample scientific evidence that systematic desensitization is an effective technique applicable to a variety of problems. One study, reported by Moore (1965), suggested that the spectrum of problems potentially amenable to successful treatment using this technique may be very broad indeed. Moore worked with asthmatic adults and children and found

---

[3] As Woy and Efran (1972) noted, somewhat conflicting results regarding the importance of expectancy in systematic desensitization have appeared in the literature. For example, Oliveau, Agras, Leitenberg, Moore, and Wright (1969) and Leitenberg, Agras, Barlow, and Oliveau (1969) found expectancy effects; whereas McGlynn and Mapp (1970) and McGlynn and Williams (1970) did not. More recently, Persely and Leventhal (1972) and Borkovec (1972) have reported such effects. However, it should be pointed out that in the studies where expectancy effects were reported, significant effects of systematic desensitization in the absence of positive instructions, were also the rule.

that desensitization was superior to the control techniques in effecting improvement in maximum peak flow, a common measure of the severity of an attack. Obviously, this is not to suggest that all cases of asthma will show improvement following desensitization. However, it does suggest that there may be many problem areas not usually characterized as "phobic" that may be dealt with using desensitization.

Desensitization in Groups

In all of the just summarized studies, subjects were treated individually. Group desensitization has the obvious advantage of allowing more individuals in need of help to receive treatment. As in the case of individual treatment, experimental evidence supporting the effectiveness of desensitization in groups is impressive. The first such report came from Lazarus (1961), who worked with patients who were mainly either height phobic, claustrophic, or sexually impotent males. Subjects received either group desensitization, traditional interpretation, or traditional interpretation plus relaxation. Based upon self-report, a much larger number of individuals receiving group desensitization showed improvement than individuals in either of the other two conditions. One of the more remarkable aspects of this study was the use of very stringent behavioral tests given to participants who indicated they had improved. One month after the completion of therapy, the height phobics were required to stand on the roof of an 8-story building and count cars passing in the street below for 2 minutes; and claustrophobics had to remain in a small cubicle for 5 minutes without distress. Lazarus reported that all but two participants (among both height phobics and claustrophobics) were able to complete their task.

Since the publication of the Lazarus study, a sizable number of studies have been reported in which group desensitization was shown to be effective. Representative of these are Rachman's (1966a,b) study with spider phobics, Paul and Shannon's (1966) study with college students suffering from interpersonal anxiety, and the Taylor (1971) study, aimed at the alleviation of test anxiety. Thus, it seems clear that desensitization is effective in groups, just as it is when applied on an individual basis.

Automated Desensitization

Automated desensitization refers to the presentation of the desensitization instructions to the subject in some sort of mechanical fashion (most commonly a tape recorder), with little or no contact with a live therapist. Several studies (Melamed & Lang, 1967; Kahn & Quinlan,

1967; Lang, Melamed, & Hart, 1970; Donner & Guerney, 1969) have provided evidence suggesting that automated desensitization may be a highly effective therapeutic procedure. The technique presented by Cotler (1970) illustrates the mechanics of automated desensitization.

Subjects were snake phobics selected on the basis of a questionnaire and a behavioral-avoidance test. During a second session, the subject was presented with an explanation of desensitization and a statement of the purpose of the study, all on tape. An experimenter then answered any questions concerning the tape; and if the subject desired to participate, a future appointment was arranged. For the remainder of the treatment, the subject had no contact whatsoever with a live experimenter or therapist.

Over the next several sessions, the subject was given relaxation and visualization instructions, as well as instructions on how to use the automated apparatus, all on tape. In subsequent sessions, a standard 16-item hierarchy was presented, again on tape. The subject controlled the progress of the tape with five buttons located near his hand. He was to use the first button whenever he wanted to visualize a hierarchy scene or concentrate on relaxation. Buttons two and three were to be pressed when the subject could imagine the hierarchy scene with little or no anxiety, and depressing the buttons advanced the tape to a higher item in the hierarchy. Buttons four or five were to be depressed when the subject experienced higher levels of anxiety while imagining the hierarchy scene, and this had the effect of recycling the tape to a previously presented set of relaxation instructions. This procedure was continued until the subject was able to imagine all hierarchy scenes with minimal anxiety.

Using this highly mechanical procedure, Cotler found that subjects experienced a marked reduction in self-rating of anxiety in the presence of a harmless snake, and an appreciable increase in the tendency to approach the snake, with the improvement lasting through the 1 month follow-up. Control subjects showed little or nor improvement.

The positive results obtained with automated desensitization are important for two reasons. First, there is an obvious practical gain over treatment with a live therapist in that the patient can receive treatment at his own convenience, with the number of patients receiving simultaneous desensitization limited only by the number of automated devices available. Second, that automated desensitization can be quite successful strengthens the view that the desensitization procedure itself is therapeutically valid. If the positive results obtained with a live therapist, for example, reflected nothing more than a desire to please the therapist, one would hardly expect success with automated procedures and no therapist present.

The Theory of Desensitization

The Wolpian View

Wolpe (1958, 1969) considers desensitization as an instance of counterconditioning. Counterconditioning in this context means the substitution of an emotional response that is appropriate or adaptive to a given situation for one that is maladaptive. According to Wolpe (1958, 1969), in most instances the maladaptive emotion is anxiety. Anxiety as an emotional state has been dealt with in a variety of ways by different authors; however, Wolpe is quite specific in his use of the term: *anxiety* is primarily a pattern of activity of the sympathetic nervous system when an individual is exposed to some sort of threat. Traditionally anatomists have divided the human nervous system into three parts: the central nervous system, which includes nerves of the brain and spinal cord; the somatic nervous system, which serves the various senses, as well as so-called voluntary muscles; and the autonomic nervous system, which innervates the heart, glands, blood vessels, and other internal organs. Anatomists further divide the autonomic nervous system into two parts: the sympathetic nervous system and the parasympathetic nervous system. It is activity of the sympathetic nervous system that both laymen and scientists tend to associate with heightened emotionality. Bodily changes associated with increased autonomic activity include increased blood pressure and pulse, decreased blood circulation to the stomach, increased blood circulation to the large voluntary muscles, dryness of the mouth, and dilation of the pupils, as well as a variety of other changes. For Wolpe, these types of bodily changes taken together are the basis of the anxiety response.

Wolpe assumes that individuals learn to experience anxiety in the presence of certain stimuli through a process of classical, or Pavlovian, conditioning. For instance, a young child might be expected to have no particular feelings, positive or negative, in the presence of dogs. But if that child is bitten by a dog, anxiety associated with the experience might be expected to become conditioned to stimuli associated with the dog; for example, the sight of that particular dog. By a process of generalization, the child might experience anxiety in the presence of other dogs. The feeling of discomfort that the child would experience upon seeing a dog would have as its basis anxiety, which would motivate the child to attempt to avoid the dog.

Wolpe's theoretical interpretation of desensitization is relatively straightforward. If while experiencing stimuli usually giving rise to anxiety the person can be made to experience a response that inhibits anxiety, the effect will be a reduction in the amount of anxiety elicited by those stimuli. Wolpe used the term *reciprocal inhibition* (a term borrowed from the physiologist Sherrington, 1906) to characterize the inhibition of anxiety by some competing response. As we have suggested, there are a variety of responses that Wolpe assumes are capable of inhibiting anxiety. The ones most often used in reciprocal inhibition therapy include relaxation, assertive behavior, and sexual behavior. Physiologically, these classes of behaviors are assumed to have one principal thing in common: each is associated with a predominance of *parasympathetic* nervous activity. It is further assumed that heightened activity of the parasympathetic nervous system reciprocally inhibits activity of the sympathetic nervous system. Since sympathetic nervous activity is thought to serve as the basis for anxiety, it follows that responses such as relaxation, assertion, and sexual behavior ought to be able to inhibit anxiety.

While there is little doubt that desensitization is an extremely effective therapeutic procedure, the theoretical basis that Wolpe has provided is not without flaws. Perhaps the most serious flaw relates to his conception of anxiety as arising from sympathetic nervous activity.

There is evidence that the presentation of symbolic phobic material results in heightened sympathetic activity (Grossberg & Wilson, 1968; Rimm & Bottrell, 1969) and that relaxation induction effects a reduction in sympathetic activity, along with a reduction in the amount of anxiety the individual reports (Paul, 1969d; Paul & Trimble, 1970; Rimm, Kennedy, Miller, & Tchida, 1971). However, one must ask whether such changes in the level of sympathetic nervous activity (or the associated bodily changes) *cause* corresponding changes in felt discomfort and avoidance behavior.

One way to attempt to answer this question is to manipulate the level of sympathetic activity and see what effect this has on avoidance behavior. Wynne and Solomon (1955) surgically deactivated the sympathetic nervous system in dogs who had previously learned to avoid a painful shock whenever a warning stimulus was presented. If sympathetic activity serves as the primary motive for avoidance, the obvious prediction would be that the dogs would immediately cease making the avoidance response in the presence of the warning stimulus. The results were that the dogs showed very little tendency to reduce their level of avoidance behavior.

For obvious reasons, controlled experiments of this nature are not possible with human subjects. However, a bodily state identical to that resulting from sympathetic activity can be produced with an injection of epinephrine (also called adrenalin). In fact, when an individual is under stress, the adrenal glands release greater amounts of this hormone directly into the bloodstream, which has the effect of causing sympathetic-induced changes to continue over an extended period of time. Thus, if anxiety-like discomfort in man is caused by sympathetic activity, as Wolpe suggests, an injection of epinephrine should cause an individual to experience an elevation in anxiety. Experiments by Schachter (Schachter & Singer, 1962; Schachter & Wheeler, 1962) and his colleagues have provided convincing evidence that this is not generally true. In one experiment, subjects given epinephrine in comparison to control subjects were made more angry or more euphoric depending on whether they were exposed to a model who behaved in an obviously angry or euphoric manner. In another study, subjects who received epinephrine prior to observing a portion of a humorous film actually laughed more than subjects in the control conditions, hardly supporting the view that sympathetic-like arousal causes people to feel more anxious! It would appear, then, that in human beings, sympathetic nervous activity does not *cause* a person to experience a particular type of emotion (such as anxiety, anger, or joy), although once such a state is initiated by external circumstances, heightened sympathetic activity might well tend to exaggerate, or amplify, such an emotional state.

It follows that anxiety is not simply an elevated state of sympathetic nervous arousal, contrary to Wolpe's view. This greatly weakens one of Wolpe's main theoretical contentions: that activities such as muscle relaxation reduce anxiety by promoting a state of parasympathetic dominance that inhibits sympathetic activity. However, one must still account for why procedures such as deep muscle relaxation do result in anxiety reduction, and further, how this phenomenon relates to desensitization.

Other Theories of Desensitization

Wolpe assumed that in desensitization, anxiety is reduced by reciprocal inhibition at the level of the autonomic nervous system. One can still retain the concept of reciprocal inhibition in accounting for the effects of desensitization, as Bandura (1969) has suggested, by assuming that the inhibition of anxiety occurs in some part of the brain itself. It can be speculated that muscle relaxation in some way activates an antianxiety mechanism within the brain and that external stimuli correlated with activation of this mechanism lose their ability to evoke anxiety.

An interpretation of anxiety similar to that put forth by Jacobson (1938) stresses the importance of muscle tension per se in the anxiety state. Here it is assumed that neural messages fed back to the brain from tensed muscles constitute the basis of felt anxiety. It is further assumed that feedback from flaccid muscles is incompatible with anxiety. In desensitization, a generalized state of muscle relaxation is induced; and it is plausible to assume that stimuli paired with such a state would become less anxiety provoking.

While such an interpretation of anxiety may at best be an over-simplification, it is interesting that the layman frequently describes his response to an aversive experience by referring to muscular tension. For example, an obnoxious individual may be described as a "pain in the neck," and the anticipation of a trying event may evoke, "oh my aching back." An individual may characterize his response to a frightening experience with "my stomach was tied in knots," with the obvious connotation of painful discomfort. While anxiety is not usually thought of as focalized physical pain, it is possible that more diffuse, generalized muscular tension does indeed contribute directly to the anxiety state. Any response that reduces muscular tension would be expected to decrease anxiety. Unfortunately, such an interpretation of anxiety fails to account for why assertiveness or sexual arousal appear to reduce anxiety, since neither response is apparently marked by muscular relaxation.

Nawas, Fishman, and Pucel (1970) assumed that muscle relaxation when used in connection with desensitization acts as a distractor, shutting out the maladaptive anxiety response. Nawas *et al.* (1970) further assumed that two other processes also contribute to the success of desensitization. One is "toleration," wherein the individual becomes accustomed to the formerly noxious stimulus (noxious visual image) by being oriented to it in a graduated fashion. The other is "exhaustion," wherein repeated exposure results in the fatiguing of the maladaptive anxiety state.

There are several additional interpretations of desensitization that have a somewhat more cognitive basis. The role of cognitive factors is considered in Chapter X. For the present, these points of view are presented in summary form. London (1964) assumed that in desensitization, the subject learns to discriminate between the actual feared stimulus and the stimulus as imagined. He learns as well that experiencing images of frightening events does not lead to dire consequences. Both elements are assumed to contribute to therapeutic success. Ellis (1962) assumed that anxiety and avoidance behavior result primarily from self-verbalizations of an irrational nature. Such self-verbalizations are discouraged in desensitization, which possibly accounts for why desensitization is effective. Some writers have stressed the importance of expectations in accounting for the success of desensitization (see Wilkins, 1971), while others have emphasized the importance of the manner in which individuals interpret their own emotional responding in controlling phobic behavior (see Valins & Ray, 1967).

In conclusion, there is obviously no shortage of theoretical accounts of desensitization put forth as alternatives to Wolpe's interpretation. While each has some degree of plausibility, at this time none has attained anything approaching universal acceptance. It is quite within the realm of

possibility that a variety of different, potentially therapeutic components are combined in desensitization, with individuals differing in respect to how much they gain from each of the components. For example, one client may benefit primarily from learning how to relax his muscles in the presence of a formerly fearful stimulus; whereas for another client, the implicit discouraging of obsessional thoughts may be the most crucial element; and for a third client, learning that imagining a fearful stimulus does not have catastrophic consequences may be critical. Whatever theoretical explanation (or explanations) proves ultimately to be most valid, the reader is reminded that systematic desensitization is a highly successful therapy technique having very substantial empirical support.

III

Assertive Training

Assertive behavior is interpersonal behavior involving the honest and relatively straightforward expression of feelings. Simply stated, *assertive training* includes *any* therapeutic procedure aimed at increasing the client's ability to engage in such behavior in a socially appropriate manner. Behavioral goals usually include the expression of negative feelings such as anger and resentment, but often assertive procedures are employed to facilitate the expression of positive feelings such as affection or praise.

Increased assertiveness is assumed to benefit the client in two significant ways. First, it is thought that behaving in a more assertive fashion will instill in the client a greater feeling of well-being. In fact, as we have indicated in Chapter II, Wolpe (1958, 1969) believed that assertive responding is very similar to deep muscle relaxation in its ability to reciprocally inhibit anxiety. Subjective reports from clients undergoing assertive training have tended to corroborate the view that assertion does indeed inhibit anxiety, although this issue is taken up again in a subsequent section. Second, it is assumed that by behaving in a more assertive manner, the client will be better able to achieve significant social (as well as material) rewards and, thus obtain more satisfaction from life.

Achieving these important goals requires a good deal more than unreflective and spontaneous emoting. Thus, the therapist must devote considerable attention to likely interpersonal consequences of engaging in assertive-like behaviors. In particular, the therapist must take special pains to minimize the likelihood that the client's newly found assertiveness will be met with seriously punishing or destructive consequences. For instance, the therapist would not normally encourage his client to tell his boss to "go to hell," or to make blatant sexual overtures to a stranger on a streetcar. While it is possible that such expressions of feeling may result in momentary satisfaction or relief for the client, as interpersonal strategies they are liable to be met with disastrous consequences.

It is clear, then, that assertive training involves more than merely providing instruction and practice in the spontaneous expression of feelings (although this is usually a *part* of therapy). To illustrate: in the therapy session, a client might repeatedly and diligently rehearse asking his employer for a much-deserved raise, or asking a beautiful girl for a date. When implemented, such behaviors would involve the expression of feelings and might normally be relatively direct. Such behavior would qualify as *assertive*, but, given the large amount of dedicated rehearsal, it could hardly be labeled *spontaneous*. In a similar vein, contrary to what is sometimes assumed, assertive training is not *aggression* training, if aggression is taken to mean the impulsive expression of intense anger. In fact, as we shall see later in the chapter, assertive training may hold considerable promise for individuals who engage in self-defeating episodes of impulsive, antisocial aggression.

Background

Present-day assertive-training techniques are, to a considerable degree, based upon the writings of Wolpe (Wolpe, 1958, 1969; Wolpe & Lazarus, 1966) and, to a lesser extent, on the writings of Andrew Salter (1949, 1964). However, Salter's *Conditioned Reflex Therapy,* published in 1949, was the first major work extolling the virtues of assertive-type behavior. Thus, it may seem surprising that the writings of Wolpe and his followers have had considerably greater impact than those of Salter. There are several likely reasons for this. First, the psychiatric and psychological establishments were probably more amenable to considering a learning-based or behavioral approach in 1958 (when Wolpe's *Psychotherapy by Reciprocal Inhibition* was published) than in 1949, for during the intervening decade, Dollard and Miller's (1950) learning interpretation of psychodynamic theory was widely read, and Skinner's (1953) ultrabehavioristic *Science and Human Behavior* was beginning to have a noticeable impact. Second, for Wolpe, systematic desensitization and assertive training were closely tied theoretically, and the relatively early acceptance (in some quarters, at least) of desensitization certainly facilitated the acceptance of assertive training, à la Wolpe. Third, the manner in which Salter presented his views had the effect of antagonizing a good number of clinicians who otherwise might have made very effective use of his techniques. He attacked psychoanalysis with an unmitigated vengeance, and, since most clinicians of the day had at least some investment in psychoanalytic thinking, this could hardly endear Salter to them. He advocated assertive (his term was *excitatory*) procedures for virtually every conceivable psychological disorder and for every client who was seen as suffering from inhibition. In sharp contrast to Wolpe, Salter appeared to pay little heed to the consequences of spontaneous, impulsive behavior, a fact that could do little to enhance his credibility in the eyes of conservative clinicals. Thus, it would not have been difficult for many to dismiss Salter as a "wild man" and thereby fail to appreciate the considerable merit in his approach.

Salter's specific techniques were presented somewhat tersely in *Conditioned Reflex Therapy,* along with a large number of illustrative case histories. His six excitatory exercises (Salter, 1949, pp. 97–100) are presented below in summary form:

1. The use of *feeling talk,* which involves practice in expressing literally any feeling. Some of Salter's examples include: "I detest the man and everything he stands for"; "I like soup"; "Darling, I love you with all my heart"; "Now, that was stupid of me!"

2. The use of *facial talk,* which involves practicing facial expressions that normally go with different emotions

3. Practice in expressing a contradictory opinion when one disagrees

4. Practice in the use of *I* (our example: "I found the New England Fall breathtaking," rather than, "One finds the New England Fall breathtaking.")

5. Practice in agreeing when complimented (our example: "Yes, I like this tie, too," rather than, "What, this old thing!")

6. Practice in improvising

Salter's approach, in the main, appears to include the application of the above exercises in conjunction with a great amount of exhortation to the client to behave more assertively.

Wolpe was using assertive training at the time Salter's book appeared and was further encouraged in this by Salter's writings (Wolpe, 1969).

Although both Wolpe and Salter have stressed the importance of behaving in an assertive manner, there are crucial differences between their approaches. First, Wolpe did not assume that every client is primarily in need of assertive training, although it is obvious that he employed it frequently, often along with relaxation or desensitization. Second, whereas Salter viewed assertiveness (excitation) as a generalized trait, Wolpe did not. Thus, for Wolpe the mere fact that a client may have no difficulty expressing resentment or hurt to a fellow employee, in no way insures that he can behave similarly with his wife. As we shall learn in a later section, the research literature supports Wolpe on this point. Third, Wolpe was considerably more concerned with the interpersonal consequences (especially negative) of assertive acts. The particulars of the Wolpian approach (and that of Lazarus, 1971, which is similar) are incorporated into the method section of this chapter.

There are two additional writers who have contributed directly or indirectly to present-day assertive-training techniques. One is J. L. Moreno (1946, 1955), whom the reader may recognize as the founder of psychodrama. *Psychodrama* involves the staged dramatization of the real-life attitudes and conflicts of the participating clients. It strongly emphasizes spontaneity and improvisation, elements that Salter stressed. As a role-playing strategy, psychodrama is similar to one of Wolpe's principal assertive techniques, behavior rehearsal (described in the method section). However, the goals of psychodrama, including catharsis and insight, are not usually thought of as consistent with a behavioral approach.[1] The reader wishing to learn more about psychodrama is referred to J. L. Moreno (1946, 1955), Lippitt and Hubbell (1956) or Z. T. Moreno, 1965.

A second writer whose contributions are at least indirectly related to current assertive-training practices is G. Kelly (1955). (Kelly's *fixed-role therapy* is described in some detail in Chapter IV.) In brief, the approach, which is an interesting mixture of cognitive and behavioristic psychology, involves deriving a personality sketch of a fictitious individual who is free of the anxieties and behavioral inadequacies troubling the client; and the client is then instructed to assume this role. This includes behaving in a manner consistent with the role, but, in addition, adopting the fictitious person's way of perceiving the world, hopefully until the client no longer feels that he is assuming a role. The role-playing features of fixed-role therapy are rather similar to behavior rehearsal techniques used in assertive training. Although assertive training does not specifically aim at modifying cognitions, case histories suggest that individuals do indeed undergo attitude change as a consequence of treat-

[1] Both Strum (1965) and J. L. Moreno (1963) have suggested a possible rapprochement between a behavioral and psychodramatic point of view.

ment, especially in relation to self-perception. It is not at all unusual for the client who has successfully completed assertive training to describe himself as "a new person." Similarly, although the goal of fixed-role therapy is not specifically stated in terms of increased assertiveness, it appears likely that such would often be a consequence of treatment.

In contrast to systematic desensitization (Chapter II), the term *assertive training* does not represent a universally agreed upon set of procedures. We have already contrasted Wolpe's approach with that of Salter. As another instance of how therapists using assertive procedures might be in something less than perfect agreement, Wolpe (1958) included in the assertive trainer's armamentarium, Stephen Potter's "oneupmanship" (Potter, 1952). Lazarus (1971), on the other hand, specifically rejected such a technique, preferring a more straightforward approach. Nevertheless, in reviewing the literature, it is clear that there is far more agreement than disagreement regarding what assertive behavior is all about and the basic procedures designed to enhance such behavior. The methods presented in this section derive from a variety of sources, including our own experience, the writings of Wolpe (1958, 1969), Lazarus (1971), Salter (1949), and other clinicians, as well as from ideas contained in certain experimental investigations (see McFall & Marston, 1970; McFall & Lillesand, 1971). The reader may therefore view the following discussion as a rather comprehensive treatment of existing methods, rather than an exposition of a single point of view.

Method of Assertive Training

Determining the Need for Assertive Training

In our experience, individuals rarely come to a therapist asking for assertive training. As assertive training becomes more publicized, the situation will probably change, but for the present it is usually up to the therapist to inform his client of the availability of such a treatment. Normally this is done after the therapist has decided, tentatively perhaps, that assertive training might be helpful to the client. This decision is most often based on a relatively routine behavior therapy interview, although structured assessment devices such as the Wolpe-Lazarus Assertive Inventory (Wolpe & Lazarus, 1966, p. 41) may be helpful. The following are sample items from this inventory:

Do you generally express what you feel?

Are you able to contradict a domineering person?

If a friend makes what you consider to be an unreasonable request, are you able to refuse?

In a similar vein, as a diagnostic aid, Wolpe (1969) determined how his clients would respond in the following representative situations: 1) when the client has been shortchanged; 2) when the client has discovered he has purchased a damaged article; 3) when someone pushes in front in a line; 4) when a clerk waits on a customer who arrives after the client; 5) when the client orders a rare steak, which arrives well done.

Similarly, Lazarus (1971, pp. 132–133) presents a questionnaire consisting of items such as:

When a person is blatantly unfair, do you usually fail to say something about it to him?

If you had a roommate, would you insist that he or she do their fair share of cleaning?

Naturally, elements of any of these assessment tools can be readily incorporated informally into a clinical interview.

Many therapists may prefer a less structured approach, searching for indications of interpersonal difficulties from the client's interview behavior. As we have said, most clients do not ask for assertive training. But as a rule, they are willing to talk about problems they are having with others, and such problems can usually be restructured in terms of situation-specific interpersonal anxiety. If the anxiety is clearly tied to the client's inability to express his feelings in a way that is personally satisfying, as well as socially effective, assertive training is probably in order.

Often the anxiety is directly manifest when the client attempts to engage in an important interchange, as in the case of the student who becomes hopelessly flustered whenever he asks an attractive girl for a date, or the loyal employee who becomes tongue-tied when asking his boss for a much-deserved raise. Sometimes the anticipatory anxiety is so intense that the individual totally avoids the situation, leading to immediate frustration and sometimes depression. On occasion, the therapist is confronted with a client who is quite able to engage in significant interchanges without apparent anxiety, but who consistently exhibits a woeful lack of skill, which results in the failure to satisfy fundamental needs and *consequent* anxiety. For example, Rimm recently observed an interview involving a young male client despondent over his inability to establish satisfying relationships with girls. He did not appear to believe he was in any way lacking in requisite skills; however, when asked to role play a particular incident involving an initial overture to an attractive female in the college student union, his verablizations were insensitive and clumsy, and it is not surprising that the interchange ended in his rebuff.

In the above example, the client's verbal description of his own behavior when attempting romantic overtures was clearly at odds with his manner of responding when he role played a sample situation. Contradictions of this nature are not at all uncommon, and when they occur it is likely that the role-played behavior is far more accurate than the client's verbal characterization of how he typically handles such a situation. While behavior rehearsal constitutes the basis for assertive therapy, it is also an invaluable diagnostic technique, and its use is recommended. A detailed discussion of behavior rehearsal is presented in a later section.

Frequently the therapist must deal with persons whose anxiety is related to the expression of anger. Often the anxiety leads to an almost total suppression of direct expressions of hostility in the target interchange, although sometimes the individual may express anger in an ambivalent or apologetic fashion, producing an unsatisfying and ineffective performance. Inability to express anger directly leads sometimes to a passive-aggressive mode of dealing with hostility. Passive aggression is the label clinicians give to behaviors designed to punish another in some indirect fashion (often by inducing guilt). If the individual is skilled at this, he will be spared immediate retaliation on the part of his victim, who will usually fail to label his assailant's behavior as aggressive or punitive. Unfortunately for the individual regularly exhibiting passive aggression, sooner or later his victim will begin to feel resentment and avoid the assailant. Individuals exhibiting consistent patterns of passive-aggressive behavior would not be expected to have many lasting, satisfying relationships; this situation often drives them to seek therapeutic help.

Of the various types of interpersonal problems amenable to assertive training, those associated with unexpressed (or indirectly expressed) anger are among the most difficult to deal with. Persons who have considerable difficulty expressing anger often believe not only that it is wrong to express anger overtly, but that it is equally wrong to "think angry thoughts." In fact, the reader may recognize this belief as an explicit ethic of certain organized religions. Unfortunately, individuals so indoctrinated are not immune to the hurtful behavior of others, which means that they are as susceptible to anger as any of us, but they are forbidden to admit this to themselves, let alone to a therapist. Thus, the therapist is presented with a multifold task. First, he must correctly identify the degree to which his client experiences hostility in his daily interpersonal interactions. In this regard, it is helpful for the therapist to reflect on whether he, the therapist (or the "average" person) would experience anger in the situations in question, and whether the client's facial expression and tone of voice reflect anger. Some clients, when faced with the possibility that certain situations may be annoying or anger inducing, respond with "it wasn't that important," or "it isn't worth getting angry over." A high frequency of responses of this nature

may well reflect a good deal of latent anger. Nor should the therapist be misled by the statement, "When I get mad, I really blow my top," which can usually be translated to read, "Although I'm rarely justified in showing or even feeling anger, some situations clearly are so wrong and unfair that I must react."

Once the therapist has gathered sufficient evidence that unexpressed hostility is a problem, his next task is to convince the client of this, which is no minor undertaking. Telling a client who believes feeling anger is immoral that he is angry may be likened to confronting a Victorian spinster with the observation that she is oversexed. A premature confrontation would likely anger the client who might smile and nod his head in agreement, but inwardly experience a swell of resentment toward the therapist; this reaction might result in the client's terminating therapy. We recommend that feelings of trust and confidence be first established and that the subject of the client's hostile feelings be dealt with in a graduated fashion. For some clients this might mean dealing with mildly angry feelings occurring in relatively insignificant situations; while for others, the general area might be approached by using synonyms (admittedly of a euphemistic nature) for "angry," or "hostile." For example: "I get the feeling you are a bit irritated at your wife," or, "Do you find that it is somewhat annoying when your father interrupts you like that?" Finally, having persuaded the client that he has angry feelings, assertive training can commence.

Just as it is unusual to encounter a client who offers the unsolicited plea for help at expressing hostility, it is rare for clients to verbalize, spontaneously, that they feel love or affection for another, but do not know how to share these feelings—although this is certainly a common enough problem. Thus, a client might tell his therapist that he loves his spouse, but that he "doesn't have to tell her" because she "knows," that is, she can "read between the lines." In fact, not infrequently there is the implication that it is the *responsibility* of the other party to somehow know that they are loved or appreciated. It is well to point out that in any relationship involving intense feelings, subtle cues are often missed, and feelings of affection, warmth, and love occasionally, at least, must be made very explicit. Generally, however, clients seem more willing to "own up" to honest, but inadequately communicated, positive feelings than to resentment or anger, probably because the culture is far more permissive to the expression of positive feelings. On the other hand, there are many persons (men, especially) who believe that expressing love and affection is indicative of weakness. Here the therapist's task may be to turn this attitude around on the client by indicating how straightforward expressions of positive feeling are interpreted by most people as a sign of strength and confidence.

not necessarily his
task.

One emotion that may present particular diagnostic difficulties is jealousy. This label has a variety of meanings in this culture, but we are specifically referring to feelings of anxiety and resentment when threatened with losing one we love to a competitor. Extreme jealousy, especially when unfounded, has destroyed many a relationship, and therapeutic strategies for dealing with this problem might well include a combination of systematic desensitization (Chapter II) and Rational-Emotive Therapy (Chapter X).

Whereas occasional feelings of mild jealousy are inevitable and normal, many individuals refuse to admit such feelings, perhaps because they place them in the same category as pure anger or selfishness. Certain persons are imbued with an ethic of totally unselfish love that realistically cannot exist between a man and a woman engaged in a love relationship. Given normal expectations and a normal degree of possessiveness, jealousy will sometimes be experienced. Often one partner will deliberately try to induce such a feeling in the other, to test his love. If he regularly fails to respond, this may drive the other to more drastic action (for example, consummated sexual encounters, rather than casual flirting at a cocktail party) to convince the partner that, indeed, love is lacking. As an illustration, Wolpe (1958) described the case of a man whose wife was engaged in an extramarital affair that he condoned, but also resented. Only when he forcefully made his feelings known did his wife terminate the affair and most willingly, at that.

As in the case of hostility, the therapist must decide whether his client is experiencing jealousy. Again, asking himself the question, "Would the average person feel some jealousy in such a situation?" will probably prove to be of diagnostic value. Problems involved in persuading the client to acknowledge these feelings (and to see the therapeutic benefit of expressing them in a reasonable way) are similar to those raised in connection with unexpressed anger. Here, too, the gentle approach is recommended.

As we have indicated earlier in the chapter, assertiveness (or the lack of assertiveness) is not a pervasive trait. That is, a person may be quite assertive in one situation, yet tremulous and ineffective in another seemingly related set of circumstances. It is absolutely essential that the therapist be aware of this, lest he come to some premature and fallacious conclusions that will impede the course of treatment. On numerous occasions the clinician is confronted with a smiling, verbally facile client who presents the superficial picture of an individual supremely confident and competent in virtually any social interchange. The therapist might easily conclude that assertive training is the last thing such an individual requires. Yet careful interviewing (including role playing) will often reveal significant specific situations involving a woeful lack of assertiveness. This is well illustrated by the confident, boisterous businessman who is regularly intimidated by his wife or his children; or even more specifically, by his wife, when he attempts to make certain kinds of decisions; or by his children, when he attempts to apply verbal discipline. Another example is the cool and highly articulate professional woman who, while espousing the rights of women, will, upon careful questioning, admit that she is frequently the victim of unscrupulous and unsatisfying sexual conquests because she is unable to say no. On the other side of the coin, perhaps less frequently during an initial interview, the client may evidence extreme anxiety and apparent lack of self-confidence and/or social skill, not because this is his habitual manner of social interaction, but because he is quite unaccustomed to situations where he is expected to reveal highly troublesome and embarrassing facets of his personal life.

The therapist's skill in diagnosing problems related to assertiveness will be enhanced considerably if he disavows himself of the notion that people are either generally assertive or generally inhibited. In deciding whether or not to apply systematic desensitization, the therapist does not ask himself whether his client is fearful or fearless, but, rather, what he is afraid of and in what degree. Similarly, in relation to assertion training, the therapist finds out which situations evoke appropriate assertion and which situations do not. As in the implementation of any behavior therapy technique, problems are dealt with effectively only when they are seen as *situation specific*.

In summary, diagnosing problems pertaining to a lack of assertiveness may be facilitated by the use of structured assessment devices, although a precise pinpointing of areas of difficulty normally requires careful interviewing. Assertive training is usually in order when the client is unable to express his feelings in a manner both personally satisfying and socially effective. Indications for assertive training include obvious signs of interpersonal anxiety or habitual avoidance of important interpersonal interactions, as well as obvious or subtle signs that the client is experiencing intense, but unexpressed, emotions, especially anger, resentment, or jealousy. Lack of assertiveness should be seen as a behavioral deficit related to specific situations, rather than as a general personality trait.

Presenting the Concept of Assertive Training to the Client

We will assume that the therapist is now convinced that certain of his client's problems reflect a lack of assertion. The next task is to inform the client about assertive training and to enlist his cooperation. Although this has not been subject to controlled research, most writers in the area place considerable emphasis on inducing a positive, enthusiastic attitude toward assertive training prior to attempting the actual procedures. In part this is a consequence of the fact that assertive training, like most other behavior therapy techniques, requires a good deal of active participation on the part of the client, necessitating reasonable motivation. More specifically, however, the initial prospect of behaving assertively in certain situations may be frightening. It is likely that for many clients in need of assertive training, significant prior attempts (perhaps in childhood) at assertion were met with highly unpleasant consequences. While it is usually true that appropriate assertion is met with positive consequences, the client cannot be expected to know this, and it is the therapist's task to point this out, within the specific context of the client's current difficulties.

The therapist might stress the negative effect (frustration, resentment, lack of satisfaction) the client is currently experiencing, followed by a projection, by the therapist, of the feelings of personal well-being and relief, as well as increased interpersonal satisfaction, as very likely consequences of increased assertiveness. However, the obsequious, overly conforming client may well reply (perhaps to himself), "Yes, I can see that by not expressing my true feelings I am making myself unhappy and am missing out on many rewards. But what right do I have to impose my feelings on others?" Thus, aside from anticipated positive consequences, it is important to point out to the client that he does, indeed, have the right to assert himself because this is a right belonging to every human being. In making such an assertion, the therapist is clearly expressing a value judgment, albeit, one we share with most writers on the subject.

The following dialogue between a therapist and an adult male client who has admitted he is bullied by and greatly resents his brother-in-law, illustrates the above.

Therapist: "From what you've been saying, it seems clear that you feel a lot of resentment and anger toward your brother-in-law. What do you think about feeling like that? I mean, is it a good, or pleasant, way to feel?"

Client: "Well, no, really the opposite. Sometimes I feel I'm going to lose control and hit him. That would be terrible."

Therapist: "What else do you feel around him?"

Client: "Like I said, I'm pretty upset and nervous, and when I'm over at his house for dinner I don't feel like eating. I don't want to offend my sister so I do, but afterward I feel like throwing up."

Therapist: "So, in other words, your brother-in-law's way of acting makes

you angry and anxious and downright sick to your stomach?
Sounds like you are pretty miserable around him."

Client: "Yes, pretty miserable. Like I was saying, he's not the only
one, but it's worse around him."

Therapist: "Just pretend for a minute that you were the sort of person
who could tell him off whenever he was bothering you. Whenever he was on your back, bullying you the way he does. How
would you feel then?"

Client: "Well, if I did tell him off, he'd say something cruel to hurt my
feelings. It wouldn't be worth it."

Therapist: "No, wait. Suppose you were so good at telling him off that he
would actually wither under your onslaught, and would shut
up and leave you alone, and even treat you with admiration
and respect. How would you feel then?"

Client: "That is hard to imagine. If I could do it, I mean beat him at
his own game, I'd feel better. I just want him to leave me
alone, and I would enjoy visiting my sister a lot more if he
were off my back. But I don't think I could ever do it—I'm not
that way."

Therapist: "Tell me what you mean."

Client: Well, I guess I've always felt that telling people off, or attacking them, was wrong. Especially him . . . after all, he is my
sister's husband, and he's a good provider. I'm not even married, and have a lousy job. I guess I just haven't the right to
tell him off."

Therapist: "Do you think he has any more right to pick on you?"

Client: "No. But I guess way down deep I must think he does. (Pause)
But really he doesn't. It is wrong."

Therapist: "So, in other words, people don't really have the right to bully
others."

Client: (Pause) "Yes, I'll agree with that."

Therapist: "Then don't you think people who are bullied have the right
to defend themselves? Even if it means counterattacking, naturally in a reasonable and controlled way."

Client: "Well, I don't know. (Tentatively) Yes, I can see your logic. I
guess it would make sense for me to defend myself. But I
always clam up when anyone criticizes me or makes fun of
me."

Therapist: "I think there are some things we can do to help you defend
yourself and not clam up."

At this point the therapist would briefly describe the method and rationale of assertive training. He might point out that role playing re-

sponses within the "safe" confines of the consulting office can result only in increased effectiveness in interpersonal situations and that when a person is behaving assertively, it is very difficult for him to experience anxiety. Certain writers (Wolpe & Lazarus, 1966) have recommended presenting the client a sample case history, to provide him with a more concrete notion of what is in store.

Implementing Assertive Procedures

Behavior Rehearsal

By far the most commonly used assertive-training technique is *behavior rehearsal.* This technique requires that the client and therapist act out relevant interpersonal interactions. Part of the time the client plays himself, with the therapist assuming the role of a significant person in the client's life, such as a parent, employer, or spouse. In carrying out this role the therapist must portray the other person with some degree of realism. Since the client is normally the only source of information about the other person, it is impressed upon him that he must tell the therapist how to behave. Telling the client that it is "his show" and that he must "direct the play" may serve the purpose of involving him further while appealing to any latent theatrical impulses that most people seem to possess in some degree. The client might model the behavior outright, or, if this is too anxiety provoking or awkward, he might simply describe the behavior to be modeled, with the therapist filling in the details.

Having so set the stage, the client usually initiates the vignette with behavior that is *typical* for him in such a situation. The therapist responds according to his role, and this, in turn, is met with the client's response, and so on. Normally, exchanges of this nature are quite brief, and sometimes the nature of the target task is such that only the client need make any response. For example, a client may wish to learn how to deal with a salesclerk who persists in ignoring him. Here the therapist might say, "Pretend I'm that clerk. Role play what you would say (did say) to me." The client would then terminate the exchange with a single statement such as, "Excuse me, I'm sorry but . . . when you are through, would you . . . wait on me?"

As we have said, on the basis of such initial role-played behaviors, the therapist is in an excellent position to assess whether assertive training is required for the situation just acted out and, if so, to pinpoint the exact behaviors of the client in need of changing. If deficiencies are apparent, the therapist may opt to provide immediate corrective feedback (presented in a decidedly nonpunitive manner), followed by a second attempt on the part of the client. This procedure might be continued until

both client and therapist agree that the response is appropriately assertive and is accompanied by minimal anxiety. Alternatively, following the
client's initial response, the therapist might immediately model a more
adequate response that the client would then have an opportunity to imitate. However, *the most desirable strategy would probably incorporate both immediate feedback and modeling,* illustrated by the following example.

A male college student has difficulty making dates with girls. In the
present situation, he is attempting to ask for a date over the telephone.
He has introduced himself and has engaged the girl in the appropriate
amount of small talk. Both client and therapist agree that it is now time
to ask for the date.

Client: "By the way (pause) I don't suppose you want to go out Saturday night?"

Therapist: "Up to actually asking for the date you were very good. However, if I were the girl, I think I might have been a bit of-
fended when you said, 'By the way.' It's like your asking her
out is pretty casual. Also, the way you phrased the question,
you are kind of suggesting to her that she doesn't want to go
out with you. Pretend for the moment I'm you. Now, how
does this sound: "There is a movie at the Varsity Theater this
Saturday that I want to see. If you don't have other plans, I'd
very much like to take you.'

Client: "That sounded good. Like you were sure of yourself and liked
the girl, too."

Therapist: "Why don't you try it."

Client: "You know that movie at the Varsity? Well, I'd like to go, and
I'd like to take you Saturday, if you don't have anything better
to do."

Therapist: "Well, that certainly was better. Your tone of voice was especially good. But the last line, 'if you don't have anything better
to do,' sounds like you don't think you have too much to offer.
Why not run through it one more time."

Client: "I'd like to see the show at the Varsity, Saturday, and, if you
haven't made other plans, I'd like to take you."

Therapist: "Much better. Excellent, in fact. You were confident, forceful,
and sincere."

Certain of the principles discussed in Chapters V and VI are incorporated in the above dialogue.[2] One was the use of plentiful *reinforcement*

---

[2] The assertive procedures described in this chapter incorporate several well-established
principles borrowed from the operant literature (for example, the use of successive approximations). Clinical experience strongly suggests the appropriateness of these ex-

in the form of praise from the therapist. The second was the use of the *principle of successive approximations.* Following the client's first attempt at imitating the therapist, the therapist praised those components of the client's response that reflected improvement. Had the therapist insisted on a perfect performance, almost anything the client said would have missed the mark. However, by attending to *any* improvement discernible in the client's behavior, such improvement, instead of being lost, would persist through the next response. Rewarding *improvement,* rather than *absolute levels of performance,* is generally labeled *shaping,* and, as we consider in Chapters V and VI, shaping is an essential ingredient of behavior modification. Also stressed in these same chapters is the importance of dealing with relatively small segments of behavior at a time. In assertive training, this means that initially, at least, protracted monologues would not be modeled by the therapist, who would opt, instead, to work on effecting improvement in small portions of the client's behavior. Ordinarily, segments of an interaction would be dealt with sequentially, until the interaction was complete. Following this, the therapist might have the client "put together" (that is, rehearse) the entire sequence, thus simulating the interaction as it would actually occur.

Frequently, when the therapist assumes the client's role, the client models the behavior of the other person in the interaction. This technique, known as *role reversal,* is useful because it provides a more realistic context in which the therapist may model appropriate behavior for the client. Additionally, assuming the role of the other person encourages the client to experience the sorts of feelings that the other person (any person) would plausibly experience in the given situation. This is especially valuable if the client has unrealistically negative expectations regarding how other people will respond to more assertive overtures. For instance, consider the client who is reluctant to express disagreement with his employer lest it offend him. By engaging in role reversal, the client has the opportunity to observe the therapist modeling disagreement in a tactful and well-reasoned fashion and to observe his own emotional reaction to this. He may well realize, to his own surprise, that the modeled response did not elicit especially negative feelings, after all, and this would provide added impetus for trying out the new behavior, *in vivo.*

The following illustrates the technique of role reversal, as well as the procedures and principles described in the preceding discussion. The client is a teenage girl, about to graduate from high school. She is not an especially good student and has no desire to attend college, but her mother, who chronically dominates the client, is insistent.

---

trapolations. However, the reader should be advised that controlled research investigating these *specific elements* of assertive training is, in general, lacking.

Therapist: "Well, it is apparent to me that you really don't want to go to college. It is also clear that you've given it a great deal of thought. Now what happens when you discuss this with your mother?"

Client: "We don't exactly *discuss* it. She tells me what is best for me, and that I am immature and don't know my own mind, and that I'll regret not going to college for the rest of my life."

Therapist: "And how does that make you feel?"

Client: "Angry inside and pretty frustrated. I can't seem to get a word in edgewise, but if I did say what I really felt, it would hurt her, so I don't. I just go to my room and cry for a while."

Therapist: "Just to see how you do come across in this situation, let me play your mother and you be yourself. You direct the play and make sure I act like your mother. Ready? Here goes (As mother): When are you going to apply to State? You haven't done it yet, have you?"

Client: "No. You know, I don't really want to go."

Therapist: "I know you are not old enough to know your own mind! You are very immature and you'll regret not going to college the rest of your life. If I didn't love you I wouldn't say these things. Now, I insist that you apply!"

Client: (Long sigh) "Oh, all right. (Role play ended). That's actually what I'd say. To get her off my back."

Therapist: "Well, you began by telling your mother how you really felt and that sounded good. But then, after she said her piece, you backed down, angry and frustrated. Let's try reversing roles for a minute. You be your mother and I'll be you. You start."

Client: "O.K. . . . (As mother) Why haven't you applied to State College yet?"

Therapist: (As client) "To tell you the truth, mom, I've thought about it a great deal, and I don't want to go to college."

Client: (As mother) "I absolutely insist that you apply. You aren't really very grown up and you don't know your own mind. Do as I say. I love you and it's for your own good."

Therapist: (As client) "Mom, I know you care a great deal about me and that is important.[3] But, like I said, I thought it over very carefully. I wouldn't enjoy college and I know I wouldn't do well."

Therapist: "Now, why don't you try something like that? You be yourself

---

[3] Note that the therapist is modeling a response which while conveying the client's objections also conveys an awareness of the mother's feelings. Thus, the response is marked by *empathy*, an element which Jakubowski-Spector (1973a) has stressed in her approach to assertive training.

and I'll be your mother. (As mother) I insist you apply to State. I love you and it's for your own good."

Client: (As client) "I know you love me and I appreciate it. But I've thought about it a lot and know I won't do well. I really don't think it would be a good idea. I'm sure it wouldn't be."

Therapist: "That was certainly much better! How did you feel?"

Client: "A little anxious."

Therapist: "Let's try it again.

The interaction continues until the client reports little or no anxiety while engaging in the interchange.

Therapist: "Would the conversation end with that?"

Client: "No, I don't think so. She'd probably say I was a disappointment to her. That really gets to me, and she knows it, and I wouldn't know what to say."

Therapist: (As therapist) "Let's try to reverse roles again. You begin with the statement about disappointment."

Client: (As mother) "Why do you insist on disappointing me?"

Therapist: (As client) "Well, I don't want to disappoint you and, if I am, that makes me feel bad. But this is an important decision that I have to make for myself. You know I value your opinion and I don't want to seem disrespectful, but I've looked at this from all angles, and I know it would be best if I take that job instead of going to college."

Therapist: "How did that sound?"

Client: "Really good. It was like you were disarming her. Putting it that way would have made her less angry."

Therapist: "Now, you try it. Just the last part. (As mother) Why must you disappoint me?"

Client: (As client) "Well, that isn't what I want to do and I'm really sorry if I am. You know I respect your opinion very much, but this is an important decision and it has to be made by me. I've really thought it over and over and know it would be best if I took the job and didn't go to college."

Therapist: "Very good. You came across forcefully, but you didn't sound harsh or unkind. Also, your eye contact is getting much better and that is important. Did you feel anxious at all?"

Client: "No, as a matter of fact, I felt pretty good while I was talking."

Therapist: "How would your mother respond to what you just said?"

Client: "I really don't know. I've never asserted myself that much before."

Therapist: "Do you think you feel comfortable enough to try that sort of
thing out?"
Client: "Yes, but with a little more practice."
Therapist: "O.K., let's go through the whole thing now. (As mother) Why
haven't you applied to State yet?"

The above dialogue illustrates an additional important principle. *Before proceeding to the next segment of an interaction, the therapist should determine that the client can engage in the present one with little or no anxiety.* In this regard, the procedure is very much like systematic desensitization.

The Minimal Effective Response

As we have indicated, the goal of training in assertion is the appropriate expression of feelings. Deciding whether a particular act is appropriate is of course a matter of social judgment. Ordinarily the decision is made jointly by client and therapist, taking advantage of the client's specific knowledge of the target situation, and the therapist's broader experiences and objectivity. Since many of the problems the therapist will deal with specifically involve a failure on the part of the client to "stand up for his rights," some general guidelines for determining "appropriate behaviors" in such situations may be helpful. In expressing feelings such as hurt or anger, a good rule of thumb is to stress implementing the *minimal effective response.* The minimal effective response is that behavior that would ordinarily accomplish the client's goal with a minimum of effort and apparent negative emotion (and a very small likelihood of negative consequences). Consider how a person might deal with a chatty couple interfering with his enjoyment of a movie. Assume the couple has been engaged in loud whispering for about 5 minutes, and no one has yet ask them to refrain. A minimal effective response might be, "Gee, I wonder if you'd mind being a little more quiet? I'm having trouble hearing (whispered in a friendly tone of voice)." Naturally, one could engage in overkill, with a loud and angry, "If you don't shut the hell up, I'll call the usher and have you kicked out." However, a response of this nature, while it might "get the job done" would probably cause the complainant to feel guilty, unnecessarily anger or distress the target couple (who, after all, were probably quite unaware they were causing a disturbance), and irritate all innocent bystanders within earshot.

The following are frequently occurring annoying situations, with sample minimal effective responses.

A gas station attendant fails to clean your windshield: *I wonder if you'd mind getting the windshield? It's kind of dirty today.*

A waiter charges you for dessert you didn't have: *I believe you've made an error in the check. Would you mind checking it again?*

The night before an important exam, a friend drops in to chat; 20 minutes later he is going strong: *Hey, you know, I've got this exam tomorrow. But let's get together some other time and shoot the breeze.*

Your date is 30 minutes late. He offers no excuse: *I was getting a little worried* (while glancing at your watch).

A friend continually interrupts you. (With a friendly smile): *I'm sure you don't realize this, but sometimes I get kind of flustered when you interrupt.*

Escalation

Assertive responses of this relatively mild nature are quite effective in most cases, much to the amazement of many a client. Sometimes, however, they are met with unresponsiveness or even belligerence, and some steps should be taken to prepare the client for this. Once the client has shown himself to be adept at the minimal effective response, the therapist may model successively more negative or threatening counterresponses. However, the therapist should take special care to keep these *escalations* [a term borrowed from McFall and Marston (1970)] within the realm of *plausibility* and to remind the client that such counterresponses are, after all, rather unlikely to occur. This caution is important because an individual who is timorous in such situations has probably done a thorough job of intimidating himself with anticipated dreadful consequences to any assertive act on his part. The last thing the therapist would want to do is reinforce these ruminations. The following, in summary form, is an example of an escalation involving the noisy couple in the theater. In implementing this, the usual modeling-rehearsal format should be followed.

Complainant:	"I wonder if you would please be a little more quiet. I'm having difficulty hearing." (After 5 minutes of silence the chatter resumes.)
Complainant:	"Look, would you please be a bit more quiet? I simply can't hear the movie." (First-order escalation.)
Spokesman for the culprits:	"Sorry." (Silence for remainder of movie.)

However, the therapist may wish to extend this into a second-order escalation. The second complaint is met with "Jeeze, what's that guy so uptight about?"—followed by continued chatter. Now, an appropriate response might be: "Look, if you people don't quiet down, I'm simply going to call the manager," followed by: "(Extended sigh) O.K., buddy,

O.K.," and silence for the remainder of the movie. Or: "This guy gets on my nerves. Let's leave."

Note that at each step, the therapist structures things in such a way that the client's assertions are met with ultimate success. While it might be argued that in the "real world," appropriate assertiveness is not *always* met with success, in fact, it usually *is* successful, and practicing negative consequences in therapy will only reinforce already powerful tendencies toward inhibition.

The client may raise the possibility that during the course of an escalated encounter, the other person may resort to physical violence or corresponding threats. The likelihood of this happening is probably very much lower than most clients realize. People who frequently behave in a bullying manner in our experience easily succumb to verbal assertiveness, so that the interchange rarely reaches the point of physical threats or violence. This is especially true of the client who is taught to avoid "backing his opponent against the wall." This is best accomplished by having the client concentrate on ways to inform the other person that what he is doing is a source of personal inconvenience, discomfort, or, when appropriate, hurt, rather than on tactics involving personal attacks or insults.

Consider the following situation. You are in serious need of some cash, but the clerk at the convenience market you frequent refuses because he is new and he doesn't know you. You might say, "To tell you the truth, this makes me feel kind of funny. After all, I've been a good customer here for some time, and I do need the money very badly." From personal experience, this almost always works. However, in a far more foolish and impulsive vein, you might back him into a corner with: "Look, you moron, I've been cashing checks in here for more than a year." If he now complies with your request he is admitting he is a moron, and this he is not likely to do. Additionally, if he is given to violence, calling him a moron will do little to suppress this response. In fact, the source of the would-be-check-casher's discomfort in the present situation has precious little to do with any enduring "trait" (such as intelligence) the clerk might possess. It is his present behavior that is annoying, and telling him this in an objective and straightforward manner is a good deal more honest (as well as effective) than engaging in inflammatory name-calling. Similarly, for the customer who has just been shortchanged, the problem is not that the waiter is "a liar and a cheat" (although indeed he may be). The problem, that is, the event causing distress, is an irregularity in change-making behavior on the part of the waiter, and this is what is in need of correction.

The following is a summary of the main points associated with the

technique of behavior rehearsal as it is applied to a specific area of interpersonal difficulty.

1. The client enacts the behavior as he would in real life.
2. The therapist provides specific verbal feedback, stressing positive
features, and presenting inadequacies in a friendly, nonpunitive fashion.
3. The therapist models more desirable behavior, with the client assuming the other person's role when appropriate.
4. The client then attempts the response again.
5. The therapist bountifully rewards improvement. If necessary,
Steps 3 and 4 are repeated until both therapist and client are satisfied
with the response, and the client can engage in the response with little or
no anxiety.
6. The interaction, if it is at all lengthy, should be broken up into
small segments, dealt with sequentially. Following this, the client and
therapist may wish to run through the entire interaction for the purpose
of consolidating gains.
7. In an interchange involving the expression of negative feelings, the
client should be instructed to begin with a relatively mild response (the
minimum effective response). However, he should also be given
stronger responses in case the initial response is ineffective.
8. In rehearsing the expression of negative feelings, objective statements pertaining to annoying or hurtful behaviors on the part of the
other person are far superior to personal attacks, which are often irrelevant and have the effect of backing the other into a corner.

The Use of a Hierarchy

As we have seen in Chapter II, systematic desensitization requires the
use of a well-structured and carefully detailed hierarchy. The therapist
could as well develop very similar hierarchies for behavior rehearsal,
and sometimes this is done. More often, however, the behavior therapist's approach to assertive training is somewhat more informal, although it is recommended that easier items be dealt with first. Making
up a detailed hierarchy and methodically going through it is a time-con-
suming undertaking, and an experienced therapist may feel that he can
accurately gauge when the client is ready for a particular situation (even
when he has not rehearsed easier interactions).

On the other hand, for the novice to assertive training, such a hierarchy may be very valuable indeed, providing the therapist with much-
needed structure, as well as valuable diagnostic information. We are of
the opinion that the premature presentation of an item (that is, interac-

an discouraging effect

tion) can be a good deal more damaging in assertive training than in desensitization. This is especially true if the assertive item has to do with the expression of hostility. Getting the client to "tell off" his father (even in a supposedly "safe," role-playing context) when he is not ready for this, may threaten him to the point of terminating therapy. If the client's lack of assertiveness encompasses expressing negative feelings toward therapists, the therapist may be unaware of what is happening, only to discover after several subsequent meetings have been cancelled that he has "lost" the client with whom he was "doing so well." Therefore, it is specifically recommended that the newcomer to assertive training employ a desensitization-type hierarchy, at least until he feels that this procedure can ordinarily be dispensed with.

Hierarchy construction has already been described in Chapter II. Ordinarily, items will be ranked according to anxiety, as in the case of desensitization, although suggesting to the client that he rate situations according to the degree to which they irritate, frustrate, or anger him, as well, may prove to be helpful, especially if the client does not deem it appropriate to admit he is anxious in certain situations.

The following are sample hierarchies. The first two items are presented in detail, with the remainder presented in abbreviated form. The items are in order of increasing difficulty. As in desensitization, situations should be presented in realistic detail.

The first hierarchy is for an accountant who was bullied by his immediate supervisor.

1. Your supervisor is sitting at his desk. For the past 3 days you've been working overtime and you'd like to leave the office 20 minutes early to attend to your son's birthday party. You walk up to his desk and begin to make the request.

2. Your supervisor walks by as you are seated at your desk one morning. In spite of the fact that you are always punctual, he says, in a very sarcastic tone, "Were you late today?"

3. Your supervisor observes (inaccurately) that you and the others have been taking excessively long coffee breaks.

4. Your supervisor unjustly accuses a colleague of yours of acts of dishonesty.

5. You approach your supervisor to request that your vacation, scheduled for September, be changed to August.

6. You have been working overtime all week. Your supervisor requests that you do so again. You want to refuse.

7. Your supervisor makes sarcastic comments about your leaving the office early on Wednesday to meet with your psychotherapist.

8. You approach your supervisor to ask for a much-deserved raise.

9. You want to inform your supervisor that if a raise is not granted you will leave the firm.

The second hierarchy is for a 25-year-old girl having an affair with an older, married man who appears to be indifferent to her feelings.

1. Late one night, he telephones you from his apartment, insisting that you visit him immediately. He seems unconcerned with whether or not this would be inconvenient for you.

2. He was to meet you at 5:00 p.m., at the railroad station. You haven't eaten and it is cold and rainy. He shows up at 7:30, offering no excuses.

3. He phones to tell you he may not be able to see you the following weekend, offering no reason.

4. He refuses to discuss the future of your relationship.

5. You complain about his mistreatment, and he calls you a "bitch" and won't respond further.

6. He says he can't see you because Bonnie (another girl friend) is in town.

7. You want to tell him off, but fear losing him as a result.

8. You want to tell him to change or you will terminate the relationship.

9. You want to tell him you no longer wish to see him.

The Use of a Co-Therapist

We have found that assertive training may at times be considerably expedited if the client is seen by two therapists at the same time. While we know of no controlled research investigating this, the rationale behind the use of a co-therapist is highly plausible. First, the reader will, no doubt, agree that one of the most difficult aspects of assertive training has to do with deciding what precisely is an appropriately assertive response in a given situation. Certainly, in matters of social judgment, the adage "two heads are better than one" seems applicable. Second, and related to this point, the credibility of a novel response presented to the client can only be enhanced by the fact that *two* ("expert") observers agree on its appropriateness. Third, in behavior rehearsal, since there are two individuals available to assume the role of the "other person," it is far more likely that the role will be portrayed in a plausible manner. This is obviously the case when the client has difficulty asserting himself vis-à-vis members of both sexes, and one therapist is male and the other female. Co-therapists would have a similar advantage if the client had difficulty with authority figures, as well as peers, and the therapists differed markedly in age. Finally, two therapists verbally reinforcing increased assertiveness on the part of the client would be expected to have far more impact than praise from a solitary therapist.

Naturally, it is not always feasible to have co-therapists (if fees are an issue, it might be prohibitively expensive), and the standard one-to-one therapy arrangement can be quite effective. Under such circumstances, the therapist may want to enlist the help of another individual on an occasional basis (for example, the male ward psychologist may ask a nurse to assume the role of the male patient's wife).

Passive-Assertive Tactics

As Wolpe (1958) has suggested, there are situations in which overt acts of assertion, no matter how skillfully presented, may still lead to negative consequences. While such situations are probably *far less common* than most clients realize, anyone who has spent time in the military, or who has been subjected to a paranoid, tyrannical employer (at a time when job changing was not feasible) would probably agree with Wolpe. For such situations, Wolpe recommends the famous *gamesmanship techniques* of Stephen Potter (1952). Here the client is instructed in ways of gaining a psychological advantage or behavioral advantage by playing on the subtle weaknesses of his adversary. Wolpe and Lazarus (1966) report the case of an employee who was regularly subjected to long-winded and aversive speeches from one of his employers. The client was able to eliminate this behavior by engaging in various ploys, including staring at his boss's bald head (the boss was known to be self-conscious about this).

Whether a therapist wishes to implement such indirect (and admittedly "sneaky") techniques is, of course, a matter of personal preference. One well-known behavior therapist, Lazarus (1971), has explicitly disassociated himself from gamesmanship tactics, preferring a more straightforward approach. While we would not go this far, it is recommended that passive assertion be used in a highly restrictive manner. In particular, it should be reserved for situations where it is quite clear that more direct approaches would meet with seriously negative consequences, and where the client's imminent escape from the situation is blocked. The reader should be most wary of the fact that clients in need of assertive training wrongly describe many situations in just these terms, and it is the therapist's responsibility to impress upon his client that disastrous consequences are not likely to occur and/or he is free to exit from the particular situation (or relationship). Finally, in situations where passive assertive tactics are appropriate, the therapist is advised to present them within the context of more usual assertive training procedures, thus reducing the possibility that the client learns to adopt the indirect (and

usually less satisfactory and less effective) approach as a universal means of dealing with interpersonal difficulty.

Assertive Training in the Treatment of Antisocial Aggression

Thus far, we have concentrated on what might be described as conventional applications of assertive procedures. That is, we have dealt with problems of social inhibition or timidity, whether the feelings not expressed were of a negative or positive nature. It may, therefore, surprise the reader to learn that assertive training has considerable potential for another class of problems, specifically those marked by impulsive and self-defeating aggressive behavior. The reader is asked to recall the definition of *assertive behavior:* behavior marked by the appropriate expression of feeling. Just as timorous, obsequious behavior fails to convey feelings in a socially effective way (and is, therefore, nonassertive), belligerent, offensive behavior is similarly nonassertive. We have suggested that assertive training has *potential* for the treatment of such problems because its application in this area is relatively novel, although preliminary findings (presented later in this chapter) are encouraging.

Clinical experience suggests that many individuals resort to physical violence or threats of violence simply because they are deficient in the verbal skills that would accomplish their goals more effectively and without the severe negative consequences often associated with acts of extreme belligerence. This is especially true with many males in our society who have been taught to believe that a man proficient in verbal skills is somehow lacking in masculinity.

Teaching an individual to be assertive, rather than aggressive, is quite similar to teaching an individual to be assertive, rather than timid. However, the therapist may want to take particular pains to convince his client that *talking* his way through interpersonal difficulties is not a sign of lack of masculinity. One way to accomplish this is to point out that whereas physical aggression might well have been an effective way of handling problems in the past (for instance, when the client was growing up in the ghetto), such is no longer the case. Furthermore, it can be pointed out that assaultiveness can lead only to interpersonal failure and even confinement to a prison or a mental institution.

As in the case of timidity, one can employ a graduated hierarchy consisting of situations that typically give rise to aggressive behavior. However, it is likely that even for those situations evoking the most intense anger, given the appropriate coaching and modeling, the client will be able to role play appropriate behavior—without experiencing intense

anxiety. For this reason, a graduated hierarchy is probably not necessary. On the other hand, if the therapist is able to discern noticeable anxiety when the client is required to exhibit novel, nonbelligerent modes of
responding, less difficult or threatening items should be dealt with first.

The following is an excerpt from an interview that Rimm conducted
with a 23-year-old male college student. The client approached the therapist explicitly asking for help in controlling his violent outbursts. It is
interesting, and not at all unusual, for such individuals that, despite his
concern, the client has mixed feelings about expressing anger in a violent manner.

Therapist: "You mentioned you hit somebody. Tell me about it."

Client: "We were at this peace rally. Afterward we were standing
around outside this stadium and this hardhat comes up to me
and says, 'What do you blacks want, anyway?' I told him, 'the
same thing you want.' He said, in a nasty tone, 'No, you want it
all.'

Therapist: "That was a belligerent thing for him to say. How did you
handle that?"

Client: "Well, I just told him he was only expressing his own ignorance."

Therapist: "Good for you! But how did he respond?"

Client: "He didn't say anything, just looked at the ground. The bigot
knew I was right."

Therapist: "Sounds like you handled it well . . . you won."

Client: "That's not all. I started walking away. I guess maybe I felt
bad about beating him. And it must have showed. Then he
turned to this other hardhat and said, 'These black bastards
want to take over the world.' I said, 'Who said that?' but I
knew he was the one. I was really mad 'cause I'd let him off
the ropes, and this pig had to insult me again."

Therapist: "Well, then what?"

Client: (Said with a faint smile and a definite note of pride) "I
knocked the bigot down. The police came, but I got away in
time."

Therapist: "Sounds like you are kind of proud. But would it have been
worth going to jail for?"

Client: "Well, he had it coming, but I don't want to go to jail. You're
right. It wouldn't have been worth it. That's why I'm here."

Therapist: "Personally, I would have quit after I told him he was ignorant, and I certainly wouldn't have felt bad. After all, he *was*
wrong. And after that he really got insulting. Let's see how

> you could have handled that without hitting. You play the
> bigot and I'll be you."

Client: (As bigot) "These black bastards are trying to take over the
world."

Therapist: (As client) "Like I said, you are just displaying ignorance
when you say things like that. Maybe if you got to know some
black people you wouldn't think like you do."

Therapist: (As therapist) "Now, if that sounded O.K., you try it. But say it
with a lot of feeling, so it will be personally satisfying to you.
Like it really is a substitute for hitting the guy."

It is important that the therapist pinpoint *exactly* what it is that angers
or frustrates his client. In the above example, it was not the bigot's
isolated statement that infuriated the client (although such would have
been expected to give rise to anger). Rather, it was that such a statement
was made even after the client had begun to walk away as a gesture of
apology.

Problems associated with verbal aggression, while somewhat less
dramatic than the problem of physical violence, are more commonly
encountered in the clinic. Consider the following dialogue between a
father and his son.

Son: "Dad, I'm going out for a while."

Father: "If you plan to be with those pot-smoking weirdo friends of
yours, don't bother to come home."

Son: (Running out of the house) "I hate you, you rotten bastard!"

A therapist, working with the father might have modeled the following response: "Son, I know you have your own life to lead, but I'm disturbed about the effects some of your friends might have on you. Can
we talk about it?" Or, if working with the son, the therapist might
prescribe the following in response to the father's outrage: "Dad, I know
you don't like these guys, but they are not like that. Maybe if I brought
them home you could see for yourself."

Verbal aggression need not be delivered in a loud and emotional tone
of voice. Consider the following interchange. The husband has just
made a sexual advance toward his wife, but she has failed to respond. He
is, of course, hurt and frustrated, but rather than telling his mate this in
an honest and straightforward fashion, he says, in an apparently unemo-
tional tone: "I wonder if your frigidity has to do with your mannish figure." Stunned, but maintaining her composure, she replies, "That's
funny, most of our friends think you are the sort who likes men." This

example, while obviously facetious in its extremity, does illustrate aggression in lieu of genuine assertiveness. In a more assertive vein, the husband might have said "I really want you tonight. Is anything wrong?" The wife might then reply, "Lately you've been rushing things and that turns me off. Maybe if we could take our time and just go slow." Needless to say, "dirty fighting" of this nature has unnecessarily destroyed many a relationship. For a more thorough discussion of tactics of *constructive fighting,* the reader is referred to Bach and Wyden (1969).

Assertive Training in Groups

In Chapter II, evidence was presented that systematic desensitization could be effectively and economically presented within a group setting. Not surprisingly, the same would seem to hold true for assertive training, although experimental findings while encouraging, are of a preliminary nature. Aside from obvious economic considerations, there are several compelling reasons for supposing that group assertive training *ought* to be superior to individual treatment. We have already discussed the advantages of co-therapists over an individual therapist, and the arguments in favor of group assertive training are essentially the same. The group, consisting (usually) of 2 therapists and 5–10 clients, can provide a ready consensus for what is appropriately assertive in a given situation, can provide multiple models, as well as a varied assortment of "target" persons, for assertive exercises, and can provide massive social reinforcement for improved performances on the part of any member.

The principal group exercise is, of course, *behavior rehearsal.* The rules for implementing behavior rehearsal in a group are virtually identical to those holding for individual treatment. After a member presents a particular problem to the group, he is asked to role play his typical response, which is then evaluated in a nonjudgmental and friendly manner by other members of the group. Each member of the group is expected to assume some responsibility for training his fellow members, although ordinarily the therapists will provide more guidance than others in the group. After the member's initial response has been evaluated, one of the therapists might say, "Now, let's decide on what would be an appropriately assertive response in this situation." In an inexperienced group, this statement will often be met with silence, and one of the therapists may be required to provide the necessary response, although care should be taken to wean the members away from such overreliance on the therapists. Once the alternative response has been put forth, it is discussed by the group until agreement is reached that it indeed is appropriate. This response is then modeled by a group member volunteering for the task or by one of the therapists, if a volunteer is not forthcoming. Since modeling the response is a learning experience for the actor, as well as the observer, it is generally more productive if a member, rather than a therapist, acts as the model.

Initially a good deal of encouragement by the therapist may be required in modeling. Praising the model's performance will increase the likelihood that group members volunteer for such tasks in the future. What if the model's performance is inadequate? In our experience this is rare, in part because the appropriate response has already been agreed upon. But if one of the therapists does consider the performance as lacking, he might follow it up with: "That's certainly in the right ball park, but what about the following . . . ," whereupon he models the response. Once an effective response has been modeled, the member originally presenting the problem is asked to rehearse it and is praised by all members of the group for any improvement. As usual, an inquiry is made as to how the member felt. If anxiety is indicated, he is asked to repeat the response. Normally, the level of anxiety is considerably diminished during the second attempt.

Additional Group Exercises

The authors have found that for groups consisting of extremely withdrawn members (ordinarily chronic inpatients in a mental hospital), behavior rehearsal is too difficult or threatening. Here it is recommended that the group be presented with a graduated series of exercises, normally leading up to behavior rehearsal when the majority of group members are ready. *Greetings* and *free association* are intended as very nonthreatening warm-up exercises. The former exercise, greetings, simply requires that a given member turn to his neighbor, saying, "Hello _____, how are you?" The neighbor replies, "Fine _____, how are you?" The recipient then turns to a third member, and a similar exchange of greetings occurs, with the process continuing until each member has participated. Warmth, good eye contact, and a loud and assertive tone of voice are reinforced. Free association begins with a member saying a word, which is freely associated to by his neighbor; again, the exercise continues until each member has participated. Brief latencies and emphatic voicing are reinforced. In these and the remaining exercises, the therapists, participate as any other group member, although they must take particular pains to model the style of responding they wish their clients to acquire.

As Salter (1949) has noted, many individuals experience difficulty in giving and receiving compliments, and *exchanging compliments* is aimed at increasing skill (as well as comfort level) in this area. A group member turns to another member and warmly and emphatically provides the other with a compliment. Example: "Gee, _____ , I really like the way you are wearing your hair today." The recipient is encouraged to accept the compliment with some sort of positive acknowledgment. Example: "Thank you, that makes me feel good," or, "Gee, thanks, I thought I'd try something different." Self-disparaging comments (for instance, "Are you kidding, it's a mess") are gently but firmly discouraged, as are automatic and insincere countercompliments.

Positive self-statements require that each member tell the group something about himself that he particularly likes (example: "I like my sense of humor," or, "I am pleased with my taste in clothes"). *Small talk* is probably the most difficult (albeit beneficial) of the exercises. Here a member who is "it" designates two other members by name and gives them a topic for "small talk" ("Harry and Louise, discuss the weather"). As usual, good eye contact, spontaneity, and a warm, assertive tone of voice are reinforced. Quite frequently, members are initially reluctant to participate because they "have nothing to say." It should be stressed that in small talk it usually does not make a great deal of difference what is said and that the participants are by no means on trial. Often an individual who is uneasy in this exercise will assume the role of the "friendly interrogator," bombarding his partner with questions, but revealing nothing of himself. In fact, many people consider this to be good conversational style. Such behavior, however, is generally defensive in nature and ordinarily will thwart the otherwise natural tendency for small talk to evolve into a more intimate and satisfying interaction. For this reason it is discouraged.

Sometimes individuals find themselves engaged in conversations about which, *objectively,* they know very little (in sharp contrast to the chronic feeling certain people have, that they never have anything to contribute to conversations). In these situations it would be well if the individual could change the subject, and we recommend a variant of small talk requiring practice in doing just this. A smooth transition of subject (and avoidance of such hackneyed and rather rude ploys such as "Not to change the subject, but . . .") is warmly reinforced. Another potentially useful variation involves having members practice "breaking into" an ongoing conversation.

The exercises presented by no means exhaust the possibilities available to an assertive-training group. We would encourage therapists to be innovative in their approach. However, a word of caution is in order. It would be unwise to encourage group members, already deficient in the ability to make judicious social discriminations, to participate in behaviors that, outside of the group, would be subject to ridicule or censure. Thus, exercises involving intimate physical contact, the venting of rage, self-disclosures of a startling nature, blatant sexual overtures, and language that society would view as shockingly profane are to be discouraged. This is certainly not to suggest that such practices are never therapeutic. However, the individual participating in group assertive training is led to believe (often explicitly) that he will be interpersonally more effective if he engages in direct applications of what he has learned. Given this expectation, it would be nothing short of cruel to provide him with responses that would tend to shock or offend people outside the group setting.

Assertive Training versus Systematic Desensitization

Both assertive training and systematic desensitization are alike in that each provides the client with a way of reducing (or certainly coping with) maladaptive anxiety. In view of this, it is likely that there will be situations wherein the therapist may have difficulty deciding which method is more appropriate. At the outset, it is well to point out that no great harm will result if one method is used when the other would have been more effective. Nevertheless, choosing an inappropriate method of behavior therapy means wasting valuable time.

Generally speaking, when an individual is deficient in social skills (even if he is nonanxious in critical situations, which is rare), assertive training would seem to be in order. Naturally, one could desensitize the client to his social anxieties, but this would by no means guarantee that he would, if left to his own devices, acquire effective interpersonal behaviors. Assertive training has the advantage of dealing with the anxiety and overt behavioral deficiency at the same time. On the other hand, when anxiety is present in a situation that normally does not call for any active social behavior (for example, the sight of blood) desensitization would seem appropriate. This is *not* to suggest that the therapist is limited to desensitization in the treatment of such disorders. In Chapter X the reader is presented with certain so-called *cognitive* techniques that, in a clinical setting at least, have proven effective in dealing with such problems. Interestingly enough, one of these techniques, which we label *covert assertion,* bears more than a semantic relationship to standard assertive training.

Occasionally the therapist may come across an individual who shows no apparent behavioral deficiency, but who, nevertheless, complains of discomforting anxiety. The anxiety is often anticipatory in nature, and not unlike stage fright, which vanishes when the client at last begins to perform. If the level of anxiety is high enough to discourage participation in the target behavior (assuming that participation is necessary for the client), desensitization might be very helpful. However, there is often a fine line between what the client labels as "normal" excitement and "abnormal" anxiety, and many persons perform best under moderate levels of tension (regardless of how it is labeled). Desensitization would probably be followed by self-induced or externally induced resensitization in ver short order. If the client's "problem" appears to be of this nature, edu cating him to the fact that his "anxiety" is nothing more than normal excitement (shared by many others) may be the most effective strategy of all.[4]

Empirical Findings

Case Histories

In recent years a rather sizable number of case histories employing assertive-training procedures have been published. In the vast majority of these reports, assertive training was not the only method used. Frequently, relaxation training and systematic desensitization were also employed, as in the large-scale reports of Wolpe (1958) and Lazarus (1963). Thus, improvement rates for assertive training per se, based upon a large enough sample to be reliable, are not presently available. A more valid assessment of the efficacy of assertive procedures is to be found in the section to follow, which presents results of controlled experimentation. Nevertheless, as usual, case history results can provide the reader with a good deal of suggestive evidence, especially in relation to the spectrum of problems amenable to treatment. The material presented is based upon published reports wherein assertive training was the primary therapeutic intervention.

Salter (1949) presented 57 case histories in *Conditioned Reflex Therapy,* and apparently the majority were exposed to at least some of his excitatory exercises. Unfortunately, details are quite lacking. What may be of interest to the reader is the very wide variety of problems that have been dealt with, using Slater's approach. A partial list includes claustrophobia, fear of the dark, blushing, fear of public speaking, suicidal tendencies, homosexuality, and alcoholism. As we have suggested earlier, Salter's universal diagnosis is inhibition, and it is not surprising that almost any presenting complaint would be dealt with using his excitatory procedures.

Wolpe (1958) described three cases successfully treated with assertive training. The first case involved a socially insecure salesman who received treatment relevant to business and social contacts, as well as his

---

[4] For a further discussion of assertive training, specifically focusing on the problems of women, the reader is referred to Jakubowski-Spector (1973b).

wife's infidelity. The second dealt with a female who was overly dependent and submissive, especially with lovers (who ultimately rejected her). The third case was a male stutterer who typically withheld anger until he experienced an emotional outburst. For the second and third cases, follow-ups of 2 and 2½ years are reported.

Wolpe and Lazarus (1966) reported two additional case histories. The first is interesting in that the client was taught to use "one-upmanship" tactics on an employer who burdened him with lengthy and intimidating lectures. The second case, spelled out in unusual detail, dealt with an underemployed male. Treatment consisted of standard behavior rehearsal pertaining to job interviewing. Additionally, role-played interviews were taped and played back to the client. Care was taken to teach the client effective verbal strategies, but essential nonverbal elements (good eye contact and entering the interview room in an assertive, poised manner) were also dealt with. A 5-year telephone check revealed that the client now held an important position in his present firm (in contrast to "assistant chief ledger clerk," prior to treatment).

As we have suggested, in contrast to certain other forms of treatment, behavior therapy is generally rather brief. There is some evidence that this is especially true for assertive training. Wolpe (1958) has tabulated the results of behavior therapy for 88 clients and in 5 cases, assertive training was the primary focus of treatment. The mean number of interviews was approximately 16 for these cases, in contrast to a mean of over 45 interviews for all clients. Naturally, assertive training may require many more sessions, as in the case reported by Wolpe (1954) of a socially inadequate female who required 65 interviews. Occasionally, the therapist encounters an individual so "phobic" about assertion that he finds it necessary to apply desensitization along this dimension prior to implementing assertive procedures, as in a case reported by Wolpe and Lazarus (1966).

Stevenson (1959) treated 21 patients with assertive training, and 12 of the 21 patients remained much improved at a 1-year follow-up. Apparently encouragement to behave more assertively in interpersonal encounters was a major therapeutic strategy, although details are lacking. In a later report, Stevenson and Wolpe (1960) treated three sexually deviant males with assertive training. Again, pertinent details are lacking, although interestingly enough, as the patients became more assertive, their heterosexual relations improved. As we have suggested, the therapist ordinarily should not expect this sort of generalization to occur.

Lazarus and Serber (1968) presented two case histories in which desensitization was ineffective. One case involved a male who would either withdraw or become violent in the face of criticism from his wife.

Assertive training proved to be effective. The second case involved a depressed female who improved following assertive training (as well as instructions to seek employment). In their paper the reader is admonished to take care that desensitization, when it is administered, is the appropriate method of treatment.

Lazarus (1971) described three cases receiving assertive training. The first involved a lawyer who was suffering from claustrophobia and who described himself as a failure. The presentation is especially valuable in that a sizable portion of patient–therapist dialogue is included. A noteworthy feature is Lazarus's emphasis on his client's being able to communicate that the behavior of another was hurtful. That is, the client was not given training in how to "attack," but rather how to share his feelings in an honest and direct fashion. The second case involved the use of what Lazarus has called *rehearsal desensitization,* a technique similar to systematic desensitization in that a graduated hierarchy is employed. The client was a chronically depressed housewife, anxious in most interpersonal situations. She was taken through two hierarchies, the first involving progressively more assertion vis à vis one other person. The second, similar in nature, involved two or more persons. The increased assertiveness and diminished depression persisted through a 6-month follow-up. The third case represents an application of, in Lazarus's term, *training in emotional freedom* (that is, training in the expression of positive, as well as negative, feelings). For the first phase of treatment, the 19-year-old female client was given training in accepting and expressing anger, which resulted in a reduction in her depression. Phase two stressed the expression of positive feelings (for example, appreciation and physical affection). This latter case is unusual in its breadth, and it is unfortunate that details are so sparse.

Cautela (1966) described treatment with three cases of pervasive anxiety. The first case involved a young girl fearful of people; the second, a female doctoral candidate who reported having difficulties with her parents, and who had problems related to criticism and sex. The third case was a middle-aged man dominated by his wife and sexually impotent. Each of the three clients received assertive training, as well as other modes of treatment, and all showed marked and lasting improvement. What is most interesting is Cautela's observation that in every case of pervasive anxiety he had treated, assertive training was indicated. This is noteworthy because behavior therapists generally do not view this as the "treatment of choice" for pervasive anxiety (for example, Wolpe, 1958, suggests carbon-dioxide-inhalation therapy).

Hosford (1969) treated a sixth-grade girl fearful of speaking in a classroom situation. Treatment consisted of her practicing successive approximations to classroom speaking, within the therapist's office, as well as in the classroom itself. By the end of the school year, the client volunteered to give an oral classroom presentation. Varenhorst (1969) reported a rather similar case involving a school girl who was able to achieve her primary goal of participating in an art seminar (which had been especially threatening because students regularly criticized each other's work).

Serber and Nelson (1971) provided one of the few relatively large-scale applications of assertive training to hospitalized patients. Of the 14 schizophrenics receiving treatment (some also underwent systematic desensitization for phobic reactions) over a 6-week period, only 2 could be described as improved at a 6-month follow-up. The authors indicated that during the treatment period, there were signs of increased assertiveness on the part of the patients (unfortunately, no data is presented), which tended to disappear with the termination of treatment. Apparently, the patients experienced some difficulty with the role-playing exercises, consistent with our experiences with individuals from a similar population. Considering the contingencies of reinforcement that operate in most mental hospitals (that is, passive, dependent behavior tends to be rewarded), it is not surprising that the patients tended to "regress" following treatment.

With the exception of the cases reported by Salter (1949), the majority of published case histories involving the use of assertion have focused on problems related to timidity. On the other hand, assertive-type procedures have been used with a rather wide variety of clinical problems not obviously related to interpersonal timidity. For example, Seitz (1953) reported obtaining a reduction in self-mutilation of the skin in 12 of 25 patients following therapy that stressed the expression of hostility. Rimm (1967) reported using assertive procedures (including assertion to escape painful shock) to effect a lasting reduction in chronic crying spells in a hospitalized male. Walton and Mather (1963) successfully treated two compulsive males (a handwasher and an individual who had the urge to inform others of his homosexuality and to harm them with sharp objects) with a treatment that apparently primarily involved assertive training. Edwards (1972) successfully employed assertive training (following an initial treatment involving thought stopping, see Chapter X of this volume) with a male with a 10-year history of homosexual pedophilia. The pedophilia was apparently related to infrequent sexual contacts between the client and his wife. His increased assertiveness reportedly resulted in a vastly improved marital relationship.

Experimental Results for Individual Treatment

In what is evidently the first published report comparing assertive training with other treatment methods, Lazarus (1966) compared behavior rehearsal with a reflection-interpretation condition and with advice-giving. Each patient received no more than a total of four 30-minute sessions. The behavior-rehearsal condition included modeling by the therapist, practice by the patient, and relaxation induction when anxiety was indicated. Details of the two control conditions are lacking. A patient was considered improved when evidence was provided for *in vivo* behavior change. Given the brevity of treatment, the results reported by Lazarus are very impressive indeed, with 92% of the behavior rehearsal patients showing improvement, compared with 44% for the group receiving advice, and 32% for the reflection-interpretation group. Since Lazarus served as a therapist for all three conditions, it is possible that his bias as a behavior therapist may have retarded improvement in the control groups. Nevertheless, the 92% improvement rate for behavior rehearsal is quite encouraging. Unfortunately, no follow-up was reported.

Sanders (1967) worked with subjects who suffered from public-speaking anxiety. He compared the effectiveness of systematic desensitization with two forms of behavior rehearsal, both involving working through a speech-making hierarchy, graduated with respect to anxiety. For one of the two groups, the subject was told not to imagine an audience, while for the other, explicit instructions were given to imagine a critical audience. All groups, including a control group, were given training in deep muscle relaxation, as well. Treatment was conducted over six relatively brief sessions.

The principal response measures were objective performance ratings, as well as self-ratings while the subject engaged in making a speech. Sanders obtained significant improvement in objectively rated anxiety for all three treatment groups, although for self-rated anxiety, the treatment conditions, somewhat surprisingly, were no more effective than the control condition. Additionally, self-rated confidence was significantly more enhanced for each of the three treatment groups than for the control subjects, and the same was true for self-reported organization. Thus, in general, the three treatment conditions did not appreciably differ in their ability to enhance subjective and objective aspects of public-speaking behavior, although each was at least somewhat effective in comparison to a control condition. Since systematic desensitization is known to be effective in the treatment of speech anxiety (Chapter II), these results provide support for the possible therapeutic value of the two behavior rehearsal treatments, although their practical value would have been better established had Sanders conducted a follow-up.

In a well-executed study that did include a follow-up, Friedman (1968) assigned nonassertive college students to one of six conditions. In one condition, *directed role playing,* the subject was given a script defining the role of a student who was attempting to study at the library and who was faced with an antagonist attempting to interfere. In a second condition, the subject was to assume the role of the same student, but was not given a script to follow. For the third condition, the subject passively observed two confederates going through the above script. The fourth condition began with the subject again observing the confederates going through the script, followed by directed role playing, and a fifth treatment condition involved merely presenting the subject with the script. An additional control group was presented with a script unrelated to assertiveness. Each treatment condition lasted 20 minutes.

The principal response measures included self-rated and objective ratings of the subject's assertiveness when another person attempted to interfere with his efforts at putting together a puzzle. The main findings were that subjects who first observed the interaction modeled and then role played it themselves showed the greatest improvement. The remaining four treatments did not differ in terms of treatment effectiveness. These results, which held up at the 2-week follow-up provide support for behavior rehearsal (in other words, modeling followed by role playing) as it is ordinarily used in a clinical setting. Given the brevity of treatment (20 minutes), the results are striking.

In another well-executed study also characterized by extremely brief treatment, Lawrence (1970) assigned female college students to three different conditions. The first group received behavior rehearsal over two 12-minute sessions. The emphasis was on teaching the subjects to express honest disagreement. A second group received instructions pertaining to the value of assertiveness, with an emphasis on the irrational statements that nonassertive individuals say to themselves (taken from Ellis, 1962). A third group was given the same opportunity to express disagreement, but the experimenter, rather than providing feedback, merely paraphrased in a nonevaluative manner what the subject had said. The primary response measure was an objective rating of the subject's ability to disagree (consistent with her actual feelings) while engaged in an interchange with two confederates. Of the three treatment groups, the behavior-rehearsal group showed the greatest change, which persisted through a 2-week follow-up. This group also showed the greatest increase in self-rated assertiveness.

Lawrence also included a measure of the subject's ability to agree. Treatment had no appreciable effect on this measure. That is, subjects trained to express greater disagreement did not show a corresponding increase in the ability to agree (when agreement reflected their true feelings). This provides confirmation for a point raised earlier in this chapter: If a therapist wishes to increase assertiveness in a particular area, maximum attention should be devoted to practicing behaviors specific to that area. Assertiveness does not manifest itself as a broad "trait," and elevating assertiveness in one class of situation should not be expected to increase assertiveness in situations markedly different.

In addition to the above experiment, Lawrence developed a multiple-choice assertive inventory, consisting of items taken from Wolpe and Lazarus's (1966) assertive questionnaire, as well as from etiquette books. Separate forms were prepared for both males and females. A factor analysis, a standard statistical procedure for determining the extent to which a particular set of responses cluster together into traits, was performed on both forms, and the results provided no evidence for the existence of a broad trait of assertiveness.

McFall and Marston (1970) provided males and females with 4 hours of treatment. One group was given the opportunity to practice responding assertively to a variety of recorded situations, with an appropriately assertive response modeled on a portion of the trials. Additionally, subjects in this group were permitted to hear and evaluate their own responses. The second group received the same treatment, but the subjects' own responses were not fed back to them. A third placebo group received encouragement in isolating the situational determinants of nonassertiveness, as well as behaving in a more assertive manner; and a fourth group served as no-treatment controls. The chief response measures were objective ratings of assertiveness and self-ratings of anxiety while responding to recorded situations similar to (but never identical with) those used in training. Principal findings were that the subjects who had engaged in behavior rehearsal showed somewhat more assertion and less anxiety than subjects in the control groups. However, given the total treatment time (4 hours compared with 24 minutes in the Lawrence study), the effects were weak. This may reflect the fact that an assertive response was modeled only on a portion of the trials, or that the training and test situations were never precisely the same. A follow-up using the aforementioned response measures was not reported.

In a similar experiment, McFall and Lillesand (1971) assigned male and female subjects to two treatment groups and a control group. The treatment conditions were similar to those of McFall and Marston (1970), except that verbal modeling and coaching were provided on all trials. One group practiced their responses overtly, and their responses were fed back to them, as in the prior study. The second treatment group practiced their responses covertly. Treatment was conducted over two 20-minute sessions. On the average, subjects in the treatment groups showed a greater increase in assertiveness than those in the control group, with subjects who were not permitted to practice their responses overtly showing somewhat more improvement than those of the overt group. Again, a follow-up employing these same response measures was not reported.

For this study (McFall & Lillesand, 1971) and that of McFall and Marston (1970), telephone follow-ups were conducted. In the former, a confederate attempted to persuade the subject to subscribe to magazines, and in the latter study, a confederate requested that the subject volunteer to stuff envelopes for 3 hours. The results of these novel and refreshingly realistic follow-ups tended to parallel the main experimental findings, although the effects were quite weak.

Young, Rimm, and Kennedy (1973) assigned female subjects to one of four groups. The first group received two assertive-training sessions. Training consisted of having the subject respond to specific situations, followed by an appropriately assertive response modeled by the experimenter, followed in turn by the subject again responding to the same situations. A second group underwent identical training, except that appropriate assertive behaviors on the part of the subject received praise from the experimenter. A third group received a placebo treatment, and a fourth served as nontreated controls.

Both assertive groups showed a significantly greater increase in objectively rated assertiveness than either of the control groups, when tested in situations that were identical to those employed in training. For test situations that differed from those used in training, weak generalization effects were found for subjects in the first condition (that is, without reinforcement), with no generalization for subjects in the second condition (with reinforcement). On the other hand, in terms of improvement as measured by an assertive inventory (Lawrence, 1970), only condition two subjects showed significant gains, relative to the controls. Additionally, subjects in this condition tended to rate their treatment as somewhat more effective. At a subsequent telephone follow-up, this latter effect was marginally significant, with no significant group differences for a self-rating of generalized assertiveness.

While the study by Young *et al.* (1973) provides additional support for the efficacy of assertive training, the results pertaining to the role of social reinforcement are somewhat equivocal. As we have suggested earlier, the impetus for employing generous social reinforcement comes from an impressive body of operant research, as well as from clinical experience. At this stage there seems little basis for excluding reinforcment when assertive training is carried out. On the other hand, the results of the study just described point to the need for additional research in this area.

Experimental Results for Group Treatment

Research reviewed in Chapter II pointed to the effectiveness of systematic desensitization presented in a group setting. Recently, several studies have been reported that examine the effectiveness of assertive procedures applied to a group of subjects. In one such study, Lomont, Gilner, Spector, and Skinner (1969) compared the effectiveness of group assertive training with that of insight therapy. Each group met for 1½ hours per day, 5 days a week, over a 6-week period. Assertive training consisted mainly of highly structured role playing, with coaching from the therapist. Unfortunately, response measures did not include direct behavioral assessments, but were restricted to two measuring instruments normally used to assess rather broad personality dimensions, the Minnesota Multiphasic Personality Inventory (MMPI) and the Leary Interpersonal Check List. While MMPI scores did show a generally greater decrease in "pathology" for the assertive group than for the insight group, the effects were extremely weak. Given the soundness of the assertive procedures employed and the very considerable amount of treatment (in contrast to the studies cited in the previous section), it seems quite likely that more direct behavioral measures would have revealed marked improvement.

Hedquist and Weingold (1970) compared the effectiveness of group behavior rehearsal with a social-learning approach (Mainord, 1967) also administered in a group setting. Behavior rehearsal consisted of role playing with corrective feedback, coaching, and modeling, and the social-learning approach stressed problem solving within a context of honesty and responsibility. Treatment was conducted over a 6-week period. The solitary measure of therapeutic effectiveness was the subject's own report of the frequency of verbal assertive responses occurring *in vivo*. Most experimenters would not rely entirely on a subject's report of improvement, although the authors did mention performing spot checks on the validity of this measure. The results were that both treatment groups showed greater improvement than a control group, but did not differ from each other. At a 6-week follow-up, the differences between the treatment groups and the controls were no longer statistically significant, although still in the same direction.

Rathus (1972) provided three groups of female subjects (six subjects per group) with assertive training, conducted over seven weekly sessions. Training included participation in nine exercises similar to those described by Salter (1949) (for example, assertive talk, feeling talk, disagreeing, etc). Additionally, subjects were asked to practice 25 such tasks per week *in vivo*. In a second, placebo condition, three groups of females participated in a discussion of the nature of fear and child-rearing practices and were asked to observe acquaintances between sessions and apply what they had learned in brief character sketches. A third group of subjects served as nontreated controls.

On a 30-item assertiveness schedule, the experimental subjects showed significantly greater increments in assertion than the controls. While this group showed greater gains than the placebo group, the difference was not significant. A second measure involved interviewing five members from each condition. Subjects were asked how they would respond to specific situations calling for an assertive response. Results, while in the predicted direction, were not significant. On a third measure, a general fear survey inventory, the assertive subjects showed significantly greater fear reduction than the nontreated controls and slightly (nonsignificant) greater fear reduction than the placebo subjects. No follow-up was reported.

Although the study just cited provides some additional support for the value of group assertive training, the results are rather weak. From the report, it appears that at least some of the items on the assertive-response measures were not practiced during assertive training. To the extent that the dependent variables measured generalization, rather than the direct effects of treatment, one would have anticipated relatively weak results.

Although Sarason (1968) did not use the term *assertive training,* the procedures he employed with juvenile delinquents bear a definite resemblance to those described in this chapter. One group received group behavior rehearsal dealing with relevant tasks (for instance, applying for employment and talking with teachers or parole officers). Treatment was extensive, covering fifteen 40-minute sessions. A second group had appropriate behaviors described, but they were not enacted. A third group served as nontreated controls. Principal results were that in terms of staff ratings and ratings of review boards, as well as attitudinal measures, the behavior rehearsal group showed the greatest improvement, followed by the group receiving a description, followed by the controls.

In another preliminary investigation, Rimm, Keyson, and Hunziker (1971) employed the group assertive procedures presented in the method section of this chapter to a small group of adult males confined to a mental hospital primarily because of antisocial aggressive behavior. Treatment was conducted over six 1-hour sessions. A second, attention-placebo group also received 6 hours of treatment that consisted of reflection and advice-giving bearing upon the expression of anger. In terms of objective laboratory ratings of the subject's assertiveness (as opposed to verbal aggressiveness or timidity), the assertive group showed significantly greater increase in assertion than the controls. Informal follow-up observations by ward personnel and relatives tended to support the view that the assertive training resulted in less hostility and aggression.[5]

[5] Recently, Rimm, Hill, Brown, and Stuart (in press) completed a similar investigation, employing non-hospitalized male volunteers reporting a history of expressing anger in an anti-social manner. Subjects who had received 8 hours of group assertive training (primarily behavior rehearsal) were rated significantly more assertive and comfortable when presented with laboratory situations designed to illicit anger, than subjects receiving 8

Although the results of the studies conducted by Sarason and Rimm *et al.* (1971, in press) must be viewed as tentative, they are encouraging in light of the lack of success with more traditional attempts at rehabilitating persons with histories of engaging in antisocial behaviors of an aggressive or criminal nature.

In conclusion, the empirical findings, including results of case histories and experimental investigations, provide relatively convincing evidence that assertive training, primarily in the form of behavior rehearsal, is a valid and efficient treatment method. On the other hand, in terms of sheer volume, the evidence supporting systematic desensitization far exceeds that for assertive training, in part because well-controlled tests of the latter have been carried out only relatively recently. While preliminary studies suggest that assertive training may be applied in a group setting and that it may be of considerable benefit to individuals exhibiting antisocial aggression, such findings are especially in need of replication and extension.

The Theory of Assertive Training

Probably the most influential interpretation of what happens to an individual when he behaves assertively has been put forth by Wolpe (Wolpe, 1958; Wolpe & Lazarus, 1966; Wolpe, 1969). Consistent with his reciprocal-inhibition model of therapy, Wolpe assumed that assertion and anxiety are to a considerable degree incompatible. The physiological mechanisms upon which Wolpe based this assumption have already been discussed in Chapter II, with assertion taking on the same role as muscular relaxation. However, psychophysiological evidence that assertion correlates with anxiety reduction is much less direct than the evidence that relaxation results in anxiety reduction. Furthermore, what experimental evidence does exist relates to the relationship between anger and anxiety; to draw on this evidence is to assume (probably quite plausibly) that assertion and anger are on the same psychophysiological continuum.

In Chapter II we presented evidence that emotional experiences (such as fear or anger) are not *caused* by activity of the autonomic nervous system. Nevertheless, it is well established that changes in autonomic activity do correlate with emotional experiences. Moreover, there is evidence that the physiological (autonomic) patterns associated with fear and anger are at least somewhat distinguishable when objective measures are

hours of placebo group therapy. In terms of self-rated anger and comfort, subjects receiving assertive training showed significantly greater improvement than the controls. Unfortunately, follow-up data were not available.

taken. Experiments by Ax (1953), Schachter (1957), and Funkenstein (1956) revealed that when subjects were angry, in contrast to fearful, they showed a greater increase in diastolic blood pressure, a smaller increase in systolic blood pressure and a smaller increase in heart rate. In addition, skin resistance tended to increase during anger, but decrease during a state of fear. Certain writers, such as Funkenstein (1956), have suggested that whereas fear is associated with the hormone epinephrine, anger responses appear to reflect the effects of another hormone, nor-epinephrine.

Related to this, Wolf and Wolff (1942, 1947), by means of a tube inserted in the stomach of a male suffering from an ulcer, were able to directly observe the physiological response of the stomach wall when the subject was fearful or hostile, and characteristically different responses were reported.

The fact that the emotions of fear and anger give rise to somewhat different patterns of autonomic activity suggests that different brain mechanisms may be involved. If fear and anger do tend to inhibit each other (as Wolpe maintained), it is plausible to suppose that separate controlling mechanisms in the brain exist. On the other hand, separate controlling mechanisms in the brain would not necessarily imply that a person could not experience both emotions at the same time, or that one tended to inhibit the other.

Thus, direct evidence that assertion physiologically inhibits anxiety is lacking at the present time. Given that it is possible to tell when a person is anxious from his psychophysiological responses, an experiment showing that responses of this nature are weakened when the subject behaves assertively would provide the necessary direct support for the Wolpian position. As it is, patients often *report* being less anxious when they behave assertively, a finding that has also been reported in laboratory investigations of assertive training (see McFall & Marston, 1970). To date, subjective reports of this nature provide the most direct (and convincing) support for Wolpe's hypothesis relating assertion and anxiety.

Salter (1949) viewed behavioral timidity (as well as a variety of other problems) as reflecting a state of psychological inhibition that has come about as a result of Pavlovian conditioning. His therapeutic exercises are designed to replace this state of psychological inhibition with one of excitation. Although his therapeutic exercises may well have considerable practical value, his theoretical position is quite weak. First, it was based on Pavlov's outmoded conceptions of cerebral excitation and inhibition (although there is certainly nothing outmoded about Pavlovian conditioning as a type of learning). Second, it assumed a very broad trait of inhibition. Available evidence seems to indicate that lack of assertiveness is highly situation specific, making this assumption untenable.

While there are other accounts to explain why an individual may benefit psychologically from expressing his feelings (for instance, the early Freudian view of catharsis) there are presently far fewer competing points of view than is the case for assertive training's sister technique, desensitization. This, at least, is partly the case because, until recently, assertive training has received only meager attention in the laboratory, and it is not unlikely that in years to come a variety of different theoretical accounts of assertion will emerge. For the present, the reader is reminded that there is adequate support for the practical value of assertive training, from both the laboratory and the clinic.

IV

Modeling Procedures

The use of modeling procedures in behavior therapy is a relatively recent development (Bandura, 1969, 1971). The basic modeling procedure is quite simple: it involves exposing the client to one or more other individuals—actually present (live) or filmed (symbolic)—who demonstrate behaviors to be adopted by the client. As will become clear later in the chapter, exposure to models also includes exposure to the cues and situations that surround the model's behavior, so that not only the behavior, but also its relationship (appropriateness) to relevant stimuli, is demonstrated. Furthermore, the effect of a modeling procedure may be not only the adoption of certain modeled behaviors by the client, but also the changes in the affective and attitudinal correlates of these behaviors (Bandura, Blanchard, & Ritter, 1969). For example, a snake-phobic patient, after observing a model perform approach behaviors toward a snake (pick it up, let it crawl around in his lap), would be expected not only to show an increase in the approach behaviors he is willing to perform toward the snake, but also a *decrease,* or total elimination, of the fear he previously felt toward snakes.

There are four basic functions that modeling procedures serve. By the

acquisition

observation of a model, a client may learn new, appropriate behavior patterns, and modeling may thus serve an *acquisition* function. More likely, the observation of a model's behavior in various situations may provide social *facilitation* of appropriate behaviors by inducing the client to perform these behaviors, of which he was previously capable, at more appropriate times, in more appropriate ways, or toward more appropriate people. Modeling may lead to the *disinhibition* of behaviors that the client has avoided because of fear or anxiety. And, while disinhibiting behaviors, modeling may promote the *vicarious* and *direct extinction* of the fear associated with the person, animal, or object toward which the behavior was directed.

Instances of actual acquisition of totally new or novel behavior patterns by observation of a model are probably quite rare. The use of modeling to promote the initial acquisition of language in an autistic or psychotic child (Lovaas, Berberich, Kassorla, Klynn, & Meisel, 1966; Risley & Wolf, 1967) is probably an example of this. Similarly, the typical use of modeling in clinical practice usually has not been oriented toward the facilitation of behaviors already in the individual's repertoire; however, since this is a necessary procedure in some cases, we will discuss a few examples (Chittenden, 1942; O'Connor, 1969). Most of the recent work with modeling procedures has been concerned with the elimination of phobias or fearful behavior by exposure to models, and hence has been involved primarily with the disinhibition of approach behaviors toward the feared stimuli and the vicarious extinction of that fear (Bandura, Grusec, & Menlove, 1967; Bandura & Menlove, 1968; Bandura, Blanchard, & Ritter, 1969; Rimm & Mahoney, 1969; Rimm & Madieros, 1970; Ritter, 1968a,b; Ritter, 1969a–c).

The most obvious interpretation of modeling would lead one to expect that it is a technique limited to the treatment of behavior deficits; that is, for individuals whose repertoire of social behaviors are deficient such that they are unable or inhibited from behaving appropriately in certain circumstances. This is not the case, although modeling may be used to induce the acquisition, or facilitate the performance, of appropriate social behaviors. However, it may also be utilized to eliminate problem behaviors by instilling alternative behaviors that are incompatible with the problem behaviors (see Chittenden, 1942; O'Connor, 1969, to be discussed later). Furthermore, modeling is perhaps the most rapidly effective technique for eliminating fears and anxieties. There is evidence that avoidance behaviors motivated by fears are not eliminated simply by replacing them with alternative, incompatible approach behaviors, but rather, as we discuss later, exposure to fearless models produces vicarious extinction of the fear and anxiety that promotes the phobic avoidance behaviors (Bandura, Blanchard, & Ritter, 1968).

Many applications of modeling involve the participation of the client in the modeled behavior immediately following the demonstration by the model, and often reinforcement is provided for the client's successful performance. Procedures involving client participation are referred to by a variety of labels. If the modeling sequences involve the systematic, graduated presentation of increasingly difficult behaviors (as they almost always do), the term *graduated modeling* is often used. The analogy of this presentation procedure to that utilized in systematic desensitization is clear. Generally, the senses of the various terms are self-evident:

1. graduated modeling
2. guided modeling (usually gradual)
3. guided modeling with reinforcement
4. participant modeling (usually gradual)
5. modeling with guided performance (usually gradual)
6. contact desensitization

Graduated modeling, guided modeling, and guided modeling with reinforcement are terms usually used to describe procedures for the acquisition or facilitation of new patterns of behavior. Participant modeling and contact desensitization are usually reserved to describe procedures dealing with fear, anxiety, and avoidance behaviors. Clearly, of course, the systematic, gradual manner in which fearless models demonstrate progressively more daring behavior is indeed gradual or graduated, so the term graduated modeling is applicable as well, although it is not typically used. As noted above, the terms *participant modeling* and *contact desensitization* have not been differentiated in the literature except to the extent that some authors consistently use the term *participant modeling* (Rimm & Mahoney, 1969; Rimm & Madieros, 1970), while others are consistent in the use of the term *contact desensitization* (Ritter, 1968a,b; 1969a–c). Procedures termed contact desensitization invariably involve body contact with the therapist in the guiding of the client's participation. For example, in climbing a ladder following a model's demonstration, an acrophobic may be assisted in his assent by the model, who puts her hand around the client's waist (Ritter, 1969b,c); or a model, after interacting closely with a snake, may place his hand on the snake and the client place *his* hand on the model's, gradually moving it then onto the snake (Ritter, 1968a). While these may be cogent reasons for separating modeling procedures that involve physical contact with the model from modeling that involves more distant demonstration and independent participation by the client, the importance of this distinction awaits empirical confirmation.

Acquisition and Facilitation of New Behavior Patterns by Modeling

Before discussing procedures for the acquisition and facilitation of new behavior patterns, it is necessary to discuss briefly procedures for the training of imitation itself as a generalized response. In the case of severely retarded or psychotic patients, behavior patterns already established may include only repetitive, bizarre, meaningless, or self-stimulatory behavior, accompanied by attention and responsiveness to others that is minimal or totally absent. In other cases, minimal social responsiveness may not include a tendency to imitate or acquire any new behavior patterns by observing others. In these instances, training in imitation itself is a prerequisite to the use of modeling procedures to teach new behavior patterns.

Reinforcement Training of Imitative Responding

Individuals who work with severely disturbed or retarded clients, either adults or children, may encounter the problematic instance of a client who shows no propensity or ability to imitate at all. In such instances, the therapist may find it necessary to teach the client to imitate modeled responses or to use some method to increase imitation that is already at an extremely low rate. The question, then, is whether it is possible to influence the rate of imitation using reinforcement techniques.

Baer, Peterson, and Sherman (1967) worked with three 9–12-year-old severely retarded children who evidenced no imitation whatsoever in their daily interactions with others. Furthermore, when an adult approached and engaged the children in extended play, even when asked to imitate some simple response such as clapping hands or waving, these children steadfastly failed to imitate any of the responses, even though it was obvious that the responses were clearly within their ability to perform.

Training was conducted during mealtime, once or twice a day and three to five times a week. The experimenter would say "do this," and model a simple response such as raising his arm. Any response by the child that vaguely resembled arm-raising would be rewarded by food, which was delivered a spoonful at a time. The experimenter also said "good," just before putting the spoon into the subject's mouth. If the child tended to make no response, the experimenter would gently guide the child's arm through the appropriate motion and then offer the reward. Gradually such assistance, if necessary, was faded out. After each child demonstrated the reliable imitation of one response, they

tient's performance (for example, by shaping the mouth into an "O" shape for production of the "oh" sound), and reinforcing the behaviors of the patient that recreate or approximate the modeled behavior. When working with patients who have extreme deficiencies in their behavioral repertoires, it may even be necessary to utilize specific means to garner their attention and train them to be responsive to modeling cues (Baer, Peterson, & Sherman, 1967; Lovaas, 1967).

In treating psychotic children (or other patients whose behavioral repertoires are extraordinarily limited and/or whose contact with the environment is poor), initial treatment will usually be aimed toward increasing the scope of their social and intellectual capabilities, a goal that ultimately involves the development of linguistic skills. Let us consider closely the procedure utilized by Lovaas and his colleagues for the establishment of linguistic competencies in autistic children (Lovaas et al., 1966a; Lovaas, Berberich, Perloff, & Schaeffer, 1966b; Lovaas, Dumont, Klynn, & Meisel, 1966c; Lovaas, Freitag, Nelson, & Whalen, 1967).

The therapist confronts the child, sitting directly in front of him at close quarters. This placement maximizes the likelihood that the child will attend to the responses being modeled by the therapist. Continued attention is maintained by the therapist's physically reorienting the child if he turns away. Episodes of bizarre or self-stimulatory behavior are interrupted and halted by behaviors on the part of the therapist to command the child's attention, such as a sharp word or even a slap on the thigh. A film is available (Lovaas, 1966) that illustrates this procedure effectively. The film also contains striking examples of the effectiveness of these procedures. For example, in one instance a girl is being asked to name the color of a yellow crayon. As the therapist attempts to elicit this response from the girl, she behaves in an increasingly bizarre fashion, flapping her arms and grimacing. The therapist then slaps her on the thigh and again attempts to elicit the name of the color, and the girl responds "yellow" in a calm and straightforward manner.

Figure 4.1 depicts the course of verbal imitation in a previously mute autistic child. This case is especially illustrative since it demonstrates how, when the acquisition of a totally new and complex behavior pattern is required, treatment must begin with the modeling of necessary, simple components of the desired complex response (note the similarity to the successive-approximations procedure discussed in Chapter V).[1] In this instance "baby" was modeled for several days, simple sounds such as "ē" and "pa" were imitated first. Furthermore, initial imitation may not

[1] This is also similar to the procedure of graduated modeling, discussed later in this chapter. It may be instructive to consider this an example of the application of graduated modeling to cases requiring the acquisition of new behaviors (the later discussion concerns its application as a procedure to reduce fear and anxiety).

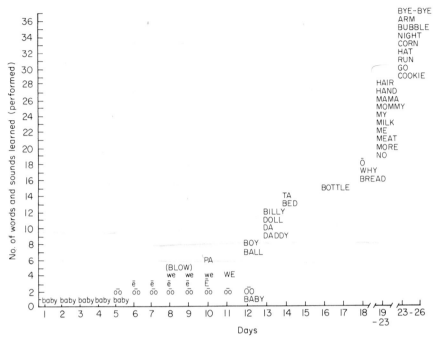

Figure 4.1 Growth of verbal imitation during the initial 26 days of treatment by an autistic child who was previously mute. From Lovaas, Berberich, Perloff, and Schaeffer, 1966.

occur immediately, and in this example even the simplest sounds were not imitated during the first 10 days of treatment. It seems possible that "pa" plus "e" were elements whose similarity to the components sounds of "baby" aided in the capability of imitating that word. Once some word imitation had occurred, the rate of subsequent imitation of new words indicated that even mute children may possess greater linguistic competence than their mutism implies. Nonetheless, the common element in the acquisition of new linguistic units, despite its rapidity, is the prior modeling of those sounds and words.

Another procedure for initial word learning described by Humphrey (1966), has been reported by Bandura (1969a). In this procedure, children sit in a darkened room and view pictures of objects projected on a screen, while hearing the appropriate word over earphones. At first the child may not be required to reproduce the words himself, and learning presumably involves the linkage of the verbally modeled labels to the visually modeled objects. Subsequently, however, the individual may be rewarded for correct productions of the acquired words. The pictures presented may include people, animals, objects, or even activities. Humphrey (1966) presents slides depicting the patients themselves (children, in this case) interacting with peers in natural settings.

The procedures discussed thus far are not limited to the treatment of autism in children. Quite similar methods have been used in the treatment of echolalic children (Risley & Wolf, 1967) or of young children whose speech is deficient or defective (Sloane, Johnston, & Harris, 1968). (The reader may wish to consult these sources for detailed procedural descriptions.)

When simple imitation occurs and when the child begins to show verbal responsiveness to commands and requests, these behaviors are typically reinforced. For example, in training competence in language skills, the initial task is the acquisition of words and sentences and the use of these words and sentences to label appropriate objects and actions. The use of contingent reward increases the likelihood that the child will attend, imitate (accurately), and subsequently utilize the acquired language skills. Lovaas (1967) has shown clearly how the use of contingent reward increases the accuracy of imitative responding (Figure 4.2, below). As may be seen in Figure 4.2, when an autistic child was rewarded for the accurate imitation of modeled responses, there was increased correct imitation, while, when reinforcement was given so that it was *not* contingent on the child's imitative responding, accurate imitation was clearly decreased.

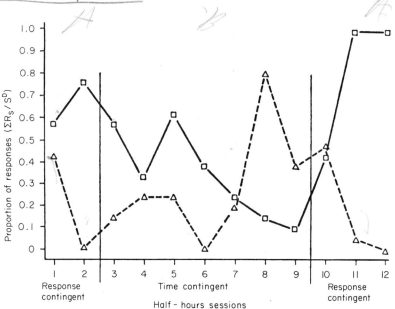

Figure 4.2 Percentages of modeled responses correctly and incorrectly reproduced by an autistic child as a function of reward contingency: during periods when rewards were contingent upon the correct reproduction of the modeled response and when they were contingent upon the passage of a certain amount of time (□——□: correct R; ▽---▽; incorrect R). From Lovaas, 1967.

The use of reinforcement accompanying modeling procedures is important in the continued expansion of language abilities into the realm of abstract conceptual function, especially as it is contained in language. For example, let us consider therapeutic procedures designed to teach a child prepositional constructions and to respond to abstract queries from others. Initially the child might be given an instruction to put a toy "on the table." If he fails to respond appropriately, the therapist may repeat the request while guiding the child's hand, with the toy, executing the behavior for him and, in the process, illustrating the "meaning" of the preposition. In this instance, we might say that the meaning is modeled by the child's observation of his own guided behavior. Subsequently, objects will be placed such that an accurate verbal description of their placement requires use of the preposition. In the process of training, various relationships (on, in, over, on top of, under, beneath, near, away from, etc.) would be modeled, a procedure that encourages the child to generalize his experience and form a rule for the usage of prepositional phrases in general. These same general procedures may be used to facilitate the child's acquisition of increasingly complex linguistic and conceptual capabilities, including verbal responding to abstract queries like "what did you do yesterday," "where are you going tomorrow," etc. Careful planning allows the initial teaching of such cognitive skills to involve particular queries that can be modeled (for example, "what did you do yesterday" at first could be responded to by acting out the answer).

Since speech is not only a linguistic-cognitive skill, but a social skill as well, language training must involve training in verbal social interaction and in appropriate spontaneous speech. Procedures for training these functions in children who were initially mute may also be applied to patients who have not been mute, but whose speech lacked social appropriateness. In this training procedure, the goals include the use of acquired language skills to express feelings and desires, to ask for and communicate information, and in general, to use speech to initiate and maintain social interaction with others. If desired objects are withheld from the child or desired activities are prevented, the occasion is created for the child to verbalize his desires, and the subsequent granting of these wishes constitutes reinforcement for the elicited verbal behavior. Narrative skills may be encouraged by having patients tell stories concerning pictures and to venture opinions, predictions, and comments concerning the persons and activities represented. Again, gradually more complex and novel recountings would be rewarded. After specific training of this sort, the individual may be guided into real social interactions with other individuals whose approval and friendly social responsiveness will continue to reinforce appropriate social verbal behavior.

We have concentrated upon the example of linguistic skills for two reasons: such skills are a prerequisite to appropriate social interaction, and the systematic application of both modeling and reinforcement procedures is a good example of the combined use of behavior techniques to work effectively with behavior problems. The combination of modeling and reinforcement procedures is effective in training appropriate social behaviors other than those intimately linked to language in a variety of types of patients. The general procedures remain the same: obtain the patient's attention, illustrate the behaviors by modeling, then, often in steps of increasing difficulty (again compare graduated modeling, discussed later in the chapter), physically guide behavior that is difficult to match, and then, reinforce first the guided behavior, then only behaviors that did not require guidance, and finally, reinforce behaviors that are initiated by the individual, without modeling, in the appropriate circumstances.

These procedures work well with a variety of patients. Although they have not yet been applied to the treatment of adult psychotics, they are clearly relevant to a variety of behavior deficits such patients often show. Lovaas and his colleagues have utilized them in the treatment of autistic children (Lovaas *et al.*, 1967). The combination of modeling and reinforcement procedures has also been utilized in the treatment of delinquents. In one instance involving delinquent boys (Sarason & Ganzer, 1969), methods of coping with common problem situations were demonstrated by models and then they were rehearsed and perfected. A variety of complex skills was included in this case, including self-control, coping with job demands, and interacting with authority figures, as well as handling negative influences from peers. In this case we may be speaking more of the use of modeling to facilitate and perfect social skills, rather than the actual acquisition of such skills.

Facilitation of Behavior Patterns by Modeling

Experiments dealing with the effectiveness of models actually present (live) and models shown on TV or film (symbolic) have consistently failed to show that either is more effective (Masters & Driscoll, 1971). Many of the techniques we discuss in the remainder of this chapter employ live models (Ritter, 1968a,b, 1969 a–c), while others utilize modeled behaviors as depicted on film or videotape (Bandura, Grusec, & Menlove, 1966; Bandura & Menlove, 1967), or even simple verbal instruction (Kelly, 1955). Perhaps due to the usual necessity (and difficulty) of obtaining the patient's attention in the treatment of behavior deficits requiring the acquisition of new behavior patterns, reports of such treatment applications of modeling (just discussed) have not tended to utilize symbolically presented models.

Modeling may be used to facilitate patterns of behavior that are seldom performed and that have been replaced by prepotent behavior patterns that have become problematic. Thus, less frequent, but more appropriate, behavior patterns may be strengthened by modeling and utilized as an incompatible response in the elimination of the more common problem behaviors. Withdrawal or isolation behaviors and, on the other extreme, aggressive behaviors are two good examples of behavior patterns that have been treated in this manner.

A recent study by O'Connor (1969) presents a good example of the use of symbolic modeling procedures to correct severe behavior deficits in young children. Children in this project all showed extreme social withdrawal, tending to isolate themselves from adults and other children. It should be noted that such a behavior problem may indicate the lack of requisite social skills *or* a fear of the avoided social interaction. Half of the children observed a sound film that vividly portrayed a variety of social interactions between a child and others. A number of interaction scenes were depicted, with each successive one containing increasingly energetic activity (graduated modeling). In each depicted activity sequence, a child model was first shown observing the social activity from a distance, then later joining in and interacting with other children. A second group of socially isolated children observed a control film that did not contain a graded series of social interactions and portrayed no behaviors particularly incompatible with isolate, withdrawn behaviors. O'Connor also observed nonisolate children in the same environment to obtain a measure of "normal" social activity.

Following these treatments, the children were given the opportunity for social interaction, and the extent of their participation was measured, as may be seen in Figure 4.3. Children who had not observed the film depicting social interaction remained quite withdrawn, showing no improvement in their social skills at all. Children who had observed the modeling films, however, showed an impressive gain in the number of social behaviors displayed, and displayed a frequency of social interactions that approached (and even surpassed slightly) the nonisolate base line frequency. One criticism of the study is that the measure of behavior change occurred *immediately* following the experimental manipulation, and there was no long-term follow-up. However, the reinforcing value of the skills acquired makes it likely that the social interaction behaviors would be maintained by the children.

In another treatment study, this one completed long before modeling was a recognized behavior therapy technique, Chittenden (1942) used symbolic models to alter children's hyperaggressive reactions to frustra-

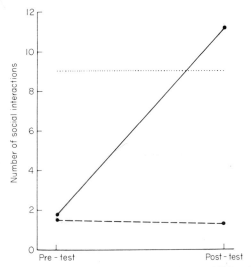

Figure 4.3   Extent of social interaction shown by withdrawn children before and after a treatment session which utilized symbolic modeling (———). The dashed line (– – –) illustrates the behavior of control group children who saw no filmed models. The dotted line (·····) represents the amount of social interaction displayed by nonwithdrawn children who were observed at the time of the pre-test. From O'Connor, 1969.

tion, replacing them with cooperative, constructive behavior in the same circumstances. The children selected for treatment were excessively domineering and hyperaggressive. Tests of aggressive tendencies, and for the relative lack of cooperative behaviors, included 1) situations in which two children were placed in a room with but a single valued and attractive toy and 2) behavior observations of the children in a nursery school setting. The "treatment" for one group of these hyperaggressive children involved the observation and discussion of eleven 15-minute playlets involving dolls. In each little play, dolls representing preschool children were depicted in interpersonal conflicts common to preschool children, and the plot of the playlet then demonstrated both an aggressive and a nonaggressive, cooperative solution to the problem. Also of importance is the fact that the *consequences* of these two solutions differed radically: aggression was shown to lead to unpleasant consequences, while cooperation was depicted to result in rewarding circumstances (compare Bandura, 1965). For example, in one playlet involving the conflict of two boys over a wagon, the aggressive solution depicted a fight over the wagon during which the wagon was broken. The cooperative solution involved the two boys' taking turns playing with the wagon, obviously enjoying themselves as they played.

The results, as shown in Figure 4.4, are quite clear. Compared with a

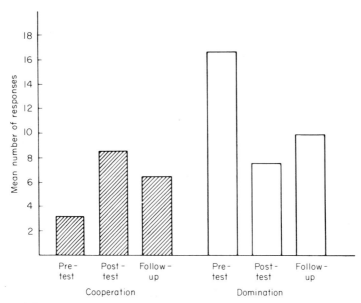

Figure 4.4 Amount of cooperative and dominating behavior displayed by hyperaggressive children in a nursery school before and after exposure to symbolic modeling treatment. (Drawn from data reported by Chittenden, 1942.)

pretest measure of both cooperativeness and aggressiveness, children were much less domineering and substantially more cooperative after viewing the series of playlets. These observations were made in a situation during which children found themselves in a room with another child, but with only one toy. Furthermore, other observations were made, and these also found an increase in cooperativeness and a decrease in aggression, which extended to typical "real life" social situations. Another important aspect of this experiment was the inclusion of a follow-up observation conducted 30 days after the treatment. Ratings of behavior in the nursery school situation at this time indicated that the decrements in aggressiveness and increases in cooperation were being maintained in actual social situations. Modeling procedures, it should be noted, may also be adapted for use in modifying the aggressive behavior of older children (Gittelman, 1965). This procedure includes the enactment of irritating and aggression-provoking situations along with the modeling of nonaggressive ways of coping with them.

Fixed-Role and Exaggerated-Role Therapy

Some techniques of therapy, not generally considered behavior therapies, rely heavily on modeling procedures. Consider, for example, the *fixed-role* and *exaggerated-role* therapies proposed by George Kelly (1955). In fixed-role therapy, the therapist, often with some collaboration by the client, composes a role sketch that includes desired behavior patterns. This sketch, and some role playing by the therapist, constitute a model for the client. In a fixed-role sketch, the role a client is to assume includes overt behaviors, as well as behaviors that are less available to observation by others, such as feelings, attitudes, and points of view. If a client cannot change his attitude or point of view upon request, he may still be able to adopt overt behaviors that are in line with the views and feelings he hopes to achieve as a result of therapy. Fortunately, there is a strong tendency for changes in behavior to *evoke* changes in attitudes and other cognitive activities (Festinger, 1964; Bandura, Blanchard, & Ritter, 1969); hence, changes in overt behavior may be the desired therapeutic procedure to gain attitudinal change.

Nonetheless, role sketches that the client is to adopt generally contain descriptions of both behaviors *and* attitudes whose adoption by the client is the goal of therapy. The client is to adopt the behavior patterns in the sketch over an extended period of time, often several weeks. The behavior patterns in the sketch are often at great variance with the client's typical behaviors, and some difficulty is usually encountered. The client is instructed to act *like* a person whom the character sketch would fit, not to try to *be* him. There is stress on the experimental, simulatory aspect of the role adoption in order to minimize the threat the client might feel about oralizing broad changes in his life style.

A fixed-role sketch (Kelly, 1955) is presented below; it was developed for a college-age client who came for therapy because of severe self-consciousness. He was extremely ill at ease with others, compulsive in his attempts to be errorless in the completion of every task, and subject to swings of mood, from cool placidity to hyperirritability. In this sketch, since the role is to be considered practically as an entire personality, the central character is given a new name: Kenneth Norton. The client, then, is to assume the role of Kenneth Norton . . . . to behave and feel as though he *were* Kenneth Norton. Note how the fixed-role sketch describes Kenneth Norton's behavior and feelings in great detail, specifying just exactly how the client is to act when he assumes this role. For example, the client was quite self-concerned, gave many examples of his tendency to introspect, to examine his every motive. Kelly (1955), in composing the fixed-role sketch, rolled this into a single behavior prescription (and, in this case, *proscription*): Be so concerned with other people that there is no time left to examine yourself. Note also how satisfying and enjoyable certain of their behaviors will be to the client. Thus, the role even includes what stimuli are to be reinforcing for the person.

FIXED-ROLE SKETCH: Kenneth Norton

Kenneth Norton is the kind of man who, after a few minutes of conversa-tion, somehow makes you feel that he must have known you intimately for a long time. This comes about, not by any particular questions that he asks, but by the understanding way in which he listens. It is as if he had a knack of see-ing the world through your eyes. The things which you have come to see as being important he, too, soon seems to sense as similarly important. Thus he catches not only your words but the punctuations of feeling with which they are formed and the little accents of meaning with which they are chosen.

Kenneth Norton's complete absorption in the thoughts of the people with whom he holds conversations appears to leave no place for any feelings of self-consciousness regarding himself. If indeed he has such feelings at all, they obviously run a poor second to his eagerness to see the world through other people's eyes. Nor does this mean that he is ashamed of himself; rather it means that he is too much involved with the fascinating worlds of other peo-ple with whom he is surrounded to give more than a passing thought to soul-searching criticisms of himself. Some people might, of course, consider this it-self to be a kind of fault. Be that as it may, this is the kind of fellow Kenneth Norton is, and this behavior represents the Norton brand of sincerity.

Girls he finds attractive for many reasons, not the least of which is the ex-citing opportunity they provide for his understanding the feminine point of view. Unlike some men, he does not "throw the ladies a line" but, so skillful a listener is he, soon he has them throwing him one—and he is thoroughly en-joying it.

With his own parents and in his own home he is somewhat more expressive of his own ideas and feelings. Thus his parents are given an opportunity to share and supplement his new enthusiasms and accomplishments [Kelly, 1955, pp. 374–375].

With practice, clients can adopt prescribed roles such as these. Thus, their behaviors are changed for at least a short period of time. However, one is still faced with the problem of maintaining such changes in behav-ior. It is seen as important that new behavior patterns be practiced in as many different approximate contexts as possible, and care should be taken to help the client "try them out"—first in situations that will allow the new behaviors to be reinforced. In the case of Kenneth Norton, Kelly (1955) reported the following anecdote indicating that the role be-haviors of Kenneth Norton met with positive consequences in at least one instance when the client met a girl, a former classmate after a movie:

The girl works in the candy counter in the lobby (of the theatre) and she and he had a twenty-five- to thirty-five-minute talk. She seemed quite inter-ested in him and the role worked better with her than with anyone else. In fact, by the time the conversation was finished she was paying him several compliments, saying that he had changed since he had gone away to college, obviously implying a change for the better. The conversation was so rewarding to the client that he did not leave until the manager of the movie came along and implied that he was taking too much of her time [p. 394].[2]

Kelly's (1955) fixed-role therapy is more sweeping than other role-therapy techniques, perhaps because Kelly's procedure is embedded within an entire theory of personality. Often therapists with a behavioral bent will make use of what is known as *exaggerated-role training,* a procedure of instructing patients deliberately to adopt prescribed, but limited, roles that are designed to correct highly specific behavioral problems. Wolpe and Lazarus (1966) described the case of a college student who complained of severe feelings of uneasiness when dining at his girl friend's house. The problem became exacerbated when, during dinner, his mouth would become so dry that he could not swallow his food. The following short role was prescribed:

> *The next time you dine at her house I want you to act as if you were a wealthy and important businessman . . . not 22-year-old Peter. As you sit at the table, I want you to look at each person and see him as you think he would appear in the eyes of this mature and wealthy businessman* [p. 134].

In this case, we may surmise that the use of the "label" *businessman* was sufficient to produce in the client a clear notion of all the attendant social behaviors that would characterize a businessman at the dinner table. More important, perhaps, than the client's success in acting out all those behaviors a businessman does perform, is his success in avoiding anxiety, which certainly would *not* have characterized an effective businessman. It seems likely that by behaving like a businessman (including the cognitive aspects that were embodied in that role, such as a feeling of competence or superiority) many internal stimuli eliciting the anxiety were removed. Probably it was not the sight of his girl friend or her father which produced anxiety, but rather the client's thoughts in that situation: "What can I say to impress them, how do I talk to her father when I don't even know him," etc. Thus, it seems reasonable that the therapist determine the cognitive components of any set of maladaptive behaviors so he may, if using role therapy, devise a role that includes cognitive components that supplant those which elicit anxiety or other maladaptive behaviors.

[2] This and the extract on the opposite page are reprinted from *The Psychology of Personal Constructs,* Vol. II, Clinical Diagnosis and Psycho-Therapy by George A. Kelly, Ph.D. By permission of W. W. Norton & Company, Inc. Copyright 1955 by George A. Kelly.

Disinhibition and the Vicarious Extinction of Fear and Anxiety by Modeling

There are several components that may enter into an overall modeling procedure designed to eliminate fears and anxieties and to allow free performance of patterns of behavior that had been inhibited. These components are often combined to maximize the effectiveness of treatment, as will become obvious in the discussion to follow. Nevertheless, for the sake of clarity, we discuss the three primary procedural concerns separately; we then provide two detailed examples of the use of modeling techniques to treat quite divergent behavior problems involving fear and avoidance behaviors.

Graduated Modeling

In a manner quite similar to the systematic exposure sequencing in desensitization, it is usually best to expose fearful clients to models who perform behaviors that are progressively more and more threatening, as perceived by the client. To expose snake-phobic individuals to a professional snake handler interacting closely with a giant anaconda would do little to lower the person's fears, and he would very likely avoid even observing the model if his fears were particularly intense (Bandura, 1971). Similarly, the observation of such a scene would be likely to elicit intense emotional responding in the observing client, which would not dissipate during observation (compare the discussion of implosive therapy or flooding/response prevention, Chapter VIII; Bandura, 1971) and which might promote avoidance behaviors (looking away, shutting eyes, etc.) during the modeling sequence. For these reasons it is generally deemed best to graduate, or order, the behavior patterns performed by the model so that sequences that are minimally anxiety provoking to the client are performed first. It is noteworthy, however, that some investigators (for example, Bandura, 1971) feel that the graduated modeling procedure is an aid to the effectiveness of modeling, but not a prerequisite, and repeated exposure to the model's performances of highly anxiety-provoking behavior patterns might also prove effective, though they might also require a longer series of treatment sessions.

Bandura, Grusec, and Menlove (1967) treated children who were extraordinarily fearful of dogs by exposing them to peer models who fearlessly interacted progressively more closely with a dog. Treatment consisted of eight 10-minute sessions held over the brief period of 4 days. Groups of four children observed the model, whose sequence of behaviors lasted only 3 minutes during each session. During the first sessions, the model's behaviors included patting the dog (which was confined in a pen) and feeding her. Beginning with the fifth session, the modeled tasks were performed outside the pen, and the model walked the dog around the room. During the last two sessions, the model climbed into the pen with the dog and continued his friendly interactions with her.

Since the purpose of the study was to evaluate the effectiveness of graduated modeling, there were several treatment procedures utilized by these investigators: two modeling procedures and two control conditions. In one modeling condition, the context of treatment was positive, designed to buoy the children's spirits and generally make them happy and relaxed (responses presumably incompatible with fear). Thus, in that modeling condition the children were met with a party atmosphere (hats, prizes, games) prior to the modeling sequence. In a second condition no attempt was made to alter the children's general affective state: they simply sat at a table and observed the model. In two control conditions the party atmosphere was created, but there was no modeling sequence, the dog simply being present in the room (penned during the first sessions, on a leash afterward) in one control condition and absent in the other.

The children's fear of dogs was assessed by means of an approach test in which they were exposed to a live dog and asked to approach it, feed

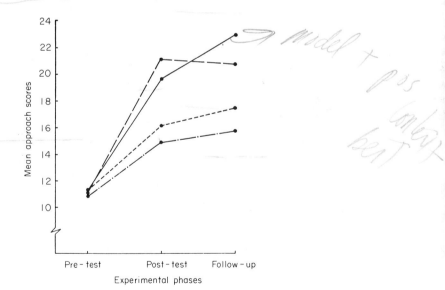

Figure 4.5 Mean approach scores achieved by children before and after various treatment conditions and after a follow-up period of 1 month (●——●: model + positive context; ●— —●: model + neutral context; ●– · –●: dog + positive context; ●– –●: positive context). From Bandura, Grusec, and Menlove, 1967.

it, and spend time alone with it in a room. Their behavior was assessed prior to treatment, immediately following the completion of 10 treatment sessions, and then 30 days later. During the posttest and follow-up test assessments, children were exposed not only to the dog used during treatment, but also to a dog of vastly different appearance. Figure 4.5 illustrates the effectiveness of these various treatment procedures. It is quite clear that the context in which the modeling occurred had little effect upon the effectiveness of the modeling procedure, and there was no effectiveness from simple exposure to a dog in the positive atmosphere, or from exposure to the positive context alone. There was clear evidence of the generalized effectiveness of treatment, as well. Children in the modeling condition were more likely to perform extremely threatening behaviors (remaining alone in the room with either dog) than were children in either control condition.

The Use of Multiple Models

The use of multiple models is one procedure that may promote generalization of treatment effects. While single models might be presumed by the client to have some special talents that allow them to be fearless, this is less likely to be the case among a group of divergent models (Bandura, 1971). Furthermore, multiple models are likely to vary slightly in the ways in which they demonstrate fearless behavior, thus providing greater latitude of behavior possibilities for the client.

As we noted earlier, the symbolic presentation of models is generally no less effective than the use of models actually present. An advantage of symbolic presentation is that the same modeling sequences may be presented to a number of clients at different times without requiring the services of the model in each instance. Consequently, more elaborate procedures involving equipment and numerous individuals may be filmed, relieving the client or therapist from the organizational and financial burden of assembling them repeatedly for various clients. This allows, then, the economical presentation of multiple models.

It is not surprising, in light of these considerations, that the effectiveness of multiple models for fear reduction has been tested by exposing individuals to films of various models demonstrating fearless behavior. In a study similar to that described in the preceding section, Bandura and Menlove (1968) exposed dog-phobic children to a series of eight 3-minute films that depicted models interacting with a dog in gradually more threatening ways. One group saw films that included models of both sexes and varying ages interacting with a variety of dogs of all sizes and degrees of fearsomeness (these factors increased gradually as treatment proceeded). In a control condition, the children saw films of Disneyland and Marineland.

The children's actual avoidance behaviors were tested prior to treatment, immediately following treatment, and 30 days later. As Figure 4.6 illustrates, the two modeling conditions were more effective than the control in increasing the children's capabilities to fearlessly interact with a dog. The effect of multiple modeling is most apparent when one examines the data concerning children's capabilities for performing the terminal interaction behavior in the assessment scale: to remain alone in

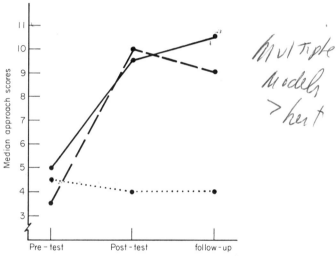

Figure 4.6 Median approach scores achieved by children in the treatment and control conditions before and after treatment and after the follow-up period (●——●: multiple model; ●— —●: single model; ●·····●: control group). From Bandura and Menlove, 1968.

a room confined in the pen with the dog. Figure 4.7 illustrates these data. It is clear the multiple-model procedure was the only one that actually induced such fearless behavior, and its effectiveness was, if anything, improved after the 30-day follow-up.

Participant Modeling and Contact Desensitization

There are several terms in the literature which are used indiscriminately, it seems, to describe basically the same modeling procedure: participant modeling, modeling with guided participation, demonstration plus participation, and contact desensitization. There is some tendency

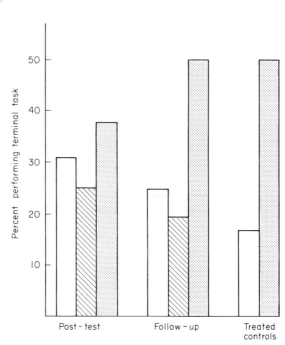

Figure 4.7 Proportions of children from each treatment condition who performed the terminal approach behavior immediately following treatment and 1 month later. (The behavior of the Treated Controls was assessed immediately after their treatment, which occurred during the follow-up period.) [▨: multiple model; ▧: single model; □: control.] From Bandura and Menlove, 1968.

for one or the other term to be used consistently by a particular author, and as such it may indicate a preference of terms, rather than an actual difference in procedure. As we noted earlier, it would appear that a major factor determining the use of the term *contact desensitization* is the inclusion of actual physical contact between the therapist and client. In general, all terms may be reduced to the general procedure of *demonstration plus participation*, and the participatory portion typically involves guidance by the therapist, either verbal or by actual physical contact. For the remainder of this chapter we use the general term *participant modeling* to refer to the general technique of modeled demonstration plus client participation, employing other terms only when describing the work of investigators who prefer those terms (for example, Ritter, 1969 a–c).

Before turning to a detailed description of participant modeling procedures, it is well to consider the factors that seem responsible for the effectiveness of the technique (studies bearing upon this question are presented in a subsequent section). A primary factor is clearly that of *vi-*

carious extinction. Observing a model perform a feared behavior in the *absence* of dire consequences constitutes a learning situation in which the cues that tend to induce avoidance behavior are present, but the avoidance behavior does not occur. Furthermore, to the extent that anxiety generated by the observation of the feared stimulus (for example, a snake) or behavior (for example, approaching the snake with a gloved hand) is minimal, it may dissipate during the performance, thus allowing the client to be relatively free of anxiety in the presence of the stimulus, reducing the tendency for that stimulus to evoke anxiety.

Another factor that has been inadequately stressed in the literature is the *acquisition of technical knowledge and information* via modeling. In the extinction of a snake phobia, the client learns technical details concerning how to handle a snake gently but effectively so it will not get away; in treating a water phobia (described later in the chapter), technical skills of swimming, treading water, floating, etc. are undoubtedly important and fear-reducing. Information may also serve an important function in reducing fear or revulsion, as in the case when a client learns, by experience, that a snake is not slimy or deathly cold, does not immediately strike, etc. Technical skills may be acquired by observation, but polished during the participation procedure; information is conveyed by both the observation of the model's behavior and the client's direct experience during participation.

The acquisition of technical knowledge and information is intimately related to the direct *acquisition of skills* during the demonstration phase, skills that are likely to reduce anxiety due to not knowing how to behave and that also improve the likelihood that the client will successfully participate in the feared activity, thus providing needed practice and reinforcement (success) for those newly acquired behaviors. Similarly, the acquisition of information is related to another factor, namely the *direct extinction of fear*, which tends to occur when anticipated dire consequences fail to materialize during the participation phase. The disconfirmation of such expectancies, accompanied by a diminution in level of anxiety, reduces the degree to which the stimulus continues to evoke that anxiety.

Finally, the continued *presence of the therapist* is an important factor for at least three reasons. First, his presence provides support, social (emotional) and/or physical (contact) during the participation phase. Second, the continued presence of the therapist also allows social reinforcement to be given following each successful participatory act. Third, the continued presence of the therapist is likely to prevent or at least minimize any problems that may develop again during the participatory phase (for example, if a snake starts to escape, or an acrophobic client stumbles while on the steps of a ladder).

Research on Components of the Participant-Modeling Procedure

Blanchard (1969, 1970) isolated several components of the participant-modeling procedure and compared the individual contributions to specific and generalized behavior change. Three components were separated from a demonstration-plus-participation procedure, the modeling component, the provision of *verbal information,* and the provision of *direct contact* with the feared object. Four subjects simultaneously participated in a treatment procedure, but each subject was in a different condition. To one subject, the therapist administered a demonstration-plus-participation modeling procedure. Behind a one-way mirror, two other subjects observed. One of these who observed also listened via earphones to the verbal interchange between the therapist and the participating subject, the other observer merely watched. Of these three subjects, then, the participating subject received modeling, verbal information, and direct contact with the feared object; another subject, modeling and verbal information; and the third received only modeling. A fourth, control subject received none of these treatment procedures.

Prior to the treatment stage each subject was given a test to determine how closely he would approach a live snake. Following treatment, the subjects were twice again adminstered this test, once with the same snake that had been included in the earlier test and in the treatment procedure, and once with a different, unfamiliar snake, in order to assess the generalization of the treatment effectiveness. The terminal behavior in each assessment was the subject's picking up the snake from a glass cage with bare hands, holding it close to his face, and then allowing it to crawl around freely on his lap, with his arms at his side. Blanchard (1969, 1970) also gathered data concerning the subjects' general fear of snakes (affect) and their attitude (liking) toward snakes.

Figure 4.8 illustrates the changes in behavior, affect, and attitude produced by the various procedures. The modeling component appears to account for 60% of the observed change in behavior and 80% of the recorded changes in affect and attitude, with the guided participation contributing the remainder. It is interesting that information appeared to add nothing to the effectiveness of the general technique, but this information was limited to verbal renditions of the nonslimy nature of snakes, the harmlessness of the tongue, their poor vision, etc. Giving highly phobic people such verbal information may even prove arousing. It is still the case, certainly, that the modeling procedure and the subsequent participation provides both vicarious and first-hand information on how to handle snakes and how they do, indeed, feel and behave.

Blanchard (1969, 1970) also gathered ratings of fear arousal at several

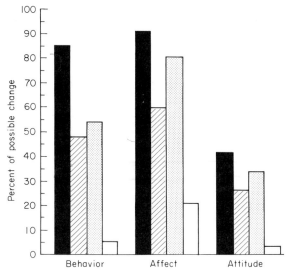

Figure 4.8 Percentages of change in approach behavior, fearfulness, and attitudes exhibited by individuals who received various components of modeling and guided participation treatment procedures (■: modeling + information + participation; ▨: modeling + information; ▥: modeling; □: control). From Blanchard, 1969.

times throughout the three modeling sequences. Figure 4.9 illustrates the effect of these procedures on arousal at the various points during treatment. Again, there is indication that the provision of extensive verbal information may prove arousing since the two procedures containing information began at a higher level of arousal. However, in all procedures there was a dramatic reduction of arousal during observation of, or *participation* with, the live snake.

In testing subsequent improvement, Blanchard (1969, 1970) measured subjects' abilities to approach the snake used in treatment and a new, generalization snake as well. The entire modeling-plus-information-plus-participation procedure proved to be the most effective in reducing fear toward the snake that was used during treatment. However, subjects who only observed the therapist modeling the desired behavior, without participating or hearing the verbal interchange, proved to be the least fearful of the new, generalization snake. Thus, there is some indication that modeling *without* participation by the client constitutes a procedure which is to be preferred when the behavior to be changed will necessarily occur in many different situations or toward many different objects, in the case of a fearful avoidance behavior. If extensive generalization must occur before changes in environmental contingencies, produced by the client's changed behavior, elicit the desired

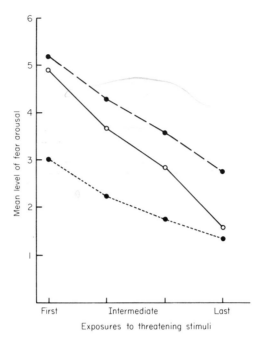

Figure 4.9   Mean degree of fear arousal elicited by approach to the feared object: level of arousal following the initial approach, and by subsequent repetitions of the approach, shown by individuals who participated in treatment or observed the treatment of others with or without informational influences (O——O: modeling + information + participation; ●——●: modeling + information; ●– – –●: modeling). From Blanchard, 1969.

behavior in new situations, the therapist may choose to conduct a rather lengthy simple modeling procedure, rather than utilize a less extensive exposure to a demonstration-plus-participation procedure.

Participant modeling is a technique that is applicable to a variety of behavior problems characterized by fear, anxiety, and powerful avoidance behavior. It has been applied to specific fears of animals (Bandura, Blanchard, & Ritter, 1969; Rimm & Mahoney, 1969; Ritter, 1968a) and fears of rather nonspecific stimuli such as height (Ritter, 1969b,c) or water (Hunziker, 1972). Throughout the range of problem behaviors to which this technique may be applied, the basic procedures remain the same: graduated demonstration plus graduated participation. The following sections present two detailed examples of participant-modeling procedures adapted for the treatment of a snake phobia and the fear of water. The basic procedures clearly may be adapted to a wide range of other behavior problems.

Example: Treatment of Fear of Snakes by Participant Modeling

Initially one must acquire a snake known to be docile and relatively unmenacing in appearance (for example, a Florida hognose). Pet store managers or other suppliers of reptiles are knowledgeable in this area.

Following an initial session or portion of a session in which the technique is generally outlined, the procedure may commence. First the client will be asked to enter the room containing the snake, which is enclosed in a glass cage on the other side of the room. The client is told that the door will remain open throughout the treatment sessions and that he may leave at any time. Following this, the client will be asked to stand (or seat himself) at whatever distance from the cage he feels comfortable (there are some constraints on this: the client should be in the room and able to view the snake and subsequent modeling interaction clearly). The therapist then slips on a pair of gloves, opens the top of the glass cage, and touches the snake briefly (but not hesitantly). If this interaction causes undue distress to the client, he may reposition himself farther away from the cage. In addition the therapist may verbally reassure the client that the snake cannot escape the cage. Similarly, throughout the entire series of modeling demonstrations the therapist/model should clearly evidence ease, confidence, a lack of hesitancy, and show warmth toward the client.

Following these introductory interactions the therapist may proceed to the major sequence of modeled interactions with the snake, which are as follows:

I. Gloved hand procedure
   1. Stroke the snake's midsection, then tail, then top of head.
   2. Raise the snake's midsection, then tail, then head.
   3. Grasp the snake gently but firmly a few inches from the head and about 6 inches from the tail, remove from the cage (taking care not to approach the client or swing the snake obviously closer to him).
   4. Comfortably handle the snake, modeling how easy and comfortable the interaction process can be, how the model is in complete control, etc. This facet of the procedure should continue for several minutes (it may be wise to time it to insure adequate length), until external indications are that the client's anxiety level is rather low.

II. Bare hand procedure.
   1–4. The above procedure should be repeated by the therapist/model using his bare hands.

Throughout the entire procedure care should be taken not to allow the client to become unduly agitated. If the client reports intense fear, or if such fearfulness is observed by the therapist, the procedure should stop, the snake be replaced in his cage with the lid, and attention be turned to giving support and reassuring the client, and perhaps some relaxation suggestions. If such an interruption is necessitated, the procedure should subsequently be started at an earlier phase in the graduated sequence than the one that evoked anxiety and followed by the careful progression through the various modeled interactions.

When these two modeling sequences have been successfully completed, the client may be asked if he feels willing to approach the snake. By this time most clients will agree; however, if they are not willing, continued demonstration sequences should be undertaken with care given to the lengthy exposures to calm, controlled, pleasant-appearing interactions with the snake. When the client agrees to approach the snake, the therapist should pick the snake up and hold it while he asks the client to don the gloves and briefly touch the snake's midsection. When the client successfully does so, reinforcement and support should be given; for example, "I'll bet that is the first time in your life you ever touched a snake. Good for you!"

The client may then be asked to stroke the midsection, then touch and stroke the tail, and finally touch and stroke the top of its head. Should the snake extend its tongue, the therapist might matter-of-factly note that it is harmless, merely a sensing device for sound waves.

When the gloved touching and stroking behaviors have been completed, the next step involves the client's holding the snake in his gloved hands. He may be instructed to place his hand loosely about the midsection of the snake and hold it there until he feels fairly comfortable (the therapist continues to support the snake). If these actions appear to cause some anxiety (or perhaps to excite) the client, it may be suggested to the client that he take a deep breath to induce some relaxation. When progress is apparent, praise should be given.

The procedure continues, with the client holding (in gloved hand) the snake's tail, then its head, and finally he may be asked to support the entire snake. This progression is not rapid, of course, with praise given for progress and time allowed at each step for the client to become comfortable. If at any point the client expresses anxiety, the therapist should immediately take the snake back (calmly) and offer reassurance before returning to the participation process. The availability of the therapist, to intervene if any problems develop, is an important part of the procedure, and the therapist should make certain that the client realizes this. Some investigators and therapists feel that it is important, at the beginning of the participation phase, to have contact between the therapist and client (Ritter, 1969b,c). In the present case, this might be accomplished by having the therapist place a bare hand on the snake's midsection, with the client placing his *gloved* hand on the therapist's hand and then sliding it off the therapist's hand and onto the snake (similar procedures should be added to other components of the modeling sequence described above). The choice of including such contact procedures appears to be a matter of the personal experience and preference of the therapist, and there are successful cases reported in the literature that did (Ritter, 1969b,c) and did not (Rimm & Mahoney, 1969) include such contact.

Example: Treatment of Water Fears by Participant Modeling

It should be clear from the above example that overcoming fears of quite specific objects includes the acquisition of approach skills, as well as the vicarious extinction of fears and anxiety. There are many instances of unreasonable fears that appear to be attached even more to the requisite behaviors involved in an activity and their individual consequences than to a particular stimulus object itself. Thus, a fear of water, which prevents the participation in, and enjoyment of, water activities may be not precisely a fear of water (since there may be little fear of showering, bathing, etc.), but of activities such as swimming in deep water, submerging the head, and so on.

Hunziker (1972) developed a 54-step procedure designed to reduce fear of water activities and allow previously fearful individuals to enjoy water-related activities. This program included 54 individualized modeled behaviors and was designed for group treatment programs. When administering such a treatment regime to groups, an attempt is typically made to include a sufficiently lengthy series of graduated stimuli to prevent even the most timid participants from experiencing overwhelming anxiety following transition from one step to the next. Clearly, if such a program is utilized in the treatment of individuals alone, it may be shortened (or perhaps lengthened) and tailored to the individual's unique pattern of fearfulness.

At each step, ideally, treatment participants should be asked to rate their level of anxiety in order to insure that anxiety reduction has accompanied each step. Any modeled sequence might be repeated if some clients indicated that anxiety is still present (at a level of, say, 4 or more on a 10-point scale). An effective adjunct, also, is to sequester one of the clients as an aide, preferably a client who is likely to do well. His demonstrated successes provide a second modeling stimulus, creating a situation of multiple models. At the therapist's choice, there may be guided participation, verbally or manually carried out, as well as reinforcement for success. Hunziker's utilization of this procedure eliminated all these factors, with clients simply trying each modeled behavior sequence after it was modeled, and yet he still found participant modeling to be more effective than modeling without such participation.

Below are listed the 54 steps proposed by Hunziker. The treatment regime is primarily designed for use in a swimming pool. Such a setting provides a body of water with an even bottom, and with depths specifically marked, and with no tides or drop offs. Furthermore, closer supervision and safety measures can be maintained in such a setting. Generalization might be assessed at an ocean beach or lakeshore, and further treatment might be required since each of these settings includes stimulus elements that may be fear provoking and that are not handled in the specific treatment program. The 54 steps:

1. Sit on the edge of the pool.
2. Sit on the edge of the pool with your feet in the water.
3. Sit on the edge of the pool and splash water on yourself.
4. Stand in the pool and hold onto the side.
5. Stand in the pool . . . away from the side.
6. Hold the side and splash water in your face.
7. Not holding the side, splash water in your face.
8. Hold the side and blow bubbles in the water.
9. Not holding the side, blow bubbles in the water.
*10–12. Hold onto the side and put your face in the water.
*13–15. Not holding the side, put your face in the water.
*16–18. Hold onto the side and completely submerge.
*19–21. Not holding the side, completely submerge.
*22–24. Hold the side and put your face in the water with one foot off the bottom.
*25–27. Hold the side and put your face in the water with both feet off the bottom.
*28–30. Hold the kick board and put your face in the water with one foot off the bottom.
*31–33. Hold the kick board and put your face in the water with both feet off the bottom.
*34–36. Hold the kick board with one hand and put your face in the water with both feet off the bottom.
*37–39. Without any support, put your face in the water and take both feet off the bottom.
40. Where the water is 12′ deep, sit on the side.
41. Where the water is 12′ deep, descend pool ladder.
42. Where the water is 12′ deep, hold onto the side.
*43–45. Where the water is 12′ deep, hold onto the side and submerge completely.

*46–48. Where the water is 12' deep, hold onto the kick board and completely submerge.
*49–51. Where the water is 12' deep, let go of the side and completely submerge.
  52. Sit on the side where the water is 12' deep and push off the side into the pool.
  53. Kneel on the side where the water is 12' deep and push off the side into the pool.
  54. Stand on the side where the water is 12' deep and jump into the pool.

NOTE: Steps 1–39 were performed in approximately 3½ feet of water.
* Each of these series of 3 steps was demonstrated by the therapist for 1 inch, 3 inches, and 5 inches of water.

Studies of the Effectiveness of Modeling Procedures

Research on modeling as a behavior therapy technique often contrasts various types of modeling procedures, rather than selecting particular modeling protocols and contrasting them with a nonmodeling technique. Ritter (1969b) drew a distinction between contact desensitization, in which the therapist manually guides or assists the client's participation; demonstration plus participation, in which any guidance is verbal only; and live modeling, with no participation. She then compared these three techniques in terms of their effectiveness for the elimination of acrophobia. Subjects exhibiting a severe degree of fear of heights were given but a single 35-minute treatment session utilizing one of these techniques. Treatment occurred on the roof of a seven-story building, a flat roof with a 41-inch concrete railing. The pace of treatment was governed by feedback from the subjects concerning how comfortable they were with the various tasks they were asked to perform. As in a desensitization procedure, whenever a subject reported feeling some discomfort, at the completion of a task, that task was repeated [there was some difference between this procedure and the typical desensitization systematicity in that a discomforting task might not be repeated until one of somewhat more difficulty had been completed successfully (Ritter, in press)].

In all procedures, the therapist first performed the behaviors to be acquired. These consisted of several behaviors. First the therapist would stand on each of five rungs of a wooden ladder for two 30-second intervals; then for two 30-second intervals she would stand on an 18-inch-high chair, and on a 29½-inch-high stool, all positioned 11 inches from the roof railing. Finally, the model would climb to the eighth rung of an elevator penthouse wall ladder, 8 feet above the roof's surface.

In the contact-desensitization procedure, the therapist, after demonstrating each behavior, assisted the subject in his performance of the modeled response. For example, in working on ladder climbing, the therapist might walk alongside the subject, an arm around his waist, while approaching the ladder. Then, as the subject ascended the ladder, the therapist might follow behind with hands placed on the subject's waist. Finally, when the subject was standing on the upper rungs of the ladder, the therapist might place her hands on the subject's legs. In the demonstration-plus-participation procedure, following the therapist's demonstration the subject would be guided verbally through his replication of the therapist's modeled behaviors. In the live modeling procedure, the therapist demonstrated the behavior while the subject sat toward the center of the roof and observed. The therapist also asked occasionally how the subject was feeling and only proceeded to model more difficult behaviors when the subject was able to observe the preceding behaviors with little or no discomfort.

Before treatment each subject was given a height avoidance test, which included the behaviors described above. Points were given for each behavior the subject could already perform, the maximum score being 44, and only those individuals accumulating 18 points or fewer were included as subjects in the experiment. Following the modeling procedures, the subjects were again administered the height avoidance test, with only a 5-minute rest period. Thus, the total time included in treatment amounted to a bare 40 minutes.

The results of this study are shown in Figure 4.10. Treatment by contact desensitization produced a greater increase in the number of fearless behaviors performed than did either of the other two procedures, and the demonstration plus participation produced a greater increase than did live modeling.

It is clear from this study that the greater the interaction between therapist and client in a modeling procedure, the greater the effectiveness of treatment. The question that remains, however, is which of the components of this interaction enhance the effectiveness of treatment. Certainly one factor is the provision of social reinforcement by the therapist as the client actually demonstrates his mastery of new behaviors. The client's own self-administered reinforcers, such as positive self-comments or feelings of pride, doubtlessly contribute to the successful acquisition and maintenance of behaviors previously feared.

It may be that the presence of the therapist and the encouragement he gives, whether verbal or physical, has a calming effect—similar to the relaxation portion of a desensitization procedure. An indication that this may be the case comes from the results of an experiment by Rimm and Madieros (1970), in which demonstration plus participation was coupled

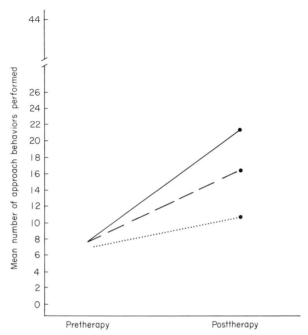

Figure 4.10 Mean number of approach behaviors shown by individuals before and after treatment by live modeling, demonstration plus participation, or contact desensitization procedures (———: contact desensitization (pretherapy = 7.6, posttherapy = 21.2); — —: demonstration + participation (pretherapy = 7.6, posttherapy = 16.6); · · · · · ·: live modeling (pretherapy = 7.0, posttherapy = 10.4). From Ritter, 1969c.

with relaxation training for one group of subjects, while another group received demonstration plus participation or relaxation training alone. The subjects, all severely frightened of snakes, showed an equally striking reduction in their snake phobias when demonstration plus participation was employed, regardless of the inclusion of relaxation training. Subjects who received relaxation training showed no substantial relief from their fears. The finding that relaxation training, which appears to be important in desensitization procedures, had no observable effect may indicate that subjects receiving demonstration-plus-participation procedures were already sufficiently calm and relaxed to allow the completion of fearful behaviors such as the actual handling of a snake. It is also possible that the effectiveness of demonstration plus participation, for reasons that remain unclear, is so powerful that the addition of ancillary techniques such as relaxation training cannot offer improvement since the effectiveness is already so great. Further research should clarify this point.

In an extensive study, Bandura, Blanchard, and Ritter (1969) compared the relative effectiveness of *symbolic modeling, live modeling plus participation,* and *desensitization* for the reduction of snake phobias. Symbolic modeling consisted of a 35-minute film depicting young children, adolescents, and adults engaging in progressively more frightening and intimate interactions with a snake. This procedure also contained elements of a desensitization procedure. Subjects were taught to induce and maintain deep relaxation throughout the period in which they viewed the movie. Furthermore, they were in control of the progression of the film and they were instructed to stop the film whenever a particular model performance was anxiety provoking, to reverse the film to the beginning of the aversive sequence, and to reinduce deep relaxation.

Desensitization utilized a 34-item hierarchy containing scenes that the subjects were to imagine while in a deep state of relaxation. These scenes ranged from relatively innocuous activities such as looking at pictures and toy replicas of snakes to the imagined handling of live snakes. In the live-modeling-plus-participation condition, subjects repeatedly observed intimate snake-interaction behaviors modeled by the experimenter. Then they were aided by joint participation from the experimenter in the performance of progressively more threatening approach responses toward a king snake. There was also a control condition in which subjects participated in the assessment procedures that were administered before and after the treatments utilized in the other conditions.

It is noteworthy that the various treatments required differing amounts of time to administer. Subjects continued in a treatment procedure until they either achieved the terminal criterion (observing the model perform the most threatening behavior or imagining the most fearful item on a hierarchy, for example), or until treatment had consumed 5.25 hours, not including time for relaxation training. The modeling treatments both took somewhat more than 2 hours, while systematic desensitization required an average of 4½ hours to achieve the criterion, a significantly longer period of time.

Following treatment, subjects were presented with the opportunity to interact with a snake, either the one included in the treatment and pretest phases or another snake of distinctively different appearance (generalization). One stringent measure of the effectiveness of a treatment is the percentage of subjects who will perform the behavior previously rated *most* threatening. Fully 92% of the subjects in the modeling-with-participation treatment condition were able to interact this closely with a snake. On the other hand, only 33% of the subjects in the symbolic modeling condition, 25% in the systematic desensitization condition, and 0% in the control condition were willing to interact so intimately with a snake. Subjects from the symbolic modeling, systematic desensitization, and control groups who would not perform the most intensely threatening interactions with a snake were subsequently given the live-modeling-with-guided-participation treatment. The average length of this subsequent treatment was 1 hour and 20 minutes. After this treatment had been administered, 96% of all subjects were able to make the most threatening approach response to the snake used during treatment, and 70% showed the complete elimination of avoidance behavior toward the generalization snake as well! These results indicate that participant modeling is a powerful and extremely rapid technique for the elimination of fears.

Before discussing this procedure further, it would be well to comment upon the relationship between behavioral and attitudinal changes that presumably result from these therapeutic techniques. In a study by Bandura *et al.* (1969) subjects were given an attitude scale concerned with their attitudes toward snakes and were also requested to fill out a semantic differential. Changes in approach behavior toward snakes were positively related to attitude change as measured by both the semantic differential $(r = .55, \ p \leq .01)$ and attitude scales $(r = .58, \ p \leq .01)$. Interestingly, there was no relationship between the degree of initial fearfulness (initial number of intensity of fears) in other areas of functioning and the degree of behavioral change with respect to the behavior problem treated. It was also found that subject's initial attitudes toward snakes did not affect the extent of improvement in their approach behavior toward snakes effected by the various treatments.

Ritter (1968) utilized a group-desensitization procedure for the elimination of snake phobias in young children. In her procedure, peer models were employed to demonstrate fearless and bold interactions with snakes. Initially, children were given an avoidance test in which they were required to move from a point 15 feet away from a caged snake to a point 1 foot away. Other tasks involved standing in front of the snake, looking down at the snake, touching the cage with a gloved hand or with a bare hand, or inserting a glove and then a bare hand into the cage up to the wrist. Further tasks involved the lifting of the snake or taking it out of the cage. Only children who could not hold the snake within the cage with a gloved hand for 5 seconds were included in the study.

Children were given two treatment sessions that lasted approximately 35 minutes each and that were spaced 1 week apart. Seven to eight children participated in each treatment group. In one condition, which involved *contact desensitization,* the children observed an adult experimenter taking a snake out of the cage, sitting with the snake, and petting it. This continued until one of the subjects appeared to be willing to participate, at which time the experimenter encouraged the child to put on a glove and to place his hand on her hand while stroking the snake.

Gradually, then, the child was encouraged to stroke the snake himself, first with a gloved hand, then with his hand bared. When several children had become bold enough to stroke the snake, the children were encouraged to take turns being therapist and client, one stroking the snake and the other beginning with his hand on the first child's and gradually moving it to the body of the snake.

In a *vicarious-desensitization condition,* there were five peer models at each session. These were boys and girls who had expressed no fear at all of snakes prior to the experiment. In each session these models were seated in a corner of the room. After the experimenter had removed the snake from the cage, she encouraged the models to perform taks that had been included in the avoidance task, such as stroking the snake with a gloved and then a bare hand, lifting the snake with first gloved and then bare hands, etc. The children who were subjects were not encouraged to participate directly with the snake. They did, however, take charge of the demonstrators, in a game, during which they sent the demonstrator from the room, called him back in, and instructed him to perform the various fearless interactions with the snake, at which time they could again observe his behavior.

Following the treatment procedures all children were again administered the snake avoidance test. There was also a control group of children who were administered the avoidance test and then, following a period of time equivalent to that consumed by the treatment for the other two groups, were readministered the avoidance test.

The behaviors required in the avoidance test, some of which were described earlier, culminated in a task requiring that the snake be held approximately 5 inches from the face for 30 seconds, after which the subject was asked to sit in a chair with his arms at his side while the snake was in his lap for 30 seconds. *All* of the items in the avoidance test were performed successfully by fully 80% of the children who received contact desensitization. Significantly fewer children in the vicarious-desensitization condition performed all of these items, whereas none of the children in the control condition performed all items. Statistical analyses revealed that children in both treatment groups evidenced highly significant increases in their abilities to interact closely with snakes when compared to children in the control conditions. It was also evident that children in the contact-desensitization condition improved in their ability to interact intimately with snakes to a significantly greater degree than did children who received vicarious desensitization.

Clearly, group procedures may be highly effective in the administration of observational learning techniques for the elimination of fears. Although little research has been done, it seems quite apparent that these techniques also lend themselves to group application for the treatment of problems in which the goal may be the addition of behaviors to the client's repertoire.

The success of the group application of behavior modification techniques reinforces the possibility of developing treatment centers on the model of "schools" that could devote concerted effort to the behavioral treatment of common problems. In such "schools," assistants could be trained to administer all assessment techniques, both behavioral and paper and pencil, as well as many of the modification procedures. Professionally trained individuals, then, could devote their time to the construction of new therapeutic programs and the evaluation of current therapeutic procedures, tasks to which their training is directly suited. As Ritter (1969b) has suggested, such an institution might include laboratories suitable for various *in vivo* and filmed treatments. In addition a team of technicians could be trained to do "on location" work when laboratory treatment would be difficult or less efficient (for example, with street crossing phobias). Information obtained from the results of *in vivo* treatment could be used as the ground work for producing the filmed and taped treatment demonstrations. Living skills film suitable for use in existing academic settings could also be developed (Ritter, 1969).

V

Contingency Management Procedures

In this chapter we examine procedures involving the contingent administration of rewarding (reinforcing) consequences or events. We also discuss the contingent administration of 1) aversive consequences that are only mildly painful and 2) aversive procedures such as the withdrawal of reinforcement following a maladaptive behavior.

The discussion also includes _time-out_ procedures, which involve the elimination of rewarding consequences typically contingent upon a behavior, as well as the removal of all other potentially rewarding stimuli that are present, but not necessarily contingent upon, the maladaptive behavior (for instance, immediately following a misbehavior, the child is sent to a quiet room with few, if any, interesting playthings). Time-out procedures may be administered by a therapist, but often their effectiveness is increased if they are controlled by individuals who populate the life space of the person under treatment and, therefore, have greater contact with him. Close attention must be given to the training of these individuals, which involves giving them some degree of expertise in the administration of the behavior-change procedures to be employed.

It is not an uncommon comment that all too frequently, clinicians focus upon the elimination, or extinction, of maladaptive behaviors and ignore the more positive goal of strengthening adaptive behaviors that are infrequent, or initiating adaptive behaviors that are absent from an individual's repertoire (Meehl, 1962). In Chapter IX, which considers techniques of aversive control, it is stressed how important it is to strengthen alternative adaptive responses whenever punishment is employed to eliminate maladaptive ones. Indeed, where possible, it is surely preferable to eliminate maladaptive behaviors by increasing the frequency of desirable, competing behaviors (which cannot be performed at the same time as the maladaptive behavior) whenever this is a viable alternative to the use of punishment, or even simple extinction procedures (withdrawal of reward). Eliminating a response by punishment may be quite ineffective if no alternative response is available, and when working with individuals whose lives are already overly replete with punishment, or who seldom enjoy reinforcement, the use of extinction procedures may alienate or depress the individual and consequently prove ineffective. Too often the therapist encounters children whose parents punish them when they misbehave, but do nothing when the children behave properly; in such cases a primary goal may be to teach the parents techniques of contingency management, which employ reinforcement, rather than punishment (Tharp & Wetzel, 1969).

As we have stressed, depending upon the nature of the presenting problem, the therapist may need to employ varying combinations of modification techniques. For example, if the problem involves the complete absence of a desirable behavior, and the behavior appears to be one that the client lacks the ability to perform, it may be necessary to shape his performance of this behavior by the procedure of *successive approximation*. In such a case observational learning techniques could be utilized to instigate some initial performances of the behavior, following which the judicious use of reward might be employed to establish the behavior firmly in the person's repertoire and insure its performance in appropriate situations (*discrimination training*). To take a second example, one may have to punish a maladaptive behavior of very high frequency in order to clear a "slot of time" into which a new behavior may be inserted. Self-destructive children often require punishment to inhibit their persistent tendency to injure themselves, or to engage in hyperactive behavior so that more human rewards—such as love and affection—may be made contingent upon more acceptable forms of behavior such as smiling, passive social contact (sitting in an adult's lap), or quiet play.

The Role of Reinforcement in the
Learning of Social Behaviors:
An "Operant Philosophy"

Although various learning theorists concerned with human behavior adopt essentially the same roster of factors that they feel are responsible for the acquisition and maintenance of human behavior, they differ in the emphasis they place, or the importance they feel any one factor may have. Thus, theorists who are primarily concerned with observational learning as a source of human social behavior are likely to argue cogently that the observation of others is a powerful, and perhaps even primary, source of behavior acquisition for the child and adult. Theorists with more of an operant bent are likely to acknowledge the utility of observational learning, but may be quick to point out that only when a behavior is rewarded will it continue to be performed, even though the observation of another person provided the original learning situation. And, similarly, they will point out that behaviors that produce contingent aversive consequences (that is, are punished) may be observed, but not adopted into the individual's own behavioral repertoire (Bandura, 1965).

Certainly, it is not our goal to argue in favor of one theory or another, nor even to take sides in the value-laden arguments concerning which process of learning is more important for the development of personality behaviors in human beings. Clearly, while the "operant philosophy" stresses the importance of reward and punishment in the acquisition, maintenance, and extinction of human behavior, it also acknowledges, at least minimally, the roles of other factors in addition to the use of reinforcement and punishment (for example, classical conditioning and observational learning).

Definitions of Terms

Reinforcement

The terms *reinforcement* and *reward* are often used synonymously, and to a considerable extent they do in fact overlap in meaning. A *positive reinforcer* is an event, behavior, or material object that will increase the frequency of any behavior upon which it is contingent (Skinner, 1969). Another person's smile or having him pay you a compliment are events that would be likely to act as reinforcers (note that we must say "likely"— although the therapist may often anticipate what will act as a reinforcer, technically he may not be certain of this until he observes that the contin-

gent presentation of the speculated reinforcer does indeed affect the behavior of the person in question) (Becker, 1971; Skinner, 1966 in
Honig). Similarly, the privilege of performing a high-frequency behavior on one's own may act as a reinforcer: children's disruptive behavior
in the classroom may be eliminated and their quiet, studious behavior
strengthened if they are allowed to be rowdy only *after* they have been
quiet for a set period of time (Premack, 1959). And finally there is the
typical, somewhat hackneyed notion of reinforcer as tangible, material
reward. While it is clear that material rewards are indeed quite effective
in the control of behavior, the social reinforcement value of another person's friendly, loving, approving, or simply attending behavior is also a
powerful factor in the control of behavior, and social reinforcement is
certainly a more common occurrence that the dispensation of material
rewards (Stevenson, 1965).

Reinforcers always *increase* the frequency of a behavior. By definition,
there are two types of reinforcers, positive and negative. A *positive reinforcer* is any stimulus event whose contingent *presentation* increases the
rate of a performance of response; a *negative reinforcer* is any event whose
contingent *withdrawal* increases the rate of performance of a response.
As Skinner (1969) has so aptly put it, "The kinds of consequences which
increase the rate (of a response) ("reinforcers") are positive or negative,
depending upon whether they reinforce when they appear or disappear
[p. 7]." As the reader will already have noted, a negative reinforcer is
usually the termination of a punishment or punishing stimulus. Chapter
IX covers the use of the contingent termination of punishment as an integral component in avoidance conditioning procedures.

Contingency

In its simplest form, to dispense a reinforcer contingently is to dispense it *following* a desired behavior (one whose frequency is to be
increased) and to take care that the reinforcer be dispensed *only* following desired behaviors. Later in the chapter we discuss principles designed to increase the effectiveness of the contingent dispensation of
reward.

There is little doubt that the contingent dispensation of reinforcement
is an effective method for controlling behavior. It has been clearly demonstrated that noncontingent reinforcement fails to control behavior,
whereas the contingent application of the same reinforcer does exert effective control (Bandura & Perloff, 1967; Hart, Reynolds, Baer, Brawley, & Harris, 1968; Redd, 1969). If an office worker receives a raise
every 3 months, regardless of the quality of his work, his performance is
less likely to improve than if he is working under a system employing

bonuses and raises based on merit (that is, contingent on good performance). Similarly, the contingent application of a stimulus or event that
has no value to an individual is ineffective in altering the behavior upon
which it is contingent (Ayllon & Azrin, 1968; Kelleher, 1966), and in
such cases one should either employ a stimulus that can be demonstrated
to have reinforcing properties, or directly establish some reinforcing
value for the neutral stimulus by pairing it with an established reinforcer
(Kelleher, 1966; Lovaas, Freitag, Kinder, Rubenstein, Schaeffer, & Simmons, 1966). Chocolate candy will not be a powerful reinforcer for the
child who dislikes, or is allergic to, chocolate, nor will the opportunity to
play baseball be an effective reinforcer for the child who dislikes physical
activity and prefers to play chess.

What Is Contingency Management?

Contingency management consists of the contingent presentation and
withdrawal of rewards and punishments. Although such procedures
may be used by the therapist himself, often it is more feasible and effective that he train others to function as contingency managers—such as
parents and teachers, individuals more closely involved in the life of the
individual under treatment than is the therapist himself. Furthermore,
as detailed in Chapter VII, a client himself may be trained in contingency management in order that he may exercise self-control over his
own problem behaviors.

Obviously there are more skills involved than the mere dispensation of
reinforcements. To take just a few examples, one must discover a number of rewards or reinforcers that can be manipulated and that are effective for the individual whose behavior is to be altered. Even prior to this
step, the therapist must determine the behaviors to be changed, their
frequency of occurrence, the situations in which they occur, and the
stimuli or reinforcers that appear to be responsible for the maintenance
of these maladaptive behaviors. These assessment procedures may also
reveal that an individual's problematic behavior may be due not to the
presence of inappropriate behaviors, but rather to the absence of appropriate behaviors. In a nutshell, assessment and pretreatment procedures
include establishing a base-line rate of frequency, instituting procedures
for measuring behavioral change, and assessing such things as the behaviors to be treated and the reinforcers to be employed in treatment.

All of these skills are involved in contingency management and make
it a complex and sophisticated procedure, even though many would feel
that a reinforcement analysis of behavior is rather simplistic.

Base-Line Measurement

In the assessment procedures that must precede any contingency manipulations, the therapist must establish the relative frequency or in-
frequency of the behavior(s) in question. This procedure is applicable to
many behavior therapy techniques, but it is perhaps most important in
the application of operant techniques, whether in the office, or home, or
in the institution. There are several sources of information concerning
the frequency of a behavior.

In what might seem the most direct assessment, the therapist may ask
the client, or simply listen to, his account of the presenting complaint.
This source of information has its problems, however, since people are
not objective observers of their own behavior (Robbins, 1963; Mischel,
1968). Experience shows that a behavior to which one objects may seem
all too frequent, even though in actuality it occurs quite rarely, and a behavior that one desires may seem never to occur. Often an individual's
concern with the frequency of a behavior makes him a less discrimi-
nating observer in that he does not notice, and, hence, cannot report, the
situations in which the behavior does or does not occur. This makes it
difficult for the therapist to move from the assessment of frequency to
the assessment of when, where, or under what conditions the behavior
tends (not) to occur, as we discuss later in the chapter (Mischel, 1968).

When the clients are children, they are often referred by their
parents, and the therapist may utilize the parental complaints as assessment information. This source is problematic since parents can speak
only for the frequency of behaviors in their presence, and they themselves may be powerful eliciting stimuli for behaviors that occur only
rarely otherwise—or that also frequently occur in other situations. The
therapist cannot tell all from the parents' report alone (Robbins, 1963).

Clients and individuals who refer clients generally do not count behaviors, draw graphs, or in other ways attempt to objectify their impressions
of behavior. Thus, it is often up to the therapist to direct them in techniques of generating good base-line data. They may be instructed in the
procedure of time-sampling (Wright, 1960). Once each 5 minutes, say, a
parent will be instructed to note simply whether the child is or is not performing the questionable behavior. Furthermore, he will be instructed
to make his observation in a certain situation; for example, in the house,
and not to count those times (or not to record them on the same sheet)
when the child performed the behavior in the yard. In the same fashion
a person may be instructed in the observation of his own behavior
(Chapter VII), although clearly the fact that he is his own observer may
well affect the behavior in question.

It is also possible to use *direct observational report* (specimen description) (Wright, 1960; Barker & Wright, 1955). In this procedure, the observer, whether he is the client himself or a parent, teacher, friend, or an observer employed by the therapist (Wahler & Erikson, 1969), simply notes the time and place for each occurrence of the behavior in question. Clearly, this technique is cumbersome, especially for a behavior that occurs with any great frequency; however, it is fairly comprehensive and may be reduced to tabular or graphic form, thereby allowing a clearer picture of the frequency of the behavior in question. The client may be asked to bring this information to the therapist, who may then plot a graph of the behavior. Furthermore, it may be desirable to have the client, his parents, teachers, or other observers plot the data as it is gathered, or perhaps once a day, thus giving them a continuing picture of the behavior in question. This procedure is especially useful during the period of behavior *change* since it may act as a powerful reinforcer for the individuals whose manipulation of contingencies is effecting the change. Incidentally, the direct observational report is also not a bad practice in the utilization of *any* technique of behavior change because it allows the rapid recognition of progress (or the lack thereof). As we discuss later, assessment is not limited to the period before behavior change, but should be an ongoing process that occurs throughout the intervention period (and afterward, during follow-up).

Clearly, the most effective technique of behavior measurement, whether for base-line data, or data regarding behavior change during and after therapy, is the utilization of trained observers to observe the client in the situations where the maladaptive behavior tends to occur (Patterson & Cobb, 1971; Wahler & Erickson, 1969). The training of competent observers is an arduous process (Patterson & Cobb, 1971), and expensive as well. Occasionally the therapist himself may act as observer; for instance, when he attends a class in which a child typically exhibits disruptive behavior, or monitors the interaction between mother and child in the waiting room (Bernal, Duryee, Pruett, & Burns, 1968) prior to an appointment. We must state unequivocally that these procedures are clearly the most accurate and were it not for economic limitations would surely be the preferred assessment technique. It is clear, however, that they are expensive and may not always be possible. To the extent that videotaping equipment is available or the therapist has the opportunity to observe behavior first-hand, even for a limited period of time, it will increase the likelihood that he has accurate information concerning the behavior in question (Bernal *et al.,* 1968).

Recording the Frequency of Behaviors

When working with problem behaviors utilizing contingency management, the therapist is often concerned, not with problems of discriminative performance of behaviors (learning to perform them in the
appropriate situations), but with problem behaviors that are present
in appropriate situations yet occur too frequently or too infrequently.

Consequently, the assessment of frequency typically occurs within a
given situation. For example, the therapist does not record the total
frequency of aggressive behavior a child may show throughout the entire day. Rather, the necessary information may include the frequency of
aggression *at home, toward parents,* or *toward other children at school* versus
toward other children at home; and so on. Thus, there are two basic considerations when setting up a program of frequency recording: 1) designating the behaviors to be recorded and the situations during which they
are to be recorded and 2) training observers (who may be the client himself, parents, teachers, or although not very likely, the therapist himself
or persons in his employ). The latter procedure should include the
provision of tallying materials and instruction in the art of constructing a
graph or chart that summarizes the frequency information.

Designating Behaviors and Situations to Record

Typically, the therapist must sift through the presenting complaints
and any observational material he may have concerning the client's behavior in order to arrive at a description of the problem behaviors and
the situations in which they seem to occur. If the evidence (information)
at this point appears reasonably complete, little may need to be done in
the way of further specification of the frequency of the problem behaviors. However, it is always a good idea, nonetheless, to gather specific
data on behavioral frequencies since these data either will confirm the
initial impressions or disconfirm them by demonstrating that the behavioral frequency is not as high or low as supposed, or that the situations
originally designated are not the ones in which the behavior occurs inappropriately, or with a maladaptively high or low frequency. Thus, the
gathering of frequency data during the early part of a modification
sequence may provide corrective feedback to an inaccurate behavioral
diagnosis.

Training Observers

Observation of frequency of occurrence should actually involve *behavioral events, units* that include the performance of a behavior *and* the

consequences that accrue. These may be recorded as separate frequencies. For example, if a child exhibits tantrum behavior at home, the therapist might first attempt to ascertain the response of the parents, although the parents may be quite accurate in reporting their own behavior in this case. Let us say that the parents have tried to ignore the tantrums, attempting a simple extinction procedure (Chapter VIII). The child reacts, however, by howling longer and longer, louder and louder until most of the time the parents give in to the child's wishes just to silence him. Undoubtedly the parents' behavior has had two effects: 1) to increase the length and loudness of the tantrum since increasing both of these characteristics has led to attention-getting (success) and thus been reinforced and 2) to increase the frequency of tantrums, or at least hold them constant, since they are usually successful in removing the frustration of desire (Bernal *et al.,* 1968).

Parents of a child such as this might be asked to fill in a chart, listing the numbers of tantrums per day and noting their response to the tantrum. They ought also be asked to estimate the amount of time the tantrum endured. Table 5.1 illustrates what such a chart might look like.

TABLE 5.1

Instances of Tantrum Behavior and Parental Responses to Tantrums Over a 7-Day Period: Sample Behavior Chart

Days	Tantrums	Duration (minutes)	Response
1	1	4	Comforted child when he slipped and banged head during crying
2	1	5	Told child to be quiet but finally gave cookie to quiet him down
	1	6	Ignored until couldn't stand it; gave cookie
3	1	5	Ignored
	2	6	Ignored
	3	8	Ignored until child took cookie himself; spanked child
4	1	4	Ignored; child stopped spontaneously
5	1	4	Company present; gave child cookie to quiet him
	2	5	Ignored; finally gave in
6	1	8	Ignored; went into bathroom, had cigarette, read magazine until child quieted himself
	2	4	Ignored; just as I was about to give in, child stopped
7	1	3	Ignored; child stopped, began to play

The sequence of behaviors in Table 5.1 is more the sort of sequence that would happen toward the end of an assessment period and toward the beginning (and throughout) a few days of "treatment," when the mother was instructed in techniques of ignoring the child's tantrum behavior. The frequency data for tantrums could then be converted into a graph (Figure 5.1), with days on the abcissa and frequency on the ordinate.

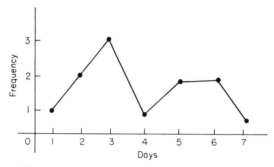

Figure 5.1 Graph of data presented in Table 5.1.

As we discuss later, this graph is actually inconclusive—there is no period of time during which the tantrum behavior occurs at a stable rate, and at the seventh day there is no reason to believe that the frequency is any different from the first; hence, there is no indication that the treatment worked. In Figure 5.2 see what the total picture might have looked like, including the period *before* Day 1 on the present graph and *after* Day 7.

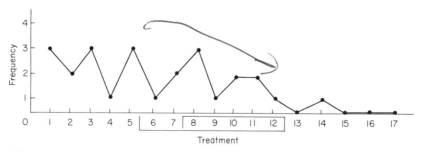

Figure 5.2 Frequency of a particular target behavior over a 17-day period. The frequencies for days 6–12 were also presented in Figure 5.1.

Typically, contingency-management techniques all involve the training of parents, teachers, and other individuals in the client's naturalistic environment to act as therapists. Part of this training must involve teaching them to observe and record behavior. Initially it will often prove wise to have these individuals read materials that introduce them to the notion of observing behaviors of individuals, not personality characteristics, and to the notions of analyzing behavior *consequences* in order to understand and change behaviors. Fortunately there are several good paperback books in this regard, which are written so that laymen can readily understand them (Patterson & Gullian, 1971; Becker, 1971). The therapist directing these "paratherapists" may wish to discuss these books with the individuals conducting the observations and contingency-management procedures and instruct them personally in the techniques he prefers for the gathering of frequency information, the skills involved in making graphs, etc. He may also provide them with the observation charts already prepared, wherein they are to record behavior observations. As new behaviors are to be modified, new charts should be prepared, and the therapist should reinstruct the observers in the observation of these particular behaviors.

Frequency Recording in Assessment, Treatment, and Follow-Up

There are three periods in the sequence of behavior modification, all of which should involve the gathering of information on the client's behavior. During *assessment,* the recording of frequency information will confirm the behavioral diagnosis, and observation in general is likely to give information concerning the maintaining stimuli, discriminative occurrence of the behavior in question, and so on. During *treatment,* continued tallying of behavior frequencies will indicate whether the modification procedures are indeed being effective. Finally, the frequency of a problem behavior (or lack thereof) should be recorded for some time following the termination of treatment to verify the continuing success of treatment.

Let us return to Figure 5.1. We noted that this record is not a good one. There are several reasons. First of all, if Days 1, 2, and 3 are a baseline period, the behavior appears to be increasing in frequency and clearly is not being performed at any stable rate. If there is any intent on the part of the therapist to determine whether improvement will be due to the treatment procedure he subsequently designs, or to other factors, treatment should not begin until a stable frequency is observed. Otherwise, in the present case, any improvement noted during treatment may be due to the ups and downs of the frequency of this behavior, which seems to be characterized by such fluctuations.[1]

---

[1] For the therapist whose primary goal is simply to lower (as in the present example) or increase the frequency of a problem behavior as quickly as possible, however, an extended base-line frequency measure may be deemed unnecessary. It is always best, however, to include base-line measurement even in these cases.

During treatment the therapist must know if the frequency of a behavior is indeed changing so that treatment may be modified if no frequency changes are being observed (or changes in the wrong direction), or so that treatment may be terminated when the desired end frequency is reached and is stable. In Figure 5.1, if treatment extended to Day 7, there is a problem in knowing whether it in fact has been effective because the behavior is still as frequent as on the first day. If treatment extended only to Day 4, apparently there was a short reoccurrence.

Since the termination of treatment may involve the client's return to his normal environment, the undesirable behaviors may well return: old contingencies that reinforce the maladaptive behaviors are reinstated, and the individual may again be exposed to models who exhibit the maladaptive behavior. Long-term follow-up periods have not been as characteristic of research on operant techniques as they have for, say, desensitization. Possibly this is because most research studies have concentrated on the effectiveness of certain techniques to produce rapid change and have not involved total treatment programs designed to influence natural contingencies in the environment, or thereby to produce enduring change. In Figure 5.1 there is little evidence of a follow-up period, and given the ups and downs of the frequency of tantrum behavior, it would not be surprising if the frequency rose again after Day 7. Without a follow-up, then, there would be no way to tell whether the cessation of treatment on Day 7 was wise or unwise.

Figure 5.2 shows what a total graph might look like.[2] If Days 8–12 (3–7 on Figure 5.1) are the treatment period, it is clear that there is an average level of 2 tantrums per day from Day 1 to Day 7, then a ragged, but fairly clear, downward trend Days 8–12, and finally a reasonably good indication that tantrums continued to be absent at the end. The reader should note that this is a hypothetical graph, and a 5-day follow-up is not a long one. Note also how even if a tantrum occurred occasionally—say, one of every 4 days—during an extended follow-up the presence of the graph would make it clear that the frequency was greatly reduced after treatment; moreover, a client keeping this graph would not be likely to misinterpret isolated, single occurrences as a full-blown reoccurrence of the problem, and thus would not likely become disheartened.

Identifying Maintaining Stimuli

Another integral part of problem behavior assessment, and again a procedure apropos in the use of nearly all behavior therapy techniques,

---

[2] Printed forms of various sorts are available. One notable source is: Behavior Research Company, Box 3351, Kansas City, Kansas 66103.

is the identification of the particular stimuli, situations, and conditions that consistently precede (elicit) the maladaptive behavior and those that consistently follow (maintaining factors, or reinforcers). Determining eliciting stimuli is often an aid, both in the subsequent assessment of maintaining reinforcers, in the discovering of exactly which stimuli comprise effective reinforcers, and in the determination and description of the social and physical environments that currently elicit the maladaptive behavior and into which more adaptive behaviors must be programmed. Often close questioning of the client will provide insight into the determinants of his behavior, although direct observation may be necessary and nearly always provides more detailed and objective information than does the client report.

The thrust of any initial questioning should be toward the last several times the behavior occurred. There is little point, at first, in seeking general, characteristic times when the behavior occurs or is absent since the client is not usually predisposed to observe his own behavior in terms of times, situations, events, or people who stimulate his behavior (unless, of course, this is not the first maladaptive behavior the therapist has treated for a particular client) (Mischel, 1968). For example, if severe procrastination were the problem, the following dialogue might take place:

Therapist: So you say that you continually defeat yourself by putting things off until it is too late?

Client: Yes . . . it really seems to be a terribly self-destructive sort of behavior. . . . I can't understand why I do it.

Therapist: Well, let's think back to the last time you kept putting something off until it was too late. Can you recall when something like this happened recently?

Client: Well, it was just this morning if you want to know the truth. I was supposed to have taken the storm windows off, now that it's getting hot. I didn't do it last night and then didn't have time to get to it this morning because I had to come here.

Therapist: What did your wife say?

Client: What did she say? She nagged at me a little last night, but not much. There was a good baseball game on that I wanted to see. But this morning she really let me have it. She said that she thought I was doing it just to hurt her, and then she cried. I comforted her and apologized and promised to take them off when I got back from here.

Therapist: Did you go through this last year, too?

Client: No, believe it or not, I took them off just as the weather began to get warm.

Therapist: What did your wife say?

Client: Nothing. Oh, yes, I believe she made a few nasty comments about how it was the first time I had taken them off early and how she hoped I had (sneeringly) "finally gotten rid of your laziness." But that's all.

It is clear from this dialogue that the consequences, in this instance, for the desired behavior were clearly less positive than the ones for procrastinating. Putting off the household chore allowed the client to watch a baseball game, and, the next morning, the wife's final pleas led to a highly reinforcing, tender scene between them. Further interviewing would be likely to uncover additional instances in which procrastination allowed immediate reinforcement that outweighed any eventual punishment for the procrastination itself.

Parents and other adults (for example, teachers, counselors, coaches) may inadvertently deter the performance of desired behaviors, especially when these behaviors are in long sequences. In teaching a child to dress himself for school, a mother may repeatedly enter the child's room while he is dressing and berate him for not being ready yet. Thus, each time the child puts on a few more clothes he is punished by his mother's complaints over his slowness, and even when completely dressed, he may face a minor scolding for having been so slow. Any reward at this time may also be inconsequential because the behavior was not performed perfectly; the effect of a small reinforcer is likely to be minimal, and, indeed, it may be completely without effect since it follows a number of punishments and comes after a long delay.

In each of these examples, it is the therapist's task to determine quite concretely the component behaviors in any general category of behavior or behavior sequence and to gather precise information concerning the rewards and punishments consequent upon these behaviors. In the second example, the therapist would discern this information from interviewing the mother or observing the mother–child interaction. And treatment, in this case, would clearly involve the training of the mother in more effective procedures of contingency management than those she already uses.

Validity Problems in Recording Behavior

As a processor of information, the human observer is probably incapable of refraining from interpretation when he observes and records behavior. The individual's theoretical bias may not only alert him to the occurrence of phenomena to be recorded, but it may also predispose him to misinterpret other, unrelated events as instances of the phenom-

enon he is to observe and record. Often, generally in experiments requiring the recording of behavior, more than one observer may be employed, and comparison of the reports of several observers constitutes
what is called rater reliability. The assumption is made that phenomena
—in this case, instances of a behavior—that are consistently reported
independently by, say, two separate observers are trustworthy and probably represent observations of events that actually occurred.

Unfortunately, this is an overinterpretation of the power of rater reliability since it implies that reliable observations (more than one observer
recording the same event) are valid observations. This does not follow,
primarily because it does not rule out the possibility that both observers
share many of the same biases and expectancies. That shared biases may
influence raters records and evaluations has been shown clearly by
O'Leary and his colleagues (Kass & O'Leary, 1970; Kent, O'Leary, Diament, & Dietz, 1973; O'Leary & Kent, 1973; Romanczyk, Kent, Diament, & O'Leary, 1973).

In one study (Kass & O'Leary, 1970), three groups of observers each
observed the same videotape of two disruptive children in a simulated
classroom. One group was told that soft reprimands were anticipated to
be effective in reducing disruptive behavior, while another group was
told that such reprimands were expected to increase disruptive behavior. The third group was given no information. It was clearly demonstrated by an analysis of the reports of these raters that each group's
expectancy tended to be confirmed in observations recorded:individual
raters expecting an increase in disruptive behavior recorded such an
increase and individual raters expecting a decrease recorded a decrease.

Lest the reader be tempted to throw up his hands in despair, we must
quickly add that there is further evidence that training individuals to
record behavior in clearly and specifically defined categories may reduce, or
even eradicate, this source of error due to shared biases. Kent et al.
(1973) found that the rater's expectancies affected his global evaluation of
the extent of behavior change he observed, but that the specific behavioral
recordings produced by the same observer did not show any effect of expectancy. Thus, one can hardly overemphasize the importance of defining target behaviors specifically and thoroughly when training individuals
to record behavior.

Assessment of Effective Reinforcers

When the decision has been made to treat a particular problem behavior by means of contingency management, at some point prior to the actual initiation of treatment, the reinforcer(s) to be utilized should be

clearly specified. In most instances, at least some of the effective reinforcers will have become clear during the assessment of maintaining
stimuli. Often such stimuli are quite general, such as attention by mother
or teacher, help given when dependent whining occurs, capitulation to
petty or veiled hostile threats, and so on. Clearly some of these reinforcers (for example, capitulation to threats) are unlikely to be useful
during the course of treatment. However, other reinforcers—positive attention, smiles, short play periods, quiet times between parent and child,
husband and wife—although rather general, may prove useful when
they are applied contingently in a therapeutic regimen. A client's statements concerning his desires for attention, recognition, social acceptance, or even small objects will prove informative in a search for
effective reinforcers.

It is clear from these considerations that the use of material reinforcers is not as common as the naive picture of a behavior modifier
suggests. Therapists do not lurk in dark corners, pockets bulging with
candies to be contingently dispensed upon the performance of desired
behaviors. For children or hospitalized patients, material or token rewards are likely to be employed with greater frequency than for the
typical adult patient, while contingency management performed in the
natural environment by parents, teachers, family members, etc. will
most likely involve social or behavioral reinforcers (smiles, attention,
verbal comments) since they are by far the most common reinforcers
in such environments (Stevenson, 1971).

When it becomes necessary to seek out and identify various reinforcers that are effective for a particular client, there are several alternative procedures. One involves the use of a *Mediation-Reinforcer Incomplete Blank* (referred to as MRB) (Tharp & Wetzel, 1969) and a
reinforcer-rating scale. The MRB is a modified incomplete-sentences test
including 34 incomplete sentence stems such as "The thing I like to do
best with my (mother/father) is _____," or, "I will do almost anything
to get _____," representing social and material reinforcers respectively. As represented here, the examples are intended for children or
adolescents, but they can easily be changed to suit clients of various ages
and walks of life. It is noteworthy that many material reinforcers and
nearly all social reinforcers will have *mediators*—persons typically delivering them—who are truly part of the reinforcing system and must be considered when designing a contingency-management program. Actually,
the mediators will typically become auxiliary therapists, who carry out
the management program in the natural environment.

When the reinforcers that have been defined as effective for a client
appear to vary in their effectiveness, it may be desirable to employ a
reinforcer-rating scale. While this is simply a scaling of reinforcer

effectiveness and may be done in a variety of ways, one procedure that has been used effectively (Tharp & Wetzel, 1969) involves the use of a 9-point scale ranging from "highly reinforcing; never fails to be effective (9)" through "reinforces fairly well; moderately effective (5)" to "has reinforcing property of a very low or undeterminate power (1)". This rating is carried out by the interviewer or primary therapist who has had initial contact with the client.

Another method of defining effective reinforcers, and the method most applicable to children or adults with limited capabilities for communication, is the *Reinforcing Event Menu* (REM) (Homme, 1971). This technique may be seen as a variant of the Mediation-Reinforcer Incomplete Blank. A REM is simply a list, or assemblage of pictures, that includes a variety of material reinforcers with their dispensors (for instance, mother giving a hug is a reinforcing *event*—the hug is a reinforcer that might be *ineffective* if delivered by another mediator), as well as pictures of activity reinforcers. When the client is actually involved in the manipulation of his own behavior, as in contingency contracting (Chapter VII), he may be allowed to select from this menu the reinforcers he wishes to work for. Clearly this technique may be used by teachers in the classroom, parents in the home, or even therapists on an inpatient ward. Token economies (Chapter VI) may be seen to utilize this principle when the therapist makes it amply clear the variety of possessions and privileges tokens may be traded for and insists that patients sample the reinforcers that may be purchased with tokens (Atthowe & Krasner, 1968).

Reinforcers and Reinforcement

When tailoring a contingency-management program to a particular individual, the therapist often attempts to utilize reinforcers (and punishers perhaps) that have proved effective for that particular individual in the past. (We have discussed the assessment of effective reinforcers in an earlier section.) When attempting to define these effective reinforcers, there are some basic types of reinforcers and reinforcing events for which to look, and often there are stimuli or events within these categories that are effective reinforcers for nearly everyone. The three types of reinforcers and reinforcing events are *material* reinforcers (Becker, 1971), *social* reinforcers (Stevenson, 1965), and *activity* reinforcers (Premack, 1959).

In the therapeutic modification of behavior, reinforcers are rarely directly dispensed to adults immediately following desired behaviors. In view of this the therapist should take great care to direct the client into environments where his new behaviors will be reinforced and thus maintained. The difficulty in guiding the client to a more favorable environment is compounded when the reinforcers are social, or perhaps activity, and not material.

For children, the therapist himself, or an agent such as a parent, teacher, or nurse, may dispense reinforcement of just about any category, material, social, or activity, and the child may be directly *placed* in environments that reinforce the devised behaviors (with adults the environment is generally *encouraged* or *directed,* but children have less freedom than adults in our society). Institutionalized adults or adults who are retarded, but not institutionalized, may be the recipients of direct reinforcement by therapists, ward personnel, or caretakers (Ayllon & Azrin, 1965; see Chapter VI). Normal adults, however, are usually the recipients of token rewards (money, gold watches, trophies, certificates, letters of commendation), which may be dispensed long after the behavior being reinforced has occurred, although usually the contingency is made quite clear.

Types of Reinforcers

Material Reinforcers.   Material reinforcers are perhaps most effective for children—or at least most common—although they have their place in adult life. Candy, toys, and food treats are often dispensed to children who have been "good," done their chores on time, and so on. Adults often receive bonuses or raises, and some business organizations also give trips as prizes for jobs well done. On a person-to-person basis, material rewards are not as common among adults, although husbands and wives probably consent more readily to let their mates buy some desired item when prior behavior has met a particular standard or preference.

The use of material and other types of reinforcers (for example, activity or negative reinforcers based on the termination of aversive events) has one rather important and desirable side effect. When the reinforcer is consistently delivered by a single individual (or group), the person (or persons) delivering the reinforcement begins to acquire a positive, reinforcing valence himself (Mowrer, 1950; Lovaas, 1968; Lovaas, Freitag, Kinder, Rubenstein, Schaeffer, & Simmons, 1966). This quality then predisposes the client to respond to the other person's presence, approval, and other behaviors as though they were reinforcers. Thus, we have the class of *social reinforcers.*

Social Reinforcers.   It seems clear that a vast majority of all reinforcing events that come to affect human behavior are social events involving the nearness, smiles, praise, or even physical contact with other individuals.

The assumption is usually made that human beings learn to value other human beings since they are consistently paired with material, unlearned reinforcers, especially in early infancy (for example, the early feeding experience, which involves being held while feeding or even being breast fed directly) (Dollard & Miller, 1950). Some authors believe that the human organism innately shows social responsivity (Bowlby, 1969). For our purposes the argument is largely academic. It remains the case, in either event, that people are, or become, responsive to people. There is some evidence, however, that individuals who are not responded to as reinforcing will become so if they are paired with established reinforcers; and autistic children, who appear to find no social contact reinforcing, may become (socially) responsive to an individual who is consistently paired with a very powerful existing reinforcer (Lovaas, 1968).

Table 5.2 presents some common social reinforcers. Certainly different individuals respond more or less (and sometimes negatively) to each of these. They are common, however, and people dispense and receive these reinforcers all the time. In most instances, these reinforcers are acquired *contingently*. Mothers are loving to their children; husbands

TABLE 5.2

Common Social Reinforcers: Examples [a]

Praise (Verbal reinforcer)

Good	Exactly	Great
That's right	Good job	Groovy
Excellent	Good thinking	That's interesting
That's clever	Thank you	I'm pleased with that

Show this to your father
Show Grandma your picture
I love you

Facial expressions

Smiling	Looking Interested
Winking	Laughing

Nearness

Walking together   Eating together   Playing games together
Talking and/or listening to each other for a while

Physical contact

Touching	Shaking hand	Sitting in lap
Hugging	Holding hand	Patting head, shoulder, or back

[a] Adapted from Becker, W. C. *Parents are teachers: A child management program.* Champaign, Illinois: Research Press Co., 1971.

are affectionate to their wives, but not during arguments or spats, and more so after behaviors or interactions pleasing to the reinforcing person. Reinforcers may be dispensed contingently without the dispensor being aware that his dispensation is indeed contingent. But our point here is that social reinforcers are quite prevalent in the natural environment, are quite powerful, and can be manipulated in order to modify behavior. It has even been proposed that the therapist's attentiveness and facial expression in more traditional, nonbehavior-modification forms of therapy is largely responsible for the changes that occur in various client behaviors (Bandura, 1962).

Activity Reinforcers. While many of the social reinforcers discussed above involve activity as well, we wish to stress in this section that the occasion, or privilege, to perform preferred activities of any sort (social or not) may be used to reinforce activities or behaviors that are less preferred. Some authors (Becker, 1971; Homme, 1971) refer to "Grandma's Rule," which states "First you work, then you play." Or, "You do what I want you to do before you get to do what you want to do." Clearly this principle has been around a long time as simple common sense, but only recently did it make its debut as a formal principle defining one type of reinforcer (Premack, 1965). Typically it is referred to as the *Premack principle.*

The Premack principle is quite simple. It states that an activity, or behavior, may be reinforced by the privilege to engage in another behavior of greater base-line frequency. Thus, sitting quietly in a classroom for a few minutes may be reinforced by the privilege of running around (Homme, deBaca, Devine, Steinhorst, & Rickert, 1963; Osborne, 1969), or studying at home may be reinforced by periods of watching TV.

Often the frequency with which a behavior is performed is an index of the degree to which it is valued. Not all valued behaviors can be performed that frequently, so there are other activities that may be reinforcing even though they are not performed as frequently as the behavior to be reinforced. Watching TV may reinforce a less frequent behavior, such as studying, for an individual who is an avid video fan. In another instance, a poor child who has little access to TV may also find watching it reinforcing even though in the past he has seen TV less frequently than he has performed the behavior to be reinforced (for example, studying). The thoughtful reader will note, as well, that a particular activity reinforcer will not reinforce all other activities. For one child, getting to study with a friend, rather than alone, might reinforce reading a new book. For another child, who reads a great deal, the opportunity to read after studying (with a friend or alone) might increase the frequency of studying.

For children, the privileges to engage in various activities may often be dictated by parents, teacher, etc., and hence these individuals can control the sequence of these activities, making more preferred ones contingent upon the performance of less preferred activities. For adults, contingency management of this sort may be placed within the control of the client (Chapter VII). After discussion with the therapist of the problematic low frequencies of some behaviors and the designation of other, more preferred activities, the client may be instructed in the sequencing of various behaviors. For example, a student with poor study habits may be told to read five pages and then go down to the student lounge for a while, or to read his five pages before 7:00 p.m. and then watch a half-hour TV show before returning to study. A writer may organize his day to work for 3 hours in the morning and then to be with his family, working in the afternoon only if he feels like it (see Chapter VII for a detailed discussion).

Table 5.3 contains examples of some common activity reinforcers. Most of these are appropriate for children, although many are not particularly age related. As we noted earlier, these are simply common reinforcers of the activity type and additional ones will most likely be specifiable with respect to any particular client.

TABLE 5.3

Activity Reinforcers [a]

Seeing a movie	Going first
Watching TV	Being thrown around in a circle by daddy
Outdoor camping	Going shopping
Going on field trips	Going out to play
Studying with a friend	Being read to
Having a friend stay overnight	Playing games with friends
Listening to music	Getting to stay up late
Having a party	

[a] Adapted from Becker, W. C. *Parents are teachers: A child management program.* Champaign, Illinois: Research Press, Co., 1971.

Types of Reinforcement

Extrinsic and Intrinsic Reinforcement. Often the question arises as to whether training an individual by means of externally administered reinforcement will enslave such a person to the use of reinforcement forever and doom him (or the behavior in question) to extinction whenever the planned reinforcement of that behavior ceases. This is clearly not the case since newly acquired desirable behaviors tend to be reinforced by others (not just the contingency managers) and will be reinforced in new situations as well (O'Leary, O'Leary, & Becker, 1967; Wahler & Erikson, 1969). Often individuals participating in a program of contingency management object to the overt use of extrinsic reinforcers as "bribery." They may feel it is a child's moral duty to empty the trash, or help with the dishes; or a wife's domestic responsibility to keep a clean house. They may feel that they were never reinforced (untrue though this may be) for the behaviors in question, so why should someone else be treated differently. Often an effective counter to this position is to draw a sharp distinction between (socially) desirable and undesirable behaviors. It can be pointed out that bribery refers to a payoff for irresponsible, undesirable, or morally offensive behaviors, while desired behaviors are often reinforced under such conceptualizations as salary, bonuses, commission, praise, approval, or even reward.

There are several procedures that help to insure the enduring effectiveness of a reinforcement-based therapy program. The procedure of *leaning* is often evoked in a reinforcement paradigm. This procedure involves very gradually omitting reinforcement that has been externally administered and is extrinsic in nature. The result of such a procedure is often, not the extinction of the behavior in question, but, rather, the adoption by the individual of intrinsic reinforcement such as feelings of pride, approval of his own behavior, or perhaps self-professed enjoyment of the behavior in question (Festinger, 1961). Many individuals dislike coffee or cigarettes at first but indulge in their consumption for other reasons (wanting to be "grown-up," needing to stay awake, etc.). In most cases, the consumption of these products eventually comes to be intrinsically reinforcing—quite powerfully so in some cases. It has long been known that individuals who engage in a particular behavior and are insufficiently rewarded for it come to prefer that behavior (Festinger, 1957; Festinger & Carlsmith, 1959; Masters & Mokros, 1973). This effect is termed "the psychology of insufficient reward" (Festinger, 1961), or "cognitive dissonance" (Festinger, 1957). Interestingly, the use of reinforcers that are intensely valued may deter learning and behavior change (Miller & Estes, 1961; Masters & Mokros, 1973), perhaps via a process of distraction: an individual's attention may become riveted to the prospect of coming rewards to such an extent that he attends only poorly to the behaviors he is learning.

There is another, even more important factor in the establishment of enduring behavior change. An important part of nearly any modification program is the guiding of an individual's behavior into natural contexts that will approve, accept, or even praise the new behaviors, thus providing maintaining factors in an everyday setting. Often, however, the client may find the first occasions of showing behavior change very difficult. Although they are well-intentioned, individuals from the client's environment may point out the change, but omit any positive comments. "Why, Mildred, you're so animated tonight. Usually you sit by yourself at parties!" Such a comment might be a powerful reinforcer for a client who has been prepared to hear such things, but another person who is still reluctant and fearful of social activity might respond to such a comment as though it were a punishment. A more sensitive individual might have followed up the preceding comment with, "It's been so nice talking to you—I enjoyed it!"

We wish to make two points here. First, there is a tendency for behaviors that have been acquired through reinforcement techniques to become intrinsically reinforcing, especially if the reinforcement manipulated during learning is effective, but not of grandiose proportions, and if it is carefully and gradually withdrawn as the behavior becomes an established part of the person's repertoire. Second, it is simply not true that all "normal" behaviors are primarily internally motivated. The social environment continually reinforces (and punishes) everyday behaviors, and a client may be guided into environments that respond appropriately to newly acquired behaviors (and away from environments that respond inappropriately).

Negative Reinforcement.   Many people equate negative reinforcement and punishment, and this is incorrect. The term *reinforcement* as we noted earlier refers to the increasing of the likelihood that a behavior will be performed, or the intensity with which it is performed (Deese & Hulse, 1967). The term *positive reinforcement* is used to describe the occurrence of some reinforcing event following the performance of some desired behavior. On the other hand, the term *negative reinforcement* describes the termination of an aversive event following the performance of some desired behavior. The addition of a positive event and the termination of an aversive event both have the same effect upon behavior: they increase the frequency of the behavior upon whose occurrence they are contingent.

Negative reinforcement is rather difficult to manipulate. In Chapter IX, on aversive control, we discuss the effects of the termination of punishment on the strengthening of avoidance responses and the enhancement of the attractiveness of a stimulus that appears just as the punishment terminates. Procedures such as these are typically employed under laboratory or clinic conditions and involve the use of electric shock or drugs. There are, however, some instances of the use of negative reinforcement in everyday life.

Parents and teachers often prefer the use of negative reinforcement and punishment even though they do so unwittingly. For example, parents may threaten a child with dire consequences, nag at him, and cease these activities only when he complies with their wishes. Children may cry, stamp their feet, or in general make a nuisance of themselves until they elicit the desired behavior from their parents, at which time they cease such aversive behavior. Children in school grunt, groan, stamp their feet, and wave their hands until they are called on, or spoken to, by the teacher. Husbands moan, groan, and become generally surly until they are given leave for a desired activity by their wives. And so on.

In some instances, the use of punishment seems based on the (often implicit) belief that the behavior in question is intrinsically rewarding; thus, the individual "deserves" nagging until the behavior is performed or punishment if it is not, but not reinforcement if it is. Children should empty trash cans from a sense of responsibility, and wives should wash dishes, cook, and clean house because they enjoy these wifely duties and the appearance of a clean house and have a responsibility to do so— compliments and thanks from the husband are unnecessary. Often parents or other individuals participating in a contingency-management program are devoted to the use of punishment; this attitude is itself difficult or impossible to change, thus rendering ineffective any contingency-management procedures. (Later in the chapter we discuss a tragic case, reported by Tharp & Wetzel, 1969.)

Schedules of Reinforcement

In both the assessment of the problem and its treatment by contingency management, it is important to determine the schedule of reinforcement that pertained for the client prior to treatment and to train the change agent in the proper, most effective utilization of reinforcement. There are several important principles to be grasped here.

Immediacy versus Delay of Reinforcement. The longer the time between the completion of a behavior and the delivery of a reinforcing consequence, the less effect the reinforcer will have (Hull, 1952; Terrell & Ware, 1961; Ware & Terrell, 1961). This is often termed the *temporal gradient of reinforcement.* Thus, if a desired behavior is of low frequency even though it generally elicits reinforcement, it is important to determine whether the reinforcement is delivered soon after the completion of the behavior. Thanking a child at night for finally making his own bed that morning is likely to be ineffective, or only slightly effective at best. Telling a child on Thursday that you are docking his allowance because of something he did (did not do) on Monday is also likely to have only a weak effect. To increase his allowance by advance notice is also a weak procedure and one that we feel is not generally characteristic of parents.

A reinforcer (or punisher) is most effective when it is delivered immediately following the completion of the desired response.

Delay of Reinforcement in Behavior Sequences.   When an individual is expected to acquire an extended sequence of behaviors (most "behaviors" are actually sequences of more elementary component behaviors), it may be necessary to insert reinforcement into the sequence while it is being learned. Often this is termed *shaping* (we discuss this procedure in a later section). Since some sequences are quite long, they are not always completed quickly, and a reinforcer delivered at the end may be relatively ineffective overall. The example cited earlier of the child getting dressed illustrates a long sequence of behaviors—but in this instance the mother used punishment, not reinforcers. Diagnostically, the therapist is faced with two questions. First, he must decide whether the behavior is actually such a long sequence that reinforcement should be given following components of the chain, as well as at the end. Second, he must ascertain whether reinforcement is being administered with little delay upon the completion of a low-frequency desired behavior.

Verbal Clarification of Behavior and the Contingent Relationship between Behavior and Reinforcer.   Behavior is clearly a complex, ongoing stream (Becker, 1971), and as such a reinforcer that suddenly appears may not have any clear contingency. There is an extensive literature concerning whether it is necessary to recognize consciously that a reinforcer is contingent in order for learning to occur (Farber, 1963; Spielberger & DeNike, 1966). We do not intend to resolve this conflict here. However, when a reinforcer follows a long sequence of behaviors, or when it is somewhat delayed following the completion of a behavior, its effectiveness may be enhanced by a clear spelling out of the contingency. "You have been a good boy today," followed by a kiss or special treat is less informative than "You mowed the lawn without being asked!" Often, too, spelling out a contingency includes specification of the behaviors involved in the sequence. "You put your underwear, socks, pants, and shirt on *all* by yourself," said with a smile while mother buttons his shirt, is likely to be more powerful than a comment before dinner that night, with a smile, the "You nearly got dressed all by yourself this morning." (Stevenson, 1971).

Discriminative cues may also be enhanced by verbal explication ("When you go play after school and don't tell me before you go, I am unhappy."). Similarly, it seems plausible that family or marital therapy often provides a forum for individuals to discover that the contingency they surmised for reinforcers or punishers is not, in truth, the intended contingency. "I thought you were crabby on those days because it was just that time of the month. I didn't know that those were the days I forgot to clean the sink after shaving." Or, "When you complained about my not cleaning the sink, I didn't know you were generally ticked-off because I didn't let you have the bathroom first and you were in a hurry. I thought you were just mad in general 'cause there are lots of times I don't clean the sink and you don't say anything." From these examples it is clear that communication skills and reinforcement skills may often be similar, and perhaps even identical, phenomena.

Incentive Value and the Power of a Reinforcer. Often individuals inadvertently assume that what is a powerful reinforcer for them is also one for others. For this and a variety of other reasons a behavior may remain at low frequency because it is reinforced by a reward of slight value to the individual. Parents who feel children should help around the house out of a "sense of responsibility" (self-dispensed reinforcement?) often expect such behavior, offering only punishment when it does *not* occur, and little, if any, reinforcement when it does. A feeling of pleasure when someone has done something may result in a smile, but nothing more, and this may not be a sufficiently powerful reinforcer to maintain the behavior. We must quickly point out that no judgments are made as to whether people *should* require more than a smile, a fond glance, or simply a sense of responsibility to reinforce behaviors. Some individuals do not respond as powerfully to praise as do others. Some people feel less pride in completing a task and may not, therefore, behave as though they have a sense of responsibility (as we have noted above, whether they *should* have this feeling is not under consideration). Thus, the fact is simply this: desired behaviors that are infrequent when followed by certain reinforcements can be increased in frequency by utilization of a more powerful or more effective (powerful for that person) reinforcer. The only caution here is that one should be careful not to employ reinforcers of such high value that they excite or distract to the point of *reducing* the learning of new behaviors (Masters & Mokros, 1973; Miller & Estes, 1961).

Shaping New Behaviors

The technique of shaping behavior is often termed *successive approximation* or *response differentiation* (Bandura, 1969). If a behavior is not exhibited by an individual, it cannot be reinforced. Shaping is simply a general procedure designed to induce the performance of new behaviors by the initial reinforcement of behaviors in the individual's repertoire that have some similarity to the desired behavior. Then, gradually, reinforcement is withdrawn from the less similar behaviors and concentrated upon the more similar ones, which progressively become more and more similar to the desired behavior until they are one and the same. For example, in teaching an autistic child or psychotic adult to talk, one might desire to teach him to say "Hi." Reinforcement, at first, would be given contingent upon utterances such as "Aye," "Bi," "Yi," "Fi," and so forth. Gradually, as these utterances became more frequent, reinforcement would be withdrawn following utterances such as "Bi" and "Fi," but retained following "Aye" and "Yi." Similarly, reinforcement must be given contingent upon utterances like "Hoo," "Ho," "Hargh," and so on—vocalizations containing the correct initial H sound. As these sounds, too, increased in frequency, note that the probability of a chance occurrence of "Hi" is increased. When vocalization resembling "Hi" occurs, reinforcement would be contingent, but would gradually be withdrawn from vocalizations less similar to the desired sound. Finally, once the sound "Hi" is of high frequency, reinforcement may be withdrawn gradually, except in those instances when the word is used appropriately—as when spoken to an approaching person. Note how the utterances successively came to approximate the desired utterance and how this particular response became differentiated from similar ones to the point where it was uttered clearly and in appropriate situations.

In a striking example of the technique, Wolf, Risely, and Mees (1964) used shaping to get a 3½-year-old autistic boy to wear glasses. Initially, a conditioned reinforcer was established by pairing the clicks of a toy noisemaker with a small bit of candy or fruit. Very quickly the child learned to approach the bowl where food was immediately delivered after the click. Initially, since the prescription of the lenses required was quite powerful and changed the visual field radically—a condition that might itself have been aversive—the child was rewarded for wearing the glasses *frames* only. Even this proved difficult since they could not be placed appropriately upon the child's head because he became active and upset when ever anyone touched his head. Furthermore, the staff of the hospital ward was reluctant to deprive the child of food, so the candy and fruit were minimally powerful reinforcers.

To counter these problems, Wolf *et al.* (1964) reported:

. . . We attempted to increase deprivational control by using breakfast as a shaping session, bits of breakfast now being dependent upon approximations to the wearing of glasses. . . . Later we added to the glasses . . . a "roll bar" which would go over the top of his head and guide the pieces up and over the ears.

After wearing the glasses was established in these sessions, it could be maintained with often less manipulable reinforcers. For example, the attendants would tell Dicky, "Put your glasses on and let's go for a walk." Dicky was usually required to wear the glasses during meals, snacks, automobile rides, walks, outdoor play, etc. If he removed the glasses, the activity was terminated.

At the time of Dicky's release from the hospital he had worn the glasses for more than 600 hours and was wearing them about 12 hours a day [pp. 309–310].

The use of shaping is not limited to simple behaviors, young children, or highly disturbed individuals. Schwitzgebel (Schwitzgebel & Kolb, 1964) has effectively used a shaping procedure to treat noninstitutionalized adolescent juvenile delinquents. In this procedure, the therapist went directly into areas of high crime rate on the pretext of hiring subjects for a research project. It was explained that the purpose of research was to find out what teenagers think and feel about things, and one of the "qualifications" for the job was that the person have a court record.

Schwitzgebel and Kolb (1964) paid adolescents $1.00 an hour to give tape-recorded "interviews." When it was noticed that the juveniles seemed to enjoy these interviews, they were gradually modified toward therapeutic ends and the payment was withdrawn. The adolescents were seen an average of three times per week for approximately 9 months in a therapy setting where the therapist was highly directive. A 3-year follow-up revealed a significant reduction in the frequence and severity of crimes they committed when compared to a matched-pair control group.

Schwitzgebel (1967) similarly elicited therapeutic cooperation of juvenile delinquents for a series of 20 interviews over a period of 2–3 months. One group of adolescents received positive consequences for statements of concern about other people and prompt arrival at the session. (for example, he might be given cigarettes, candy bars, or even cash bonuses of 25¢ to $1.00 for statements like "Joe is a good guy."). Another group received negative consequences for hostile statements about people (for example, the therapist might become inattentive or mildly disagree following expressions showing antagonism toward, or depreciation of, another person's status. The juveniles were observed in a social situation outside the therapy situation (a restaurant). When positive consequences had followed statements of concern for other people, there was a significant increase of such statements in a natural social interaction. Juveniles punished for hostile comments showed a significant decrease in such comments in the social situation. The use of contingent positive consequences also induced the adolescents to arrive promptly for their appointments.

Arrangement of Contingencies

Usually the term *schedule of reinforcement* is limited to the actual relationship between the occurrence of a response (or the passage of time) and the provision of a reinforcing event. There has been extensive research concerning the effects of various schedules of reinforcement upon the behavior of lower organisms and of man [see Ferster & Skinner (1957) and Ayllon and Azrin (1965) for extensive research reviews]. Consequently, we do not attempt an exhaustive review, but instead examine those schedules of reinforcement most prevalent in the practice of behavior modification: continuous, intermittent, ratio, and interval schedules.

Continuous Reinforcement

Under continuous reinforcement (CRF) *every* appropriate response is followed by reinforcement. Thus, this schedule also qualifies as a fixed-ratio schedule for which the ratio is 1:1 (one reinforcement for each response—FR1; see the discussion of fixed-ratio schedules later in the chapter). Under these conditions the acquisition of a particular behavior is likely to be quite rapid, but upon the cessation of reinforcement, extinction also occurs quite rapidly. Thus, a CRF schedule may be used in shaping a particular behavior, but other schedules are likely to be employed later in order to increase the "endurance" of the response. It should be noted here that the natural environment very rarely provides a CRF schedule or reinforcement for a particular behavior. More often, some or most instances of a response are reinforced, but some are not.

Intermittent Reinforcement

Under this schedule, not every response is followed by a reinforcer. All ratio (except FR1) and interval schedules are intermittent schedules. When not every response is reinforced, the behaving individual is always in extinction to some degree since extinction is supposedly the result of the repeated occurrence of a response without ensuing reinforcement. The result of an intermittent schedule is less rapid acquisition (if this schedule is used from the start) and a rather unsteady rate of responding, with rapid responding sometimes, slow responding at other times: the individual tends to pause after the delivery to a reinforcer, then begin responding at an increasingly rapid rate until another reinforcer is dispensed.

When extinction is instituted and the designated responses are no longer reinforced at all, the individual only gradually ceases to respond.

It is thought that the onset of an extinction procedure (withdrawal of contingent reinforcement) is difficult to recognize in this case since one is "used to" responding without reinforcement (there is some controversy over the proper explanation of this phenomenon; see Deese & Hulse, 1967). In practice, it is quite common to begin a training procedure utilizing a continuous schedule and gradually transform the schedule into an intermittent one (variable ratio), and then gradually, as environmental and self-managed contingencies become increasingly effective, to phase out the therapeutic reinforcement schedule completely.

Ratio Reinforcement

Most schedules of reinforcement are ratio schedules that are either *fixed* or *variable* in nature. *Fixed-ratio (FR) schedules* describe cases in which every *n*th response (second, third, fourth, etc.) is reinforced. If every second response is reinforced, the schedule is an FR2, every third an FR3, and so on. Obviously this requires close monitoring of the precise number of times a response occurs and is not very common in everyday life. In practice, however, it may be a useful way in which to "lean out" a continuous schedule (or a "rich" intermittent one, "rich" indicating that the ratio is quite small, say, 2 or 3) in a gradual, regulated way; for example, by going from FR4 to FR5 to FR7, etc.

Variable-Ratio (VR) Schedules.   By far the more common ratio reinforcement is variable-ratio. Furthermore, reinforcement dispensed in the natural environment is almost always on a VR schedule. Variable ratio means simply that the ratio between the number of responses and reinforcements changes from time to time. For example, a reinforcer may occur after three responses, then after the very next one, then not until five responses have occurred. In experiments, or under conditions where the dispensation of reinforcement is closely monitored, the therapist may describe a VR schedule by referring to the *average* number of responses that occur before a reinforcement is administered (for example, a VR3 means that even though the ratio is variable, *on the average* every 3rd response is reinforced). Variable-ratio schedules tend to produce steady and high rates of responding without the pause associated with a fixed-ratio schedule. Note how this schedule of reinforcement would be best for preventing extinction since it is usually impossible to know for sure when the next reinforcement is going to occur. This is quite necessary for human behavior, since often a desired behavior must be performed many times before it gains any reinforcement if only because it is offered occasionally (often a desirable behavior will be appropriate when there is no one around, hence reinforcment is extremely unlikely). Also, variable ratios give training in responding to highly delayed reinforcement—an occurrence that is also characteristic of natural environments.

Interval Schedules

Finally there are *interval schedules*, which may be either fixed (FI) or variable (VI). Note that the ratio schedules discussed above are "internally" controlled in the sense the reinforcement is linked to the responses made by the individual himself. Interval schedules, unlike ratio schedules, are not solely tied to an individual's rate of behavior, but are primarily concerned with the amount of time between reinforcement. Nonetheless, they do have an effect upon his behavior. Fixed-interval schedules, in which reinforcement is given after fixed periods of time, tend to produce or maintain behavior in a manner similar to that of a fixed-ratio schedule, with pauses after the receipt of each reinforcement. Variable-interval schedules produce steadier responding. Interval schedules are not particularly common in behavior therapy, except in instances such as a token economies, when for example, a fixed-interval privilege (for instance, sleeping in a single bedroom) is contingent upon some minimal behavior standards. Even in this example, the reinforcement—though itself interval in nature—is ratio, as well, since some occurrence (response rate) is necessary to maintain the privilege. Salaries, with fixed-interval paydays, recesses in schools, meals, all these are fixed-interval reinforcers in the natural environment. To be utilized in therapy procedures, however, they are typically changed to a ratio basis: behave yourself, or go to bed without dinner (a poorly specified contingency, with threatened time-out).

Reinforcement versus Punishment

It is clear that punishment may be effectively used to modify behavior (see Chapter IX) and that there may be particular behavior problems that respond better, or perhaps exclusively, to aversive procedures. And while there may be a choice between using positive reinforcement and punishment procedures, there are several good reasons for preferring reinforcement techniques (or observational learning, assertive training, or cognitive methods, etc.). First of all, when effective, alternative techniques are available, it is difficult to justify the employment of techniques which cause pain and suffering even if they, too, are effective. Second, punishment often produces a number of side effects that may be quite undesirable. And finally, while punishment may be used cautiously and effectively by the experienced behavior therapist, it is often a technique of choice by some spouses and parents, one that they use *ineffectively,* and consequently one that becomes ineffective for the individual in question. A more detailed discussion of aversive techniques is found in Chapter IX. For our present purposes let us simply cite some examples of the undesirable side effects and imprudent uses of punishment that may be encountered in contingency-management procedures.

The major side effect of punishment is the potential training it provides by reinforcing other behaviors that allow the avoidance or termination (negative reinforcement) of punishment. Ceasing to perform the behavior being punished is but one way to avoid the punishment. Becker (1971) has clearly pointed to some common alternative behaviors individuals turn to when punishment is imminent:

Cheating:	avoiding the punishment that goes with being wrong
Truancy:	avoiding or escaping the many punishments that go with school failure, poor teaching, punitive administration of school
Running away from home:	escaping the many punishments parents can use
Lying:	avoiding the punisment that follows doing something wrong
Sneaking:	avoiding being caught "misbehaving"
Hiding:	avoiding being caught

Often the persons in a client's natural environment who are to become contingency managers must be weaned from a dependence upon the use of punishment. The point is made succinctly in the case cited below, reported by Tharp and Wetzel (1969).

> *Case #56. Alan's parents were fundamentalist protestants who imposed strong limitations on their son's freedom for relatively minor offenses. When his school grades began to deteriorate they reacted by almost totally restricting him to his room and depriving him of TV, the use of the phone, etc. The father was a rigid martinet whose job kept him away from home three or four days a week. Both parents felt that anything but total submission to parental authority subverted the rules of man and God.*
>
> *Alan was a bright, conscientious, and mildly withdrawn 16-year-old, but this crushing limitation drove him to run away from home.*

He turned himself in to the juvenile probation lock-up and announced that he would rather go to the State reform school than go home. When his parents arrived he refused to go home with them and said if he were forced he would run away immediately.

Finally the boy agreed to go home after several telephone conversations among probation officers, the father, and our Project, the essence of which was that the restrictions would be lifted and our help would be immediately available.

The parents agreed to an intervention program based on weekly grade notices from Alan's teacher. On the basis of grades, Alan earned points which governed the hours he might spend away from home, watch TV, and use the phone.

The program began effectively, although the boy was suspicious since it appeared to be nonpunitive.

His suspicions soon proved well founded. Although he earned enough points to allow a greater degree of freedom than he had previously been granted, his parents meddled with the plan. Despite repeated discussion and instructions from the BA [Behavior Analyst], they insisted on searching for reasons to punish Alan. One Sunday Alan had enough points to go off with some friends, but as he started for the door his father prohibited him from leaving because he had received a low grade in one subject that week. "You haven't got time to play if you can't keep up your studies," was the way his father justified the action.

The parents were obviously adding punitive features to the program, many of which were not revealed to the BA, and the boy threatened to run away again, protesting that his father and mother were not honoring their promise not to apply restrictions. When the BA deplored these actions the parents explained that they would like an "altered" program which would eliminate the reinforcement features and the point system. "We'd want to use your program as a guideline without being so formal." "We like the weekly grade notes, because we don't have to wait six weeks for Alan's report card." (To this they might have added that such an arrangement made it possible to keep au courant with their son's failures for punitive purposes without accepting the responsibility of rewarding his successes.) [pp. 129–130].[3]

While this example may be an extreme one, it clearly points out the necessity for extensive training, and perhaps modification of contingency managers themselves, in order to secure effective results for the total program.

[3] Reprinted from Tharp, R. G. and Wetzel, R. J. *Behavior modification and the natural environment.* New York: Academic Press, 1969. Pp. 129–130.

Extinction Procedures

Extinction is the term used to describe the relatively permanent *unlearning* of a behavior (the elimination of a behavior from a person's repertoire). Extinction is often inferred from the observation that a behavior has decreased in frequency, although the *suppression* of a behavior (a temporary reduction in frequency often resulting from punishment) produces similar, if temporary, results. Extinction occurs when a behavior is performed and is *not* reinforced. Typically, the performance of a behavior is seen as necessary for extinction to occur (Hull, 1952), for only then are the internal motivating factors truly weakened. This model, which is theoretical to be sure, implies that high-intensity punishment is likely to *suppress* behavior, not extinguish it, since the behavior is performed but a very few times—only once in some instances of quite severe punishment—before it stops entirely. Thus, there is some feeling (as we discuss in Chapter IX, on Aversive Control), that punishment will be ineffective since suppressed behaviors tend to reappear, while extinguished ones do not. This thinking has led to the current stress upon the building-in of alternative behaviors that are mutually exclusive to the punished behavior. These behaviors may be established during the period of suppression that follows the sequence of punishments.

When extinction procedures are being used, there are also cogent reasons for providing reinforcement contingent upon alternative behaviors (Guthrie, 1952; Hilgard & Bower, 1966). If the performance of the behavior being extinguished requires some time for completion, the individual is obviously going to do *something* during the time previously taken up by the performance of the undesirable behavior. If this behavior is adaptive and desirable, it may be made the object of the reinforcement formerly contingent upon the undesirable behavior. This is also a good time to model, shape, or otherwise train the client in specific alternative behaviors appropriate to the situation at hand, not assuming that the individual in question will automatically emit socially desirable and adaptive behaviors once the maladaptive behavior is eliminated.

A second reason for the training of alternative behaviors while target ones are being extinguished is concerned with the individual's responses to decreased reinforcement. It is often found that the beginning of extinction (immediately following the time when reinforcement is no longer forthcoming) is accompanied by emotional responding and occasionally an *increase* in the frequency of the maladaptive response (especially high magnitude behaviors such as tantrums) (Solomon, 1964). This itself may be trying for the agents who must tolerate the behavior without responding in a manner that is reinforcing. Emotional responding, ranging from irritability to temper tantrums and crying, does tend to extinguish relatively rapidly, and one may suspect that the provision of reinforcement, now contingent upon other behaviors, is in large part responsible. At any rate, when a high-frequency behavior is being extinguished, it is almost imperative to provide reinforcement contingent upon other behaviors, both to maintain some level of behavior in the extinction settings and to avoid creating a reinforcement vacuum that is an arousing and clearly uncomfortable state of affairs. Such a reinforcement vacuum is an example, perhaps, of the time-out procedures described in the next section.

Designing a program of extinction involves the assessment of the contingencies currently operating and the planned elimination of such contingent reinforcement. Often these contingencies involve social reinforcement, and the reinforcing agents may be retrained to offer their attention, responsiveness, smiles, etc. contingently upon behaviors *other* than the undesirable one, and to stand mute, look away, or divert their attention to someone else when the maladaptive behavior occurs.

In a now classic study, Allen and Harris (1966) treated a girl whose face, neck, and various other parts of her body were covered by open sores and scabs from nearly a year's worth of scratching herself. Her mother was trained to withhold all reinforcement upon the child's scratching behavior (attention, restraining physical contact, etc.), while simultaneously reinforcing the desirable behaviors. The mother was also given instruction in leaving out the established reinforcement schedule. By the end of 6 weeks, the child's face and body were clear of all sores and scabs, and a 4-month follow-up revealed no reestablishment of the scratching behavior.

As part of a procedure to treat alcoholism, Mertens and Fuller (1964) encouraged the extinction of alcoholic drinking by instructing friends of the client to dispense their usual social behaviors (attention to client, talking, joking, general carousing) as long as he came to the local tavern and drank soft drinks only. As soon as he drank an alcoholic beverage they were immediately to withdraw all their reinforcement (ignore the client and, if necessary, leave the tavern). Note how discrimination training immediately becomes a part of extinction procedures since the client is essentially required to discriminate that a new behavior is now instrumental in obtaining reinforcement, while an old one is not.

Time-Out Procedures

Although time-out procedures are often utilized as part of a contingency-management program, technically they are actually punishments because of their generally aversive nature (Ullman & Krasner, 1969). Extinction procedures involving the social ignoring of disruptive behaviors or the withdrawal of physical reinforcement previously contingent upon an undesirable behavior may be seen as focused time-outs since they involve a planned absence of reward contingent upon a particular behavior. Actual time-out procedures involve a contingent withdrawal of all major reinforcing consequences, usually by confining an individual in a barren place devoid of people and objects of interest. Occasionally a sort of time-out may be instituted by removing the primary sources of reinforcement from the individual, rather than him from them. Some years ago an unruly child might be locked in his room —or even in a closet—in a home-remedy sort of time-out, which is seen as generally unethical today because of the potential side effects and fearfulness likely to ensue. Sending a child to his room is, again, a sort of pseudo-time-out, weakened by the presence of diversionary toys, etc., still at his command.

When a single person is a major source of reinforcement, removing that person may constitute a sort of time-out. This is especially helpful when the continued presence of that person makes it difficult to prevent an undesirable behavior from being reinforced. Thus, a mother may be instructed to get a cigarette, a good magazine, and betake herself to the bathroom, locking herself in, when her child's temper tantrum erupts, coming out only when all is quiet. This method is especially helpful when the behavior to be eliminated is an extraordinarily compelling one that all but demands attention (reinforcement) from those present.

Wolf, Risely, and Mees (1964) describe the elimination of tantrum behavior in a 3½-year-old autistic boy. The child was placed in a room by himself when he had a tantrum and was allowed to come out only when the tantrum ceased. A similar procedure was described by Williams (1959) in treating a 21-month-old child. Wahler, Winkel, Peterson, and Morrison (1965) instructed mothers in the use of time-out procedures in the elimination of obstructive and tantrum behavior while reinforcing cooperation. Time-outs for tantrum behavior were combined with the ignoring of obstructiveness. Very few time-outs were necessary in order to eliminate the tantrums and the obstructiveness was eliminated rapidly. As we stress throughout Chapter IX, punishment techniques should *always* be used in conjunction with the procedures designed to build in desirable alternative behaviors. Punishment is an adjunct to other procedures. The use of time-outs is no exception.

Achieving Long-Term, Generalized Treatment Effects: Instilling the Self-Control of Behavior

Since we devote an entire chapter to the topic of self-control (Chapter VII), we need not belabor the point here. It is clear, nevertheless, that the goal of any contingency-management program will include lasting changes in behavior that will generalize to appropriate, new situations. Toward this end, it is often desirable to include training in the self-monitoring and self-evaluation of appropriate behaviors and to induce the self-dispensation of reinforcement for such behaviors. Often this will be a natural concomitant of contingency management since the procedures themselves include the specification of appropriate behaviors and the modeling of the verbal reinforcement for their performance. It has been clearly shown that the reinforcing or criticizing behavior of a model toward an individual may induce similar behavior by that individual toward himself, and that in acquiring such self-reinforcement patterns he also learns the specific contingencies with which they are dispensed (Bandura & Kupers, 1964; Mischel & Liebert, 1966; Aronfreed, 1964; Grusec, 1966; Bandura, 1971). It is occasionally beneficial, however, to have more direct training in self-control, too (see Chapter VII).

Contingency-Management Research and Case Studies of Reinforcement Procedures

It would be impossible for us to include examples of each type of behavior problem that has been successfully treated by reinforcement techniques. Contingency-management procedures utilizing parents or teachers to treat problem behaviors exhibited by children have been used to treat depressive feelings and hyperdependency (Wahler & Pollio, 1968); extreme withdrawal (Allen, Hart, Buell, Harris, & Wolf, 1964; Brawley, Harris, Allen, Fleming, & Peterson, 1969; Johnston, Kelley, Buell, Harris, & Wolf, 1963); extreme passivity (Johnston, Kelley, Harris, & Wolf, 1966); and hyperactivity and aggression (Allen, Henke, Harris, Baer, & Reynolds, 1967; Hall, Lund, & Jackson, 1968). Patterson and his colleagues (Patterson, Ray, & Shaw, 1968) have worked extensively with family members and peer groups as effective contingency managers.

Reinforcement procedures have also been used to develop social skills and self-management abilities in severely retarded and psychotic patients. These skills include dressing and feeding oneself (Ayllon & Michael, 1959); personal grooming and responsiveness to verbal directions (Bensberg, Colwell, & Cassell, 1965; Girardeau & Spradlin, 1964; Minge & Ball, 1967; Roos, 1965); and toilet training (Giles & Wolf, 1966; Hundziak et al., 1965). Other problems treated include autism (Lovaas, 1968; Wetzel, Baker, Rooney, & Martin, 1966); mutism (Sherman, 1965; Straughen, 1968); self-mutilation (Allen & Harris, 1966); and a variety of behaviors exhibited (or not exhibited) by schizophrenic patients (King et al., 1960; Peters & Jenkins, 1954; Schaefer & Martin, 1966). Other problems shown responsive to these procedures include school phobias (Patterson, 1965); psychogenic seizures (Gardner, 1967); and psychogenic blindness (Brady & Lind, 1961). Obviously the list could go on and on. Let it suffice to say that for the therapist who decides to treat just about any sort of problem, there will be an example of a successful procedure in the published literature if he but looks for it. When a therapeutic procedure proves difficult to devise or seems ineffective, such examples can be immensely helpful.

Design of Experimental and Case Studies

Of all the techniques of behavior therapy, the manipulation of reinforcing events in contingency management is certainly the technique based on the greatest amount of empirical research in laboratory settings. Furthermore, most case studies concerned with contingency manipulations are presented in the form of research studies, as has become clear during the sections on various procedures of contingency management. This is the direct result of—or, indeed, comprises—one of the major research design contributions operant psychology has made to the field in general: the single-subject research design. The most common research procedure utilizing a single subject is the "reversal" design, in which information is gathered concerning the frequency of a target behavior in a designated situation (base line); the contingency is applied (initial intervention) and frequency continues to be recorded; the contingency is removed (reversal—similar to base line) and frequency is recorded; and finally the contingency manipulation is reinstituted and frequency is monitored for an extended period of time (reintervention and follow-up). If the frequency of the target behavior is stable during base line, changes markedly during intervention (increases if it is the recipient of reinforcement, decreases if an incompatible behavior is the recipient), returns to base-line frequency during reversal, and then increases or decreases appropriately when the contingency is reestablished—if all these criteria are clearly met, then it is concluded that the power of the contingency manipulations to affect the target behavior has been duly demonstrated.

This design is not without its critics, and many of their comments are well taken. The primary criticism that applies to all instances of this experimental design is that the use of only a single subject limits the confidence with which the results may be interpreted to be valid for adults or children (or both) *in general.* One may never be certain that the individual in question was not in some way atypical in a manner that predisposed him to respond to the contingency manipulation differently from the manner in which others would respond. The only answer to this criticism is replication, or utilization of the manipulation in a number of individual cases with successful results in each. Fortunately, the operant literature is so extensive that there are few manipulations that have not been replicated a significant number of times, enough to inspire confidence in their effectiveness.

Individual studies may still be flawed, and there are certain flaws common to single-subject studies. Some studies omit the base-line period of frequency recording. In some ways this is understandable and is comparable to the necessary, but often omitted, inclusion of a nontreated control condition on studies of drug or psychotherapy effectiveness: when a potential curative action is available, it is difficult to justify delaying (for base line) or omitting (in control) its employment, especially when the behavior problem or illness in question is extremely debilitating. Self-destructive children, to take an extreme example, might seriously injure themselves if allowed to batter themselves without restraint during a base-line period. Fortunately, however, most behavior problems are not of this nature and there is little reason not to gather the base-line frequency.

We should also reiterate at this point that the assessment of base-line information is important for the practicing therapist, too, since it is by comparison with the base-line frequency that he can assess the effectiveness of the contingency-management program he has devised for a particular client. Without such information it is difficult to determine whether parents, teachers, etc. are accurately effecting the planned contingencies, or whether the planned contingencies themselves are showing any effective control of overt behavior if they are being properly executed. Such decisions must be made if the therapist is to evaluate the effectiveness of current manipulations for future clients with similar behavior problems. This brings us to a second problem with base-line frequency data, which may apply even when it is gathered: it must be stable. Occasionally data is reported in which the base-line frequency, although quite high, let us say, is clearly declining during the base-line period. Thus, even though a subsequent manipulation appears to produce a further decline, it cannot be strongly argued that the decline present during base-line measurement would not have continued and the frequency of the behavior become reduced even if the contingency manipulation had not been instituted. Consequently, it is well to gather base-line data until a fairly stable frequency is obtained, one that appears to be neither increasing or decreasing.

One of the clearest reported examples of the reversal design in case studies is a case reported by Allen et al. (1964). This is a pleasant example, also, since it illustrates quite clearly the way in which changes in one behavior may be paralleled in an opposite way by changes in a mutually exclusive behavior, thus providing evidence that the frequency of one behavior may be manipulated in order to manipulate (indirectly) a different, but related, behavior. In this particular case, Ann, a nursery school child, was quite isolated from other children in the nursery school she attended, spending 45% of her time alone, 35% interacting with adults, 10% of her time near, but not interacting with, children, and 10% in actual interaction with other children. From an initial analysis of the situation it appeared that Ann possessed several skills that encouraged teachers to interact with her, such as advanced language and conceptual development, and long attention span for teacher-initiated projects. Furthermore, her slow, halting speech appeared to be another factor eliciting teacher attention. Initial observation also indicated that the nursery school teachers granted attention to Ann when she was with them or was playing alone, but when she was with other children they rarely interacted and offered attentions, as though it would disrupt such activities. Figure 5.3 illustrates the relative frequencies of Ann's interactions with adults and children at the nursery school.

Base-line measurement covered 5 days of observations and revealed a somewhat stable, high frequency of interaction with adults (although a downward slope is rather noticeable and 1–2 days more of observations

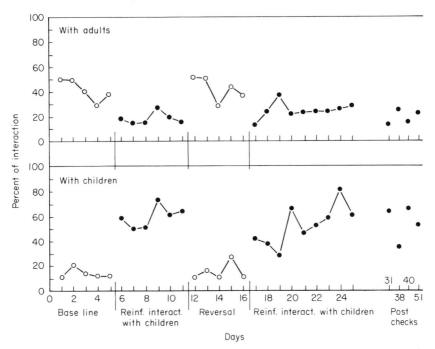

Figure 5.3 Percent of social interactions with adults and with other children shown by an isolated child as a function of reinforcement for peer interaction. From Allen *et al.*, 1964.

would have been in order) and a quite stable low frequency of interaction with children. Following base line, the nursery school teachers were instructed to pay as little attention as possible to Ann when she was engaged in solitary play or approached one of them, but to grant and actively offer such attention when she was playing with other children. As Figure 5.3 illustrates, the effects are striking and immediate. After 5 days of this contingency, the teachers were instructed to attend to her during solitary play and to respond to her when she was in their presence or made attention bids to them. Clearly, the behaviors of playing with children and interaction with adults was under the control of the nursery school teachers' attention-giving behavior, since the frequencies of these two behaviors reversed again. Finally, the original "therapeutic" contingencies were reinstituted after 5 days, and the frequencies of these two categories of behavior again changed. Follow-up checks conducted over a period of 2 weeks indicated that the changes in these two behaviors appeared to be rather enduring.

Generality and the Enduring Nature of Behavior Changes

Natural Contingencies for Newly Established Behaviors. The success of a reversal design rather paradoxically implies that behavioral changes induced by changing the contingencies of *specified* reinforcers are highly dependent upon the contingencies of delivery of those particular reinforcers, at least for the course of time and in the situation for which data are gathered. One might mistakenly conclude, however, that the results of reinforcement therapy are quite limited and potentially quite fragile. This does not appear to be the case. Certainly, if a child or adult is returned to an environment in which the contingencies are clearly in favor of the originally maladaptive behavior, this behavior is quite likely to increase in frequency again. Similarly, if the natural environment of a client is not reinforcing of a newly acquired behavior or reinforcing of a mutually exclusive alternative behavior, the newly acquired behaviors are likely to decrease in frequency.

Fortunately, a thorough analysis of the home or natural environment will allow the anticipation of such problems, and when parents, spouses, or teachers are involved in a contingency-management program, the natural environment is being altered in such a way as to encourage the continued performance of newly acquired behaviors, the continued absence of formerly problematic ones. In this sense, contingency management is often a good adjunct to other techniques of behavior therapy to insure the longevity of a therapeutic change in behavior patterns. But, in many instances such precautions are unnecessary. Most uses of contingency-management procedures are intended to establish or increase the frequency of prosocial behaviors that naturally tend to evoke reinforcing consequences. This is clearly indicated in a study by Ingram (1967).

In this experiment the goal was to increase the social interaction with peers shown by a 4-year-old boy in a nursery school setting. After a base period, contingencies were altered in an attempt to increase the extent of this child's interaction with other children. A repeated series of reversal periods were used. As illustrated in Figure 5.4, although each reversal did, at first, tend to produce a reduction in total peer interaction and cooperation, each successive setback was less pronounced until the fourth period of nonreinforcement had no effect upon the child's ongoing social interaction, and the extent of his cooperative behavior showed a slight increase. Clearly, naturalistic contingencies of peer reinforcement had become the prepotent source of maintaining reinforcement to the category of behaviors.

Some authors (Baer & Wolf, 1967) have used the rather unflattering term *behavior trap* to refer to the concept that the initial behavior manipulation (by procedures of contingency management or other therapy procedures) of a few client behaviors may provide an "entry" to an environment that provides naturalistic reinforcement contingencies that

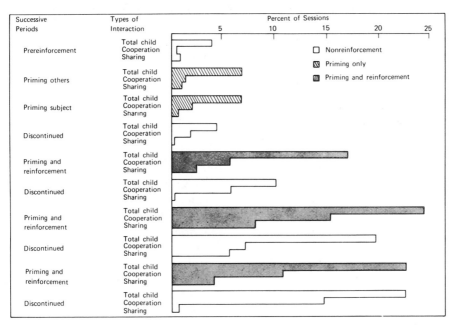

Figure 5.4 Development of cooperative and sharing behavior during periods of contingency management and periods when management procedures were discontinued. From Ingram, 1967; in Baer and Wolf, 1967.

maintain those behaviors and shape new, related ones as well. Although we have not specifically discussed this possibility up to now, it seems clear from evidence and theorizing that analysis of the environments into which the client will move following therapeutic intervention will provide information concerning the behaviors likely to gain reinforcement and thus be maintained. This means also that an attempt should be made to assess or predict how a client's current environment will respond to newly established behaviors and then if necessary, work with that environment to encourage the likelihood that therapeutically induced behaviors will be reinforced and maintained.

Generalization of Therapeutic Results. Any program of behavior change, but most especially those concerned with therapy procedures conducted in a special setting such as an office, must be concerned with the extension of newly changed behaviors to the naturalistic settings in which they are necessary and appropriate. Contingency-management procedures conducted directly in the naturalistic setting are less beset with this problem, although in many instances it is desirable that new behaviors generalize to those other situations in which they are appropriate, but which are not the domain of the contingency managers employed in the management program. In the section on naturalistic contingencies of reinforcement, it was argued that appropriate, prosocial behaviors are likely to be maintained in naturalistic situations *because* they are appropriate and desirable; thus, these behaviors elicit reinforcement and approval from a variety of social agents, such as peers, parents, teachers, nurses, and so on.

There is clear evidence that generalization does tend to occur, although typically to settings reasonably similar to those in which contingencies were originally altered during the management program. O'Leary et al. (1967) treated a 6-year-old child who was diagnosed as an "immature, braindamaged child with a superimposed neurosis." The child was demanding and aggressive toward a younger brother and tended to fight and cause general destruction of household items. Treatment was diverted toward three classes of behavior: deviant (kicking, hitting, pushing, name-calling, and throwing objects); cooperative (asking for a toy, requesting the sibling's help, conversation, and playing within 3 feet of his sibling); and isolate (playing or simply being along, with no physical, verbal, or visual contact with the sibling). Cooperative behavior was then reinforced by a therapist who put an M&M into the child's mouth and simultaneously said "good." This schedule was then thinned to become intermittent such that every fourth response was reinforced. After 5 days of treatment, token rewards were introduced (checks on a blackboard that were worth reinforcers such as candy, comics, puzzles, and other small toys). The number of checks needed for various prizes was gradually increased. Eventually it took several days to earn enough checks for a reinforcer. A time-out procedure was made contingent upon kicking, hitting, etc. Any instance of the deviant behavior was followed by isolation in the bathroom for at least 5 minutes, and the child had to be quiet for a period of at least 3 minutes before he could come out.

The percentage of time spent in cooperative play rose dramatically, essentially doubling, and after 40 days there were no instances of deviant behavior requiring the use of the time-out procedure. Isolate behavior (solitary play) increased in frequency, even though it was not specifically treated. This is an instance of the generalization of treatment effects, to behaviors different from those under treatment, but whose frequency of occurrence is unaffected by the occurrence of the maladaptive behaviors. In the present instance, the increase in isolate behavior was considered a desirable outcome since it did not prohibit cooperative behavior at other times and appeared to have taken the place of the deviant aggressive behaviors.

The various changes in this child's behaviors did not include the total elimination of all deviant behaviors in all settings. Occasionally, aggressive behaviors were reported in the school situation. However, during the year encompassing this treatment, both the parents *and teachers* in contact with this child reported marked progress. Incidents of deviant aggressive behaviors were greatly reduced in both settings, and there was evidence that following treatment there was a stable tendency to play cooperatively with a neighbor's child.

In the study by O'Leary *et al.* (1967), although there was some generalization from home-based management procedures, the generalization was not perfect. In fact, the child was placed in a classroom that utilized behavior therapy principles to establish total control over his school behaviors. A lack of generality in instances like this is not surprising since home and schools are distinctively different situations and include different social agents with whom one interacts. Wahler (1969) reported two cases involving the contingency management of oppositional behavior in a 5-year-old boy and study behavior in an 8-year-old boy. Figure 5.5 presents the results of a contingency-management program for treating the oppositional behavior of the 5-year-old boy. At first, only the parents were trained to give attention to cooperative (nonoppositional) behavior and to utilize time-out procedures contingent upon oppositional, argumentative behavior in the home. By the ninth session it may be seen that there was a great increase of cooperation at home, but no change at school. When the changed contingencies and time-out procedures were removed, the behavior reverted to base line. Finally, however,

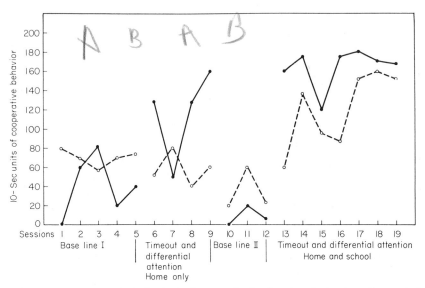

Figure 5.5 Cooperative behavior in home and school setting during base-line periods of contingency management in the home alone or in both the home and school (●——●: home behavior; O– –O: school behavior). From Wahler, 1969.

when both home and school became the setting in which contingency management occurred, cooperative behavior increased in both settings.

Effectiveness of Training in Contingency Management

Typically it will be necessary to train parents, spouses, teachers, nurses, etc. in the techniques of reinforcement delivery according to prescribed contingencies. In most instances this will involve a general introduction to behavior therapy principles, though not necessarily calling them such, since most people do not view social interaction in terms of reinforcers, punishers, and models, nor are they acquainted with the general rules of reinforcer delivery such as immediacy, schedules, time-outs, etc. There are manuals written expressly for this purpose (for example, Patterson & Guillion, 1971), and it is common therapeutic practice to insist that individuals who are to be the agents of a contingency-management program read such a manual before the therapist schedules further appointments or begins his behavioral assessment.

It is clear that the training of these agents may be accomplished effectively via thorough, but brief, training programs. One of the first reports of contingency management using an agent other than the therapist employed the psychiatric nurse as a "behavioral engineer" (Ayllon & Michael, 1959). In their procedure, Ayllon and Michael utilized psychiatric nurses to carry out contingency-management programs of extinction, reinforcement for incompatible behaviors, escape and avoidance training, and satiation. Since the nurses were on the ward in their capacity as attending staff, as was the psychologist in charge, it was not necessary to provide training sufficient to enable the agents to perform their programs of contingency management for extended periods of time in the absence of the therapist. This sort of training becomes more necessary in the treatment of noninstitutionalized clients.

In the present case, the agents were provided with a mimeographed record form. They were instructed to seek out the patient under treatment at regular intervals (time sampling) and, without interacting with him, record the behavior taking place at that time. The ongoing behaviors were simply classified in terms of a preestablished trichotomy: 1) the undesirable behavior; 2) an incompatible behavior (that could replace the undesirable one); or 3) an incompatible behavior (that could also replace the undesirable one, but was not a desirable behavior itself). This established a base frequency for any behavior to be treated.

Instruction to nurses was given at ward staff meetings for the two daytime shifts. Here is an example from Ayllon and Michael (1959) of the informal instruction regarding reinforcement and extinction (nonreinforcement) procedures:

Reinforcement is something you do for or with a patient, for example, offering candy or a cigarette. Any way you convey attention to the patient is reinforcing. Patients may be reinforced if you answer their questions, talk to them or let them know by your reaction that you are aware of their presence. The commonsense expression 'pay no attention' is perhaps closest to what must be done to discourage the patient's behavior. When we say 'do not reinforce a behavior,' we are actually saying 'ignore the behavior and act deaf and blind whenever it occurs [p. 325].' [4]

The results were dramatic for each type of procedure attempted. In one instance, a female patient persistently entered the nurses' office and distracted them. Prior to the intervention she had typically been carried bodily from the office or taken by the hand and led out. Then nurses were instructed to ignore her when she came in—to proceed as though she were not there. Figure 5.6 illustrates the steady decline in her frequency of entering the nurses' office over a 2-month treatment period.

[4] This and the extract on page 208 are reprinted from Ayllon, T., and Michael, J., The psychiatric nurse as a behavioral engineer. *Journal of the Experimental Analysis of Behavior*, 1959, **2**, 323–344. Copyright 1959 by the Society for the Experimental Analysis of Behavior, Inc. Additional information and related research can be found in *The Token Economy: A Motivational System for Therapy and Rehabilitation*, by T. Ayllon and N. H. Azrin, published by Appleton-Century-Crofts, 1968.

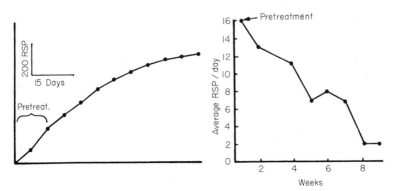

Figure 5.6 Declining frequency (extinction) of entering the nurses' office as illustrated by a cumulative record (on the left) or a conventional behavior graph (on the right). From Ayllon and Michael, 1959.

Similarly, the nurses were instructed to carry out an escape–avoidance training procedure for patients who were so "regressed" that they refused to feed themselves. These patients, two females, had to be forcefully taken to the dining area where they would then permit themselves to be spoon-fed. One patient was in the hospital 7 months, the other, 28 years. Since both patients were neat in appearance, the following procedure was devised:

> Continue spoonfeeding the patient; but from now on, do it in such a careless way that the patient will have a few drops of food fall on her dress. Be sure not to overdo the food dropping, since what we want to convey to the patient is that it is difficult to spoonfeed a grown-up person, and not that we are mean to her. What we expect is that the patient will find it difficult to depend on your skill to feed her. You will still be feeding her, but you will simply be less efficient in doing a good job of it. As the patient likes having her clothes clean, she will have to choose between feeding herself and keeping her clothes clean, or being fed by others and risking getting her clothes soiled. Whenever she eats on her own, be sure to stay with her for a while (3 minutes is enough), talking to her, or simply being seated with her. We do this to reinforce her eating on her own. In the experience of the patient, people become nicer when she eats on her own [pp. 330–331].

Figure 5.7 presents the progress of one of these two patients. During an 8-day base-line period, this patient ate 5 meals on her own, refused 7 meals, and had to be spoon-fed for 12. By the end of treatment she tended to feed herself all meals that she did not refuse. The treatment was similarly successful for the other patient. It is interesting to note that when this patient left the hospital her weight had risen from 99 to 120 pounds. Furthermore, upon admission, her refusal to eat was accompanied by paranoid beliefs and statements that the food was poi-

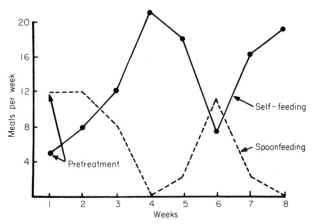

Figure 5.7 Frequency of self-feeding and spoonfeeding by a psychotic patient during 8 weeks of contingency management in which spoonfeeding was done in an aversive fashion by the staff. From Ayllon and Michael, 1959.

soned. Though no treatment was directed toward these beliefs, as the patient began to eat on her own, her claims that the food was poisoned ceased entirely.

The idea that parents should be included in the treatment of the child is not new, although only recently has any attention been turned to the training of the parent as agent or mediator in the charge of his child's behavior (Prince, 1961; Russo, 1964; Straughan, 1964; Wahler, Winkel, Peterson, & Morrison, 1965). In procedures of this sort, greater training is required since much of the actual contingency management must be effected during extended periods of time between consultation appointments. Some therapists require telephone check-ins daily, during which they can answer questions, direct reinforcing activities, and so on. Often the behavior of noninstitutionalized clients is so varied and occurs in so many different contexts that it is difficult to prescribe a "reinforcing regimen" that can be applied automatically, or with little training or practice.

A classic example of the successful employment of contingency-management procedures using mothers as agents is that of Wahler et al. (1965). The procedures employed occasionally require a good deal of space and the use of observers whose time and availability may be expensive and difficult to secure. However, in actual clinical practice, observers may be replaced by parental or client report (not a particularly desirable alternative), by closed-circuit TV and videotape recording of the client *and* agent's behavior (most preferred), or perhaps by therapist observation of the client's behavior. Wahler's procedure included two sessions devoted to the classification of mother–child interaction during which the mother was instructed to play with her child in a play room "just as you would at home." Two observers recorded the mother and child's behaviors and these records were analyzed for 1) the child's deviant behavior; 2) the child's behavior(s) that was incompatible with the problem behavior; and 3) the mother's ways of reacting to the various incompatible behaviors.

Following this step the therapist instituted training to modify the mother's reaction to the various behaviors. In general, Wahler's procedures always involved the elimination of a problem behavior by strengthening an incompatible one. The mother was shown the base-line data and given an interpretation of it (the problem behaviors, incompatible behaviors, her reactions and their effects, etc.). She was then instructed that in future play sessions she was to ignore completely the problem behavior and respond in any approving way to the incompatible behaviors only. A signal light was provided in the play room and it was explained that this light was an aid to help her respond: She was to keep an eye on the light and respond in an approving way *only* when it was lighted. Thus, the light was a device to aid in teaching the mother procedures of effective contingency management while she was actually interacting with her child. The mother and child were still observed during interaction and when it became clear she was responding accurately, the use of the signal light was discontinued.

Wahler, Winkel, Peterson, and Morrison (1965) reported the successful treatment of several young children with a variety of problems. One child exhibited extreme dependency, which, when thwarted, led to aggressive outbreaks of hitting and kicking in nursery school. Another child exhibited extreme "stubbornness," or oppositional behavior, toward her parents, refusing to cooperate or obey their requests. A third child was oppositional to the point of commanding his parents, who acquiesced and allowed him to determine his own bedtime, foods, and even when the parents would play with him. In each case the mother was carefully taught to ignore the problem behavior and to respond with exhilarant approval and acceptance toward incompatible behaviors.

For example, in treating the oppositional child, the mother was instructed to ignore any stubborn behaviors, but to respond warmly whenever he exhibited any sort of cooperation; since a reduction in oppositional behavior was not proceeding rapidly, Wahler *et al.* (1965) also instructed the mother in the use of a time-out procedure: Following each stubborn response, the child was to be put in a room adjacent to the playroom and left alone for 5 minutes. If he exhibited tantrum behavior, he was left alone in the room until the tantrum ceased (negative reinforcement contingent upon quieting down).

Figure 5.8 illustrates the cumulative recording of *oppositional* and cooperative responses during periods of treatment and reversal (stub-

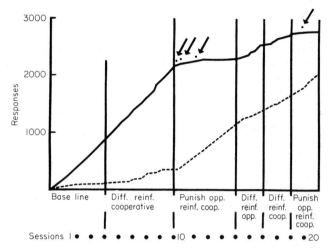

Figure 5.8 Cumulative record of oppositional and cooperative behavior over a baseline period and sessions utilizing various types of contingency management (———: oppositional; – – –: cooperative). From Wahler *et al.,* 1965.

bornness was complied to, as during base lines). A horizontal line of the graph indicates 0 frequency (no new responses), a climbing line indicates repeated instances of response (the sharper the incline of the line, the greater the frequency of responses). Arrows indicate times when the mother used time-outs. Clearly the mother had gained control over oppositional behavior by the judicious use of ignoring and punishing on the one hand (with time-outs); on the other, consistently warm responses to cooperation insured that the child continued to emit cooperative behavior.

In a laudatory and successful attempt to provide psychological services to a rural, poverty-ridden area, Wahler (1969) established a community program based upon contingency-management procedures to handle child behavior problems in a population of 100,000 residents. A county health clinic with but a single social worker was the source. First of all, Wahler, who was a consulting psychologist to the clinic, spending a maximum of 10 hours a month there, initiated a drive to recruit volunteer workers. In the treatment of an individual case, a child, his immediate family, and any other closely involved persons (for example, teachers) were interviewed by the clinic's professional staff. The intent of the interview was to establish fairly objective descriptions of the problem behaviors and the consequences that typically followed instances of these behaviors. The behavioral diagnosis produced by the interview thus included a list of the problem behaviors, plus a compilation of likely reinforcers.

The volunteer worker was then familiarized with the interview data. He was also introduced to the principles of contingency management. It was stressed that the deviant behaviors were probably being maintained by social reinforcement from individuals in the child's environment. Then a brief verbal essay was given on principles of reinforcement, punishment, and extinction, and finally a therapeutic regimen was devised by considering which social agents in the child's environment were most likely responsible for the maintenance of the deviant behavior and how their reinforcing contingencies might be changed in order to modify the child's behavior.

The volunteer worker was first to obtain at least two 1-hour observations of the child's behavior to confirm the hypotheses drawn from the interview, and other contact was made with those social agents whose reinforcing behavior seemed most easily modifiable and were also likely to produce changes in the child's behaviors. These contacts included both the consulting psychologist and the volunteer worker. As a volunteer worker became more experienced, he met with the social agents alone and then held separate meetings with the consulting psychologist. At first both the psychologist and the worker met with the social agents at biweekly intervals. Throughout treatment the volunteer worker made 1-hour observations of the child's behavior once each week.

During 2 years of operation, 66 cases were treated, involving one or more problem behaviors. Table 5.4 reports the general outcome in terms of general reduction of the frequencies of various problem behaviors. For each category there was a significant reduction of frequency of problem behavior. Furthermore, the average length of treatment declined significantly, from an average of 19 weeks per case prior to the initiation of the contingency-reward program, to an average of only 5 weeks.

Although it is desirable to train contingency managers by observing them in direct contact with the individuals whose behaviors are to be changed, it is not unusual to work with the contingency managers alone. Mothers who themselves have come to treatment may be given instruction in management techniques to improve the behavior of their children and reduce their own stresses at home. Mira (1970) reported the results of a massive contingency-management program in which 82 cases were treated by contingency management. In this particular instance all referrals were children, and in most of the cases only a parent or teacher was seen (only 11% of the cases involved both manager and child attending sessions in which management training was given and practiced).

The manager learned first to delineate the troublesome behavior, which involved instruction in describing behaviors in noninterpretive ways. Then they learned to record the frequencies of the target behaviors

TABLE 5.4

Mean Number of Problem-Behavior Episodes before and after Treatment[a]

Behavior	Mean variance				F test	t test	Corrected t test	Number of cases
	Pre-treatment		Post-treatment					
Classroom disruptive behavior	25.77	128.70	7.77	27.83	4.62[b]		4.03[b]	35
Classroom study behavior	51.68	660.22	95.12	1366.68	2.28[b]		10.70[b]	50
School absences (days absent)	7.60	5.69	1.66	4.67	1.22	2.68		15
Home study behavior	13.49	120.35	59.67	1075.00	8.93[b]		8.37[b]	45
Home disruptive behavior	29.87	259.10	9.88	76.40	3.39[b]		7.87[b]	52

[a] Adapted from Wahler, R. G., and Erickson, M., Child behavior therapy: A community program in Appalachia. *Behavior Research and Therapy*, 1969, **7**, 76.

[b] $p < .05$.

on a standard behavior record form that is commercially available. Finally, the managers were trained in the contingent application of reinforcing consequences that were appropriate to the person involved and the setting in which the problem behavior occurred. The frequency was still recorded in order to assess the effectiveness of the technique.

In this program, the behaviors treated included self-care skills (dressing, feeding, going to the toilet); inappropriate social behavior (lying, screaming, hitting, throwing furniture); educational or rehabilitation behaviors (wearing hearing aids, doing physical-therapy exercises, completing academic assignments); and self-mutilation (teeth grinding, skin picking, head banging). As we have noted, the manager tended to complain about behaviors they wished the child to stop doing, and therapists were required to turn the therapy program toward problems of acceleration—what the managers wished the child *would* do. Drooling was "eliminated" by teaching a child to swallow; running off was "eliminated" by teaching a child to walk beside his mother during shopping.

To be classified as successful, a manager had to complete two management goals (behavior changes) successfully, and success was measured by the use of independent observations and recorded changes in the child's behavior, and not solely on verbal reports of the managers: 15% of the managers successfully modified the sample presenting troublesome behavior and then dropped out of the program; 46% of the managers who came at least once did successfully modify at least two problem behaviors. Interestingly, teachers, school social workers, and psychiatrists were no more successful than parents in learning to become effective contingency managers.

Fear Reduction

Although reinforcement is usually seen in a procedure to increase the frequency or intensity of voluntary responses, it can also be used to eliminate maladaptive fears. Studies demonstrating the effectiveness of operant procedures also provide the few instances of comparative effectiveness of reinforcement and modeling or desensitization procedures since the latter are also applicable to problems of fear reduction. However, results of comparative studies should be interpreted guardedly because it is difficult to determine how many reinforced trials are equivalent to how many desensitization trials or modeled trials and to institute modeling procedures completely devoid of reinforcement.

Barlow, Agras, Leitenberg, and Wincze (1970) reported two studies comparing shaping procedures with desensitization and participant-modeling techniques. In the first study, clients were given systematic desensitization treatment utilizing deep muscle relaxation and received mild social reinforcement ("very good," or, "you're doing fine") after the successful completion of each item in the hierarchy. A second group of subjects were instructed to enter a room that was across the hall from the therapist's office and that contained a snake in a glass cage. They were to enter this room alone and practice approaching the snake according to a preestablished hierarchy of approach responses. On a given trial, when the client had approached as closely as she chose, she was to return to the therapist and report how many hierarchy items she had completed on that trial. The therapist then gave praise ("good . . . congratulations!" or, "you're doing much better . . . that's fine") for report of improvement. If the client did not improve after three or more trials, her report was met by a blank stare and a change in conversation. Although both groups improved in terms of how closely they would approach the snake in an actual behavioral test, there was significantly greater improvement for the shaping group than for the desensitization group. On a physiological measure of fear (galvanic skin response), to imagined scenes of snakes and to the real snake, it was found that treatment procedures reduced fearful arousal to imagined scenes of snakes, but only shaping produced any significant reduction in arousal to the sight of a real snake.

In a second study, clients in one treatment condition underwent the shaping procedure in which the therapist remained in his office. A second group of clients was accompanied by the therapist to the room containing the snake, but he did not interact with the client, and any praise was given only after they had returned to the therapist's office. A third group of clients was also accompanied by the therapist, who also modeled the desired behaviors in the room containing the snake. In this study all clients but one were able to perform the most trying task on the behavioral fear measure, picking up the live snake and holding it for 30 seconds, after fewer than 10 treatment sessions. In terms of the number of trials required to reach the criterion, the clients treated with shaping procedures alone (therapist not present) were slowest; clients accompanied by the therapist modeling the desired behaviors was most rapid in defeating their fears.

Rimm and Mahoney (1969) employed procedures of participant modeling and monetary reward in order to eliminate snake-phobic behavior. Participant modeling proved to be a successful treatment procedure; however, the adult clients were unable to show improvement when offered increasing monetary rewards for performing a systematically graduated series of approach responses toward a harmless snake of threatening appearance.

It is clear from these studies that in many instances reinforcement procedures can be effective in the treatment of both fearful behavior and fear itself in the presence of a formerly frightening stimulus. Yet it would be unfair to conclude that any single technique has been demonstrated more effective than any other. The shaping procedure involved the actual presence of a snake, whereas the desensitization manipulation did not; and there is some evidence that desensitization in the presence of a real stimulus is more effective than the alternative use of imagination (Barlow, Leitenberg, & Agras, 1969). Furthermore, few of these techniques were "pure" examples of a specific procedure. The most effective technique in the Barlow *et al.* (1970) report included aspects of systematic desensitization (the gradual exposure to the feared stimulus), contingent reinforcement, and modeling.

VI

Contingency Management in Institutional Settings

We now turn our attention to the use of operant techniques in institutions such as the mental hospital, the house of detention for delinquent individuals, the school, and even the home. The principles behind the use of these techniques in such settings remains the same—and indeed the techniques themselves are identical. Often, however, since the institutional environment is more controllable than a naturalistic one, the precision with which techniques are applied may be enhanced by extensive staff training, and reinforcement systems such as token economies may be established since nearly all reinforcing events may be managed by the therapist and his co-workers (contingency managers). Nevertheless, in other units (such as the family) procedures often labeled institutional—such as the token economy—may also be applied.

At this point we must make a distinction between the application of operant techniques in the treatment of an *individual* who merely happens to be hospitalized or incarcerated for some reason, and the use of *group* contingencies, operant techniques that make use of the fact that an individual is in a residential institution or is actually being treated in a group setting. In the former instance, all the techniques discussed in Chapter V, and the rules and regulations for their application, would apply; we have already discussed several research reports concerned with the use of these techniques in the treatment of institutionalized individuals. This chapter is concerned with techniques specifically designed for the institutional setting and that generally take advantage of the group environment and extent of control characteristic of such environments. Given this emphasis, we concentrate on *reinforcement economies* in which a large proportion of the available reinforcers are controlled, typically through the use of or medium of exchange such as a token.

Token Economies: Introduction

Token economies are surely rarer in institutions concerned with the treatment of behavior disorders than they are outside. Indeed, any national economy with a currency system is in every sense a token economy: any currency consists by definition of token or symbolic "reinforcers" that may be exchanged for items that truly constitute a more direct form of reinforcement (Winkler, 1970). While the individual in society works to earn tokens with which he purchases his dwelling place, food, recreation, etc., most institutions provide such comforts noncontingently and hence cease to encourage many adaptive behaviors that are appropriate and effective in the natural environment (Gelfand, Gelfand, & Dobson, 1967). Thus, the concept of a token economy both is and is not an innovation, depending upon whether or not it is considered in the context of a treatment institution.

The use of token rewards constitutes the primary procedure with which we are concerned in this chapter. Consequently, let us begin with a general description of procedures. In setting up a token economy, there are three basic considerations. First, as in all operant modification procedures, it is necessary to *identify the target behaviors* (Tharp & Wetzel, 1969; Bandura, 1969). Little further needs to be said concerning this prerequisite except that such response identification will clearly be necessary in the later determination of reinforcement rate, or magnitude, and whether procedures of response cost [1] will be necessary. Obviously, response cost is applicable only when there are behaviors to be elimi-

---

[1] Response-cost procedures involve the *removal* of a reinforcer contingent upon a designated response. Docking pay for late arrival or denying a privilege because of misbehavior are both examples of response cost; see Chapter IX for an extended discussion.

nated or when, as treatment progresses, behaviors learned initially are to be phased out in favor of others that were too difficult, complex, or undesired at the beginning of treatment. For example, a patient who spends much of his time in bed may be allowed to purchase bedtime by earning tokens in some other activity. As treatment progresses and he spends more and more time out of bed earning tokens, the cost of bedtime may also be raised with little or no inflation in the number of tokens earned for the performance of desired behaviors.

Second, the therapist must *define the currency* (Bandura, 1969; Baer & Sherman, 1969). This is generally simple and may depend in large part upon the resources of the institution to provide tangible tokens. In the past, items such as poker chips, points on a tally sheet, gold stars, numbers shown on an electric counter, plastic slips resembling credit cards, or holes punched in a ticket have served as tokens.

Finally, the therapist must *devise an exchange system*. This poses a twofold problem. Initially it must be determined exactly what items or privileges for which tokens may be exchanged and how often exchanges may take place. If exchange is allowed but once a year, it is unlikely that a token system will succeed since the value of the token is sure to become obscured in the waiting (Baer & Sherman, 1969; Ayllon & Azrin, 1968a). As in all instances employing reinforcement techniques, effective reinforcers must be defined, and these may well vary depending upon the population being treated (Birnbrauer, Bijou, Wolf, & Kidder, 1965). Examples of such reinforcers—termed *back-up reinforcers*—include tangibles such as money, food, or toys, or intangibles like behavior privileges (ward privileges, passes, special trips to movies, shows, pools, etc.). Note how the latter is a direct utilization of the Premack principle concerning the use of preferred activities as reinforcers.

A second important aspect of the exchange system concerns the establishment of a *rates* of exchange. Here we are speaking of two rates of exchange, the number of tokens earned by the performance of a nonpreferred activity, and the number of tokens required to be surrendered in payment for a desired item or privilege. Each of these may change during the course of a treatment regimen. At first, nonpreferred behaviors should earn large numbers of rewards, enough so that extensive numbers of nonpreferred behaviors are not required to earn minimally valued items or privileges. Cases and research studies cited throughout the chapter contain examples of exchange rates found to be effective.

Advantages and Disadvantages of Token-Reinforcement Systems

The establishment of a system of token rewards, even though it is a difficult undertaking, contains a number of inherent advantages. First of all, the individual under treatment may select the specific back-up reinforcer he considers himself to be working for. Essentially, all individuals are continually presented with a "menu" of reinforcing events (Homme, 1971) and can, at any time, be working for the reinforcer of their own choice. The use of a menu removes the necessity of determining a single reinforcer that has some value for all individuals under treatment or the tedious process of defining different reinforcers for each person (although often this is a worthwhile procedure nonetheless; see Birnbrauer *et al.,* 1965). This leads us to a second advantage, namely that the use of easily managed tokens removes the necessity for the contingent dispensation of bulky, messy, or otherwise unmanageable reinforcing events. Perhaps the primary advantage, however, is the ability, by manipulating the rate of exchange, to allow individuals to work over extended periods of time for single, highly potent reinforcers; at the same time, the staff is able to dispense immediate, tangible (if basically symbolic) reinforcement after each response with very short temporal delays. Both of these factors serve to increase the effectiveness of the reinforcer.

Certainly there are disadvantages to token systems, but it is generally conceded that they far outweigh the advantages. Typically (except for permanently institutionalized individuals), any particular token system is not the usual system of reinforcement that prevails outside the institution or even within an institution outside a specific treatment program (for example, in schools where a token system may be used to promote studying one subject but not another). Clearly, to increase generalization an individual's reliance upon a token system should be phased out once the requisite behaviors are established and the token reinforcers replaced by reinforcers most appropriate to the natural environment, such as social reinforcement or money (Fairweather, 1964). Even token systems relying upon money must fade out money as reinforcers for activities not reinforced by money in the natural environment. Another disadvantage concerns the process of exchange. The institution or staff monitoring the token system must maintain a supply of exchange items, a store, in effect (Baer & Sherman, 1969). Again, the use of money as the unit of exchange reduces this problem.

A major difficulty and, as such, a disadvantage concerns the initial establishment of the token system, especially as it applies to each individual. Often individuals must be taught to value the token, to discriminate that they have exchange value (Atthowe & Krasner, 1968; Ayllon & Azrin, 1968a). Sometimes supplying a verbal explanation will suffice. At other times, as with severely retarded individuals or some psychotics, it is necessary to shape the individual in the use of the token system (Baer & Sherman, 1969). Often this is done by a sort of free distribution before actual contingencies are put into effect, which requires the individual to earn his token rewards.

One of the initial decisions that must be made concerns the use of group-wide or individualized contingency systems. In a group-wide system, all patients earn tokens at the same rate for any particular behavior and are required to pay the same number of tokens for the same privilege or desired item. In an individualized token economy, the rate of pay and exchange may be different for all patients involved. Patients just beginning the system may be required to pay fewer tokens for a particular privilege and at the same time earn more for various behaviors than do more seasoned patients whose rate of performing appropriate behaviors has already improved. Clearly, the group contingency is more easily administered, although its effectiveness for some patients may be reduced since it is not tailored to their individual behavioral capabilities. It seems rigid, however, to assume that a group contingency cannot have individual components injected into it. Liberman (1968) describes an instance of a woman who screamed loudly at a lunch table after being accidentally pushed by a table mate. The decision was made to impose upon her an immediate fine of one token each time this occurred. It seems likely that individualized components such as these could easily be handled within the context of a group contingency system.

Procedural Details in the Establishment of a Token Economy

Considerations in the Establishment of a Token System. Token economies are truly complicated social and economic systems whose construction can be summarized, but not fully represented, in a single chapter. Fortunately, there are two excellent descriptions of token economies that describe in great detail the procedures, rules, and general considerations for such systems and that have been written in a specific, concrete manner that will facilitate the reinstitution of such systems in any institutional ward (Ayllon & Azrin, 1968a; Schaefer & Martin, 1969). While these two volumes share a great deal in common, Ayllon and Azrin (1968a) present a good overview of a single token economy, including a series of experiments demonstrating the effectiveness of various procedures. Schaefer and Martin (1969) describe their system at Patton State Hospital in California in similar rigorous detail, but concentrate upon specific methods of implementation, rather than the system as a whole.

In their account, Ayllon and Azrin (1968a) organize much of their presentation around a series of "rules" to be followed in establishing and maintaining an effective token system. Several of these rules summarize what we feel are the most basic considerations and consequently we limit our discussion to them. It should be noted that many of these recommendations are equally applicable in the use of contingency-management procedures with individual clients, including the training of contingency managers since in the present instance, ward personnel of necessity become contingency managers as they enforce the contingency inherent in the token economy.

There are certain procedural details that are helpful in the establishment of any token economy. Although the individual case will surely necessitate slight modifications, depending upon whether it is a token system for an individual group, institutional ward, or freer environment, and so on, the basic considerations and recommended procedures remain somewhat the same. Some authors (see Ayllon & Azrin, 1968a) have abbreviated these procedures into a set of "rules" governing the coordination of staff efforts toward the observation, elicitation, and reinforcement of desired behaviors. We would prefer to call them not "rules," but, rather, simply recommendations for procedures that have proved effective in the establishment and maintenance of reinforcement programs, including token economies, for groups, as well as individuals.

Control over the Dispensation of Reinforcement. The typical contingencies that spontaneously exist in an institution are often related to the bizarre or unusual behavior of the patient (Gelfand, Gelfand, & Dobson, 1967; Birnbrauer *et al.*, 1965). Extreme self-mutilating behavior may be reinforced by personal physical restraint given by ward attendants, and a paranoid ideation is likely to get a response from at least somebody on the ward. Furthermore, many powerful reinforcers such as food or cigarettes are often dispensed noncontingently, and an attempt to make reinforcers such as these contingent upon appropriate behavior are often resisted by staff and hospital administrators alike (Lucero, Vail, & Scherber, 1968). As the case study by Ayllon and Michael (1959), reported in Chapter V, clearly shows, the effectiveness of any contingency-based program of behavior change will be enhanced as a function of the power of the reinforcers employed. Token economies are no exception, and most (see the examples to be described later in the chapter) insist that powerful reinforcers, such as food and private rooms, be purchased with tokens earned for appropriate behaviors.

Staff Coordination. All staff members in contact with a patient form opinions regarding the important aspects of the case that they base upon their own observations of the patient. Everyone observes a slightly different aspect of any patient's total behavior system, and thus different staff members may come to strikingly different conclusions concerning the problem and may present these conclusions to the patient, thereby promoting confusion. As Ayllon and Azrin (1968a) have so succinctly put it:

One staff member may tell a patient she is not cooperative enough. Another that she has not yet learned to live with herself. Other contradictory objectives often given: she must not form too dependent a relationship on others vs. she must learn to be more dependent or to relate more to others; she must not be rigid vs. she must show more perseverance; she must show more diversity of actions vs. she must develop a better concentration on one thing; she must have a better personal appearance vs. she must not be so obsessed with personal appearance; she must learn to acquiesce to authority figures vs. she must show more independence of action. [p. 196–197]

As the suggestions to follow clearly indicate, the behavior of staff members toward the patient must be coordinated and follow closely specified procedures for observing, recording, and responding to (reinforcing) target behaviors.

Defining Target Behaviors: Response Specification. Perhaps the most basic recommendation is that the particular behaviors in question, both those to be changed and the eventually desired behaviors, must be specified as concretely and elaborately as possible in ways that require but a minimum of interpretation by staff or patient (see Chapter V for a more complete discussion of this point). For example, uncooperative behavior may be many things; however, when defined as "responds willingly to requests regarding the taking of medication," a certain behavior is clearly specified and differentiated from all manner of other behaviors that are also uncooperative, but are not part of the particular set of problem behaviors characterizing patients on a certain ward. Schaefer and Martin (1969) have noted how "good personal hygiene" becomes:

no dirt on feet	clean fingernails
no dirt on legs or knees	nicely combed hair
no dirt on hands or arms	daily change of underwear
no dirt on neck or face	clean socks or stockings
no evidence of body odor	neat and recent shave (men)
no residue in the navel	suitable cosmetics (women)

This is a long list, and certainly the *total* number of criteria would constitute an extremely long chain of behaviors to require from a patient who performs few of them at first, or at the onset of his experience with a token system. Note, however, the extreme specificity of each item.

Often a token economy in a hospital may be designed both to increase the highly regressed patient's adjustment to the hospital and, via such improved adjustment, to increase his command of appropriate personal and social behaviors. The tasks (behavior sequences, behavior chains, "jobs") required of patients vary from maintaining standards of personal hygiene and grooming to the actual fulfillment of jobs both on and off the ward. There are several factors that must be coordinated: how a patient gains access to a task, what the rate of "pay" (tokens per unit time) shall be, and the amount of time he must spend at a task before it is considered completed (assuming the quality of the work is adequate) and deserving of reinforcement. We have noted how the target behaviors must be clearly specified. This should include the further specification of what constitutes adequate performance. (Determination of the rate of pay is discussed in a subsequent section.) For the moment we can offer no concrete, proved recommendations for the manner in which behaviors or tasks are selected for inclusion; we can make only the obvious points that the list should specifically include the desired and change-worthy behaviors, and the desired behaviors selected should be within the eventual competence of the patients participating in the economy.

Specification of Behaviors That Are Positive Alternatives to Problem Behaviors. At this early point, it is worth commenting on the preponderance of discussions and examples that will concentrate more upon the *elimination* of problem behaviors than upon the more positive *development* of appropriate behavior patterns: in general, there is probably more concern with the "don'ts" than with the "dos." We meet this problem in disguised form in another chapter, too, that concerned with aversive control (Chapter IX), in which it is repeatedly emphasized that alternative behaviors must be provided when a problem behavior is to be eliminated from the individual's repertoire (in that case typically by punishment or punishment-related techniques).

It is difficult to overemphasize the importance of positive training and yet this aspect of therapy often becomes obscured by the common necessity to eliminate some set of problem behaviors. In a management procedure designed to eliminate problem behaviors there will still be clear, positive contingencies for desired behaviors that are currently infrequent (in many instances they may be opposite—or mutually exclusive of—to the problem behavior), but these contingencies are not as emphasized (to readers or to the patients being treated) as the negative contingencies assessed against the problem behaviors. Thus, in the rules and contingencies governing Achievement Place (Bailey, Wolf, & Phillips, 1970), to be discussed in detail later in the chapter, a variety of behaviors received points but an even more clearly specified set of negative behaviors lost points for the boys. In this particular instance, many of the negative behaviors could have been rephrased, resulting in a more positive and less punitive-appearing contingency-management program. For example, the list of rules presented might have been rephrased as follows:

1. Ask permission if you wish to leave your seat.
2. Talk with your classmates before class and ask permission if you must talk while in class.

3. Focus your attention on the teacher, the board, and the work on your desk in order to avoid daydreaming or gazing out the window.

4. Position your desk properly at the beginning of class and leave it that way.

5. Work quietly.

6. Focus your attention on your own work so as to avoid disturbing others.

7. Work for the whole period.

Although it is a disadvantage that these rephrasings are so long, note that they are all positive in nature, specifying the behavior desired and in many instances also specifying, but in a positive way, the problem behavior to be eliminated. In this way positive behaviors that are mutually exclusive alternatives to the problem behaviors are clearly spelled out, thus aiding their adoption and the concurrent elimination of the problem behaviors. This is perhaps the most compelling reason to design a contingency-management procedure for an individual or in an institution in a positive manner, clearly specifying the desired behaviors, as well as the problem ones.

Specifying Reinforcers. Another necessary procedure, similar to the clear identification of desired and changeworthy behaviors, is to specify concretely and elaborately the reinforcer to be administered. Within a strictly token economy this is a second-order process, involving the communication to the patient of various "real" reinforcers he can purchase with his earned tokens.

Often there is the problem of determining what items for which tokens may be redeemed constitute reinforcers. Since individuals differ in their reinforcer preference, a wide variety of items maximizes the likelihood that tokens will come to have potency as reinforcers for all patients. In many instances it is wise to vary the forms of a known reinforcer in order to discover slight variants that themselves can act as "new" reinforcers. In their token economy, Ayllon and Azrin (1968a), were able to maximize the continued effectiveness of a variety of reinforcers as a result of this technique. Prior to the installation of the token economy, patients had used bulk tobacco and rolled their own cigarettes. Variation showed that brand, filter versus nonfilter, and even smoking versus chewing tobacco were all reinforcers of varying potency for different patients. Similarly, flavors of soda pop, colors of bedspreads, floor mats, and throw cushions, and even whether one "purchased" low or high beds were preferences that varied among the patients. The larger the variety of reinforcers for which tokens may be traded, the greater the likelihood that tokens will be of maximal value for each and every participant in the economy.

Observation of ward patients can be an important source of information concerning general behavior patterns that are of high frequency from all or most patients. This information is important in determining activity reinforcers that may be utilized as privileges exchangeable for tokens. Occasionally the therapist encounters patients whose behavior is so regressed that they appear to value few, if any, items and certainly no activities. (As we have noted, the use of activities or privileges to perform activities as reinforcers requires that the activity in question be performed more frequently than the behavior to be reinforced; see the discussion of activity reinforcers and the Premack principle in Chapter V.) Ayllon and Azrin (1968b) have demonstrated that *enforced sampling of activities* is an effective way to increase their reinforcing properties as seen in the frequency with which patients will exchange hard-earned tokens to purchase them.

In three instances, these investigators demonstrated the effectiveness of procedures designed to increase the value of outdoor walks, music, and movies as reinforcers. Each of these behaviors was minimally attractive to the ward patients at first. However, patients were required to sample each activity before deciding whether or not to spend tokens in order to participate more fully. For example, patients were required to assemble outside before deciding whether or not to pay for a walk. Those who decided not to pay then returned indoors. There was a music room in the ward, and in a second experiment patients were assembled for 3 minutes just outside the door to this room before deciding whether to pay in order to enter. The door to the room was left slightly ajar so that the music could be heard. In a third study, patients viewed 5 minutes of a weekly ward movie before being invited to view the remainder for the price of a token. In all studies patients were given the opportunity to purchase any of the activities for a period of several weeks prior to the sampling procedure, and then, after the sampling had been required for several weeks, sampling was discontinued and the patients' continued rate of purchasing of the activities was observed. As Figure 6.1 clearly shows, sampling markedly increased the rate of purchasing of the sampled activities and even after it was discontinued, the activities continued to be purchased at a much higher rate then prior to the sampling experience. Clearly, such a sampling procedure may prove invaluable when one deals with the patients who appear to find few, if any, activities reinforcing.

Specification of the Contingency and Magnitude of Reinforcement. How *many* tokens, smiles, ignorings (turning one's back and walking off, or simply changing the subject); *when* to reinforce, *whom* to reinforce with *which* reinforcers—all these points must be crystal clear to the staff that

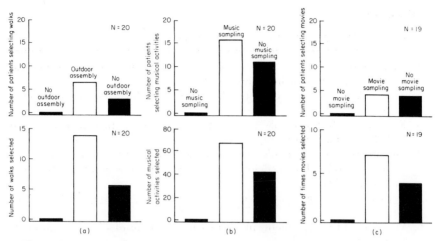

Figure 6.1 Numbers of patients selecting various activities and numbers of activities selected as a function of reinforcer sampling: Outdoor activity (walks), listening to music, and watching movies. From Ayllon and Azrin, 1968b.

implements the contingencies of the token economy. Some authors (see Ayllon & Azrin, 1965) recommend the use of automated devices to deliver the tokens and record the fact of that delivery wherever possible. In any event, since reinforcement is the heart of the procedure, they strongly recommend that systematic, direct observation of the reinforcement procedures be used to coordinate and assure the proper implementation of the contingencies. Table 6.1 contains a summary of the several "rules" suggested by Ayllon and Azrin (1968a), with asterisks marking the ones that we discuss in some detail in the text.

Laws of supply and demand are as important in the token economy as they are in the economy of nations. Jobs that are strenuous, tedious, or that take a long time may be desiring of higher pay. However, if these jobs are attractive for other reasons as well, resulting in their being preferred by a majority of patients, they may be devalued—reduced to lower pay—in order to encourage patients to select other jobs (or they may themselves be used as reinforcers). Occasionally it may be feasible to adjust the number of tokens earned for a specific task for each patient, awarding a higher number of tokens for those tasks least preferred or deemed most therapeutic for that particular patient (Ayllon & Azrin, 1968a). Also, sometimes the qualifications for a job will not permit all patients to sign up for it, and this exclusivity may merit greater token reward. Ayllon and Azrin (1968a) have reported that the job of tour guide through the ward required only 10 minutes of a patient's time, but earned 10 tokens; yet a popular job such as sweeping the floor, although physically demanding and requiring about 3 hours, earned only 5.

TABLE 6.1

Rules for the Use of Incentives in Mental Hospitals [a]

---

1. Dimension of behavior rule: describe the behavior in specific terms that require a minimum of interpretation.[b]
2. Target-behavior rule: describe the desired performance in behavioral terms.
3. Relevance of behavior rule: teach only those behaviors that will continue to be reinforced after training.[b]
4. Probability of behavior rule: observe what the individual does when the opportunity exists. Those activities that are very probable at a given time will serve as reinforcers.
5. Verbal-request rule: act immediately upon every verbal request for a reinforcer.
6. Variation of reinforcement rule: use many variations of a known reinforcer to discover new ones.[b]
7. Conditioned-reinforcement rule: provide a distinctive and tangible stimulus event to bridge any delay between the desired response and the delivery of the reinforcer.
8. Multiple-reinforcer rule: use many different types of reinforcing stimuli with a given individual.
9. Compatibility of reinforcers rule: schedule reinforcing activities so that they occur at different times.
10. Reinforcer-sampling rule: before using an event or stimulus as a reinforcer, require sampling of the reinforcer in the situation in which it is to be used.[b]
11. Reinforcer-exposure rule: at the moment of reinforcer availability, display all the stimuli that typically occur during reinforcer utilization; if possible, have the individual actively utilizing the reinforcer.
12. Behavior-effect rule: arrange the situation so that the behavior produces some enduring change in the physical environment.
13. Time-and-place rule: specify the time and place of the response occurrence and the reinforcement delivery.[b]
14. Individual-responsibility rule: assign one and only one individual to act as the reinforcing agent for a given occasion.
15. Dimensions of reinforcement rule: specify in physical terms as many dimensions of the reinforcer as possible.[b]
16. Automated-reinforcement procedure: use automated means to deliver and record the reinforcing event whenever possible.[b]
17. Direct-supervision rule: provide systematic and direct observation of the reinforcement procedure.
18. Procedure for multiple reinforcing agents: use different individuals to implement the delivery of reinforcement.
19. Recipient of reinforcement procedure: use the report of the recipient of the reinforcer as an additional check on the reinforcement transaction.
20. Response-shaping rule: in developing a desired response chain, begin by reinforcing an existing response that has a component relation to the target

---

Table 6.1 (*continued*)

behavior; then reinforce variations of the component that are in the direction of the target behavior.[b]

21. Response-sampling rule: require the individual to perform at least the initial portions of a desired response.

22. Prompting-shaping rule: in developing a desired response chain, begin by verbally prompting and reinforcing an existing response that has a component relation to the target behavior; then prompt verbally and reinforce variations of the component that are in the direction of the target behavior.[b]

23. Response-exposure rule: have the learner observe another individual performing the desired response.[b]

[a] Reprinted from *The Token Economy: A Motivational System for Therapy and Rehabilitation.* Appleton-Century-Crofts, New York, 1968. Copyright © 1968 by Meredith Corporation.

[b] These rules are discussed in detail in the text.

Clearly there is some latitude in the number of tokens arbitrarily assigned to a job. On most token economy wards, however, a minimum number of tokens must be earned each week to "pay" for room and board. Certainly the number of tokens earned by the performance of various tasks must be adjusted so that a patient is not immediately faced with an 80-hour work week or doomed to failure because the only jobs at which he may earn sufficient tokens are beyond his present competence or level of motivation.

Another contingency decision involves the determination of the number of tokens that must be traded for each back-up reinforcer. This question is clearly correlated to the problem of determining how many tokens a job earns since both considerations affect a patient's access to the back-up reinforcers. Supply and demand are important here, as well. If the bus to town is of limited capacity, the "cost" of town passes may be high, whereas if the opportunity to play ping pong is unlimited, the cost may be low (Ayllon & Azrin, 1968a). On an individual level, the cost for a particular reinforcer may be reduced to encourage a particular patient to partake of that item or activity. An obvious example would be when visits with the ward psychologist may be purchased with tokens, a high price might prevail for talkative patients while the cost would be nil for patients who are relatively uncommunicative (Ayllon & Azrin, 1968a).

Fading Procedures. Since it is the goal of most therapy programs that the particular, intentional contingencies that constitute the program be eventually withdrawn while the changed behavior patterns continue to persist, it is wise to select for change—at least at first—behaviors that will continue to be reinforced after training. We have discussed this earlier in terms of the effects of natural contingencies in maintaining socially desirable behaviors once they have been shaped. In a developing token economy, it would also be poor judgment to train patients at first in behaviors that the staff reinforce (as part of training) and that earn tokens, but that the patients themselves do not respond to favorably. A ward of patients used to discussing their problems or engaging in "sick talk" (overt hallucinations, communicated paranoid ideation, etc.) would not constitute a good environment for the early and rapid introduction of contingencies encouraging nothing but "well talk."

It is not uncommon for token economies to include progressive liberation from the token system as behavioral improvement is noted. In the example cited in Table 6.6 not all patients on a given ward were included in the token economy, and it was clearly specified from the start that it was the goal of that token program to "promote" individuals to a regular ward routine.

Later in the chapter we discuss the transitional lodge program of Fairweather (1964), in which psychotic patients were eventually assigned to a transitional, out-of-hospital lodge where they honed their skills of responding appropriately within the reinforcement economy, token and real, that characterizes productive life within our society. We also discuss the work of Phillips, Phillips, Fixen, and Wolf (1971) with delinquents; these authors have described an effective procedure for fading out token rewards for academic achievement behavior.

There are probably some risks in any rather abrupt termination of a token program (or the graduation of an individual from that program) since the maintenance of new behavior patterns becomes solely dependent upon naturalistic contingencies or self-dispensed reinforcers (for example, pride, a sense of accomplishment, or self-scheduling in which privileges such as recreational activities are embarked upon only after the completion of a specific behavior pattern). Consequently, it seems most advisable that a token program—or an individual's participation in it—be gradually faded out as appropriate behavior patterns are developed. This may be done by increasing the length of time between token administrations or redemptions, by decreasing the number of token rewards earned by target behaviors, by increasing the number of tokens required to earn the back-up reinforcers, or by some combination of these procedures. There is no research on this point, but when utilizing the procedures of decreasing the number of tokens earned, or when increasing the number of tokens required to purchase a given back-up reinforcer, it would seem advisable to begin to make the back-up reinforcers freely available to a limited extent; in this way, fading out the token program would not necessitate the deprivation of back-up reinforcers or the frantic performance of appropriate behavior at an inappropriately high rate necessary to guarantee the continued availability of the back-up reinforcers.

Institutional Applications of Contingency-Management Procedures

Token Economies: Some Brief Examples

Let us turn first to a few examples of the implementation of token-economy procedures. Schaefer and Martin (1969) employed token systems that were very much oriented toward each individual patient. Table 6.2 contains treatment programs for two patients treated by these authors. Note how the behaviors are simple, specific, and clearly have reference to the behavior problems characterizing each particular patient.

Schaefer and Martin (1969) also used jobs as sources of token reinforcement. Their purpose was, of course, to benefit the patient and not simply to obtain cheap labor. Toward this end, one goal was to enable the patients to complete the entire task or job by himself—an extended chain of behaviors—without reinforcement or reminders in the midst of the job sequence. Table 6.3 presents two job descriptions for a patient at different phases of his treatment. Note how, via fading techniques, greater and greater reliance was placed upon the patient himself for remembering the equipment he needed and the various individual tasks included in the total job.

Ayllon and Azrin (1968a) used a large number of on and off ward jobs for which patients could earn tokens. Table 6.4 lists some of the on-ward jobs and the number of tokens they earned, while Table 6.5 lists the off-ward jobs. Many of these jobs may be available in any large institution. Ayllon and Azrin allowed patients to select the jobs they wished to perform. Each job was described to a patient, with attention given to details about the time, place, and number of tokens earned by successful completion. They allowed patients to sign up for a job at any time and, initially, to keep signing up for a job as long as they liked. They recommended, however, that patients be encouraged or forced to rotate from job to job to prevent the bored, rote, stereotyped performance that comes to characterize performance of a particular job after a time.

Although token economies with many considerations for individual patients may be elaborated and lengthy, an economy for a total ward may sometimes be described quite succinctly. Table 6.6 is an account of the token economy—in terms of information presented (in written form) to the patient—at a Veterans Administration hospital (Petrik, 1971).

TABLE 6.2

Sample Treatment Program Form [a]

Name————

Date————

Behavior	Reinforcer	Schedule	Control stimuli
Smiling	Tokens	Each time detected	As part of greeting
Talking to other patients	Tokens	Each time detected	
Sitting	Tokens	Each time detected	Patient must be with others; not alone
Reading (patient looking at printed material)	Tokens	Each time detected	Appropriate time and place; especially not in group meetings or at medications
Grooming—hair	Tokens or praise	Each time detected	Only when hair is not pulled tightly against head; prefer "feminine"
Completion of specific assignment	Tokens or free trip out-of-doors	Each time detected	Prior to reinforcement patient must say something positive about the job she completed

Example of treatment program displayed as wall chart for quick reference.

Current Treatment Plan for: Helen

Behavior	Reinforcer	Schedule	Control Stimulus
talking softly	*tokens*	*each time*	*especially in groups*
working	*1 token per task*	*once each day*	*at 9:00 am*
combed hair	*1 cigarette*	*each hour*	*9:00 am to 9:00 pm*

[a] Reprinted from Schaefer, H. H. and Martin, P. L. *Behavior therapy.* New York: McGraw-Hill, 1969.

TABLE 6.3

Job	Dorm cleaner [a]	Time	9:00–9:30 am

Equipment	
	1 Dust mop
	1 Dust rag
	1 Dust pan
	1 Cleaning rag
	1 Pail of water

Requirements
1. Pick up equipment at 9:00
2. Dust all ledges, partitions and sills (every day)
3. Dust-mop entire dorm floor except area under beds
4. Shake out dust rag and dust mop outside behind the ward
5. Empty and clean water pail
6. Rinse out cleaning rag
7. Turn in all equipment at 9:30 or before
8. Wash insides of all dorm windows (each Saturday)

[a] Job description of dorm cleaner during early phase.

Job	Dorm Cleaner [b]	Time	9:00–9:30 am

Equipment	
	1 Dust mop
	1 — —
	1 Dust ___
	1 Cleaning rag
	1 ___ of water

Requirements
1. Pick up at ___ o'clock
2. Dust all partitions, ledges and ___
3. — — — — — — — — —
   — —
4. Shake out dust rag and dust mop outside behind the ward
5. Empty and ___ ___
6. Rinse out ___ rag
7. Turn in all equipment at about ___
8. Wash insides of all dorm windows (each ___)

[b] Job description of dorm cleaner during later phase.
[c] Reprinted from Schaefer, H. H. and Martin, P. L. *Behavior therapy.* New York: McGraw-Hill, 1969.

TABLE 6.4

Types and Number of On-Ward Jobs [a]

Types of jobs	Number of jobs	Duration (minutes)	Tokens paid
Dietary assistant			
1. Kitchen chores	3	10	1
Patient assembles necessary supplies on table. Puts one pat of butter between two slices of bread for all patients. Squeezes juice from fruit left over from meals. Puts supplies away. Cleans table used.			
2. Coffee urn	1	10	2
Patient assembles cleaning compound and implements. Washes 5-gallon coffee urn using brush and cleaning compound. Rinses inside, washes, and dries outside. Puts implements away.			
3. Ice carrier	1	10	2
Patient goes with attendant to area adjacent to ward where ice machine is located, taking along 10-gallon ice container. Scoops flaked ice from machine into container and carries it to the kitchen.			
4. Shakers	2	10	2
Patient assembles salt, sugar, and empty shakers on table, fills shakers, and puts supplies away.			
5. Pots and pans	3	10	6
Patient runs water into sink, adds soap, washes, and rinses all pans used for each meal. Stacks pans and leaves them to be put through automatic dishwasher.			
6. Steam table	3	10	5
Patient assembles cleaning supplies. Washes and dries all compartments used for food. Cleans and dries outside of table. Places all pans in proper place on steam table.			
7. Meal server [b]	6	60	10
Patient puts food into proper compartments on steam table. Assembles paper napkins and silver on counter			

(*continued*)

Table 6.4 (*continued*)

Types of jobs	Number of jobs	Duration (minutes)	Tokens paid
Dietary assistant (continued)			
placed at beginning of serving line, puts tablecloths, napkins, salt and sugar shakers on tables. Prepares proper beverage for each meal, putting ice in glasses for cold beverages and drawing coffee from urn. Prepares proper utensils for dirty dishes and garbage. Dips food, places food and beverage on trays. Gives patients their trays. After the meal is over, dietary workers empty all leftover food and garbage, place all trays, glasses and silver used on cabinets ready for the dishwasher.			
8. Dishwasher [b] Patient prepares dishwater, fills automatic dishwasher. Washes dishes, silver, and glasses. Operates automatic dishwasher, washes cabinets, sinks, and tables, and puts everything away. Patient counts silver (knives, forks, and spoons) for all patients and places them in containers ready for next meal.	9	45	17
Waitress			
1. Meals Empties trays left on tables and washes tables between each of four meal groups.	6	10	2
2. Commissary Cleans tables, washes cups and glasses used at commissary. Places cups and glasses in rack ready for automatic dishwasher.	3	10	5
Sales clerk assistant			
1. Commissary Assembles commissary items. Displays candy, cigarettes, tobacco, cosmetics, dresses, and other variety store items so that they can be seen by all. Pre-	3	30	3

(*continued*)

Table 6.4 (*continued*)

Types of jobs	Number of jobs	Duration (minutes)	Tokens paid
Sales clerk assistant (*continued*)			
pares ice, glasses, and cups for hot and cold beverages. Asks patient what she wishes to buy. Collects the tokens from patient and tells the secretary the name of the patient and the amount spent. Puts commissary supplies away.			
Secretarial assistant			
1. Tooth brushing [b]	1	30	3
Assists with oral hygiene. Writes names of patients brushing teeth.			
2. Exercises [b]	2	30	3
Assists recreational assistant with exercises. Writes names of patients participating in exercises.			
3. Commissary [b]	3	30	5
Assists sales clerk assistant. Writes names of patients at commissary, records number of tokens patient spent. Totals all tokens spent.			
Ward cleaning assistant			
1. Halls and rooms	24	30	3
Sweep and mop floors, dust furniture and walls in seven rooms and hall.			
2. Special	1	30	4
Cleans after incontinent patients.			
3. Dormitories [b]	1	180	8
Supplies each of five dormitories with the necessary cleaning implements. Fills buckets with cleaning water and delivers bucket of water, broom, mop and dust pan to each dormitory at a designated time. Picks up cleaning supplies and implements after a 30-minute interval.			
Assistant janitor			
1. Supplies	1	10	1
Places ward supplies in supply cabinets and drawers.			

(*continued*)

Table 6.4 (*continued*)

Types of jobs	Number of jobs	Duration (minutes)	Tokens paid
Assistant janitor (*continued*)			
2. Trash	3	5	2
Carries empty soft drink bottles to storage area, empties waste-paper baskets throughout the ward, and carries paper to container adjacent to building. Carries mops used during the day outside to dry.			
3. Porch [b]	2	10	2
Sweeps and washes walk adjacent to building. Washes garbage cans with soap and water.			
4. Washroom janitor	1	20	3
Obtains necessary cleaning supplies and implements from utility room. Cleans four wash basins and four toilet bowls with cleanser and brush. Returns cleaning supplies and implements to utility room.			
Laundry assistant			
1. Hose	1	15	1
Match and fold clean anklets and stockings.			
2. Delivery	1	10	2
Carries bags of dirty clothing and linens from ward to outside linen house adjacent to building.			
3. Folding [b]	2	30	3
Folds and stacks clean linens in neat stacks and takes it to the clothing room.			
4. Pick-up service [b]	1	60	8
Sorts dirty clothing and linens and puts items into bags marked for each item.			
Grooming assistant			
1. Clothing care	1	15	1
Patient sets up ironing board and iron. Irons clothing that belongs to patients other than self. Folds clothing neatly. Returns ironed clothing, iron,			

(*continued*)

Table 6.4 (*continued*)

Types of jobs	Number of jobs	Duration (minutes)	Tokens paid
Grooming assistant (continued)			
and ironing board to nurses station.			
2. Personal hygiene [b]	3	60	3
Patient takes basket with grooming aids, gargle, paper cups, lipstick, comb, hairbrush, and powder into patients' washroom. Patient stays with grooming basket and assists any who need help with their grooming before each meal. Returns grooming basket after the meal has ended.			
3. Oral hygiene [b]	1	20	3
Assembles toothpaste, toothbrushes, gargle solution, and paper cups. Pours gargle into cups and dispenses toothpaste or gargle to all patients.			
4. Personal [b]	1	30	3
Patient assists selected patients who need extra aid with personal grooming.			
5. Bath [b]	2	45	4
Patient assists with baths, washing, shampooing, and drying. Cleans tub after each bath.			
6. Beauty aids [b]	1	30	4
Assists in shampooing, setting, and combing hair for patients who desire special service.			
Recreational assistant			
1. Walks [b]	1	20	3
Assists ward staff when taking group of patients on walks. Walks in front of group.			
2. Exercise [b]	1	20	3
Operates record player and leads patients in exercises.			
3. Movie projectionist	1	90	10
Sets up movie projector and shows movie to patients. Changes reels and rewinds tape.			

(*continued*)

Table 6.4 (*continued*)

Types of jobs	Number of jobs	Duration (minutes)	Tokens paid
Special services			
1. Errands	1	20	6
Leaves the ward on official errands throughout the hospital grounds, delivering messages and picking up supplies and records pertaining to the ward.			
2. Tour guide	1	15	10
Gives visitors a 15-minute tour of the ward explaining about the activities and token system. Answers visitors' questions about the ward.			
3. Nursing assistant [b]	1	10	10
Assists staff with the preparation of patients to be seen by the medical doctor. Assists staff with the control of undesired interaction between patients.			
Self-care activities			
1. Grooming			1
Combs hair, wears: dress, slip, panties, bra, stockings, and shoes (three times daily).			
2. Bathing			1
Takes a bath at time designated for bath (once weekly).			
3. Tooth Brushing			1
Brushes teeth or gargles at the time designated for tooth brushing (once daily).			
4. Exercises			1
Participates in exercises conducted by the exercise assistant (twice daily).			
5. Bed making			1
Makes own bed and cleans area around and under bed.			

[a] This Table and Table 6.5 are reprinted from Ayllon, T. and Azrin, N. H. The measurement and reinforcement of behavior of psychotics. *Journal of the Experimental Analysis of Behavior*, 1965, **8**, 357–383. Additional information and related research can be found in *The Token Economy: A Motivational System for Therapy and Rehabilitation* by T. Ayllon and N. H. Azrin published by Appleton-Century-Crofts, 1968.

[b] Job requires two or more patients for its completion.

TABLE 6.5

Types and Number of Off-Ward Jobs

Types of jobs	Number of jobs	Duration (hours daily)	Tokens paid for each job
Dietary worker Helps serve meals for 85 patients and cleans tables after meals.	1	6	70
Clerical Types and answers the telephone. Calls hospital personnel to the telephone.	2	6	70
Laboratory Cleans cage pans, fills water bottles and cleans floor in laboratory.	2	6	70
Laundry Helps to run sheets, pillow cases and towels through mangle at hospital laundry. Also folds linens.	3	6	70

TABLE 6.6 [a]

The Token Economy

In order to more clearly teach responsible behavior, this ward has a Token Economy. You can *earn* over 200 tokens weekly for being responsible in three areas: Appearance—Work Assignment—Use of Free Time and Social Skills. Bonus tokens for other behaviors are also available. How tokens may be *spent* is explained later in the handout.

How to Earn Tokens

I. Appearance: Possible 12 tokens daily or 84 weekly.

a. *Personal Appearance:* Five areas will be inspected at about 8:00 A.M. and 4:15 P.M. daily. You will receive one token for each of the following areas which are satisfactory:

How to earn tokens (*continued*)

1. Hair—neatly combed and clean.
2. Face and hands—clean shave, clean face and hands.
3. Shirt—clean, buttoned, tucked in, good repair, clean undershirt.
4. Trousers—clean, pressed, zippered, good repair, belt, proper fit.
5. Shoes and socks—clean, tied, good repair, shined, pulled up socks.

b. *Bed and Locker Appearance:* Checked daily at 8:00 A.M. One token for each if satisfactory.

c. *Comments:* Not all patients will be required to stand close personal inspection but everyone is subject to a five token penalty for inappropriate appearance at any time. Wearing pajamas in public areas before 9:00 P.M. daily is considered inappropriate and the five token penalty applies. Persons not required to stand daily inspection will receive 84 tokens credited to their account at weekly token counting time. Persons on close personal inspection will receive tokens at the time of inspection unless they have deficiencies to correct. Each person has 15 minutes to correct the deficiencies and report back to the inspector and if the corrections are made, he will receive tokens as earned on the initial inspection. Failure to correct the deficiency in 15 minutes results in loss of all tokens for that inspection. There is a ten token penalty for still being in bed at 8:00 A.M., seven days a week.

II. Work: Four tokens per satisfactory hour as recorded on time card, or about 100 per week. Ten token penalty for missing work assignment each half day. Penalty for missing three consecutive half days on assignment is to lose all earned tokens to that time and go on daily food plan. No token credit for work assignment at a time when other appointments are scheduled, e.g., groups and ward meetings. You are required to know the name of your work supervisor and to inform him if you will be absent from work.

III. Use of Free Time and Social Skills: Possible ten tokens per evening or 70 tokens per week. Constructive use of free time and social skills will be judged daily for the entire evening period from about 4:00 P.M. to 9:00 P.M. Tokens are given according to a general impression of the whole evening activity as follows:

Tokens:

0 Little or no activity alone, e.g., sitting alone in chair, in bed, or in chair sleeping.
2 Minimal activity alone, e.g., watching TV, listening to radio, reading.
5 Part of the evening spent on minimal activity, and part of the evening spent participating more with others.
10 Participation most of the evening in activities with others, e.g., playing pool, cards, conversation, going to off-ward activities, such as dances or bowling.

(*continued*)

Table 6.6 (*continued*)

How to earn tokens (*continued*)

Comments: Use of inappropriate talk, including statements implying lack of responsibility for change, will limit ratings to two or zero. No tokens given to anyone in pajamas.

BONUS TOKENS AS FOLLOWS

1. *Attendance at Group Meetings*—Two tokens for attendance and up to three more for appropriate participation; also three for being at doctor's rounds. Five token penalty for missing groups without adequate excuse.

2. *Dayroom and Porch Clean-up*—Two men will be assigned daily and should finish the clean-up by 8:00 A.M. and 6:30 P.M. Five tokens per man for satisfactory work. Penalty for unsatisfactory ward appearance is no TV until the next inspection period.

3. *Other Behavior*—Tokens will be available from staff for satisfactory performance of other tasks such as laundry sorting, better personal hygiene, and cleaning except for routine ward cleaning which is everyone's responsibility.

4. *Watching 10:00 P.M. News*—Two tokens at 10:30 for persons watching entire newscast and who can satisfactorily report some news they viewed.

5. *Explaining Token Economy to Guests*—You may earn ten tokens for touring guests and explaining the program.

HOW YOU MAY SPEND TOKENS

Tokens must be spent for board and room just like outside the hospital. In addition, tokens can be converted into weekly cash allowance, passes, and privileges of various kinds.

1. *Room and Board*—Your first obligation is to spend 140 tokens per week for room and board. These tokens will be collected Thursday afternoon for the next week beginning on Friday. If you do not have the necessary 140 tokens you will be placed on a daily food payment plan. In order to make the beginning stages of the Token Economy somewhat easier, you will pay 15 tokens daily for food, however, after your second Thursday on the ward (after about 10 days) you will be required to pay 20 tokens daily or 140 for the entire week. You must pay the full amount for an entire day and you will receive all meals on a given day after payment is made in full.

Comments: Earning 20 tokens daily for room and board is not difficult, but it does make you responsible for some constructive behavior in order to receive your food. You can earn 12 tokens daily for appearance, up to 10 daily for social interaction and about 20 for an average day on assignment, or about 40 tokens per day.

In order to reward persons who have been doing well but haven't many tokens left at the end of the week because of the required daily food payment, there are two plans.

Table 6.6 (*continued*)

How you may spend tokens (*continued*)

a. If you earned 225 or more tokens in the previous week, the staff will return to you the full amount of tokens paid for daily food during the previous week.

b. If you earned 150 or more tokens in the previous week, the staff will return to you ⅔ of the tokens you paid for daily food during the previous week.

2. *Weekly Cash Allowance*—You may exchange tokens for funds from your account at the rate of ten tokens per dollar. Except for persons on canteen books, drawing funds more than once a week will be at the rate of 15 tokens per dollar. Persons on canteen books may exchange tokens for books at the same rate, ten tokens for one dollar.

3. *Passes*

a. *Continuous passes into town:* You may request a continuous Saturday, Sunday, and holiday pass, or an evening pass, and if it is approved, you may use it without a token charge, unless:

    1. You are on daily food.

    2. You must stand personal inspection.

    3. You do not take medication satisfactorily.

(You must correct these problems before you are eligible for a continuous pass).

b. *Weekend or overnight passes:* You may request a weekend or overnight pass prior to the weekly team meeting, and if the pass is approved, you may use it according to the following guidelines:

    1. The usual weekend pass from after work Friday afternoon until Sunday evening is 60 tokens including $10.00 of your funds.

    2. Funds over $10.00 within limits, are available at three tokens per dollar.

    3. In order to receive money at this rate, you must be gone from the hospital at least 24 hours, otherwise you will be required to pay additional tokens at the usual rate for weekly cash allowance.

    4. If you sign up for a pass, but don't have enough tokens, you will be fined 20 tokens, so plan carefully.

    5. Recreational passes during duty hours are 20 additional tokens for each ½ day. You must clear with your work supervisor before you may use a pass during duty hours.

4. *Other Cost Items*—

a. Sleeping on bed during work hours (weekdays 8:00 A.M. to 11:00 A.M.) and (1:00 P.M. to 3:30 P.M.) five token penalty if you get up, or 10 tokens per hour if you choose to rest. This does not apply if a physician agrees you are sick and prescribes bed rest.

b. Missing roll call or being late for medication: five token penalty, more for repeat offenders.

c. Smoking in small bedrooms, 20 tokens and transfer to dorm, smoking in dorm, 20 tokens, more for repeat offenders.

d. Hitting another person or damaging property: 20 token penalty for the first offense and more for repeat offenders.

(continued)

Table 6.6 (*continued*)

How you may spend tokens (*continued*)

    e. Persons off grounds without a valid pass lose all tokens in their possession or banked at that time and are placed on daily food.

    f. Inability to pay any token fine results in loss of advanced room and board payment, and being placed on daily food.

GOOD LUCK! WE HOPE TO PROMOTE YOU OFF THE
TOKEN PLAN AS SOON AS POSSIBLE!

---

    [a] Reprinted from Petrik, N. The token economy. Unpublished manual, Veterans Administration Hospital, St. Cloud, Minnesota, 1971.

Effectiveness of Contingent Reinforcement in Groups

    Fortunately, there is ample evidence of the effectiveness of contingencies on the behavior of both groups and individuals (Ayllon & Azrin, 1968a). Ayllon and Azrin (1968a) compared the total number of hours spent each day performing on-ward activities when token rewards were contingent upon such activities and when there was no reinforcement (contingent or noncontingent). Figure 6.2 clearly indicates that reinforcement was a powerful determinant of the amount of time spent in these activities. Furthermore, these authors compared the amount of time spent in such rehabilitive activities when there was contingent reinforcement and when reinforcement continued, but was no longer contingent upon performance. Figure 6.2 depicts these results, which confirm that the contingency of rewards is a major factor promoting the patient's continued performance of these activities.

Effectiveness of Group Contingencies

    Group contingencies involve the dispensation of reinforcers to an *entire* group contingent upon the behavior of the total group (for example, average performance such as average number of spelling words correct for a school class, or average number of necessary jobs completed on a hospital ward) or contingent upon the behavior of a single member of that group. Such contingencies have powerful effects upon the behavior of individuals. Wolf and Risley (1967) used group contingencies in treating the classroom disruptive behavior of a child. Casting their treatment regime in the form of an experiment, they measured the amount of disruptive behavior displayed during periods of no special reinforcement, during periods when the girl received 5 points for her proper behavior, and during periods when she *and her immediate peers* individually

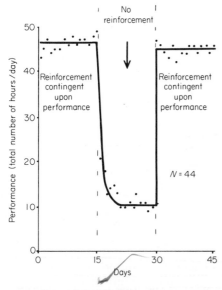

Figure 6.2 Numbers of hours per day during which schizophrenic patients participated in "on-ward" activities during periods when reinforcers (activities and privileges) were made contingent on these activities and when such reinforcers were freely available (non-contingent). From Ayllon and Azrin, 1965.

earned only 1 point for her proper behavior. Even though the amount of reinforcement per child was least when the girl and her peers all received reinforcement, this condition proved most effective in controlling the disruptive behavior. It seems that the peers exercised additional influence over the girl's behavior when they, too, were brought into the contingency system.

Glaser and Kraus (1966) also employed a group contingency in a laboratory investigation. They found that total group behavior responds in a manner similar to individual behavior when total group performance is the criterion for reinforcement of all group members. When total team performance was reinforced, the output of the entire group increased, and when such reinforcement was omitted, total team output declined. When any single member of the group was reinforced following his own correct response, there was often a decrease in performance level by the total group and by individual members as well.

The Lodge System: Incorporating Patients into the Natural Environment

In several contexts we express concern over the problem of generalizing treatment results from the office or institution to the natural environment. The extent to which token economies recreate the economic and vocational nature of the natural environment increases the likelihood that their effectiveness will enable patients to rejoin the community on a permanent basis. There are still a number of impediments to perfect generalization. For example, the token economy typically resides within the structure of the institutional setting and the behavioral interactions of patients or inmates are limited to other patients, inmates, or the staff members from the institution. Furthermore, the token system mimics, but is not identical to, the reward system in society. Such problems are not insurmountable, and they do not entirely dissipate the potential effectiveness of a token, or other reinforcement-based, system within the institutional setting. Still, the extent to which any treatment regimen can be extended to include behavior in the natural environment seems likely to enhance its effectiveness.

Fortunately, there is a clear example of at least one way a treatment program for institutionalized psychotics can be extended into the natural environment via the establishment of a treatment-related setting within the community. Fairweather and his colleagues (Fairweather, Sanders, Maynard, & Cressler, 1969) established a lodge environment (the lodge was formerly a motel) within the community into which patients were transferred after they had achieved a minimal level of social competence. Within the hospital setting, after patients had developed a variety of vocational, self-care, and social skills, which enhanced group cohesiveness, patients were either discharged to the community directly or into a lodge setting. The lodge was not a half-way house and was not staffed by any professional personnel. Patients in the lodge were responsible for their own behavior, including financial affairs, the purchasing and cooking of food, and even (with the advice of a local physician) the dispensation of required medications. The patients living at the lodge were also in charge of operating an independent business providing custodial services, painting, hauling, and yardwork for commercial and private customers in the community.

At the beginning of the lodge's existence, the daily operations were supervised by a staff member. This was rapidly eliminated as the patients proved themselves capable of managing their own affairs; the introduction of many new patients to the lodge setting over a 3-year period proved that the initial supervision was probably unnecessary except when a lodge is being established. The business operated by lodge members was actually quite profitable, turning a profit of $52,000 in fewer than 3 years. One of the responsibilities of lodge members was the dispensation of this income as "wages." Weekly there was an allocation of funds to various lodge members, with the amounts dependent upon the extent of personal responsibility a patient had within the group enterprise and the extent of his productivity. *not a patient!!*

The lodge was established as part of a therapeutic experiment concerned with the importance of training patients in community-relevant skills by means of involving them in the natural environment. Consequently, since it was an experiment, there was a control group of patients who had received the benefits of hospital training in the skills mentioned above, and who were eligible for outpatient treatment following discharge, but who did not participate in the lodge setting. Measurements were taken to establish patients' capabilities for continued independent existence within the community. There were a substantial number of patients involved, approximately 75 in the lodge group and 75 control patients at the beginning of the study. The lodge was in operation for 33 months and the experiment extended over a period of 40 months, yielding a follow-up period of 7 months.

One important criterion for any hospital program is the ability of discharged patients to remain productive members of the community. Figure 6.3 illustrates the percentages of time patients from the lodge and control groups remained in the community during the 40 months after formally leaving the hospital. As long as the lodge was in full operation, nearly 100% of the lodge patients were active in the community (presumably through lodge activities), while only 20–30% of the control

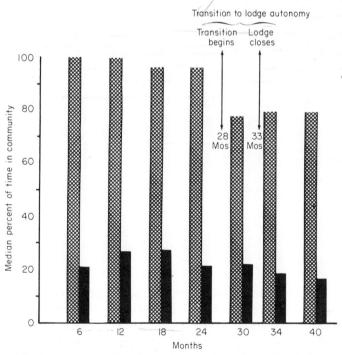

Figure 6.3 Percentages of time that patients in the lodge and typical treatment programs spent in the community over a 40-month period (lodge group: ⊠; control group: ■). From Fairweather *et al.*, 1969.

patients continued such community involvement. Furthermore, after the lodge closed, the percentage of time in the community remained near the 80% level for lodge patients, while it dropped slightly, to less than 20%, for the control patients.

Another important result from participation in the lodge program was an increase in the ability to become and remain gainfully employed. As illustrated in Figure 6.4, after the lodge had closed, more than 3 years after the initiation of the program, nearly 40% of the lodge patients were employed full time, whereas fewer than 3% of the control patients

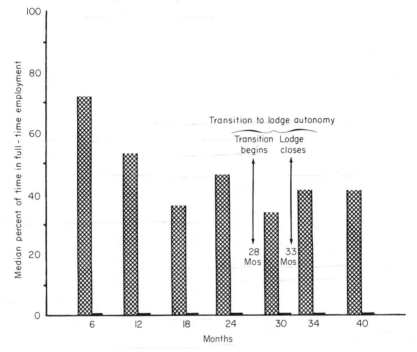

Figure 6.4 Percentages of time that patients in the lodge and typical hospital programs were employed full-time over a 40-month period (lodge group: ▨; control group: ■).From Fairweather *et al.,* 1969.

were so employed. On all comparisons, the lodge patients were clearly and significantly more adapted and integrated into community living, and their continued ability to remain as productive members of the community is the definition of a successful outcome for an institutional treatment program.

Treatment of Institutionalized Psychotics

In describing the design of token economies we have repeatedly referred to two well-known token economies designed primarily for in-patient psychotic adults: the token system at Anna State Hospital in Illinois (Ayllon & Azrin, 1968a), and at Patton State Hospital in California (Schaefer & Martin, 1969). We shall not reiterate descriptions of these programs. At the same time, there is a third token economy system designed for psychotic patients that antedates both Ayllon and Azrin (1968a) and Schaefer and Martin (1969). Since it was cast primarily in the format of a large social experiment, we have deferred discussion of it until now. We are referring to the work of Fairweather and his colleagues at the Palo Alto (California) Veterans Administration hospital (Fairweather, Simon, Gebhard, Weningarten, Holland, Sanders, Stone, & Reahl, 1960; Fairweather & Simon, 1963; Fairweather, 1964; Fairweather, Sanders, Maynard, & Cressler, 1969).

Fairweather's concern for the effective treatment of institutionalized psychotics appears to have risen from follow-up studies indicating the general ineffectiveness of all treatment programs. In their earliest work, Fairweather and colleagues found that nearly 70% of chronic psychotic patients return to the hospital within 18 months after discharge, regardless of the brand of treatment received while in the hospital (Fairweather et al., 1960; Fairweather & Simon, 1963). Fairweather speculated that a primary reason for the ineffectiveness of treatment programs was the general lack of procedures designed to train marketable skills, increased self-direction, appropriate interpersonal behavior—generally, to establish the competence in social interactions and vocational activity that is necessary for an independent life outside of the hospital. Given these considerations, Fairweather (1964) designed a group treatment program intended to establish, within the hospital, behavior competencies in social skills, problem-solving, and general self-management.

The patients involved were generally diagnosed as schizophrenic, matched on the basis of diagnosis, age, and length of hospitalization. One group of patients received the conventional hospital program of treatment, while the remainder participated in a program involving patient-lead problem solving groups. Although the treatment regimes for each group were relatively constant over the 27-week period, at mid-point the two sets of staff members switched wards in a control for possible effects due to specific staff characteristics.

Generally the treatment programs were quite similar, except for 2 hours each day when the one group held group work assignments and decision-making sessions. In addition, there was an incentive system in which patients received money and pass privileges as contingent rewards for the development of social and self-directive behavior, which was divided into four levels, each progressively more complex.

It was left to the groups to evaluate and modify the behavior of a single member. The staff did not interfere in this process and the group met each day to discuss how individual members were proceeding in the development of competence and to decide ways in which an individual's progress could be fostered. Once each week the group met with the staff and gave their recommendations concerning their evaluation of each member's competence, actions taken over problem behavior, and the suggested passes and monetary rewards for individual patients. The staff then acted upon these recommendations (it could approve or disapprove each one) and, on some occasions, rewarded or penalized the *entire group* as a function of the appropriateness of the group's decision-making behavior. It should be noted that although the monetary and pass privilege rewards were important in the early part of the experimental treatment program, subsequently there was strong evidence that the patients were rewarded by self-reinforcement (pride, perhaps) of their own accomplishments, and there were clear indications of social approval and disapproval for various behaviors.

The experiment lasted for a period of 27 weeks, and behavioral measures were gathered throughout this period and again 6 months after its termination. Results clearly indicated that the experimental program with its contingent rewards for interpersonal responding was inclined to produce improved patient behavior in a variety of areas. As Figure 6.5 shows, toward the end of the treatment phase, the patients on the experimental ward came to show much less pathological behavior during periods of observation. Furthermore, patients on this ward were much more likely to be observed in interaction with groups of three or more other individuals (Figure 6.6). Finally, as Figure 6.7 shows, patients from the experimental ward were less likely to be silent, as a group, during the weekly ward meetings and were more likely to participate on an individual basis in these meetings.

But these are behaviors relevant to the hospital setting and the treatment programs itself. What of generalized effects? There were striking ones. Patients on the experimental ward stayed in the hospital less time, and upon follow-up it was found that they more often spent time with their friends and were more likely to be gainfully employed.

Treatment of Delinquent Children and Adolescents

In the literature, most reports concerning the behavioral treatment of delinquents describe practices appropriate to the classroom or to a cot-

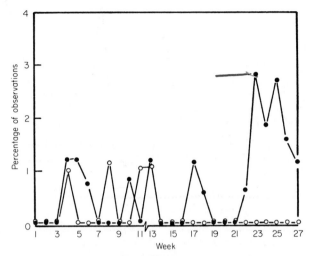

Figure 6.5 Changes in behavior achieved by patients receiving treatment designed to establish problem-solving and self-management skills (small group ward) as contrasted with changes shown by patients in a traditional hospital treatment program: percentage of observations during which patients displayed pathological behavior (traditional ward: ●——●; small group ward: ○——○). From Fairweather, 1964.

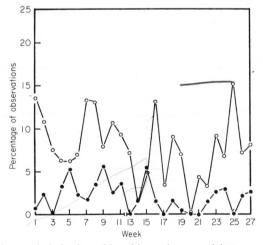

Figure 6.6 Changes in behavior achieved by patients receiving treatment designed to establish problem-solving and self-management skills (small group ward) as contrasted with changes shown by patients in a traditional hospital treatment program: percentage of observations during which patients engaged in social interactions involving three or more patients (traditional ward: ●——●; small group ward: ○——○). From Fairweather, 1964.

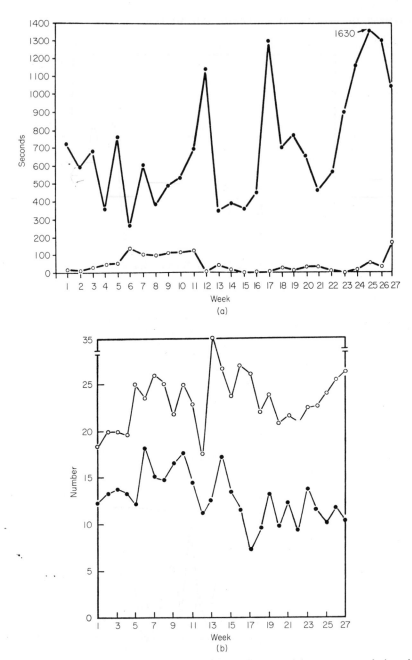

Figure 6.7 Changes in behavior achieved by patients receiving treatment designed to establish problem-solving and self-management skills (small group ward) as contrasted with changes shown by patients in a traditional hospital treatment program: (a) total time each group of patients remained silent during weekly ward meeting, and (b) the average number of patients participating in the weekly ward meeting discussions (traditional ward: ●——●; small group ward: ○——○). From Fairweather, 1964.

Glaser-Ventura (CYA)

tage system of institutionalization (5–20 delinquent or predelinquent children housed in a "cottage" with a small resident staff, occasionally a married couple). In this section we concentrate on procedures relevant to these settings. Most procedures discussed, however, are acknowledged to be drawn from the token economy (as described above), especially the work of Ayllon and Azrin (1968a) (Phillips, 1968; Bailey, Wolf, & Phillips, 1970; Phillips *et al.*, 1971). Clearly, then, it would take only a slight adaptation of the token economy as described, in the preceding section, for institutionalized psychotics to make it applicable to delinquents in a large institution. And we have already discussed the use of operant techniques to work with individual delinquents on an outpatient, or counseling, basis (Slack, 1960; Schwitzgebel, 1960, 1963; Schwitzgebel & Kolb, 1964).

Recently there has been a trend away from the use of large reformatories toward the establishment of homelike, small residential units. An outstanding example of such a unit employing token economy principles with delinquent and predelinquent boys is Achievement Place, a cottage style rehabilitation unit to which boys are remanded by the court after being judged "predelinquent" (guilty of minor offenses, but deemed likely to advance to more serious crimes). The techniques and procedures utilized at Achievement Place have been described several times in the literature (Bailey *et al.*, 1970; Phillips, 1968; Phillips *et al.*, 1971) as they have been applied to various problems and as they have evolved to become more effective in the face of these problems.

The tokens used in this system were quite simple: points were earned upon the performance of various target behaviors. Typically the target behaviors selected were social, self-care, and academic behaviors and competencies. At first the system was on a weekly basis, with tokens being exchanged once a week for desired reinforcers. Later, however, a daily point system was invoked because of irregularities that developed in the boys' behaviors: the 2 or 3 days following cashing in of points were characterized by a decrease in target behaviors and consequently fewer points earned (characteristic of an interval schedule, which the weekly cashing in amounted to—superimposed upon the typically continuous schedule of awarding points after cash performance of a target behavior). In the final system, points were cashed in each day, but the privileges (reinforcers) purchased could not be used the next day until a minimum number of points were earned on that day. Points were tallied on index cards that the boys carried with them. The prices of privileges were typically kept constant, but occasionally they were changed as the value or importance of the privilege seemed to vary (watching TV cost more in winter). Over all, the system was designed so that an individual who performed all the target behaviors expected of him and who lost a minimum number of points in fines could obtain all desired privileges without performing extra tasks.

In the Achievement Place economy, points could be both earned and lost. Table 6.7 presents the various target behaviors that were desirable and undesirable, and the points they earned or lost (this is from a weekly cash-in system requiring approximately 7000 points to "live well"). Most of the target behaviors, both those earning and those losing points, were formalized and explicit and were listed on the house bulletin board. Few contingencies were not so explicit, although there were some of this sort (for example, boys might earn or lose points for good or poor manners while guests were at the house). Finally, there were some privileges that had no point price, but were auctioned off once a week. An example of

TABLE 6.7

Behaviors and the Number of Points They Earn or Lose [a]

Behaviors Earning Points	Points
1. Watching news on TV or reading the newspaper	300 per day
2. Cleaning and maintaining neatness in one's room	500 per day
3. Keeping one's person neat and clean	500 per day
4. Reading books	5–10 per page
5. Aiding house parents in various household tasks	20–1000 per task
6. Doing dishes	500–1000 per meal
7. Being well dressed for an evening meal	100–500 per meal
8. Performing homework	500 per day
9. Obtaining desirable grades on school report cards	500–1000 per grade
10. Turning out lights when not in use	25 per light

Behaviors Losing Points	
1. Failing grades on the report card	500–1000 per grade
2. Speaking aggressively	20–50 per response
3. Forgetting to wash hands before meals	100–300 per meal
4. Arguing	300 per response
5. Disobeying	100–1000 per response
6. Being late	10 per minute
7. Displaying poor manners	50–100 per response
8. Engaging in poor posture	50–100 per response
9. Using poor grammar	20–50 per response
10. Stealing, lying, or cheating	10,000 per response

[a] Reprinted from Phillips, E. L. Achievement place: Token reinforcement procedures on a home-style setting for "pre-delinquent" boys. *Journal of Applied Behavior Analysis,* 1968, **1,** 215.

one such privilege, which stressed responsible interpersonal behavior, was the position of "manager" over other boys in the execution of some household task for a week. Such a manager would be personally responsible for the maintenance of bathrooms, the basement, the yard, and had the authority to award or withdraw points from the boys who worked under his direction. The manager himself, however, earned or lost points as a function of the house parents' judgment concerning the quality of the job he directed.

The token system at Achievement Place was designed to influence various target behaviors (and could, of course, be adapted to any number of potential target behaviors if it were desired to incorporate them into the system), and data were gathered to monitor its effectiveness (Phillips, 1968; Phillips et al., 1971). Typically base-line data were gathered concerning the frequency of the behavior under no constraints; then some constraint, often the use of tokens, was inserted; then perhaps another procedure for comparison was inserted; then back to base line or the use of threats; and finally a return to the effective procedure.

One target behavior at the outset (Phillips, 1968) was the use of aggressive statements. Often aggressiveness was noted in court, academic, or in psychological reports, but typically there was no real evidence of aggressive *behavior,* but rather, aggressive *statements.* ("I'll kill you," or "I'll smash that car if it gets in my way"). Consequently, aggressive statements were monitored for a 3-hour period daily. During base line no constraints were imposed. Then came a period during which the house parents "corrected" the boys ("Stop that kind of talk"). Subsequently fines were levied for a period of time, 20 points per statement, and this was followed by a period of no fines, but threats ("If you boys continue to use that aggressive talk I will have no other choice but to take away points"). Finally the fines were reinstated. Figure 6.8 shows the results. Clearly, the use of fines gained complete control over the emission of aggressive statements. Other experimental monitoring and manipulations concerned bathroom cleaning, punctuality, completion of homework, bad grammar (Phillips, 1968), promptness, room cleaning, saving money, and keeping up on current events by watching the news (Phillips et al., 1971). In the latter instance, "news quizzes" were introduced, which could be answered by watching (and learning from) the evening news. Various manipulations included the possibility of earning:

1. 100 points for each question correctly answered
2. 600 points for each correct answer
3. 600 points earned for each correct answer if 40% of the quiz were answered correctly and otherwise a loss of 600 points for each incorrect answer

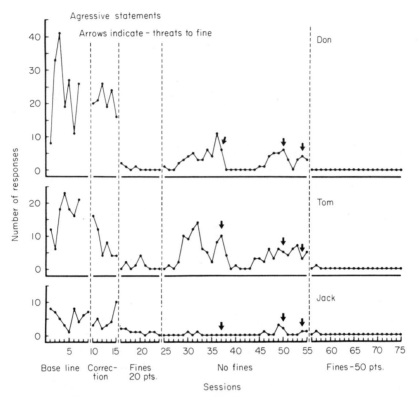

Figure 6.8 Number of aggressive statements by each of three youths under various conditions: base line, correction, 20 point fines, no fines, and 50 point fines. From Phillips, 1968.

4. 600 points lost for each incorrect answer but no points gained for correct ones

As Figure 6.9 indicates, a combined reward-fine system appeared most effective, and when only rewards were used, 600 tokens were not consistently any more effective than 100 tokens, nor was a punitive "fine only" system as good as the reward-fine combined system. It was also clear that the reward-fine procedure had a greater effect upon watching the news since by the end of that period 100% of the boys watched the news each evening.

Reinforcement procedures have also been used to improve the academic behavior of delinquents. Completion of homework, bad grammar (Phillips, 1968), and keeping up on current events (Phillips *et al.*, 1971) are examples of academically relevant behaviors that can be manipulated within the home-style treatment situation. The reinforcement sys-

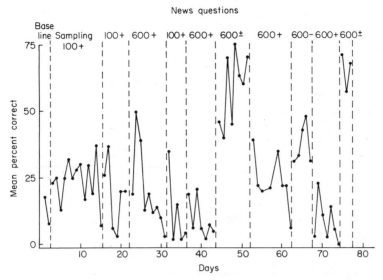

Figure 6.9 Mean percent correct answers on daily news quiz as a function of various contingency management procedures for watching the news program. From Phillips *et al.*, 1971.

tem can also be expanded to cover the school setting (Bailey *et al.*, 1970; Meichenbaum, Bowers, & Ross, 1968). Bailey *et al.* (1970) presents two experimental case studies in which the poor academic behavior of delinquent children was improved via reinforcement techniques. In one instance five boys were placed in a special classroom and worked on mathematics during a summer session. A number of rules governed behavior in this classroom and were communicated to the boys:

1. Do not leave seat without permission.
2. Do not talk without permission.
3. Do not look out the windows.
4. Do not tilt the desks.
5. Do not make noise.
6. Do not disturb others.
7. You should work for the whole period.

These "rules" were derived from complaints of the boys' public school teachers.

After a period of base-line measurement of rule violation, several manipulations were sequentially applied. The boys were required to carry a daily report card home (to Achievement Place), on which the teacher supposedly checked "yes" or "no" for each of the rules: 1000 points were to be awarded if all checks were for "yes," the points to be spent for three popular privileges (snacks, TV, outdoor privileges); a single "no" lost them these privileges, and 6000 points were required to earn them back. In fact, the teacher rated *all* boys "yes" for all rules, without regard to their actual rule obedience. Following this procedure, there was a period during which a child could violate a rule 10% of the time he was observed and still receive a "yes" (the boys were watched by observers during classtime through a one-way window, and these observers, not the teacher, made the yes and no decisions). Next there was a period when yeses were not required to earn the privileges. And finally the procedure with observers (and yeses required for privileges) was reinstated. Figure 6.10 shows the results of this experiment. Only the periods when the boys' rule-obeying behavior was accurately assessed and reinforced did their class performance improve. During the final period, rule violators were essentially absent and studying occurred at all times during the class period.

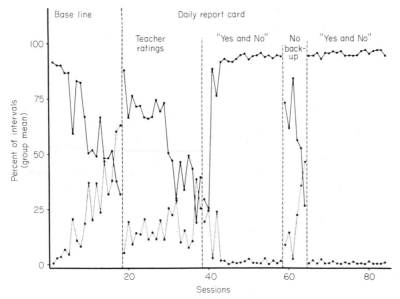

Figure 6.10   Amount of time (mean percent of intervals) spent in studying or rule violations during base line and as a function of contingent ("yes and no") or noncontingent ("yes only") teacher evaluations (a single "no" led to a point loss) and whether a point-loss did or did not ("no back-up") lead to deprivation of privileges. From Bailey *et al.*, 1970.

Phillips *et al.* (1971) reported several other successful applications of a treatment- or home-based contingency upon academic performance. One case is worth citing because in it the investigators eventually reduced the number of days per week the student earned privileges from his daily report card. The daily report card with all yeses could earn the privileges just mentioned. During some periods of the study, the report card was dispensed with entirely, and at the end instead of five daily report cards per week, the boys brought one to the home on only 2 of the 5 days (Tuesdays and Fridays). Figure 6.11 illustrates the results. Clearly, the daily report card and attendant contingent rewards were effective in increasing study behavior, and although there was greater variability, this improved studying was maintained when the frequency of the use of the contingency system was reduced.

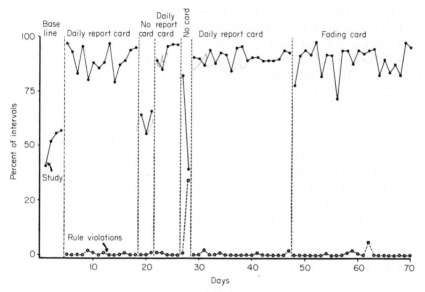

Figure 6.11 Effect of contingent reinforcement based on a daily report card as a determinant of study behavior and rule violations: base-line period, periods of daily report cards and of no report cards, and a period during which report cards were utilized only twice weekly. From Bailey *et al.*, 1970.

The Use of Contingency Management with More Highly Disturbed and Disruptive Behavior

Up to now we have been concerned with the operant treatment of less highly disturbed behaviors shown by delinquents in institutional, small group settings. Clearly, the principles of contingency management and the token economy are applicable to the reformatory setting and for the control of more highly deviant behaviors than we have yet discussed in this section. Let us close our discussion of delinquency, then, with a case study illustrating the use of contingency-management techniques to treat delinquent behavior in the reformatory setting (Burchard & Tyler, 1965).

This case recorded in Burchard and Tyler (1965), involves a 13-year-old boy who was institutionalized since he was 9 years old for offenses including stealing, starting fires, bed wetting, and cruelty to animals and small children. Upon various occasions this child was diagnosed as psychopathic and even schizophrenic. After commitment to the institution, it had been recommended that the child be given regressive therapy: ". . . that he should be regressed to the point of taking a bottle from his therapist . . . and that if he could be brought to smearing feces, it would surely be good for him [p. 246]." After 2 years of unsuccessful regressive therapy, contingency-management procedures were instituted.

During the year immediately prior to the contingency-management intervention, the child had spent 200 days in an isolation room for a variety of offenses including glue sniffing, attempted escape, breaking and entering, and smearing paint on the walls and curtains of his room. It was most obvious that the use of the isolation room as a punisher by the untrained staff was completely ineffective! Indeed, it was discovered that the staff felt sorry for the isolated child and brought him snacks in the isolation room. The isolation room also allowed boys in adjacent rooms to communicate with each other.

The contingency intervention lasted 5 months, during which time the child was taken off all medication and given no other psychotherapy. Upon displaying any unacceptable behavior, the child was placed in the isolation room. The child was to remain in isolation for 3 hours unless the offense occurred in late evening, in which case he was isolated until 7:00 A.M. The following instructions were given to the staff to insure their proper use of this time and procedure:

Whenever Donny displays any unacceptable behaviour, he is to be immediately placed in isolation. Unacceptable behaviour is defined as any behaviour which would normally require a sanction, verbal or otherwise. If you don't feel the behaviour should warrant isolation, then the behaviour should be ignored. However, if any action is taken to modify or eliminate the behaviour, it should be isolation. The use of isolation should be on an all-or-none basis; that is he should never be threatened with the possibility of being sent to isolation. He should be sent to isolation in a "matter-of-fact" manner. He should be told in simple terms why he is being sent and any further verbal interactions with Donny should be held to a minimum. It is important that you do not become too emotionally involved with Donny. Anyone who feels guilty or for some other reason does not send Donny to isolation when his behaviour warrants it is not participating in the treatment plan. As long as Donny is "fouling up", the more he is sent to isolation, the more effective the treatment programme will be [p. 246].[2]

[2] Reprinted from Burchard, J. and Tyler, V. Jr. The modification of delinquent behavior through operant conditioning. *Behaviour Research and Therapy*, 1965, **2**, 246.

Also, to remove the possibility of reinforcing communication with other boys during periods of isolation, a radio was installed immediately above the isolation room and was played from 7 A.M. to 10 P.M., masking any possible communication between rooms. The room contained only a metal bed with no mattress, and a toilet (a mattress was added when the child had to spend the night). Finally, whenever any unacceptable acting-out behavior occurred during isolation, the period of isolation was extended by 1 hour.

On the positive side, contingencies were established to promote acceptable behavior. For each hour during the day that the child was *not* in isolation, he received a token and if he stayed out over night, he was given 3 tokens upon waking up. These tokens could be exchanged for cigarettes, soda pop, trips to town, movies, etc. The opportunity to exchange tokens was given daily. The system evolved with improving behavior. After a while (2 months), the child was required to stay out of isolation for 2 hours, not just 1, in order to gain a token, and there was a *bonus* of 7 tokens for each 24-hour period completed without isolation. Finally, the time-out period was shortened to 2 hours, thus allowing the child greater time with the staff and other inmates.

Isolation was used relatively rarely, 18 times in the first month of treatment and only 12 times in the last. Still, there was a clear effect upon the child's behavior. In addition to the slight (33%) decline in the use of isolation, the offenses for which it was invoked became much less serious. During the first month of treatment these included glue sniffing (twice), stealing while on a field trip, stealing from the staff, fighting, and sniffing from a stolen bottle of bleach. During the fifth month the offenses included running in the dormitory, disrupting the classroom at school, and insolence to staff.

Contingency Management of Retarded Individuals

Typically, the contingency management of the retarded has been applied less to behavior management than to the actual teaching of new skills. Most often, the skills desired by staff members and seen as most advantageous to the patients are those of toilet training (Giles & Wolf, 1966; Hundziak, Mowrer, & Watson, 1965) and general self-help skills, including self-dressing, self-feeding, and responsiveness to verbal commands (which is an aid to further social training) (Bensberg, 1965; Bensberg, Colwell, & Cassel, 1965; Girargeau & Spradlin, 1964; Minge & Ball, 1967; Roos, 1965).

The use of operant procedures in toilet training retarded individuals has proved effective, and even when it is conducted in a special room with its own commode, the training generalizes to the ward or cottage facilities (Giles & Wolf, 1964); nevertheless, some investigators recommend installation of commodes in wards and classrooms and the gradual transfer of these commodes to the real rest room in order to facilitate elimination control when outside the rest room itself (Hundziak et al., 1965). In any event, the usual procedure has been to place the child on the commode and reward any elimination immediately with either candy or some other tangible reward delivered by an automatic device (Hundziak et al., 1965), or by more behavioral rewards such as praise, showers, privileges, etc. determined by the preferences of the individual being trained (Giles & Wolf, 1964). The effectiveness of operant measures to control eliminative behavior should not be underplayed, especially since these behaviors often are difficult to control because of neurological involvement: neurological examinations indicate that soiling and bed wetting among severely retarded patients may be correlated highly with the degree of damage to the central nervous system (Hundziak et al., 1965).

Training in self-help skills is more complex since a number of skills are being shaped simultaneously or in rapid succession. Furthermore, the reports in the literature are typically concerned with quite severely retarded individuals (10–25 IQ). The usual procedures involve shaping the specific self-help skills desired by means of successive approximations to the total chain of behaviors desired. For example, Minge and Ball (1967, pp. 865–866) utilized the following succession of responses to teach severely retarded girls to stand up and get undressed utilizing food and praise as reinforcers:

Standing up
I. Stands up, with technician providing
    a. gentle lift under arm or shoulder plus spoken direction.
    b. a light touch and gesture plus spoken direction.
    c. upward gesture plus spoken direction.
    d. spoken direction only.
II. Stands up with technician at least 5 feet away, giving
    a. upward gesture plus spoken direction.
    b. spoken direction only.

Undressing: Pants
I. Use elastic-banded cotton pants. Child should be seated, with pants nearly off; over one foot only. She removes them, with technician
    a. placing patient's hands on pants and helping pull them off, plus spoken direction.
    b. pointing to pants, plus spoken direction.
    c. giving spoken direction only.
II. Patient is seated with pants at both knees. She removes them, with technician
    a. pointing at pants, plus spoken direction.

     b. giving spoken direction only.
  III. Patient either seated or standing, pants all the way up. She takes them
     off when the technician
     a. points at the pants, plus spoken direction.
     b. gives spoken direction only.[3]

It is noteworthy that initially patients were given food reinforcers in addition to their meals, but these rewards soon proved to have little potency. Consequently, the patients were deprived of one or even two meals a day in order to increase the potency of food as a contingent reinforcer. Interestingly, though this was necessary to enable the training, none of the patients showed any loss of weight, indicating that meal deprivation may not be as harsh a procedure as it at first sounds.

  Bensberg et al. (1965) worked with severely retarded boys, training one patient at a time during two 15–30-minute sessions daily. Behaviors shaped included dressing and undressing, toileting, washing hands and face (and other personal grooming), and self-feeding. At the beginning of the training the four patients to be trained had an average score of 27.9 on a test of social maturity, while a three-patient control group's average score was 28.5. After 3 months, the trained patients average score was 59.5 compared to an average of 34.2 for the control group. All trained patients were amenable to simple verbal instruction by the end of 8 months of training. It should also be noted that the staff, as well as the patients, benefit from the results of contingency training in self-care. Bensberg et al. (1965) found that "Those employees who actually had contact with the [patients] . . . were tremendously heartened by the project. Their job changed from drab, custodial care to one of active participation in helping . . . [p. 678]."

  Although we have concentrated our discussion upon the use of contingency management to promote the acquisition of adaptive behaviors in retardates, this is not to say that these techniques cannot be used to control disruptive behavior when it characterizes retarded individuals. It is clear from the above discussion that positive reinforcement is effective for retarded individuals, and there is growing evidence that time-out is an effective punishing technique (Bostow & Bailey, 1969; Hamilton, Stephens, & Allen, 1967).

  Hamilton et al. (1967) effectively controlled the aggressive and destructive behavior of severely retarded patients by confining them to a barren time-out area for periods ranging from 30 minutes to 2 hours contingent upon each incident of poor behavior. Bostow and Bailey (1969) described the modification of disruptive and aggressive behaviors

[3] Reprinted from Minge, M. R. and Ball, T. S. Teaching of self-help skills to profoundly retarded patients. *American Journal of Mental Deficiency,* 1967, **71,** 864–868.

using positive reinforcement and time-out procedures. In one case the loud and abusive verbal behavior of a 58-year-old retarded woman was controlled by wheeling her to a corner of the ward and depositing her carefully on the floor after each abusive outburst. She was lifted into the wheelchair only after 2 minutes had passed and there was a 15-second period of silence. Furthermore she was given a treat, a favorite object, or attention when she remained quiet. As a test, the manipulation was omitted for a period (a return to base line) and then reinstated. As Figure 6.12 illustrates, the time-outs plus positive reinforcement were quite effective in eliminating the abusive verbalization (screaming). It is also noteworthy that the administration of a tranquilizer (Prolixin En-

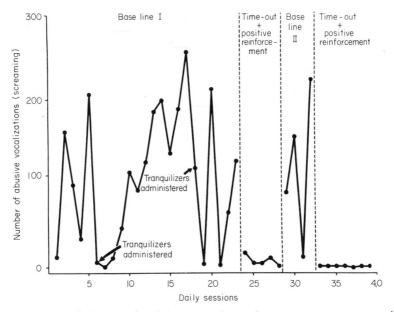

Figure 6.12 Elimination of verbal tantrums by contingency management procedures involving time-out from reinforcement and positive reinforcement for quiet behavior. From Bostow and Bailey, 1969.

anthate) was ineffective in controlling the patient's vocal outbursts; a comparison of the effectiveness of the tranquilizer and the contingency procedures is obvious from Figure 6.11.

In a second case described by Bostow and Bailey, the aggressive behavior of a 7-year-old retarded boy was effectively controlled by the same procedures. In this case the time-out consisted of being placed in a specially constructed booth (4 feet × 2 feet × 5 feet 5 inches high), which was closed on all sides, but open at the top. Time-out was contingent upon aggression toward other children in the playroom. Whenever 2 minutes passed without an aggressive response, the boy was given a small amount of milk, a carbonated drink, or a bite of cookie. Not only were these procedures dramatically effective in decreasing aggressive behavior, but the decrease in aggressive behaviors was apparently accompanied by an increase in positive, acceptable social interactions. During the treatment phases the child was observed to approach other children occasionally and to hug and embrace them.

Contingency Management in the Shaping of Symbolic Skills and Educability

The use of reinforcement techniques in the area of remedial education has two distinct levels. On the most basic level, investigators, primarily Staats and his colleagues (Staats, 1965; Staats & Butterfield, 1965; Staats, Finley, Minke, & Wolf, 1964; Staats, Minke, Goodwin, & Landeen, 1967), have been concerned with the teaching of reading skills, including the necessarily complex visual and verbal discriminations, to individuals often regarded as uneducable for reasons of temperament rather than retardation. Other investigations (Hall, Lund, & Jackson, 1968; Goodwin, 1966; Wolf, Giles, & Hall, 1968; Birnbrauer, Bijou, Wolf, & Kidder, 1965 to name but a few) have concentrated upon increasing the effective learning skills of children and adolescents in the classroom. There has also been work on procedures to control disruptive behavior in the classroom (O'Leary & Becker, 1967; O'Leary, Becker, Evans, & Saudargas, 1969; Ward & Baker, 1968; McAllister, Stachowick, Baer, & Conderman, 1969; Osborne, 1969; Patterson, Jones, Whittier, & Wright, 1965), procedures that indirectly affect the successful attainment of educational goals.

Contingency-Management Procedures for the Training of Reading Skills

Reading is a complex perceptual and symbolic activity, one that underlies the attainment of most educational goals. Staats (1965) has developed a training program in the laboratory that has proved to be quite effective in the training of preschoolers to read for the first time (Staats, Finley, Minke, & Wolf, 1964; Staats, Minke, Finley, Wolf, & Brooks, 1964) and for remedial training relevant to the education problems of older children and adolescents (Staats & Butterfield, 1965). Staats's procedure is primarily one of discrimination training since different words are often similar in many ways (for example, compliment, complement; ability, agility, utility; tall, ball, fall, call, wall, hall, mall). Initially, when the procedure is applied to individuals with few, if any, language skills, a child might be rewarded for the imitation of words or single sounds (vowels) spoken by the experimenter (see the example of training in verbal imitation in Chapter IV; Risley & Wolf, 1967; Sloane, Johnston, & Harris, 1968). Once this training is completed, the child learns to match words with verbal objects. A printed word will be displayed with several drawings of objects, one of which is named by the word, and the word is pronounced for the child. When children have learned, utilizing standard reinforcement techniques, to identify and pronounce the word, the actual training of reading begins. In this portion of training, a target word is to be matched with one of three other printed words. The target word is pronounced, and when the child correctly pronounces it himself and identifies it, he immediately receives a token reinforcer that can be exchanged at a later time.

After the reading of words is well established, this same procedure is utilized to train the reading of sentences (which have previously been learned auditorally, and even short paragraphs). Every correct response is followed by immediate reinforcement, although as proficiency increases, the schedule may be leaned (Staats et al., 1967). Whenever an incorrect response is made, the entire learning sequence is repeated until the child gets it right and is reinforced. Errors can be minimized by the use of cuing procedures (not prompting by giving the desired response), or by making the alternative choices highly discriminable from the correct choice at first, and on subsequent trials fading out this sort of support, making the similarities between correct and incorrect responses choices greater (Rocha e Silva & Ferster, 1966). Staats et al. (1967) demonstrated that once reading is established, the extent of reinforcement can be reduced drastically. In this study, the amount of reinforcement per response was reduced to 25% of its original level by increasing the amount of work required for reinforcement. Children actually continued to increase their rate of reading and to tackle more difficult reading material even after this change in amount of reinforcement had been effected.

In a well-known case study, Staats and Butterfield (1965) applied these procedures to a 14-year-old delinquent boy who had been labeled retarded, incorrigible, and uneducable. After 8½ years of school, his reading achievement was at the second-grade level and he had not earned a single passing grade in any subject. Vocabulary items were learned utilizing presentation on index cards. Training then proceeded to oral reading of paragraphs, and then silent reading, with subsequent testing on content. Tokens were dispensed contingently, and could be redeemed for various reinforcers including money. Treatment encompassed only

40 hours and was administered by a probation officer. Reinforcers for which tokens were redeemed cost a total of $20.31. Nevertheless, reading skills were acquired at a surprisingly rapid rate, including increased skills at reading new words when first encountered. The overall effects of training were evident in this boy's reading achievement scores. As Figure 6.13 illustrates, there was a staggering effect of the short period of training compared to the boy's niggardly development during the prior 8 years.

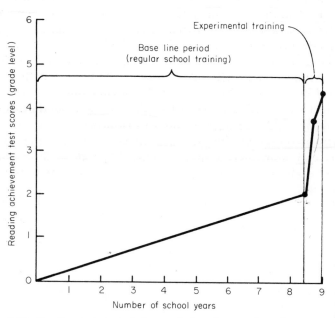

Figure 6.13   Reading test scores before and after the use of contingency management procedures to teach reading: during 8½ years of regular classroom instruction and following 4½ months of contingency management instruction. From Staats and Butterfield, 1965.

Contingency Management in the Classroom

In the classroom setting contingency management can be applied to studying, attention, and other directly educational behaviors, as well as to the elimination of disruptive behaviors that somewhat indirectly affect the educational process.

Several studies have indicated the effectiveness of contingency procedures to improve accurate learning directly. Lovitt, Guppy, and Blattner (1969) utilized free time and listening to the radio as reinforcers for spelling accuracy in a fourth-grade class. During a base-line period there was a median of 12 perfect spelling papers per week. Then a free-time contingency system was introduced in which those pupils receiving perfect scores on one day (there were four tests each week) were relieved from having to take the spelling tests for the remainder of the week. During this period there was a median of 25.5 perfect papers per week, a highly significant increase. In the third phase, the same contingency was in effect, with the additional stipulation that on any day when 100% of the students received perfect scores the entire class could listen to the radio for 15 minutes. For this phase there was a median of 30 perfect papers per week, a significant increase over Phase 2. Figure 6.14 depicts the results of this study.

This is clearly not an isolated result. Evans and Oswalt (1968) found that peer influence may also play a powerful role (as may be inferred from the effectiveness of Phase 3 in the study by Lovitt *et al.* (1969) peers with perfect scores still wanted to listen to the radio so they may have pressured the children with less than perfect scores).

This report presented four studies in which reinforcing activities for the entire class (early recess, story reading, early noon dismissal) were contingent upon the improved performance of from one to three indi-

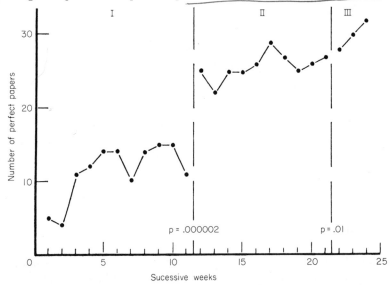

Figure 6.14 Number of perfect papers for each week throughout three consecutive experimental phases: I: traditional classroom instruction in spelling; II: perfect papers rewarded by release from any further spelling tests that week; III: same as phase II with one additional reinforcer—whenever the entire class had perfect papers all children were allowed to listen to the radio for 15 minutes. The *p* values indicate the significance level for any difference between adjacent phases. From Lovitt *et al.*, 1969.

viduals whose work was judged by the teacher to be less than their ability would suggest. In all cases but one, the target children showed significant improvement when the contingencies were placed in effect. The one instance wherein the contingency appeared ineffective involved the requirement that a child doing poor work in social science answer a question correctly to gain early class dismissal for afternoon recess. A similar procedure had proved effective when the reward was early dismissal for morning recess. Perhaps afternoon recess, because of shorter afternoon sessions, is less reinforcing than is morning recess. Even more plausibly, it may have been that the age of the children was the determining factor. Teachers reported that fourth-grade peers made several attempts to influence the target child, while no such attempts were observed among sixth graders. Interestingly, the two studies with the most striking effects involved fourth graders, whereas one of the two involving sixth graders showed only minimal improvement in the target child's performance, and the other showed none at all.

In a frequently cited report, Wolf (1968) described a series of studies concerning an after-school remedial education program for low-achieving fifth- and sixth-grade children. Tokens similar to trading stamps were used. Some tokens could be traded for money and tangible articles, some for weekly activities, and some for more long-range goals such as clothes, inexpensive watches, or even a bicycle. Token rewards were earned for work completed in the regular classroom (the better the grade, the greater the number of tokens), for homework and other assignments from the remedial classroom, and for the grades shown on the 6-week report cards from the regular school. On report card grades, students in the remedial classroom showed nearly a full grade point gain over a control group.

In a study similar to that by Wolf et al. (1968), Chadwick and Day (1971) worked with underachieving elementary students assigned to an experimental classroom. Percentage of time spent at work, work output per minute, and accuracy were measured during three phases, a base-line period, a treatment period involving both token and social reinforcement, and a treatment period involving only the social reinforcement. Students spent time working on workbook assignments and exercises. With the combined token and social reinforcement, the percentage of time at work, rate per hour, and accuracy all substantially increased, as shown in Figure 6.15. In addition, after termination of the token reinforcement, even though the amount of time at work decreased, rate and accuracy of work were maintained.

There are a number of studies indicating that reinforcement procedures may be effectively used to maximize pupil's attending behavior, but must involve the contingency management of individual students

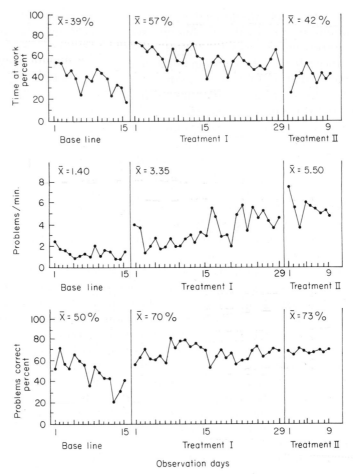

Figure 6.15   Percent of time spent working, rate of work output, and accuracy of work: (top) number of minutes spent working on assignments divided by the total time assigned to the task; (middle) the number of exercises and problems completed divided by the total number of minutes spent working; (bottom) the number of problems and exercises completed correctly divided by the total attempted (both correct and incorrect). From Chadwick and Day, 1971.

(Walker & Buckley, 1968; Bushell, Wrobel, & Michaelis, 1968; Zimmerman, Zimmerman, & Russell, 1969). These procedures are similar to the procedures we have previously discussed. Packard (1970) reported the successful training of teachers in the kindergarten, third-, fifth-, and sixth-grade classes to shape the attending behavior of their classes by reinforcing the entire class: criteria were set up, and class reinforcement was determined by the teacher's own judgment of the degree of atten-

tion and whether it met the criterion (for example, "Your attention as a class today reached 60%; this is 2% short of our goal so nobody gets any extra points today"). In addition to the teacher's rating, Packard gathered independent observations and recordings of the amount of attending time spent by randomly selected individual students and by the class as a whole. The results were reasonably similar for all classes, and Figure 6.16 depicts the results for the sixth graders.

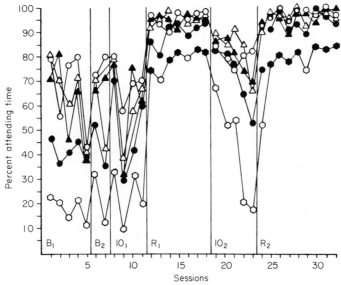

Figure 6.16 Percent of time children spent attending to relevant items (written and verbal information, the teacher, etc.) as a function of contingency management by the teacher: base-line periods (B_1, B_2), instructions to pay attention (IO_1, IO_2), and contingent reinforcement for attention (points which could be exchanged for privileges) (R_1, R_2) (○: Child A; ●: Child B; △: Child C; ▲: Child D; ⊙: Class ⬤: Class, reinforced). From Packard, 1970.

Contingency-Management Procedures in the Control of Classroom Disruptive Behavior

Often the control of disruptive behavior in the classroom involves the training of teachers in contingency-management procedures to be applied to individual children. Ward and Baker (1968) trained three elementary school teachers to identify problem behavior instances in four children identified as having behavior problems. They learned to cite specific incidents of inappropriate behaviors (and not to say "he's *always* bad") and to identify *when* to reinforce *which* appropriate behavior. Teacher attention for task-relevant behaviors and the ignoring of undesirable behavior were the therapeutic procedures involved. Overall, the total amount of teacher attention remained the same, but it was redistributed to be applied contingently to task-relevant behavior. There was a significant decline in deviant, disruptive behavior; moreover, the problem children no longer differed significantly from controls in terms of the number of incidences of problem behaviors, although they had had a significantly greater rate of such incidences prior to treatment.

O'Leary and Becker (1967) and O'Leary *et al.* (1969) utilized a token reinforcement program to reduce the disruptive classroom behaviors of elementary school children. O'Leary *et al.* (1969), trying a variety of other techniques as well, found that classroom rules written on the blackboard were ineffective, as was structuring the day into 30-minute sessions, or even praising appropriate behavior and ignoring inappropriate or disruptive behavior. When all these techniques were combined, the disruptive behaviors of one child appeared to be controlled, but not the others. However, a token system in which tokens were dispensed according to how well the children followed the rules on the blackboard was

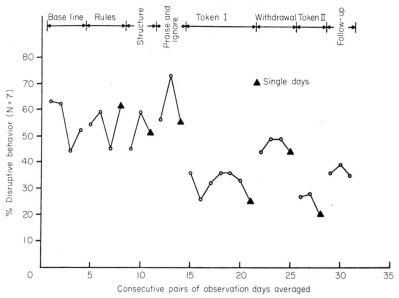

Figure 6.17 Average percentage of disruptive behavior displayed by seven children under various contingency management procedures: Base line, rules, educational structure, contingent praise and ignoring of behavior, contingent dispensation of tokens, the withdrawal of this contingency and its subsequent reinstatement, and during a follow-up period. From O'Leary *et al.,* 1969.

effective in controlling the disruptive behavior of six out of the seven children. Tokens also reflected, wherever possible, the quality of a child's classroom discussion and the accuracy of his schoolwork. Figure 6.17 depicts the data for all children combined. Even though the tokens were not contingent solely upon the absence of disruptive behavior, this behavior was clearly controlled.

The use of reinforcement techniques has been applied, not only to mild disruptive behavior in the elementary classroom as discussed above, but also to tantrum behavior (Carlson, Arnold, Becker, & Madsen, 1968), generally hyperactive behavior (Patterson *et al.*, 1965), and even inappropriate socializing in a high school English class (McAllister *et al.*, 1969). Occasionally such programs prove expensive (the total cost was approximately $125.00 in the case of O'Leary *et al.*, 1969), and token programs are sometimes attacked as being too impersonal (for example, Staats's reading procedure implemented in the school system could be almost completely automated). However, when well-designed, according to principles of contingency management and when adequately executed, there seems no doubt as to the effectiveness of token systems, and there seem to be few, if any, limitations in terms of the problems to which they may be applied.

VII

Operant Methods in Self-Control

This chapter is concerned with the application of the methods described in Chapters V and VI to problems associated with self-control. It is important to point out that the practitioner is by no means restricted to operant procedures in treating problems of self-control. As Cautela (1969) has pointed out, many of the standard behavior techniques (including most of those described in this text) lend themselves to self-administration. This is especially true for thought stopping and covert assertion, described in detail in Chapter X, and the reader wanting a broader understanding of the implementation of self-control procedures is advised to familiarize himself with that material, along with the material covered in the present chapter. On the other hand, in terms of clinical practice and research, behaviorists have generally tended to emphasize an operant approach to self-control (stressing stimulus control and the use of positive reinforcers), and it is this aspect of the psychology of self-management that is dealt with here.

Problems of self-control usually fall into one of two categories (Kanfer & Phillips, 1970). In the first, the client is engaging in a behavior pattern that is self-defeating or injurious. A few examples of problems of this nature often encountered in the clinic include eating patterns leading to obesity, excessive smoking or drinking, and indiscriminate sexual behavior. For problems in this category, it is the task of the therapist to help his client *reduce* the probability of occurrence of such behaviors. In the second category, the client is suffering because he is engaging in certain behaviors only very infrequently. Common examples include problems such as the inability to study, the failure to initiate social contacts, a low frequency of helping others, and sexual inactivity. Here it is the therapist's goal to aid the client in *increasing* the probability of such responses.

In actual practice, a given self-control program involves simultaneous efforts to increase the likelihood of certain types of responses, while decreasing other types of responses. To illustrate, most obese individuals eat excessive amounts of high-calorie food, and the primary goal of the therapist and client is to reduce this behavior. One way is to have the client reward himself for failing to engage in excessive eating. Another way is to attempt to strengthen responses that would compete with eating. For example, the client might be encouraged to take a walk at a time when he would normally engage in eating (Stuart, 1967). In a similar vein, Watson and Tharp (1972) reported a case of a male student who spent most of his study time in the library, looking at girls. By eliminating the competing response of girl watching (by having the student study in his room), as well as by allowing for reinforcement of study behavior, the amount of studying was effectively increased. Both examples illustrate a strategy common to most self-control programs: the simultaneous strengthening of desirable behaviors and weakening of competing undesirable behaviors.

Background

The idea of applying operant technology to problems associated with self-control is certainly not new. Skinner provided a rudimentary conceptual analysis of self-control, as well as a variety of techniques, in 1953, and, during the early and mid-1960s, a small number of writers (see Ferster, Nurnberger, & Levitt, 1962; Goldiamond, 1965; Homme, 1965) did make significant inroads into the application of operant principles to problems of this nature. On the other hand, only in very recent years have therapists, in general, begun to appreciate the vast potential inherent in such an approach. In fact, as recently as the mid-1960s, widely read behavioristic texts such as Eysenck (1964) and Ullmann and

Krasner (1965) entirely ignored the area of self-control. That this state of affairs has changed dramatically in a relatively short period of time is seen in the substantial space devoted to self-control in texts such as Franks (1969) and Kanfer and Phillips (1970), and in the recent appearance of texts devoted exclusively to the psychology of self-control (Watson & Tharp, 1972; Thoreson & Mahoney, 1974).

There are several factors that probably have contributed to the initial wariness on the part of many behaviorists dealing with issues related to self-control. First, when we think of self-control, we almost automatically think of such terms as *willpower* or *strength of character*. Concepts of this nature may be meaningful to the theologian, but certainly not to the deterministically minded psychologist. Second, self-control connotes control from within the individual, that is, control emanating from nonobservable mental processes. In Chapter I we dealt with the unfavorable reaction toward "mentalistic" analyses displayed by many behaviorists. Third, self-control, when one does attempt to deal with it in operant terms, implies self-reinforcement. That is, the individual has free access to reward, but does not partake of it until he has performed some desired response. Skinner (1953) has suggested the necessity for accounting for why a person would behave in this manner (when the most obvious response would be immediate self-reinforcement). He then raises a far more basic question: will self-reinforcement increase the probability of the behaviors that precede it? Skinner's intimation was that indeed it might not.

That self-control is now viewed as a legitimate area of investigation is certainly due, in part, to the fact that the aforementioned issues have been dealt with in a reasonably satisfactory manner. First, it is now clear that self-control can be viewed in terms of the systematic manipulation of antecedent stimulus events and response consequences, rather than as a mystical exercise in willpower. Second, as we have suggested in Chapter I, developments in cognitive psychology over the past few decades have pointed to the value of postulating inferred "mental" states provided, of course, that such theorizing leads to testable hypothesis about human behavior. Third, recent research (for example, Bandura & Perloff, 1967) has demonstrated that one of the mechanisms most fundamental to self-control, self-reinforcement, can alter the likelihood that a person will behave in a certain manner.

Applying Operant Procedures to Problems of Self-Control

When to Implement a Self-Control Program

In principal, the therapist can apply self-control procedures to almost any behavioral problem provided that the client has the intelligence sufficient to comprehend and carry out such a program (which is probably almost always the case). For instance, consider the male who becomes tongue-tied whenever he approaches an attractive female. A therapist might provide him with instructions in self-control procedures, stressing the maintenance of careful records, attending to those stimuli in the environment that typically give rise to such responding, and possible rewards that the client might provide for himself following more adequate approach responses to attractive females. Before long, it is likely that the client will report some progress, and eventually he may be making frequent and effective overtures to females.

However, while such a therapeutic approach might well be effective, it is naive, because it ignores the fact that there is a potential immediate and potent external reinforcer in every target situation, namely, a positive response (for example, a smile) on the part of the woman. In other words, there are important *short-term* (as well as long-term) rewards for behaving in a certain manner in such a situation. A more reasonable therapeutic strategy would involve simply providing direct instruction (behavior rehearsal, Chapter III) in how to behave in such situations. Once the client has acquired such skills, these behaviors will be maintained (perhaps intermittently) by powerful external rewards.

Now, consider the case of the student who seeks professional help because he seems unable to study. He reports that studying is a "drag," although he thinks he would like to do well in school (receive good grades). The therapist might make the assumption that all that is required is to provide instruction in how to study (that is, taking effective notes, rehearsing, reciting, etc.) However, this is naive because it assumes that there is some significant short-term gain in studying in a more efficient manner. Such may be the case for the student who does not have a study problem, but it is probably not true for the person in question. It is quite unlikely that, after 10 minutes of effective study behavior, the professor will burst into the room, saying "Terrific! Here is your A," or even that a friend will happen on the scene and commend the student for more efficient studying. For this individual, in the short run, there is little in the natural environment to maintain more effective study behaviors. Here is a case where training in self-control is a preferred method of treatment, because one of the main things it would provide for this individual is immediate incentives for engaging in more desirable behavior. Such incentives would be expected to bridge the temporal gap between responding and long-term, naturally occurring reinforcements (good grades, praise from parents, a rewarding job).

While there are no hard-and-fast rules, the foregoing examples suggest some general guidelines. When a client is behaving in a self-defeating manner, and there are no immediate and potent reinforcers in the natural environment for behaving otherwise, a self-control regimen might well be the most feasible treatment. Problems that would seem to lie in this category include low frequencies of so-called self-improvement behaviors, associated with relatively long-term rewards; for instance, academic studying, practicing a musical instrument, participation in strenuous exercise programs, the novice practicing his golf swing. Other problems include overeating, excessive drinking or smoking, and the inability to save money. This list is certainly not exhaustive and it is presented merely to provide the reader with a general feel for the types of problems amenable to self-control programs. As we have implied earlier, when the nature of the problem is such that appropriate behavior change is likely to be reinforced by the natural environment with a relatively minimal delay, therapeutic strategies other than self-control would probably prove to be more efficient. Naturally, there is nothing to preclude combining the implementation of a self-control program with other therapeutic interventions. For example, the alcoholic might undergo the avoidance conditioning procedures of Chapter IX while receiving training in self-control.

Introducing the Self-Control Program

Having decided that self-control is an appropriate method of treatment for the client's problem, the therapist's next task is to orient the client. The method of orientation here is quite similar to that described in Chapter V. The client receives what is tantamount to a brief course in the experimental analysis of behavior. As in Chapter V such an orientation is a very important part of the overall treatment program, because the primary therapist is the client himself, who must become skilled in the application of relevant learning principles. As was clear in Chapter V, this task is not especially formidable, since the principles involved are relatively few in number and not unduly complicated. Ordinarily, it can be accomplished in one or two treatment sessions, although it is expected that the client's understanding and skills will increase as the program unfolds.

One of the major points to be made during this first session is that it is of no use whatsoever for the client to think of himself as lacking in willpower or backbone. Viewing himself in such terms can only sabotage his efforts at self-control, for, what is the point of trying to change if one's difficulties emanate from an immutable state of inner weakness. No doubt the client can point invidiously to certain people he knows who appear to have no particular difficulty in most areas of self-control, intimating that they are "strong," whereas he is "weak." It must be stressed that what such an individual possesses is not strength or moral fiber, but, rather, a fortunate learning history that enables him, probably without very much effort, to behave in a way that allows a life of considerable personal satisfaction. The problem with the client is not that he is not trying hard enough, but that he has not yet learned to employ the most effective tactics. Naturally, the therapist's role is to teach the client these tactics.

Self-Control Principles

The therapist may now introduce the principles of operant conditioning. He might begin with a discussion of *stimulus control*, pointing out that behavior does not occur in a vacuum, but is under lawful stimulus control. The obese person is not observed to be gorging himself all the time, nor is it likely that the person with a study problem never studies. It may be that the person with the weight problem eats excessively only when he is alone in his apartment and before retiring, or that the student has no difficulty studying when in his dormitory room, but is distracted when he attempts to study in the fraternity house when his friends are around, or at the library when an attractive girl is in view. Certain of the controlling stimuli may be internal (most often related to states of deprivation or anxiety). To help get the point across, the client should be requested to provide specific situations in which he is most likely to exhibit the problem behavior.

If behavior is under stimulus control, it should be possible for a person to weaken or eliminate undesirable responses and strengthen desirable responses by changing his stimulus environment. The student distracted from studying in the library would be expected to fare better in an isolated room. The alcoholic who is a solitary drinker should attempt to place himself in social situations at those times he is most likely to drink. The housewife who spends excessive amounts of money on clothes should attempt to avoid stimuli, such as fashion magazines, that tend to cue such behavior. In these examples, the individual would be taking advantage of already existing stimulus-response relationships. *He places himself in a different situation, or in some manner changes the environment, and behaves more adaptively.*

Other methods of stimulus control may involve building in appropriate stimulus–response connections. One such method is *narrowing*, or tightening, stimulus control (Ferster, Nurnberger, & Levitt, 1962). An overall pattern of behavior may be especially maladaptive because it is practiced in a wide variety of situations. Certain obese individuals perhaps have acquired the habit of eating while watching TV, listening to the radio, or reading the newspaper. Narrowing means restricting the behavior to a limited set of stimuli. For example, eating might be limited to the dinner table at certain times of day, with the TV off (Stuart, 1967, 1971).

Another method of building in stimulus control may be used when an adaptive behavior is not strongly conditioned to any set of environmental cues. The technique of *cue strengthening* requires that conditions be made favorable for the person to practice the response in a specific situation. A good example would be the student whose study behavior is virtually absent. He might be encouraged to study in a certain specified location (Fox, 1962) so that stimuli associated with that location come to trigger study behavior.

The therapist might now discuss the importance of the *response consequences* on the maintenance of behavior. People behave so as to maximize positive reinforcements (food, praise, money, etc.) and to minimize negative reinforcement (pain, criticism). Perhaps the most important point to be made is that reinforcements are far more effective when they are immediate, and that self-control problems always involve behaviors that have immediate positive consequences (gratification or relief), but long-term negative consequence. So-called addictive behaviors illustrate this principle very well. To the nonsmoker, the inveterate cigarette smoker may appear to be acting out a Freudian death wish every time he lights up. From the smoker's point of view, however, the anticipation of satisfaction as he takes a cigarette from his pack far exceeds whatever feelings of dread are associated with the notions of some likelihood of serious illness many, many years hence. The therapist might now have the client describe one immediate reinforcer that seems to be maintaining the behavior he wishes to change, and one long-term advantage of changing.

The client may have some difficulty identifying potent reinforcers in his environment, and some coaching on the part of the therapist may be in order. He might provide the client with a list of common reinforcers (food, money, talking with friends, going to the movies, cigarettes, etc.). It should be stressed that the reinforcer be readily available and that it be powerful enough to serve as an incentive for doing things that might seem somewhat distasteful. It might be pointed out that reinforcers are not very effective under conditions of satiation (for instance, food is a poor reinforcer after a heavy meal). The Premack principle (Chapter V) may be of considerable value in helping the client identify reinforcers. As the reader will recall, this principle states that high probability behaviors may be used to reinforce responses which occur less frequently. To illustrate, the student who very frequently watches TV may make this high-probability behavior contingent upon engaging in a specified amount of low-probability study behavior.

Next, the therapist might discuss the *alternative,* or *competing, responses.* Such responses keep a person from doing something else in a specified situation. They may be adaptive, as in the case of the obese person taking a walk when he would normally snack. Or they may be maladaptive, as in the case of the individual who watches girls in the library instead of studying. If the client's stated problem involves failure to engage in adaptive behavior (say, a study problem), he should be asked to think of one response that he typically makes which interferes with such behavior.

Whenever a client engages in a particular self-defeating behavior, that behavior is actually the *termination of a sequence of responses,* chained together. To illustrate, consider the alcoholic who does his drinking in a particular neighborhood tavern between the hours of 10 in the evening and 2 in the morning. On a given evening, he looks at the clock and it is 9:45: this cues searching for the car keys, getting in the car, and driving toward the tavern. The closer he gets to his destination the more likely he is to encounter additional stimuli reminding him of the tavern, his first drink, and the feeling he will have after a couple of drinks. By the time he enters the tavern and sits at the bar, he is likely to be overwhelmed by a multitude of cues (any one of which is strongly conditioned to drinking: the bartender, the sight of whiskey bottles, the smell of alcohol, the sight of one or more drinking partners). Naturally, the first drink will act as an additional powerful stimulus for further drinking. Had this person been able to interrupt this behavioral chain at any point prior, say, to having consumed three or four drinks, for that evening, at least, he would not be a problem drinker. Both in terms of the number of cues tending to elicit drinking, and the immediacy of reinforcement (the effects of alcohol), it is clear that the likelihood of interrupting this chain is far greater if efforts at self-control occur early, rather than late, in the sequence. It may be that as the person progresses in the self-control program, he will be able to interrupt the chain at a point much closer to the terminal behavior. However, for the relative novice, writers in the area tend to agree on the following important principle. *Self-control procedures are most easily implemented early in a response chain.*

The point just made may seem rather obvious, yet many persons with serious self-control problems appear oblivious to it. This can be seen in a dieting obese person who regularly lunches with gluttonous friends, or the philandering husband who, bent on reform, tests his resolve by having a drink with his attractive secretary in her apartment. Certain people seem to believe that the mark of self-control is the ability to withstand any and all temptation. In fact, it is far more correct to say the mark of self-control is the ability to minimize temptation by early interruption of such behavioral chains.

In Chapters V and VI we emphasize the fundamental importance of the principle of shaping in the modification of behavior. To shape a particular behavior means to begin by rewarding crude approximations, gradually increasing the demands put upon the subject until he is responding in a desired manner. It is a truism that in order to reinforce and thereby strengthen a response (whether it be a desirable response or one that competes with undesirable behavior), the response must first occur. Thus, throughout the program, *response requirements must be modest enough to make it very likely that the client meet his ongoing behavioral goals.* It is common for clients to specify initial goals that are far too stringent. For example, Watson and Tharp (1972) described a case of a college male who desired to reduce the frequency of nail biting. His plan required that he not bite his nails all day, in order to reinforce himself with the evening meal and a visit to his girl friend's that night. As Watson and Tharp have pointed out, demands of this magnitude can only decrease the likelihood of success.

Individuals with control problems often have an all-or-nothing attitude about their problem behavior. Contrary to what is commonly believed, in our experience they are often ultra-perfectionistic, stubbornly refusing to reinforce themselves for anything less than total improvement. This is illustrated in the case of a hospitalized alcoholic treated by Rimm. His religious background led him to believe that drinking in any amount was sinful. Another person might have strengthened the behavior of having only one drink by self-reinforcement for a competing response (for example, leaving the tavern). He could not, however, because having only one drink was no more deserving of reward than having a dozen. The very brief treatment consisted merely of helping him view drinking on a continuum so that he was in a position to reward himself for drinking less on any given occasion. He was soon discharged from the hospital and at a follow-up several months later, he was handling a responsible job and reported no problem with alcohol. He indicated that his new attitude about drinking had been a major factor in his improvement.

Self-control programs usually incorporate all of the principles we have specified. The two techniques described in the following sections are used less frequently, and are not a necessary part of every such program. Naturally, the client should be oriented to these techniques only if they are to be employed in his specific program.

Coverant Control

We have already indicated the importance of the early interruption of behavioral chains leading to undesirable consequences. While certain behaviors (for instance, nail biting) have a certain "automatic" quality, in many cases we are quite aware of thoughts we have that regularly

precede certain responses. Often these thoughts are in the form of in-
tentions ("I'm going to eat that piece of cheesecake"), desires ("I really
want a martini"), or plans ("If I put 50 cents in the machine, I'll get a
pack of cigarettes"). Just as one can prevent the occurrence of maladaptive terminal behaviors by early interruption of overt behaviors in the
chain, it can be argued that a similar objective could be accomplished by
blocking *covert* responses early in the chain. This is precisely the objective
of *coverant control* (Homme, 1965). A coverant, by definition, is a covert
operant. It is a "mental" response that is not observable, but that is subject to the same principles of behavior modification used with overt
responses. In particular, it is under stimulus control (although the eliciting stimuli may be other coverants), it may be prevented by incompatible
coverants, and its probability of occurrence is affected by reinforcements
that follow it.

Homme (1965) has described the technique of coverant control as it is
applied to cigarette smoking. First, the client makes a list of thoughts
(self-verbalizations) relating to smoking that he personally finds aversive.
The thoughts might relate to long-term health hazards (lung cancer,
coronary disease) or more immediate aversive consequences (bad
breath, discolored teeth). Second, the client selects a reinforcer (Homme
is partial to the Premack high-probability-event concept of reinforcement) that is readily available. The actual procedure is as follows: When
the client experiences the urge to smoke, rather than engaging in the
usual coverants, for instance, "I really want to smoke," he engages in an
antismoking coverant such as "Smoking makes it hard to breathe," or
"I'll die of lung cancer if I smoke." If a prosmoking coverant leads to
overt smoking, presumably an antismoking coverant will have the opposite effect. Since there is nothing inherently reinforcing about engaging in the antismoking coverant, it is necessary that the response be
reinforced if it is not to extinguish. Therefore, the client is instructed
to provide such reinforcement immediately after engaging in the antismoking response.

Naturally, the technique may be applied to other problems associated
with appetitive behavior such as overeating (and undereating). Homme
described how the technique may be applied to the strengthening of attitudinal behaviors. For example, a person lacking in confidence is assumed to engage in "confident" coverants with a very low probability.
Here the therapist has the client make a list of reasons why he should be
confident (in other words, a list of his personal assets). The client is then
instructed to provide immediate reinforcement whenever he engages in
such confident coverants.

Homme's technique of coverant control has much in common with the
cognitive techniques (that is, techniques concerned with manipulating

thoughts) described in Chapter X. While there is a lack of direct empirical evidence supporting Homme's approach, the findings reported in Chapter X do strongly suggest that thoughts can exert control of feelings and overt behaviors, and that accepted psychological principles can be employed to manipulate thoughts.

The Use of Contracts

A self-control program involves at least an implicit contract between the therapist and client, wherein the client receives approval for achieving the various subgoals. However, formal contractual agreements usually involve more tangible rewards, for example, money refunded from cash deposits according to the degree of progress (see Harris & Bruner, 1971). Contracts may be arranged between the client and a person or persons other than the therapist. The essence of such contracts is the assumption of a reciprocal exchange of rewards, contingent upon certain actions on the part of each party (Tooley & Pratt, 1967). For example, a husband may agree to cut down on his smoking in exchange for better housekeeping on the part of his spouse. The terms of the contract should be very explicit. Thus, in the above example, the husband might contract to reduce his cigarette consumption by 10 cigarettes per day, on the understanding that the living room be tidy when he arrives home from work. Although contracts may be used by themselves, they may also be incorporated into a broader self-control program employing other principles mentioned in this chapter.

Whether the therapist chooses to incorporate formal contractual procedures is a matter of preference, although there are cases for which they might be especially appropriate (for example, when a husband and wife are counseled together). For persons less adept at delaying gratification (that is, individuals who tend to self-reward in a noncontingent manner), contractual management that involves external reinforcement may be very helpful. Many individuals in our culture have been conditioned to view contract obligations as virtually sacred. For such persons, the inclusion of some type of formal contractual understanding in the overall program might be a very valuable addition.

In the summary, the following are the basic operant principles with which the client should have some familiarity prior to dealing with his specific problem.

1. Self-control is not a matter of willpower. Instead, it comes about as a result of judicious manipulation of antecedent and consequent events, in accord with established principles of learning.

2. The client should take advantage of the fact that behavior is under stimulus control by employing any of the following tactics:

a. Physically changing the stimulus environment.

b. Narrowing the range of stimuli eliciting undesirable behaviors.

c. Strengthening the connection between certain stimuli and desirable behaviors. *cuing*

3. The client should determine events that are potent rewards and administer them immediately after responding appropriately.

4. The client should determine which responses are competing with, and thereby inhibiting, desirable behavior, with the goal of weakening them. He should determine which responses might serve as healthy alternatives to undesirable ways of behaving, with the goal of strengthening them.

5. The client should attempt to interrupt behavior chains leading to undesirable responses as early as possible in the chain.

6. Step-wise behavioral goals in a self-control program should always be easily attainable. That is, the client should deliberately plan to achieve his overall goal in a very gradual manner.

Auxiliary Principles

7. Thoughts exert a certain amount of control over behavior. Thoughts may be thought of as internal behaviors subject to the same principles of learning applicable to overt behavior.

8. Contracts involving exchange of reinforcers may be arranged between client and therapist, or between the client and some other party. Such contracts may serve as an additional basis for motivation.

Having introduced certain fundamental principles, the therapist might now provide the client with a brief overview of the treatment program in store for him. The program will begin with the client's establishing a base line of the undesired behavior, during which time he is to make *no efforts* at modifying his behavior (the procedures for collecting base-line data are presented in the next section). Ordinarily, this will require 1–2 weeks, and during this period, the client will make careful note of the stimuli controlling the undesirable behavior, possible reinforcers, and adaptive and maladaptive competing responses. Research (see McFall, 1970) indicates that sometimes the mere act of monitoring one's behavior results in a change in frequency of the target response. It is probably a good idea to advise the client of this, lest he automatically attribute such changes to external factors and prematurely incorporate this information into the treatment program.

At the termination of the base-line period, the client and therapist will be in a position to use the information collected during the period, to prepare a written program, specifying short- and long-term behavioral goals and how such goals are to be achieved.

Collecting Base-Line Data

It is important that the client keep a careful quantitative record of the degree to which he is engaging in the target behavior during the baseline period. It is equally important that, whenever feasible, he record the environmental events prior to, and following, his engaging in the target behavior (or, when appropriate, the events surrounding his failure to engage in the target response).

Keeping accurate records during base-line and treatment periods is a crucial part of a self-control program. This allows for accurate specification of the nature and magnitude of the problem, permitting client and therapist to set up realistic continuing treatment goals. In setting up the program, information pertaining to circumstances under which the target behavior does or does not occur is absolutely essential, and such records are the source of this information. Equally important, accurate records permit the client to observe progress, even when it is very small. In the absence of this information, the client might well conclude that the program was not working when it actually was, and this could well result in his dropping out of treatment.

The client may require some coaching in the most effective way to quantify the target behavior (Watson & Tharp, 1972). Some behaviors, such as cigarette smoking, lend themselves most naturally to a simple counting procedure. Others, such as eating, require a measure representing amount. Naturally, in the case of food, records must indicate what is eaten, as well as how much. For still others, time engaged in the target behavior may be the most reasonable measure (for example, studying; sleeping during the day).

For target behaviors having a very high frequency (smoking, nail biting), some type of portable counter might be helpful. If none is available the client might take a coin from one pocket and place it in another each time he engages in the response (Watson & Tharp, 1972). Behaviors of this nature (such as smoking) are sometimes performed unconsciously and, in such instances, it might be helpful to have the client deliberately practice the response with a great deal of concentration, in order to increase his awareness of its occurrence (Watson & Tharp, 1972).

Knowledge of antecedent and consequent events is important in developing the self-control program. For behaviors having a relatively low frequency (sexual encounters, engaging in serious arguments), it is possible to record these events for every occurrence of the target behavior. For high-frequency behaviors this may not be feasible. For example, consider the heavy smoker who consumes three packs (60 cigarettes) a day. While counting might not be especially difficult, recording events surrounding each cigarette would be impossible. On the other hand, by periodic examination of the rate of smoking, it should not be difficult for the client to ascertain ongoing events or experiences that tend to correlate with gross changes in the rate of smoking. A person who is heard to say, "I smoke a lot when I'm studying for exams," is doing precisely this.

Whether the client chooses to employ a small notebook or mechanical counting procedure for reliable, on-the-spot observations, he will want to transcribe the data collected each day onto more permanent records that he and the therapist can use during the planning and implementation stages of the program. Data sheets, such as the one presented below, are useful for this purpose (see Figure 7.1).

Day	Time	Frequency or amount	Antecedents, consequences, or correlated events
Monday	8 – 10 am	4	Awoke, had 1, had remainder after drinking coffee; coughed afterward
	10 – 12 am	6	After heavy housecleaning, lit up while resting; no coughing
	12 – 2 pm	3	Right after lunch; felt relaxed
	Total for Monday	34	

Figure 7.1 Sample of portion of one day's record for housewife with a smoking problem.

Keeping accurate records can be a rather tedious task. As Watson and Tharp (1972) have suggested, it is probably a good idea to have the client reward himself for this behavior, lest it undergo extinction, which would seriously jeopardize the entire program.

Thus far, we have dealt with general principles applicable to any self-control problem. In the section to follow, we describe specific programs for dealing with two common problems, obesity, and academic underachievement resulting from poor study habits.

Self-Control and Obesity

It is likely that most people in our culture (certainly persons over 30) have been confronted with the problem of obesity in some degree, at least. In the main, attempts at dealing with this problem have been described as "spectacularly unsuccessful" (Harris, 1969, p. 263).[1] The

---

[1] Certain recent investigations (Foreyt & Kennedy, 1971; Janda & Rimm, 1972; see Chapter IX) suggest the possible value of aversive conditioning in the treatment of obesity.

generally dismal state of affairs has been summarized by Stunkard (1958) . . . "most obese persons will not stay in treatment for obesity. Of those who stay in treatment, most will not lose weight and, of those who do lose weight, most will regain it [p. 27]." On the other hand, recent investigations employing self-control procedures (Harris, 1969; Stuart, 1967, 1971) have provided some basis for optimism. The results of these and related investigations are presented in a later section. The following procedures are derived principally from the writings of Ferster *et al.* (1962), Stuart (1967, 1971), and Harris (1969), as well as the experience of Rimm and Masters.

It is assumed the client and therapist will meet once a week for 30 minutes to 1 hour. If necessary, several clients may be seen in a group. During the first session or two, the aforementioned learning principles are discussed.

Base-Line Period

A 2-week period is recommended. In keeping records, the type and amount of food eaten must be recorded, as well as the events surrounding eating. Daily weight records must be kept. Since body weight may vary several pounds over a single day, weight should be taken twice, before breakfast and after the evening meal. An ordinary bathroom scale is adequate, although the same scale should be used throughout the program.

Treatment Goals

During an early session, at the end of the base-line period, treatment goals are established. The most immediate goal is a reasonable weekly weight loss, a minimum of 1 pound but probably no more than 2 pounds per week. A second goal to be established is the total number of pounds the client wishes to lose. If the client is vague on this point, a readily available weight chart may be helpful. At the most general level, the purpose, or goal, of treatment is to establish enduring eating habits that will maintain the desirable weight level. In this regard, the current procedures differ markedly from so-called "crash diets," which may be very effective in bringing about very rapid weight loss, but which in no way insure that the weight will not be regained. In addition, crash diets may be aversive to the client (causing him to believe that weight control is necessarily a painful experience), and certain such diets may have a deleterious effect on the client's health. The self-control approach to dieting, with its emphasis on small increments in weight loss, the intake of a variety of nutritious and palatable foods, and psychological interventions that make engaging in appropriate eating behaviors relatively easy (and sometimes pleasant), is a rather painless approach to dieting.

Diet Selection

While most individuals have some notion of which foods are especially fattening, misconceptions (primarily relating to caloric content) can sabotage any diet. While it is not necessary for therapist and client to become expert nutritionists, knowledge of certain fundamentals will be quite helpful. Familiarity with any elementary text on nutrition or, for that matter, a dietary cookbook (for example, Nidetch's Weight Watchers' Cookbook, Hearthside Press, 1966) will suffice. In planning the diet, it is recommended that a food-exchange procedure (Stuart, 1971) be employed. This involves listing a sizable number of foods of comparable nutritional value, from each of several general categories. Meals are then based upon selections from differing categories, allowing for greater flexibility.

Self-Control Techniques

1. *Removing Undesirable Foods from the House.* This includes foods (except those very low in calories) that require no preparation, for instance, breadstuffs, cheese, and many canned goods (Stuart, 1967). Since the purpose of this is to increase the time and effort involved in unplanned eating, this goal may also be accomplished by freezing prepared foods (such as leftovers), making it impossible to eat them impulsively.

2. *Modifying Consummatory Behavior.* In order to decrease the rate of food consumption, while possibly increasing sensual satisfaction associated with eating, it is recommended (Harris, 1969; Stuart, 1971) that after taking a mouthful, the utensils be returned to the table until that mouthful is swallowed. Additionally, short breaks (5 minutes) during the meal may help provide the client with the comforting realization that he does not *have to eat* in the presence of food. Such periods of abstinence may facilitate his becoming aware of feelings of satiety, especially if they occur during the latter part of the meal (Harris, 1969).

3. *Stimulus Narrowing.* In order to decrease the number of stimuli eliciting eating behavior, the client is to eat in only one place, such as the kitchen. Food is allowed in no other room in the house. The client is to engage in no other activity (such as watching TV, listening to the radio, carrying on a conversation, reading). The client should be informed that

obese people are especially susceptible to environmental, as opposed to viscerally cued, eating (Schachter, 1971).

4. *Changing the Stimulus Environment.*   The client should take advantage of his particular learning history by exposing himself to stimuli that tend to inhibit eating. For example, if he is too embarrassed to gorge himself when others are around, he should attempt to eat only in the presence of others. If stimuli associated with the program (such as the diet plan, or food, or weight charts) have a similar suppressing effect, they should be in plain view.

5. *Reinforcement.*   The client should provide self-reward for improvements in eating behavior (eating smaller portions, eating the right foods, etc.). The client may also wish to enlist the help of friends or relatives, requesting that they provide social reinforcement for such improvement.

6. *Competing Responses.*   At times when impulsive or otherwise inappropriate eating is likely to occur, the client should engage in competing behavior. Competing responses (for example, going for a walk) either decrease the availability of food or the desire for food (smoking a cigarette, for obvious reasons, not strongly recommended, or drinking a large glass of water or diet soda). If the competing response is not inherently pleasurable, it should be self-rewarded, although the ideal alternative response is reinforcing in and of itself. The competing response should be initiated as early as possible in the chain that otherwise would lead to eating. The therapist may wish to employ the Homme technique for strengthening thoughts that compete with eating.

7. *Incorporating Shaping Principles.*   As in the case of all operantly based-self-control programs, care must be taken not to overload the client with treatment requirements, at any given point in time. The most reasonable way to proceed is to have the client incorporate the above procedures gradually, perhaps one or two per week (Stuart, 1967). Since it is important for the client to experience success at each stage of the program, it is recommended that the procedures be presented in order of increasing difficulty. This may be most easily accomplished by having the client rank the various tasks as to the likelihood that he can successfully carry them out.

   The reader may wonder why the shaping principle is not applied to the amount of weight lost from week to week. While large increments in weight loss might come about naturally during the latter stages of treatment, programming this into treatment would require planning on initial weekly changes on the order of a few ounces, which could easily be obscured by a variety of uncontrollable factors (for example, a relatively minor change in water retention).

Weekly Sessions

Initially (perhaps over the first month after the base-line period) treatment sessions will be devoted to setting up the program. Thereafter, meetings will be devoted to monitoring the client's progress and making modifications in the program, when necessary. After the program is well underway, client and therapist may decide that weekly meetings are no longer necessary, opting to meet every 2 weeks, or perhaps even once a month. However, until the client's weight goal has been reached, there is the danger that prolonged periods between meetings may increase the likelihood that he will lapse into some of his former eating habits. The therapist, after all, is a potent dispenser of reinforcements, as well as a technical advisor. Once the client has begun to approximate the desired weight, naturally occurring reinforcements should do much to maintain appropriate eating behaviors. Additionally, it is easier for most individuals to remain on a maintenance diet than on a reduction diet.

Other Techniques: Covert Sensitization

Stuart (1967) employed covert sensitization with two subjects who had particular difficulty controlling eating between meals. The technique, described in detail in Chapter IX, may be used to reduce the attractiveness of certain especially troublesome foods or eating habits. Depending on how the procedure is presented to the client, it may be perceived as an externally imposed conditioning procedure, or it may be seen as another method of self-control. Viewing covert sensitization as a self-control procedure would seem to be more consistent with the long-term treatment goals discussed in a previous section. To facilitate this attitude on the part of the client, the therapist might begin by presenting one or two scenes, with the remainder of the scenes verbalized by the client himself.

Use of Contracts

Certain authors (Harris & Bruner, 1971) have reported somewhat successful attempts at controlling obesity with contractual procedures. After the client and therapist agree on the total weight to be lost, the client deposits a fixed amount of money per pound with the therapist who, in turn, refunds this amount each time a pound is lost. In the

Harris and Bruner study, the amount was either 50 cents or one dollar. Naturally, the more affluent the client, the greater expenditure per pound, in order to insure that the procedure generates an effective level of motivation. Although the contract procedure may be employed by itself, it is reasonable to suppose that it would be most effective when combined with the more standard self-control program.

Exercise

Certain therapists such as Stuart (1971) stress the role of strenuous exercises (aerobics, Cooper, 1968) in a reducing program. As the nutritionist Mayer (1968) has pointed out, inactivity is a major factor accounting for obesity in modern society. While we would by no means discourage the ambitious client from incorporating a regular exercise program into his weight-control regimen, the reader should be aware that a great deal of vigorous exercise is required to lose even 1 pound. Aerobic exercises (swimming, running, vigorous walking) involve high levels of effort over relatively extended periods of time. Requiring that the client engage in such activity on a daily basis, while at the same time fulfilling the regular requirements of the self-control program, may overburden him, resulting in his abandoning treatment. An alternative might be to have the client begin his exercise program *after* the client has lost the desired weight and has gained control over his eating habits.

Self-Control and Study Behavior

The practitioner, especially the school psychologist, or the member of a university counseling service, frequently encounters the student with a study problem. Often the difficulty is a function of insufficient time devoted to studying and inefficient study habits. For such a student, participation in the kind of program presented below may be precisely what is needed. Naturally, the therapist should look for other contributing factors. The student may have unrealistic long-term goals (straight A's at a highly competitive university), which give rise to apathy when he becomes aware they will not be met. Such a case is illustrated in Chapter X in the section dealing with Rational-Emotive Therapy. Another factor, which may be of increasing importance with the current emphasis on providing higher education for members of minority groups, is a serious lack of adequate academic preparation. Rimm, in teaching undergraduate statistics for psychology majors, has often encountered persons in this category who fail simply because they do not have the mathematical background to compete with their classmates. In such cases, remediation is the most reasonable course of action. Some individuals may be so lacking in verbal intelligence that even the most efficient study habits cannot overcome this deficiency (hopefully, the school counselor, therapist, or parent will not reach such a conclusion based upon limited evidence, such as a single administration of an IQ test). Certain students may have been coerced by their parents into attending school and would much prefer to engage in alternative constructive activities. Such individuals might benefit considerably from assertive training, with the goal of "standing up" to the coercive agents (Chapter III). Finally, as the experienced therapist in an academic setting is well aware, often students with problems not related to academic matters will use a study problem as a relatively "safe" entry into therapy, hoping that the therapist will ask questions that are more pertinent to what is troubling them. If, after careful consultation with the client, the aforementioned factors can be ruled out as major causes of poor academic performance, the therapist may turn to self-control methods.

The procedures to be presented in this section are adapted principally from the writings of Fox (1962), Goldiamond (1965), Beneke and Harris (1972), and Watson and Tharp (1972).

Base Line

A period of 1 week is probably adequate. The client should record the total time allocated to studying during a given time, the total time spent in actual studying, where the behavior occurred, and surrounding events (distractions, reinforcements for studying, competing responses). With this information, the therapist can determine to what extent the problem is one of poor stimulus control, inadequate reinforcement, or ineptitude in dealing with the subject matter.

Treatment Goals

As with obesity, goals exist at several levels. Long-term goals are: a better appreciation for the subject matter, adequate grades in present and future coursework, graduation, etc. Short-term goals involve the successful completion of periods of effective study. Initially, periods of study should be relatively short (perhaps 10–20 minutes), depending upon the individual and the material, with the duration increasing a few minutes each day. Many persons with study problems set short-term goals that are unrealistically high. Consider the student taking an algebra course. He does not like algebra and is somewhat behind. He decides that he must complete 3 hours of uninterrupted study (alternatively, three 20-page chapters) before he will allow himself to feel good about himself, to visit a friend, etc. After 20 minutes, his mind begins to wander. He experiences particular difficulty solving a problem. His level of frustration is rising rapidly and now, 10 minutes later, he slams his book closed, exclaiming "What's the use; I'll never make it." This is the latest in a long series of failure experiences and can only serve to strengthen his distaste for the subject matter. Had he set up a more realistic goal (10 or 15 minutes of studying, or solving a small number of algebra problems) he would probably have achieved it, reinforced himself accordingly, and increased the likelihood of wanting to study in the future.

Frequently, unrealistic goals arise from the necessity of covering an entire term's material the night before the final examination. While the student in this predicament might be given a few tips on efficient study techniques (presented below) this is not the time to begin the self-control program, with its emphasis on attaining modest, stepwise goals. A far more propitious time would be the beginning of the new term.

Self-Control Techniques

1. Changing the Stimulus Environment.   Most often this involves selecting a study area where undesirable competing behaviors are unlikely to occur. If the client tends to be distracted by other people while at the library or fraternity house, he must find another location where he may study in solitude. On the other hand, he may regularly avoid studying by sleeping, in which case a more suitable locale might *be* the library, where such behavior is less likely to occur. For most people, however, a quiet, well-lighted room is most desirable.

2. Cue Strengthening.   The student should select one study area (a desk) in the room, which is to be used exclusively for studying. Only those materials directly relevant to the study task at hand should be on the desk. In time, stimuli associated with the study area will become powerful, discriminative stimuli for studying.

3. Reinforcement.   The initial subgoal of 10–20 minutes is based on the assumption that most people can study for such durations without experiencing aversive consequences such as boredom. Naturally, the precise duration will have to be tailored to the individual, based upon his self-report. The major point is that he should attempt to avoid exceeding his limit at any stage in the program. Overstudying leads to aversive consequences that only negatively reinforce studying. Fox (1962) has suggested that once the student begins to experience discomfort, he should leave the area, but before doing so, he should complete some easy part of the lesson (rereading a page). It is probably best, however, that he leave *before* experiencing discomfort.

The client should reward himself immediately after completing the desired segment of study behavior. Rewards might include a piece of candy, calling a friend, etc. As Watson and Tharp (1972) have suggested, a good reinforcer might be engaging in the behavior that in the past has competed with studying ("girl-watching," is their example). At what point the client should return to the study area must be worked out on an individual basis. Certain individuals may be sufficiently "revitalized" after a break of only a few minutes, whereas for others, initially at least, no more than one or two study periods per day can be tolerated. As a rule of thumb, if during a given day, successive study periods tend to be shorter and shorter, the rest intervals are probably too brief.

Improving Study Efficiency.   Thus far we have discussed methods for increasing the amount of time the client spends in study behavior. Now we shall focus on tactics of studying designed to increase what the client is able to learn over a fixed period of time.

The SQ3R method (Fox, 1962; Beneke & Harris, 1972, based on Robinson, 1946) is one means for increasing study efficiency. The client is instructed to begin by *surveying* (S) the material to be covered, attending to chapter and section headings and summaries and to concluding paragraphs. Following this cursory survey, the client is then to take the first subheading or introductory sentence and turn it into a *question* (Q), proceeding to *read* (R) the material to follow, in order to answer the question. For example, the above subheading might be transformed into: "What are the specific ways for increasing study efficiency?" (Q). After the section has been read (R), the client is to engage in *recitation* (R) of the material, which would involve answering the above question (for example, "The SQ3R method is one way to increase efficiency. It involves . . ."). The last phase involves *reviewing* (R) the material. Thus, SQ3R stands for Survey, Question, Read, Recite, and Review.

Beneke and Harris (1972) discuss two additional aspects of overall academic skill—the taking of notes, and examination performance. As they point out, students tend to err in one of two directions. Either they attempt to take notes verbatim (which means they are so busy writing, they miss essential points,) or they fail to take any notes. Beneke and Harris suggest using outlines and then revising the notes the same day. However, some people have difficulty in outlining, and it might be very helpful for the therapist to present a tape of a portion of a typical lecture, having the client make notes in outline form and then, afterward, presenting him with a good outline of the same material.

Debilitating text anxiety is a commonly observed phenomena. A variety of methods for dealing with this problem (for instance, systematic desensitization) are to be found elsewhere in this text. Unrelated to anxiety, the client may be in need of instruction in testmanship. For example, for essay questions, the client might be asked to write answers (beginning with a brief outline of what is to be said, under simulated examination conditions). He might also be provided with sample answers as models. For objective exams, he might be instructed to go through the exam fairly rapidly, answering only questions he is reasonably certain of (thus providing him with an initial success experience and insuring that he not get bogged down by a few difficult items). Following this, he might go through the exam again, this time answering questions he is moderately sure of, and so on. It should be pointed out that the desirability of guessing depends on whether the test involves a penalty for guessing.

Empirical Findings

The following are representative case histories employing many of the aforementioned procedures. They illustrate the broad range of problems that have been treated with these methods. Naturally, given the limitations of the case history approach, the results can be taken as only suggestive.

Case Histories

In an early report describing the application of operantly based self-control procedures, Ferster *et al.* (1962) treated three mildly obese nurses. The treatment, which was similar to that described in a previous section, stressed stimulus control, the development of verbal behaviors for controlling eating, meal interruption, and the consumption of appropriate foods. The results of the 3-month treatment were weight losses of approximately 5, 12, and 14 pounds, with the loss maintained over a follow-up some 4 months. Goldiamond (1965) reported treating an obese young man. Initially, treatment stressed stimulus narrowing (for example, not eating while watching TV). Later, appropriate content of meals was emphasized. Goldiamond reported that when he met the client 3 months later, he was considerably slimmer.

Fox (1962) provided one of the first reported applications of self-control procedures to study problems. The treatment, essentially that described in the previous section, is presented for only one of five students who received treatment, with a particular emphasis on studying for a physics course. Results for the five are rather impressive. Each student continued in the program for the entire quarter and, during the second quarter, reported continuing to use the methods. All showed improvement in academic achievement, varying from one to four letter grades. Goldiamond (1965) described two additional case histories involving study problems. In one case, a female would become sleepy whenever she attempted to study. Treatment consisted of instructing her to increase the level of illumination in the room, to turn away from the bed when she studied, and to participate in no other activity at her desk. After 1 week she reported studying for 10 minutes. She was reinforced for this and encouraged to increase the amount and, eventually, was studying regularly 3 hours per day. A second case involved a college junior with an adequate IQ who was failing out of school. Goldiamond had him reinstated, on the proviso that he work with the student. Treatment, which stressed better study habits, was associated with only minor improvement, attributed to very poor early academic preparation.

Nurnberger and Zimmerman (1970) described the treatment of a 31-year-old assistant professor who, in spite of pressure to complete his dissertation, had failed to write a single page. He also suffered from a variety of other problems, including insomnia and a distaste for sex. The treatment plan, which dealt with the writing of the dissertation, required that the client deposit sizable postdated checks with the therapist. The checks, which were made out to charities, would be sent unless the client wrote a preselected number of pages. The plan was initially successful but, by the ninth week, writing had slowed down. Subsequently, checks were made out to organizations that the client had found particularly distasteful (for example, the Ku Klux Klan, the American Nazi Party). The revised program was highly successful and, within a few months, he had completed a first draft and much of a final draft. A 10-month follow-up revealed that the thesis was completed, with the client to receive his doctorate 2 months later. His relationship with his wife reportedly was improved, and he was enjoying sex on a regular basis.

Several attempts at employing self-control procedures to deal with excessive cigarette smoking have been reported. Tooley and Pratt (1967) described a three-phased treatment of heavy smoking with a married couple. Both partners were professional people and each was smoking heavily for over 25 years. The first five sessions were devoted to covert sensitization. Following this treatment, both clients were smoking 10–11 cigarettes per day (down from 50 for the husband, 35 for the wife). Next, coverant control was introduced, with coffee- and water-drinking used to reinforce low-probability anti-smoking coverants. After 5 days (which included one additional covert sensitization treatment) the husband was down to five cigarettes, and the wife was down to just one. In the next phase, both partners agreed to a contract wherein they would not smoke in each other's presence. The husband dropped to two cigarettes per day and the wife dropped to zero. The husband then contracted to smoke only one cigarette per day and, later, not to smoke at

all. From the authors' comments, the program was completely successful, although the duration of the follow-up is not indicated.

Nolan (1968) employed his wife as the subject in a smoking study. The
method, based upon Goldiamond (1965) required that she smoke only
in a special "smoking chair," which was situated such that she could not
readily watch television or carry on a conversation from it. Other
members of the household did not approach or converse with her when
she was in the chair, and reading materials were out of reach. Within a
few days she had gone from 30 cigarettes per day to 12. During the second week, the chair was taken to the cellar, with smoking showing an additional reduction to 5 cigarettes per day. After a period during which a
slight increase was noted, the client, in disgust, quit altogether, and 6
months later was still totally abstinent. In a similar report, Robert (1969)
employed himself as the subject. Having made the observation that he
rarely smoked in the bathroom, smoking was restricted to this location.
During the first week, the smoking rate, which was over 22 per day,
decreased to fewer than 10. Added restrictions of not talking or reading
while smoking appeared to effect some additional reduction and, following an illness, he ceased to smoke altogether. Seven months later he was
still abstinent. Needless to say, the choice of subjects in these two reports
tends to confound the results.

Bergin (1969), using a technique somewhat similar to thought stopping (Chapter X), emphasized the interruption of thoughts that typically
lead to impulsive smoking behavior. In one such case, an acquaintance
was able to abstain from smoking for 2 weeks (a record for this individual) after only one treatment session (continued treatment was not possible). The second was a neurotic inpatient who was experiencing serious
physical problems as a result of a long history of chain smoking, which
he was totally unable to control. One treatment session resulted in the
client's abstaining for several days, which was most unusual for him.

As we have suggested, self-control procedures are potentially applicable to a wide variety of problems. For example, Goldiamond (1965)
described the imaginative use of self-control principles in marriage
counseling. In one case, 2 years prior to seeking treatment, the wife had
committed adultery with her husband's best friend. Since then, the husband regularly screamed at her, followed by long periods of sulking.
After instruction in behavior analysis, the couple was told to rearrange
the furniture and use of the rooms in the home (thereby altering some
of the stimuli that had cued the husband's behavior). To facilitate
nonangry interchanges, the following tactic was used. The couple was instructed to go out to dinner and tip the waitress with a $20 bill that was
previously attached to an index card. The word *farm* written on the card
was intended to cue a discussion of a mother-in-law's unusual ideas

about farming, which was known to be a safe subject for discourse. Stimulus narrowing is illustrated in the instructions to the husband to sulk only on a special stool located in the garage. The amount of sulking reportedly went from a high of 7 hours of sulking to zero, in approximately 3 weeks. Finally, to provide a cue for improved sexual relations, a yellow light was placed in the bedroom and the couple was instructed to turn it on when they were feeling amorous. The remaining sessions involved additional discussions of behavior analysis, at the end of which no sulking was reported and the "partners were able to commune."

A second marital case involved a professional young couple who were having sex on the average of twice a year. The husband, an ambitious executive taking evening courses, appeared to have little time or inclination for sex. The therapist suggested he "schedule" his wife for two evenings a week, but this was not very successful. Since both parties valued being well groomed, it was then suggested that his visits to the barber (and the wife's visits to the beautician) be made contingent on keeping the above appointments. After an initial failure, the couple kept their appointments (presumably having sex, although this is not made explicit) on a regular basis.

Bergin (1969) treated two homosexuals, both desiring to change their sexual orientations. One case involved a 24-year-old male who had a 10-year history of compulsive homosexual fantasy and behavior. While he enjoyed the sexual act, he felt disgust afterward, and desired developing an adequate heterosexual adjustment. Since he was fearful of women, part of the 35 hours of treatment was devoted to assertive training (Chapter III) which had no effect on his homosexual behavior. The remainder of treatment was primarily concerned with interrupting thought patterns that led to homosexual consummation. It was determined that strong homosexual urges frequently began with the client's seeing a male in a public place, followed by an exchange of glances, mild emotion and fantasy, establishing visual contact, increasing arousal, verbal interchanges, etc., and, eventually, consummatory behavior. He was instructed to interrupt the sequence as soon as he became aware of it, by switching to competing thoughts and activities. Initially, complying with these instructions was quite difficult, but during the later stages of treatment, he reported being able to control his homosexual behavior with increasing ease. At a 2-year follow-up, he was free from the problem, and was successfully married.

A second case, very similar to the first, involved a 24-year-old female homosexual, also fearful of heterosexual contacts. Treatment consisted of desensitization, along with the above self-control procedure. The client was seen 41 times over an 8-month period. The treatment was quite successful, and at a 10-month follow-up, she was married.

Todd (1972) employed Homme's (1965) coverant control technique in two cases of depression. The first case was a 49-year-old physician's wife with a history of three suicide attempts. The overall treatment plan involved broad-spectrum behavior therapy (including desensitization and behavior rehearsal). However, the therapist considered success in total treatment to be dependent upon initial removal of the client's severe depression. To this end, with considerable prompting from the therapist, she was able to come up with six positive self-referential statements. Since smoking was a high-probability response, the client was instructed to read one or two of these statements prior to lighting a cigarette. To facilitate this, it was arranged for the list of statements to be clearly visible whenever cigarette smoking occurred. Within 1 week, her depression was considerably reduced and she had increased the number of positive statements to 14. By the end of the second week she reported feeling so much better (she now had 21 items on her list), it was decided to embark on the broader behavior therapy program. Three years after the completion of a total of 41 sessions, the client continued to make a good social adjustment, was active in the community, and reported no serious depression since the termination of treatment.

The second case involved a 27-year-old male college student who had previously undergone successful desensitization for severe test anxiety. Although his grades were excellent, he doubted his ability to deal with graduate work, and was reluctant to engage in classroom discussions lest he reveal his inadequacy. Treatment consisted of assertive training, instruction in the operant approach to self-control, and application of Homme's technique. With respect to the latter technique, a list of 10 items relating to personal accomplishments (assumed to reflect basic abilities) was constructed. Since the client's student employment required frequent telephoning, this high-probability behavior was made contingent on reading one or two of the above items. Todd reported that within 6 weeks, the client was enjoying classroom discussions and apparently doing well. Six months after the completion of therapy (15 sessions) the client was performing very well in graduate school.

Experimental Findings

The Efficacy of Self-Reinforcement.   In Chapters V and VI the importance of external reinforcement in strengthening behavior was made abundantly clear. We now direct our attention to something very fundamental to the psychology of self-control. Specifically, we deal with the question of whether a person can provide self-reinforcement in a way that can modify his own patterns of behavior.

Until relatively recently, psychologists have tended to ignore the role of self-reward. Bandura (1969) has suggested that this has been a result of the traditional concern with animal learning, since animals presumably do not engage in the kind of self-evaluative behavior usually associated with a self-reinforcement in human beings. The paramount question is whether or not self-enforcement works; that is, whether or not it strengthens behavior. On one hand, the answer ought to be in the affirmative, since the same stimulus–response-reinforcement paradigm is involved, as when reinforcement is administered externally. On the other hand, if a reward, in order to be effective, must be truly *contingent* upon making a certain response, one might expect self-reinforcement to be a pointless exercise. This is because the individual is not really required to make the response to receive reinforcement. He has control over the reward source and is free to provide himself with reinforcement without going to the trouble of engaging in any certain behavior. Thus, there are theoretical reasons arguing for and against the efficacy of self-reinforcement. Fortunately, controlled experiments have provided information pertaining to this very important question.

In one study, Bandura and Perloff (1967) compared the effectiveness of self-imposed and externally imposed reinforcement on an effortful wheel-turning task. The subjects, ranging in age from 7 to 10 years, were assigned to four groups. The self-reinforcement subjects selected their own standard of performance and rewarded themselves whenever they attained the standard. Reward was in the form of token that the children were told would be exchanged for prizes, with more tokens buying more valuable prizes. Each child in the externally imposed reinforcement condition was yoked to a self-reinforcement child with respect to number of tokens received. Thus, these two groups did not differ in the amount of reinforcement received. A third group received tokens noncontingently, that is, they first received their tokens and then performed the task. A fourth group of children received no tokens.

The main finding was that the self-administered and externally administered reinforcement groups did not differ in terms of the total number of cranking responses, but that both showed significantly more such responses than the noncontingent-reinforcement and nonreinforcement groups. In other words, children who were free to provide themselves with as many tokens as they wished, on any given trial, worked about as hard per token as children whose reward was externally imposed. Interestingly, children in the self-determined reinforcement condition rather consistently selected performance standards (that is, ratio of responses to tokens received) a good deal higher than the minimum required by the experiment. It should be pointed out that the experimenters went to great pains to minimize social pressures. The children performed the task alone and were led to believe they were not being observed. Children in the self-reinforcement condition selected their standard after the experimenter had left the room, and deposited their tokens in banks placed in a sealed paper bag that was to be collected by a second experimenter.

Lovitt and Curtiss (1969) described an experiment involving a 12-year-old student. For 12 days he received points for a variety of academic behaviors, with the teacher determining the number of points per task (points could be exchanged for the privilege of engaging in reinforcing behaviors). During the second stage, which lasted 22 days, the student determined the number of points per task, and during the third stage, lasting 7 days, the teacher again controlled the contingencies. The experimenters report a median number of academic responses of 1.65, 2.50, and 1.9 for the three stages. The experiment was then repeated on the same student, with very similar results. Again, maximum performance was associated with self-imposed contingencies. In a third experiment, it was found that the rate of reinforcement when student determined, was slightly lower than when teacher determined, suggesting that findings of the first two experiments were not an artifact of larger magnitudes of reward under the self-imposed conditions.

Glynn (1970) assigned ninth-grade girls to four groups. One group received tokens over a 10-day period for correct answers to multiple-choice items covering history and geography material. The number of tokens per correct answer was determined by the experimenter. A second group was instructed to impose their own standards. A third group, yoked to the second with respect to number of tokens, served as a noncontingent control; and a fourth group received no tokens. The principal finding, similar to that reported by Bandura and Perloff (1967), was that the experimenter and self-determined reinforcement groups did not differ, but both were significantly superior to the control groups in terms of multiple-choice test performance. During subsequent token phases (now self-determined) and withdrawal phases, Groups 1 and 2 tended to show somewhat superior performance. Throughout the experiment, the self-reinforced group tended to make more correct responses per token than the other groups. That is, as in the Bandura and Perloff study, self-reinforcement was associated with stringent performance standards.

The findings just cited indicate that self-reinforcement can be effective in strengthening and maintaining behaviors. From a practical point, it is of considerable interest that self-reinforcement is "inexpensive." That is, subjects tend to work hard for their rewards. Naturally, individuals vary greatly with respect to standards of self-reward. Clearly, such standards are acquired through learning, probably in large measure through imitation of adult and peer models (Bandura & Kupers, 1964;

Bandura & Whalen, 1966; Marston, 1965; Mischel & Liebert, 1966). The work of Bandura, Grusec, and Menlove (1967a) suggests that one potent method of teaching high standards of self-reward is to provide a model for such behavior, with the model's response receiving social approval.

The reader may be surprised to learn that it is possible, even with pigeons, to train very high work requirements per self-reward, in part, by punishing noncontingent self-feeding (Mahoney & Bandura, 1972).

The Treatment of Obesity.   In recent years several studies have reported generally positive results using operantly based self-control procedures with overweight subjects. Some of the studies have been lacking in adequate controls. Nevertheless, the findings to be presented strongly suggest the value of this treatment approach, particularly when viewed within the broader context of research on obesity, with its predominantly negative results.

Stuart (1967) presented the results of a self-control program, with eight obese women. The women were seen three times per week over the first 4–5 weeks, followed by sessions every other week for the next 12 weeks, and maintenance sessions as needed. The treatment, similar to that presented in the method section, began with instruction in learning principles. Specific techniques were presented in stepwise fashion over the next five sessions, beginning with merely interrupting the meal for a few minutes, followed by removing food from the house, stimulus narrowing, methods for slowing down eating, and, finally, engaging in competing behaviors. The remaining treatment sessions were devoted to refinement of methods and therapist reinforcement for progress, except in the case of two clients who received covert sensitization for eating between meals. The results over a 12-month period are strikingly consistent across clients, with each showing an approximately linear decrease in weight. Total weight loss was appreciable, ranging from 26 to 47 pounds (mean, 37.8 pounds) although none of the subjects consistently met the treatment goal of 1–2 pounds per week, the average approximating ¾ pound.

Harris (1969) employed self-control procedures with obese male and female subjects who were seen in groups twice a week for 2 months. A second group of subjects (a control group) was merely asked to lose weight on their own and given calorie charts. In addition to the standard self-control procedures, subjects in the first group were presented with findings of Schachter (1971) and his associates, which stressed the importance of external control of eating in obese individuals. They also received relaxation training, with relaxation offered as an alternative to eating. Approximately 2½ months into treatment, half of the subjects in this group received covert sensitization related to improper eating habits, with the remaining half continuing to receive the above treatment.

In terms of weight loss, as determined by a final weighing 4 months after the study began, the subjects in the treatment group showed significantly greater improvement (10.6 pounds) than the control subjects, who actually showed a slight increase in average weight. Whereas all 14 of the treatment subjects showed at least some weight loss, 3 of 7 controls gained weight. Additional decrements in weight were not associated with the covert-sensitization treatment. However, the reader is referred to the Janda and Rimm study (Chapter IX), which demonstrated positive effects when this procedure was employed with obese subjects.

In one of the better controlled obesity studies, Wollersheim (1970) compared the effectiveness of social pressure, social pressure combined with insight, and social pressure combined with training in self-control. The social pressure treatment emphasized motivation and commitment. Subjects were weighed in front of the group, with weight decrements receiving social approval, and increments receiving mild negative reinforcement. Throughout a given session, each subject was required to wear a tag reflecting weight change during the prior week. Although group discussions dealt with factors relating to obesity, care was taken not to provide information relative to techniques for eating less.

Insight therapy stressed obtaining an understanding into underlying factors, focusing on historical elaboration. Subjects in this condition also received relaxation training, on the rationale that this would facilitate gaining insight. Again subjects were dissuaded from discussing ways of eating less.

The self-control procedures were presented in graduated fashion over six sessions, beginning with building positive associations relating to controlling eating behaviors. The next session dealt with stimulus control and the manipulation of deprivation and satiation. Session 3 stressed reward for self-control and imagined negative consequences for overeating. Session 4 dealt with alternative responses and reinforcers, session 5 with chaining, and Session 6 with the use of aversive imagery (presumably a variant of covert sensitization).

Following 10 sessions of treatment, the group receiving only social pressure, lost an average of 5.40 pounds, and the insight group lost 6.90 pounds. These groups did not differ significantly, but both showed significantly less weight loss than the self-control subjects, who averaged 10.33 pounds. All three groups showed significant improvement relative to a fourth waiting-list control group, which gained 2.39 pounds. The weight loss noted in the self-control group approximates the 1 pound per week minimum goal often employed in such programs (although subjects in the present study had been encouraged initially to lose 2 pounds per week). Given their initial average weight of 153.61 pounds, a weight loss of over 10 pounds is not unappreciable. At an 8-week follow-up, all groups showed slight weight increases (on the order of 1–2 pounds). On an inventory pertaining to eating habits, only the self-control subjects showed significant changes in the positive direction, with the effect considerably weaker at the time of the follow-up. On a variety of anxiety scales (not relating to eating) the groups did not differ at the time of posttreatment. Wollersheim correctly took this as evidence for lack of symptom substitution. That weight loss is not generally associated with increments in anxiety has been found elsewhere (for example, Janda & Rimm, 1972, Chapter IX), casting doubt on the widespread belief that overeating is primarily an anxiety-reducing ritual.

In a pilot investigation, Stuart (1971) employed his "three-dimensional" program for obesity, stressing diet selection, standard self-control techniques, and acrobatic exercises, incorporated into the pattern of the client's everyday life. The subjects, women whose base-line weight varied from 171 to 212 pounds, were divided into two groups. One group, which was seen twice weekly for 15 weeks, was provided with diet and exercise information and instruction in principles of self-control. The second group was given the same diet and exercise information, but did not receive training in self-control procedures, until 15 weeks had passed. Although both groups appeared to have lost some weight by the end of the first 15 weeks, this is difficult to interpret, since weight was also declining somewhat during the 5-week base-line period. Follow-up data is rather impressive. Approximately 11 months after treatment had begun, the first group had lost an average of 35 pounds, and the second an average of 21 pounds.

Hall (1972) compared the effectiveness of a standard self-control procedure (including coverant control) with a procedure wherein the experimenter provided up to $20 for the purchase of a reinforcing item "symbolizing weight loss." At the beginning of treatment, $5 was provided, with the remaining $15 given to the subject if she met the weight-loss goal at the end of a 5-week period. Half the subjects participated in the first procedure for 5 weeks, and the second for the remaining 5, with the order of treatment reversed for the remaining subjects. In general, subjects tended to lose more weight (approximately 1 pound per week) under the monetary incentive condition, although the average of about .6 lbs. per week under self-control is not inconsistent with previous findings. Unfortunately, no statistical comparisons are presented. Improvement tended to be maintained at a relatively brief 1-month follow-up. Since all subjects received both treatments, it is not possible to determine which treatment by itself would have led to the most long-term benefit.

Mahoney, Moura, and Wade (1973) assigned overweight subjects to five groups. All subjects initially deposited $10, which was refundable at the conclusion of treatment, 4 weeks later. The self-reward group contributed another $11. At each of seven weigh-ins, they awarded themselves a portion of this money, the amount being a function of weight lost, as well as the degree to which they had been engaging in thoughts and behaviors related to weight loss. The self-punishment group began with a portion of money that was returned to the experimenter when weight was not lost or when the subject failed to engage in related thoughts and behaviors. A third group engaged in both self-reward and self-punishment, combining the above conditions. A fourth group merely recorded weight and adaptive and maladaptive eating habits; and a fifth group, an information-control group, received the same stimulus-control booklet given other groups, but underwent no additional treatment.

Only the self-reward group lost significantly more weight (6.4 pounds) than the self-monitoring and information-control groups (0.8 lbs. and 1.4 pounds respectively). At a 4-month follow-up, both self-reward subjects and subjects who had engaged in self-reward plus self-punishment had lost significantly more weight (11.5 pounds and 12.0 pounds) than the two control groups (4.5 pounds and 3.2 pounds.) These results point to the importance of self-reinforcement in the treatment of obesity, while at the same time calling into question the value of self-punishment.

The results of self-control studies concerned with obesity have not been uniformly positive. For example, Tyler and Straughan (1970) compared the effectiveness of coverant control with Mees's (1966) breath-holding technique. The latter technique requires that the subject imagine some tempting food and then hold his breath for a period of time. The seven, hourly treatment sessions, spread over 9 weeks, led to only nominal weight loss for both groups, comparable to a third, non-treated control group. Treatment was administered in groups. If equal numbers were assigned to each group (the authors are not clear on this), treatment would have involved dealing with 19 subjects simultaneously. Groups of this size might not have been conducive to providing adequate levels of individual attention, perhaps accounting for the negative results.

Harris and Bruner (1971) compared the effectiveness of eight sessions of instruction in self-control (almost identical to Harris, 1969) with a contract treatment similar to the Mahoney et al. (1973) self-reinforcement condition. After making an initial deposit, the subjects received 50 cents or one dollar for each pound lost, until all the money was refunded. At the end of treatment, the self-control subjects had lost an average of 7.4 pounds, compared with 13.4 pounds for the contract group (the difference was significant). However, by the end of a 10-

month follow-up, net weight loss was down to 3.5 pounds for the self-control subjects while the contract group had actually gained 2.75 pounds. A second study compared self-control with an attention-control group. Both groups showed negligible weight losses, a finding inconsistent with previous reports.

In conclusion, the results of the majority of the studies employing self-control procedures with obese subjects have been positive. Although Harris and Bruner (1971) found the initial improvement was lost over the 1-year follow-up, Stuart (1967, 1971) found that his subjects continued to lose weight over prolonged periods of time. While motivation is built into the self-control regimen, the individual inclined toward obesity is presented with omnipresent temptation. It may be that a series of "maintenance" treatments (Stuart, 1967) could provide whatever increments in motivation (and technical knowledge) necessary to overcome this temptation.

Self-Control Techniques Applied to Other Problem Areas.   Cigarette smoking, like overeating, is widespread, is clearly a health hazard, and is not readily eliminated through psychological interventions.

A potentially misleading aspect of the research findings pertaining to smoking is that significant reductions are often reported. However, as reviews by Keutzer *et al.* (1968), and Bernstein (1969) have pointed out, when several treatments are compared (including a placebo condition in some instances), subjects in each condition show approximately the same rate of reduction (see Keutzer, 1968; Koenig & Masters, 1965; Ober, 1966; Janis & Miller, 1968). That this short-term gain may be appreciable in magnitude is seen in a study by Lawson and May (1970), which compared covert sensitization, coverant control, contractual management, and a nondirective supportive treatment. At the end of the 5-week treatment period, subjects in all conditions were smoking at the rate of approximately 30% of base line. The most parsimonious interpretation of these and other findings is that smoking rate is highly sensitive to nonspecific factors of a placebo nature. If this is so, one would expect a high rate of relapse, given a long-term follow-up, which is precisely what Bernstein (1968) found, using follow-ups of 5–16 weeks. As Bernstein (1969) has noted, such long-term follow-ups are rare in smoking research, in spite of the fact that they are crucial if the findings are to have any practical significance.

Even when it seems clear that the specific treatment contributed to smoking reduction, there is no guarantee that the effects will endure. Powell and Azrin (1968) provided three smokers with a special cigarette case that delivered painful electric shock when opened. Six subjects had volunteered, but three dropped out before the shock contingency was put into effect). For all three subjects, the hourly rate of cigarette consumption decreased as shock intensity increased. However, after shock was removed, smoking returned to base-line level. Also, there was a tendency for subjects not to wear the shock apparatus at high levels of shock.

These same authors (Azrin & Powell, 1968) offer a second procedure that appears to hold more promise than the former. Here, heavy smokers were provided with a cigarette case that automatically locked after a cigarette was taken. Duration of the interval was gradually increased to about 1 hour, over periods ranging from 7 to 13 weeks. At the end of the experiment, each of the five subjects was smoking no more than one-half the original number of cigarettes (about 12 per day). Two of the participants underwent a brief control procedure involving another locking cigarette case for which they (and not the experimenter) set the duration of the interval. Cigarette consumption did not decrease when the control device was used. Although smoking rate returned to its original level immediately after the imposed delay was eliminated, it is significant that subjects did continue in the experiment until the goal of 1-hour delays was met (7–13 weeks). The subjects apparently did not find the procedure particularly aversive, and continued use might well have resulted in maintenance of the improvement noted. The special cigarette case might prove to be particularly useful as part of a broader self-control program. For instance, the individual who chain smokes only when he reads or writes (or when, by prior agreement, he is seated in his "smoking chair") might experience a substantial reduction in smoking were he to use the case at such times.

Another study, demonstrating improvement over and above that found for a placebo condition, is reported by Sachs, Bean, and Morrow (1970). Treatments included self-control that required subjects to discontinue smoking in successively more difficult situations, covert sensitization, and an attention placebo that involved a discussion of smoking records, stressing the importance of awareness of smoking patterns. By the third week, a significant treatment effect was found. Whereas the base-line rate of smoking was approximately 16 for all groups, the covert-sensitization group now averaged 3.5, the self-control group averaged 5.6, and the placebo group showed a mean of 11.0 cigarettes per day. At a 1-month follow-up, the comparable means were 6.9, 8.9, and 13.5, with both covert-sensitization and self-control conditions still significantly below the base-line rate, no longer true for the attention-placebo group. It is of interest that at both 3 weeks and at the follow-up, five of the eight covert-sensitization subjects were abstinent, whereas none of the self-control subjects were down to no cigarettes per day. Given the nature of the respective treatments, it is not surprising that the self-control subjects showed a more gradual change in smoking behavior. Also, it should be pointed out that the self-control regimen used by Sachs *et al.* (1970) is very limited, considering the many self-control measures available. As a whole, the results of this study are promising, although, as the authors point out, the participants initially were not heavy smokers.

Chapman, Smith, and Layden (1971) provided subjects with extensive aversive conditioning (electric shock), along with instruction in self-control. The latter included engaging in emotional statements pertaining to dangers of smoking, and advantages of not smoking, stimulus narrowing, individual instruction for situations where smoking was most likely, changing to a least-preferred brand, role playing in how to refuse cigarettes, and engaging in competing responses. At the end of the 5-day treatment, 11 of 12 subjects were not smoking at all. However, at a 1-month follow-up, only a third of the subjects were still abstinent. A second experiment differed from the first chiefly in that a longer post-treatment monitoring period was employed. That is, subjects in the first experiment had agreed to record daily consumption of cigarettes for 3 weeks, whereas in the second, the period was extended to 12 weeks. Also, subjects in the second experiment were told that treatment would continue until no smoking had occurred for 48 consecutive hours. Considering the aversive conditioning involved, this might have been a potent motivator. Only 1 of the 11 subjects was still smoking at the end of treatment. At a 3-month follow-up, 9 of 11 were abstinent, and at 12 months, 6 of 11 were abstinent. While the results of the second study appear to be rather promising, interpretation would have been facilitated by the inclusion of adequate control groups. Although the authors stress the role of aversive conditioning, they provide no means for assessing its relative contribution. One positive feature is the use of observers other than the subjects themselves as a check on the reliability of the subjects' reported rate of smoking.

Given the findings we have just reported, it is not possible to come to any firm conclusion regarding the value of self-control procedures in producing long-term reductions in smoking. While certain findings (see Sachs *et al.*, 1970) are clearly suggestive, additional research is needed. Perhaps the most compelling reason for believing in the self-control approach is that many, many people have succeeded in giving up smoking voluntarily (that is, in the absence of obvious, direct coercion, and when no external agent was likely to dispense immediate and powerful rewards for abstinence). Surely, in such cases, techniques somewhat akin to those reported earlier in the chapter must have been employed. Detailed interviews with such individuals might provide much in the way of valuable information.

The case histories presented by Fox (1962) and Goldiamond (1965), and the studies of Lovitt and Curtiss (1969) and Glynn (1970) (reported in previous sections) suggest that academic performance may be improved through self-control procedures, In a further investigation, Beneke and Harris (1972) provided college students with a self-control program similar to that described in the method section. One group of subjects participated in biweekly group meetings, with 1 lesson presented per session, through 11 sessions. A second group was instructed to work on the 11 sessions on their own. Sessions dealt with stimulus control, reinforcement, the SQ3R method (described earlier in the chapter), taking effective lecture notes, and examination skills. The principal response measure was change in grade-point average. A significant relation was found between number of sessions completed and grade-point average, with subjects completing zero sessions losing 0.02 points, subjects in the one- to six-session category gaining 0.15 points, and subjects in the seven- (or more) session category gaining .78 points (on a 4-point system, with A equal to 4 points). These figures are based upon performance during three consecutive semesters following treatment. No significant differences were found between individual and group subjects. These results are certainly suggestive, although lack of adequate controls makes it impossible to rule out the role of motivational factors in accounting for the relationship between sessions completed and academic improvement. As the authors point out, a major problem encountered in their study was the high dropout rate (only 17% completed all 11 sessions). Greater incentives for continued participation might have improved the outcome.

Rehm and Marston (1968) experimentally investigated the effects of a self-control technique on a population of college males who reported anxiety in connection with meeting and dating girls. One group of subjects engaged in a self-reinforcement procedure, wherein they awarded themselves varying numbers of points, according to the degree of *in vivo* approach-behavior manifested. Treatment goals were individualized, with zero points awarded when obvious avoidance or escape occurred, with the maximum number of points (3) awarded when the subject rated his performance as good. Tasks were undertaken in hierarchical fashion, with one level of difficulty attempted per week. One control group received nondirective low-level interpretation, while a second control group received no therapy. Instead, each week they were questioned as to how they viewed their problem, whether change had occurred, and how they were working on their problem. On two measures of anxiety and verbal output associated with the subject's response to taped situations involving interaction with girls, subjects in the self-reinforcement condition (that is, self-control) showed significantly more improvement than the control subjects, although the differences were not great. On a questionnaire asking the subject to rate anticipated discomfort for a variety of relevant interactions, self-reward subjects showed significantly greater reductions in discomfort than did control subjects. Similar results were obtained on a measure of general anxiety (the Manifest Anxiety Scale). Also, subjects in the self-reinforcement condition showed significantly more dating behavior than the control subjects. In general, the results tended to hold up at a follow-up 7–9 months later. We would not necessarily recommend a self-control approach to problems of this nature, in view of the availability of other techniques such as assertive training (Chapter III) and desensitization (Chapter II).

In this section, we have presented experimental evidence dealing with self-control approaches to obesity, smoking, academic behavior, and social interactions. The findings on obesity would seem to be the most encouraging, perhaps because this problem area has been researched somewhat more thoroughly. Clearly, in all areas, more well-controlled research is needed if self-control methodology is to be provided with the sound scientific foundation associated with certain other behavior therapy approaches, such as systematic desensitization. In particular, research is needed that is aimed at assessing the value of the many treatment components found in the typical self-control program.

VIII

Extinction Procedures

In this chapter we discuss a number of techniques designed to eliminate or reduce the frequency of problem behaviors. We use the term *extinction* to describe the elimination of such behaviors, and it should be noted that this usage is not totally true to the most accepted definition of the process of extinction as it is differentiated from other, topologically similar processes (such as *response suppression*). Extinction refers to the reduction in frequency of a behavior as a function of occurrences that are nonreinforced (Woodworth & Schlosberg, 1954). By this definition, techniques such as *response prevention* or *extinction via contingency management* (in which managers are trained to avoid reinforcing problem behaviors) qualify as extinction techniques; other techniques, on the other hand, such as *negative practice* and, possibly, *satiation,* appear more interpretable in terms of their capability to *suppress* the performance of problem behaviors while not actually promoting any "unlearning."

There are a number of techniques that promote the reduction in frequency of problem behaviors that we discuss elsewhere in the text: 1) desensitization may be interpreted to reduce the frequency of avoidance behaviors (in this chapter we discuss *graduated extinction* and aspects of *implosive therapy,* both of which bear some resemblance to desensitization); 2) the contingent use of punishment reduces the frequency of problem behaviors by suppression (in this chapter negative practice and satiation may be interpreted to work in this way also); and 3) modeling with guided participation eliminates avoidance behavior and resembles the procedures of both systematic desensitization and graduated extinction. Clearly, then, the factor unifying the techniques presented here is the elimination of problem behaviors, even though the theoretical rationales vary considerably. We discuss seven basic procedures: extinction by contingency management procedures, graduated extinction, covert extinction, negative practice, stimulus satiation, implosive therapy, and flooding, or response prevention.

Contingency Management

In many ways the simplest and most direct procedures for extinguishing problem behaviors involve contingency management (see Chapters V and VI). In these procedures, contingent reinforcers that appear to be maintaining the problem behaviors are eliminated, typically by instructing the social agents in the individual's environment to change their patterns of reinforcing behaviors toward the individual under treatment. An ancillary procedure that is often employed involves the simultaneous reinforcement of an alternative, more acceptable behavior, perhaps with the same reinforcers as those which previously maintained the problem behavior. As we discuss Chapters V, VI, and IX, on contingency management, contingency management in institutional settings, and aversive control, it is usually preferable to include the shaping of alternative responses in order to enhance the individual's repertoire of appropriate behaviors, so that he continues to have behaviors that will elicit the customary, valued reinforcers from the environment.

The Withdrawal of Contingent Reinforcement

The literature contains few instances of the use of contingent reinforcement alone, since this procedure involves no specification of alternative behaviors. In some instances, however, it is clear that the person being treated is already capable of the performance of alternative, more appropriate behaviors, and it is expected that no "behavioral vacuum" is likely to be created by the extinction of the problem behavior. In one instance, extinction procedures were applied to the aggressive, demanding, dependency behaviors exhibited by a young boy (Williams, 1959, 1962). These behaviors had developed during an extensive illness during which the child required special care and attention. In this particular case, after the child recovered from his illness, the parents attempted to extinguish these behaviors by withdrawing some of the attention he had previously enjoyed. The child, however, protested so intensely that the parents were forced to continue the excessive attention and, by yielding to the boy's demands, may have inadvertently reinforced the increased intensity of his protests. In treating the child's bedtime tantrums (Williams, 1959), the parents were instructed to put the child to bed each night in a calm fashion and, once all bedtime routines were completed and there were obviously no problems, to ignore his subsequent raging protests. As depicted in Figure 8.1, the tantrums disappeared in very short order—a matter of days.

The reader will note that for the tantrums at bedtime, there is an alternative "behavior," namely going to sleep, which is clearly in the child's behavior repertoire; this alternative behavior made it unnecessary to specify and reinforce some other behavior as an alternative to the tantrums.

In treating other disruptive demanding behaviors, such as food throwing at mealtimes, the parents were instructed to remove the child from his high-chair whenever he intentionally spilled or threw food (Williams, 1962). Although the child had to be removed from the table 12 times consecutively, at the initiation of this treatment regimen, the food-throwing behavior was entirely extinguished within 7 meals. Here, of course, eating was the logical alternative behavior, again, one that was within the child's repertoire.

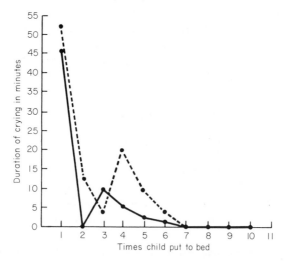

Figure 8.1   Duration of crying in two successive extinction programs (●——●: first extinction; ●– – –●: second extinction). From Williams, 1959.

In executing any program of behavior extinction, the procedures must be assiduously and consistently employed if they are to be effective. This is well illustrated by the case described above. Some time after the bedtime tantrum behaviors were extinguished, the child received some attention from an aunt when he mildly protested being put to bed, and the bedtime raging was soon completely reinstated. A second extinction procedure was conducted, with, as shown in Figure 8.1, rapid success. One should remain mindful, however, that the permanence of an extinction procedure relies on the *continued nonreinforcement* of random occurrences of the problem behavior. Thus, all individuals who come in contact with the patient must be instructed in the management of their own reinforcing behavior, and each individual must be consistent in his continued avoidance of inadvertent reinforcement of the behavior under treatment.

In another case, Walton (1960) treated a woman suffering from neurodermatitis, which was maintained by her persistent scratching of her skin. The condition was one of long standing, and the scratching appeared to be reinforced by the attention the patient received because of her skin disorder. For example, her fiancé frequently helped the patient apply ointments to the irritated areas. The family members and fiancé were instructed to ignore all aspects of the dermatitis and to cease their ministrations to the patient. The scratching behavior was extinguished, and by the end of 3 months the neurodermatitis had disappeared completely. There was no recurrence over a 4-year follow-up.

Finally, Ayllon and Haughton (1964) treated excessive somatic complaints of two hospitalized patients. Figure 8.2 shows the course of extinction for these behaviors in each of the two patients. In order to test the efficacy of the extinction procedures, periods of ignoring the somatic complaints were alternated with periods during which the complaints were reinforced. The effects were striking. In both cases the complaints declined sharply when they went unreinforced. In the case of the patient whose behavior is recorded in Figure 8.2a, the slight rise in frequency during the final extinction period occurred when she was visited by a relative who presumably attended to the psychotic verbalizations.

Clearly, there are two primary processes in the establishment of an extinction regimen: 1) determining the effective, maintaining reinforcers and 2) manipulation of the behavior of agents who appear to be delivering the reinforcers that maintain the problem behavior. The latter, of course, is a problem of training contingency managers (see Chapter VI). Determining the maintaining reinforcers is also considered in Chapter V, but it deserves special mention here. Often behaviors that are candidates for extinction have been on a schedule of supposed punishment by parents, teachers, friends, colleagues, etc. In truth, however, the verbal reprimands, glaring looks, or whatever stimuli the agents considered

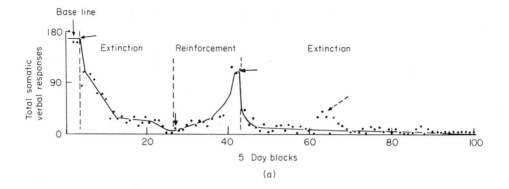

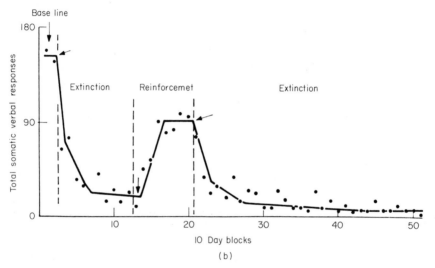

Figure 8.2   Frequency of somatic complaints during a base-line period and when such complaints were ignored or rewarded with attention: two patients. For one patient, the temporary increase in somatic complaints (noted by the arrows) in the final extinction period occurred at the time of a visit by a relative. From Ayllon and Haughton, 1964.

aversive may have been the reinforcers that maintained the behavior. In an example discussed later in the chapter, Madsen, Becker, Thomas, Koser, and Plager (1968) demonstrated that children who exhibited disruptive behavior in the classroom by standing, actually stood up *less* when the teachers were instructed to *cease* their exhortations for the children to "sit down!" and instead ignore the standing behavior (the reader may wish to refer to Figure 8.3).

The Withdrawal of Contingent Reinforcement and the Reinforcement of Alternative Behaviors

As we noted earlier, it is fairly unlikely that an extinction program will include only the elimination of reinforcement without the concurrent shaping of alternative behaviors which are appropriate. As with the use of punishment in the elimination of problem behavior (see Chapter IX), the provision of an alternative response is likely to increase the effectiveness of other procedures for the elimination of problem behaviors. A good example of this is contained in the study by Madsen *et al.* (1968) that was cited earlier. In treating behaviors disruptive of classroom decorum, these authors instructed teachers to ignore children's standing behavior, rather than attempting to control it with punitive reprimands and commands to "sit down!" As indicated by Figure 8.3, periods when the teachers ignored the problem behaviors were characterized by a lower likelihood of such behaviors. However, when teachers were later instructed to praise the alternative, desired behavior of sitting down, the rate of standing was lowest of all.

Ayllon and his colleagues (Ayllon & Michael, 1959; Ayllon & Haughton, 1964) reported many examples of the effectiveness of rein-

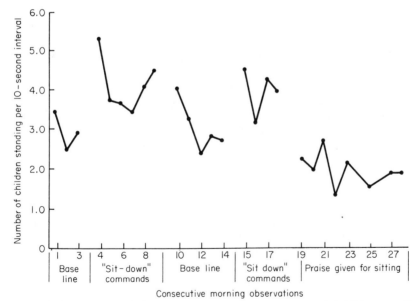

Figure 8.3 Extinction of positively reinforced behavior. Number of children standing during class time: base-line periods, periods when standing received verbal admonishment, and periods when incompatible behavior was positively reinforced. Madsen *et al.*, 1968.

forcement withdrawal and the shaping of alternative responses in the control of problem behaviors. In one case, (Ayllon & Michael, 1959), a female patient's psychotic verbalizations appeared to be maintained despite verbal and physical punishment (from other patients), simply because the nurses often listened carefully to these strange verbalizations in an attempt to "get at the roots of her problems." When the nurses were instructed not to attend to the psychotic talk and, simultaneously, to reinforce any verbalizations that made sense, the percentage of verbalizations that were clearly psychotic declined from 91% to less than 25%.

Ayllon and Haughton (1964) treated the psychotic verbalizations exhibited by three female patients by instructing ward staff to withhold social and tangible reinforcement from these patients whenever they were engaging in psychotic talk. Figure 8.4 shows the effectiveness of this extinction regimen for one of these patients. Initially, the staff was instructed

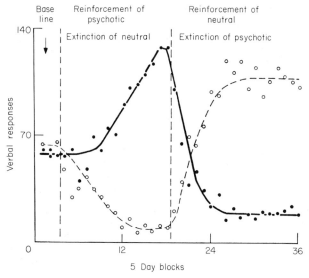

Figure 8.4 Influence of reinforcement or extinction of psychotic talk upon incidence of neutral speech and the influence of reinforcement or extinction of neutral speech upon the incidence of psychotic talk (●——●: psychotic verbal response; ○——○: neutral verbal response). From Ayllon and Haughton, 1964.

to reinforce psychotic verbalizations and to ignore, look bored, etc., whenever more normal verbalizations were occurring. Then, to demonstrate the effectiveness of these contingencies, they were to reverse the procedure, ignoring the problem verbalizations and attending to the normal ones. It is clear from the frequencies shown in Figure 8.4 that these procedures were effective in increasing normal talk and extinguishing psychotic verbalizations.

Graduated Extinction

Graduated extinction is a technique designed to eliminate avoidance and fearful behaviors by the gradual reexposure of the individual to the fear-evoking stimuli. The careful reader will note the similarity of this procedure to that of desensitization (Chapter II) and to the techniques of implosion and flooding, or response prevention, discussed later in this chapter. Graduated extinction differs from these procedures in several ways. For example, there is no competing response that comes to replace the response of anxiety; while desensitization, at least by one interpretation (Wolpe, 1958, 1969), proposes that relaxation provides a competing response to anxiety and arousal. Similarly, there is no assumption of psychodynamic determinants as there is in the theorizing behind implosive therapy, nor is any specific care taken to prevent avoidance responses or to direct the treatment procedure only to behaviors that are presumed to have been acquired via the process of avoidance conditioning [see the discussion of implosive and (flooding) response-prevention therapies].

Actually, graduated extinction may be seen as a technique of response prevention in which fearful, avoidance responses are not prevented by physically restraining the individual or by having him recreate fearful stimuli and situations in his imagination without, at the same time, avoiding or escaping from them. Rather, graduated extinction proceeds by the systematic presentation of aversive stimuli, beginning with extremely weak versions that do not elicit avoidance or defensive behavior and gradually moving on to more aversive scenes; avoidance behavior may be prevented by always presenting stimuli that are too weak to elicit the avoidance behavior. After minimally aversive stimuli have been presented, it is assumed that slightly more aversive stimuli will no longer elicit the avoidance behaviors, although if presented initially, avoidance would have occurred (Bandura, 1969). An alternative interpretation states that the initial presentations of minimally aversive stimuli allow for the occurrence of behaviors that are alternatives to avoidance behaviors, and that these competing responses are likely to generalize to other situations and complex stimuli that are somewhat more aversive (Bandura, 1969).

The use of the graduated-extinction technique is not new. Herzberg (1941) treated a patient suffering from agoraphobia of such intensity that she refused to leave the house alone. Treatment initially consisted of assigning the woman to walk by herself in a park, a sort of outing she did not fear greatly. The settings for her walks were gradually expanded to streets, first quiet and then busy ones, until finally she was able to walk almost anywhere she wished without experiencing her previously debilitating anxieties. There have been several other reports of the successful use of this technique with patients suffering from agoraphobias (Jones, 1956; Meyer, 1957; White, 1962).

Grossberg (1965) treated a woman who was unable to complete graduation requirements from college because she was unable to complete a required public-speaking course. Prior to treatment by graduated extinction she had received tranquilizers, group therapy with other individuals troubled by speech phobias, and 30 hours of individual psychotherapy. Grossberg treated the problem with 17 sessions, during which the woman faced progressively larger audiences and delivered speeches that gradually became longer and longer. Indeed, in the beginning the patient merely read passages from books to the therapist alone, both in his office and in a small empty classroom. Gradually an audience was introduced, and on different sessions the classrooms in which the speeches were delivered were varied to induce greater generalization (other generalization-encouraging procedures included having the patient imagine she was speaking to her public-speaking class). The patient first sought treatment after she was required to deliver a 1-minute speech; after treatment she was able to complete six required speeches, and she received a B in the speech class.

The details of the process of designing a graduated-extinction program need not be specified further. In essence, this technique requires only that the therapist be adept in devising a series of behavior prescriptions, systematically arranged in a hierarchy that proceeds from behaviors so minimally anxiety provoking or inhibiting that they can be performed with reasonable ease to behaviors successively more anxiety provoking.

There has been very little research on the use of graduated extinction other than that which can be drawn from the literature on systematic desensitization (see Chapter II). Often in studies of component factors within the desensitization procedure, a control condition is included that involves the presentation of the serialized hierarchy of anxiety-provoking stimuli in the absence of relaxation instructions. The results of such studies, as they reflect upon the efficacy of a graduated-extinction procedure, are mixed. The reader should note that studies such as these are generally concerned with the extinction of fear responses to *imagined stimuli* and not with the extinction of fear to the actual performance of *behaviors*. Davison (1968) found that snake phobics who were administered the same hierarchy of items as those imagined by desensitization subjects, but without relaxation instructions, showed smaller decrements in fear and would not approach the feared object as closely as would desensitized subjects. Krapfl (1967), also studying snake-phobic subjects, found no difference between a variety of treatment conditions immediately following treatment, but after a 6-week follow-up period, desensitization and graduated exposure to stimuli (graduated extinction) produced greater approach responses than did the random presentation of fear-provoking items or two control procedures.

The results of several studies (Davison, 1968; Schubot, 1966) indicate that the graduated presentation of stimuli produces greater levels of anxiety in subjects than does desensitization (graduated presentation of stimuli, coupled with relaxation). It must be remembered again that these studies are concerned with stimuli, and not responses. The finding that anxiety levels are greater when relaxation is omitted may imply that treatment via graduated extinction should proceed even more carefully, methodically, and slowly than the presentation of the hierarchy in systematic desensitization. Indeed, this caution may be responsible for the negative findings reported by Davison (1968). In this study, the speed with which subjects were able to advance through the hierarchy in the desensitization condition determined how rapidly subjects were advanced through the hierarchies in the graduated-extinction condition. Thus, the desensitization condition was tailored to the individual subjects, while the graduated extinction one was not, and progress in the latter condition may have been too rapid.

There are a number of studies with animals that indicate the potential effectiveness of graduated extinction. It has been clearly shown that graduated exposure to aversive stimuli produces a more rapid elimination of emotional responding than if they are presented at full intensity, without any graduated introduction (Kimball & Kendall, 1953; Poppen, 1968). A stimulus that elicits one response (for example, anxiety) can come to evoke an entirely different response if it is initially imbedded in the context of a number of other stimuli that evoke the new response—and then these latter stimuli are gradually removed until only the new stimulus remains (Terrace, 1966).

Poppen (1970) compared a number of procedures, including graduated counterconditioning (similar to desensitization, but with a competing response other than relaxation), graduated extinction, flooding, nongraduated counterconditioning and regular extinction, in terms of their efficacy for reducing the inhibition of rats to press a bar after such pressing had been punished by shock. In this experiment, the treatment procedures were carried out as follows. Initially, a tone was paired with shock so that eventually it alone would suppress a bar-pressing response. In the graduated-extinction condition, subjects heard the tone initially at quite a low intensity, then the intensity was gradually increased. In the graduated-counterconditioning condition-only group, the tone was presented at its full intensity (used during training) and was accompanied by food rewards. And in the flooding procedure, the aversive stimulus was presented at its full intensity for durations of 10 minutes at a time. The effects of these various treatments are shown in Figure 8.5.

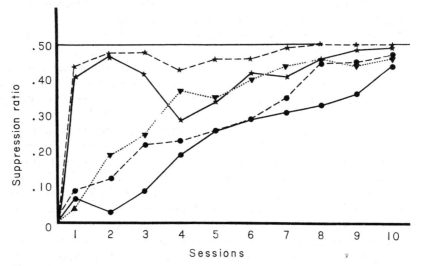

Figure 8.5 Recovery from response suppression displayed by subjects in each of 5 treatment conditions during 10 extinction sessions. Suppression ratio: a value of 0 indicates complete suppression of the response, and a value of .5 indicates freedom from response inhibition (★– – –★: graduated counterconditioning; ★——★: graduated extinction; ▼······▼: flooding; ●– – –●: counterconditioning; ●——●: regular extinction). From Poppen, 1970.

The regular extinction procedure was least effective in producing rapid recovery of the suppressed response. Graduated extinction and graduated counterconditioning both showed the most rapid alleviation of the response suppression, and each produced the greatest improvement in the very first session. Only after 10 sessions had the other techniques come to produce equivalent amounts of release from the response suppression induced by the prior aversive experience.

Covert Extinction

Covert extinction is one of a "family" of techniques in which the reinforcing, nonreinforcing, or punitive consequences to a behavior are imagined. Covert sensitization, a technique discussed in Chapter IX, involves the imagination of a problem behavior and a noxious or aversive correlate that persists in imagination as long as the problem behavior is imagined to be occurring. *Covert positive reinforcement* (Cautela, Steffen, & Wish, 1970; Cautela, Walsh, & Wish, 1971; Flannery, 1970; Kropp, 1971) requires that the patient imagine a behavior and then that he be reinforced for it. *Covert negative reinforcement* requires that a patient imagine himself to be in an anxiety-provoking situation and then, just as the anxiety peaks, shift to an imagined scene in which he is performing a behavior, the frequency of which is to be increased. For example, a client might imagine he is tied to a chair with a snake about to strike and then, when this image is vivid and truly anxiety provoking, he shifts to a scene in which he is delivering a public address before a large audience. Clearly, this is a procedure of covert, or imaginal, avoidance conditioning.

Covert extinction requires the client to imagine himself performing a problem behavior and then to imagine that a common reinforcing stimulus does *not* occur. Thus, covertly, the client "performs" behaviors in the absence of contingent reinforcement, conditions that have been shown to be effective in promoting the extinction of overt behaviors. Like systematic desensitization, implosive therapy, and other behavior therapy techniques involving the patient's imagination, covert extinction initially includes the therapist's verbal descriptions of scenes to be imagined. Initially, the client may be told the rationale behind extinction procedures, that his problem behavior is being maintained by reinforcement from the environment, and that treatment will involve the elimination of that reinforcement in the imagination (Cautela, 1971). Then, the client will be given several covert-extinction trials in the office and given "homework" assignments, trials he is to perform by himself between sessions.

To take an example, a client who complains of stuttering in social situations may be asked first to imagine that he is in a common situation, that he stutters, and that the stuttering evokes no response from others:

You are sitting in your school cafeteria. Choose a place in which you usually sit. (Pause) You can hear and see students walking around, eating and talking. (Pause) You are eating your favorite lunch. (Pause) There is an empty seat near you. (Pause) A pretty blonde girl comes over and asks you if she can sit down. (Pause) You stammer, 'Ya..ya..ya..yes.' She absolutely reacts in no way to your stuttering [Cautela, 1971, p. 193–194].

After the client has gone through the total scene he may be quizzed to determine if the scene was vivid and real. Then he may be asked to imagine it on his own, without the therapist's verbal descriptions. He is asked to signal the therapist, for example, by raising the little finger on one hand, when the scene is finished, and the therapist may again ask about its clarity (Cautela, 1971).

Guided by laboratory evidence that extinction is most rapid when extinction trials are massed (Pavlov, 1927; Lawson, 1960), it is proposed that each therapy session have as many as 20 imagined scenes, 10 with the therapist verbalizing the scene, 10 with the client on his own. Furthermore, the client is required to practice the scene 10 times each night at home and to modify the scene on some trials, to encourage extinction effects in a variety of situations. These procedures are justified by reference to laboratory studies of the effects of massed practice, distributed practice (Pavlov, 1927), generalization of extinction (Kimble, 1961), and secondary extinction (Pavlov, 1927). However, these citations appear to be post hoc, and there have been no studies indicating the effectiveness of these various procedures, although they do seem reasonable. Actual clinical sessions are usually concentrated upon specific important situations involving the problem behavior until all such common situations have been covered. To continue Cautela's example, a stutterer may be given scenes "such as stuttering in response to a professor's question, stuttering whenever the patient is asked directions, and stuttering over the phone (in this case, he is assured that there is absolutely no reaction on the other end) [Cautela, 1971, p. 194]."

Covert extinction has been proposed as a behavior therapy only recently (Cautela, 1971), and there has been little research on its effectiveness and extremely few case studies. Cautela (1971) has given the following examples of scenes utilized in the treatment of a variety of problem behaviors:

1. A hospitalized patient was considered functionally blind, i.e., he claimed he could not see, but observation by a number of individuals indicated that the patient had almost normal vision. . . . Evidently, many situations had become . . . discriminative stimuli . . . for not focusing on a particular object, since not focusing was reinforced by helping behavior. The staff was advised to tell the patient that even though he did not realize it, he was being made helpless by people paying attention to him when he was stumbling around, etc. A staff member presented scenes to the patient in which he was to imagine that he was stumbling over or couldn't find a chair, but that no one helped him or talked to him.

2. In a training school, a boy's disruptive behavior was reinforced by the laughter of his classmates and the attention of his teacher. . . . In the case described here, the teacher and students would not cooperate with the therapist by ignoring the boy's disruptive behavior. Therefore, covert extinction was employed. The boy was asked to imagine performing the disruptive behavior, but no one noticed him. The disruptive behavior was eliminated in three weeks.

3. In many cases of multiple phobias, the husband, wife, or parents of the patient cannot follow the instructions not to reinforce certain behavior because they feel it would be cruel or that the patient would become angry. In these cases, the patients are asked to imagine that they are expressing the phobic behavior, but that no reinforcement is provided by others. The following is a typical example of treatment of fear of being left alone:

You are home with your husband. He says he wants to go bowling. You tell him you don't want him to go because you are afraid of being left alone. But he says, "I'm sorry. I'm going anyway." and he leaves you alone.

4. A homosexual who was reinforced for going into "gay" bars by admiring glances and approaches by other homosexuals was given the following scene:

I want you to imagine you are walking into your favorite bar. You hear the music and the noise of talking and glasses tinkling. You expect to be noticed, but no one notices you. They all act as if you weren't even there. It seems very strange . . . they pay no attention to you at all. This procedure can be combined with covert sensitization toward sexual urges toward males. [p. 195–196].[1]

Although covert extinction is a technique of recent derivation and thus far generally untested, it is included in this discussion because of the strong evidence that other techniques involving imagined stimuli (systematic desensitization, implosive therapy, covert sensitization; see Chapter X on cognitive methods) are effective in the modification of problem behaviors. Clearly, the technique awaits empirical validation, as do other covert-treatment procedures such as covert positive reinforcement and covert negative reinforcement. In the available evidence (clinical case studies), there is no indication of any ill effects consequent upon the use of covert-extinction procedures, although it is conceivable that there might be some. For example, if an individual's stuttering is provoked by the anticipation of other people's response, that portion of the covert-extinction scene describing the initial social encounter and consequent stuttering might so sensitize the individual that he would find it difficult to imagine the nonresponse of that other person. Implied here is the possibility of a hierarchical covert-extinction procedure, although this possibility has received no attention in the literature as yet. For the time being, covert extinction is probably a technique the behavior therapist should have in his armamentarium, but it remains for future research to clarify the true extent of its effectiveness.

Negative Practice

Theoretically there might be some discussion as to whether *negative practice* constitutes a technique designed to extinguish (as opposed to

---

[1] Reprinted from Cautela, J. R. Covert extinction. *Behavior Therapy*, 1971, **2**, 192–200. Copyright 1971 by Academic Press and reprinted by permission.

suppress) behaviors. Nonetheless, it is one that has often been employed to eliminate small motor behaviors, usually tics, without the prominent establishment of some observable alternative response. Consequently we include it in our discussion of extinction procedures.

In 1932, Knight Dunlap published a book entitled *Habits, Their Making and Unmaking,* in which he propounded a treatment procedure for the elimination of small motor habits that had become problematic. The technique ran quite clearly against "common sense" in that Dunlap proposed practicing the behaviors, not to perfect their performance, but to eliminate them; hence the term *negative* practice. Actually, in Dunlap's original presentation of the technique and reports of successful application, negative practice was not limited to small motor acts such as tics and stuttering (to which its application is generally limited today), but included the treatment of enuresis, homosexuality, and masturbation, as well as tics, typing errors, stuttering, and speech blocking.

Theoretical and empirical support for the procedure of *massing practice* in order to extinguish behaviors came primarily from a different source, experimental psychology (Hull, 1943). Hull proposed that one consequence of the repeated performance of a behavior is the build-up of fatigue, which was aversive to the organism. On the other hand, one consequence of any rest period is the dissipation of this fatigue, which was pleasurable and thus constituted a negative reinforcer (see Chapter V). The fatigue and other aversive events associated with practice eventually predispose the organism to inhibit further practice (reactive inhibition) and since the aversive effects of fatigue and boredom occur *simultaneously* with the performance of the practiced behavior, they become conditioned to them (classical conditioning), thus attaching aversive properties to the behaviors themselves (conditioned inhibition). Since reactive inhibition (fatigue) dissipates after the practiced behavior is ceased, the negative reinforcement of such dissipation is paired with the "act" of "not-performing-the-practiced-response." Thus, lengthy practice produces inhibition of the practiced behavior and reinforces the "habit" of *not* responding. Consequently, extensive practice may eventually eliminate the behavior practiced.

Within his theory of behavior, Hull hypothesized the construct of *reactive inhibition,* symbolized I_r. Since I_r builds up as a function of the repeated performance of an act, Hull proposed that by the process of classical conditioning, the response of inhibition might become conditioned to the performance of the act and the cues that elicited the act, since it was paired with them; he termed such inhibition *conditioned inhibition,* symbolized ${}_sI_r$. The build-up of conditioned inhibition is maximized when a behavior is performed in such rapid succession that the reactive inhibition from one response has not dissipated when the behavior begins to occur again, thus allowing such inhibition to become conditioned to the beginning of the behavior and to the eliciting cues. Finally, when such conditioned inhibition has become powerful enough to prevent the behavior from occurring at all, it is effectively extinguished (actually, suppressed). Since the repetition of motor acts is more likely to produce fatigue and other aversive consequences than is the repeated performance of less "tangible" behaviors (for example, thoughts), the concept of negative practice is usually reserved to describe the treatment of problem motor behaviors (for example, tics) by forced repetition (massed practice). As we see later in this chapter, proponents of implosive therapy and (flooding) response prevention, which also involve the repetitive presentation of stimuli and the repetitive elicitation of the response of anxiety, account for the proposed effectiveness of these techniques in terms of different theoretical rationales.

In applying the technique of negative practice to the treatment of a problem behavior, the essential procedure is the patient's repeated performance of the act with little rest. Unfortunately, there is no rule of thumb for determining the duration of periods of repeated performance or the duration of rest periods. In one study that varied these two factors, Yates (1958) treated a patient who suffered from four different tics—an eyeblink tic, a throat-clearing tic, a nasal tic (explosive exhalation), and a complex stomach contraction–breathing tic. Initially the patient practiced her tics for 1 minute and then rested for 1 minute; there were two sessions per day (one with the therapist, one at home), with five practice trials in each session. In subsequent experiments with the same patient, the periods of massed practice were extended to 15 minutes and even 1 hour, and the rest periods extended to 15 minutes, 1 hour, several days, and even up to several weeks. Figure 8.6 shows the patient's ability to produce the tics voluntarily over the course of 300 sessions that included all of the different experimental lengths of practice and rests.[2] The decline in the ability to perform the tics is relatively uniform across all the sessions, giving no indication that any procedural variation was more effective than any other. This study is, of course, actually an extensive case study and contains a number of methodological problems such as the lack of counterbalancing of the order in which the various lengths of practice and rest were enforced. Nevertheless, there is evidence that the technique can be effective, even though it is not possible to recommend durations of practice and rest periods that maximize success. As may be seen in other case studies, there is little consistency in the durations that have been employed.

[2] Although these data represent the patient's ability to reproduce the tic voluntarily, she also reported a significant decline in the involuntary occurrence of those tics in social situations outside the treatment situation.

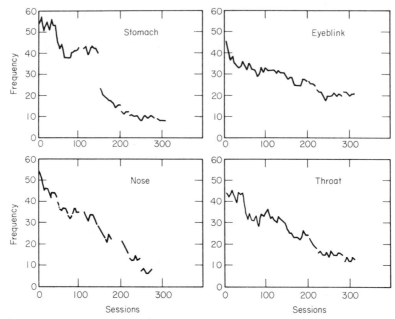

Figure 8.6 Frequency of the voluntary performance of four tics during treatment by massed practice. From Yates, 1958.

Early studies and case histories report the use of negative practice to treat a variety of small motor behaviors such as errors in piano or organ playing (Wakeham, 1928, 1930), spelling errors in typing (Holsopple & Varicouse, 1929; Poindexter, 1936; Ruhl, 1935), or simple maze learning (Kellogg & White, 1935). These early reports were poorly executed, and the results were thoroughly mixed, some positive (Wakeham, 1930; Holsopple & Varicouse, 1929; Kellogg & White, 1935) and some negative (Wakeham, 1928; Poindexter, 1936; Ruhl, 1935). Nevertheless, there was some indication in these early studies that negative practice does not apply to all behavior problems, especially those which themselves may be interpreted to involve inhibition. For example, Fishman (1937) treated two cases of speech blocking (inability to speak for a short time after beginning to say something) and three cases of stammering. Following treatment by negative practice, both speech-blocking patients showed *increases* in the frequency of their problem, while the stutterers all showed improvement. Case (1940) treated 39 stutterers, achieving total remission of stuttering in common social situations for the 10 individuals who completed the treatment regimen. He also treated three cases of speech blockage, which became worse as a result of treatment (Case, 1940). Rutherford (1940) used negative practice to eliminate grimacing and unusual body movements made by cerebral palsied children when they spoke. Negative practice also improved their speech.

There has continued to be a mixture of positive and negative results for negative practice in more recent literature. Yates (1958) (see the description of this case earlier in the section) achieved what appeared to be positive results in the treatment of tics; the treatment of the same patient by Jones (1960) revealed no increase in the prevalence of the tic upon transfer to a new therapist. However, Jones noted that there was not a perfect generalization of treatment effects from the voluntary reproduction of a tic in the clinical setting to involuntary occurrences in the natural environment: "Despite the improvement, . . . the patient is still a tiquer. Her tics are far less noticeable, are more easily brought under control and cause far less social embarrassment, but can be temporarily exacerbated by illness and by social and vocational frustrations [Jones, 1960, p. 257]."

Walton (1961) treated a young boy with multiple tics, giving prolonged periods of negative practice on the primary tic and shorter periods on the others. Walton also used a sedative drug to induce the earlier occurrence of involuntary rest periods (times during the period of practice when the patient can no longer produce the response even though he tries). Treatment produced a significant reduction in the involuntary performance of the tics that was maintained over a 1-year follow-up period. Walton also treated another child with an 11-year history of headshaking plus two other tics (hiccoughing and explosive exhaling) with 109 sessions of massed practice, which ranged from ½ to 1½ hours in duration (Walton, 1964). A sedative drug was also employed in the treatment of this child. Treatment achieved a significant reduction in the frequency of the tics over a 5-month follow-up period.

Lazarus (1960) successfully treated a child whose stuttering was also accompanied by unusual head and mouth movements. Clark (1966) applied the technique of massed practice to three patients suffering from the Gilles de la Tourette syndrome (involuntary explosions of obscene utterances), two of whom remained free of symptoms over a 4-year follow-up period. Mogel and Schiff (1966) described the extinction of a young girl's problematic behavior of "head bumping" after a single treatment session involving 2 minutes of massed practice. Apparently, the voluntary performance of this behavior in the presence of the therapist proved quite embarrassing, and the success of this procedure might as easily be understood in terms of punishment. It is noteworthy, of course, that since many clients are embarrassed by their tics, any embarrassment that accompanies the sessions of negative practice may prove to be an additional factor in successful treatment. This hypothesis would predict differential effectiveness for negative-practice treatment regimens that involved extensive use of home (solitary) practice sessions in addition to office sessions.

There is one fairly recent case study in which negative practice failed to be successful, despite the fact that the behaviors treated were similar to those treated successfully by other therapists (Feldman & Werry, 1966). In terms of design and data collection, this is one of the better studies of the effects of negative practice. The patient, an adolescent boy, had two tics, one of which was treated (a head jerk) and one was left to be an untreated control (an eyeblink tic). Furthermore, data comprised the number of *involuntary* performances of the tic during the first 15 minutes of each treatment session, which served as a "warm-up period" and during which no negative practice (voluntary performance of the tic) occurred. Feldman and Werry found that negative practice produced a significant increase in both the treated and untreated tics, and an old tic, which had been gone for some time, reappeared. The practice sessions were 5 minutes in length, and the tic was practiced only once per session. The patient was instructed to practice two other times each day; thus, the practice periods were 5 minutes in length and the rest periods quite long and probably variable.

Some authors (see Yates, 1970) feel this study casts serious doubt on the effectiveness of negative practice. It is, of course, more a case study than an actual experiment, and the time lengths and frequencies of the practice and rest periods are not particularly similar to those employed in other cases reported in the literature (see cases just described). Furthermore, the head-jerk motion in the treated tic caused dizziness, and this factor limited the length of the massed-practice sessions. No rationale is given, however, for the use of only one practice session per treatment session or the decision to have only three sessions per day, unless the dizziness produced by practicing the tic was of long duration.

Like the other techniques discussed in this chapter, the therapeutic use of negative practice has produced mixed results, and there has been very little research concerning the overall effectiveness of the technique or the possibility that it should be applied only to certain classes of disorders—for example, those behavioral problems that do not themselves include response inhibition. It seems reasonable to propose that caution be used in the employment of this technique, not because there is the possibility it will be ineffective, as much as because there are indications that with some classes of behavior (for example, speech blocking), negative practice actually exacerbates the problem. Overall, the technique appears to have merit, and it is hoped that sufficient research will be conducted within the next few years to allow more extensive evaluation of this technique.

Stimulus Satiation

Stimulus satiation is one of the less common techniques of response elimination, but it nonetheless deserves mention. Related to drive theories of behavior (for example, Hull, 1943), the technique of satiation is designed to reduce the attractiveness of stimuli whose valence is so positive that they motivate behaviors that allow the individual to observe, touch, smell, or possess the stimuli (see Chapter IX for a more detailed discussion of changing the valence of stimuli). The procedure of satiation involves the repeated presentation of such stimuli to the client until the attractiveness of the stimuli is reduced.

The most famous example of the use of satiation is a case, reported by Ayllon (1963), involving a psychotic patient who had hoarded towels throughout her 9-year hospitalization. Although the staff consistently removed hoarded towels from her room, the patient managed to keep on hand 19–29 towels. The program of satiation involved allowing the patient to keep towels in her room and, furthermore, delivering additional towels to her. Towels were handed to the patient in her room, without any comment. Initially she received 7 towels each day, but within 3 weeks the number was increased to 60 per day. During the first week, whenever a towel was delivered the patient would say, "Oh, you found it for me, thank you." By the second week she typically announced that she did not need any more, and by the third week she was asking that the towels be taken away. Nevertheless, satiation continued, and by the sixth week the patient was removing the towels from her room herself. Figure 8.7 shows the number of towels in the patient's room at various weeks before, during, and following treatment.

In many instances, stimulus satiation is totally confounded with negative practice since a particular behavior on the part of the patient may be necessary to provide the stimulus. For example, in treating problematic smoking behavior, patients may be required to chain smoke for extended periods of time, thus massing the practice of the minor motor behaviors in the overall act of smoking. Marrone, Merksamer, and Salzberg (1970) treated smoking behavior by having patients chain smoke for either 10 or 20 hours straight. They found that either treatment produced equivalent results immediately following treatment in terms of total abstinence from smoking. However, at the end of a 4-month follow-up period, the group that had received the longer satiation (practice) period showed greater abstinence than the group that had received the shorter treatment; the latter group did not differ from a nontreatment control.

Clearly, there is also the possibility that aversive control is operating in this instance. Other investigators have utilized a satiation procedure in

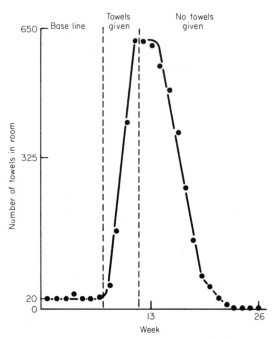

Figure 8.7 Number of towels hoarded during a base line-period, a satiation period when towels were given to the patient; and following the satiation period (second base line). From Ayllon, 1963.

the treatment of smoking, but in the context of aversive control. In these studies, patients are exposed to hot, smoke-filled air, often from an external source, while going through the motor behaviors of smoking (Wilde, 1964; Franks, Fried, & Ashem, 1966). There is clearly a satiation with respect to the stimulus of smoke; however, the aversive nature of the smoke is typically cited for any success achieved by this procedure. Furthermore, data are not typically reported on the extent to which the attractiveness of smoke as a stimulus is altered.

There has been little research on the process of satiation other than that done in the laboratory with children (Gewirtz & Baer, 1958a,b) and animals (Woodworth & Schlosberg, 1954). Despite the paucity of reports in the literature, satiation appears to be a technique worth considering, especially as an alternative to aversive counterconditioning, when the inappropriately attractive stimulus is one that may be readily dispensed to the point of saturation (for example, towels may be so dispensed, but there is no evidence that sexual behavior toward inappropriate objects might be eliminated by enforced exposure and interaction with these objects). Certainly, however, research is needed to specify the categories of stimuli and of behavior that respond to this technique and any procedural details that determine the effectiveness of the procedure. Caution should be exercised in any decision to employ this technique, although unlike many other extinction techniques (described in this chapter), there is no indication in the published literature that satiation may achieve negative results such as the exacerbation of the behavior under treatment. The published literature is sparse, however, so that this possibility cannot be ruled out.

Implosive Therapy

Implosive therapy is a technique designed to eliminate avoidance behaviors by the process of extinction. The first description of the procedure and use of the term *implosion* appeared in 1961, in a public presentation by Thomas Stampfl. The first written discussion of the technique appeared a few years later (London, 1964), and since that time there have been numerous theoretical and research papers on the technique (see, Hogan, 1963, 1966, 1968, 1969; Hogan & Kirchner, 1967; Kirchner & Hogan, 1966; Levis, 1966; Levis & Carrera, 1967; Stampfl, 1967; Stampfl & Levis, 1967a,b, 1968; DeMoor, 1970; Borkovec, 1972; Barrett, 1969; Boulougouris, Marks, & Marset, 1971; Mealiea & Nawas, 1971; Miller & Levis, 1971; Fazio, 1970; Hodgson & Rachman, 1970; Morganstern, 1973).

In implosive theory, the avoidance of anxiety-generating situations and behaviors is the object of treatment. It is assumed (Stampfl & Levis, 1967a; Hogan, 1969) that such avoidance behaviors are learned because they keep a person from experiencing anxiety (compare anxiety- or aversion-relief therapy procedures, Chapter IX). Such defensive avoidance behavior is usually learned in childhood, from situations in which an individual was punished, rejected, or deprived in some manner (for example, aversive environmental events such as being cut or burned or falling down; parental punishment such as slapping, spanking, or deprivation; or peer-group experiences such as being bullied, ostracised, or pummeled). Although these assumptions, as well as others that we discuss later, are reasonably similar to those held by more psychodynamically oriented theorists, learning principles are invoked to account for the initial acquisition of such anxieties and to justify the various procedural details of implosive theory. Following the two-factor theory of learning from aversive consequences (Solomon, 1964; Mowrer, 1960), it is proposed that various behaviors, feared situations, or phobic objects are persistently avoided and that such avoidance behaviors are consistently covertly reinforced by the termination of anxiety each time these behaviors, situations, and objects or people are avoided.

In order for extinction of avoidance responses to occur, the patient must be prevented from performing the avoidance behavior, if only in his imagination, and be forced to experience the intense anxiety in the absence of any real aversive consequences. When such anxiety is experienced without the occurrence of actual aversive consequences, such consequences will cease to be anticipated, and the anxiety will dissipate. The avoided behaviors and stimuli will now be perceived without any attendant anxiety, and the tendency for these behaviors and stimuli to evoke anxiety will undergo extinction. In the words of Stampfl and Levis (1967a):

> The fundamental hypothesis is that a sufficient condition for the extinction of anxiety is to re-present, reinstate, or symbolically reproduce the stimuli (cues) to which the anxiety response has been conditioned, in the absence of primary reinforcement (the actual punishment, rejection, or deprivation) [pp. 498–499].

In theory, and somewhat in actual procedure, implosive therapy is similar to flooding, or response-prevention techniques (discussed in a later section). There are several distinct differences, however. Implosive therapy is based upon clearly specified assumptions concerning the psycho-dynamics of the individual under treatment. Earlier we noted that childhood trauma is proposed to be the source of most avoidance behaviors. Within the theory of implosive treatment, it is further specified that imagery in treatment is usually directed toward usual conflict areas that the therapist, from experience, knows concern most individuals (Hogan, 1968). These areas of conflict include, according to Hogan (1968), "fears, rejections, prior humiliations or deprivations, or conflicts related to expression of fear of aggression, sexual problems of various types, and guilt related behavior [p. 423]." Stampfl (Stampfl & Levis, 1968) has explicitly stated that the concerns of various psychosexual stages postulated by Freud (toilet training, anal experiences, infantile sexuality, aggression, etc.) are the substance of treatment.

Like several other behavior therapies, implosive therapy includes the use of visual imagery, rather than the actual performance of avoided behaviors, or the exposure to feared stimuli. It would appear that this is a necessary procedure of treatment since the therapist, in his attempts to evoke the maximum amount of anxiety, is likely to describe images that include projected traumata clearly beyond actual experience (see the descriptions presented later in the section). There is some theoretical inconsistency at this point since the technique is supposed to induce the patient to recreate the original life trauma, while in actual practice the trauma which the patient is to imagine transcends that of actual human experience. One may speculate that such imagined elaboration may be seen as necessary for the induction of a level of anxiety equivalent to that which presumably accompanied the original traumatic experience.

Typically, in implosive therapy, scenes of avoided behaviors and stimuli are presented in a hierarchical fashion, beginning with less anxiety-provoking items. While this would appear to be in the manner of desensitization, it should be clear from the case excerpts that follow that the initial steps in an implosive-therapy hierarchy still elicit intense anxiety. Flooding, or response-prevention techniques require that images related to specific behavioral problems must be presented for sufficiently long periods to allow the dissipation of anxiety (Baum, 1970; Siegeltuch & Baum, 1971; Rachman, 1969), and it has been found that presentations that are too short may produce increased *sensitization* to the feared stimuli and behaviors (Rachman, 1969; Baum, 1970). The theory of implosive therapy makes no specification regarding the dissipation of anxiety, only that anxiety must be experienced without any actual aversive consequences.

In the practice of implosive therapy, it is important to prevent the patient from engaging in any avoidance behavior or otherwise limiting the effectiveness of the reinstitution and magnification of the anxiety associated with the imagined scenes (Hogan, 1969). Psychotics have been observed to interrupt their participation in a therapy session by rolling up their eyes and dissociating; less disturbed patients may ask questions or in some other verbal way interrupt the provocation of anxiety. In any event, should such dissociation occur, the therapist is obligated to stop the client at this point and to begin the presentation again. The therapist must constantly monitor the responses of the patient, interpret those responses, and act accordingly. If foot wiggling or other body movement occurs, which may dilute the experience of anxiety, it must be stopped. Although crying is often a part of a genuine emotional reaction, if the therapist judges it to be an attempt to elicit sympathy, it should be ignored.

Let us now turn to some examples of implosive procedures. We shall rely heavily upon actual transcripts here since the theatrical nature of the presentation, designed to maximize anxiety and incorporate all possible cues involved in the initial learning experience, cannot be overemphasized. As one researcher (Hogan, 1968) has noted, the patient's involvement is limited only by the creativity of the therapist, who may imitate the growls and roars of animals, touch the patient's arm as an animal is described slithering over his body, or even use electrical devices, such as a fan to simulate a buzz saw mutilating his body.

Stampfl and Levis (1967) have outlined in detail the areas of conflict that generally comprise the domain for implosive treatment, ". . . usual conflict areas which [the therapist] knows, from experience, concern most individuals [p. 423]." The eight primary areas of concern and the elements of relevant implosive scenes are:

Orality. Many scenes will be destructive (see "Aggression," below), involving the eating, biting, spitting, sucking of various objects, including other human beings (cannibalism).

Anality. General anal scenes involving anal retention and expulsion (see Erikson, 1950), often in social situations.

Sexual Concerns. In addition to dynamically oriented oedipal and primal scene depictions, this area includes scenes of castration, cunnilingus, fellatio, homosexuality, bestiality, etc.

Aggression. Scenes include interactions with others in which the patient expresses anger, hostility, and aggression. The target is usually a parent, sibling, spouse, or other significant figure. It is usual to include body mutilation, including the death of the patient himself.

Initial treatment sequences dealing with hostility are often life history related. I will ask the person to describe an incident when he was very angry and frustrated by another person (usually the mother, father, or a teacher). The themes are then developed around his emotional verbalizations toward this person. You request that he say the words as he pictures the scene. As I build the emotion I have him attack the source of his frustration with bites, kicks, and curses. I have him imagine a scene in which he takes a knife or hatchet and cuts out the victim's eyes and tongue, mutilates his body and destroys his sexual organs. In another sequence, the client might be requested to picture himself as a wild leopard savagely ripping and clawing his victim. Underlying such a creation would be our emphasis on loss of control by the person and the complete expression of impulse [Hogan, 1969, p. 180].

Rejection. In this area, scenes depict the patient being deprived, abandoned, rejected, shamed or left helpless.

"Shut your eyes and imagine that you are a baby in your crib. You are in a dark, shabby, dirty room. You are alone and afraid. You are hungry and wet. You call for your mother, but no one comes. If only someone would change you; if only they would feed you and wrap you in a warm blanket. You look out the window of your room into the house next door, where a mother and father are giving another baby love, warmth and affection. Look how they love the baby. You are crying for your mother now. "Please mother, please come and love me." But no one comes. Finally, you hear some steps. They come closer, and closer, and closer. You hear someone outside your door. The door slowly opens. Your heart beats with excitement. There is your mother coming to love you. She is unbuttoning her blouse. She takes out her breast to feed you. Then she squirts your warm milk on the floor and steps in it. Look, see her dirty heel mark in your milk. She shouts, "I would rather waste my milk than to give it to you. I wish you were never born; I never wanted you." [Hogan, 1969, p. 181].

Loss of Impulse Control. These scenes are centered about problems of impulse control. Patients are to imagine scenes in which they clearly lose control and act out sexual or aggressive impulses. Incorporated also are scenes of the consequences of such impulsive acting out, such as being relegated to the back ward of a mental hospital for life.

Guilt. These scenes generally depict the patient confessing his responsibility for a variety of wrongdoings that may have been described in other implosive sessions. He may imagine himself in a court room with his parents and loved ones present, or in front of God. God or the court may then condemn him to eternal hell, or sentence him to death, and the attendent execution is then visualized. Thematically the punishment is generally related to the unpardonable sins confessed by the patient.

Central or Autonomic Nervous System Reactivity. The patient may be required to imagine aspects of his own responsivity that may themselves heighten his anxiety. Thus, scenes may depict his own heart racing, perspiration pouring forth from his body, muscular tension, or involuntary incontinence.

Stampfl and Levis (1967) feel that most of these areas will be touched upon during the treatment of any particular client. Certainly, within any one area the total scene depicted will overlap with other areas: for example, sexual behaviors will certainly elicit moral judgments from others, and the imaginary performance of inhibited sexual, aggressive, oral, anal, etc. behaviors is likely to be equated with a loss of control. Furthermore, single scenes may combine multiple elements. One implosively oriented therapist was asked how he would respond via implosive treatment to the following dream reported in treatment:

The client would be in bed for his night's sleep. As he was falling asleep, he would imagine that he saw some shadows in his room; then, there were some sounds; then, a shadowy figure would become apparent. This figure would move toward the client, and the face would become bathed in light. At that point a knife would be seen in the figure's hand; he would come toward the client about to attack. The client would try to resist by kicking out and at this point he would wake up, often on the floor as a result of his 'struggle.' [Hogan, 1969, p. 182].

The therapist replied that he would explore *all* of the following scene themes:

In a theoretical discussion one of my colleagues asked me what themes I would implode if a client reported such a dream during treatment. I stated that I would try *all* of the following possibilities: (1) A male figure assaults the patient, beating him up, and then he is cut up in the manner described in the section on aggression. (2) The patient is masturbating. His parents catch him. He is then punished for this behavior by a threatening, rejecting authoritative father. (3) The client is the victim of a homosexual assault in which he is helpless. (4) A male figure castrates the patient with a knife. He then uses the patient as if he were a female sexual partner. In fact, you might have the client picture himself playing this fe-male role [Hogan, 1969, p. 182].[3]

In order to give the reader some idea of the emotional intensity of the implosive themes, the following transcription is excerpted from the treatment of a snake-phobic individual (Hogan, 1968; Hogan & Kirch-ner, 1967). Prior to the therapeutic interaction quoted below, the treat-ment method had been explained to the client, and in discussions with the patient the therapist had gleaned specific material that he could in-corporate into imagery later in the session. Note the intensity of the description and the total involvement that the therapist tries to elicit from the client:

"Close your eyes again. Picture the snake out in front of you, now make your-self pick it up. Reach down, pick it up, put it in your lap, feel it wiggling around in your lap, leave your hand on it, put your hand out and feel it wiggling around. Kind of explore its body with your fingers and hand. You don't like to do it, make yourself do it. Make yourself do it. Really grab onto the snake. Squeeze it a little bit, feel it. Feel it kind of start to wind around your hand. Let it. Leave your hand there, feel it touching your hand and winding around it, curling around your wrist."

In this second excerpt the level of anxiety is raised and the tempo of the presentation is increased.

"Okay, now put your finger out towards the snake and feel his head coming up. No, it is in your lap, and it is coming up. Its head [is] towards your finger and it is starting to bite at your finger. Let it, let it bite at your finger. Put your finger out, let it bite, let it bite at your finger, feel its fangs go right down into your finger. Oooh, feel the pain going right up your arm and into your shoulder. You want to pull your hand away, but leave it there. Let the snake kind of gnaw at your finger. Feel it gnawing, look at the blood dripping off your finger. Feel it in you stomach and the pain going up your arm. Try to picture your bleeding finger. And the teeth of the snake are stuck right in your finger, right down to the bone. And it is crunching like on your finger there. Let it. Feel it biting, it is biting at your finger, it is biting, now it is coiling around your finger, and it is biting at your hand. Again and again and again. All over your hand, feel it. Now squeeze the snake with your hand. Make it bite you harder. Squeeze it. Make it bite you. Squeeze it hard, squeeze it. Let it bite you, squeeze it hard, squeeze it hard. Okay, slowly put the snake out in front of you. Now pick him up again. Put it in your lap. Let it wiggle around. Uhuh—leave your hand on him. Let him wiggle around your hand and touch it; snap at it."

In the third section the level of anxiety is increased as the animal begins to at-tack the person's face or vital organs. This material is closer to the real fears of such *S*s.

[3] This extract and the three extracts on the previous pages (336–337) are reprinted from Hogan, R. A. Implosively oriented behavior modification: Therapy considerations. *Behav-iour Research and Therapy*, 1969, **7**, 177–184. Reproduced with the permission of Microform International Marketing Corporation exclusive copyright licensee of Pergamon Press Journal back files.

"Okay, feel him coiling around your hand again, touching you, slimy, now he is going up on your shoulder and he crawls there and he [is] sitting on your chest and he is looking you right in the eye. He is big and he is black and he is ugly and he's coiled up and he is ready to strike and he is looking at you. Picture his face, look at his eyes, look at those long sharp fangs. He is staring at you, he is evil looking, he is slimy, he is ready to strike at your face. Feel him sitting there, just staring at you. Those long sharp teeth with the blood on them. He strikes out at you, (T slaps hands). Feel him bite at your face. Feel him bite at your face, let him bite; let him bite; just relax and let him bite; let him bite at your face, let him bite; let him bite at your face; feel his fangs go right into your cheeks; and the blood is coming out on your face now. And the poison is going into your body and you are getting sick and nauseated and he is striking at your face again and again. Now he coils up on this shoulder and he is ready to strike again at your face. Feel him bite, put your head down towards him, put your head down, let him bite at your face, let him bite as much as he wants. Feel him bite, he is putting his head, his little head up by your ear and he is snapping at your ear. Feel him snap at your ear. Now he is going up by your eyes and he is starting to bite at your eyes, feel him bite at your eyes. Feel him bite, let him bite, feel his fangs go into your eyes and he is pulling at them and tearing at them and ripping at them. Picture what your face looks like. Get that sick feeling in your stomach and now he is gnawing at your nose, and biting at your mouth. Just take a deep breath and let him do it. Now he is coiling around your neck, slimy and wet and dirty and he is squeezing you. He is choking you, feel him choke you, feel the breath come out of you, that sick feeling in your stomach. He snaps out at you, feel him snap at you. Now he is crawling across your face. Can you feel him? He is wet and slimy and he's touching your face, he is crawling up into your hair. Feel him up in your hair, coiled around up there. Take a deep breath and try to get that sickening feeling, he is up there in your hair. Put your hand up there by your hair, by him and let him snap at your hand. Pick him up now in your hand and bring him down by your face and squeeze him; squeeze him real hard and make him bite you. Put your hand up by your face; make him bite you, make him bite; look at those fangs; he is going to bite; put your hand right up by your face. Let him bite you. Let him bite you. Are you letting him bite? Let him bite. Now just relax your hand and he is mad and enraged, feel him come out and bite at you, feel him snap at you (T slaps hands). Feel him snap at you. Feel him snap; that sick feeling in your stomach, feel him biting you; he is gnawing at your cheeks now feel him, bluhh——and just picture how ugly you're looking and terrible and he's enraged and he's biting and biting and biting and biting and biting and biting and biting." And later, the following scene: "Feel it up by your eye and it is going to bite it, it is going to pull it right out. Feel it is biting your eye and it is going to pull your eye right out and down on your cheek. It is kind of gnawing on it and eating it, eating at your eye. Your little eye is down on your cheek and it is gnawing and biting at your eye. Picture it. Now it is crawling into you eye socket and wiggling around in there, feel it wiggling and wiggling up in your head. Feel it wiggling around, uhhhh uhhhh, feel it wiggling. And now it wiggles out of your eye, and now it is wiggling up into your nose. Feel it crawling right up into your nose, into your head, wiggling around and it is gnawing out through the other eye, from the inside. Feel it biting its way out."

(For the most I do not let the S verbalize at will, because speech is often used as a defense to avoid anxiety. I am satisfied with a nod of the head or a brief comment to verify a clinical hypothesis. The reader will note that the T frequently goes right on after a comment by the client.)

T. "Now I want to picture that you are walking along through the woods, and you are kind of scared and frightened because you have the feeling that something terrible is going to happen to you. You are walking along, and you are all alone, and it is getting dark, and you get that feeling in your stomach, that kind of uhuhuh-feeling, try to get that. Okay and you trip and fall into a big pit. And there are thousands of snakes there and they are staring at you. Can you feel them staring at you? And they are starting to crawl towards you and you can't move. Your legs hurt and you are helpless and you are there on the ground and they are starting to crawl on you. Feel them, they are crawling all over you and starting to bite you now. Are you letting them bite you? Let them bite you. Do you have that scared feeling in your stomach?"

S. "Yeah."

T. "Try to make it worse, take a breath and make it worse. Picture yourself there in the pit, try to describe it."

S. "To you?"

T. "Yes."

S. "Well, all those things are slimy and they just keep going over me all the time, wiggling, oooh."

T. "Touching you, biting you, try to get that helpless feeling like you can't win, and just give up and let them crawl all over you. Don't even fight them any more. Let them crawl as much as they want. And now there is a big giant snake, it is as big as a man and it is staring at you and it is looking at you; it's ugly and it's black and it has got horrible eyes and long fangs, and it is coming towards you. It is standing on its tail and it is looking down at you, looking down on you. I want you to get that feeling, like you are a helpless little rabbit, and it's coming toward you, closer and closer; feel it coming towards you. Horrible, evil, ugly, slimy, and it's looking down on you, ready to strike at you. Feel it in your stomach, feel it coming, oooh, it is getting closer and closer and it snaps out at you. Feel it biting at your head now, it is biting at your head; it opens its giant mouth and it has your whole head inside of its mouth. And it is biting your head right off. Feel it; feel it biting, the fangs going right through your neck. Feel it, and now it is starting to swallow you whole. It is pulling you right inside its body, feel yourself being pulled and dragged into its body. Feel yourself inside, helpless, lost, and now you are starting to turn into a snake. Feel yourself turning into a slimy snake. And you are crawling out of its mouth. All the other snakes see you. And they start to attack you. Feel them; they are coming to bite and rip you apart. Do you know how animals attack each other? Look at the snakes attacking you, feel them biting you, ripping you to shreads." (In dealing with a client, rather than a research S, greater emphasis would be placed on sexual cues. The large snake in this sequence might sexually violate the S and/or mutilate her sexual organs. The snake, a symbol of male sexuality, was used in this research only on a symbolic level.)

"Can you see the snake out in front of you again? Reach out and pick it up. Put it up by your face, make it bite you. Feel that scared feeling? Put it closer to your face, let it bite your lips. Are you letting it? Put out your tongue. Let it bite your tongue. Now let loose of it. And it jumps down in your stomach. And it is down in your stomach and it is wiggling around down there. Feel it jumping around and biting in your stomach, and laying eggs, and now thousands of little snakes are in your stomach and they are crawling around, slimy and wiggly, feel them inside you. They are biting at your heart and your lungs. Feel them crawling up into your lungs, they are shredding your lungs and biting and ripping and they are swimming in the blood in your stomach, kind of swishing their tails around, uhhhh—horrible little snakes, slimy, wormy, crawly, feel them. You are getting sick to your stomach, take a deep breath, feel them, inside you, wiggling around. Can you feel them down there? Biting at your heart, feel them biting and gnaw-ing at your heart. Crawling in and out of your mouth now, feel them crawling in and out of you. They are inside and outside of you, biting you, all over your body, feel them, just destroying you, cutting you up in little pieces. Biting you, feel them biting you. Pick up that snake again now, out in front of you, make yourself reach out. He snaps at you. Pick it up anyhow, pick it up, put it up by your face. Put it up by your eyes, right up by your eyes; feel it gnaw and bite at your eyes. Do you get the scared feeling? Let it bite, squeeze it, make it bite, now let it loose, let it bite at your eyes. Uhhh—Now it is wiggling around and it is com-ing by your ear. It has got a little head, a little slimy head and it is putting its head in your ear. It is kind of wiggling inside of your head now. Feel it crawl in there and crawl around and it is biting at your brains, chewing and gnawing, and bit-ing and ripping, feel it, inside of you. And now it is turning into a giant snake and it is slowly coiling around you, feel it coil around you and it is tightening; squeezing you; feel it squeezing you, uhhh—feel the bones crunching, biting at your face, and squeezing you. Just give up, quit fighting it. Can you feel it biting you?"

(With clinical cases this next sequence would include greater sexual emphasis. I might have the snake swallowed by the S, and later it might exit from her vagina. I would have her play a male sexual role, or she might be castrated in an attempt to relive, in imagery, a Freudian-related conflict.)

T. "I want you to picture yourself getting ready to get into your bed and there in your bed are thousands of snakes. Can you see them there crawling around in your bed? I want you to lay down with them. Get down with them. Feel yourself moving around with the snakes and they are crawling all over you. And you are moving and turning in bed and they are touching you. Feel them crawling on you, touching you, slimy and slithering. Feel yourself turn over in your bed, and they are under you and on you and around you, and touching your face and in your hair. And they are crawling across your face. Can you feel them touch you? Describe the feeling."

S. "Kind of cold."

T. "Feel, you are now cold and clammy like a snake and they are touching you with their cold, clammy, wet, slimy, drippy, cold bodies that are wiggling and touching your skin and feel them. Uhhhh how can you feel them touch you. They are touching you. Can you feel them touch you? Move around so you can get greater contact. Move your body like that woman in the Seely ad and feel them touch you, uhhh, wiggly and slimy, they are crawling on you, on your face. Uhhh!"

Because of this *S*'s overt responses to the series of imagery in which we had her swallow the snake, and in view of our clinical judgement that she had oral conflicts, (she is overweight and seemed to be an oral aggressive personality) we included the material in this final section.

T. "Squeeze it now, softly, kind of get the squish of it. Feel it bite, feel it bite. Squeeze it harder. Does that bother you to do that? Kind of knead its body like it was dough. Stick your nails into it and break open its skin. Feel its insides start to squish out. Squish it between your fingers. Kind of squish it up now in little pieces like it was dough. Squish it, take that sloushy stuff and put it up by your face. Go on up by your face. Rub it on your face quickly. Feel it, uhhhh you don't like that part of it do you? Put it down, uhhhhhhh, squish it some more. Now rub your hands in that mess, and put that by your face and leave it there. Up by your nose, uhhh smell it, feel it. It is cold come on, put it on your face. You are pulling away from it, okay put your hand down. Pick up the snake; pick it up, put it up by your mouth. Bite its head off. Bite its head. Bite it! Bite it! Did you bite it? Chew its head. Feel it. Chew it! Chew it! Chew it! Chew it hard. You are not chewing it. Chew it. Not swallow it, uhhh, it is inside you, the poison and uhhh it is dripping down in your stomach. Do you feel it in your stomach? Its head is down there. It is laying in your stomach, the head is biting now, it is biting down in your stomach. It is moving around and biting. Feel it down in your stomach. Uhhh! It is wiggling around, it is wiggling by itself, that head. Pick up another snake, pick it up. Bite its head off, bite it. Now chew it. Chew it! Chew it! Chew it! Chew it! Chew it! Feel its crunching in your mouth. Feel its crunching hard, bite it, swallow it; uhhhh it's down in your stomach, can you feel that sick feeling in your stomach? Uhhhhhhh they are wiggling around down there. They are wiggling around down there. They are getting longer and they are wiggling and they are touching you and they are slimy and your stomach is cold and wet. Pick up another and bite it. Bite its head, chew it, slowly, chew it slowly, chew it. Uhhhhh uhhhhh you are biting into its eyes. Go on, bite, and into the top of its head, and swallow it, slowly swallow it. Very good, pick up another one, Bite it! Bite it! Chew it! Chew it! Swallow it. Pick up another one, this time bite its body, bite it, uhhhh uhhhh now chew it, swallow it, feel them crawling and jumping around in your stomach, uhhhh do you get that sick feeling, that scared feeling? Uhhhh the poison's inside you, it is cold, and clammy and wet, how can you stand that in your stomach? Uhhh that snake juice and pieces of snake-flesh and eyes and teeth and heads rolling in your stomach. Can you feel them down there? Uhhhh feel them in your stomach, wiggling and turning. Feel it; it is inside you. Can you feel it crawling around? Feel it in your stomach. Just let it, quit fighting it. Just let it crawl around in there. Quit fighting it. Feel it wiggle. It has got a mind of its own. It is just wiggling around and biting. It's teeth are biting; can you feel its teeth? [pp. 427–431]" [4]

[4] Reprinted from Hogan, R. A. The implosive technique. *Behaviour Research and Therapy*, 1968, **6**, 423–431. Reproduced with the permission of Microform International Marketing Corporation exclusive copyright licensee of Pergamon Press Journal back files.

Research on Implosive Therapy

In general, research on the effectiveness of implosive therapy has been mixed in its support for the effectiveness of the technique. Using the MMPI as a criterion for therapy effectiveness, Levis and Carerra (1967) found that outpatients treated by 8-hour-long sessions of implosive therapy had a larger number of T scores drop into the normal range than did patients who received conventional treatment or no treatment at all. This study did not indicate, of course, the degree to which problem behaviors were modified, nor does it propose any theoretical rationale for the capability of implosive therapy to induce changes in paper-and-pencil measures of mental status, such as the MMPI. The instrument was chosen primarily because it was a common instrument in other studies evaluating psychotherapy effectiveness (for example, Barron & Leary, 1955; Gallagher, 1953; Kaufmann, 1950; Mogar & Savage, 1964; Schofield, 1950, 1953).

Hogan and Kirchner (1967) treated clients with intense fears of rats, utilizing a single implosive therapy session, or relaxation training paired with neutral imagery. Clients treated with implosive therapy were to imagine touching a rat, having a rat nibble at their fingers, then the rat might bite them on the arm and eventually sink its fangs into their neck, claw about in their hair, and eventually even devour their eyes. The single treatment session lasted, on the average, only 39 minutes. Following treatment, 20 of 21 subjects treated with implosive therapy opened the cage of a live rat, and 14 of the 21 actually picked up the rat. Only 3 of the 22 control-group subjects would open the cage, and 7 refused even to enter the room. Physiological monitoring during treatment indicated that the pulse rate declined during the session, indicating that anxiety was abating and that extinction might thus be occurring.

Fazio (1970) compared implosive therapy with irrelevant imagery and discussion in the treatment of roach phobias. Subjects treated with irrelevant imagery and discussion were given implosive therapy with respect to irrelevant fears (being attacked by a bear, burned by a forest fire, etc.) and discussions of the feared insect, its living habits, and how harmless it really was. Fazio found that the irrelevant imagery and discussion was more effective than implosive therapy or implosive therapy plus discussion in enabling subjects to touch or hold a live roach. It is noteworthy that these were three treatment sessions of one-half hour each, and that all therapy was delivered via a tape recorder. In a second study including groups treated by implosive therapy, irrelevant imagery implosion only, or discussion only, Fazio found that discussion only produced the greatest increase in approach behaviors toward the feared insects. Indeed, of three implosive-therapy subjects who were treated even though they were not judged phobic, two became sensitized to roaches as a result of treatment. As we discuss later, this latter result may indicate that the implosive therapy sessions were too short (Mealiea & Nawas, 1971; Hodgson & Rachman, 1970).

Hodgson and Rachman (1970) attempted to reduce anxiety associated with snakes by exposure to anxiety-provoking images that were unrelated to the snake phobia. One group of subjects (adolescent girls) heard a 40-minute tape describing interactions with a snake, similar to the one cited earlier in this chapter. In a second condition, subjects heard descriptions of terrible scenes unrelated to snakes (for example, automobile crashes) for 30 minutes and then only the last 10 minutes of the implosion tape. In another condition this same sequence was given, but the last 10 minutes of the implosion tape were heard 24 hours after the irrelevant implosive-imagery session. Finally, there was one condition involving 40 minutes of pleasant, nonanxiety-provoking images. There was no positive effect found for implosive therapy. In fact, on a self-rated fear inventory, implosive-therapy subjects subsequently reported an increase in fear of snakes, while subjects who heard the 40 minutes of pleasant images reported a decrease. Furthermore, subjects who heard the 10 minutes of implosive therapy immediately following unrelated anxiety-provoking images reported a decrease in fear, whereas those who heard the 10 minutes of implosive therapy after a 24-hour interim period reported an increase. In discussing their failure to find the strikingly positive effects of implosive therapy that other investigators had found (for example, Hogan & Kirchner, 1967), Hodgson and Rachman noted that there appeared to be a greater probability of improvement being evidenced by subjects who were tested some time after the end of the implosive-therapy session, when anxiety generated during the treatment session had dissipated to some degree. It should be further noted that Hogan and Kirchner (1967) did not use tapes, as did both Fazio (1970) and Hodgson and Rachman (1970), and they found that imagery and timing effective with one subject was not necessarily effective with another, an observation that would seem to preclude the use of taped implosive descriptions.

There have been a number of studies contrasting the effectiveness of implosive therapy with that of systematic desensitization (Barrett, 1967, 1969; Borkovec, 1970, 1972; Carek, 1969; Jacobson, 1970; McGlynn, 1968; Mealiea & Nawas, 1971; Willis, 1968; Willis & Edwards, 1969). Again, these studies have produced seemingly conflicting results, and are unanimous only in that none of them showed implosive therapy to be superior to systematic desensitization. Mealiea and Nawas (1971) matched 50 snake-phobic college women on a behavior avoidance test and fear thermometer scale and then assigned them to conditions involving treatment by systematic desensitization, by implosive therapy, or to one of three control conditions. Subjects received five 30-minute sessions. Following treatment and on a follow-up test 1 month later, only subjects treated with systematic desensitization showed a significant decrease in phobic behavior. Subjects treated with implosive therapy did not differ from subjects in the control conditions.

In a study of similar design, Willis (1968; Willis & Edwards, 1969) found that systematic desensitization was significantly more effective than implosive therapy in reducing avoidance behavior in mice-phobic female college students. Subjects treated with implosive therapy showed no less avoidance behavior than subjects in a control condition.

Barrett (1967, 1969) found no difference in the effectiveness of systematic desensitization and implosive therapy, but he still concluded that systematic desensitization was a preferable form of treatment for the reduction of fears. In this study both systematic desensitization and implosive therapy produced significant decrements in avoidance behavior (a noteworthy finding since this is one of the few comparative studies in which implosive therapy produced results different from that of a control group), but the effect of implosive therapy was found to be more variable. That is, while there was a significant degree of average improvement in the implosive-therapy group, some of the subjects improved a great deal, while others improved hardly at all. On the other side of the coin, Barrett concluded that implosive therapy was more "efficient" than systematic desensitization since the same amount of average improvement was accomplished in only 45% of the time required by systematic desensitization: systematic desensitization subjects received 4 training sessions and up to 11 systematic-desensitization sessions; implosive-therapy subjects received two 50-minute interviews followed by up to two sessions of implosive therapy (of unspecified duration).

A number of studies have reported no differences between systematic desensitization and implosive therapy (Borkovec, 1970; Carek, 1969; Jacobson, 1970; McGlynn, 1968). In a well-designed study, Borkovec (1970; 1972) contrasted the effectiveness of systematic desensitization and implosive therapy under two conditions of expectancy, in which subjects were either led to believe that the therapy they were receiving was being effective (they were shown false physiological "data" indicating reductions in fear) or in which subjects were shown false physiological records, but not led to believe that this was at all indicative of the progress of therapy. In this study it was found that systematic desensitization and implosive therapy both produced decreases in pulse rate in the presence of the phobic object. However, there was no indication that either type of therapy increased subjects' actual approach behaviors toward the phobic object, although there was an effect due to expectancy: subjects who thought that the treatment was reducing their fear showed greater increases in approach behavior than subjects having no such expectation, and subjects with a positive expectancy touched the object more rapidly during the posttest than did no-expectancy subjects.

A Tentative Evaluation of Implosive Therapy

Although the initial reports of the effectiveness of implosive therapy were quite glowing (Hogan & Kirchner, 1967; Levis & Carrera, 1967; Stampfl, 1967), the total body of research has not been particularly positive in supporting the effectiveness of this technique. Furthermore, there has been a great deal of criticism concerning not only the effectiveness of implosive therapy, but also the proposed theory (Stampfl & Levis, 1967a) underlying it (Morganstern, 1973). Finally, the methodological sophistication of most of the research in this area is quite poor, making any conclusions from the research literature exceedingly difficult (Morganstern, 1973).

Theoretically, the incorporation of psychodynamic themes into the implosive imagery is an important part of therapeutic procedure: it promotes the description of stimuli that are truly related to the hypothesized original traumatic learning situation. However, Hogan, (1968, 1969) one of the most prolific of implosive therapists, uses little if any direct psychodynamic imagery in his treatment procedure (see the extensive example cited earlier). Since Hogan (Hogan & Kirchner, 1967), claims such striking successes this would seem to indicate that the psychodynamic content of implosive themes may be unnecessary, but this has not been directly tested.

Both systematic desensitization and implosive therapy propose that patients must be prevented from making avoidance responses, and that the low (systematic desensitization) or high (implosive therapy) levels of anxiety must be replaced with nonanxious responses (systematic desensitization) or allowed to extinguish when an expected aversive event fails to occur (implosive therapy). However, Borkovec (1970, 1972) included a control condition in which subjects were instructed to make imaginary avoidance responses when imagining implosive scenes. This group also showed some reduction in arousal to the feared stimulus and did not show the increased arousal that implosive-therapy theory would predict.

There are a number of aspects of the implosive procedure that vary from study to study, but whose effects have not been investigated systematically. The inclusion of psychodynamic themes is one. Another involves the hierarchical presentation of the implosive scenes (Stampfl & Levis, 1967a). No clear rationale is presented for the hierarchical presentation of scenes other than that scenes higher on the hierarchy are likely to be close to the actual scene of the original trauma and consequently have been repressed. Presumably, then, it would have been difficult or impossible for the client to imagine them earlier because of such repression, which is eliminated as scenes lower on the hierarchy lose their tendency to provoke anxiety. Some investigators have included the hierarchical presentation of scenes (Barrett, 1967, 1969; Borkovec, 1970, 1972; Hogan & Kirchner, 1967; Levis & Carerra, 1967), while others have omitted this part of the procedure (Mealiea & Nawas, 1971); it is nevertheless impossible to evaluate the effectiveness of their procedures from the study results since the studies differed in a number of ways.

There are a variety of possible alternative explanations to the effectiveness of implosive therapy that have also been ignored in the literature. For example, in many presentations of implosive scenes the subject is asked to imagine various approach behaviors toward the feared object (e.g., Fazio, 1970). This includes the covert and symbolic modeling of such approach behaviors, a technique entirely unrelated to the basic theoretical notions of implosive therapy and more similar to systematic desensitization since emphasis is placed upon the observation of symbolic stimuli in the absence of anxiety (see Chapter II).

Another generally uncontrolled factor in studies on implosive therapy (and many other techniques, as well) is the presence of cognitive factors that might affect approach behaviors toward phobic objects, thus influencing the behavior outcome interpreted as due to other aspects of the therapy. The study by Borkovec (1970, 1972) cited earlier indicates that a client's expectancy of success may be one such important cognitive factor. Furthermore, Borkovec found that expectancies that treatment was effective were more closely related to overt behavioral measures of fear than to physiological measures of fear, such as pulse rate, which were affected by both implosive therapy and systematic-desensitization treatments. This indicates that cognitive components in any treatment regimen may have effects independent of other components of treatment. The evidence here, too, is somewhat mixed. Dee (1970) found that implosive therapy preceded by positive instructions was somewhat more effective than implosive therapy without such instructions. On the other hand, Layne (1970) found no expectancy effect in a study in which implosive therapy itself produced no significant effect.

Finally, an important variable that has been little studied within individual experiments is that of the length of the exposure time to the implosive stimulus. There is some indication that exposures (session lengths) that are too short are likely to produce sensitization, rather than a reduction in anxiety (Eysenck, 1968; Staub, 1968; Wolpe, 1958, 1969). While there has been no research on this question with respect to implosive therapy, some investigators have broached the question in studying the effectiveness of flooding, or response-prevention procedures (Rachman, 1969; Siegeltuch & Baum, 1971).

Another untested assumption in implosive therapy concerns the necessity of presenting descriptions of the fear-eliciting stimuli which are dramatic and clearly unlikely to be, or have been, encountered in the normal occurrence of events (having snakes gouge your eyes out, swallowing them, finding yourself sexually involved with a parent). In implosive therapy the necessity for such scenes is usually derived from the emphasis upon psychodynamic themes, from the argument that such intense scenes do, somehow, approximate the original traumatic learning situation, or from the assumption that there are repressed memories and fears that can be approximated by such creative descriptions. In practice, the presence of psychodynamic scenes and the creative dramatization of hypothesized repressed material are two ways in which the procedures of implosive therapy differ from those of flooding (response prevention). Consequently, let us now turn to a discussion of that technique before concluding our evaluation of both implosive therapy and flooding procedures.

Flooding and Response Prevention

Flooding and *response prevention* are two names for the general technique of exposing an individual to anxiety-provoking stimuli while preventing the occurrence of avoidance responses. As we noted earlier, the theoretical rationale for these techniques is generally the same as that for implosive therapy. The techniques differ in that flooding/response prevention does not involve the psychodynamic interpretations common to implosive therapy, nor does it include the extensive and theatrical thematic elaborations in the presentation of the phobic stimuli. In some instances, especially in experimental work with animals, exposure may be to the actual feared stimuli, rather than to imagined versions. Obviously, the extreme situations commonly presented in implosive therapy do not lend themselves to *in vivo* presentations.

The technique of flooding/response prevention has its roots in experimental work on the establishment and extinction of avoidance responses, work that contributed also to the techniques of aversive control involving avoidance learning (see Chapter IX) (Solomon, Kamin, & Wynn, 1953; Solomon, 1964). Interestingly, this work appeared just prior to the original statements of implosive therapy (Stampfl, 1961), and it is cited in the theoretical statements concerning the mechanisms underlying extinction during implosive therapy (Stampfl & Levis, 1967). Briefly, in his work on avoidance conditioning, Solomon (Solomon, Kamin & Wynn, 1953; Solomon, 1964) found that if an unavoidable shock is preceded by some sort of warning signal (for instance, a light), that light comes to evoke intense emotional responding in the organism being conditioned (presumably because of the anticipation of the aversive stimulus). If that organism is then given the opportunity to escape the shock, say, by jumping out of the portion of the cage containing the grid, then very quickly it begins to make that escape response as soon as the light that signals impending shock comes on. At that time, of course, the escape response has become an avoidance response since it occurs prior to the onset of shock and allows the organism to avoid the punishment.

Once such an avoidance response has been established, Solomon found that the animal would continue to avoid the potential shock for hundreds and hundreds of trials, never waiting long enough to ascertain whether the shock would actually occur. This is, of course, one characteristic of avoidance responses: they are quite persistent, and since they do not include "reality testing," they may persist long after the supposedly avoided aversive consequences have actually ceased to exist. In the theoretical model of flooding/response prevention and implosive therapy, such avoidance responses might have been established long before the individual comes for treatment, perhaps as early as childhood.

Discovering the persistent nature of the avoidance response, Solomon naturally became interested in what procedures, if any, would successfully modify this response. One effective procedure he found (Solomon, Kamin, & Wynn, 1953) was to introduce the animal into the area from which he typically escaped in order to avoid the shock, to actuate the stimulus that supposedly signaled the future onset of shock, but then to prevent the animal from leaving that area and omit the aversive event (shock). Presumably, after a number of trials in which the avoidance response was prevented, the light (the cue that elicited anxiety) no longer elicited anxiety, and when the animal was not prevented from performing the avoidance response, it in fact refrained from avoidance behaviors and appeared calm and nonanxious. Further research on the effectiveness of this technique has explored various parameters promoting effective extinction of avoidance responding, such as the length of each trial during which the organism is prevented from performing the avoidance response (Baum, 1966, 1968, 1969a, 1970).

The use of the term *flooding* (Polin, 1959) appeared about the time implosive therapy was being developed, and the first use of the technique on human clients was reported by Malleson (1959) in that same year. Using a hierarchy similar to that employed in systematic desensitization, Malleson instructed patients to feel more and more frightened, not relaxed, as he progressed through the hierarchy. At first there was an increase in distress, following which Malleson reported that clients showed a recovery of composure and eventually a complete cure. A flooding technique was also reported by Boulougouris and Marks (1969), accompanied by complete recoveries by phobic patients.

Essentially all of the subsequent reports on the use of flooding have come from experiments designed to test the efficacy of this procedure. These studies have been plagued by methodological deficiencies (Morganstern, 1973), as have been the studies of implosive therapy. And, in a manner similar to implosive therapy, the studies of flooding have also produced confliction results.

Wolpin and Raines (1966) presented flooding subjects with the top item of a fear hierarchy throughout four treatment sessions. Subjects in two other conditions either visualized, progressively, a 20-item hierarchy with no relaxation or completed the hierarchy while deliberately tensing their muscles. *All* subjects were subsequently able to handle the phobic object (a snake) after the four treatment sessions, and five out of six subjects could still hold the phobic object 3–5 weeks later. There were only two subjects in each condition, making generalization from this study rather precarious.

There has been one extensive series of studies that reflects upon various parameters of the flooding/response-prevention technique, utilizing animals as subjects (Baum, 1966, 1968, 1969a, 1970; Baum & Poser, 1971; Siegeltuch & Baum, 1971). While caution must be taken in generalizing such results to human beings, Baum (Baum, 1966, 1968, 1969a) has found consistently that procedures of response prevention can extinguish experimentally established avoidance responses. In one study it was apparent that the presence of fearless models can result in "social facilitation" during the flooding experience and hasten recovery of normal behaviors in fear-producing situations (Baum, 1969b; see Chapter IV on modeling procedures). Indeed, Baum tends to interpret the effectiveness of models in terms of vicarious response prevention (Baum, 1970; see Chapter IV). He has also found that the more non-fear-related behavior the animal engages in during flooding, the more effective the flooding/response-prevention treatment (Baum & Poser, 1971). Baum has also found that short durations of response prevention (5 minutes) are effective in treating avoidance behaviors established by typical avoidance conditioning (the animal was allowed to escape the shock on initial trials and then learned to avoid the shock by escaping prior to its onset). However, when avoidance learning was preceded by a series of unavoidable shocks, only a response-prevention period of long duration (30 minutes) was effective in extinguishing the avoidance response. In an earlier study, Baum (1969a) showed that 1-minute response-prevention periods were ineffective in eliminating avoidance responses, while periods of 3 or 5 minutes allowed successful extinction to occur.

Lederhendler and Baum (1970) have demonstrated not only the increased effectiveness of longer response-prevention periods, but also that extinction is facilitated when the animals are forced to move about and explore during the period of response prevention. The authors interpreted these results to indicate that the occurrence of "nonfear" behaviors (approach behaviors or relaxation, for example) may be important factors in the successful employment of flooding/response-prevention procedures.

There have been several studies comparing flooding/response prevention with systematic desensitization in terms of effectiveness and brevity of treatment. Strahley (1965) found flooding more effective than systematic desensitization, although there was no no-treatment control in this study. Brock (1967), in an experimental analogue study, found no significant differences in effectiveness between flooding/response prevention and systematic desensitization, but again the no-treatment control was absent. DeMoor (1970) found both flooding/response prevention and systematic desensitization to be effective in reducing fear, with some suggestion that systematic desensitization produced better results at a later, follow-up test. As with the other studies, however, there are problems with this experiment in the use of inappropriately short periods of relaxation training in systematic desensitization and fairly short periods of flooding as well (though they were four times as long as the periods of relaxation training). In working with speech-anxious college students, Calef and MacLean (1970) found that flooding and systematic desensitization both produced improvements on the Taylor Manifest Anxiety Scale and a personal-report scale of speaker confidence, but no measure of actual public-speaking behavior was included.

Rachman (1966) treated three subjects with spider phobias with flooding/response-prevention and compared them to three subjects treated earlier by systematic desensitization and three subjects in a no-treatment control. In Rachman's flooding/response-prevention procedure, subjects were to imagine fear-provoking scenes for 2 minutes while the therapist "vivified" the experience through verbal elaboration. There were 10 trials per session for 20 minutes of flooding. This study found that flooding produced no improvement on either an actual avoidance test or on the fear thermometer, while systematic desensitization did result in improvement.

Finally, in a well-designed and well-executed study, Boulougouris, Marks, and Marset (1971) gave phobic clients 6 sessions of flooding, followed by 6 sessions of systematic desensitization, or 12 sessions in the reverse order. After the initial six sessions they found that flooding produced greater improvement in terms of ratings by therapist and an independent medical assessor on both total phobic behavior and behavior related to the phobia under treatment, and in terms of skin conductance measures of anxiety during a discussion of the phobic object. After all 12 sessions combined, measures taken immediately after either the first 6 or second 6 flooding sessions, or the first 6 or second 6 systematic desensitization sessions, showed flooding to have produced greater improvement than systematic desensitization on 5 out of 7 measures of anxiety and phobic behavior; in terms of mean scores, flooding showed greater positive effects than systematic desensitization on all 7.

Evidence for the Clinical Effectiveness of Implosive Therapy and Flooding

There is no question that the results of studies concerned with the effectiveness of implosive therapy and flooding/response prevention are quite mixed, and the studies themselves tend generally to be so methodologically poor as to be inconclusive (Morganstern, 1973).

In general, however, the studies evaluating the effectiveness of flooding procedures are generally better designed and executed than those evaluating implosive therapy. Unfortunately, however, there are few studies of flooding involving human patients (as opposed to animals), so the effectiveness of flooding must be interpreted cautiously.

 Although the techniques appear to have generated some positive results, more research is clearly necessary before specific statements can be made with regard to their effectiveness. In the absence of such research, the clinician should consider carefully any inclination to employ these techniques. If they are utilized, it seems most prudent that therapeutic procedures be matched carefully—to the point of identity—with those presented in the literature, including even the details of the therapist's monologue in implosive therapy (see the earlier example in this chapter). Tapes exist modeling the styles of presentation. Still, the possibility of inadvertent sensitization and other potential ill effects demands that the use of implosive therapy and flooding/response prevention be accompanied with caution as least as great as that accompanying the use of techniques of aversive control (see Chapter IX).

IX

Aversive Control

In this chapter we are concerned with two types of procedures: 1) procedures that decrease the likelihood, or *frequency,* of a designated behavior and 2) procedures that reduce the *attractiveness* of certain behaviors and the stimuli that elicit them. Often the second procedure is not associated with the use of punishing consequences, so we should elucidate a bit. To give a brief example, a child who snitches cookies between meals may be punished, when caught, by a slap on the hands or by the removal of some valued privilege because of his misdemeanor. When a person is diagnosed as alcoholic and overimbibes much in the manner of a child overeating cookies (but obviously with more debilitating results), the procedure of choice may not be punishment for drinking, but rather the use of some technique that will reduce his enjoyment of (and desire for) liquor. As we shall see later, an effective procedure toward this end is the *pairing* of an unpleasant, aversive event with the taste, smell, and observation of liquor (in a "punishment" paradigm the unpleasant event would *follow* the act of drinking; we shall discuss the importance of timing and how this relates to the definition of various types of punishment later).

Definitions of Terms

Some initial definitions are now in order. The reader may recall from Chapters V and VI, on the use of operant procedures, that two types of reinforcers are defined, that is, positive and negative. The contingent application of a positive reinforcer, or the contingent termination or withdrawal of a negative reinforcer increases the frequency of a response. In this chapter we define the opposites of these two procedures as constituting *punishment*. Punishment may be defined as the *withdrawal* of a positive reinforcer or the *application* of a negative reinforcer. Stated somewhat differently, punishment involves the withdrawal of a positive or rewarding stimulus, or the application of an aversive, unpleasant stimulus (Hilgard & Bower, 1966). In the example given previously, the two potential punishments were the deprivation of a valued privilege (withdrawal of a positive reinforcer) or the occurrence of an aversive event such as a slap on the hand (the application of a negative reinforcer). Throughout this chapter the terms *punishment, aversive stimulus* (stimuli), and *aversive event* are used interchangeably since even the mere withdrawal of positive reinforcers is generally seen as aversive (Krasner & Ullmann, 1965).

In this chapter we discuss another procedure of aversive control, namely *aversive counterconditioning*. While punishment includes the contingent, *consequent* application of a negative reinforcer, aversive counterconditioning involves the *simultaneous* application of a negative reinforcer (aversive event) *at the same time* the individual is perceiving the stimuli that elicit the problem behaviors, or *at the same time* that the individual is performing the problem behavior. The goal of this procedure is also the elimination of a problem behavior, not by suppressing performance, but by altering the effectiveness or the *valence* of the eliciting stimulus; that is, rather than by affecting the problem behavior itself. It is termed aversive counterconditioning for theoretical, rather than descriptive, reasons. It is assumed that the effectiveness of this technique is due to the classical conditioning of the internal discomfort produced by the aversive stimulus to the perceptual derivatives (sight, sound, smell, taste) of the stimulus (or response) so that eventually the stimulus (or response) alone is no longer attractive and may now in fact produce feelings of discomfort similar to those produced by the aversive stimulus. (This model is discussed later in the section on theoretical concerns.)

The procedure is termed *aversive* because of the nature of the aversive stimulus typically employed (emetics, electric shock, paralyzing drugs, imagination of noxious scenes). It is termed *counterconditioning* since it is theoretically assumed that the original, positive, appetitive value of the stimulus was learned (conditioned); this procedure replaces or counters that learning by substituting the discomfort and desires for avoidance that accompany the aversive stimulus. The reader will note the similarity between this analysis and one theoretical conceptualization (Wolpe's) of the effects of desensitization (relaxation responses replace anxiety responses through a process of counterconditioning).

Escape Training and Avoidance Learning

The effects of aversive events upon behavior may be varied strikingly by controlling the timing between the occurrence of a behavior and the beginning and end of an aversive event. For the present discussion we define punishment as the contingent presentation of an aversive event following a behavior. Thus, the presentation of an aversive stimulus, or the withdrawal of some positive state of affairs, both qualify as punishers. Often a behavior may be performed and be completed before the punishment begins. In these cases the aversive event comprising the punishment has both its onset and offset in the absence of the punished behavior. There is no generally accepted label for this procedure, so we shall simply label it punishment.

In some instances a punishing event may begin after a behavior has been initiated, but before the behavior terminates, and terminating the behavior may also terminate the punishment. This is one example of *escape* training, that is, terminating the punishment behavior allows escape from the aversive stimulation comprising the punishment. A child who is caught unaware raiding the cookie jar and gets his hand slapped may inadvertently receive escape training since the slap is over just as he removes his hand from the cookie jar. A different child might not get his hand slapped, but, rather, be placed in a corner to sit and mull over his sin. This punishment, although occurring after the termination of the problem behavior, may also lead to escape training: this particular mother might be satisfied that a lesson was learned when an apology was rendered and terminate the punishment (a time-out procedure, as we see later). Therefore, an apology would be an active response (terminating the problem behavior, in the first example, may be termed passive) that allows escape from the punishment.

In the course of social interaction, it is often possible for individuals not only to terminate punishment by ceasing the disapproved behavior or performing another response, but indeed to *avoid* punishment by ceasing that particular behavior, or by ceasing the behavior and performing an immediate alternative behavior, as well, *prior* to the onset of the punishment. The adventuresome child referred to above might be able to avoid punishment if he quickly pulls his hand from the cookie jar before his mother reaches him. This is not escape training since the punishment never occurs. If his mother is more strict, however, simply stopping the cookie snitching may not be sufficient; nevertheless, a quickly and abjectly rendered apology might warm the cockles of her heart sufficiently to allay the punishment. Thus, an apology becomes an active behavior (as opposed to passively stopping snitching) that serves to allow the avoidance of punishment.

Responses that allow the avoidance of punishment are extraordinarily resistant to extinction—that is, they often persist for long, long periods of time even though there is no obvious reinforcement occurring to account for their longevity (Solomon, 1964; Solomon, Kamin, & Wynn, 1953). In the next section we discuss a possible reason for this characteristic of avoidance responses: the termination of punishment is a very powerful negative reinforcer, and to the extent that the anticipation of punishment, generated by involvement in an activity that usually results in punishment, is itself an aversive experience (some would label it anxiety) (Dollard & Miller, 1950), an avoidance response carries with it its own reinforcer.

Whenever a behavior is performed that generates anxiety because it has generally been punished in the past, the performance of an avoidance response, which has prevented punishment in the past, will serve to reduce that anxiety and thus be reinforced—even if in the present situation there was no possibility of punishment. It is noteworthy that there are two forms of negative reinforcement that may occur, depending upon the situation. Any response that terminates punishment (which is already in effect) will be reinforced by the termination of that punishment—but the punishment must be in effect. Any response that terminates the anxiety of anticipating punishment will be reinforced even if the punishment is not actually forthcoming. Hence, in the latter instance the negative reinforcement exists *within* the individual and will generally accompany the performance of the avoidance behavior, while in the former instance only when punishment actually occurs will negative reinforcement be experienced following the escape response. This is seen as a fundamental difference between escape learning and avoidance learning: negative reinforcement is an integral component of both escape and avoidance behaviors, but escape behaviors depend upon the environment to provide and then terminate the punishment, while avoidance behaviors carry their own reinforcing consequences with them, so to speak, since the anxiety and its termination are events occurring within the individual.

Later in the chapter we discuss a proposed difference between the procedures of aversion-relief and anxiety-relief, defining aversion relief as the training of a new response by the termination of an aversive event (escape training), and anxiety relief as the training of a new response by allowing that response to avoid anticipated punishment (avoidance training). Table 9.1 presents a schematic representation of the general relations among the occurrences of problem behaviors, punishments, and alternative (avoidance) behaviors. This table is illustrative only—it does not exhaust all the temporal relations that exist among these three variables.

Historical Perspective

The interested reader may wish to reread the historical review presented in Chapter V (contingency management procedures). This review traces the influence of early investigators upon the subsequent research and theorizing concerned with principles of reinforcement.

Often there is a tendency to interpret the definition of negative reinforcers as punishers to mean that the application of a negative reinforcer promotes learning. This is not the case, and an analysis of the effects of punishment is not at all that simple. Skinner's first coherent presentation of "operant psychology" appeared in 1938. In 1944, in a series of brilliant studies, W. K. Estes (1944) explored the effects of punishment in an attempt to clarify this portion of the operant model. Estes came to some striking conclusions that were accepted without question or limitation until quite recently. Stated most simply, it was generally concluded from Estes's experiments that punishment led to the *suppression* of the performance of a behavior, but *not* to its *unlearning*. The general conclusion was reached that a response may not be eliminated from an organism's repertoire by punishment alone. Furthermore, the response suppression that is seen may be due to the aversive character or emotional concomitants of the punishing stimulus and not to the effects of contingent application alone. Estes found that regularly presenting an aversive stimulus every 30 seconds reduced responding to the same degree as did the contingent presentation of punishment.

For some time (20 years) after the publication of these results there was a tendency to minimize the usefulness of punishment. Research continued, primarily in laboratory settings, but it was not until the publication of a thorough research review by another eminent researcher, R. L. Solomon (1964), that attention again was given to punishment and aversive stimulation as an important, if unpleasant, aspect of experience, which could have powerful and lasting effects upon behavior.[1]

---

[1] Note that in this historical review we are concentrating upon punishment, not aversive counterconditioning, and, within the concept of punishment, upon the delivery of aversive stimuli, not upon the withdrawal of positive reward. This omission reflects a lack of theoretical concern that has characterized the literature and is not intended to undermine the importance of these procedures.

TABLE 9.1

Temporal Relations in Techniques of Aversive Control

Label	Procedure	Time[a]	Type of learning
	Simple punishment		
Punishment (including covert sensitization)	Problem behavior		
	Punishment		Passive escape learning
	Alternative behavior (none)		
	Punishment plus aversive counterconditioning		
Aversion-relief conditioning (including relief version of covert sensitization)	Problem behaviors and inappropriate stimuli		
	Punishment		Active escape learning
	Alternative behaviors and appropriate stimuli		

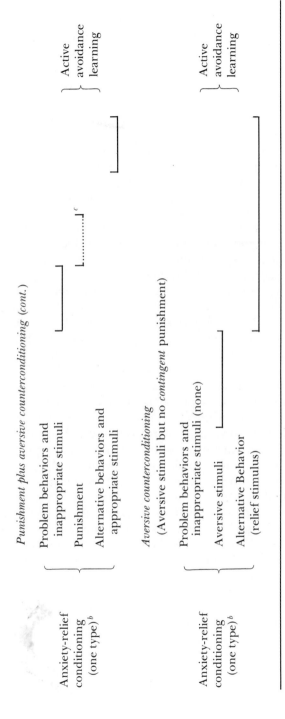

Punishment plus aversive counterconditioning (cont.)

Problem behaviors and
inappropriate stimuli

Punishment

Alternative behaviors and
appropriate stimuli

Anxiety-relief
conditioning
(one type)[b]

Active
avoidance
learning

Aversive counterconditioning
(Aversive stimuli but no *contingent* punishment)

Problem behaviors and
inappropriate stimuli (none)

Aversive stimuli

Alternative Behavior
(relief stimulus)

Anxiety-relief
conditioning
(one type)[b]

Active
avoidance
learning

[a] ⌐ = onset; ⌐ = offset or termination.
[b] See text.
[c] Dotted line = sometimes punishment occurs; sometimes it does not.

In his review, Solomon (1964) attempted to systematize the conclusions that could be drawn from the research on punishment up to that time. He began from the basic observation that individuals learn in order to *avoid* punishment and then proposed that all punishment learning (including what is usually termed *escape*) might be termed avoidance learning.

According to Solomon one may systematize punishment learning into two classes: *passive* avoidance learning (or conditioning) and *active* avoidance learning. The common observation that punishment inhibits a response exemplifies passive avoidance learning: one learns *not* to respond in order to avoid the aversive stimulus that comprises the punishment. There is also active avoidance learning, in which an individual learns to *do* something, an alternative behavior, in order to avoid the punishment. The individual who is repeatedly punished for wasting time, rather than cleaning his room or office, may develop feelings of discomfort when he is in a messy surrounding and find that only by cleaning the room does he again feel comfortable.

This latter example brings us to a theoretical conceptualization of punishment that is reasonably prevalent (Solomon, 1964; Mowrer, 1960). This theory is termed the *two-factor* or *two-process* theory of punishment. The first process, basically one of classical conditioning, involves the strong association of the aversive experience (and its internal correlates, presumably strong anxiety, or at least discomfort) with the stimuli that are present at the time and in the situation of the punished response. After several punishments, simply being in the particular situation and feeling the motivation to perform the response (observing the evoking stimuli) may make the individual feel anxious and prevent the response. In passive avoidance learning, the individual does not perform the behavior and may do nothing at all. On the other hand, however, one might not simply become inactive, but rather perform some behavior that is instrumental in avoiding the punishment. Typically, in the initial learning of either type of avoidance behavior, the behavior learned (either passively doing nothing, or actively performing an alternative behavior) is instrumental in *terminating* the punishment; and later it is discovered that performing the behavior prior to the punishment will prevent the punishment from occurring at all. A child may learn that when he is caught doing something he is not supposed to, he can avoid the punishment if he immediately stops (passive avoidance) and lowers his head, looks sad, apologizes, etc. (active avoidance behaviors).

In this conceptualization there are two types of learning occurring. First of all, the individual comes to associate the internal components of the aversive response with the stimuli present at, and prior to, the time of behavior. This is seen as a process of classical conditioning in which the internal responses of fear and anxiety in their physiological forms come to be evoked by the surrounding stimuli since they are consistently evoked in the presence of these stimuli. Some authors might see it as inversely analogous to the way in which relaxation comes to replace anxiety in the procedure of desensitization (see Chapter II).

The second process is one of operant conditioning. Any behavior that removes some or all of these stimuli will decrease the anxiety and consequently be reinforced (negative reinforcement—see Chapter V). Since the situation now automatically evokes the aversive anxiety responses within the individual, the avoidance response automatically carries with it its own reinforcer and supposedly is reinforced every time it occurs. Similarly, since the punished response is part of the stimulus environment (to the extent that one monitors his own behaviors), if the punishment overlaps with the behavior at all, the behavior itself will come to elicit anxiety and guilt (internal aversive states that may be seen as punishers accompanying the punished response).

The conditioning of anxiety to the stimuli that evoke a response is likely to alter the attractiveness and value placed upon the perceiving (viewing, hearing, smelling, touching) of these stimuli. This may provide an invaluable aid in the treatment of behavior disorders for which a powerfully evocative stimulus is an important component of the performance of the response (for example, sexual deviation or alcoholism). Similarly, the provision of specified new stimuli immediately upon the termination of the punishing aversive stimulus pairs these stimuli with the strong positive components of this "relief" (Mowrer, 1960) that is, the powerfully reinforcing aspects involved in negative reinforcement).

Positive and Negative Concerns in the Use of Aversive-Control Techniques

The pros and cons of employing aversive control should be considered carefully since there is a deserved general distaste for intentionally caused pain or discomfort, and the potential for harm that accompanies some aversive stimuli cannot be taken lightly. Society has generally frowned upon the intentional infliction of pain except under certain well-specified conditions and in the hand of particular agents. Parents may spank their children with little formal justification, but the schools are essentially prevented from using this technique of punishment. Parents may send their children to bed without supper, but institutions are occasionally prevented from depriving patients of cigarettes or meals even when the attempt is not to punish, but to create more powerful reinforcers (Lucero, Vail, & Scherber, 1968). Until recently, legal authorities could order the execution of individuals (as military authorities still may during time of war), but the use of torture (following which the individual survives) has long been prohibited. Certainly there are many inconsistencies in the formal, legal, and informal, societal sanctions granted certain forms of punishment, and it is quite unfortunate that so many obviously inhumane practices continue to have any sanction at all, especially when it is clear that they are ineffective in controlling behavior that truly must be controlled. To take a particularly heinous example, the old Blue Laws of Connecticut specified that a father could kill a disobedient son (Blue Laws of Connecticut, 1861, Section 14, p. 69)!

The use of aversive control will always involve the infliction of pain, physical or mental. Like suicide, which may be assumed to have the tacit approval of the person who attempts it, mere approval by a client for the use of aversive techniques does not immediately justify them. Clearly, however, a client's informed approval is necessary before application of these techniques can be considered. The only true justification for the eventual use of aversive procedures is the likelihood that they will be effective in changing a person's behavior in the desired direction, leaving no residual ill effects, again either physical or mental. Such cautions in the use of aversive techniques point to the single negative aspect of aversive control: more than any other type of behavior modification procedure, aversive techniques have an inherently greater possibility of causing physical harm to a client if they are used incorrectly. Note, however, that they contain the possibility, not probability, of causing harm. Aversive control need not employ punishing consequences at an intensity likely to harm an individual; however, when *misused,* harm is often a possible result. Also, some aversive techniques, such as having an individual imagine unpleasant circumstances, do not have the potentiality for harm that other techniques involving the administration of electric shock or drugs do. But the point is clear: the use of aversive techniques *must* be carefully considered and monitored in order to insure that the client is in no physical danger.

Highly disturbed children and adults may occasionally develop patterns of self-destructive behavior, which cause extensive physical harm. Paradoxically, it appears that these behaviors are often maintained by the attention of parents or institutional staff who offer interpersonal contact when physically restraining these patients. Indication that the physical contact by the caretakers is responsible for these behaviors comes from studies showing that self-abusing behavior does indeed decrease in frequency when it ceases to elicit attention and care from others (Lovaas, Freitag, Gold, & Kassorla, 1965; Lovaas & Simmons, 1969).

A basic problem with handling self-destructive behaviors by simple nonreinforcement or extinction procedures is the length of time an extinction procedure requires. Often, also, there is an increase in the frequency of the behavior at the time when reinforcement is initially withdrawn. While these factors may be tolerated when less dangerous responses are under treatment, self-destructive behavior in psychotic patients often reaches such proportions that the patient's life is endangered. For example, it is not uncommon that self-destructive children break their own noses, keep their eyes constantly blackened, tear out their nails, or even tear large quantities of flesh from their bodies by gnawing, scratching, or gouging with objects. One self-destructive boy hit himself 2750 times in the space of 1½ hours when restraints were removed and an extinction procedure was instituted.

In the treatment of deviant responses requiring rapid inhibition, intense punishment is an extremely effective procedure. More "humane" treatment of self-destructive patients often involves long-term hospitalization (that is, for life) during which time the patient is almost continuously restrained. Restraint procedures used include "camisoles" (straight jackets) or tying the patient's arms and legs to the head and foot of a bed, thus effectively keeping him from injuring himself. Such restraints, however, have severely debilitating effects themselves, including demineralization of bones, shortening of tendons, and an increasing loss of movement ability. Clearly, nonpunitive treatment of patients is not always more "humane" than aversive procedures. As we discuss later, a very few intense punishments can effectively eliminate maladaptive behaviors and provide the opportunity for training in alternative behaviors that are adaptive.

Although there is great concern in our society over the use of aversive consequences outside the legal or family domains, not all of this concern centers about the possibility of harm to the individual. Some concern is over the possibility of inadvertent changes in behavior, which may be accomplished rapidly and out of a therapist's control because of the powerful effects of aversive techniques. However, the fact that the use of negative consequences may be a powerful procedure of behavior therapy need not be a liability. Indeed, while it does make necessary the use of extreme care during application, the fact that aversive events may exert rapid and decisive control over behavior is a primary advantage of this technique, as well. Experiences resulting from the abuse of powerful drugs are often highly rewarding and the effects of such immediate rewards often outweigh later negative consequences, resulting in frequent, habitual drug usage. Similarly, sexual deviations immediately provide their own maintaining rewarding consequences of great strength. Behaviors that are intimately linked to highly rewarding, maintaining consequences may require the manipulation of extremely aversive consequences if they are to be brought under control. Since drug use, whether it be the ingestion of illegal drugs or inappropriately high consumption of alcohol, may quickly cause physical damage, it may be necessary to use a modification procedure that produces rapid change or control, as in the case of self-destructive behaviors discussed above. Therefore, aversive techniques may be appropriate for gaining control over behaviors that are either highly rewarding or physically damaging, when control is unlikely to be achieved by other means, or when it must be achieved quickly in order to prevent further damaging effects from the client's current behavior.

Thus, similar characteristics of aversive techniques may be both liabilities or assets, depending upon the nature of the behavioral problem at hand or the capability of the person employing the techniques. Even when they are appropriately and carefully employed, however, there are certain potential problems that may arise following the use of aversive procedures. Such problems, of course, may be prevented or minimized given the use of proper precautions.

Conditioned Emotional Responses and Inappropriate Avoidance Responses

Intense punishment has the capacity to condition anxiety as a response consequent to all stimuli and responses present at the time of punishment (aversive counterconditioning). Any response that serves to terminate the punishment or to remove the anxiety-evoking stimuli will be reinforced by the termination of that anxiety. Hence, there is the possibility that avoidance responses that, in effect, carry their own reinforcement (the termination of the internal state of anxiety) will develop and become powerful new responses to the stimuli that previously elicited the punished response, as well as other stimuli that are present during punishment. In everyday experience one may feel discomfort when entering a room in which an unfortunate aversive experience has occurred. Another example may be seen in the behavior of a dog who becomes hand-shy after punishment administered by his master's hand, rather than by a rolled-up newspaper.

In the presentation of aversive stimuli during a behavior therapy procedure, avoidance responses are often carefully prevented or, as in anxiety-relief procedures, the response intended to replace the undesirable one may be presented as an avoidance response to the aversive stimulus. Consider the earlier example of the treatment of a male homosexual who is shocked during the presentation of a slide of a nude male, but who can, by pressing a button, both terminate the shock and replace the male slide with one of a nude female. This procedure constitutes escape training with some aversive counterconditioning, as well (since the shock overlaps with the viewing of the male slide). In avoidance-conditioning procedures, such a client would be given a signal denoting the impending shock and could avoid the shock entirely by pressing the button and summoning the female picture. The careful prevention of the possibility of undesirable avoidance responses by the provision of desirable ones can easily eliminate this potential problem. Also, the use of aversive techniques other than punishment (for example, withdrawal of positive reinforcers) is not as likely to produce avoidance behaviors.

Punishment intensity is another factor that may enter into the possible development of a conditioned emotional response. As noted earlier, in aversive counterconditioning, the aversive stimulus is presented during the performance of the undesired response or during the presentation of stimuli that usually evoke the undesired response; the purpose of this procedure is to alter the valence of these stimuli or responses by conditioning the emotional concomitants of punishment directly to them. In this case, obviously, the therapist would want punishment of sufficient intensity to elicit an emotional response because the emotional response would not be problematic: it is the desired outcome. Even in this case, however, punishment of too great an intensity may drive the client from therapy: an emotional response may have been conditioned to the entire therapy situation! One may, of course, err in the other direction, as well, by administering an aversive stimulus whose intensity is too mild. In this case the desired counterconditioning, or inhibition of behavior, will not be accomplished. The stimulus must be truly aversive to accomplish the desired ends. Careful consideration on the part of the therapist is necessary in selecting the proper intensity. Granting the necessity to avoid physical harm, a rule of thumb might be to adjust the intensity (awareness) of the punishment employed to the maximum that will be endured by the client.

In contrasting techniques of positive (reinforcement) and aversive control, it has also been proposed that punishment is generally inefficient because aversive stimuli of high intensity create a general disruption in behavior and thereby impede learning. Undoubtedly this is to some extent true, but the problem is not unique to aversive control. It has long been known that reinforcement of high magnitude disrupts learning (Miller & Estes, 1961), and recent work indicates that the retention of acquired behavior patterns and preference for these patterns is also disrupted by the use of high-magnitude rewards (Masters & Mokros, 1973).

Behavioral Rigidity

Another potential problem is the development of the desired behavior in such strength that it becomes a rigid part of the person's repertoire

and may not be replaced, temporarily or permanently, by different behaviors when they are more appropriate. When working with children,
often the behavior problems presented are those of behaviors that are
appropriate for adults, but judged inappropriate when displayed by
children. For example, sexual curiosity or exploratory sexual behavior
by children may be deemed quite undesirable and severely punished.
While such punishment may effectively inhibit the sexual behavior, a
child who is severely punished for exploratory sexual behavior may develop anxiety as a generalized response to sexual behavior and stimuli.
Later in life, when sexual behavior is deemed appropriate and even
desirable, such a person may find himself impotent, inhibited, or simply
unmotivated toward appropriate sexual encounters. At this point, the
results of prior "successful" behavior therapy may become grist for
further modification procedures!

Often the suppression of behavior by punishment is extremely transi-
tory, and the behavior may reappear within a relatively short period of
time unless other modification procedures have established behaviors alternative to the punished ones. However, some classes of behavior seem
extremely sensitive to punishment. Behaviors related to an organism's
survival (*consummatory behaviors*) such as eating, drinking, and sexual behavior are extremely sensitive to punishment, and caution should be
used when working with such behaviors, especially if some flexibility and
not blanket inhibition is desired.

Generalization of Punishment Effects and the Availability of Alternative Behaviors

When a behavior is punished within a given stimulus context, care
should be taken to provide an alternative behavior deemed appropriate
and acceptable. Suppression of a behavior by punishment may produce
either extensive behavioral inhibition—the individual will do nothing at
all in the relevant stimulus context—or, if no specific alternative is
provided, the next behavior in the individual's personal hierarchy may
appear, and this behavior may not be appropriate either. For example, if
a child were punished for physically assaultive behavior toward his
parents when he did not get his own way, the assaultive behavior might
drop out, but the child might yell, stomp out of the room, or even cry (a
response typical of an earlier period in his development). Modeling the
appropriate skills of asking with tact and politeness would be good ac-
companiments to such treatment since they would probably meet with
some modicum of success from appreciative adults and become relatively enduring components of the child's behavioral repertoire.

Aside from the inclusion of training in acceptable alternative behaviors, the therapist may prevent the uncontrolled generalization of punishment effects by labeling clearly the behaviors being punished and designating the alternative behaviors that are acceptable and that will not elicit negative consequences. Discriminations may also be encouraged by clear labeling that designates not only the appropriate and inappropriate behaviors, but also the times, places conditions, and people in whose presence the desired behaviors will be deemed appropriate and elicit reinforcement rather than punishment.

Negative Modeling

Another problem that may arise from the use of aversive techniques is the acquisition, by the client, of various skills and predilections for personally administering similar aversive stimuli to others. Thus, a child who is punished physically by his parents for assaultive behavior in the home may in fact be quite well behaved at home, while being quite physically aggressive toward his peers and adults in other situations. This problem is most likely to arise when children are involved and when the modification procedures occur in a naturalistic environment such as the home. (As such, they are discussed in greater detail in the chapter on contingency management.)

As we must stress throughout this chapter, *AVERSIVE TECHNIQUES, ESPECIALLY PUNISHMENT, ARE RARELY UTILIZED ALONE; THEIR EFFECTIVENESS WILL BE MAXIMIZED AND POTENTIAL PROBLEMS MINIMIZED WHEN THEY ARE USED IN CONJUNCTION WITH OTHER TECHNIQUES DESIGNED TO PROMOTE MORE EFFECTIVE BEHAVIOR PATTERNS.* Such combined procedures can hasten the change process, while also complementing improvements in the person's behavior by the elimination of undesired behaviors with the simultaneous addition of desired ones.

Procedures of Aversive Control

For the sake of the current presentation, we wish to define several procedures of aversive control that differ primarily in the timing with which an aversive event occurs relative to a problem behavior and/or perception of eliciting stimuli and whether alternative responses are provided in some temporal relationship to the aversive event.

Contingent Aversive Control: Punishment

The use of contingent punishment is the most common aversive technique employed in naturalistic socialization and is often incorrectly viewed as the essential, or only, method of aversive control. There are several ways in which punishment may be employed. First of all, punishment may be administered immediately following the occurrence of a problem behavior. This procedure typically produces rapid suppression of the punished behavior, although the behavior may begin to recur if there is no alternative behavior that the individual may perform successfully in situations that usually elicit the problem behavior. It is also important that punishment occur immediately following the problem behavior since the longer the lag between the termination of behavior and the occurrence of punishment, the less effective the punishment will be in suppressing the behavior (Azrin & Holz, 1966).

It is also possible that punishment may be applied *while* the behavior is actually occurring. If this is done, it is equally important that the punishment be terminated as soon as the behavior terminates. Reference to the theoretical analysis of punishment and aversive experiences presented earlier will reveal that this timing is important since the negative reinforcement inherent in the termination of a punishment will reinforce the act of terminating the problem behavior. It is also likely in this procedure that since the aversive event and the problem behavior overlap in time, the problem behavior will acquire some aversive valence by virtue of having been paired with the aversive event. A caution so obvious it hardly bears mentioning: some problem behaviors may well be exacerbated by the use of punishment. Obviously, in such cases, punishment should not be employed. Examples of such behaviors might include certain aggressive responses for which punishment might well be seen as counteraggression and serve as an inappropriate model, thus increasing subsequent aggression (Bandura & Walters, 1959) or tantrum behavior (Burchard & Tyler, 1965; Carlson, Arnold, Becker, & Madsen, 1968).

Generally, there are four procedures related to the use of punishment for the suppression of problem behavior; these procedures are noted in Table 9.2. For greatest effectiveness, a contingent aversive stimulus should be of maximal appropriate intensity from the start, should be of the greatest intensity possible (but not so intense as to inflict physical damage, totally disrupt behavior, or produce a conditioned emotional response), should follow a problem behavior immediately, and should follow every occurrence of a problem behavior.

TABLE 9.2

Variables Related to the Administration of Contingent Punishment

---

I. *Manner of introduction of punishment*
   The introduction of punishment at full intensity maximizes its effectiveness (Azrin, Holz, & Hake, 1963; Masserman, 1946; Brethower & Reynolds, 1962). An abrupt, substantial increase in the current intensity of an aversive stimulus will increase the degree of behavioral suppression (Azrin, 1959, 1960; Holz & Azrin, 1963).

II. *Intensity of punishment*
   The greater the intensity of the aversive stimulus, the greater the suppression of behavior produced (see section on conditioned emotional responses, however) (Estes, 1944; Azrin, 1958, 1959; Holz & Azrin, 1962).

III. *Immediacy of punishment*
   A contingent aversive stimulus should be applied immediately following a problem behavior (Azrin & Holz, 1966; Azrin, 1956).

IV. *Scheduling of punishment*
   A continuous schedule of punishment (aversive stimulation following each instance of the problem behavior) is more effective than intermittent punishment (Estes, 1944; Zimmerman & Ferster, 1963; Azrin, Holz, & Hake, 1963).

Aversive Counterconditioning: Anxiety Relief and Aversion Relief

As we have repeatedly pointed out, any stimulus that is present during the termination of an aversive stimulus (for instance, stimuli that have distinct offsets, such as shock) will come to have a positive valence: that is, it will be accompanied by feelings of "relief" (Mowrer, 1960). Theoretically, the conceptualization is that any stimulus that is repeatedly paired with the positive sensations accompanying the termination of punishment will, by a process of classical conditioning, come to evoke these same feelings even in different situations (Mowrer, 1960). A stimulus that has negative valence (for example, the nude female figure for a homosexual) will come to have positive valence if it is repeatedly paired with the powerful feelings of relief that accompany the termination of a strongly aversive stimulus. Similarly, a neutral stimulus, one that was neither pleasing, comforting, distasteful, nor nauseating, will come to have positive properties.

The *anxiety-relief* procedure is intended to transform a neutral stimulus into one which evokes such strong positive feelings that it can overcome and displace feelings of anxiety. We have emphasized the problem of generalizing treatment effects beyond the treatment room. Anxiety-relief procedures are typically utilized in cases where anxiety is the primary problem. By taking a verbal stimulus, such as the word *calm,* and associating it with the termination of punishment, one can create a stimulus that a client may provide for himself when faced with an anxiety-provoking situation outside the therapy room, a stimulus that can reduce or even nullify the feelings of anxiety so that adaptive behavior and relearning can occur. The use of verbal stimuli has distinct advantages since they can be thought, rather than said aloud, thus enabling the patient to control his own behavior without the notice of others (see Chapter VIII for other procedures of self-control).

The procedure for establishing anxiety-relief conditioning is quite simple. Typically, a continuous shock is delivered to a client for as long as he can bear it. The client is instructed to allow the shock to continue until he can simply bear it no longer, at which time he is to say a particular word (for example, "calm") aloud. As the word is uttered, the current is terminated. This procedure may be repeated a number of times over a series of sessions. Its effectiveness may be enhanced by slightly increasing the level of shock on each trial. An alternative procedure is to begin with a mild level of shock and to increase the intensity gradually as the current stays on, with the client saying the designated word when the intensity has reached the maximum the client can bear. In any event, care should be taken to utilize a level of shock that is truly aversive to the client and to increase the level whenever the client reports that he is adapting to the point that the aversiveness of the stimulus seems to be decreased.

The *aversion-relief* procedure is also best employed when the aversive stimulus employed has a sharp offset. In this procedure, when the client performs his problem behavior or when he views a stimulus that is inappropriately attractive to him, a punisher (such as shock) is presented. He then ceases the behavior (or the therapist prevents the client from continued observation of the stimulus) while the punishment continues, and then a short time after the behavior has ceased, or the stimulus is gone, the punishment is terminated. Any behavior performed, or stimulus perceived, by the client at the time when the punishment is terminated will come to have positive properties. Thus, in the case where the client performs a behavior and then is punished, it is well to terminate the punishment as quickly as possible after the behavior ceases so that the process of terminating the problem behavior, as well as the immediately succeeding behavior, will come to have positive properties.

When treatment is designed primarily to alter the valence of a stimulus, the shock should be continued for a while after the stimulus is no longer visible so that any remaining image of the stimulus continues to be paired with the punishment, and inconsequential responses such as shutting the eyes, turning the head, etc. do not accidentally acquire relief properties. In the latter cases, treatment might not alter the valence of the stimulus, but rather instil peculiar avoidance responses whereby the client would avoid looking at the objects in the stimulus class even though he still found them attractive.

Adding the "relief" procedure to contingent-punishment procedures is quite simple. It involves the presentation of a stimulus or the evocation of a behavior just at the moment of punishment termination. The stimuli or behaviors would be chosen from the general classes of socially approved, adaptive behaviors that the client does not perform or value, and that typically are mutually exclusive with the behavior or stimulus attraction under treatment. Thus, homosexuals may be shown pictures of nude males accompanied by the onset and duration of shock. Subsequently they may activate a switch that terminates the slides, or the therapist may darken the screen just as the shock terminates. Simultaneously a slide depicting a nude female may appear, paired with the termination of that shock. An alcoholic might be shocked immediately as he quaffs a mouthful of bourbon, but the shock might be terminated immediately as he spits out the bourbon.

Initially, aversion relief is actually an escape procedure, and after this technique has been employed for several treatment sessions, or trials, a client may be allowed to *avoid* the aversive stimulus by requesting or otherwise self-administering the termination of the display of inappropriate stimuli and the onset of the relief stimuli *before* the punishing event has occurred. For example, after the inappropriate stimuli are displayed, the client may have 8 seconds before a shock will occur, during which time he can terminate the display, institute the display of more appropriate items, and in doing so avoid the shock (Feldman & MacCulloch, 1971). Even though punishment may not occur (because the client terminates the display), this period tends to be quite anxiety provoking because of the imminent aversive event. Furthermore, the avoidance response (say, pressing a button that terminates the slide of a nude male and substitutes one of a nude female) does not always produce immediate results. The time period during which the inappropriate stimuli and shock can be avoided varies from trial to trial: 6½ seconds on some trials, 4½ on others, and up to 7½ on others. These procedures promote even more intense anxiety and heighten the subsequent feeling of relief (when the slide is removed and shock avoided). Since the purpose of all these aspects of this technique is to produce anxiety, and since it is the internal experience of anxiety that comprises the aversive event, the label, anxiety-relief conditioning, seems appropriate to this procedure. Additionally, such a label differentiates this technique, which is based on *avoidance* training, from aversion-relief procedures, which are based upon *escape* training.[2]

It should be noted that in the use of the anticipatory avoidance technique (for example, in which a homosexual client may terminate his viewing of a nude male slide prior to experiencing an aversive stimulus and by so doing avoid that unpleasant experience), it has not been demonstrated that the aversion-relief effect actually operates (MacDonough, 1972). It is clearly a basic theoretical premise, however, that anxiety increases as the client views the slide (and the shock approaches), and that the termination of the viewing of that slide produces a decrement in anxiety, which is a highly positive event paired with current stimuli (for instance, the presentation of a slide of a nude female) and one which may reinforce the act of terminating the availability of the prohibited stimulus and attention to it.

The Use of Symbolic Behavior in Aversive Procedures

Occasionally, symbolic, or imagined, representations of the behavior or of the stimuli that elicit the problem behavior will be items to which aversive procedures are applied. Thus, although some therapists have homosexual patients masturbate to homosexual and heterosexual fantasies during treatment, this is not a common procedure, and there is no instance of which we are aware in which actual homosexual activity was performed during treatment. Consequently, the treatment of homosexuality typically involves the presentation of symbolic stimuli such as slides of nude males.

Furthermore, only portions of a behavior sequence may be used during treatment. Consider, for example, the alcoholic patient who slowly but surely becomes intoxicated as he drinks and is shocked contingently. In this case the typical procedure is to have the individual take a sip of an alcoholic beverage and then spit it into a basin immediately upon the termination of shock.

In treating a variety of disorders some therapists employ only words that suggest the changeworthy behavior or describe situations or stimuli associated with it. Thus, a male homosexual might be confronted with the words "sodomy," "man in bed with me," or "gay bar," during shock; and then with "woman's breasts," "woman in bed with me," or "girl friend," immediately upon the termination of shock (an aversion-relief procedure with anxiety-relief components, as well, since thinking

---

[2] It should be noted that another term used to describe this technique is *anticipatory avoidance* (Feldman & MacCulloch, 1971).

"woman in bed with me" will surely reduce his anxiety when he advances to that stage of heterosexual behavior).

It seems likely that the use of symbolic representations in any therapy, while effective to a good degree, may not be as effective as if the true stimulus or behavior were employed. In some instances, however, the symbolic stimuli employed may in fact be the ones operative in real life. The fantasy of a nude male or a picture of one may in fact be a common stimulus for sexual arousal in an active homosexual or even more so for a homosexual who wishes to alter his behavior and consequently is less active with real partners, depending more upon masturbation to homosexual fantasies for sexual outlet. The point remains, however, that even though the use of real stimuli and behaviors may enhance the effectiveness of a modification technique, symbolic representation of stimuli and behaviors is often the only alternative available to a therapist.

The extent to which such symbolic representations may be effective is demonstrated in the effectiveness of systematic desensitization, which uses imaginal stimuli (see Chapter II). Furthermore, in the section of this chapter on covert sensitization (see also the sections on implosive therapy, in Chapter VIII), it is seen that imagined circumstances that are highly aversive may be effectively employed as the aversive stimulus in place of "real" stimuli of an aversive nature—such as electric shock or emetic drugs.

Counterconditioning and Sensitization

In the application of techniques of aversive control, one common goal is the reduction of the attractiveness of inappropriate stimuli and behaviors. This goal is usually achieved by having an aversive stimulus occur at the same time as the performance of the problem behavior or the perception of the inappropriate stimuli. Thus, the procedure may be seen as one of counterconditioning in which attractive valences of inappropriate behavior and stimuli are replaced by the overpowering aversive qualities of the simultaneously presented aversive stimulus, presumably by the process of classical conditioning (Mowrer, 1960). This procedure may also be seen as one of sensitization: the individual becomes "sensitized" in that he learns to feel anxious when performing the problem behavior or viewing (tasting, smelling, etc.) the stimuli associated with the problem behavior (see Chapter II for a discussion of one view of desensitization as a counterconditioning procedure; see also Bandura, 1969). The procedure of covert sensitization is the only technique that uses the term *sensitization* in its formal label. However, other counterconditioning procedures utilizing nonimaginal aversive stimuli might well be labeled techniques of *overt* sensitization.

The remainder of this chapter is organized according to the type of aversive stimulus used. These stimuli include electric shock, emetic and paralytic drugs, and the imagination of aversive scenes (covert sensitization). Within each section, case histories are described, which illustrate the treatment of different behavior disorders by the application of various specific procedures (contingent punishment, aversion relief, anxiety relief).

Procedural Examples: The Use of Electric Shock in Aversive Control

Electric shock is a powerful punishing, aversive stimulus and has many advantages over other punishing stimuli used in aversive control. Excepting covert sensitization procedures, shock is the punishment most easily employed since it requires little special equipment other than the inductorium device used to supply the electric current. Obviously, severe electric shock can cause skin burns of serious proportions if applied inappropriately. However, sufficient care in making certain that the client is in good health, the use of an inductorium device specially designed for the purpose of aversive control with human beings,[3] and

---

[3] There are a number of references in the literature concerning proper equipment for the delivery of electric shock as an aversive stimulus. The interested reader should consult the following references:

Galbraith, Byrich, & Rutledge (1970): telemetric delivery of electric shock
Royer, Rynearson, Rice, & Upper (1971): grid for delivery of shock to soles of feet
Pfeiffer & Johnson (1968): electrode for delivery of shock to arm
Lafayette Instrument Company Catalogue #270.

As an indication of the measures taken to insure the safety of electrical devices to deliver shock, the following paragraph from the Lafayette Instrument Company catalogue describes their inductorium.

82400 Master Shock Supply
Two outstanding features of this instrument have made it the most popular shock source in its category. First, the actual subject current is indicated on the front panel. No approximations or indirect methods are required. This is accomplished by a precision meter and solid state metering circuit. Second, the 82400 is certified safe for human use. Great care in its design and construction insure that no leakage current whatsoever can flow from the unit. The initiate circuit is totally isolated from the line and shock voltage circuits. Thus a shock hazard cannot exist. In addition, only the 0–1 ma output terminals appear on the front panel. The 0–5 ma output is on the rear panel.
SPECIFICATIONS:
  Line Voltage: 105/125V AC 50/60 Hz
  Current Range: 0–5 milliamperes
  Meter Ranges: 0–1 or 0–5 MA RMS

the appropriate placement of the electrodes (typically the forearm, fingers, back of legs, or feet) will minimize potential dangers.

As an aversive stimulus, shock has several distinct advantages (Rachman, 1965). It has a highly discrete and controllable onset and offset so that the timing of the onset of punishment and its termination may be precisely linked to the occurrence and termination of a problem behavior. A clear offset also facilitates the pairing of new stimuli, or alternative behaviors, with termination of punishment in order to increase their attractiveness, as in anxiety-relief and aversion-relief procedures. The intensity of shock is generally adjustable so that the aversiveness of the stimulus may be varied in accord with clients' individual differences in sensitivity. There are, of course, disadvantages, too (Rachman & Teasdale, 1969), most of which are concerned with the high degree of aversiveness of electric shock, which may produce aggression or drive patients from therapy if the level of shock employed is too extreme.

Several types of inductoria and electrodes are available. Some dispense current via electrodes that may be connected to a client's fingers, leg, soles of feet, or forearms. These devices typically operate directly from house current. Other devices are battery operated (see the telemetric unit listed in note 3) and provide the client some freedom of movement. This is occasionally necessary when, for example, the client is an active child, or when the behavior to be controlled, for example, is sufficiently motoric to require that the client not be hampered by temporarily attached electrodes and wires. Obviously, the administration of the aversive stimulus from a portable device involves care on the part of the therapist to insure delivery within a short time following the response and to an appropriate part of the body. Battery-operated devices are also used for the self-dispensation of shock. These devices may be carried by the client, who may self-dispense shocks when undesired thoughts or motives occur, or when a changeworthy behavior seems imminent. In these cases, the client must be carefully instructed in the procedures of timing and the identification of instances when self-administered aversive consequences are appropriate (see Bucher & Fabricatore, 1970).

Before giving some actual examples of cases, let us consider the general procedures involved in the application of shock as an aversive technique. When shock is to be used as a *contingent punisher* with no attempt to alter stimulus valences or establish an avoidance condition, the procedure is quite simple. Whether in the home, or in a clinical setting, the

---

Meter Accuracy: 3% of full scale
Internal Source Voltage: 2600V AC
Internal Resistance: 2.4 megohms @1 MA output
    400 kilohms @5 MA output

client should be provided with stimuli that elicit the changeworthy behavior. Thus, if smoking is to be treated, the client may be given a package of cigarettes and directly asked to smoke (Koenig & Masters, 1965). Or he may be asked to form an image of smoking so realistic that he can nearly experience the actual sensations. As in an example to be presented in greater detail later, a client with tendencies toward transvestism might be given women's clothing articles, which are attractive to him, and instructed to begin to put them on. These responses, once performed, may then be followed by shock, either on a continuous schedule (that is, every time they are performed) or on an intermittent schedule (that is, every third time or every fourth time, on the average).

Some responses are not so directly under the client's control, and in these instances the therapist must arrange for presentation of the stimuli that evoke the response. For example, later we discuss the case of an infant who tended to vomit following eating with such frequency and regularity that his life was endangered. In this instance, the treatment could be conducted only after a meal had been eaten, and the therapist could either provide the food himself, or work with the child following mealtimes in the naturalistic setting.

Whereas contingent punishment can be applied as long as the response may be elicited in the presence of the punishing agent (granted the agent may be the client himself), *avoidance conditioning* can be utilized only when the onset of a response can be anticipated and when there is some method of inhibiting the behavior (passive), or performing an alternative behavior (active) in order to avoid the punishment. Clearly, the vomiting behavior of the infant just discussed would be difficult to treat with an avoidance-conditioning procedure, while the transvestism behavior, discussed earlier, is under greater voluntary control and could be treated via avoidance conditioning. In that case, had avoidance conditioning been employed, the client might first have been asked to don women's clothing and then, after some signal such as a bell, been given a specified period of time during which to remove the clothing or suffer a shock. Since avoidance-conditioning procedures produce behavioral change that is quite resistant to extinction (Solomon, 1964), it may be advisable to utilize this procedure whenever the behavior in question can be fitted to the paradigm, especially when the behavior is one itself reinforcing and highly motivated, and the goal of therapy is to attach anxiety to the problem behavior.

Some procedures may be said to involve *escape training*. The paradigm for escape training is one in which a behavior begins, is punished, and the punishing stimulus continues until the individual ceases the behavior and possibly performs an alternative behavior, at which time the aversive stimulus terminates. In this procedure, punishment may not be avoided, but rapid execution of a behavior incompatible with the one punished will bring about termination of the punishment. Consequently, curing the problem behavior and any alternative behaviors that occur are strongly reinforced by the termination of pain and anxiety accompanying the punishment.

Usually, aversion-relief procedures are initially procedures of escape training. For example, a homosexual may be shocked while viewing slides of nude males. He is given control over the termination of punishment, however, since by pressing a button he can simultaneously terminate the shock (escape) and substitute a slide of a nude female for the male slide (Feldman, & MacCulloch, 1965; Feldman & MacCulloch, 1971). After some trials with this procedure, the client may gradually be allowed to avoid the shock by switching slides before the shock actually occurs. Thus, escape training may be faded into avoidance conditioning. As we must repeatedly point out, this procedure is one primarily designed to influence subsequent behavior by reducing the attractiveness of problem behaviors and stimuli and increasing the attractiveness of alternative, acceptable behaviors and stimuli. Since the timing of the occurrences of behaviors and the onset and termination of punishers is so important in these procedures, electric shock is an extremely effective aversive stimulus.

Contingent punishment appears to be most effective when it occurs 0.5 seconds following a response (Hull, 1952). Most cases described in the literature have attempted to deliver the punishment with this approximate latency, especially in cases that do not involve long chains of behavior. When the treatment is applied in a clinical setting, this delay can often be established precisely by the use of timing equipment. However, when punishment is applied in more naturalistic settings such as the home, often the person employing the punishment must estimate the time lag or simply apply the punishment as rapidly as possible following the behavior. It is unlikely in such cases that the punisher could be applied any more rapidly than 0.5 seconds following a response, and great care should be taken to prevent lag of much more than a few seconds since the effect of punishment decreases rapidly as the lag between response and punishment is increased.

There are no clear guidelines concerning the duration of punishment. Shock is so extremely aversive to most individuals that it seems clear the duration ought to be quite brief. Longer durations become so aversive as to create conditioned emotional responses or to drive clients from therapy, neither of which effects is ethical or desirable. As with all aversive stimuli we discuss, it is possible for clients to form a clear discrimination between the therapy situation and other situations in which the behavior is likely to occur, or between the therapist and other individuals who must exercise control over the client's behavior. As we see in the following examples, the use of portable inductoria allows treatment to proceed within the diverse situations in which problem behaviors are likely to occur, and the use of multiple therapists may prove effective in encouraging the generalization of behavioral extinction when initial results indicate that the behavior is inhibited only in the presence of the therapist, or in the clinical setting.

While these are many of the concerns most important in the use of shock as an aversive technique, actual procedures vary slightly depending upon the behavior under treatment. Problem behaviors may be frequent and discrete, as in the case of a stutter response to certain letters, or the self-destructive behavior of a psychotic child. At other times the problem may require the alteration of the valence of behaviors and associated stimuli, as in the treatment of homosexuality or alcoholism, and the problem behavior is of lesser frequency and unlikely to occur in the therapy situation. Since the behavior under treatment affects the manner of procedures by which aversive control is utilized, let us turn to some examples of successful cases that have employed electric shock as the aversive stimulus. The reader should note that in many of these examples, the aversive technique is employed in combination with other, more positive means of behavior change, although in several cases, aversive techniques were used only after positive techniques had failed.

The Use of Electric Shock as a Contingent Punishment

In the treatment of a case of transvestism, Blakemore, Thorpe, Barker, Conway, and Lavin (1963) employed contingent electric shock, which was administered while the patient was donning women's attire. Treatment sessions were administered at 30-minute intervals, spaced throughout each treatment day (which lasted from 9:00 in the morning to late afternoon). Treatment lasted 6 days. Each session included five "trials," when the client would be donning female attire. During this time he stood upon a rubber mat into which had been imbedded an electrical grid. A hand-operated generator could deliver a powerful electrical stimulus (120 VAC, 10,000 ohms resistance; amperage unspecified), and punishment consisted of two hand turns of the generator. At some point during each trial, after a varying number of female articles was put on, the patient either received a shock or heard a buzzer, following either of which he was to begin undressing in preparation for the next trial. The shock and buzzer were randomly ordered, so that punishment was on an intermittent schedule, a procedure that appears to maximize the anxiety components of punishment and readily promotes generalization of training to situations and times when it is clear that shock is not likely to ensue. In the present example, the patient did not know how long it would be before he received the signal to undress, whether this would be the shock or buzzer, or the frequency with which these would occur over the various trials.

Although treatment lasted only 6 days, the patient found it quite unpleasant and stressful, and there was a clear decline in his level of motivation. Consequently, after 4 days of treatment, a 2-day intervening "vacation" was prescribed, following which treatment resumed and was completed. Even during this 2-day period, cross-dressing was avoided several times in situations that would have stimulated the patient to cross-dress in earlier times. When the total of 6 days of treatment was concluded, a 6-month follow-up revealed that no transvestism occurred and that the patient had no desire whatsoever to engage in what had been his most satisfying sexual outlet.

Behavior that is self-injurious or that is likely to produce self-injury is often difficult to eliminate because of social reinforcement from individuals charged with the patient's care. Vomiting, head banging, self-pummeling, and other forms of self-mutilation are likely to bring sympathetic reinforcement from the environment, which has the effect of maintaining the behavior even though such caretakers may be thoroughly convinced that they are providing the needed love or security, the lack of which, they believe, is responsible for the bizarre, self-destructive behavior. Children who have become particularly adept at self-mutilation, or other individuals who are on the verge of permanent damage or even death, often require some initial form of treatment that will immediately eliminate the self-destructive behavior. Hence, even though it may be postulated that the behaviors are being maintained by contingent social reinforcement, procedures only mildly aversive (ignoring, or time-out procedures) may be inadvisable since they do not decrease a behavior's frequency as rapidly as punishment, and often the onset of extinction procedures produces an *increase* in the dangerous behavior.

Bucher and Lovaas (1968) worked with a 7-year-old psychotic boy who had shown self-mutilating behaviors since the age of 2. He typically was kept in physical restraints and when they were removed he was likely to hit himself nearly 2000 times in the space of just 1 hour. When electric shock was applied contingently to such destructive behavior, only 4 treatment sessions and 12 shocks were required to eliminate this behavior almost entirely. In another case reported by the same authors, head banging by a psychotic girl was reliably eliminated after a total of only 15 contingent shocks. It is interesting to note that the self-destructive behavior by these children was not the only behavior affected by the treatment. Following treatment, the children whined less and showed much greater tendencies to attend to their therapists. This latter result can pave the way for other forms of treatment, which may involve social reinforcement or modeling.

A case reported by Risley (1968) provides a good example of the effectiveness of shock as a punisher when other aversive techniques (for instance, time-out, verbal rebuke) have been tried, and of the use of parents or caretakers as therapists for behaviors exhibited primarily in situations other than the office or clinic setting. A 6-year-old hyperactive girl enjoyed climbing to the point where she continually climbed any and all objects within her reach and had suffered many injuries from falls while climbing. A treatment program involving the ignoring of climbing activities and reinforcing incompatible responses had failed to change her behavior. Brief physical isolation had also proved ineffective. A program combining shock with verbal reprimand was instituted, wherein immediately following the actual beginning of climbing the therapist quickly approached the child and delivered a powerful shock through a prod-like device, while saying sharply "no!" When the therapist had clearly established control over the climbing behavior, the mother was trained in the employment of these procedures so that the behavior change could be incorporated into the home situation. This was necessary since the cessation of climbing in the therapy situation was accompanied by no change at all in the frequency of climbing at home. It was also found that if the child were placed in the therapy room, prior to a session, without the therapist being present, she would climb even though after the therapist entered there would be no climbing at all.

These latter findings point to one of the problems of any behavior change procedure, which is perhaps most exaggerated in the use of aversive techniques, namely, the generalization of the behavior change from the therapy situation into the naturalistic environment. In the present instance, climbing prior to therapy sessions was almost entirely eliminated in a single session. During the time when the child was alone in the room, the therapist inconspicuously observed the child while she was alone and when she began to climb, he entered the room shouting "no," applied the shock, and left again. Climbing at home continued at the rate of 29 precipitous scaling behaviors a day. The therapist went to the home to instruct the mother in the use of the shock device. Within 4 days, climbing at home was reduced from 29 to an average of 2 instances a day, and within a few weeks it disappeared entirely.

During this period, shock was also applied to eliminate the girl's propensity to strike her 3-year-old brother with objects, push him down stairs, and generally aggress against him. No information was available concerning the frequency with which these behaviors occurred, but following 20 days of treatment with the mother applying contingent shock, these behaviors ceased entirely and remained absent for the entire 2-month period during which the child was observed following the treatment.

It is noteworthy that during the entire period of treatment, the child did not exhibit any aggressive behavior that appeared to be a consequence of the use of shock, and, as noted above, the aggressive behavior toward her little brother decreased when contingent shock was applied. Risley does not mention whether the mother had any initial objection to the use of shock as an aversive technique she was to apply herself. During the period of treatment in the home setting, after shock had eliminated climbing (it had been absent on 14 of 15 days), the mother was instructed to discontinue the use of shock and to spank the child whenever she climbed. During this period climbing again appeared in the child's repertoire and seemed to be increasing in frequency. The mother stated that she felt spanking the child was more unpleasant and was "brutalizing" for both herself and for the child than the shock had been because it was so obviously ineffective.

Clearly, in the training of mothers and other nonprofessionals in the use of aversive techniques, care should be taken to note that methods which replace the ineffective use of other more common punishers are more humane than the continued use of the ineffective procedures. Many therapists (like the mother in the case study above) feel that a minimal number of mild shocks is more humane than the continual, but ineffective, spanking or shaming of a child. Often this may also be the case in instances requiring the use of more powerful aversive stimuli. Lovaas and Simmons (1969) found that restraining self-destructive children for prolonged periods of time produces physical damage including demineralization, shortening of tendons, and arrested motor development. Many individuals feel that such physical debilitation and the prolonged use of strait jackets or practices such as tying a self-destructive child's feet and arms to his bed are more morally reprehensible than the application of short-term procedures of aversive control.

It is not necessary that the behavior under treatment be one over which the client has voluntary control, or that the client be of any minimum age. Sachs and Mayball (1971) reduced the incidence of spasms and involuntary movements in a cerebral palsied individual from more than 100 per hour to the low rate of 6 per hour. Lang and Melamed (1969) eliminated rhuminative vomiting in a 9-month-old infant; Galbraith et al. (1970) did so with a 13-year-old retarded boy; and Kohlenberg (1970) effectively treated similar behavior in a severely retarded 21-year-old adult.

In the case treated by Lang and Melamed (1969), the infant tended to regurgitate small amounts of food all during the day and to vomit most of his food within 10 minutes after feeding. It was possible to recognize the imminent onset of vomiting by observing the vigorous throat movements that would precede vomiting and that occurred at no other time. Since vomiting occurred only after feeding, not during it, the use of aversive techniques was seen as appropriate since there would be little possibility that actual feeding behavior would be affected by the administration of contingent punishment.

In the treatment of this infant, 1-second electric shocks were administered to the leg. The intensity level was set by two criteria: The shock was judged painful by the therapists and was sufficient to elicit signs of distress in the infant. The 1-second shocks were delivered at 1-second intervals beginning at the start of vomiting and terminating only when vomiting had ceased. Both the observation of a nurse and electromyographic recording of muscle activity were used to determine the onset of vomiting.

By the end of the first session of aversive procedures, the frequency and duration of vomiting had decreased markedly from earlier levels. After a second session it was clear that the infant had learned to anticipate shocks, and he also had begun to avoid the shock by curling his foot. This latter behavior necessitated the therapists' moving the electrodes from the bottom of the foot to the calf. Following this maneuver, the vomiting quickly showed a decrease, and by the end of the sixth session, vomiting no longer occurred. After 2 days of nontreatment, there was some indication that the vomiting was beginning to recur. However, after 3 further days of treatment sessions, the response was reliably eliminated; 6 months later the infant still showed no tendency to vomit following feeding and had regained his normal weight.

In the case treated by Kohlenberg (1970), a severely retarded adult woman had exhibited vomiting following every meal for a period of 3 months, reducing her weight to 74 pounds. Treatment was given during a 1½-hour period following each meal, over a series of three days. When observation of the patient's stomach indicated that vomiting was about to occur, a 1-second shock was administered to the thigh, utilizing a shock-prod device. After the 3-day treatment, a milder aversive-control procedure was added. If any vomitus was observed on the patient following a meal, her activity was restricted for a period of 1 hour by confining her to a chair. Whereas vomiting had occurred following every meal for a period of 3 months prior to treatment, during a 25-day follow-up, after treatment vomiting occurred only 11 times out of a total of 75 meals. The therapist noted that the vomiting that did occur was much less severe, and during this 25-day period there was a 10.5 pound weight gain.

A variety of investigators have found positive results in treating alcoholics with shock as a contingent punishment for drinking (Vogler, Lunde, Johnson, & Martin, 1970; Vogler, Lunde, & Martin, 1971). Furthermore, not all treatment procedures are designed to produce total abstinence. Lovebond and Caddy (1970) trained alcoholics to discriminate levels of alcohol in their bloodstream (0.00–0.08%) and administered strong electric shock contingent upon drinking only after the blood-alcohol level exceeded 0.65%. Over a follow-up period ranging from 16 to 60 weeks, 21 of the 28 patients completing treatment continued drinking at a moderate, socially acceptable level; while for the remaining 7 patients, success was somewhat more limited. These results are encouraging although they must be accepted as tentative since Mills, Sobell, and Schaefer (1971) were less successful in training alcoholics to drink moderately. It should be noted, however, that Mills *et al.* (1971) utilized contingent shock to train alcoholics to drink in a manner typical of social drinkers (small sips, not gulps; mixed drinks, not straight liquor) and did not include training in the self-assessment of blood-alcohol level. Furthermore, Lovebond and Caddy (1970) were careful to stress self-control factors and to enlist the cooperation of a family member in the treatment in an attempt to improve generalization.

The Use of Electric Shock in Anxiety Relief and Aversion Relief

Although the aversive treatment of alcoholism does not usually employ shock as the aversive stimulus, it can be used in the treatment of this disorder. Blake (1965) reported the successful use of a combination of relaxation and shock procedures in the treatment of alcoholism. In this procedure, the client is placed in a room and separated from the therapist by a one-way vision screen. Electrodes for the delivery of shock are attached to the forearm of the client. The client is given the liquor of his choice, a glass, and some water, and told to mix his drink as he prefers it. He is then told to sip his drink, but not to swallow any of it. Prior to this time the therapist and client have established a level of shock that is above the threshold level at which the client begins to report that the shock is unpleasant and painful. Following each sip, a shock may be applied and the client may terminate this shock by spitting out his mouthful of alcohol into a bowl. Half the time, on a random schedule, the client receives a shock, and half the time a green light comes on, signaling that there will be no shock and that he is to spit the liquor into the bowl. Blake's procedure usually lasts over a period of only 4–8 days and involves an investment of about 5 hours per client.

The relaxation Blake uses in addition to aversive procedures is not intended to involve systematic desensitization. Clients are simply instructed in the use of muscular relaxation techniques (Jacobson 1938) and told to use such relaxation as a means to control general tension and to induce natural sleep at night. With this combination of relaxation training and aversive conditionings, Blake has reported that up to 54% of his clients remain abstinent over a period of 6 months, 52% over a 12-month period.

Aversive procedures have also been used in cases of drug abuse involving drugs other than alcohol. As with alcohol, the treatment procedures occasionally employ relaxation training as well, perhaps as a potential substitute for the drug-induced relaxation. Lesser (1967) worked with a 21-year-old college senior who wished to eliminate his drug habit, which involved the self-administration of morphine two or three times a week. The client was not completely addicted, but was at an earlier time. He was successful at eliminating his addiction by dropping out of school and locking himself in a hotel room until the withdrawal symptoms were past. A few years prior to the administration of behavior therapy techniques, the client had received 6 months of psychoanalytically oriented psychotherapy.

Before utilizing aversive techniques, the client was trained in relaxation techniques and given some minor assertive training. The assertive training allowed some new recreational behaviors such as attending college dances, behaviors that may be interpreted, like the relaxation, as potential alternatives to the relaxation and enjoyment obtained from the use of drugs. Relaxation and assertive training did allow the client to foreswear the use of drugs for a period of time, but they proved insufficient to produce total abstinence. Consequently, it was reasoned that aversive procedures were indicated as measures to associate anxiety with drug administration. It is noteworthy that the use of other techniques prior to the use of aversive procedures provided a number of alternative, if not incompatible, behaviors.

In the present instance, aversive procedures were designed to associate anxiety with various aspects of injecting drugs. After the client had described in detail his procedure of injecting drugs, he was asked to bring in the equipment he typically used: a hypodermic syringe and rubber nipple, which he used to squeeze dissolved morphine through the needle. The injection procedure was analyzed into five steps. In each treatment routine, the client was asked to imagine a particular step and to signal when he had a clear image in his mind. Two of the five steps involved the client's picking up the syringe or nipple while imagining. Once the client signaled that he had a clear image, the shock commenced and ceased only when the client said "stop," indicating that he had ceased to visualize the step, and after he had dropped any object he may have picked up as part of the sequence.

For this particular case the aversive procedure was administered twice a week, with the client going through the five steps three times each session (for a total of 15 shocks). Each step was shocked for the first 16 sessions, and from then on a partial schedule of punishment was instituted. It is interesting to note that after eight sessions of aversive procedures, the client accepted an opportunity to take drugs. He reported that he did not get the expected "good feeling" and was disappointed that he had yielded. Apparently, any lack of success of the aversive procedures to inhibit the behavior is more than overcome by their successful elimination of the positive value of the drug effects. Follow-ups after 7 and 10 months indicated that the client had successfully avoided hard drugs. He did continue to smoke marijuana upon occasion, but had never considered stopping its use when undertaking therapy. Continued use of marijuana did not appear to hamper the successful avoidance of more dangerous drugs.

As we have noted, avoidance procedures have most often been employed to behavior problems such as homosexuality, various sexual deviations, or alcoholism, problems for which the typical eliciting stimulus is attractive and compelling to the client. While the basic procedure remains the same, there is a fairly wide variation among different behavior therapists in the exact procedural details utilized in their standard treatment of a particular disorder. Consequently, we discuss several treatment procedures that have been applied to the treatment of homosexuality, with positive results.

Two authors (Feldman & MacCulloch, 1965; Feldman & MacCulloch, 1971) have presented detailed treatment procedures for the treatment of homosexual individuals, male and female, who wish to change their sexual proclivities. In this procedure the client views slides (and short movie clips) from a chair, with electrodes attached to his leg ("posterior tibial group of muscles, avoiding the tibia and the lateral peroneal nerve"). Provision was made for the use of current at either of two preset levels in order to avoid habituation to a stimulus of one particular level of intensity. The client was provided with a switch that controlled the slide projector, although the therapist had final control (see below). The apparatus is depicted in Figure 9.1. [Feldman and MacCulloch (1971) have presented other detailed diagrams of the construction of the treatment apparatus.]

Initially clients were given a large series of pictures of clothed and nude males and asked to rate their degrees of attractiveness. Eventually, a number of these, including pictures brought in by the client, were arranged into a hierarchy. After this step, a hierarchy of female slides was also formulated, and the two hierarchies were melded into a series of pairs, with the *least* attractive male slide paired with the *most* attractive female slide, and so on. Patients who had pictures of their own, which were

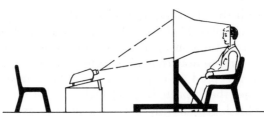

Figure 9.1 A diagram of the setting and apparatus utilized by Feldman and Mac-Culloch in the electrical aversion treatment of homosexuality. From Feldman and Mac-Culloch, 1971.

appropriate (for example, a lover, wife, girl friend), contributed these pictures and they, too, were made into slides and included in the procedure. In later versions (Feldman & MacCulloch, 1971), short film clips were included, as well as slides.

The level of shock was determined by increasing the current gradually up to the point identified by the patient as unpleasant. The slides were presented on a small screen in a quiet, darkened room. The client was informed that he would see a male slide and after several seconds he might receive a shock. He was further informed that he could turn off the slide by pressing a switch, and that the moment the slide was no longer visible, the shock would no longer be forthcoming (or would terminate if it had already commenced). However, it was stressed that the slide should remain on the screen so long as the client found it sexually attractive.

When the first slide was then presented, if the client switched it off within 8 seconds he was not shocked. If he left it on, after 8 seconds a shock was given. If the client did not immediately terminate the shock, the intensity of the shock was increased until he did so (this rarely occurred). If the client waited until shock had begun, terminating the slide was termed an escape response. Typically, the first several exposures to the slide resulted in escape responses; next there were some escape trials and some trials when the client pressed the switch prior to shock (anticipatory avoidance); and then there was a series of trials with consistent avoidance. At this point (after three consecutive avoidance trials), the procedure became more complex. Some of the subsequent avoidance attempts were successful, and shock was avoided; some were not successful: the slide remained on, and after 8 seconds the client received a brief shock; and some of the avoidance attempts received delayed success (the slide did not leave the screen for 4½, 6, or 7½ seconds after coming on, these delay times being varied randomly). Immediate success, nonsuccess, and delayed-success trials were interspersed randomly.

Feldman and MacCulloch (1971) reported that clients felt relief when the slide to be avoided actually disappeared from view (this is a common report, cited also by Birk, Huddleston, Millers, & Cohlers, 1971). Consequently, a corollary to the procedure described above included having a female slide appear upon the termination of the male slide (and, of course, vice versa when treating female homosexuals). This did not happen on each trial (a procedure the authors felt leads to better generalization), and the therapist was in control of the termination of the female slides. The client could, however, request the return of the female slide (and a correlated delay in the beginning of the next trial), and randomly this request was or was not granted.

Treatment began with the least attractive male slide and the most attractive female slide. After a client was continuously and quickly rejecting a male slide, the next slide pair was introduced. Table 9.3 presents the schedules of successful, unsuccessful, and delayed-success trials that these authors utilized in one outcome study (Feldman & MacCulloch, 1971). To keep clients from learning the schedules, each session began at a different point within the schedule. There were approximately 25 trials per session, and each session lasted about 20 minutes. The length of time between sessions varied with the patient's schedule.

The four programs noted in Table 9.3 and summarized in Table 9.4 represent a series of gradual progressions. The patient was moved from one to another as he progressed. The frequency with which the female slide appeared on successful avoidance trials (when requested) I went from 100% to 33%. This was intended to establish firmly the behavior of requesting the female slide and to allow maintenance of this behavior despite decreasing success. The maximum number of requested reappearances of the female slide rose from one to three across the first three programs, and then decreased to two for the fourth program. This also was intended to develop the habit of performing active approach behaviors to female stimuli. To accustom the client to viewing female figures, the length of the presentation of the female slide was increased from 4 seconds to 12 seconds across the four programs, and its reappearance increased from 4 to 12 seconds as well.

We discuss the results of Feldman and MacCulloch's outcome studies in greater detail later in the chapter. It is noteworthy at this point, however, to report that of eight clients who received this treatment regimen and no other, seven were successfully avoiding homosexual behavior 3 months following treatment, and one engaged only in homosexual fantasy. This treatment procedure was only one of several in an evaluative study reported in the final section of this chapter. When clients who were unsuccessfully treated by one or more other treatment procedures were given the anticipatory avoidance regimen, the success rate was far lower, and only one out of six patients could be counted as a success. This latter ratio may be an extreme underestimate to the extent that only

TABLE 9.3

Four Programs Used in the Treatment of Homosexuals (Feldman & MacCulloch, 1971)

	Program 1			Program 2			Program 3			Program 4		
A [a]	B [b]	C [c]	D [d]	B	C	D	B	C	D	B	C	D
			(secs)			(secs)			(secs)			(secs)
1.	D4½	2	20	D4½	3	20	R	—	20	R	3	20
2.	R	2	35	D4½	—	35	R	1	35	R	—	35
3.	D6	2	20	D6	1	20	R	1	20	D4½	1	20
4.	R	2	25	R	3	25	D4½	4	25	D6	—	25
5.	NR	—	15	NR	—	15	NR	—	15	R	1	15
6.	D4½	2	35	D7½	—	35	R	—	35	R	—	35
7.	D7½	2	25	D6	—	25	D4½	—	25	D4½	—	25
8.	NR	—	40	NR	—	40	D6	1	40	D4½	—	40
9.	NR	—	30	R	1	30	D7½	—	30	R	1	30
10.	R	2	40	R	3	40	D6	4	40	R	—	40
11.	NR	—	20	R	—	20	D4½	—	20	R	—	20
12.	R	2	25	D4½	1	25	R	—	25	R	—	25
13.	NR	—	35	NR	—	35	D4½	1	35	D7½	1	35
14.	R	2	25	R	—	25	R	—	25	R	—	25
15.	R	2	15	R	1	15	R	4	15	R	—	15
16.	D6	2	40	D4½	3	40	D6	—	40	D7½	—	40
17.	D7½	2	30	D6	—	30	R	—	30	D6	—	30
18.	NR	—	15	D7½	3	15	R	4	15	D7½	—	15
19.	D4½	2	35	R	—	35	R	—	35	D4½	3	35
20.	R	2	20	R	3	20	R	1	20	R	—	20
21.	NR	—	30	NR	—	30	NR	—	30	R	1	30
22.	R	2	40	R	—	40	D7½	—	40	D6	—	40
23.	NR	—	30	D7½	3	30	D7½	4	30	D6	3	30
24.	D7½	2	15	R	3	15	D6	—	15	D7½	—	15
	(Female stimulus time 4 sec both for initial appearance and reappearance)			(Female stimulus time 8 sec)			(Female stimulus time 12 sec)			(Female stimulus time 12 sec)		

[a] A = trial number.
[b] B = trial type: D = delayed; R = reinforced; NR = nonreinforced (shock).
[c] C = number of female requests granted.
[d] D = intertrial interval.

TABLE 9.4

Summary of Variations in the Four Programs Used by Feldman & MacCulloch (1971)

Variable	Program[a]			
	1	2	3	4
Nonreinforced trials	8	4	2	0
Reinforced trials	8	10	11	12
Delay trials	8	10	11	12
Trials on which initial F[b] allowed	16	12	10	8
Exposure of initial F	4 sec	8 sec	12 sec	12 sec
No. of reappearances of F per trial	1	2	3	2
No. of trials on which F reappears	16	8	5	3
Exposure of return F	4 sec	8 sec	12 sec	12 sec

[a] Patient must avoid within 4 seconds on 3 trials in succession at the beginning of each new slide before going on to a program.

[b] F = Female slide.

the more difficult and trenchant cases were included, ones that had been treated unsuccessfully by other treatment procedures. Indeed, Feldman and MacCulloch felt that their anticipatory avoidance procedure was most applicable to patients who had had some form of heterosexual experience prior to treatment, however minimal, and for whom some heterosexual interest was present, again however minimal. These authors classify homosexuals into two categories on this basis, primary homosexuals (having no heterosexual interest or skills) and secondary (having such interest and skills). They reported that most failures, especially clients who had already had another form of treatment, could be classified as primary homosexuals.

This classification brings us again to a point that must be stressed over and over in the context of aversive control, namely the importance of the availability (or training in) alternative modes of behavior. In the present instance, although Feldman and MacCulloch's technique contained procedures designed to increase the attractiveness of female stimuli, there was no provision for the acquisition of the requisite skills needed for proper social and sexual interactions with the opposite sex. Provision of training in these behavior patterns would surely increase the success of such therapy and might eradicate the proposed importance of a distinction between primary and secondary homosexuals.

While the treatment of transvestism and fetishism often includes the presence of the actual inappropriate sexual stimuli, and transvestites are generally required to cross-dress or at least view pictures of themselves in female attire, the treatment of overt homosexuality does not generally include the presentation of real stimuli or the performance of overt sexual behavior during treatment. If overt sexual behavior is incorporated into treatment, one might expect more powerful effects since such treatment would indeed be *in vivo*. Few cases reported in the literature have included sexual behavior (including masturbation) during the aversive-conditioning phase. In one case that included sexual responding as part of an adjunct to aversive-control procedures, the inclusion of such behavior appeared to limit generalization. Thorpe, Schmidt, and Castell (1963) had a client masturbate while viewing pictures of semi-nude females as an adjunct to the usual aversive-control procedures. In this case it appears that the prior aversive procedures must not have been successful since the client subsequently reported heterosexual fantasies while masturbating, but his interpersonal sexual behavior remained homosexual. It remains clear, however, that the pairing of sexual arousal and climax arrived at via masturbation with heterosexual stimuli can be an effective procedure of positive counterconditioning that can be used in addition to the pairing of heterosexual stimuli with the termination of punishment during the aversive conditioning.

Procedural Examples: The Use of Drugs in Aversive Control

Drugs seldom have a discrete onset and offset in their effects, nor are their effects typically of brief duration. For these reasons, perhaps, there have been no reports of the use of aversive drug effects as contingent punishment. Consequently, most of the literature we present is concerned with the use of drugs in aversion-relief and anxiety-relief procedures. The reader should note, however, that in some instances there may be a contingent punishment effect present: for instance, when an alcoholic client tastes whiskey as his drug-induced nausea mounts, the peak nausea may occur after he has finished his first tasting and thus act as a contingent punisher for that act.

The Use of Drugs in Anxiety Relief and Aversion Relief

A variety of drugs have been used to produce aversive states that may be made contingent upon, or paired with, problem behaviors or stimuli that are inappropriately attractive. The most common class of drugs used are *emetics,* notably apomorphine hydrochloride or emetine hydrochloride. Occasionally, given proper respirating equipment, curare-type, short-term paralytic drugs may be used, which cause a temporary inability to breathe—a condition that is extremely aversive.

It should be clear that the use of drugs in aversive treatment requires even more equipment and preparation than the use of shock, and occasionally requires the hospitalization of the patient. Provision must be made for the collection and disposal of emesis if emetics are used, and medical supervision is ethically mandatory since drugs are typically injected and may have undesirable side effects. For example, frequent use of emetine can produce cardiovascular problems (Barker, Thorpe, Blakemore, Lavin, & Conway, 1961). Side effects of this magnitude clearly reduce the desirability of the use of such drugs when any alternative procedures involving less risk may be available.

There are several other problems with the use of drugs in aversive control. As we noted earlier, drug-induced aversive states have a relatively gradual onset and offset, thus making it difficult to have the onset contingent upon a response, or the offset simultaneous with the presentation of a relief stimulus. Furthermore, it has been clearly shown (Fromer & Berkowitz, 1964) that aversive stimuli that have a gradual onset produce weaker avoidance responses than do stimuli whose onset is clear and abrupt.

Despite its other disadvantages, emetine is generally favored over apomorphine since the latter is a central depressant. It has been found that central depressant drugs retard conditioning and are not as effective in aversive procedures (Franks, 1966). When apomorphine is used, however, its depressant effects may be counteracted by the simultaneous administration of a stimulant such as caffeine (Freund, 1960) or dexamphetamine sulphate (Lavin, Thorpe, Barker, Blakemore, & Conway, 1961).

Aversive control utilizing drugs was employed most often in the treatment of alcoholism. There is no clear reason for this limitation. Perhaps the delayed aversive effects of drugs are less of an impediment when treating abusive use of other drugs whose effects are also somewhat delayed and not of clearly specifiable onset. Along this line, one might expect that the use of emetics and other drugs producing uncomfortable physical states would be extremely effective in the treatment of narcotic drug abuse involving either the oral or injected ingestion of drugs. Such a use of this technique has not yet become common, however.

The use of drug-induced aversive states in the treatment of alcoholism is not new. Procedures involving electric shock were reported as early as 1934 (Kantorovich, 1934), and the systematic application of drugs began a few years later (Voegtlin, 1940; Lemere, Voegtlin, Broz, O'Hallaren, & Tupper, 1942a,b). Recent methods of treatment still resemble these original procedures, typically involving from four to seven sessions devoted to associating the sight, smell, and taste of alcohol with drug-induced nausea.

In a typical treatment regimen, the client will first be given a verbal description of the treatment procedures, and any questions he may have are answered. Often a client is required to drink only liquids on the treatment day. Also, he may be given a stimulant drug such as benzedrine sulphate, which is intended to augment the conditioning procedure and offset any narcotic effects produced by the emetic drug (say, if apomorphine were used). Since there are many aspects to the presentation of alcohol (smell, sight, taste), treatment typically proceeds in a darkened, soundproofed room, and the client is confronted by an array of liquors clearly lighted in order to focus his attention on them.

At the beginning of a treatment session, the client will be given two large (10 ounce) glasses of a warm salt solution containing 1½ grains of emetine and 1 gram of salt, all dissolved in the 20 ounces of water. Following this procedure, the client will be given an injection containing both emetine hydrochloride and 1½ grains of ephedrine sulphate.

After a few minutes nausea will begin, and the client should be given several ounces of whiskey in a glass (because of its properties as a gastric irritant, whiskey is to be preferred at first, although there are compelling reasons to utilize a variety of beverages, certainly the client's favorite ones if vomiting is likely to occur without the irritation produced by the whiskey). It is important for treatment eventually to encompass a variety of alcoholic beverages. Several authors (Lemere & Voegtlin, 1940; Quinn & Henbest, 1967) have reported cases in which an aversion was established to the alcoholic beverages used in the aversive procedures, but the client subsequently switched his alcoholic preferences to those which had not been included in the treatment. For each beverage presented, the client is to smell, taste, swill around in his mouth, and then (for some therapists) swallow the liquor, following which vomiting usually occurs.

Some authors (see Voegtlin) continue treatment at this point, prolonging the nausea. Following vomiting, Voegtlin and his associates (Voegtlin, 1940; Voegtlin, Lemere, Broz, & O'Hallaren, 1941; Voegtlin, Semere, Broz, & O'Hallaren, 1942; Lemere & Voegtlin, 1940; Lemere, Voegtlin, Broz, O'Hallaren, & Tupper, 1942a,b) have recommended giving the client a glass of "near beer," containing tartar emetic in order to prolong the nausea. As treatment progresses, subsequent sessions may include an increase in the dosage of injected emetine, increases in the length of treatment sessions, and a variety of alcoholic beverages to enhance generalization.

Many other authors have adopted Voegtlin's general procedure, although often their procedures are not as severe. Furthermore, several minor modifications have been proposed, including pretreatment interviews and hospitalization during treatment (Shadel, 1944) and the elimination of the client's swallowing of the alcohol during the treatment session (Kant, 1944a,b) since, unless it is immediately regurgitated, its own effects are likely to impede successful treatment.

Occasionally reports appear describing the drug treatment of homosexuality. McConaghy (1971) compared emetic aversion and aversion relief involving shock in the treatment of 40 men who complained of homosexual feelings and behavior. In the drug-treatment regimen, patients were given injections of apomorphine, which induced nausea of about 10 minutes duration, but no vomiting. Approximately 1 minute before the onset of nausea the patient switched on a slide showing a nude male. Before the nausea reached its maximum level the slide was switched off. The drug treatment included 28 sessions, which were given at 2-hour intervals over a period of 5 days (the patients were hospitalized for the duration of treatment). In the aversion-relief treatment, shock was made contingent upon the patient's reading of homosexually oriented words and phrases that he found attractive. These words and phrases were read at 10-second intervals. Following the reading of 14 of these words and phrases, the patient viewed 1 that was illustrative of heterosexual activity for 40 seconds, and was not shocked. The total procedure occurred five times within each treatment session. There were three treatment sessions daily for 5 days.

There were no significant differences in the effectiveness of these two types of treatment. Following treatment, sexual arousal to pictures of nude men was significantly lower than to slides of nude women, which was not the case in a no-treatment control condition. This tendency had not changed after an entire year. One year following treatment, 50% of the patients reported a decrease in homosexual leanings, and 50% (not necessarily the same individuals) reported an increase in heterosexual feelings; 25% reported that they engaged in no homosexual behavior, and 25% (again, not necessarily the same individuals) reported that they had commenced heterosexual intercourse or now engaged in it more frequently.)

Although emetics are by far the most common class of drugs employed in aversive control, the use of drug invoking paralysis has been reported. The drug typically used is succinylcholine chloride dyhydrate, which produces a total paralysis of the respiratory system, including, of course, the cessation of breathing, which lasts approximately 60–90 seconds (Sanderson, Campbell, & Laverty, 1963; Campbell, Sanderson, & Laverty, 1964). The onset and offset of the drug's effects are more clearcut and controllable than those of the emetic drugs, providing an increased possibility of anxiety-relief conditioning procedures. The anxiety produced by this procedure is quite intense, involving a sense of extreme terror and often including the belief that one is going to die.

In the application of this procedure, the client is connected to a polygraph monitoring his GSR (Galvanic Skin Response) respiration, heart rate, and muscle tension. A respirator is always kept at hand. The client is then placed on a stretcher and the needle of a saline drip bottle inserted into a vein of his forearm. The drip is left running slowly, and the drugs can be injected directly into the tube running from the saline bottle to the needle. Often clients are given injections of atropine to prevent excessive salivation during the period of paralysis, which might interfere with subsequent breathing. However, the paralytic agent also produces cardiac irregularities in some subjects, and since atropine also acts upon the heart, it is not always advisable to use this drug. Obviously, this procedure requires extensive care in its administration, and should never be considered unless all undesirable consequences can be anticipated and controlled.

In the aversive treatment of a behavior problem such as alcoholism, the therapist should prepare an alcoholic beverage prior to the administration of the drug. The client may be given a bottle containing some of his favorite alcoholic beverage to hold and be asked to smell it, look at it, and taste it, then hand it back to the therapist. This is done several times without the administration of the paralytic agent. These trials involve approximately 10–15 seconds and are repeated approximately once a minute. After these trials, however, the succinylcholine is injected into the drip. As soon as the drug enters the bloodstream, there is a characteristic change in GSR, indicating that the effect is imminent. The therapist then hands the bottle to the client and just as the bottle is put to the lips, the drug usually takes effect. The therapist then holds the bottle to the client's lips and puts a few drops of it into the client's mouth. The bottle is taken away as soon as signs of regular breathing begin to reappear.

Procedural Examples: The Use of Response Cost as Contingent Punishment in Aversive Control

Response cost is a punishment procedure involving contingent withdrawal of a reward (Kazdin, 1972a). Since it is generally observed that people find the loss of such a reward an aversive experience, response cost is generally classified as a punishment, and it has indeed proved to be the case that behaviors are effectively suppressed by this procedure.

Response cost in the form of "fines" is often a component of token economies (see Chapter VI), although in recent years it has been applied in the treatment of individuals as well (Elliott & Tighe, 1968; Kazdin, 1972a; Siegel, Lenske, & Broen, 1969). The concept of response cost should not be confused with that of time-out from reinforcement (see Chapter V). Although the absence of rewards in time-out procedures and during extinction (see Chapter VIII) may be judged aversive, there is no actual withdrawal or removal of an already accrued reward, while such removal is the crux of the response-cost procedure.

There are two basic procedures for the enactment of a response-cost technique. In some instances (and this may be more appropriate for laboratory studies than for clinical application), the individual may be given some amount of reward, such as a preset number of tokens, and then he loses some tokens when he performs inappropriate behaviors. Perhaps more realistically, response cost may be imbedded within a procedure of contingency management in which the individual gains rewards for appropriate behaviors and loses rewards for inappropriate action. It is easy to see how this latter procedure would maximize an individual's discriminations between behaviors that are appropriate and inappropriate, while at the same time encouraging the performance of appropriate behaviors and the suppression of inappropriate behaviors.

Wolf, Hanley, King, Lachowicz, and Giles (1970) utilized a response-cost procedure to control the hyperactive behavior of an individual child within a classroom. Points were given out, noncontingently, before class began, and out-of-seat behavior resulted in a loss of points. The out-of-seat behavior ceased rapidly, and the response-cost procedure proved even more effective when it was generalized to the entire class, whereby all points remaining at the end of a class were shared by all the members of the class, not just the individual child. Sulzbacher and Houser (1968) utilized points that were worth minutes of recess to suppress obscene gestures. In a procedure similar to covert sensitization (see the next section), Weiner (1965) has shown that *imagined* loss of reward is nearly as effective as actual reward loss.

The effectiveness of response-cost procedures has been clearly demonstrated in a number of settings. Phillips (1968) included response-cost procedures in a token system for predelinquent boys. While threats, corrective feedback, and simple instructions proved ineffective in decreasing verbal aggression, tardiness, and poor grammar, the inclusion of response-cost procedures reliably decreased the frequencies of such behaviors. Response cost has also been a small component in token economy systems, although its effectiveness has rarely been evaluated (see Atthowe & Krasner, 1968; Ayllon & Azrin, 1968; Heap, Boblitt, Moore, & Hord, 1970; Packard, 1970; Steffy, Hart, Craw, Torney, & Marlett, 1969). When its effectiveness has been evaluated, response-cost procedures have been found effective in suppressing a variety of aggressive and rule-violating behaviors in hospitalized patients (Winkler, 1970; Upper, 1971).

We have noted elsewhere the possible importance of the magnitudes of rewards (see Chapters V and VI) and punishers in determining the effectiveness of contingency-management and aversive-control procedures. Interestingly, there is no indication thus far in the research literature that the magnitude of response cost has any systematic effects upon the effectiveness of the procedure. Elliott and Tighe (1968) included a response-cost procedure in their treatment program for cigarette smokers. Clients lost great sums of money for smoking and were able to earn it back by progressively longer periods of abstinence (self-reported). After 16 weeks of treatment, fully 84% of the subjects were abstinent, and of these 75% claimed that it was the fear of losing money that enabled them to abstain from smoking. There are, of course, problems with this particular study since there was no control group with which abstinence rates might be contrasted, and the use of self-report to determine the giving or withdrawal of rewards may have induced patients to change their reports, not their actual behavior. Although Elliott and Tighe (1968) utilized a large sum of money (up to $65.00) in their response-cost procedure, Siegel, Lenske, and Broen (1969) effectively suppressed speech disfluencies in college students by levying fines of only one cent.

Studies of the effectiveness of response-cost procedures indicate that it is a powerful manipulation. For example, experimental studies have shown that response-cost procedures may lead to suppression effects that are as persistent as those following the use of electric shock as a punisher (Azrin & Holz, 1966), and response cost appears to allow less recovery of suppressed responses than do other punishment procedures (McMillan, 1967; Tolman & Mueller, 1964). Several investigators have found that after response-cost procedures are discontinued, there is little tendency for the punished response to recover to its original frequency after periods of time up to several months (Siegel, Lenske, & Broen, 1969; Kazdin, 1972b; Phillips, 1968; Harmatz & Lapuc, 1968; Kazdin, 1971) nevertheless, there are other reports in the literature citing recovery of the problem behavior when the response-cost procedure was discontinued (Birnbrauer, Wolf, Kidder, & Tague, 1965; Burchard, 1967; Phillips, Fixen, & Wolf, 1971; Sulzbacher & Houser, 1968; Winkler, 1970; Wolf *et al.*, 1970).

Although research on response-cost procedures is not yet extensive, there have been several studies contrasting the effectiveness of response cost with other procedures for the suppression of problem behaviors. Phillips *et al.* (1971) found that a combination of token reinforcement and response cost (fines) resulted in better attention to current events (televised news) than did either procedure alone (this program is discussed in greater detail in Chapter VI).

Bucher and Hawkins (1971) and Panek (1970) found that positive reinforcement and response-cost procedures were of essentially equal effectiveness in the control of disruptive behaviors by children and associative responding by schizophrenics. Harmatz and Lapuc (1968) utilized response cost, group therapy, and diet-only in treating obese patients. Response cost involved a loss of money whenever a week went by without some weight loss, while group therapy patients were given praise when weight losses were reported, and generally discussed dynamic processes underlying obesity. Following 6 weeks of treatment, group-therapy and response-cost procedures were equally effective in promoting weight loss. After a 1-month follow-up period, however, it was found that group-therapy patients had regained weight and no longer differed from the diet-only group, while response-cost patients treated with response-cost procedures had actually continued to *lose* weight.

In a study comparing response cost with other forms of punishment, Schmauk (1970) contrasted the effects of response cost (money loss), physical punishment (shock), and social disapproval in the learning of an avoidance task by normal individuals and individuals diagnosed as sociopaths. It was found that the normal individuals learned equally well under all conditions of punishment. However, although it is typically found that sociopathic individuals learn less well than normals, under response-cost conditions they learned equally well; yet under other conditions of punishment, their learning was less efficient than that of normal individuals.

It seems well documented that response-cost procedures constitute an effective form of aversive control. Furthermore, it is clearly a procedure that may be easily integrated with more positive forms of control, especially contingency-management procedures (indeed, response cost itself is a form of contingency management). The literature indicates that response cost may produce relatively enduring behavior suppression, with little likelihood of negative side effects such as disruption of ongoing behavior (Bandura, 1969; Leitenberg, 1965), emotional responding (Schmauk, 1970), or escaping the therapy situation (Phillips *et al.,* 1971; Baron & Kaufman, 1966; Leitenberg, 1965).

The Use of Cognitive Stimuli in Aversive Control

Covert Sensitization

Covert sensitization involves the use of imagery that includes aversive elements, as well as the imagined depiction of problem behaviors. The simultaneous inclusion of these two factors (aversion and the problem

behaviors) is designed to alter the valence of the behavior and any relevant imagined stimuli in a manner similar to the aversive procedures,
discussed earlier, which involve physical aversive stimulation.

The technique of covert sensitization is of relatively recent origin,
(Cautela, 1966). During its short history, however, it has been successfully applied to a wide variety of behavior disorders, including alcoholism (Anant, 1968; Ashem & Donner, 1966; Cautela, 1967, 1970,
1971; Cautela & Wisocki, 1969); obesity (Cautela, 1966; Janda & Rimm,
1972; Stuart, 1967); homosexuality and pedophilia (Barlow, Leitenberg,
& Agras, 1969); fetishism (Kolvin, 1967); transvestite fantasies (Gershman, 1970); sadistic fantasies (Davison, 1968); gasoline sniffing
(Kolvin, 1967); delinquent behavior (Cautela, 1967); self-destructive behavior (Cautela & Baron, 1969); and smoking (Irey, 1972; Lawson &
May, 1970; Mullen, 1968; Tooley & Pratt, 1967; Wagner & Bragg,
1970).

In the application of covert sensitization, the therapist must generate a
scene for the client to imagine, which combines the problem behavior,
relevant stimuli, and aversive aspects, as well, into a coherent image, or
train of images. Since problems treated by aversive procedures often involve problem behaviors that are highly motivated and quite intrinsically
reinforcing and that are generally elicited powerfully by stimuli themselves quite attractive, treatment by covert sensitization is often performed systematically, much in the manner of systematic desensitization,
or modeling with guided participation. Thus, at the beginning of treatment, the client might be asked to imagine a highly aversive scene and to
combine it with a scene in which the problem behavior is only weakly
elicited by the imagined stimuli or in which the behavior is not totally satisfying. Furthermore, some work may be required in advance, such as
testing out various aversive images in order to find one that the client
can imagine easily and clearly and that he finds most aversive.

Davison (1968) has provided a good example of the systematic application of covert-sensitization procedures in his account of the treatment
of sadistic sexual fantasies in a young man. The client was referred
because his sexual gratification was comprised primarily of masturbation
to fantasies of sadistic torture as it was inflicted upon young women. The
total treatment of this client involved both positive conditioning (instructing the client to masturbate to pictures and images of females in
nonsadistic contexts) and covert sensitization to the sadistic fantasies.
Therefore, as with the application of aversive procedures in general,
care was taken to provide alternative modes of responding, and the aversive procedures were combined with others of a more positive nature.

The aversive images utilized must indeed be aversive. Typically, the
client is given a description of a thoroughly nauseating scene that involves urine, feces, or bodily harm. Some adjustment may be necessary
to find the scene that is maximally aversive to a particular client. For ex-

ample, Davison (1968) originally instructed his client to imagine a typical sadistic scene (an attractive young girl tied to stakes in the ground and tearfully struggling to escape). While imagining this scene, the client was first instructed to imagine that as he looked upon this situation someone was bringing a smoldering branding iron toward his eyes, so close that his eyebrows became singed. When this proved unsuccessful, a second image was described, in which he was kicked viciously in the groin by an angry-looking karate expert. This image also proved to be only mildly aversive. Finally, the client was instructed to imagine himself viewing the poor struggling girl while peering over a bowl of "soup" comprised of urine with feces floating on top, all of which was steaming forth an utterly nauseating stench. When this proved effectively aversive (the client displayed facial expressions and groans indicating that it was so), he was instructed to imagine leaning over the bowl, drinking from it, and the accompanying nausea, observing the struggling girl all the while.

Occasionally the aversive imagery may draw from a client's actual aversive experiences while performing the changeworthy behavior. Miller (1963) reported the treatment of a homosexual whose past experiences had left him nauseated following the performance of fellatio with an uncircumcised partner because of the prevalent odors and taste of urine and perspiration. After several sessions in which the description of these experiences were used as the aversive component of scenes involving homosexual contacts, the client reported that he felt nauseated during the performance of homosexual behavior and eventually ceased his homosexual contacts. As in the case reported by Davison (1968), Miller (1963) combined the aversive procedures with procedures designed to increase the attractiveness of women, and the client reported increasing attraction to and dating of women as treatment progressed.

The problem of finding an aversive scene of sufficient intensity may be helped by the systematic application of relaxation training along with the aversive imagery and by the use of a series of images in which the aversive aspects are decreased and the client imagines himself ceasing the undesirable behavior or leaving a situation just as he begins to feel nauseated or frightened; finally the client imagines relief and relaxation when he pictures himself away from the original scene, performing an entirely different behavior. A good application of this procedure is reported by Barlow et al. (1969). These authors treated two clients, a pedophilic and a homosexual, utilizing only covert sensitization. The homosexual client, in one instance, was asked to imagine himself approaching and entering the apartment of a male friend. One scene he has to imagine went as follows:

As you get closer to the door you notice a queasy feeling in the pit of the stomach. You open the door and see Bill lying on the bed naked and you can sense that puke is filling up your stomach and forcing its way up to your throat. You walk over to Bill and you can see him clearly, as you reach out for him you can taste the puke, bitter and sticky and acidy on your tongue, you start gagging and retching and chunks of vomit are coming out of your mouth and nose, dropping onto your shirt and all over Bill's skin [p. 598].

These authors included eight imagined scenes in each treatment session. The one described above would have been one of the first, and would have been expanded to last from 30 to 60 seconds. During the final four scenes, however, the procedure would differ considerably. For example, the client might be asked to imagine himself approaching a male who was a potential sex partner and just beginning to feel nauseated. At that point he would visualize himself turning around and walking away from the encounter, feeling more and more relieved and relaxed as he did so. At the beginning of each session, the client was given relaxation instruction, so that the removal of the aversive image and its attendant discomfort would leave him in a pleasant, comfortable state.

It is possible to cast covert-sensitization procedures into an avoidance-conditioning or aversion-relief approach. (Cautela, 1967; Irey, 1972). The two scenes described below are from a covert-sensitization treatment of smoking. Irey (1972) utilized these scenes in treatment sessions that included 10 presentations of the sensitization scene, alternating with 10 presentations of the sensitization scene, which alternated with 10 presentations of the aversion-relief scene:

Sensitization scene:

Now I want you to imagine that you've just had your supper and have just decided to have an after-dinner cigarette, a —— (name of favorite brand). As you are about to reach for the pack, you get a funny feeling in the pit of your stomach. You start to feel queasy, nauseous and sick all over. As you pick up the pack, you can feel food particles inching up your throat. You're just about to vomit. As you pull a cigarette out of the pack, the food comes up into your mouth. You try to keep your mouth closed because you are afraid that you'll spit food out all over the place. You bring the cigarette up to your mouth. As you're about to open your mouth, you puke; you vomit all over your hands, the cigarette, the pack. It goes all over the table, all over the people sitting at the table. Your eyes are watering. Snot and mucous are all over your mouth and nose. Your hands feel sticky and slimy. There's an awful smell and a horrible sour taste in your mouth. As you look at this mess, you just can't help but vomit again and again until only watery stuff is coming out. Finally, nothing more will come up but you've got the dry heaves and just can't stop retching. It feels like the inside of your stomach is tearing loose. As you look up, everybody is staring at you with shocked expressions. You turn away from the cigarette pack and immediately you start to feel better. You run out of the room, and as you run out, you feel better and better. You wash and clean yourself up, and it feels wonderful.

Avoidance (relief) scene:
    You've just finished eating supper and decide to have an after-dinner ciga-
rette. As soon as you make that decision, you start to get that funny feeling in the
pit of your stomach, again. You say to yourself, "Oh, no; I won't have that cigarette." Then you immediately feel calm, comfortable, and relaxed [p. 89].[4]

    The evidence that has appeared in the literature does indicate that
procedures involving aversive imagery are quite effective. For example,
in the cases reported by Barlow *et al.* (1969), the therapists asked their
clients to keep a diary of the urges they felt to perform pedophilic or
homosexual acts, and the homosexual client was actually instructed to
visit bars several times a week, recording instances when he felt attracted
to other men. When the clients came in for treatment, they were also
asked to complete a card sort in which they were to rank verbal descriptions of scenes used in the sensitization procedure in terms of their attractiveness. During actual treatment, there were no sensitization trials
during the first 5 days in order to establish a base line. Then there was a
period of treatment of 6–9 days during which time sensitization was
carried out. Following this stage, there were several treatment sessions
where the scenes were presented without the aversive portions of the
images, and finally a series of sessions when the aversive portions of the
images were reintroduced. Figure 9.2 depicts the results of these procedures for the pedophilic client, and the results were similar for the
homosexual one.
    It is clear that the aversive portion of the treatment was necessary and
effective. The fact that the client's urges and attractiveness ratings rose
during the extinction period is an important indication that the pairing
of the noxious portions of the images with the attractive portions is important. During the extinction, all the other psychotherapeutic variables
remained, such as therapeutic instructions, patient expectancies of improvement, and the rapport between patient and therapist. Clearly,
covert sensitization can be an effective procedure for aversive control,
and we hope that the practical application of this technique, along with
research concerning its short- and long-term effectiveness, will increase.
    Although reports of the use of covert sensitization in the treatment of
obesity often includes the simultaneous use of other techniques as well,
(Stuart, 1967; Harris, 1969), Janda and Rimm (1972) reported an experiment that indicates the power of sensitization procedures when used as
the sole method of treatment. In this study, overweight individuals were

[4] Reprinted from Irey, Paul A. Covert sensitization of cigarette smokers with high and
low extroversion scores. Unpublished Master of Arts Thesis, Southern Illinois University
at Carbondale, 1972. Adopted from Cautela, Joseph R. Covert sensitization. *Psychological
Reports*, 1967, 74.

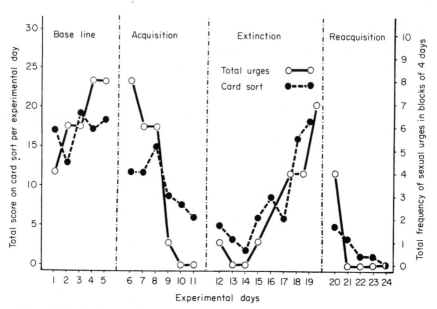

Figure 9.2 Total attractiveness score on card sort and total frequency of pedophilic urges in blocks of 4 days surrounding each treatment session. From Barlow *et al.*, 1969.

given six weekly treatment sessions involving covert sensitization. All subjects received training in deep muscle relaxation (Cautela, 1966). At the beginning of each treatment, the subjects weighed in, but received no praise or punishment for weight losses or gains. Using a scene involving stomach discomfort and eventual vomiting, subjects were required to imagine approaching various foods that were to be eliminated from their diets and to imagine, without descriptively induced discomfort, proudly eating meals that did include only approved foods. This procedure was designed to increase subjects' discriminations between acceptable and forbidden foods. Finally, there were aversion-relief scenes in which subjects imagined approaching forbidden foods, feeling ill, and then feeling better after turning away from the food. Each session included 15 scenes, 5 of each of the above 3 types.

There were two other groups of subjects in this study. In an attention-control condition, designed to control for the effect of attention to one's weight upon possible weight loss, subjects weighed in for each of six sessions and then talked with the therapist about anxiety-producing situations, with the therapist responding in a nondirective, reflective fashion. These subjects also received training in relaxation, and practiced it during each session. In a simple control group, overweight subjects simply reported to the health service weekly.

At the termination of treatment, subjects treated with covert sensitization showed a mean weight loss of 9.5 pounds. Subjects in the attention-control and simple control conditions showed losses of 4.5 and 0.7 pounds respectively. After a 6-week follow-up period, subjects in the simple control condition showed little change in their weight (further loss of 0.2 lbs.), and subjects in the attention-control condition showed a weight *increase* of 2.3 pounds. Within the covert-sensitization group, there was a relatively high correlation between the subject's rating of his discomfort to the imagined scenes and the amount of his weight loss ($r = .53$). The subjects reporting the highest degree of discomfort lost an average of 17.3 pounds during treatment, and after the follow-up period their mean loss was an impressive 21 pounds.

Empirical Findings

Treatment of Sexual Deviations

While there has been some indication in the literature of occasional failures in the use of aversive procedures in the treatment of sexual deviations (Freund, 1960; Solyom & Miller, 1967), the empirical literature generally reflects a reasonable degree of success and includes studies incorporating generally adequate follow-up periods (Cooper, Gelder, & Marks, 1965; MacCulloch & Feldman, 1967).

In the treatment of homosexuality,[5] Freund (1960) found that homosexuals who referred themselves for treatment had a greater likelihood of successful treatment than did homosexuals referred by courts or rela-

---

[5] Three points must be made clear with respect to our discussion of the various treatments of homosexuality. First, we assume that the individuals in treatment are individuals for whom the best treatment goal will indeed be the cessation of homosexual behavior. It is certainly possible that an individual with homosexual preferences might voluntarily submit himself to treatment in order to adjust more comfortably to his homosexuality (there is a growing number of states in which homosexual behavior between consenting adults is legal).

Second, we recognize that there may be individuals for whom heterosexuality would be so difficult a goal to achieve, that other treatment goals might be constructed. For example, Masters treated a middle-aged man with a lengthy history of pedophilic behavior. This individual had never had any sort of heterosexual experience and found the idea of such behavior extraordinarily distasteful. Although he had not had extensive homosexual contact with individuals his own age, he found this much less aversive, and the treatment subsequently involved directing the gentleman into a comfortable homosexual existence free from pedophilic desires.

Finally, it is impossible to overemphasize the importance of training in appropriate heterosexual behaviors (see Chapter III, on assertive training; Bandura, 1969; Feldman & MacCulloch, 1971; Bancroft, 1969).

tives: 45% of homosexuals who referred themselves adopted enduring heterosexual orientations, while only 6% of homosexuals referred by others did so. Feldman and MacCulloch and their colleagues (Feldman & MacCulloch, 1965; MacCulloch, Feldman, & Pinschof, 1965) found that 10 of 16 homosexuals treated showed an enduring heterosexual orientation during follow-up periods ranging from 2 to 14 months, and that the results were most promising when the clients were relatively young. Srnec and Freund (1953) utilized drugs in an aversive-conditioning procedure and reported success for 10 of 25 clients treated. This treatment procedure also included positive training in that the aversive portion of the procedure was followed by sexually arousing heterosexual films viewed while the client was physiologically aroused by testosterone injections.

Therapists using automated aversive treatment also have reported reasonable, but not staggering, success rates. Chapel (1970) found that 8 of 12 patients treated utilizing an automated procedure showed a predominately heterosexual adjustment 6 months following the termination of treatment and were experiencing no difficulty in maintaining such an adjustment. MacCulloch, Birtles, and Feldman (1971) found that automated aversive-treatment procedures were more effective than general psychotherapy.

Feldman and MacCulloch (1971) reported one of the more extensive follow-up studies on the effectiveness of anticipatory avoidance procedures in the treatment of homosexuality. In one study these authors contrasted the anticipatory avoidance procedure (described earlier in this chapter) with a procedure they termed *classical conditioning,* and with a third procedure termed *psychotherapy,* which included discussions with patients concerning their sexual problems and their attitudes toward females. The avoidance procedure differed from the classical conditioning procedure primarily in terms of the possibility for the client to avoid an aversive stimulus by actively choosing to terminate the homosexual stimulus display. While this was possible in the avoidance procedure, hence its name, the classical-conditioning procedure gave the clients no control over the stimulus display or the occurrence of the aversive stimulus. In this procedure the slide of a nude male was displayed just prior to the onset of shock, and both the shock and the slide of the nude male terminated simultaneously. Also simultaneous with the termination of shock was the onset of a slide of a nude female. Thus, this procedure was basically one of aversion relief, as we have defined it in this chapter.

As noted earlier, Feldman and MacCulloch (1971) defined two categories of homosexual individuals according to their prior experiences and enjoyment of heterosexual interaction. Those who have had no heterosexual experiences, or for whom the experiences (or heterosexual fantasies) were unenjoyable are termed *primary* homosexuals. The *secondary* homosexual is one who has experienced satisfactory heterosexual relations at some time in his history.

In a follow-up study, there were 10 patients assigned to each treatment group: 2 primary and 8 secondary homosexuals to the anticipatory avoidance condition; 3 primary and 7 secondary homosexuals to the classical-conditioning condition; and 4 primary and 6 secondary homosexuals to the psychotherapy condition. After these treatment regimens were applied to the patients initially assigned to each condition, those patients who did not respond favorably were given one of the other forms of treatment utilized in the study; and occasionally if this failed, the third form of treatment was utilized.

Looking at the success rate after the initial form of therapy only, it was found that six of the eight secondary homosexuals treated by the anticipatory avoidance technique were successful (free from any homosexual activity) after a follow-up period of nearly 1 year (46.2 weeks, average). Of the two primary homosexuals treated by this procedure, only one was considered a success at the final follow-up. Six of the seven secondary homosexuals treated by the classical-conditioning technique were considered successes after the follow-up, but only one of the three primary homosexuals could be so classified. In the psychotherapy condition, only two of the six secondary homosexuals were initially considered successes, and one of these relapsed before the final follow-up. Of the four primary homosexuals in this group, all four were judged failures, both immediately following treatment and after the follow-up period.

MacCulloch and Feldman (1967) also conducted an earlier study of the effectiveness of the anticipatory avoidance-treatment procedure involving 43 homosexual patients. This treatment procedure utilized a program of successful-, unsuccessful-, and delayed-success avoidance trials much less sophisticated than the one described earlier in this chapter, which was used in the outcome study reported above. Nonetheless, these authors reported a success rate of 60% among this sample of patients up to 1 year following treatment. These patients received an average of 18–20 sessions, each of 20–25 minutes duration.

The success rates reported by Feldman and MacCulloch (1971) are higher than those reported by most other investigators using behavioral techniques. The range of success reported for a variety of behavioral techniques, including aversion therapy (Freund, 1960; Schmidt, Castell, & Brown, 1965; Brierley, 1964; Solyom & Miller, 1967; McGuire & Vallance, 1964), aversion therapy and desensitization combined (Levin *et al.*, 1967), desensitization (Stevenson & Wolpe, 1960), and sensitization techniques (Gold & Neufeld, 1965; Barlow *et al.*, 1969), is from 0% (Solyom & Miller, 1965) to 100% (Stevenson & Wolpe, 1960). It is difficult to ascertain which figures are particularly trustworthy since most of the reports just cited have significant limitations in the extent of data cited, and often the procedures utilized ("rough shock," in one instance; Brierley, 1964) are poorly described and hence quite unclear. In this sense, the two follow-up studies reported by Feldman and MacCulloch (1971) represent a great improvement in the detail with which follow-up data are reported and with which the actual therapeutic procedures are described. It seems safe to conclude that carefully designed and executed aversion-treatment procedures are likely to have a fairly good degree of success in the treatment of homosexuality, and in line with the lack of obvious superiority of the anticipatory avoidance procedure over classical conditioning (aversion relief), it seems reasonable to conclude that the aversion-relief component of an aversive-control procedure is the most effective component [this seems to be a safe conclusion despite the lack of clarity concerning the true nature of the aversion-relief "effect" in the anticipatory avoidance procedure (MacDonough, 1972)].

Birk *et al.* (1971) reported a long-term follow-up study (2 years) of homosexual men treated with an anticipatory avoidance procedure similar to that of Feldman and MacCulloch (1971). Their basic treatment procedure also included extensive group therapy for 1 year prior to behavior therapy procedures; these discussions centered about heterosexual fears. Eight homosexual men were assigned to an avoidance-conditioning group and eight to a placebo condition. In the avoidance-conditioning procedure, a shock to the leg was used as the aversive stimulus. The duration of shock, 1–4 seconds, was varied from trial to trial. All trials began with a picture of a male displayed for periods of 2–15 seconds.

In avoidance trials, the client could press a switch that terminated the picture (replacing it with a picture of a female) and prevented the shock from occurring (or terminated the shock if it were already occurring). In classical-conditioning trials, of which there were three to five within the 25 trials that constituted a single session, the avoidance switch was deactivated and the shock was unavoidable (similar to Feldman and MacCulloch's "unsuccessful" trials). This is termed *classical conditioning* since the male picture continued to be displayed while anxiety mounted in the patient as he discovered the avoidance switch was inoperative and shock was imminent. On delayed escape trials, again three to five trials within a session, the avoidance switch was inoperative, but was then activated after 2–4 seconds of shock had occurred (that is, while the shock was continuing). The authors reported that in these instances, the patients experienced intense feelings of relief with escape from shock and upon the appearance of the female picture. In what were termed delayed-avoidance trials, which occurred one to three times a session after a patient had begun switching off the male slide consistently and rapidly, the avoidance switch was inoperative for 2–8 seconds during the display of the male picture; then it was activated so that the client could still avoid the shock by rapid responding.

The effectiveness of the anticipatory avoidance procedure was compared to that of a placebo control condition in which the shock was replaced by a small light. Eight homosexual clients were told that this was an *associative-conditioning* technique in which they were encouraged to make an active response (pressing the avoidance switch) that would terminate the viewing of a male picture and present a picture of a woman. The occurrence of the light was to be a signal indicating whether avoidance had occurred within a present time period.

Table 9.5 shows the success of the two procedures using a Kinsey rating scale. An assessment of improvement immediately following the behavior therapy phase of treatment is contained in the upper portion of the table. As that time there was a highly significant tendency for the patients treated by aversive-control procedures to have changed to a more heterosexual orientation than did patients in the placebo condition. After a follow-up period of 1 year, however, the differences between the behaviors of patients in these two groups was no longer significant.

While this finding may be disappointing, it seems likely that the degree of relapse may be attributed to the failure of the current treatment procedure to deal actively and adequately with the lack of heterosexual behaviors and outlets available to these patients. Figure 9.3 illustrates the changes in both homosexual and heterosexual behaviors from pretreatment to posttreatment for the two treatment groups. While there are large and significant differences between the aversive control and placebo groups with respect to changes in homosexual behavior, none of the changes in heterosexual behavior even approaches significance.

At first it may still seem difficult to account for the lack of stability in behavior changes achieved by these authors in the light of the more stable changes reported by Feldman and MacCulloch (1971), who originated the treatment procedures from which Birk *et al.* (1971) adapted their own. Recall that it was reported that group treatment was carried on for 1 year prior to the behavior therapy. Of even greater significance is the fact that it continued for the year between the termination of behavior therapy and the 1-year follow-up assessment. One may speculate that the presence of this treatment might have been a factor in the relapses during the follow-up period. For example, within a treatment group, a small number of patients who are unsuccessfully treated might serve as models for other patients, with their accounts of homosexual behavior and heterosexual fears and problems disinhibiting homosexual desires (see Chapter IV on modeling). Indeed, the authors reported that

TABLE 9.5

Kinsey Change During Conditioning[a]

Aversive Control Group [b]			Placebo Group [b]		
Original rating	Final rating	Improvement	Original rating	Final rating	Improvement
6	1	+5	5	4	+1
6	5	+1	6	6	0
5	2	+3	6	6	0
4	1	+3	6	6	0
6	6	0	6	5	+1
6	0	+6	6	6	0
6	1	+5	6	6	0
3	3	0	6	6	0
Total		+23			+2

Durable Kinsey Change 1 Year After Conditioning

Aversive Control Group [b]			Placebo Group [b]		
Original rating	Final rating	Improvement	Original rating	Final rating	Improvement
6	2	+4	5	5	0
6	5	+1	6	6	0
5	6	−1	6	5	+1
4	5	−1	6	6	0
6	6	0	6	3	+3
6	0	+6	6	6	0
6	3	+3	6	5	+1
3	3	0	6	6	0
Total		+12			+5

[a] Reprinted from Birk, L., Huddleston, W., Miller, E., and Cohler, B. Avoidance conditioning for homosexuality. *Archives of General Psychiatry,* 1971, **25,** 319. Copyright 1971, American Medical Association.

[b] Kinsey change was assessed "using both psychologic reaction and overt experience." Ratings: 0 = exclusively heterosexual without homosexual feelings; 1 = predominantly heterosexual, only incidentally homosexual; 2 = predominantly heterosexual but more than incidentally homosexual; 3 = equally heterosexual and homosexual; 4 = predominantly homosexual but more than incidentally heterosexual; 5 = predominantly homosexual, only incidentally heterosexual; 6 = exclusively homosexual.

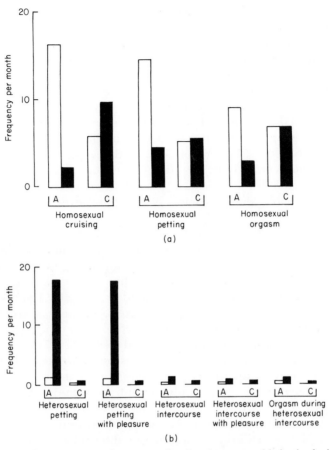

Figure 9.3 Mean changes in frequency of various homosexual behavior by individuals receiving aversive conditioning and placebo control treatment procedures. From Birk *et al.*, 1971.

one-half the patients in each of two therapy groups were from the placebo control condition and one-half from the anticipatory avoidance condition, so that from the very start, fully 50% of the patients in each group were destined to show no significant change in homosexual proclivities.

In general, reports concerning aversive procedures in the treatment of homosexuality indicate that success in modifying this behavior problem is slightly less extensive than the success reported for transvestism or fetishism. Treatment of transvestism typically involves the client's viewing of pictures of himself in female attire (Barker *et al.*, 1961) or actually cross-dressing during treatment (Glynn & Harper, 1961). Drug-induced aversion has been applied during treatment of this disorder, with success reported over follow-up periods of 3–7 months (Barker *et al.,* 1961; Glynn & Harper, 1961). One study reported the treatment of transvestism utilizing apomorphine in a treatment regimen of 39 sessions. Of 13 transvestites treated, 7 were reported as "apparently cured" during follow-up periods ranging from 8 months to 7 years (Morganstern, Pearce, & Rees, 1965). Drug-induced aversive procedures have generally been abandoned in favor of shock procedures, primarily for the advantages of better timing and the consequent availability of anxiety-relief treatment procedures. In general, these studies report a high degree of success, although most of the literature consists of case studies for which there is no possibility of calculating success "rates" (Blakemore *et al.,* 1963a; Clark, 1965; Marks & Gelder, 1967: Thorpe, Schmidt, Brown, & Castell, 1964).

Fetishism is a reasonably rare disorder, or perhaps it is rarely reported since to some degree, normal male sexual arousal is stimulated by a variety of items. Over all, successful treatment appears a common outcome in the case of fetishism and has included the use of both drug-induced aversive states (Raymond, 1956; Raymond & O'Keefe, 1965; Cooper, 1964) and electric shock aversion (McGuire & Vallance, 1964; Barker, 1965; Kushner, 1965; Marks & Gelder, 1967).

In the treatment of a fetishist, Marks and Gelder (1967) were successful in removing the patient's sexual responsiveness to the various fetish objects, while leaving unaffected his responsiveness toward appropriate sexual stimuli (for example, a photograph of a nude woman). The measures of sexual arousal typically employed in empirical studies of sexual deviations include increases in penile blood volume (these may be seen as incipient erections), the presence or absence of total erections, or the latency between presentation of a stimulus and the occurrence of an erection. In the case treated by Marks and Gelder, the inappropriate sexual stimuli were treated with aversive-control procedures one at a time. After 20 treatment trials to the first inappropriate stimulus (panties), the patient showed no responsiveness to that stimulus, but undiminished responsiveness to the other inappropriate stimuli (pajamas, skirts and blouses, and slips). As the counterconditioning procedures were applied to the other items, they each, in turn, lost their capacity to induce sexual arousal. Figures 9.4 and 9.5 present the results. Note that throughout, the responsiveness to appropriate stimuli (nude women) remained undiminished. In Figure 9.4 it may be seen that within the series of treatments of each sexually arousing stimulus the latencies between the presentation of the stimulus and the onset of erection became progressively longer until the erection no longer occurred, and the stimuli were thus judged to be no longer sexually arousing.

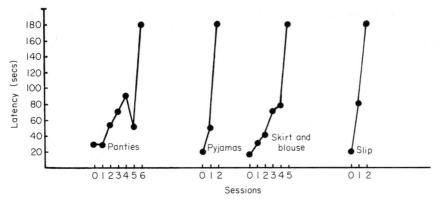

Figure 9.4   Erection latency at the end of each aversion session. Changes in the latency of erection-responses shown by a transvestite to different feminine garments during aversive counterconditioning treatment. From Marks and Gelder, 1967.

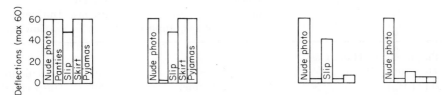

Figure 9.5   Erections after 1-minute exposure to stimulus. Changes in the frequency of erection-responses shown by a transvestite to different feminine garments during aversive counterconditioning treatment. From Marks and Gelder, 1967.

Finally, although little evaluative research has appeared in the literature, it seems apparent that aversive techniques may be employed effectively in the treatment of exhibitionism (Evans, 1968; Kushner & Sandler, 1966), although there have been several reports of other techniques, notably assertive training and desensitization (Wolpe, 1958; Bond & Hutchinson, 1960).

Treatment of Alcoholism

Studies of the effectiveness of aversive procedures in the treatment of alcoholism have tended to employ complete abstinence as the criterion for remission. This reflects the widely accepted assumption that alcoholics can never maintain a controlled pattern of drinking. Some investigators (Davies, 1962; Kendell, 1965) have reported indications that a small percentage of alcoholics, even alcoholics whose alcoholism was extreme and of long standing, can resume moderate drinking following treatment. We report the results of studies in terms of the extent to which clients show complete abstinence following treatment. The rates reported would be somewhat higher if those showing moderate drinking only were also included; however, the validity of indicators used to assess "moderate drinking" (typically the client's own verbal report) is open to question.

Table 9.6 documents the results of a number of outcome studies concerned with the treatment of alcoholism by aversive procedures either alone or in combination with other treatment methods. Although there is a good deal of variability in the abstinence rates reported, only three of the studies reported show rates lower than 50%. The variance in these

TABLE 9.6

Aversion Treatment of Alcoholism: Outcome Studies [a]

Investigator	Number of cases	Aversive stimulus	Complete abstinence (%)	Duration of follow-up
Edlin, Johnson, Hletko, & Heilbrunn (1945)	63	Emetine	30	3–10 months
Kant (1945)	31	Emetine	80	Unspecified
Lemere & Voegtlin (1950)	4096	Emetine	51	1–10 years
Miller, Dvorak, & Turner (1960)	10	Emetine	80	8 months
Shanahan & Hornick (1946)	24	Emetine	70	9 months
Thimann (1949)	275	Emetine	51	3–7 years
Wallace (1949)	31	Emetine	42	4–17 months
DeMorsier & Feldmann (1950)	150	Apomorphine	46	8–31 months
Mestrallet & Lang (1959)	183	Apomorphine	41	
Ruck (1956)		Apomorphine	50	1.5 years
Kantorovich (1934)	20	Electric shock	82	3 weeks–20 months
Blake (1967)	25	Electric shock	23	12 months
	37	Electric shock with relaxation training	48	12 months
Miller (1959)	24	Verbally induced aversion	83	9 months
Anant (1967)	26	Verbally induced aversion	96	8–15 months
Ashem & Donner (1968)	15	Verbally induced aversion	40	6 months

[a] From *Principles of Behavior Modification* by Albert Bandura. Copyright © 1969 by Holt, Rinehart and Winston, Inc. Reprinted by permission of Holt, Rinehart and Winston, Inc.

reports probably reflects the differing lengths of follow-up periods during which abstinence was assessed. The general picture is one in which abstinence is quite high during the time immediately following treatment, then a very sharp increase in incidence of reversion to drinking 6–12 months following treatment, with only gradually increasing reversion thereafter.

The work of Voegtlin and his colleagues deserves some special mention for several reasons. In accepting clients for treatment, all were offered treatment with aversive procedures and only those whose physical condition prevented such treatment (4%), or who refused such treat-

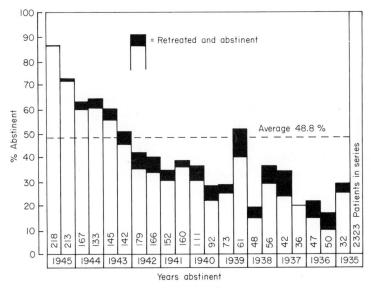

Figure 9.6 Percentage of total abstinence following the aversive conditioning treatment of alcoholism: by 6-month intervals over a 10-year follow-up period. From Voegtlin and Broz, 1949.

ment (5%) were excluded. Thus, Voegtlin's sample of clients covered a wide age range and included nearly all socioeconomic levels and nearly all occupational groups. Furthermore, follow-up periods ranged from 1 to a maximum of 10 years! Results from the treatment of 2392 clients are depicted in Figure 9.6 (Voegtlin & Broz, 1949).

The overall abstinence rate for the sample of individuals represented in Figure 9.6 is better than 48%. This figure is for all clients regardless of the length of follow-up: 70–85% of the clients remained abstinent during the first year following treatment, while after 10 years, 25–30% were still completely abstinent. The extensiveness of Voegtlin's study allowed him to study various correlates of successful abstinence following aversion treatment. Clients who continued to associate with friends who drank were quite likely to resume drinking. Those who joined abstinence organizations showed high rates of abstinence (87%), while those who did not were much more likely to revert (40% showed continued abstinence). Wealthy clients were more likely to remain abstinent (62%) than were middle class (49%), and middle-class clients were more successful than clients who were charity cases (20%). Age was also an important factor, with clients under 25 showing the lowest rates of abstinence (23%). Finally, clients who had a history of reasonably continuous employment showed good abstinence (71%), while those whose employment was less stable did poorly (21%).

There is some indication that supplementary treatment sessions are important for the long-term success of aversive procedures in the control of behavior. Voegtlin, Lemere, Broz, & O'Hallaren (1941) studied the effectiveness of supplementary treatment during the first year following the original treatment. Patients were given from one to four supplementary treatment sessions at 30, 60, and then every 90 days following the original treatment. Clients given these supplementary sessions showed consistently lower rates of remission than did clients not offered the opportunity for supplementary treatment. In another study (Voegtlin, Lemere, Broz, & O'Hallaren, 1942), it was found that 91% of clients who agreed to participate in periodic retreatment remained abstinent by the end of 1 year, while 71% of those who declined such supplementary treatment were similarly successful.

X

Cognitive Methods

In this chapter we deal with cognitive methods for effecting changes in maladaptive behavior and emotion. Cognitive psychology is specifically concerned with thinking processes. Hence, a cognitive method aims at modifying feelings and actions by influencing the client's patterns of thought. Actually, any of the more traditional forms of psychotherapy are highly cognitive in nature. For example, the methods of psychoanalysis, including intense introspection, free association, and dream interpretation are based upon an examination of the client's cognitions. However, as Beck (1970) has pointed out, cognitive therapy, as it has evolved in recent years, is markedly different from the more traditional, dynamically based methods of treatment in several significant respects. First, the therapeutic interview is more structured. Second, treatment tends to focus on overt symptoms to a far greater degree. Third, little attention is devoted to the client's childhood experiences. Fourth, relatively little heed is given to traditional constructs such as infantile sexuality, the unconscious, etc. Finally, it is not assumed that insight into the origins of a problem is necessary for its alleviation. As Beck has indicated, these characteristics, which set cognitive therapy apart from the traditional approaches, are shared by behavior therapy, as well.

In characterizing the methods described in this chapter as cognitive, we do not mean to suggest that the techniques presented in the preceding chapters are exclusively behavioral. For example, the importance of thinking and introspection are clear in desensitization and in implosive therapy. In fact, even for the ultrabehavioral operant methods, the degree to which observed behavior change is mediated by awareness of the contingencies remains a highly controversial subject (Spielberger & DeNike, 1966; Kennedy, 1970, 1971). Thus, the basis for including a particular method in this discussion is somewhat arbitrary. On the other hand, in terms of their exclusive focus on thought processes, these methods are relatively more cognitive than methods previously examined. Finally, the methods to be presented by no means represent an exhaustive list of the possible cognitive strategies that behaviorally oriented therapists might employ. For instance, many behavior therapists employ hypnosis from time to time, usually in an adjunctive manner. Needless to say, an adequate consideration of hypnosis would require a separate volume.[Lazarus (1971) has provided a variety of additional cognitive techniques (for example, "time projection," "face saving") that the reader may find of interest.]

Rational–Emotive Therapy

Rational-Emotive Therapy (Ellis, 1957, 1962), is derived directly from a theory that assumes that psychological disorders arise from faulty or irrational patterns of thinking. The thought patterns that typically manifest themselves in chains of preconscious, implicit verbalizations arise from assumptions comprising the individual's basic belief system.[1]

Ellis's view of the primacy of preconscious (as well as conscious thinking) is at sharp odds with that of classic psychoanalysis with its paramount emphasis on the unconscious, although both approaches stress the fundamental role of primitive, magical, or irrational thinking in the development of psychopathology. Early in his professional career, Ellis (a clinical psychologist) subscribed to the prevailing dynamic point of view but, over the years, evolved an approach that was increasingly more oriented away from the acquisition of "historical" insight and toward here-and-now cognitive factors that directly mediate maladaptive behaviors and emotions. According to Ellis (1962), an ever-increasing success rate in the clinic resulted from his efforts at modifying his approach.

---

[1] As Meichenbaum (1971b) has pointed out, there is actually a relatively long history of treatment approaches stressing the importance of belief systems and self-verbalizations [see Korzybski, (1933)]. Meichenbaum quotes Shaffer (1947) who defined therapy as a "learning process through which a person acquires an ability to speak to himself in appropriate ways so as to control his own conduct [p. 463]."

Despite the fact that Rational-Emotive Therapy (referred to as RET) has been readily available for public consumption for hardly a decade, it has already gained a remarkable number of enthusiastic adherents. While the popularity of RET may be partially attributed to the enthusiasm and productivity of its founder, in our view, there are more fundamental reasons for its widespread acceptance. First, for many practitioners (and many laymen), the basic assumption that what an individual says to himself has a major bearing on the way he feels and acts is incontrovertible. Second, the chief method of RET, direct (and nonsubtle) attempt on the part of the therapist to modify these self-verbalizations, is a plausible therapeutic corollary to the first assumption. Third, both in terms of theory and practice, Ellis's style of exposition is clear and explicit. Many therapists (justifiably or not) have felt sufficiently knowledgeable in RET to begin to apply it to clients after merely reading the definitive *Reason and Emotion in Psychotherapy* (Ellis, 1962). Kelly's (1955) Fixed-Role Therapy bears a remarkable similarity to RET, in terms of its philosophical basis, as well as its here-and-now action orientation. Nevertheless, Kelly's manner of presentation, while logically appealing, is quite esoteric, and this may in part account for why Kelly's impact on practitioners has not been nearly as great as that of Ellis.

The essence of RET is seen in the *A-B-C-D-E* paradigm (Ellis, 1971a). *A* refers to some real, external event to which the individual is exposed. *B* refers to the chain of thoughts (self-verbalizations) that he goes through in response to *A;* and *C* symbolizes the emotions and behaviors that are a consequence of *B*. *D* stands for the therapist's efforts at modifying what occurs at *B;* and *E* stands for the presumably beneficial emotional and behavioral consequences. To illustrate, consider the depressed client who complains to the therapist that no one "loves" him, providing objective evidence that this is, indeed, the case. In particular, the client describes the event that precipitated his present depression: his girl friend telephoned to inform him she wished to end the relationship. This is event *A*. The therapist now sets about determining the nature of *B*, the client's chain of thoughts that followed *A*. Initially the client may not be totally aware of these crucial self-verbalizations, in which case some degree of probing and encouragement on the part of the therapist is required. On the other hand, the client may be able to verbalize them quite readily. In either case, assume that the sequence of thoughts is as follows: "She no longer loves me . . . nobody does . . . I'm a worthless nothing . . . that's simply terrible." After engaging in this pattern of thinking, the client, now at *C*, is expected to experience considerable negative emotion (anxiety, anger, depression) and behave accordingly.

The therapist's interventions (*D*) consist of direct efforts at having the client examine, in a scientifically critical manner, the validity or rationality of the self-statements at point B. In particular, he helps the client in making the very critical discrimination between those statements at B that are objectively true (for example "she no longer loves me . . . nobody does") and those that may be irrational (for example, "I'm worthless").

Once the client makes this discrimination, the therapist may ask him to provide evidence that the second B statement does, in fact, follow logically from the first, as follows:

You are telling yourself that you are presently unloved, which may be true, and which means that you are lonely and sexually frustrated and so on, which is too bad, but then you are telling yourself that *because* you are unloved, you are worthless. Can you tell me how the second idea follows from the first?

Sooner or later the client will come to the realization that the second statement does not follow from the first, at which point he is expected to engage in alternative and more flexible ways of thinking. For example, with some coaching from the therapist he may now say to himself:

It is true she no longer loves me. No one does. I certainly want this person (or somebody) to love me, but I don't really *need* love. There is nothing terrible about her rejecting me, or nobody loving me, and it certainly doesn't imply that I'm worthless.

The client is now in a position to experience the more positive emotions and consequent behaviors symbolized by E.

In summary, event A (an objective occurrence) impinges on the individual, giving rise to self-verbalizations at B, some of which are irrational and self-defeating and lead to negative emotions and related behaviors at C. The Rational therapist, at point D, helps the client to examine the logical relationship among the self-verbalizations at B, resulting in the elimination of irrational thinking and a consequent amelioration of suffering at point E.

While in the consulting room, the client may indicate quite strongly that he is convinced of the irrational and self-defeating nature of certain of his self-verbalizations, also indicating alternative, healthier ways of thinking. However, it is likely that client will tend to revert to his habitual ruminative patterns between therapy sessions (especially early in therapy), and the RET therapist takes steps to minimize this. One tactic involves having the client verbalize how he would handle negative feelings when the therapist is not present. For example, the therapist might say, "Now, suppose tomorrow you notice yourself beginning to feel anxious or depressed because your girl friend rejected you. What would you do to make yourself feel better?" This allows for an additional check on the client's self-verbalizations and serves as added encouragement to practice rational thinking on his own.

Homework is an important element of Rational-Emotive Therapy. The client might be asked to read relevant chapters in Ellis and Harper's (1968) *Guide to Rational Living* (for the above individual, the chapters dealing with the need for approval and self-worth). In addition, the client might be asked to write down those situations that give rise to negative emotions, indicating the irrational self-verbalizations he was engaging in at the time, as well as what he said to himself to counter such thoughts. Part of the next therapy session would be devoted to discussing these notes, with the therapist providing corrective comments when necessary. Through homework assignments the client is also asked to confront things he fears, so as to provide direct evidence that the objects of his habitual ruminations are not really "terrible" or "awful."

According to Ellis (1971a), irrational beliefs cannot be empirically verified; that is, they are neither subject to proof nor disproof.[2] The sorts of beliefs of primary concern to RET frequently pertain to some form of moralistic imperative or dictum supposedly defining the basis for human worth. Since, according to Ellis (1971a), personal worth is not a "ratable" entity, any such belief is reduced to an arbitrary assumption. Thus, the belief that one is worthless because he is unloved or because he is not a professional success can in no way be judged true because it is meaningless. Similarly, the belief that another individual (for example, a convicted murderer) is in an absolute or basic sense worthless, cannot be taken as correct. Any words used to evaluate the absolute or ultimate worth of a person are meaningless. Criminals are not *bad* or *evil* in the sense that they are deserving of punishment or damnation (although Ellis is not suggesting that society should not protect itself from their misdeeds), nor are Jonas Salk and Martin Luther King to be considered *good* people (although society is wise to reward the works of such individuals). In short, for Ellis there can be neither saints nor sinners.

Another general class of beliefs central to RET pertains to presumed human *needs*. Needs, in this context, do not refer to the readily identifiable necessities for physical survival. A standard text on the psychology of personality would describe them as "psychological" needs. However, the term *need* carries the implication of serious and concrete negative consequences if left unfulfilled. Yet an individual expressing such a need ("I need to be respected") ordinarily expresses no clear notion of the

---

[2] Unless Ellis arbitrarily restricts his definition of "irrational," there are beliefs prevalent in most subcultures that external observers would label as irrational *because* of empirical disconformation (for example, masturbation causes mental illness).

consequences of not having this need met. For the rational therapist, words such as "want" or "desire" are far more meaningful and accurate ("I want, desire, would enjoy, would prefer to be, respected . . ."). At first blush, the reader may conclude that an attempt to foster in the client the ability to discriminate between a want, or desire, and a need is to engage in quibbling semantics. However, if, as RET assumes, individuals are drastically affected by the content of their beliefs, the psychological consequences of perceiving that a basic need is going unfulfilled are far more dire than those arising from the knowledge that a nonessential desire is being frustrated.

Ellis (1962) has provided a list of 11 irrational beliefs common to this culture, most of which fall readily into the "should" or "should not," or "need" categories. Slightly paraphrased, they are:

1. One should be loved, or approved of, by almost everyone.
2. In order to be worthwhile, one should be competent in almost all respects.
3. Some people are intrinsically bad and deserve punishment.
4. Things should always be exactly the way we want them to be (that is, it is terrible when they are not).
5. Individuals have little internal control over their personal happiness or misery.
6. If there is some possibility that something may be dangerous, one should worry about it a great deal.
7. It is easier to avoid than to face difficulties and responsibilities inherent in living.
8. A person should be (that is, needs to be) dependent on other, stronger individuals.
9. A person's present and future behavior is irreversibly dependent on significant past events.
10. A person should become extremely upset over the problems of others.
11. Every problem has (should have; must have) an ideal solution, and it is catastrophic when this solution is not found.

Ellis (1962) also has provided the reader with a detailed account of why each of these beliefs is irrational and "self defeating." For example, believing that one should be loved by almost everyone is irrational because it is arbitrary, and self-defeating because it will usually lead to frustration and disappointment. Naturally, it is possible to hold irrational beliefs that are not self-defeating simply because they have little or no bearing on one's everyday life. The belief that man is created in the image of God is by Ellis's criterion clearly irrational, but this belief, *if taken in isolation,* would not be expected to have positive or negative emotional consequences.

The Method of RET

In most general terms, the therapist's task (Ellis, 1971a) is threefold. He first determines precipitating external events. Second, he determines the specific thought patterns (and underlying beliefs) that constitute the internal response to these events and give rise to negative emotions. Third, he assists the client in altering these beliefs and thought patterns. The first task is usually accomplished by relatively standard interviewing techniques. As we have suggested, clients often bring quite specific complaints to the clinic, but when they are of a nonspecific nature (for instance, depression), it is usually not difficult to determine what external events correlated with the onset of the disorder. The therapist's next task involves determining his client's internalized response to this event. To illustrate, consider the following client-therapist dialogue. The client, a college freshman, describes himself as apathetic and depressed:

Therapist: How long have you had these feelings of depression?
Client: Ever since the beginning of this quarter, I think.
Therapist: Can you tell me what is bothering you?
Client: Everything is . . . I don't know . . . a bunch of shit. I don't seem to care about anything anymore. I don't even care about school anymore, and that used to mean a lot to me.
Therapist: How are you doing in school, gradewise?
Client: Lousy. This quarter I've studied a total of 2 hours.
Therapist: Let's see. Fall quarter was your first at Stanford? How were your grades then?
Client: Shitty; had a 2.3 average. C average. And I worked hard, too. I feel like shoving the whole thing.
Therapist: Maybe this is part of what is getting you down. How did you do in high school?
Client: Graduated with almost a 4.0. I thought I'd set the world on fire at Stanford, and I'm doing rotten.
Therapist: What does that make you, in your eyes?
Client: I'm a failure. . . . I'll never get accepted to a decent medical school with grades like that. I'll probably end up pumping gas in Salinas . . . that's all I'm good for. I feel worthless.
Therapist: Sounds like you've been saying to yourself, "I'm a failure . . . I'm worthless" on account of your *C* average last quarter. That would be enough to depress anybody.

Client: It's true. I've got to do well and I'm not.

Therapist: So, you believe that in order for you to consider yourself a worthwhile person, you've got to succeed at something . . . like making A's at Stanford?

Client: A person's got to be good at something to be worth a damn. School was the only thing I was ever much good at in the first place.

The client came from a small high school where competition was lacking and making good grades was relatively easy. Now, at a university that admits only top students, he can perform at only an average level relative to his peers. At this point the therapist begins to challenge certain of the client's beliefs.

Therapist: I'd like to point out that you're competing against some of the best students in the country, and they don't care very much about grading on the curve there. An average performance among outstanding people isn't really average, after all, is it?

Client: I know what you are getting at, but that doesn't help too much. Any decent medical school requires at least a *B* + average, and I've got to get into medical school. That's been my goal ever since I was a kid.

Therapist: Now, wait a minute! You say you *have* to go to medical school. Sounds like you think not going to medical school is against the law. Is that so?

Client: Well, not exactly. You know what I mean.

Therapist: I'm not sure. Do you really mean that you want very much to go to medical school? Because that is very different from believing that you *must* go to medical school. If you think you have to go to medical school, you are going to treat it like it's a life or death thing, which it isn't. But you believe that it is and that is likely to be a major reason why you're depressed.

Client: I can see your point, but even if I agreed with you, there's my family. They wouldn't agree with you.

Therapist: What do you mean?

Client: They are big on my being successful. All my life my parents have been telling me that the whole family is counting on my being a doctor.

Therapist: O.K., but that is their belief. Does it have to be yours?

Client: I just can't let them down.

Therapist: What would happen if you did?

Client: They'd be hurt and disappointed. Sometimes I almost think they wouldn't like me any more. That would be awful!

Therapist: Well the worst possible thing that could happen if you don't go to medical school is that your father and mother wouldn't like you, and might even reject you. You aren't even sure this would happen.

Therapist: But, even if they did, does it follow that it would be awful? Could you prove that, logically, I mean?

Client: It's lousy when your own family rejects you.

Therapist: I still can't see the logical connection between their rejecting you and things being awful or even lousy. I would agree that it wouldn't exactly be a pleasant state of affairs. You are equating rejecting with catastrophe, and I'd like you to try and convince me one follows from the other.

Client: They wouldn't even want me around . . . like I was a worthless shit. And that would be rotten.

Therapist: Well, there you go again, telling yourself that because they would reject you, which means they wouldn't want you around, you are a worthless shit. Again, I don't see the logic.

Client: It would make me feel that way.

Therapist: No, I emphatically disagree . . . it's *you* who would make you feel that way. By saying those same things to yourself.

Client: But I believe it's true.

Therapist: I'm still waiting for some logical basis for your belief that rejection means you are worthless, or not going to medical school means you're a shit.

Client: O.K., I agree about the medical school bit. I don't *have* to go. But about my parents . . . that's heavy. As far as reasons are concerned . . . (long pause) . . . I started to say I need them for emotional support but, as I think about it, I get a hell of a lot more from a couple of good buddies here at school than I ever got from them. They are pretty cold, especially Mom.

Therapist: O.K. . . . What else might be terrible about being rejected by your parents?

Client: I was thinking . . . where would I go over the holidays? But I don't spend that much time at home anyway, come to think of it. But, there is money . . . this place is damned expensive, and I don't have a scholarship. If they cut off funds, that would be a disaster.

Therapist: There you go again . . . catastrophizing. Prove to me that it would be a disaster.

Client: Well, maybe I was exaggerating a bit. It would be tough, though I suppose I could apply for support, or get a job maybe. In fact, I know I could. But then it would take longer to get through school, and that would be shitty.

Therapist: Now you are beginning to make a lot of sense. I agree that it would be shitty . . . but certainly not terrible.

Client: You know, for the first time in weeks I think I feel a little better. Kind of like there is a load off my mind. Is that possible?

Therapist: I don't see why not, but I'm wondering what would happen if you'd start feeling depressed tonight or tomorrow . . . how would you deal with it?

Note: At this point, the therapist is attempting to insure that the client is prepared to deal with bouts of depression between therapy sessions. Following this, the aforementioned homework would be assigned.

The material presented in this section is intended to provide the reader with a general introduction to the theory and method of RET. The therapist seriously interested in implementing RET is advised to refer to any one of the many primary sources currently available, including *Reason and Emotion in Psychotherapy* (Ellis, 1962) and *Growth Through Reason* (Ellis, 1971a), for a variety of cases presented in great detail. Tapes of RET sessions are also available and are recommended. The reader should be forewarned that the therapeutic style of Ellis, and certain of his co-workers, is forceful, almost to the point of being overpowering or intimidating. It is likely that this element has contributed to the belief, in certain quarters, that RET is authoritarian. We, as well as Ellis (1971a), disagree with this view. Indeed, it is not in the nature of the authoritarian therapist to provide a logical rationale for virtually every statement or suggestion made to his client, which is precisely what RET therapists do. On the other hand, one is quite justified in questioning whether Ellis's particularly blunt style is a necessary therapeutic ingredient. For example, Ellis (1971c) admonished his client with ". . . You're making your wants into necessities—not desires. Which they are! I *want* a million dollars; therefore, I should have it. And I don't have it; therefore I'm a shit! I *want* to be straight; right now I'm gay (we're just assuming that you were); now, do those things follow [p. 110; italics in original]?" In our experience certain clients are "turned off" by so direct a style. The therapist might have made the same point, but in a somewhat lower key, as follows:

Therapist: "It sounds like maybe you are telling yourself that because you want to be straight you should be straight, but since you aren't, you aren't worth very much. To tell you the truth, I guess I just don't see the logic in that, if that is what you are thinking. Because to me that's sort of like saying 'I want a millions dollars; therefore, I should have it. Since I don't, I'm a pretty awful person.' What do you think?"

Naturally, whether the forceful style modeled by Ellis and others does facilitate therapy can be resolved only empirically, although it seems likely that it would depend in part on the particular client.

Empirical Findings

Case Histories.   In an early report, Ellis (1957) summarized the results of 172 case histories, all treated by the author. Of this number, 16 cases were treated with orthodox psychoanalysis, 78 received psychoanalytic psychotherapy, and 78 received RET. As we have indicated, Ellis's therapeutic orientation gradually changed over a period of several years, and the type of treatment a particular client received reflected his therapeutic bias at the time. Of the first group, 50% reportedly showed definite improvement, with a mean of 93 treatment sessions. The corresponding figure for patients receiving psychoanalytic psychotherapy was 63%, in an average of 35 sessions. The group receiving rational psychotherapy, according to Ellis, showed an improvement rate of 90%, with an average of 26 sessions. The cases in the psychoanalytic psychotherapy sample and rational-therapy sample were selected so as to be matched on potentially important variables of age, sex, education, and diagnosis. In view of this procedure and the considerably larger sample involved, the more valid comparison is between these two groups. Although these results would seem to provide support for RET, any such conclusion must be qualified by the possible existence of biases on the part of the author (a fact Ellis freely admits).

Each of the case histories reviewed below are presented in *Growth Through Reason* (Ellis, 1971a). They are presented as an indication of the types of clinical problems treated successfully with RET. Geis (1971) treated a 17-year-old culturally deprived high school student, who had been referred because of suicidal ideation, depression, and a tendency to be highly perfectionistic, along with an intense fear of failure. Over the course of approximately nine sessions, his level of confidence increased and his depression diminished. During the last session, he indicated that he could now get along without additional therapy, and a 5-year follow-up revealed that he was doing well in school, had a reasonably active social life (prior to treatment he had never dated), and continued to be less perfectionistic.

Ellis (1971c) worked with a 26-year-old commercial artist who was obsessed with thoughts of becoming a homosexual, in spite of having a steady girl with whom he had a good sexual relationship. Ellis structured his problem in terms of an excessive fear of rejection, thoughts of worthlessness, and unrealistically high goals. In relation to thoughts of homosexuality, his anxieties arose not from a high likelihood of his becoming a fixed homosexual, but rather from perceived dire consequences were such ever to occur. Treatment focused upon self-acceptance (including accepting the possibility of homosexuality) and by the sixth session the client reported that he was improved. By Session 13, the client was ready to discontinue therapy and at a 6-month follow-up, he reported that he was no longer obsessed with thoughts of becoming a homosexual, that his relationship with his girl friend was better than ever, and that he continued to be a good deal more self-accepting.

A second case reported by Ellis (1971b) dealt with a 23-year-old girl who suffered severe guilt feelings because she failed to adhere to rules laid down by her narrow-minded, overly religious, and perfectionistic parents. Her own perfectionism prevented her from engaging in creative writing (despite her obvious talent) and interfered with her relationships with men. During treatment she was encouraged to examine her views on religion, sexual behavior, perfection, and the need to be loved. By the end of four individual sessions and several group sessions, she reported that she was doing well and could manage without additional treatment. A 12-year follow-up revealed that she had entered into, and maintained, a healthy marriage, was involved in writing successful books, and was finding considerable satisfaction in her work.

Gullo (1971) treated a husband and wife who had not engaged in successful intercourse, despite the fact they had been married for 13 years. The difficulty related primarily to the husband's impotence, which Gullo attributed to his fear of failure, as well as sexual puritanism. In addition to the standard RET didactic approach, Gullo provided suggestions for more effective sex play, as well as a program for encouraging his clients to continue to work on solving their sex problem (including suggesting that they not have meals until they had read a list of the advantages of dealing with their problem). By the sixth session, they reported having frequent successful intercourse, and at a 2-year follow-up, they had a child and reported that they continued to have successful intercourse.

The above case histories have a common theme of perfectionism and fear of failure and consequent rejection. For Ellis and his followers, attitudes of this general nature serve as the basis for most maladaptive responding, and it is not surprising that individual case histories would be conceptualized in such terms. For additional case history material, the reader is referred to Ellis's journal, *Rational Living*, as well as the remainder of case reports in *Growth Through Reason*.

Experimental Results.   Research dealing with Rational-Emotive Therapy may be divided into two categories. The first deals with whether self-verbalizations do indeed exert some control over the way we feel and behave. In one study (Rimm & Litvak, 1969), subjects from a normal college population were required to read to themselves triads of sentences that, according to Ellis (1962, 1971a), should lead to maladaptive responding (for instance, "My grades may not be good enough this semester . . . I might fail out of school . . . that would be awful.") As a control condition, other subjects were required to read neutral triads of sentences to themselves (for instance, "Inventors are imaginative . . . Edison was an inventor; therefore, he was imaginative."). As expected, subjects in the experimental group experienced significantly more emotional arousal (as measured by respiratory changes) than did control subjects.

In two studies (Meichenbaum, 1971a; Meichenbaum & Goodman, 1969), it was found that young children whose approach to problem solving was marked by impulsivity tended to engage in less self-regulatory speech than other children less impulsive in their problem-solving behavior. These findings, taken along with the results of a number of other investigations (see Velten, 1968; Loeb, Beck, Diggory, & Tuthill, 1967), support the view that cognitive activities, such as self-verbalization, exert a definite effect on behavior.

The second category of research deals with direct attempts at modifying behavior, using RET principles. In one such study, Maes and Heimann (1970) compared the effectiveness of RET, client-centered therapy, and systematic desensitization with test-anxious high school students. Treatments were administered during 10 training sessions covering a 5-week period. Response measures included an anxiety self-report, heart rate, and galvanic skin response. Following treatment, the subject was required to imagine he was about to take an examination, at which time the anxiety inventory was administered. Following this, he was given a concept-mastery test (described as an intelligence test), and as he responded, physiological measures were taken. Although the anxiety inventory failed to distinguish among the treatment groups, for both physiological measures, desensitization and RET subjects showed significantly less emotional reactivity than either the client-centered subjects, or subjects in a fourth, nontreated control group. No follow-up was reported.

In an extremely thorough investigation, Meichenbaum, Gilmore, and Fedoravicius (1971) compared the effectiveness of group RET with group desensitization in treating speech anxiety. A third group of subjects received group desensitization followed by a combination of RET and group desensitization. A fourth group served as attention controls, and a fifth were waiting-list controls. Treatment was carried out over eight 1-hour sessions.

Principal response measures, objective and self-ratings, were made in connection with test speeches occurring prior to, and following, treatment. The main findings were that subjects receiving desensitization only, or RET only, showed the greatest improvement. In fact, their level of speech performance following treatment generally matched that of an additional group of low speech-anxious subjects included in order to provide a standard for adaptive responding in such a situation. Subjects receiving the combination of RET and desensitization did not differ from attention-control subjects in their degree of improvement, and waiting-list controls showed the least improvement. The authors attributed the lack of improvement in the RET plus desensitization group to the insufficient amount of time devoted to each of the component procedures. Self-report follow-up measures taken 3 months after treatment indicated that improvement had been maintained.

In Chapter II we indicated that desensitization appeared most effective for clients manifesting relatively few phobias. Results of the above-cited study tend to support this: subjects who experienced anxiety in a wide variety of interpersonal situations benefited little from desensitization, whereas subjects whose anxiety was restricted to public-speaking situations improved noticeably. On the other hand, subjects who were anxious in many interpersonal situations benefited considerably from RET. It may well be that cognitively oriented procedures such as RET (and thought stopping, presented in the section to follow) are more appropriate to clients suffering from multiple fears than techniques such as desensitization or extinction.

Trexler and Karst (1972), also working with speech-anxious individuals, compared the effectiveness of RET with that of a relaxation treatment (viewed by the experimenters as a placebo control). A third group of subjects served as nontreated controls. Treatment was carried out during four group sessions spaced several days apart. The somewhat complex experimental design allowed for 3-minute test speeches made prior to treatment, immediately after treatment, and after some delay. Of the several response measures employed, subjects receiving RET showed significantly greater improvement than the placebo and control groups on an irrational belief scale adapted from Ellis (Jones, 1969), and on a scale measuring self-confidence while speaking. Since all subjects ultimately received RET, it was possible to increase the statistical power of the tests employed by combining pairs of groups having received RET and comparing them to a third group that had not yet undergone this treatment. The results of this more sensitive analysis revealed the superiority of RET on most of the other measures used, including objective ratings of anxiety while speaking, and anxiety concerning speaking in general. Additionally, there was evidence that the effect of RET had generalized to certain problem areas unrelated to public speaking. A questionnaire follow-up made 6–7 months after the completion of the study suggested that improvement had been maintained.

The experimental findings we have reviewed, in concert with favorable outcomes obtained in the clinic, provide rather convincing evidence that Ellis's rational-emotive approach can be effective in modifying maladaptive behavior and emotions. Further empirical corroboration for the important role of implicit verbalizations as mediators of inappropriate and self-defeating behavior is to be found in the section on thought stopping.

Thought Stopping

Quite often the therapist comes across a client who suffers considerable distress resulting from thoughts that he has difficulty controlling. When sufficiently chronic, disorders of this nature are characterized as obsessions, although experience suggests that almost everyone is "obsessive" to some degree. The so-called "worry wart" is an example of an obsessive individual whom most people regard as relatively normal. A clinically more interesting example is the individual obsessed with thoughts of "going insane," totally in the absence of supporting evidence. In both cases, the individual engages in a good deal of anxiety-producing rumination about events that objectively are very unlikely to occur. Lazarus (1971) aptly described the object of such fears as "low probability catastrophes [p. 230]." This sort of thinking or worrying is not oriented toward problem solving and is clearly self-defeating. For example, Lazarus described a patient who was obsessed with the thought of choking to death on something lodged in his windpipe. For this person, eating became an extremely aversive experience. We (and doubtless the reader) have encountered many, many individuals who appear to make themselves miserable whenever driving or riding in a car or flying in an airplane, visiting a dentist, etc. because they chronically dwell upon highly negative, but very unlikely, events associated with these activities. Certain writers, such as Ellis (1962), take the position that most, if not all, phobic reactions have at their core, irrational, obsessive thoughts. Naturally, this is debatable, although it may be significant that both desensitization and assertive training, which are among the most successful methods for dealing with phobic behavior, have the effect of discouraging obsessive thoughts. In desensitization, the client is asked to suppress intrusive thoughts of this nature, and in assertive training, the client is provided with responses that would tend to compete with self-defeating obsessions.

According to Wolpe (1969) thought stopping was introduced by Bain in 1928, although Taylor (in a personal communication to Wolpe in 1955) is apparently responsible for its adoption by present-day behavior therapists. The basic technique is extremely straightforward. The client is asked to concentrate on the anxiety-inducing thoughts, and, after a short period of time, the therapist suddenly and emphatically says "stop" (any loud noise or even painful electric shock may also suffice). After this procedure has been repeated several times (and the client reports that his thoughts were indeed interrupted or blocked), the locus of control is shifted from the therapist to the client. Specifically, the client is taught to emit a subvocal "stop" whenever he begins to engage in a self-defeating rumination.

To illustrate the method in detail, Rimm (1973) treated a female student who became extremely nervous whenever she rode in an automobile. The difficulty began some months before when she had witnessed an automobile accident. One could easily have employed systematic desensitization in this case; however, the student was specifically selected as a demonstration subject for thought stopping (when asked to volunteer, she was told only that it was an "experimental" technique that "might" be helpful). At the beginning of treatment, the only information the therapist had was that she experienced anxiety while riding in a car. The therapist assumed that the anxiety was generated by self-defeating thoughts, and the first task was to get at the content of such thoughts, as illustrated below:

Therapist: So, this has been going on for several months. Give me an example, of a specific situation when you feel especially tense.

Client: The other day I was riding with my husband. We were on Route 13, west of Carbondale and there was the little girl by the road. I was afraid she would run out.

Therapist: What kind of driver is your husband? Is he safe?

Client: Yes. He knows what he's doing when he is behind the wheel.

Therapist: Has he ever been in an accident? Does he keep his eyes on the road? Does he drive fast?

Client: Never had an accident. He keeps his eyes open and doesn't drive faster than anyone else.

Therapist: I just wanted to establish that the problem wasn't your husband's driving, which apparently it isn't. Well, if he knows what he's doing, how is it that you are getting nervous when you ride with him?

Client: I don't know; I just do. I can't help it.

Therapist: I'd like to get at the particular thoughts you are thinking when you get nervous, like on Route 13, with the little girl.

Client: I don't think I was thinking anything.

Therapist: Close your eyes and imagine the situation as it actually happened. You're on Route 13 and there's the little girl by the road. Tell me what thoughts or images cross your mind. Like you are actually in the situation.

Client: (Pause) Well, I'm feeling O.K. and then I see the girl and I wonder if Bob has seen her and then I think "she is gonna run out and he won't see her." At that point I couldn't help it, I screamed out loud "Watch out!" It made my husband mad.

Note: The therapist first established that the client's fears were not tied to unusual driving habits on the part of her husband. Note also that the client initially had difficulty recalling specific self-verbalizations and images occurring in the target situation, and a small amount of probing was necessary. After the therapist had established what the client was thinking in other driving situations associated with intense anxiety (in our experience five or six such situations are sufficient), he might then attempt to point out to the client that such thoughts are really unnecessary and self-defeating:

Therapist: I can see why it might be a good thing to get a bit uptight if the driver looked like he was about to go to sleep, or if he obviously didn't see some warning sign, because then you'd be motivated to alert him of what was happening. But in all of these situations you've mentioned, it doesn't sound like there is any need for you to get anxious, and the anxiety just makes you feel bad and not ride in a car, which is darned inconvenient.

Client: Yeah, I see what you mean. But it's hard not to think those thoughts.

The client is now prepared for the thought-stopping procedure. It is convenient to break down the treatment into four distinct phases.

Phase I. Therapist's interruption of overt thoughts.

Therapist: Imagine yourself riding in the car with Bob driving on Route 13 and the little girl is standing by the road . . . close your eyes and imagine it really clearly. As you do, you will notice thoughts cropping up, some related to your problem, some not. Say all of these thoughts out loud, including the healthy or neutral ones.

Client: (Long pause) Well, I'm thinking I've got to get home and get dinner. There is Murdale Shopping Center . . . need to do

Therapist: some shopping. I wonder what that little girl is doing by the road. What if she were to suddenly step out in front of . . .

Therapist: STOP! Let me explain. This is a conditioning procedure aimed at helping you break the habit of thinking thoughts like that. Was the thought interrupted?

Client: You startled me. Yeah, kind of.

Therapist: O.K. Let's try it again.

Client: But I know you are gonna say "stop." Does that matter?

Therapist: No, not really. The important thing is that we inhibit those self-defeating thoughts of yours.

Note: The therapist took pains to encourage "normal," as well as obsessive thinking. This allowed him to interrupt the thoughts that client and therapist agreed were irrational, while permitting a normal flow of healthy thinking. The therapist continues the above procedure until the client indicates that the thoughts indeed were blocked.

Phase II. Therapist's interruption of covert thoughts.

Therapist: Now, this time, imagine the same scene and think all those thoughts to yourself as you would in the actual situation. But the moment, the very second you find yourself *beginning* to think one of those obsessive thoughts, signal by raising your finger. If, because of what we did before, it's hard to think those sorts of thoughts, force yourself a little.

Client: O.K. (Long pause, and then she raises her finger.)

Therapist: STOP! Well, did it work?

Client: Yes, it did.

Therapist: Just for good measure, let's try one more time.

As in Phase I, the procedure is continued until the thoughts are effectively blocked.

Phase III. Client's overt interruption of covert thoughts.

Therapist: Now, we want to begin to get you to be able to control your own thinking. Once again, imagine the Route 13 situation, again as realistically and clearly as you can. But this time when you begin to have one of those irrational thoughts, say "stop" aloud, as *emphatically* as you can.

Client: (Long pause, then in a weak voice) "Stop."

Therapist: Did it work?

Client: Maybe. I'm not sure.

Therapist: Let's try again, but this time, really belt it out. Like this: "STOP!!!" Like you are ordering yourself to stop.

Client: (Long pause) "STOP" (in a loud, authoritative tone).

Therapist: That sounded good. What happened?

Client: Really seemed to work that time.

In our experience, the client's initial efforts at telling himself to "stop" are usually feeble and unconvincing (presumably to the client, himself). Encouragement and additional modeling are helpful.

Phase IV. Client's covert interruption of covert thoughts.

Therapist: Since it really wouldn't do for you to scream "stop" every time you began to have an uncomfortable thought . . . I mean, it certainly wouldn't help your husband's driving if you did . . . I now want you to do exactly what you did, but say "stop" to yourself. Not aloud. Actually tighten your vocal chords and move your tongue as if you were saying it out loud. Remember to be as emphatic as you possibly can. Go ahead and try it.

Client: (Closes her eyes . . . 20 seconds pass. She opens them.)

Therapist: What happened this time?

Client: It seemed to work.

Therapist: O.K. One more time for good measure.

After the client has been taught to block out these unwanted thoughts, he is encouraged to practice the exercise on his own, especially in the target situations (in this case, when riding in a car).

Covert Assertion

While obsessive trains of thought would seem to be of a cause of heightened levels of anxiety and even panic, clinical experience suggests that such thought patterns themselves may be partially triggered by low to moderate levels of tension. The client, in the preceding example of thought stopping, was probably somewhat anxious even before she observed the child standing by the side of the road. Instructing her in how to curtail, or prevent, obsessive thoughts would be expected to eliminate the peak emotion responses associated with such thinking, but would not be expected to eliminate anxiety conditioned to other cues associated with the driving situation. One method we have found helpful in reducing such residual anxiety is covert assertion. In Chapter III we discussed the possible inhibitory effect that assertion has upon anxiety. While as-

sertive responses are ordinarily overt, covert (subvocal) assertions might
be expected to effect a similar reduction in anxiety. In fact, the effectiveness of thought stopping may be due in part to the assertivelike quality of the client's subvocal "stop!"

After the client has successfully completed the thought-stopping procedure, he is asked to indicate positive, assertive-like statements that
would be appropriate to the particular situation. He is then asked to
imagine himself in that situation, to stop any obsessive thoughts that
might occur, and *immediately* thereafter to make the assertive statement
in a forceful, almost exuberant manner. As a check on the degree of affect, it is probably well to have the client verbalize the statement aloud
prior to having him practice the assertion covertly.

The method is illustrated in the following example (Rimm, in press).
The client is a 22-year-old male who is obsessed with the idea of having a
"mental breakdown." His notion of a mental breakdown is vague,
though apparently related to feelings of helplessness and a good deal of
crying. There is no evidence of psychotic behavior or thinking. His obsession appears, in part, to be related to his mother's brief confinement
to a mental hospital when the client was 17 years of age. The therapist
has already successfully applied the above thought-stopping procedure.

Therapist: From what you said before, you now agree that obsessing on
the possibility of a nervous breakdown is irrational and self-
defeating. In relation to so-called mental illness, what is the
reality of the situation?

Client: I'm not sure what you mean . . . I guess I'm normal, if that is
what you're getting at.

Therapist: Exactly. But if you wanted to reassure somebody like you that
they were normal, in really emphatic terms, what would you
say? In other words, what would make you feel really good?

Client: (Pause) Something like "Screw it! I'm really normal."

Therapist: O.K. Then, this time, place yourself in the same situation as
before. When you find you're just beginning to have one of
those obsessive thoughts say "stop" to yourself and then aloud
say "Screw it! I'm really normal."

Client: (Long pause) Screw it. I'm perfectly normal.

Therapist: Good. But let's do it again, and this time really say it forcefully, putting your guts into it. Also, smiling when you say
things like that sometimes helps. Will you try again?

Client: (Long pause. Then, in an emphatic tone, and with a smile)
Screw it! I'm perfectly normal!

Therapist: How did it work? How do you feel right now?

Client: Fine. It's kind of hard to tell, but I think saying that helped.

Therapist: Now, let's do exactly the same thing as before. But this time say that sentence to yourself. Don't say it aloud, but say it to yourself with a lot of feeling, and again smile. Also, taking a deep breath before you say it helps. Go ahead.

Client: (Long pause . . . takes a deep breath and smiles.)

Therapist: Well?

Client: Yeah, I feel good.

Therapist: Just for good measure, tell me some other things you could say to yourself that are in the same sort of vein. So you won't get bored saying the same thing over and over.

Client: Maybe something like "I've got a terrifically healthy head on my shoulders." I know that sounds funny, but it would make me feel good, or maybe, "I'm mentally competent."

Therapist: Let's try the same thing with these sentences, and then you can practice on your own.

Note: The therapist stressed having several covert assertive responses. The same response, used over and over, might lose some of its positive affect through extinction.

Sometimes people find themselves in situations that present a fair degree of objective danger. For instance, suppose someone is driving on a mountain road and rain begins to fall, making the road quite slippery. Several cars are close behind him and there is no opportunity to pull over. Assume that he is a highly skilled driver. In such a situation it is obvious that a certain amount of tension is essential. On the other hand, dwelling on thoughts and images of the car sliding off the road, crashing into the canyon, and bursting into flames would be expected to create a near-panic condition that would only make the situation that much more dangerous.[3] If, in this sort of situation, the client is given to engaging in such ruminations, thought stopping and covert assertion might be helpful, but the content of the assertive statements should be realistic. It would be foolhardy to try to teach the client to say "This road is perfectly safe." Instead, the client might be instructed to say, "I'm a very good driver. If I stay alert, I've nothing to fear."

The content of the assertive response does not have to be specifically tied to the content of the obsession. Consider the case of the individual who typically dwells on the plane crashing whenever he is a passenger. Naturally, he could be taught to say "The pilot really knows what he is doing," or "These 747's are super-safe airplanes," but the

---

[3] Thoughts and images of this nature clearly have an implosive flavor, and it may be that for certain individuals implosive therapy (carried out in a consulting room) would be effective in reducing intense anxiety *in vivo*. However, the situation as we have presented it is hardly the place to begin to engage in self-implosion.

therapist might also wish to have him focus on some positive stimulus in the immediate environment. For one individual, saying to himself "What a fantastically beautiful cloud formation" might be helpful (although for another, this might only remind him he is 35,000 feet above solid ground). For most males, observing that the stewardess (or an attractive female passenger) is really beautiful (sexy, exciting), followed by "I'd really love to make love to her," and related fantasies, would be distracting and anxiety reducing. Moreover, the assertions need not be restricted to the present situation. The client might dwell on the satisfaction he would have obtained in telling a former boss to "go to hell," or he might think about some future event, such as the fantastic restaurant he is to visit that evening.

The following is a synopsis of the entire sequence of thought stopping and covert assertion:

1. Irrational self-verbalizations (and images) are established, and the client is persuaded of their self-defeating nature.
2. Client closes eyes and imagines target situation, verbalizing his thoughts aloud. Therapist shouts "Stop" at beginning of obsessive thought.
3. Same as above, except the client does not say his thoughts aloud but signals when he begins to obsess.
4. Client verbalizes to himself and shouts "STOP" aloud when he begins to obsess.
5. Same as above except client says "Stop" to himself.
6. Client provides therapist with appropriate assertive statements.
7. Immediately after the client has said "Stop" to himself, he engages in an assertive statement in an emphatic loud voice.
8. Same as above, except the client makes the assertive statement to himself.

Empirical Findings

Case Histories.   Although thought stopping, as it is described in the literature (Cautela, 1969; Lazarus, 1971; Wolpe, 1958, 1969), employs the therapist's abrupt command to "stop" as the punishing or distracting event, many of the published case histories use other forms of stimulation, most often painful electric shock. An early exception to this is a case, treated by Taylor (1955, cited in Wolpe, 1958), of long-standing anxiety and insomnia, in which considerable improvement followed four sessions of thought stopping. Presumably, the method employed was similar to that described by Wolpe (1958).

McGuire and Vallance (1964) successfully eliminated a 29-year-old male's unfounded obsessions regarding his wife's fidelity. Their technique initially involved presenting electric shock when the client engaged in his obsessional thinking. During the second and third session, the client controlled the occurrence and strength of the shock, and, following this, he employed a portable shock apparatus at home.

Mahoney (1971) treated a 22-year-old male obsessed with having brain damage, being persecuted, and being "odd," with self-administered aversive stimulation. The client was instructed to snap his wrist with a rubber band on the occasion of an obsessional thought and, by the sixth week of treatment, the ruminations, reportedly, were virtually nonexistent. Additionally, the client was instructed to make cigarette smoking contingent on his engaging in positive thoughts (the content of which would tend to compete with the obsessional thoughts). A sharp increase in positive thoughts was reported and the cigarette contingency was gradually faded out. At a 4-month follow-up, the client continued to be free of his previous obsessions.

Yamagami (1971) employed a sequence of thought-stopping strategies with a 24-year-old male graduate student with an 8-year history of obsessional color naming. For each of the four treatment variations, the client was presented with colored sticks, typically cues for color naming. In variation one, the therapist shouted "STOP" 1–3 minutes after the client signaled having an obsessive thought. Variation two provided the addition of an imagined pleasant scene. In variation three, electric shock was substituted for the therapist's "stop," and variation four involved pairing electric shock and "stop." The rationale for the variety of strategies is not made clear. Over the 17 treatment sessions, the frequency of color naming went from about 100 instances per day to 5. Additionally, a decrease in other obsessions was reported. One month after treatment had ended, the color obsession reportedly was completely gone and at a 7-month follow-up it had failed to recur, and the other obsessions were decreasing.

Wolpe (1971) reported the case of a 35-year-old woman suffering from interpersonal anxiety and marital difficulties, who was obsessed with negative thoughts about herself. Initially, thought stopping (with the therapist shouting "STOP") was somewhat successful, but soon the client exhibited a disinclination to employ the technique. While no outcome was reported, the report is nevertheless interesting in that it provides a transcript in which the therapist attempts to deal with the client's resistance to the treatment (which was to involve the use of a portable shock apparatus). As we have suggested, clients having a familiarity with more traditional forms of therapy, often have a set to "talk" about their difficulties, rather than to work on them in a problem-solving fashion, and this was apparently the case with Wolpe's client. From the report, much of the session was devoted to Wolpe's attempts at pointing out the self-defeating nature of the client's obsessions, and how much better she would feel were she to use the technique to free herself of them.

Recently, Rimm (1973) described the use of the aforementioned thought stopping-covert assertion technique with six individuals whose problems in general would ordinarily be labeled as phobic, rather than obsessional. The first case involved a 24-year-old female student seeking treatment of insomnia. Upon questioning, it became apparent that her insomnia was related to anxiety concerning the possibility that someone, possibly lurking in her closet, might harm her. Following one treatment session the client reported much less difficulty sleeping. During the next session she was instructed in an *in vivo* extinction procedure requiring that she deliberately keep her closet door open all night. At the next session, 2 weeks later, she indicated she was having no difficulty whatsoever sleeping. At a 6-week follow-up, improvement was reportedly maintained.

The second client, a 25-year-old female experienced considerable anxiety at the sight of actual mutilation (that is, dead animals) or movies depicting mutilation. After three sessions of treatment she reported that anxiety in such situations was greatly diminished. A 4-week follow-up revealed additional progress.

The third case involved a 19-year-old female who became extremely anxious whenever riding in an automobile, especially in situations involving highway driving. She reported considerable improvement after two treatment sessions. At a 10-month follow-up she indicated that the improvement had been maintained (strongly corroborated by her husband). The fourth case, a 21-year-old male student, suffered from the fear of having a "nervous breakdown" (in the absence of supporting evidence). Prior to treatment the client experienced such unwanted thoughts approximately 20 times per week. After four sessions this figure was halved.

The fifth case involved a 20-year-old female enuretic. The client typically avoided going to the bathroom at night, lest she be attacked by some stranger in the darkened house. The week following the initial thought stopping-covert assertion treatment she reported no enuretic episodes. The next session, however, she reported that she had been enuretic twice. At this time she received retraining in the technique and during the subsequent month was going to the bathroom rather regularly at night, and reported only two enuretic episodes (in contrast to an average of approximately six episodes per month prior to treatment).

The final case involved a 23-year-old male who had suffered from an elevator phobia. He reported some improvement after the first of two sessions, and following the second session he reported an almost total lack of anxiety and a return of pleasant sensations he had formerly associated with riding in an elevator. At a 10-month follow-up he indicated that improvement had been maintained.

Although thought stopping ordinarily concentrates on the client's self-verbalizations, some individuals suffer from disturbing and seemingly uncontrollable visual images. For example, the flight phobic might visualize a plane crashing and burning, while engaging in related verbal ruminations or, conceivably, he might experience such images in the absence of verbal obsessions. Several case histories have specifically focused on suppressing painful and self-defeating imagery. In one such report, Kushner and Sandler (1966) treated a 48-year-old male who experienced visual suicidal ideation daily. Specific images were paired with electric shock over a large number of trials. The treatment, which effected a reduction in such ideation, held up at a 3-month follow-up. Agras (1967) treated a 25-year-old chronic schizophrenic who had a long history of compulsively breaking glass. The patient was instructed to visualize himself breaking glass, at which time he received shock. As treatment progressed, the latency of the glass-breaking imagery increased and after a total of 52 sessions of treatment, the client reported he no longer had the urge to break glass. Glass-breaking behavior was almost totally eliminated, with improvement maintained at the 18-month follow-up.

In a highly novel application of a thought-stopping procedure, Bucher and Fabricatore (1970) treated a 47-year-old paranoid schizophrenic who had a 5-year history of hearing critical and obscene voices. At the beginning of treatment the patient reported experiencing such hallucinations four or more times per day. He was provided with a portable shock apparatus and instructed to shock himself when the hallucinations occurred. By the ninth day of treatment, considerable suppression of the hallucinations was reported, with improvement persisting through the 36th day, when the client was discharged (against his will). Two weeks later he returned, intoxicated, apparently once again hallucinating. At that time he indicated that he did not wish to leave the hospital and obtain work because of the voices.

Experimental Results. Meichenbaum (1971b) employed a method with snake phobics that, in many respects, is similar to the thought-stopping covert assertion procedure described earlier in this chapter. The Meichenbaum procedure combined Wolpe's anxiety-relief training with training in appropriate self-verbalization. Anxiety-relief conditioning, as presented by Wolpe (1958, 1969) involves providing the subject with painful electric shock, which he may terminate by saying aloud a word

such as "calm," the rationale being that "calm" will become a more powerful conditioned stimulus for relaxation. In Meichenbaum's procedure,
subjects were encouraged to engage in verbalizations (and experience
images) typically occurring in the presence of a snake. Such verbalizations were followed by shock, but, in addition, subjects were provided
with training in verbalizations incompatible with snake avoidance (for instance, "relax," or, "I can touch it"), which were followed by shock offset.
Treatment was carried out over five sessions.

In terms of both behavioral and self-report measures, subjects in the
verbalization-and-shock group showed greater improvement than a
group receiving training in engaging in competing verbalizations only.
Surprisingly, a third group, similar to the first, except that healthy verbalizations were shocked, while fear-inducing verbalizations terminated
shock, showed a degree of improvement similar to the first group.
Meichenbaum indicated the difficulty in fitting these results into a standard conditioning paradigm, which would lead to the prediction that the
third group actually show *greater* snake avoidance after treatment. It
may be that the experience of shock alone provided the subjects with
training in coping with sudden elevations in anxiety and that this training generalized to snakes. The plausibility of this interpretation is
supported by an additional study by Meichenbaum (1971b) in which
subjects receiving explicit training in coping with unexpected shock
(through relaxation, slow breathing, and appropriate self-verbalizations)
showed greater reduction in fear responses to rats and snakes than subjects receiving anxiety relief or desensitization.

Recently, Rimm, Saunders, and Westel (1973) provided snake phobic
females with one hour of the aforementioned thought-stopping covert
assertion treatment. A second group of subjects received a one hour
placebo treatment which involved a discussion of snake phobias and
other fears, and a third group served as nontreated controls. In terms of
snake avoidance behavior and subjective fear ratings a significant treatment effect favoring the thought-stopping covert assertion procedure
was obtained. Improvement persisted through a two week follow-up.
Since this treatment involved nothing more aversive than presenting the
subject with a loud "stop" (certainly far less aversive than electric shock),
it is more difficult to account for these results than those of Meichenbaum (1971b) in terms of generalized coping with sudden elevations in
anxiety.

Obviously, empirical evidence specifically dealing with attempts at
blocking undesirable, obsessional thinking is somewhat limited. However, available results tend to be most encouraging. Furthermore, these
findings, in concert with those of the several RET studies presented
earlier in this chapter leave little doubt that cognitions, especially self-

verbalizations, do exert a marked degree of control over human emotions and behavior and that cognitions can be readily modified.

The Theory of Thought Stopping

The suppression of covert responses is generally assumed to proceed by the same mechanism involved in the suppression of overt forms of behavior. Therefore, much of the discussion pertaining to punishment presented in Chapter IX would seem applicable to thought stopping. One question that may be raised whenever aversive conditioning is employed concerns the status of the so-called "noxious" stimulus. Within the context of thought stopping there are at least three possibilities. The self-verbalization "stop" can indeed function as a punishment, negatively valancing, and thereby suppressing obsessional thinking. If this is true, then painful self-administered electric shock might be expected to be a more effective stimulus than the word "stop" because it is more aversive. On the other hand, if the aversive stimulus is functioning as a distractor, increasing the likelihood of the occurrence of competing, nonobsessive thought chains, rather than as a punisher, the abrupt "stop" might be just as effective as painful physical stimulation and would certainly be more convenient. A third possibility, already presented, that would definitely favor the use of self-verbalizations over physical stimuli such as shock, is that "stop" is in the nature of an assertive response. Here it is assumed that the assertion "stop" inhibits the anxiety that drives the obsession.

The mechanisms we have just discussed are not necessarily mutually exclusive. Thus, an emphatic "stop" might be distracting, while, at the same time, antagonistic to anxiety because of its assertive properties. On the other hand, it is difficult to see how a stimulus event could be effective because it conditions anxiety as a punisher, while, at the same time, reduces anxiety because it is an assertion. Experimentation systematically varying the nature, as well as intensity, of the disrupting stimuli, should help to uncover the mechanism underlying thought stopping, as well as provide information having immediate practical value in the clinic.

The theoretical basis for applying covert assertion does not differ from that presented in Chapter III, in relation to overt assertive responding. Assertive behaviors, whether overt or covert, are assumed to suppress anxiety. However, there are other interpretations. It is possible that the covert statement functions merely to compete with and block further ruminating, in which case its assertive content is irrelevant. On the other hand, it is possible that content is all important, not because it is assertive, but because it is logically inconsistent with the content of the obsession. It would be a relatively simple matter to provide an empirical test of the relative merits of these three hypotheses by varying the content, as well as the effect, of the covert verbalizations. As we have suggested, however, the researcher's more immediate task is to determine whether covert assertion does indeed provide for greater improvement than would be obtained by thought stopping alone.

The Maintenance of Obsessional Thinking

Most theoretical accounts of the maintenance of patterns of obsessive thinking (as well as compulsive behavior) assume that the obsession functions as an anxiety-reducing ritual (Metzner, 1963; Taylor, 1963; Walton & Mather, 1963, 1964). Such accounts are consistent with the widely accepted view that reinforcement is necessary for the maintenance of most behaviors and that reinforcing events are usually drive reducing (in this case, anxiety reducing). Without doubt, there are a great many instances wherein engaging in ritualistic self-verbalization does reduce subjective anxiety (prayer might be a good example). However, among any clinical population there are numerous examples in which obsessive thinking appears to have precisely the opposite effect. The examples included earlier in this section would seem to fall into this category and one can only speculate as to the "reinforcing" events that maintain obsessive patterns in such cases. It may be that the initial phase of an obsessive episode does elevate anxiety and that this is followed by a second anxiety-reducing thought (or behavior), which reduces anxiety, thereby reinforcing the entire sequence of events. For example, the thought, "I'm going to murder so and so," might give rise to intense anxiety, which in turn would be followed by "I'd never do that," and a feeling of marked relief, which would tend to strengthen the initial thought, as well as the final thought. However, in our view, this account is not very plausible for two reasons. First, if the only effect of the initial thought were to cause a sharp increase in anxiety, it seems likely that the aversiveness of this experience would rapidly result in the future suppression of such thoughts. Second, the assumed reinforcing event, anxiety reduction following the second "reassuring" thought, occurs some time after the conclusion of the initial thought (how long would depend on the duration of the reassuring thought), but delays of even 3 or 4 seconds might be expected to attenuate the ability of anxiety reduction to strengthen the initial anxiety-inducing thought.

The question is not what maintains the counterobsessive or reassuring components of the obsessional sequence (this could easily be relief from anxiety), but rather what accounts for the occurrence and maintenance of the initial anxiety-enhancing phase. There are two factors that may contribute to such responding. First, studies (Pollitt, 1960; Ingram, 1961) have indicated that classical obsessional neurotics tend to have high IQs and high socioeconomic status. Individuals in such a population would be expected to have received considerable social and economic reward for engaging in inordinate amounts of thinking, ordinarily of an objective problem-solving nature. When such an individual experiences a "bad," or uncomfortable, thought, he might be less likely than most others to attempt to "put it out of his mind," since, in his experience, virtually anything can be "thought through" to a satisfactory conclusion. Second, often anxiety-inducing obsessions have a highly aggressive content. It may be that the *immediate* effect of such obsessional thinking is anxiety *reduction* because the individual has engaged in a response that has assertive-like properties. For example, in response to being mistreated by another, one might say "I'm going to murder . . . so and so," and experience momentary satisfaction at such a prospect. However, one might then think, "My God, what if I did," and the prospect of acting on the initial thought might give rise to very intense anxiety. If this analysis is correct, it suggests that individuals suffering from anxiety-inducing obsessions might benefit from the assertive-training (that is overt assertion) procedures described in Chapter III. In fact, as was reported in Chapter III, Walton and Mather (1963) successfully treated a male obsessed with thoughts of informing others of his homosexuality, and thoughts of harming others with sharp objects, with assertive training.

The Psychology of Attribution

The empirical findings presented in the previous sections of this chapter point very strongly to the important role of cognitions, especially self-verbalizations, in influencing human behavior. We now turn to a particular class of cognitions, known as *attributions*. An attribution is an account of, or an explanation for, an observed event; that is, a perceived cause of something that happens. A high water table in the summer may be attributed to excessive snowfall the previous winter. A horse finishing first in the Kentucky Derby may be attributed to good breeding and training, as well as expert jockeying.

Impersonal attributions (such as the examples just cited) ordinarily have little effect on our behavior. On the other hand, attributions that we provide for the behavior of people may have a very profound effect on the way we feel and behave. Consider the following example: A loving husband learns that his supposedly devoted wife has recently had an affair. The degree to which he will be hurt and depressed, and whether or not he will seek to terminate the marriage, will depend in large measure on the attributions he places on her behavior. If he attributes her unfaithfulness to the fact that he has been devoting too much time to his work and thereby ignoring her, he will probably choose to stay married and spend more time with his spouse. Such an attribution might do much to decrease the pain resulting from his discovery. However, if the husband attributes her behavior to feelings of indifference for him, or deep affection for her lover, it is not unlikely that he will seek a divorce, as well as experience heightened pain.

If the attributions we place on the behavior of others are as important to us as everyday experience would suggest, what about the attributions we place on our own behavior and feelings? The remainder of this section is concerned with just this question. Our emphasis on self-attribution, as opposed to interpersonal attribution, is not based upon the assumption that self-attributions are the more important of the two (although this may be the case). It so happens that during the past decade a sizable amount of research on self-attribution has appeared, which is both theoretically interesting and which has potential relevance to clinical problems.

Experimental Findings and Clinical Applications

Most of the methods or approaches presented throughout this text originated in the clinic and, subsequently, received laboratory support. The psychology of self-attribution, as employed by behaviorists at any rate, did indeed originate in the laboratory, with social psychologists, rather than clinicians providing much of the basic experimentation. The analysis and manipulation of self-attribution in the clinic setting is not (as yet, at least) based upon some widespread and generally accepted prescription, but rather upon whatever the therapist can glean from the existing experimental literature. For this reason, we depart from our usual format and present several representative experiments, with a discussion of related clinical applications following each experiment.

One of the earliest series of experiments emphasizing the importance of self-attribution was conducted by Stanley Schachter and his associates. In one such experiment (Schachter & Singer, 1962), injections of the sympathetic nervous mimetic, epinephrine, were found to enhance emotional responding, but the nature (that is, content) of the response was dictated by external events to which the subject was exposed. However, the effect of epinephrine was considerably *weakened* for those subjects who were told in advance about the true effects of the drug. Presumably, a subject in this condition, who perceived a marked increase in arousal when confronted with an emotion-elevating situation (for example, the stooge modeling intense anger at the experiment in which both he and the subject were participating), would attribute this not to the situation, but, rather, to the drug. Such a subject might say to himself, "I'm feeling kind of worked up, but I'm not really angry . . . it's just the drug they gave me," which would have the effect of attenuating emotional responding. On the other hand, a subject not provided with information about the effects of epinephrine might have said to himself, "I really feel uptight . . . it's this damned, stupid experiment!" which would be expected to enhance emotional responding.

As a rather obvious clinical extension of the above finding, consider the plight of a person who is totally ignorant of the effects of a drug such as LSD, and unknowingly ingests the drug. During the subsequent episode he is likely to conclude that he has, for no apparent reason, "gone crazy," and even after the effects subside, he may be plagued with the agonizing fear that he might enter such a state at any time. Needless to say, providing him with a more accurate attribution ("You're really not crazy at all . . . it's this drug you took") could have only a calming, therapeutic effect.

As a less drastic, but far more common, example of the value of "reattribution therapy," some years ago Rimm treated a female outpatient who was chronically concerned with her overall psychological functioning. On this particular day she voiced special concern over her recent, heightened irritability. During the course of the therapy session the therapist learned that lately she had been drinking 8–10 bottles of diet cola per day, and the therapist immediately suggested that this provided quite enough caffeine to account for her newly acquired symptoms. The attribution "I'm uptight because of all that coke" was far more reassuring than "I'm so nervous lately . . . maybe I'm gonna have another breakdown."

The short-term debilitating effects of massive doses of alcohol on male sexual functioning are well established on anecdotal, if not experimental, grounds.[4] Consider the relatively inexperienced male who, not atypically, becomes "plastered" on his wedding night, but is conscious enough to attempt intercourse. Not surprisingly, he is impotent. If he is ignorant of the lore connecting impotency and inebriation he will seek another attribution: "My God, this woman doesn't turn me on," or, more likely, "There is something wrong with me sexually . . . I'm not a man." If unquestioned, the latter attribution could lead to chronic sexual impairment. Reattribution therapy would provide him with a self-verbalization such as "What could I expect . . . I was drunk."

[4] In fact, recent research (Rubin, 1973, personal communication) has demonstrated diminution in male sexual potency following alcohol ingestion.

Recently, a friend of Rimm reported an incident pointing to the power of reattribution even when incorrect. The friend's girl friend worried a great deal about the difficulty she often encountered in experiencing sexual arousal; she was inclined to attribute this to some deep-seated psychological problem. On a particular evening she did not respond to his sexual advances, expressing her usual concern about her "sex problem." Quite innocently he suggested that maybe she was not excited because she had a great deal to drink the night before. She responded that she did feel hung over and that maybe he was correct; whereupon she immediately experienced sexual desire (suggesting that his attribution was indeed incorrect) and enjoyed intercourse. While this experience did not result in a permanent "cure" for her problem, it is conceivable that had she been provided with situational (as opposed to personality) attributions during her initial sexual experiences, the problem might not have developed in the first place.

As a final illustration, consider a salesman suffering from undetected hypoglycemia, a fluctuating low blood sugar condition (Keele & Neil, 1961). The symptoms vary from discomfort and irritability to extreme emotionality and even a comotose state (equivalent to insulin shock). Before an important sales meeting in which he is to make a presentation, the salesman has two cups of well-sugared coffee and several cigarettes. Concentrated doses of sugar, as well as stimulants such as caffeine and nicotine, are thought to be related to attacks of hypoglycemia. The hypoglycemic attack reaches its apex as the salesman is about to make his presentation. He becomes extremely nervous and comes across badly. If he does not have a backlog of successes in such situations, he is likely to attribute his poor performance to some basic psychological failing (I can't make public speeches . . . I am afraid of audiences. . . . . I'm not cut out for sales work), which would be expected to influence adversely future performance. Naturally, treatment should include a visit to an endocrinologist, changing dietary habits, etc., but should also include a dose of reattribution: "What happened to you the other day at the sales meeting was nothing but low blood sugar . . . lay off the sweets, smokes, and coffee, and see the difference."

There is considerable anecdotal evidence that an individual's ability to withstand painful stimulation is partly a function of his attitudes or cognitions. Nisbett and Schachter (1966) and Davison and Valins (1969) provide direct experimental support for this view. In the Nisbett and Schachter experiment, among subjects who were given a placebo pill and informed that they were about to receive mild shock, individuals who were given reason to believe that the emotional arousal concomitant to shock was actually a side effect of the pill, tolerated four times the shock amperage tolerated by a group not provided with such information.

Davison and Valins obtained measures of tolerance to shock and then administered a placebo that subjects were told might affect skin sensitivity. Following this, subjects were again administered shock, but this time at a reduced level, leading them to believe they could now tolerate more shock. Half the subjects were then told the drug was a placebo, and their reaction to shock was again assessed. Subjects in this condition tolerated significantly more shock than those subjects who still believed the heightened tolerance for shock had resulted from a drug. Thus, in the Nisbett and Schachter study, a subject who was in the position to say to himself, "I feel emotional but it's just because of that harmless pill," could withstand greater pain; whereas, in the Davison and Valins study, providing subjects with the cognition "It wasn't the drug after all. . . . I really can take more pain" had a similar effect.

The practicing clinician is rarely asked to help a client increase his tolerance for physical pain. On the other hand, it is commonplace for the practitioner to attempt to help his client increase his ability to tolerate, or cope with, anxiety-inducing situations, and, for this reason, the aforementioned findings would appear to have some relevance. The implications of the Nisbett and Schachter (1966) study are similar to those of the study by Schachter and Singer (1962). Inducing a person to attribute a mildly aversive internal state to some neutral and impersonal causative agent can do much to minimize the power of that internal state to cue self-defeating thinking and behavior. For instance, informing a client that nervousness, or perhaps his high blood pressure, is caused by excessive smoking and coffee consumption, and not by his employment situation (which he is not in a position to alter), may have the effect of increasing his ability to cope with his job.

A primary impetus for the Davison and Valins (1969) study was the authors' awareness of the difficulty many mental patients have in maintaining improvement when drugs such as tranquilizers are withdrawn. In a modified application of their procedure, the therapist might gradually substitute a placebo substance for the patient's actual medication and, after he has been successfully weaned, inform him that indeed for several days or weeks he has been functioning quite well with little or no medication. Aside from obvious ethical considerations such a regimen could be used only once per patient (and probably only once on a given ward since the deception would probably be well publicized). The point of the Davison and Valins study was not that deception should be used to induce certain cognitions, but, rather, that such cognitions, however induced, might be expected to enhance a person's ability to cope with stress. A therapist's task might involve nothing more than pointing to instances in the past when the client handled a stressful situation particularly well without the aid of drugs. In addition, the therapist might persuade the patient to engage in a voluntary drug withdrawal program. During the withdrawal period, and afterward, the therapist would take special pains to point out again instances when the patient is coping especially well, emphasizing that he must now attribute this only to "the kind of person" he is, rather than to an external controlling agent such as a drug.

Storms and Nisbett (1970) provided insomniacs a placebo drug with some subjects led to believe the drug would elevate arousal, while others were led to believe it would reduce arousal. The expectation was that subjects in the arousal condition would attribute their state of emotionality to the drug rather than to emotionally toned cognitions whereas, subjects in the relaxation condition would tend to focus even more on their sleep "problem," since the drug was clearly not working. As expected, subjects in the arousal condition did get to sleep earlier, although these subjects did not show a reduction in self-reported discomfort.

The result of this procedure is interesting in that it is counter to the usual placebo effect. Storms and Nisbett (1970) suggest that the subject who suffers from chronic high levels of arousal is acutely aware of his typical level of tension and is more likely to perceive that a drug is having only a negligible effect. As in any technique involving deception, direct clinical applications are highly questionable on ethical grounds and on practical grounds as well, since exposure of the deception might destroy the therapeutic relationship. On the other hand, it is likely that a skilled therapist can provide his client with attributions for his insomnia that will be more conducive to sleep than existing ones and that have a reasonable probability of being correct (for example, interpersonal difficulties over which the client has little control). We are not suggesting that reattribution is the treatment of choice for insomnia (or, for that matter, for any other problems presented in this section). For many insomniacs, some combination of relaxation, desensitization, and thought stopping might be far more effective.

Valins (1966) conducted a study in which male subjects viewed slides of females. Although all subjects were exposed to bogus heart-rate feedback, for some the sounds were explicitly identified as the beating of the subject's heart, while others were not provided with such a set. Valins found that among those subjects who thought they were listening to their own heart beats, the slides associated with a change in heart rate tended to be rated as more attractive than those associated with no change in heart rate. Valins did conduct a follow-up (a feature all too rare in attribution research), reporting that the experimental effect was maintained over the 4–5 week period.

In a somewhat related study, Valins and Ray (1967) found that subjects who were fed bogus heart-rate feedback (identified as heart rate) indicating that they were less fearful of harmless snakes than of electric shock subsequently showed less reluctance to approach a snake than subjects who heard the same feedback, but were told it was irrelevant. However, the experimental effect was rather weak, and two attempted replications (Sushinsky & Bootzin, 1970; Kent, Wilson, & Nelson, 1972) were unsuccessful, whereas a third (Gaupp, Stern, & Galbraith, 1972) suggested an alternative anxiety-relief interpretation (that is, the shock slide was paired with electric shock, allowing the snake slide to become a cue for anxiety relief).

In the aforementioned studies, rather than manipulating the actual state of arousal, as in the Schachter and Singer (1962) study, or labels for extinguishing states of arousal, the perceived level of physiological arousal was manipulated. The subjects were free to provide whatever attributions they chose for the perceived changes in heart rate. Subjects in the Valins (1966) study could easily have concluded that the particular slides "causing emotional changes" must therefore have been the more attractive of the series. The usual objections on ethical, as well as practical, grounds would probably discourage practitioners from attempting a direct application of this procedure. However, it is useful for the clinician to be aware of the importance of how an individual labels his own emotional responding. For example, consider the case of the highly inexperienced teenage male on his first date. Some time during the course of the evening it is likely that he will experience heightened emotional arousal (perhaps some combination of sexual excitement and anxiety). If he attributes his heightened heart rate, halting respiration, and sweaty palms to the fact that he is really "turned on" to his female companion, this might serve to strengthen his view of himself as a healthy, normal male, increasing his confidence in future encounters. On the other hand, if he attributes his arousal to being "uptight," he may conclude that indeed he has some basic problem in the area of heterosexual relationships.

References

Agras, W. S. Behavior therapy in the management of chronic schizophrenia. *American Journal of Psychiatry,* 1967, **124,** 240–243.

Alexander, F., & French, T. M. *Psychoanalytic therapy.* New York: Ronald Press, 1946.

Allen, K. E., & Harris, F. R. Elimination of a child's excessive scratching by training the mother in reinforcement procedures. *Behaviour Research and Therapy,* 1966, **4,** 79–84.

Allen, K. E., Hart, B. M., Buell, J. S., Harris, F. R., & Wolf, M. M. Effects of social reinforcement on isolate behavior of a nursery school child. *Child Development,* 1964, **35,** 511–518.

Allen, K. E., Henke, L. B., Harris, F. R.. Baer, D. M., & Reynolds, N. J. Control of hyperactivity by social reinforcement of attending behavior. *Journal of Educational Psychology,* 1967, **58,** 231–237.

Anant, S. S. The use of verbal aversion (negative conditioning) with an alcoholic: A case report. *Behaviour Research and Therapy,* 1968, **6,** 695–696.

Appel, K. G., Amper, J. M., & Schefler, G. G. Prognosis in psychiatry. *American Medical Association Archives of Neurology Psychiatry,* 1961, **70,** 459–468.

Aronfreed, J. The origin of self-criticism. *Psychological Review,* 1964, **71,** 193–218.

Ashem, B. & Donner, L. Covert sensitization with alcoholics: a controlled replication. *Behaviour Research and Therapy,* 1966, **6,** 7–12.

Astin, A. W. The functional autonomy of psychotherapy. *American Psychologist,* 1961, **16,** 75–78.

Atthowe, J. M., Jr. & Krasner, L. Preliminary report on the application of contingent reinforcement procedures (token economy) on a "chronic" psychiatric ward. *Journal of Abnormal Psychology,* 1968, **73,** 37–43.

Ax, A. F. The physiological differentiation between fear and anger in humans. *Psychosomatic Medicine,* 1953, **15,** 433–442.

Ayllon, T. Intensive treatment of psychotic behavior by stimulus satiation and food reinforcement. *Behaviour Research and Therapy,* 1963, **1,** 53–62.

Ayllon, T. & Azrin, N. H. The measurement and reinforcement of behavior of psychotics. *Journal of the Experimental Analysis of Behavior,* 1965, **8,** 357–383.

Ayllon, T. & Azrin, N. H. *The token economy: A motivational system for therapy and rehabilitation.* New York: Appleton, 1968. (a)

Ayllon, T. & Azrin, N. H. Reinforcement sampling: A technique for increasing the behavior of mental patients. *Journal of Applied Behavior Analysis,* 1968, **1,** 13–20. (b)

Ayllon, T. & Haughton, E. Modification of symptomatic verbal behavior of mental patients. *Behaviour Research and Therapy,* 1964, **2,** 87–97.

Ayllon, T. & Michael, J. The psychiatric nurse as a behavioral engineer. *Journal of the Experimental Analysis of Behavior,* 1959, **2,** 323–334.

Azrin, N. H., & Holz, W. C. Punishment. In W. K. Honig (Ed.), *Operant behavior: Areas of research and application.* New York: Appleton, 1966.

Azrin, N. H., & Powell, J. Behavioral engineering: the reduction of smoking behavior by a conditioning apparatus and procedure. *Journal of Applied Behavior Analysis,* 1968, **1,** 193–200.

Bach, G. R., & Wyden, P. *The intimate enemy.* New York: Morrow, 1969.

Baer, D. M., Peterson, R. F., & Sherman, J. A. The development of imitation by reinforcing behavioral similarity to a model. *Journal of the Experimental Analysis of Behavior,* 1967, **10,** 405–416.

Baer, D. M. & Sherman, J. A. Appraisal of operant therapy techniques with children and adults. In C. M. Franks (Ed.), *Behavior therapy: Appraisal and status.* New York: McGraw-Hill, 1969.

Baer, D. M., & Wolf, M. M. The entry into natural communities of reinforcement. Paper presented at the American Psychological Association, Washington, D.C., September 1967.

Bailey, J. S., Wolf, M. M., & Phillips, E. L. Home-based reinforcement and the modification of pre-delinquents' classroom behavior. *Journal of Applied Behavior Analysis,* 1970, **3,** 223–233.

Bain, J. A. *Thought control in everyday life.* Funk and Wagnals, 1928.

Bancroft, J. H. J. Aversion therapy for homosexuality. *British Journal of Psychiatry,* 1969, **115,** 1417–1431.

Bandura, A. Social Learning Through Imitation. In M. R. Jones (Ed.), *Nebraska symposium on motivation, 1962.* Lincoln, Nebraska: Univ. of Nebraska Press, 1962.

Bandura, A. Influence of models' reinforcement contingencies on the acquisition of imitative responses. *Journal of Personality and Social Psychology,* 1965, **1,** 589–595.

Bandura, A. *Principles of behavior modification.* New York: Holt, 1969.

Bandura, A. Psychotherapy based on modeling principles. In A. E. Bergin & S. L. Garfield (Eds.), *Handbook of psychotherapy and behavior change.* New York: Wiley, 1971.

Bandura, A., Blanchard, E. B., & Ritter, R. The relative efficacy of desensitization and modeling approaches for inducing behavioral, affective, and attitudinal changes. *Journal of Personality and Social Psychology,* 1969, **13,** 173–199.

Bandura, A., Grusec, J. E., & Menlove, F. L. Some social determinants of self-monitoring reinforcement systems. *Journal of Personality and Social Psychology,* 1967, **5,** 449–455. (a)

Bandura, A., Grusec, J. E., & Menlove, F. L. Vicarious extinction of avoidance behavior. *Journal of Personality and Social Psychology,* 1967, **5,** 16–23. (b)

Bandura, A. & Kupers, C. J. Transmission of patterns of self-reinforcement through modeling. *Journal of Abnormal and Social Psychology,* 1964, **69,** 1–9.

Bandura, A. & Menlove, F. L. Factors determining vicarious extinction of avoidance behavior through symbolic modeling. *Journal of Personality and Social Psychology,* 1968, **8,** 99–108.

Bandura, A., & Perloff, B. Relative efficacy of self-monitored and externally imposed reinforcement systems. *Journal of Personality and Social Psychology,* 1967, **7,** 111–116.

Bandura, A. & Walters, R. H. *Adolescent aggression.* New York: Ronald, 1959.

Bandura, A., & Whalen, C. K. The influence of antecedent reinforcement and divergent modeling cues on patterns of self-reward. *Journal of Personality and Social Psychology,* 1966, **3,** 373–382.

Barker, J. C. Behavior therapy for transvestism: A comparison of pharmicological and electrical aversion techniques. *British Medical Journal,* 1965, **111,** 268–276.

Barker, J. C., Thorpe, J. G., Blakemore, C. B., Lavin, N. I., & Conway, C. G. Behaviour therapy in a case of transvestism. *Lancet,* 1961, **1,** 510.

Barker, R. G. & Wright, H. F. *Midwest and its children: The psychological ecology of an American town.* New York: Harper, 1955.

Barlow, D. H., Agras, W. S., Leitenberg, H., & Wincze, J. P., An experimental analysis of the effectiveness of 'shaping' in reducing maladaptive avoidance behavior: An analogue study. *Behaviour Research and Therapy,* 1970, **8,** 165–173.

Barlow, D. H., Leitenberg, H., & Agras, W. S. Experimental control of sexual deviation through manipulation of the noxious scene in covert sensitization. *Journal of Abnormal Psychology,* 1969, **74,** 596–601.

Baron, A. & Kaufman, A. Human, free-operant avoidance of "time-out" from monetary reinforcement. *Journal of the Experimental Analysis of Behavior,* 1966, **9,** 557–565.

Barrett, C. L. Systematic desensitization therapy (SDT) versus implosive therapy (IT): A comparative study of two methods of reducing the snake phobic behavior of otherwise normal adults. Unpublished doctoral dissertation, University of Louisville, 1967.

Barrett, C. L. Systematic desensitization versus implosive therapy. *Journal of Abnormal Psychology,* 1969, **74,** 587–592.

Barron, F. & Leary, T. Changes in psychoneurotic patients with and without psychotherapy. *Journal of Consulting Psychology,* 1955, **19,** 239–245.

Baum, M. Rapid extinction of an avoidance response following a period of response prevention in the avoidance apparatus. *Psychological Reports,* 1966, **18,** 59–64.

Baum, M. Efficacy of response prevention (flooding) in facilitating the extinction of an avoidance response in rats: the effect of overtraining the response. *Behaviour Research and Therapy,* 1968, **6,** 197–203.

Baum, M. Extinction of an avoidance response following response prevention: Some parametric investigations. *Canadian Journal of Psychology,* 1969, **23,** 1–10. (a)

Baum, M. Extinction of an avoidance response motivated by intense fear: Social facilitation of the action of response prevention (flooding) in rats. *Behaviour Research and Therapy,* 1969, **7,** 57–62. (b)

Baum, M. Dissociation of respondent and operant processes in avoidance learning. *Journal of Comparative and Physiological Psychology,* 1969, **67,** 83–88. (c)

Baum, M. Extinction of avoidance responding through response prevention (flooding). *Psychological Bulletin,* 1970, **74,** 276–284.

Baum, M. & Poser, E. G. Comparison of flooding procedures in animals and man. *Behaviour Research and Therapy,* 1971, **9,** 249–254.

Beck, A. T. Cognitive therapy: Nature and relation to behavior therapy. *Behavior Therapy,* 1970, **1,** 184–200.

Becker, W. C. *Parents are teachers.* Champaign, Illinois: Research Press, 1971.

Beneke, W. N., & Harris, M. B. Teaching self-control of study behavior. *Behaviour Research and Therapy,* 1972, **10,** 35–41.

Bensberg, G. J. (Ed.) *Teaching the mentally retarded: A Handbook for ward personnel.* Atlanta: Southern Regional Education Board, 1965.

Bensberg, G. J., Colwell, C. N., & Cassel, R. H. Teaching the profoundly retarded self-help activities by behavior shaping techniques. *American Journal of Mental Deficiency,* 1965, **69,** 674–679.

Bergin, A. E. The effect of dissonant persuasive communications upon changes in a self-referring attitude. *Journal of Personality,* 1962, **30,** 423–438.

Bergin, A. E. Some implications of psychotherapy research for therapeutic practice. *Journal of Abnormal Psychology,* 1966, **71,** 235–246.

Bergin, A. E. A self-regulation technique for impulse control disorders. *Psychotherapy: Theory, Research and Practice,* 1969, **6,** 113–118.

Bernal, M. E., Duryee, J. S., Pruett, H. L., & Burns, B. J. Behavior modification and the brat syndrome. *Journal of Consulting and Clinical Psychology,* 1968 **32,** 447–455.

Bernstein, D. A. The modification of smoking behavior. Unpublished doctoral dissertation, Northwestern University, 1968.

Bernstein, D. A. Modification of smoking behavior: An evaluative review. *Psychological Bulletin,* 1969, **71,** 418–440.

Birk, L., Huddleston, W., Millers, E., & Cohler, B. Avoidance conditioning for homosexuality. *Archives of General Psychiatry,* 1971, **25,** 314–323.

Birnbrauer, J. S., Bijou, S. W., Wolf, M. M., & Kidder, J. D. Programmed instruction in the classroom. In L. P. Ullman & L. Krasner (Eds.), *Case studies in behavior modification.* New York: Holt, 1965.

Birnbrauer, J. S., Wolf, M. M., Kidder, J., & Tague, C. E. Classroom behavior of retarded pupils with token reinforcement. *Journal of Experimental Child Psychology,* 1965, **2,** 219–235.

Blake, B. G. The application of behaviour therapy to the treatment of alcoholism. *Behaviour Research and Therapy,* 1965, **3,** 75–85.

Blakemore, C. B., Thorpe, J. G., Barker, J. C., Conway, C. G., & Lavin, N. I. The application of faradic aversion conditioning in a case of transvestism. *Behaviour Research and Therapy,* 1963, **1,** 29–34.

Blanchard, E. B. The relative contributions of modeling, informational influences, and physical contact in the extinction of phobic behavior. Unpublished doctoral dissertation, Stanford University, 1969.

Blanchard, E. B. The relative contributions of modeling, information influences, and physical contact in the extinction of phobic behavior. *Journal of Abnormal Psychology,* 1970, **76,** 55–61.

Bond, I. K. & Hutchison, H. C. Application of reciprocal inhibition therapy to exhibitionism. *Canadian Medical Association Journal,* 1960, **83,** 23–25.

Borkovec, T. D. The comparative effectiveness of systematic desensitization and implosive therapy and the effect of expectancy manipulation on the elimination of fear. Unpublished doctoral dissertation, University of Illinois, 1970.

Borkovec, T. D. Effects of expectancy on the outcome of systematic desensitization and implosive treatments for analogue anxiety. *Behavior Therapy,* 1972, **3,** 29–40.

Bostow, Darrel, E., & Bailey, J. B. Modification of severe disruptive and aggressive behavior using brief timeout and reinforcement procedures. *Journal of Applied Behavior Analysis,* 1969, **2,** 31–37.

Boulougouris, J. & Marks, I. M. Implosion (flooding): A new treatment for phobias. *British Medical Journal,* 1969, **2,** 721–723.

Boulougouris, J., Marks, I. M., & Marset, P. Superiority of flooding (implosion) to desensitization for reducing pathological fear. *Behaviour Research and Therapy,* 1971, **9,** 7–16.

Bower, G. Mental imagery and memory. Colloquium, Arizona State University, May, 1967.

Bower, G. H., Clark, M. C., Lesgold, A. M., & Winenz, D. Hierarchical retrieval schemes in recall of categorized word lists. *Journal of Verbal Learning and Verbal Behavior,* 1969, **8,** 323–343.

Bowlby, J. *Attachment and loss:* Vol. I. *Attachment.* New York: Basic Books, 1969.

Brady, J. P. Brevital-relaxation treatment of frigidity. *Behaviour Research and Therapy,* 1966, **4,** 71–77.

Brady, J. P. Comments on methohexitone-aided systematic desensitization. *Behaviour Research and Therapy,* 1967, **5,** 259–260.

Brady, J. & Lind, D. L. Experimental analysis of hysterical blindness. *Archives of General Psychiatry,* 1961, **4,** 321–339.

Brawley, E. R., Harris, F. R., Allen, K. E., Fleming, R. S., & Peterson, R. F. Behavior modification of an autistic child. *Behavioral Science,* 1969, **14,** 87–97.

Breger, L., & McGaugh, J. L. Critique and reformulation of "learning theory" approaches to psychotherapy and neurosis. *Psychological Bulletin,* 1965, **63,** 338–358.

Brierley, H. Electrical aversion therapy. *British Medical Journal,* 1964, **1,** 631.

Brock, L. D. The efficacy of various extinction procedures on a conditioned avoidance response in humans: an experimental analogue. Unpublished doctoral dissertation, Southern Illinois University, 1967.

Bucher, B. & Fabricatore, J. Use of patient-administered shock to suppress hallucinations. *Behavior Therapy,* 1970, **1,** 382–385.

Bucher, B. & Hawkins, J. Comparison of response cost and token reinforcement systems in a class for academic underachievers. Paper presented at the Association for the Advancement of Behavior Therapy, Washington, D.C., September 1971.

Bucher, B. & Lovaas, O. I. Use of aversive stimulation in behavior modification. In M. R. Jones (Ed.), *Miami symposium on the prediction of behavior 1967: Aversive stimulation.* Coral Gables, Florida: Univ. of Miami Press, 1968.

Burchard, J. D. Systematic socialization: A programmed environment for the habilitation of antisocial retardates. *Psychological Record,* 1967, **17,** 461–476.

Burchard, J., & Tyler, V. Jr. The modification of delinquent behaviour through operant conditioning. *Behaviour Research and Therapy,* 1965, **2,** 245–250.

Bushell, D. Jr., Wrobel, P. A., & Michaelis, M. L. Applying "group" contingencies to the classroom study behavior of preschool children. *Journal of Applied Behavior Analysis,* 1968, **1,** 55–61.

Cahoon, D. D. Symptom substitution and the behavior therapies: Reappraisal. *Psychological Bulletin,* 1968, **69,** 149–156.

Calef, R. A., & MacLean, G. D. A comparison of reciprocal inhibition and reactive inhibition therapies in the treatment of speech anxiety. *Behavior Therapy,* 1970, **1,** 51–58.

Campbell, D., Sanderson, R. E., & Laverty, S. G. Characteristics of a conditioned response in human subjects during extinction trials following a single traumatic conditioning trial. *Journal of Abnormal and Social Psychology,* 1964, **68,** 627–639.

Carek, R. G. A comparison of two behavioral therapy techniques in the treatment of rat "phobias." Unpublished doctoral dissertation, University of Iowa, 1969.

Carlson, C. S., Arnold, C. R., Becker, W. C., & Madsen, C. H. The elimination of tantrum behavior of a child in an elementary classroom. *Behaviour Research and Therapy,* 1968, **6,** 117–119.

Case, H. M. Stuttering and speech blocking: A comparative study of maladjustment. Unpublished doctoral dissertation, University of California, Los Angeles, 1940.

Cautela, J. R. A behavior therapy approach to pervasive anxiety. *Behaviour Research and Therapy,* 1966, **4,** 99–109. (a)

Cautela, J. R. Treatment of compulsive behavior by covert sensitization. *Psychological Record,* 1966, **16,** 33–41. (b)

Cautela, J. R. Covert sensitization. *Psychological Reports,* 1967, **74,** 459–468.

Cautela, J. R. Behavior therapy and self-control: Techniques and implications. In C. M. Franks (Ed.), *Behavior therapy: Appraisal and status.* New York: McGraw-Hill, 1969.

Cautela, J. R. The use of covert sensitization in the treatment of alcoholism. *Psychotherapy: Theory, Research and Practice,* 1970, **7,** 86–90.

Cautela, J. R. Covert extinction. *Behavior Therapy,* 1971, **2,** 192–200.

Cautela, J. R. Covert sensitization for the treatment of sexual deviations. *Psychological Record,* 1971, **21,** 37–48.

Cautela, J. R. & Baron, M. G. The behavior therapy treatment of self-destructive behavior. Unpublished study, Boston College, 1969.

Cautela, J. R., Steffen, J., & Wish, P. An experimental test of covert reinforcement. Paper delivered at the 78th annual convention of the American Psychological Association. Miami, Florida, August 1970.

Cautela, J. R., Walsh, K., & Wish, P. The use of covert reinforcement to modify attitudes toward retardates. *Journal of Psychology,* 1971, **77,** 257–260.

Cautela, J. R. & Wisocki, P. A. The use of male and female therapists in the treatment of homosexual behavior. In I. R. Rubin & C. Franks, (Eds.), *Advances in behavior therapy.* New York: Academic Press, 1969.

Chadwick, B. A., & Day, R. C. Systematic reinforcement: Academic performance of underachieving students. *Journal of Applied Behavior Analysis,* 1971, **4,** 311–319.

Chapel, J. L. Behaviour modification techniques with children and adolescents. *Canadian Psychiatric Association Journal,* 1970, **15,** 315–318.

Chapman, R. F., Smith, J. W., & Layden, T. A. Elimination of cigarette smoking by punishment and self-management training. *Behaviour Research and Therapy,* 1971, **9,** 255–264.

Chittenden, G. E. An experimental study in measuring and modifying assertive behavior in young children. *Monographs of the Society for Research in Child Development,* 1942, **7,** (Whole No. 31).

Clark, D. F. A note on avoidance conditioning techniques in sexual disorder. *Behaviour Research and Therapy,* 1965, **3,** 203–206.

Clark, D. F. Behavior therapy of Gilles de la Tourette's syndrome. *British Journal of Psychiatry,* 1967, **113,** 375–381.

Cook, S. W. The psychologist of the future: Scientist, professional or both. In J. R. Braun (Ed.) *Clinical psychology in transition* (rev. ed.). Cleveland: The World Pub. Co., 1966.

Cooper, A. J. A case of fetishism and impotence treated by behaviour therapy. *British Journal of Psychiatry,* 1964, **109,** 649–652.

Cooper, J. E., Gelder, M. G., & Marks, I. M. Results of behaviour therapy in seventy-seven psychiatric patients. *British Medical Journal,* 1965, **1,** 1222–1225.

Cooper, K. H. *Aroebics.* New York: Bantam Books, 1968.

Cotler, S. B. Sex differences and generalization of anxiety reduction with automated desensitization and minimal therapist interaction. *Behaviour Research and Therapy,* 1970, **8,** 273–285.

Davies, D. L. Normal drinking in recovered alcohol addicts. *Quarterly Journal of Studies on Alcohol,* 1962, **23,** 94–104.

Davison, G. C. Elimination of a sadistic fantasy by a client-controlled counter-conditioning technique: A case study. *Journal of Abnormal and Social Psychology,* 1968, **73,** 84–90. (a)

Davison, G. C. Systematic desensitization as a counterconditioning process. *Journal of Abnormal Psychology,* 1968, **73,** 91–99. (b)

Davison, G. C. & Valins, S. Maintenance of self-attributed and drug-attributed behavior change. *Journal of Personality and Social Psychology,* 1969, **11,** 25–33.

Davison, G. C., & Wilson, G. T. Critique of "Desensitization: Social and cognitive factors underlying the effectiveness of Wolpe's procedure." *Psychological Bulletin,* 1972, **78,** 28–31.

Dee, C. K. Instructions and the extinction of a learned fear in the context of taped implosive therapy. Unpublished doctoral dissertation, University of Iowa, 1970.

Deese, J. & Hulse, S. H. *The psychology of learning.* New York: McGraw-Hill, 1967.

De Moor, W. Systematic desensitization versus prolonged high intensity stimulation (flooding). *Journal of Behaviour Therapy and Experimental Psychiatry,* 1970, **1,** 45–52.

Dollard, J., & Miller, N. E. *Personality and psychotherapy.* New York: McGraw-Hill, 1950.

Donner, L., & Guerney, B. G. Automated group desensitization for test anxiety. *Behaviour Research and Therapy,* 1969, **7,** 1–13.

Dunlap, K. *Habits, their making and unmaking.* New York: Liveright, 1932.

Edwards, N. B. Case conference: Assertive training in a case of homosexual pedophilia. *Journal of Behavior Therapy and Experimental Psychiatry,* 1972, **3,** 55–63.

Einstein, A. *The meaning of relativity.* Princeton, New Jersey: Princeton Univ. Press, 1953.

Elliott, R. & Tighe, T. Breaking the cigarette habit: Effects of a technique involving threatened loss of money. *Psychological Record,* 1968, **18,** 503–513.

Ellis, A. Outcome of employing three techniques of psychotherapy. *Journal of Clinical Psychology,* 1957, **13,** 344–350.

Ellis, A. *Reason and emotion in psychotherapy.* New York: Lyle Stuart, 1962.

Ellis, A. *Growth through reason.* Palo Alto, California: Science & Behavior Books, 1971. (a)

Ellis, A. A twenty-three-year-old girl guilty about not following her parents' rules. In A. Ellis, ed., *Growth through reason,* Palo Alto, California: Science & Behavior Books, 1971. Pp. 223–286. (b)

Ellis, A. A young male who is afraid of becoming a fixed homosexual. In A. Ellis, ed., *Growth through reason.* Palo Alto, California: Science & Behavior Books, 1971. Pp. 102–122. (c)

Ellis, A., & Harper, R. A. *Guide to rational living.* New York: Lyle Stuart, 1968.

Emery, J. R. & Krumboltz, J. D. Standard versus individualized hierarchies in desensitization to reduce test anxiety. *Journal of Counseling Psychology,* 1967, **14,** 204–209.

Erikson, E. H. *Childhood and Society.* New York: Norton, 1950.

Estes, W. K. An experimental study of punishment. *Psychological Monographs,* 1944, **57** (Whole No. 263).

Evans, D. R. Masturbatory fantasy and sexual deviation. *Behaviour Research and Therapy,* 1968, **6,** 17–19.

Evans, G. W., & Oswalt, G. L. Acceleration of academic progress through the manipulation of peer influence. *Behaviour Research and Therapy,* 1968, **6,** 189–195.

Eysenck, H. J. The effects of psychotherapy: An evaluation. *Journal of Consulting Psychology,* 1952, **16,** 319–324.

Eysenck, H. J. Learning theory and behaviour therapy. *Journal of Mental Science,* 1959, **105,** 61–75.

Eysenck, H. J. (Ed.) *Behaviour therapy and the neuroses.* Oxford: Pergamon Press, 1960.

Eysenck, H. J. *Experiments in behavior therapy.* Oxford: Pergamon Press, 1964.

Eysenck, H. J. A theory of the incubation of anxiety/fear responses. *Behaviour Research and Therapy,* 1968, **6,** 309–322.

Fairweather, G. W. *Social psychology in treating mental illness: An experimental approach.* New York: Wiley, 1964.

Fairweather, G. W., Sanders, D. H., Maynard, H., & Cressler, D. L. *Community life for the mentally ill: An alternative to institutional care.* Chicago: Aldine, 1969.

Fairweather, G. W. & Simon, R. A further follow-up comparison of psychotherapeutic programs. *Journal of Consulting Psychology,* 1963, **27,** 186.

Fairweather, G. W., Simon, R., Gebhard, M. E., Weingarten, E., Holland, J. I., Sanders, R., Stone, G. B., & Reahl, J. E. Relative effectiveness of psychotherapeutic programs: A multicriteria comparison of four programs for three different patient groups. *Psychological Monographs,* 1960, **74** (Whole No. 492).

Farber, I. E. The things people say to themselves. *American Psychologist,* 1963, **18,** 185–197.

Farina, A., Gliha, D., Boudreau, L. A., Allen, J. G., & Sherman, M. Mental illness and the impact of believing others know about it. *Journal of Abnormal Psychology,* 1971, **77,** 1–5.

Farina, A., & Ring, K. The influence of perceived mental illness on interpersonal relations. *Journal of Abnormal Psychology,* 1965, **70,** 47–51.

Fazio, A. F. Treatment components in implosive therapy. *Journal of Abnormal Psychology,* 1970, **76,** 211–219.

Feldman, M. P. & MacCulloch, M. J. The application of anticipatory avoidance learning to the treatment of homosexuality: I. Theory, technique and preliminary results. *Behaviour Research and Therapy,* 1965, **2,** 165–183.

Feldman, M. P. & MacCulloch, M. J. *Homosexual behaviour: Therapy and assessment.* Oxford: Pergamon Press, 1971.

Feldman, R. B. & Werry, J. S. An unsuccessful attempt to treat a tiqueur by massed practice. *Behaviour Research and Therapy,* 1966, **4,** 111–117.

Fenichel, O. *The psychoanalytic theory of neurosis.* New York: Norton, 1945.

Ferster, C. B. & Skinner, B. F. *Schedules of reinforcement.* New York: Appleton, 1957.

Ferster, C. B., Nurnberger, J. I., & Levitt, E. B. The control of eating. *Journal of Mathematics,* 1962, **1,** 87–109.

Festinger, L. *A theory of cognitive dissonance.* Stanford, California: Stanford Univ. Press, 1957.

Festinger, L. The psychological effects of insufficient rewards. *American Psychologist,* 1961, **16,** 1–11.

Festinger, L. Behavioral support for opinion change. *Public Opinion Quarterly,* 1964, **28,** 404–417.

Festinger, L. & Carlsmith, J. M. Cognitive consequences of forced compliance. *Journal of Abnormal and Social Psychology,* 1959, **58,** 203–210.

Fishman, H. C. A study of the efficiency of negative practice as a corrective for stammering. *Journal of Speech Disorders,* 1937, **2,** 67–72.

Flannery, R. An investigation of differential effectiveness of office vs. *in vivo* therapy of a simple phobia: An outcome study. Unpublished doctoral dissertation, University of Windsor, 1970.

Foreyt, J. P., & Kennedy, W. A. Treatment of overweight by aversion therapy. *Behaviour Research and Therapy,* 1971, **9,** 29–34.

Fox, L. Effecting the use of efficient study habits. *Journal of Mathematics,* 1962, **1,** 75–86.

Franks, C. M. Behavior therapy, the principles of conditioning and the treatment of the alcoholic. *Quarterly Journal of Studies of Alcohol,* 1963, **24,** 511–529.

Franks, C. M. Conditioning and conditioned aversion therapies in the treatment of the alcoholic. *International Journal of Addictions,* 1966, **1,** 61–98.

Franks, C. M. (Ed.) *Behavior therapy: Appraisal and status.* New York: McGraw-Hill, 1969. (a)

Franks, C. M. (Ed.) Introduction: Behavior therapy and its Pavlovian origins: Review and perspectives. In *Behavior therapy: Appraisal and status.* New York: McGraw-Hill, 1969. (b)

Franks, C. M., Fried, R., & Ashem, B. An improved apparatus for the aversive conditioning of cigarette smokers. *Behaviour Research and Therapy,* 1966, **4,** 301–308.

Franzini, L. R., & Tilker, H. A. On the terminological confusion between behavior therapy and behavior modification. *Behavior Therapy,* 1972, **3,** 279–282.

Freud, S. Two encyclopedic articles: Psycho-analysis. *Standard Edition,* 1922, 1923, **18,** 235–254.

Freud, S. *The problem of anxiety.* New York: Norton, 1936.

Freund, K. Some problems in the treatment of homosexuality. In H. J. Eysenck (Ed.), *Behaviour therapy and the neuroses.* Oxford: Pergamon, 1960.

Freund, K. A laboratory method for diagnosing predominance of homo-hetero-erotic interest in the male. *Behaviour Research and Therapy,* 1963, **1,** 85–93.

Friedman, P. H. The effects of modeling and role playing on assertive behavior. Unpublished doctoral dissertation, University of Wisconsin, 1968.

Fromer, R. & Berkowitz, L. Effect of sudden and gradual shock onset on the conditioned fear response. *Journal of Comparative and Physiological Psychology,* 1964, **57,** 154–155.

Funkenstein, D. H. Nor-epinephrine-like and epinephrine-like substances in relation to human behavior. *Journal of Nervous and Mental Disease,* 1956, **124,** 58–67.

Galbraith, D. A., Byrick, R. J., & Rutledge, J. T. An aversive conditioning approach to the inhibition of chronic vomiting. *Canadian Psychiatric Association Journal,* 1970, **15,** 311–313.

Gallagher, J. J. MMPI changes concomitant with client-centered therapy. *Journal of Consulting Psychology,* 1953, **17,** 443–446.

Garcia, E., Baer, D. M., & Firestone, I. The development of generalized imitation within topographically determined boundaries. *Journal of Applied Behavior Analysis,* 1971, **4,** 101–112.

Gardner, J. E. Behavior therapy treatment approach to a psychogenic seizure case. *Journal of Consulting Psychology,* 1967, **31,** 209–212.

Garfield, Z. H., Darwin, P. L., Singer, B. A., & McBreaty, J. F. Effect of "in vivo" training on experimental desensitization of a phobia. *Psychological Reports,* 1967, **20,** 515–519.

Gaupp, L. A., Stern, R. M., & Galbraith, G. G. False heart-rate feedback and reciprocal inhibition by aversion relief in the treatment of snake avoidance behavior. *Behavior Therapy,* 1972, **3,** 7–20.

Geer, J. H., & Katkin, E. S. Treatment of insomnia using a variant of systematic desensitization: A case report. *Journal of Abnormal Psychology,* 1966, **71,** 161–164.

Geis, H. J. Rational emotive therapy with a culturally deprived teenager. In A. Ellis, ed., *Growth through reason,* Palo Alto, California: Science & Behavior Books, 1971. Pp. 46–107.

Gelfand, D. M., Gelfand, S., & Dobson, W. R. Unprogrammed reinforcement of patients' behavior in a mental hospital. *Behaviour Research and Therapy,* 1967, **5,** 201–207.

Gershman, L. Case conference: A transvestite fantasy treated by thought-stopping, covert sensitization, and aversive shock. *Journal of Behavior Therapy and Experimental Psychiatry,* 1970, **1,** 153–161.

Gewirtz, J. L. & Baer, D. M. The effect of brief social deprivation on behaviors for a social reinforcer. *Journal of Abnormal and Social Psychology,* 1958, **56,** 549–556. (a)

Gewirtz, J. L. & Baer, D. M. Deprivation and satiation of social reinforcers as drive conditions. *Journal of Abnormal and Social Psychology,* 1958, **57,** 165–172. (b)

Giles, D. K. & Wolf, M. M. Toilet training in institutionalized, severe retardates: an application of operant behavior modification techniques. *American Journal of Mental Deficiency,* 1966, **70,** 766–780.

Gill, M. M. (Ed.) *The collected papers of David Rapaport.* New York: Basic Books, 1967.

Girargeau, F. L. & Spradlin, J. E. Token rewards in a cottage program. *Mental Retardation,* 1964, **2,** 345–351.

Gittelman, M. Behavior rehearsal as a technique in child treatment. *Journal of Child Psychology and Psychiatry,* 1965, **6,** 251–255.

Glaser, R. & Kraus, D. J. A reinforcement analysis of group performance. *Psychological Monographs,* 1966, **80** (Whole No. 13).

Glynn, E. L. Classroom applications of self-determined reinforcement. *Journal of Applied Behavior Analysis.* 1970, **3,** 123–132.

Glynn, J. D. & Harper, P. Behaviour therapy in transvestism. *Lancet,* 1961, **1,** 619.

Gold, S. & Neufeld, I. L. A learning approach to the treatment of homosexuality. *Behaviour Research and Therapy,* 1965, **3,** 201–204.

Goldiamond, I. Self-control procedures in personal behavior problems. *Psychological Reports,* 1965, **17,** 851–868.

Goodwin, D. L. Training teachers in reinforcement techniques to increase pupil task-oriented behavior: An experimental evaluation. Stanford, California: Stanford University, 1966. (Mimeograph)

Greenspoon, J. The reinforcing effect of two spoken sounds on the frequency of two responses. *American Journal of Psychology,* 1955, **68,** 409–416.

Greenspoon, J. Verbal conditioning in clinical psychology. In A. J. Bachrach (Ed.), *Experimental foundations of clinical psychology.* New York: Basic Books, 1962.

Grinker, R. R., & Spiegel, J. P. *War neurosis.* New York: Blakiston, 1945.

Grossberg, J. M. Successful behavior therapy in a case of speech phobia ("stage fright"). *Journal of Speech and Hearing Disorders,* 1965, **30,** 285–288.

Grossberg, J. M., & Wilson, H. K. Physiological changes accompanying the visualization of fearful and neutral situations. *Journal of Personality and Social Psychology,* 1968, **10,** 124–133.

Grusec, J. Some antecedents of self-criticism. *Journal of Personality and Social Psychology,* 1966, **4,** 244–252.

Gullo, J. M. A husband and wife who have not had intercourse during thirteen years of marriage. In A. Ellis (Ed.), *Growth through reason.* Palo Alto, California: Science & Behavior Books, 1971. Pp. 147–178.

Guthrie, E. R. *The psychology of learning.* New York: Harper, 1952.

Hain, J. D., Butcher, H. G., & Stevenson, I. Systematic desensitization therapy: An analysis of results in twenty-seven patients. *British Journal of Psychiatry,* 1966, **112,** 295–307.

Hall, R. V., Lund, D., & Jackson, D. Effects of teacher attention on study behavior. *Journal of Applied Behavior Analysis,* 1968, **1,** 1–12.

Hall, S. M. Self-control and therapist control in the behavioral treatment of overweight women. *Behaviour Research and Therapy,* 1972, **10,** 59–68.

Hamilton, J., Stephens, L., & Allen, P. Controlling aggressive and destructive behavior in severely retarded institutionalized residents. *American Journal of Mental Deficiency,* 1967, **71,** 852–856.

Harmatz, M. G. & Lapuc, P. Behavior modification of overeating in a psychiatric population. *Journal of Consulting and Clinical Psychology,* 1968, **32,** 583–587.

Harris, M. B. Self-directed program for weight control: A pilot study. *Journal of Abnormal Psychology,* 1969, **74,** 263–270.

Harris, M. B., & Bruner, C. G. A comparison of a self-control and a contract procedure for weight control, *Behaviour Research and Therapy,* 1971, **9,** 347–354.

Hart, B. M., Reynolds, N. J., Baer, D. M., Brawley, E. R., & Harris, F. R. Effect of contingent and non-contingent social reinforcement on the cooperative play of a preschool child. *Journal of Applied Behavior Analysis,* 1968, **1,** 73–76.

Heap, R. F., Bobblitt, W. E., Moore, C. H., & Hord, J. E. Behavior-milieu therapy with chronic neuropsychiatric patients. *Journal of Abnormal Psychology,* 1970, **76,** 349–354.

Hedquist, F. J., & Weingold, B. K. Behavioral group counseling with socially anxious and unassertive college students. *Journal of Counseling Psychology,* 1970, **17,** 237–242.

Heine, R. W. A comparison of patients' reports on psychotherapeutic experience with psychoanalytic, nondirective and Adlerian therapists. *American Journal of Psychotherapy,* 1953, **7,** 16–23.

Herzberg, A. Short treatment of neuroses by graduated tasks. *British Journal of Medical Psychology,* 1941, **19,** 36–51.

Hilgard, E. R. & Bower, G. H. *Theories of learning.* New York: Appleton, 1966.

Hodgson, R. J. & Rachman, S. An experimental investigation of the implosion technique. *Behaviour Research and Therapy,* 1970, **8,** 21–27.

Hogan, R. A. The implosive technique: A process of reeducation through the application of principles of learning for emotionally disturbed individuals. Unpublished doctoral dissertation, Case Western Reserve University, 1963.

Hogan, R. A. Implosive therapy in the short term treatment of psychotics. *Psychotherapy: Theory, Research, and Practice,* 1966, **3,** 25–32.

Hogan, R. A. The implosive technique. *Behaviour Research and Therapy,* 1968, **6,** 423–432.

Hogan, R. A. Implosively oriented behavior modification: Therapy considerations. *Behaviour Research and Therapy,* 1969, **7,** 177–184.

Hogan, R. A. & Kirchner, J. H. A preliminary report of the extinction of learned fears via short term implosive therapy. *Journal of Abnormal Psychology,* 1967, **72,** 106–111.

Holsopple, J. Q. & Vanouse, I. A note on the beta hypothesis of learning. *School Sociology,* 1929, **29,** 15–16.

Homme, L. E. Perspectives in psychology: XXIV. Control of coverants, the operants of the mind. *Psychological Record,* 1965, **15,** 501–511.

Homme, L. *How to use contingency contracting in the classroom.* Champaign, Illinois: Research Press, 1971.

Homme, L. E., deBaca, P. C., Devine, J. V., Steinhorst, R., & Rickert, E. J. Use of the Premack principle in controlling the behavior of nursery school children. *Journal of the Experimental Analysis of Behavior,* 1963, **6,** 544.

Hosford, R. E. Overcoming fear of speaking in a group. In Krumboltz, J. D. & Thoresen, C. E. (Eds.), *Behavioral Counseling.* New York: Holt, 1969.

Hull, C. L. *Principles of behavior.* New York: Appleton, 1943.

Hull, C. L. *A behavior system.* New Haven, Connecticut: Yale Univ. Press, 1952.

Humphrey, J. Personal Communication, 1966.

Hundziak, M., Mowrer, R. A., & Watson, L. S., Jr. Operant conditioning in toilet training of severely mentally retarded boys. *American Journal of Mental Deficiency,* 1965, **70,** 120–124.

Hunziker, J. C. The use of participant modeling in the treatment of water phobias. Unpublished master's thesis, Arizona State University, 1972.

Ingram, E. M., Discriminative and reinforcing functions in the experimental development of social behavior in a preschool child. Unpublished master's thesis, University of Kansas, 1967.

Ingram, I. M. Obsessional illness in mental hospital patients. *Journal of Mental Science,* 1961, **107,** 382–402.

Irey, P. A. Covert sensitization of cigarette smokers with high and low extraversion scores. Unpublished master's thesis, Southern Illinois University, 1972.

Jacobson, E. *Progressive relaxation.* Chicago: Univ. of Chicago Press, 1938.

Jacobson, H. A. Reciprocal inhibition and implosive therapy: A comparative study of a fear of snakes. Unpublished doctoral dissertation, Memphis State University, 1970.

Jakubowski-Spector, P. Assertive training for women. Colloquium presented at Southern Illinois University, Carbondale, Illinois, April 1973. (a)

Jakubowski-Spector, P. Facilitating the growth of women through assertive training. *The Counseling Psychologist,* 1973, **4,** 75–86. (b)

Janda, H. L., & Rimm, D. C. Covert sensitization in the treatment of obesity. *Journal of Abnormal Psychology,* 1972, **80,** 37–42.

Janis, I. L., & Miller, J. C. Factors influencing tolerance for deprivation. In National Clearinghouse for Smoking and Health, *Directory of ongoing research in smoking and health.* Arlington, Virginia: United States Public Health Service, 1968.

Johnson, S. M. The effects of desensitization and relaxation in the treatment of test anxiety. Unpublished master's thesis, Northwestern University, 1966.

Johnston, M. S., Kelley, C. S., Buell, J. S., Harris, F. F., & Wolf, M. M. Effects of positive social reinforcement on isolate behavior of a nursery school child. Unpublished manuscript, University of Washington, 1963.

Johnston, M. S., Kelley, C. S., Harris, F. R., & Wolf, M. M. An application of reinforcement principles to development of motor skills of a young child. *Child Development,* 1966, **37,** 379–387.

Jones, H. G. The application of conditioning and learning techniques to the treatment of a psychiatric patient. *Journal of Abnormal and Social Psychology,* 1956, **52,** 414–419.

Jones, H. G. Continuation of Yates' treatment of a tiquer. In H. J. Eysenck (Ed.), *Behaviour therapy and the neuroses.* Oxford: Pergamon, 1960.

Jones, M. C. The elimination of children's fears. *Journal of Experimental Psychology,* 1924, **7,** 382–390.

Jones, R. G. A factored measure of Ellis' irrational belief system, with personality and maladjustment correlates. Doctoral dissertation, Texas Technological College, University Microfilms, 1969. No. 69-6443.

Kahn, M., & Quinlan, P. Desensitization with varying degrees of therapist contact. Paper presented at the Annual Meeting of the Association for the Advancement of Behavior Therapy. Washington, D.C., September 1967.

Kanfer, F. H., & Phillips, J. S. A survey of current behavior therapies and a proposal for classification. In C. M. Franks (Ed.), *Behavior therapy: Appraisal and status*. New York: McGraw-Hill, 1969.

Kanfer, F. H., & Phillips, J. S. *Learning foundations of behavior therapy*. New York: Wiley, 1970.

Kant, F. Further modifications in the technique of conditioned-reflex treatment of alcohol addiction. *Quarterly Journal of Studies on Alcoholism,* 1944, **5,** 228–232. (a)

Kant, F. The conditioned-reflex treatment in the light of our knowledge of alcohol addiction. *Quarterly Journal of Studies on Alcoholism,* 1944, **5,** 371–377. (b)

Kantorovich, N. V. An attempt of curing alcoholism by associated reflexes. *Novoye Refleksologii nervnoy i Fiziologii Sistemy,* 1928, **3,** 436–445. [Cited by Razran, G. H. S. Conditioned withdrawal responses with shock as the conditioning stimulus in adult human subjects. *Psychological Bulletin,* 1934, **31,** 111–143.]

Kaufmann, P. Changes in the MMPI as a function of psychiatric therapy. *Journal of Consulting Psychology,* 1950, **70,** 337–342.

Kass, R. E. & O'Leary, K. D. The effects of observer bias in field-experimental settings. Paper presented at a Symposium "Behavior Analysis in Education," University of Kansas, April 9, 1970.

Kazdin, A. E. Response cost: The removal of conditioned reinforcers for therapeutic change. *Behavior Therapy,* 1972, **3,** 533–546.

Kazdin, A. E. The effect of response cost and aversive stimulation in suppressing punished and nonpublished speech disfluencies. *Behavior Therapy,* 1973, **4**(1), 73–82.

Keele, C. A., & Neil, E. *Samson Wright's applied physiology,* 10th ed. London: Oxford Univ. Press, 1961.

Kelleher, R. T. Chaining and conditioned reinforcement. In W. K. Honig (Ed.), *Operant Behavior: Areas of research and application*. New York: Appleton, 1966.

Kellogg, W. N. & White, R. E. A maze test of Dunlap's theory of learning. *Journal of Comparative Psychology,* 1935, **19,** 119–148.

Kelly, G. A. *The psychology of personal constructs*. New York: Norton, 1955.

Kendell, R. E. Normal drinking by former alcohol addicts. *Quarterly Journal of Studies on Alcoholism,* 1965, **26,** 247–257.

Kennedy, T. D. Verbal conditioning without awareness. The use of programmed reinforcement and recurring assessment of awareness. *Journal of Experimental Psychology,* 1970, **84,** 487–494.

Kennedy, T. D. Reinforcement frequency, task characteristics, and interval of awareness assessment as factors in verbal conditioning without awareness. *Journal of Experimental Psychology,* 1971, **88,** 103–112.

Kent, R. N., O'Leary, K. D., Diament, C., & Dietz, A. Expectation biases in observational evaluation of therapeutic change. Unpublished manuscript, State University of New York at Stony Brook, 1973.

Kent, R. N., Wilson, T., & Nelson, R. Effects of false heart-rate feedback on avoidance behavior: An investigation of "cognitive desensitization." *Behavior Therapy,* 1972, **3,**1–6.

Keutzer, C. S. Behavior modification of smoking: The experimental investigation of diverse techniques. *Behaviour Research and Therapy,* 1968, **6,** 137–157.

Keutzer, C. S., Lichtenstein, E., & Mees, H. L. Modification of smoking behavior: A review. *Psychological Bulletin,* 1968, **70,** 520–533.

Kiesler, D. J. Some myths of psychotherapy research and the search for a paradigm. *Psychological Bulletin,* 1966, **65,** 110–136.

Kimble, G. A. *Hilgard and Marquis' conditioning and learning.* New York: Appleton, 1961.

Kimble, G. A., & Kendall, J. W. Jr. A comparison of two methods of producing experimental extinction. *Journal of Experimental Psychology,* 1953, **45,** 87–90.

King, G. F., Armitage, S. G., & Tilton, J. R. A therapeutic approach to schizophrenics of extreme pathology. *Journal of Abnormal and Social Psychology,* 1960, **61,** 276–286.

Kintsch, W. *Learning, memory and conceptual processes.* New York: Wiley, 1970.

Kirchner, J. H. & Hogan, R. A. The therapist variable in the implosion of phobias. *Psychotherapy: Theory, Research and Practice,* 1966, **3,** 102–104.

Koenig, K. P., & Masters, J. Experimental treatment of habitual smoking. *Behaviour Research and Therapy,* 1965, **3,** 235–243.

Kohlenberg, R. J. The punishment of persistent vomiting: A case study. *Journal of Applied Behavior Analysis,* 1970, **3,** 241–245.

Kolvin, I. "Aversive imagery" treatment in adolescents. *Behaviour Research and Therapy,* 1967, **5,** 245–248.

Korzybski, A. *Science and sanity.* Lancaster, Pennsylvania: Lancaster Press, 1933.

Kraft, T., & Al-Issa, I. Alcoholism treated by desensitization: A case report. *Behaviour Research and Therapy,* 1967, **5,** 69–70.

Krapfl, J. E. Differential ordering of stimulus presentation and semi-automated versus live treatment in the systematic desensitization of snake phobia. Unpublished doctoral dissertation, University of Missouri, 1967.

Krasner, L., & Ullmann, L. P. (Eds.). *Research in behavior modification.* New York: Holt, 1965.

Kropp, H., Calhoon, B., & Verrier, R. Modification of the "self-concept" of emotionally disturbed children by covert reinforcement. *Behavior Therapy,* 1971, **2,** 201–204.

Krueger, J. R. An early instance of conditioning from the Chinese dynastic histories. *Psychological Reports,* 1961, **9,** 117.

Kushner, M. The reduction of a long-standing fetish by means of aversive conditioning. In L. P. Ullmann & L. Krasner (Eds.), *Case studies in behavior modification.* New York: Holt, 1965.

Kushner, M., & Sandler, J. Aversion therapy and the concept of punishment. *Behaviour Research and Therapy,* 1966, **4,** 179–186.

Lang, P. J., & Lazovik, A. D. Experimental desensitization of a phobia. *Journal of Abnormal and Social Psychology,* 1963, **66,** 519–525.

Lang, P. J., Lazovik, A. D., & Reynolds, D. J. Desensitization, suggestibility, and pseudotherapy. *Journal of Abnormal Psychology,* 1965, **70,** 395–402.

Lang, P. J. & Melamed, B. G. Avoidance conditioning therapy of an infant with chronic ruminative vomiting. *Journal of Abnormal Psychology,* 1969, **74,** 1–8.

Lang, P. J., Melamed, B. G., & Hart, J. A psychophysiological analysis of fear modification using an automated desensitization procedure. *Journal of Abnormal Psychology,* 1970, **76,** 220–234.

Lavin, N. I., Thorpe, J. G., Barker, J. C., Blakemore, C. B., & Conway, C. G. Behavior therapy in a case of transvestism. *Journal of Nervous and Mental Disease,* 1961, **133,** 346–353.

Lawrence, P. S. The assessment and modification of assertive behavior. Unpublished doctoral dissertation, Arizona State University, 1970.

Lawson, D. M., & May, R. B. Three procedures for the extinction of smoking behavior. *Psychological Record,* 1970, **20,** 151–157.

Lawson, R. *Learning and behavior.* New York: Macmillan, 1960.

Layne, C. C. The effects of suggestion in implosive therapy for fear of rats. Unpublished doctoral dissertation, Southern Illinois University, 1970.

Lazarus, A. A. Objective psychotherapy in the treatment of dysphemia. *Journal of South African Logopedic Society,* 1960, **6,** 8–10.

Lazarus, A. A. Group therapy of phobic disorders by systematic desensitization. *Journal of Abnormal and Social Psychology,* 1961, **63,** 505–510.

Lazarus, A. A. The results of behavior therapy in 126 cases of severe neurosis. *Behaviour Research and Therapy,* 1963, **1,** 69–79.

Lazarus, A. A. Crucial procedural factors in desensitization therapy. *Behaviour Research and Therapy,* 1964, **2,** 65–70.

Lazarus, A. A. Behavior rehearsal vs. nondirective therapy vs. advice in effecting behavior change. *Behaviour Research and Therapy,* 1966, **4,** 209–212.

Lazarus, A. A. *Behavior therapy and beyond.* New York: McGraw-Hill, 1971.

Lazarus, A. A., & Rachman, S. The use of systematic desensitization in psychotherapy. *South African Medical Journal,* 1957, **31,** 934–937.

Lazarus, A. A., & Serber, M. Is systematic desensitization being misapplied? *Psychological Reports,* 1968, **23,** 215–218.

Leitenberg, H. Is time-out from positive reinforcement an aversive event? A review of the experimental evidence. *Psychological Bulletin,* 1965, **64,** 428–441.

Leitenberg, H., Agras, W. S., Barlow, D. H., & Oliveau, D. C. Contributions of selective positive reinforcement and therapeutic instructions to systematic desensitization. *Journal of Abnormal Psychology,* 1969, **74,** 113–118.

Lemere, F. & Voegtlin, W. L. Conditioned reflex therapy of alcoholic addiction: Specificity of conditioning against chronic alcoholism. *California and Western Medicine,* 1940, **53,** 268–269.

Lemere, F., Voegtlin, W. L., Broz, W. R., O'Halleren, P., & Tupper, W. E. Conditioned reflex treatment of chronic alcoholism: VII. Technic. *Diseases of the Nervous System,* 1942, **3,** 243–247. (a)

Lemere, F., Voegtlin, W. L., Broz, W. R., O'Hallaren, P., & Tupper, W. E. The conditioned reflex treatment of chronic alcoholism: VIII. A review of six years' experience with this treatment of 1526 patients. *Journal of the American Medical Association,* 1942, **120,** 269–270. (b)

Lesser, E. Behavior therapy with a narcotics user: a case report. *Behaviour Research and Therapy,* 1967, **5,** 251–252.

Levin, S., Hirsch, I. S., Shugar, G., & Kakar, R. Treatment of a homosexual problem with avoidance conditioning and reciprocal inhibition. Unpublished manuscript, Lafayette Clinic, Detroit, 1967.

Levine, G., & Burke, C. J. *Mathematical model techniques for learning theories.* New York: Academic Press, 1972.

Levis, D. J. Implosive therapy, Part II: The subhuman analogue, the strategy, and the technique. In S. G. Armitage (Ed.), *Behavior modification techniques in the treatment of emotional disorders.* Battle Creek, Michigan: Veterans Administration Publication, 1967.

Levis, D. J. & Carrera, R. N. Effects of 10 hours of implosive therapy in the treatment of outpatients: A preliminary report. *Journal of Abnormal Psychology,* 1967, **72,** 504–508.

Levitt, E. E. Psychotherapy with children: A further evaluation. *Behaviour Research and Therapy,* 1963, **1,** 45–51.

Liberman, R. A view of behavior modification projects in California. *Behaviour Research and Therapy,* 1968, **6,** 331–341.

Lippit, R., & Hubbell, A. Role playing for personnel and guidance workers: Review of the literature with suggestions for application. *Group Psychotherapy,* 1956, **9,** 89–114.

Loeb, A., Beck, A. T., Diggory, J. C., & Tuthill, R. Expectancy, level of aspiration, performance, and self-evaluation in depression. *Proceedings of the Annual Convention, American Psychological Association,* 1967, **2,** 193–194.

Lomont, J. F., Gilner, F. H., Spector, N. J., & Skinner, K. K. Group assertion training and group insight therapies. *Psychological Reports,* 1969, **25,** 463–470.

London, P. *The modes and morals of psychotherapy.* New York: Holt, 1964.

Lovaas, O. I. *Reinforcement therapy.* (16 mm sound film.) Philadelphia: Smith, Kline, & French Laboratories, 1966.

Lovaas, O. I. A behavior therapy approach to the treatment of childhood schizophrenia. In J. P. Hill (Ed.), *Minnesota Symposium on Child Psychology,* Vol. 1. Minneapolis, Minnesota: Univ. of Minnesota Press, 1967.

Lovaas, O. I., Some studies in the treatment of childhood schizophrenia. In J. M. Schlien (Ed.), *Research in psychotherapy,* Washington, D.C.: American Psychological Association, 1968.

Lovaas, O. I., Berberich, J. P., Kassorla, I. C., Klynn, G. A., & Meisel, J. Establishment of a texting and labeling vocabulary in schizophrenic children. Unpublished manuscript, University of California, Los Angeles, 1966. (a)

Lovaas, O. I. Berberich, J. P., Perloff, B. F. & Schaeffer, B. Acquisition of imitative speech by schizophrenic children. *Science,* 1966, **151,** 705–707. (b)

Lovaas, O. I., Dumont, D. A., Klynn, G. A., & Meisel, J. Establishment of appropriate response to, and use of, certain prepositions and pronouns in schizophrenic children. Unpublished manuscript, University of California, Los Angeles, 1966. (c)

Lovaas, O. I., Freitag, G., Kinder, M. I., Rubenstein, B. D., Schaeffer, B. & Simmons, J. Q. Establishment of social reinforcers in two schizophrenic children on the basis of food. *Journal of Experimental Child Psychology,* 1966, **4,** 109–125. (d)

Lovaas, O. I., Freitag, G., Gold, V. J., & Kassorla, I. C. Experimental studies in childhood schizophrenia: Analysis of self-destructive behavior *Journal of Experimental Child Psychology,* 1965, **2,** 67–84.

Lovaas, O. I., Freitag, L., Nelson, K., & Whalen, C. The establishment of imitation and its use for the development of complex behavior in schizophrenic children. *Behaviour Research and Therapy,* 1967, **5,** 171–181.

Lovaas, O. I. & Simmons, J. Q. Manipulation of self-destruction in three retarded children. *Journal of Applied Behavior Analysis,* 1969, **2,** 143–157.

Lovibond, S. H. & Caddy, G. Discriminated aversive control in the moderation of alcoholics' drinking behavior. *Behavior Therapy,* 1970, **1,** 437–444.

Lovitt, T. C., & Curtiss, K. A. Academic response rate as a function of teacher and self-imposed contingencies. *Journal of Applied Behavioral Analysis,* 1969, **2,** 49–53.

Lovitt, T. C., Guppy, T. E., & Blattner, J. E., The use of free-time contingency with fourth graders to increase spelling accuracy. *Behaviour Research and Therapy*, 1969, **7**, 151–156.

Lucero, R. J., Vail, D. J., & Scherber, J. Regulating operant-conditioning programs. *Hospital and Community Psychiatry*, 1968, **19**, 53–54.

MacCulloch, M. J., Birtles, C. J., & Feldman, M. P. Anticipatory avoidance learning for the treatment of homosexuality: Recent developments and an automatic aversion therapy system. *Behavior Therapy*, 1971, **2**, 151–169.

MacCulloch, M. J. & Feldman, M. P. Aversion therapy in the management of 43 homosexuals. *British Medical Journal*, 1967, **2**, 594–597.

MacCulloch, M. J., Feldman, M. P., & Pinschof, J. S. The application of anticipatory avoidance learning to the treatment of homosexuality—II. Avoidance response latencies and pulse rate changes. *Behaviour Research and Therapy*, 1965, **3**, 21–43.

MacDonough, T. S. A critique of the first Feldman and MacCulloch avoidance conditioning treatment for homosexuals. *Behavior Therapy*, 1972, **3**, 104–111.

Madsen, C. H. Jr., Becker, W. C., Thomas, D. R., Koser, L., & Plager, E. An analysis of the reinforcing function of "sit down" commands. In R. K. Parker (Ed.), *Readings in Educational Psychology*. Boston: Allyn & Bacon, 1968.

Madsen, C. H., & Ullmann, L. P. Innovations in the desensitization of frigidity. *Behaviour Research and Therapy*, 1967, **5**, 67–68.

Maes, W. R., & Heimann, R. A. The comparison of three approaches to the reduction of test anxiety in high school students. Unpublished manuscript, Arizona State University, October 1970.

Mahoney, M. J. The self-management of covert behavior: A case study. *Behavior Therapy*, 1971, **2**, 575–578.

Mahoney, M. J., & Bandura, A. Self-reinforcement in pigeons. *Learning and Motivation*, 1972, **3**, 293–303.

Mahoney, M. J., Moura, N., & Wade, T. The relative efficacy of self-reward, self-punishment, and self-monitoring techniques for weight loss. *Journal of Consulting and Clinical Psychology*, 1973, **40**, 404–407.

Mainord, W. A. Therapy-52. Unpublished manuscript, University of Louisville, 1967.

Malleson, N. Panic and phobia. *Lancet*, 1959, **1**, 225–227.

Malmo, R. B. Activation. In A. J. Bachrach (Ed.), *Experimental foundations of clinical psychology*. New York: Basic Books, 1962.

Marcia, J. E., Rubin, B. M., & Efran, J. S. Systematic desensitization: Expectancy change or counterconditioning? *Journal of Abnormal Psychology*, 1969, **74**, 382–387.

Marks, I. M. & Gelder, M. G. Transvestism and fetishism: Clinical and psychological changes during faradic aversion. *British Journal of Psychiatry*, 1967, **113**, 711–729.

Marquis, J. N., & Morgan, W. K. *A guidebook for systematic desensitization.* Palo Alto, California: Veterans Administration Hospital, 1969.

Marrone, R. L., Merksamer, M. A., & Salzberg, P. M. A short duration group treatment of smoking behavior by stimulus saturation. *Behaviour Research and Therapy,* 1970, **8,** 347–352.

Marston, A. R. Imitation, self-reinforcement, and reinforcement of another person. *Journal of Personality and Social Psychology,* 1965, **2,** 225–261.

Masserman, J. H. *Behavior and neurosis.* Chicago: Univ. of Chicago Press, 1943.

Masters, J. C. & Driscoll, S. A. Children's "imitation" as a function of the presence or absence of a model and the description of his instrumental behaviors. *Child Development,* 1971, **42,** 161–170.

Masters, J. C. & Mokros, J. R. Effects of incentive magnitude upon discriminative learning and choice preference in young children. *Child Development,* 1973, **44,** 225–231.

Masters, J. C. & Morris, R. J. Effects of contingent and noncontingent reinforcement upon generalized imitation. *Child Development,* 1971, **42,** 385–397.

Masters, W. H., & Johnson, V. E. *Human sexual inadequacy,* Boston: Little, Brown, 1970.

Mayer, J. *Overweight: Causes, cost and control.* Englewood Cliffs, New Jersey: Prentice-Hall, 1968.

McAllister, L. W., Stachowiak, J. G., Baer, D. M., & Conderman, L. The application of operant conditioning techniques in a secondary school classroom. *Journal of Applied Behavior Analysis,* 1969, **2,** 277–285.

McConaghy, N. Aversive therapy of homosexuality: measures of efficacy. *American Journal of Psychiatry,* 1971, **127,** 141–144.

McFall, R. M. The effects of self-monitoring on normal smoking behavior. *Journal of Consulting and Clinical Psychology,* 1970, **35,** 135–142.

McFall, R. M., & Lillesand, D. B. Behavior rehearsal with modeling and coaching in assertion training. *Journal of Abnormal Psychology,* 1971, **77,** 313–323.

McFall, R. M., & Marston, A. R. An experimental investigation of behavior rehearsal in assertive training. *Journal of Abnormal Psychology,* 1970, **76,** 295–303.

McGlynn, F. D. Systematic desensitization, implosive therapy and the aversiveness of imaginal hierarchy items. Unpublished doctoral dissertation, University of Missouri, 1968.

McGlynn, F. D., & Mapp, R. H. Systematic desensitization of snake-avoidance following three types of suggestion. *Behaviour Research and Therapy,* 1970, **81,** 197–201.

McGlynn, F. D., & Williams, C. W. Systematic desensitization of snake-avoidance under three conditions of suggestion. *Journal of Behavior Therapy and Experimental Psychiatry,* 1970, **1,** 97–101.

McGuire, R. J., & Vallance, M. Aversion therapy by electric shock, a simple technique. *British Medical Journal,* 1964, **1**, 151–152.

McMillan, D. E. A comparison of the punishing effects of response-produced shock and response-produced time out. *Journal of the Experimental Analysis of Behavior,* 1967, **10**, 439–449.

Mealiea, W. L., & Nawas, M. M. The comparative effectiveness of systematic desensitization and implosive therapy in the treatment of snake phobia. *Journal of Behavior Therapy and Experimental Psychiatry,* 1971, **2**, 85–94.

Meehl, P. E. Psychopathology and purpose. In P. H. Hoch and J. Zubin (Eds.), *The future of psychiatry.* New York: Grune & Stratton, 1962.

Mees, H. Placebo effects in aversive control: A preliminary report. Paper read at joint Oregon-Washington State Psychological Association, Ocean Shores, Washington, 1966.

Meichenbaum, D. H. The nature and modification of impulsive children: Training impulsive children to talk to themselves. *Research Report No. 23, Department of Psychology,* University of Waterloo, Waterloo, Ontario, Canada, 1971. (a)

Meichenbaum, D. H. Cognitive factors in behavior modification. *Research Report No. 25, Department of Psychology,* University of Waterloo, Waterloo, Ontario, Canada, 1971. (b)

Meichenbaum, D. H., Bowers, K. S., & Ross, R. R. Modification of classroom behavior of institutionalized female adolescent offenders. *Behaviour Research and Therapy,* 1968, **6**, 343–353.

Meichenbaum, D. H., Gilmore, J., & Fedoravicius, A. Group insight vs. group desensitization in treating speech anxiety. *Journal of Consulting and Clinical Psychology,* 1971, **36**, 410–421.

Meichenbaum, D., & Goodman, J. Reflection-impulsivity and verbal control of motor behavior. *Child Development,* 1969, **40**, 785–797.

Melamed, B., & Lang, P. J. Study of the automated desensitization of fear. Paper presentation at the Midwestern Psychological Association, Chicago, May 1967.

Mertens, G. C. & Fuller, G. B. *The therapist's manual.* Mimeograph, Willmar State Hospital, Willmar Minnesota, 1964.

Metzner, R. Some experimental analogues of obsession. *Behaviour Research and Therapy,* 1963, **1**, 231–236.

Meyer, V. The treatment of two phobic patients on the basis of learning principles. *Journal of Abnormal and Social Psychology,* 1957, **55**, 261–266.

Miller, B. V. & Levis, D. J. The effects of varying short visual exposure times to a phobic test stimulus on subsequent avoidance behavior. *Behaviour Research and Therapy,* 1971, **9**, 17–21.

Miller, H. R., & Nawas, M. M. Control of aversive stimulus termination in systematic desensitization. *Behaviour Research and Therapy,* 1970, **8**, 57–61.

Miller, L. B. & Estes, B. W. Monetary reward and motivation in discrimination learning. *Journal of Experimental Psychology,* 1961, **6,** 501–504.

Miller, M. M. Hypnotic-aversion treatment of homosexuality. *Journal of the National Medical Association,* 1963, **55,** 411–415.

Mills, K. C., Sobell, M. B., & Schaefer, H. H. Training social drinking as an alternative to abstinence for alcoholics. *Behavior Therapy,* 1971, **2,** 18–27.

Minge, M. R. & Ball, T. S. Teaching of self-help skills to profoundly retarded patients. *American Journal of Mental Deficiency,* 1967, **71,** 864–868.

Mira, M., Results of a behavior modification training program for parents and teachers. *Behaviour Research and Therapy,* 1970, **8,** 309–311.

Mischel, W. *Personality and assessment.* New York: Wiley, 1968.

Mischel, W., & Liebert, R. M. Effects of discrepancies between observed and imposed reward criteria on their acquisition and transmission. *Journal of Personality and Social Psychology,* 1966, **3,** 45–53.

Mogar, R. E. & Savage, C. Personality change associated with psychodelic (LSD) therapy: A preliminary report. *Psychotherapy: Theory, Research and Practice,* 1964, **1,** 154–162.

Mogel, S. & Schiff, W. "Extinction" of a head-bumping symptom of eight years' duration in two minutes: A case report. *Behaviour Research and Therapy,* 1967, **5,** 131–132.

Moore, N. Behavior therapy in bronchial asthma: A controlled study. *Journal of Psychosomatic Research,* 1965, **9,** 257–276.

Moreno, J. L. *Psychodrama,* Vol. 1. New York: Beacon House, 1946.

Moreno, J. L. The discovery of the spontaneous man with special emphasis upon the technique of role reversal. *Group Psychotherapy,* 1955, **8,** 103–129.

Moreno, J. L. Behavior therapy. *American Journal of Psychiatry,* 1963, **120,** 194–196.

Moreno, Z. T. Psychodramatic rules, techniques and adjunctive methods. *Group Psychotherapy,* 1965, **18,** 73–86.

Morganstern, F. S., Pearce, J. F., & Rees, W. L. Predicting the outcome of behaviour therapy by psychological tests. *Behaviour Research and Therapy,* 1965, **2,** 191–200.

Morganstern, K. P. Implosive therapy and flooding procedures: A critical review. *Psychological Bulletin,* 1972, **79,** 318–334.

Mowrer, O. H. Identification: A link between learning theory and psychotherapy. In *Learning theory and personality dynamics.* New York: Ronald Press, 1950. Pp. 69–94.

Mowrer, O. H. *Learning theory and the symbolic processes.* New York: Wiley, 1960.

Mullen, F. G. The effect of covert sensitization on smoking behavior. Unpublished study, Queens College, Charlottesville, North Carolina, 1968.

Nawas, M. M., Fishman, S. T., & Pucel, J. C. A standardized desensitization program applicable to group and individual treatment. *Behaviour Research and Therapy,* 1970, **8,** 49–56.

Nawas, M. M., Welsch, W. V., & Fishman, S. T. The comparative effectiveness of pairing aversive imagery with relaxation, neutral tasks and muscular tension in reducing snake phobia. *Behaviour Research and Therapy,* 1970, **6,** 63–68.

Nidetch, J. *Weight watchers' cookbook.* New York: Hearthside Press, 1966.

Nisbett, R., & Schacter, S. Cognitive manipulations of pain. *Journal of Experimental Social Psychology,* 1966, **2,** 227–236.

Nolan, J. D. Self-control procedures in the modification of smoking behavior. *Journal of Consulting and Clinical Psychology,* 1968, **32,** 92–93.

Nurnberger, J. I., & Zimmerman, J. Applied analysis of human behavior: An alternative to conventional motivational inferences and unconscious determination in therapeutic programming. *Behavior Therapy,* 1970, **1,** 1–3.

Ober, D. C. The modification of smoking behavior. Unpublished doctoral dissertation, University of Illinois, 1966.

O'Brien, F., Azrin, N. H., & Bugle, C. Training profoundly retarded children to stop crawling. *Journal of Applied Behavior Analysis,* 1972, **5,** 131–137.

O'Brien, F., Bugle, C., & Azrin, N. H. Training and maintaining a retarded child's proper eating. *Journal of Applied Behavior Analysis,* 1972, **5,** 67–72.

O'Connor, R. D. Modification of social withdrawal through symbolic modeling. *Journal of Applied Behavior Analysis,* 1969, **2,** 15–22.

O'Leary, K. D. & Becker, W. C. Behavior modification of an adjustment class: A token reinforcement program. *Exceptional Children,* 1967, **33,** 637–642.

O'Leary, K. D., Becker, W. C., Evans, M. B., & Saudargas, R. A. A token reinforcement program in a public school: A replication and systematic analysis. *Journal of Applied Behavior Analysis,* 1969, **2,** 3–13.

O'Leary, K. D. & Kent, R. N. Behavior modification for social action: Research tactics and problems. In Hamerlynck, C. L. *et al.* (Eds.), *Critical Issues in Research and Practice.* Champaign, Illinois: Research Press, 1973.

O'Leary, K. D., O'Leary, S., & Becker, W. C. Modification of a deviant sibling interaction pattern in the home. *Behaviour Research and Therapy,* 1967, **5,** 113–120.

Oliveau, D. C., Agras, W. S., Leitenberg, H., Moore, R. C., & Wright, D. E. Systematic desensitization, therapeutically oriented instructions and selective positive reinforcement. *Behaviour Research and Therapy,* 1969, **7,** 27–33.

Orne, M. On the social psychology of the psychological experiment: With particular reference to demand characteristics and their implications. *American Psychologist,* 1962, **17,** 776–783.

Osborne, J. G., Free-time as a reinforcer in the management of classroom behavior. *Journal of Applied Behavior Analysis,* 1969, **2,** 113–118.

Packard, R. G. The control of "classroom attention": A group contingency for complex behavior. *Journal of Applied Behavior Analysis,* 1970, **3,** 13–28.

Paivio, A., & Yuille, J. C. Mediation instructions and word attributes in paired-associate learning. *Psychonomic Science,* 1967, **8,** 65–66.

Panek, D. M. Word association learning by chronic schizophrenics on a token economy ward under conditions of reward and punishment. *Journal of Clinical Psychology,* 1970, **26,** 163–167.

Patterson, G. R., A learning theory approach to the treatment of the school phobic child. In L. P. Ullmann and L. Krasner (Eds.), *Case studies in behavior modification.* New York: Holt, 1965.

Patterson, G. R. & Cobb, J. A. A dyadic analysis of "aggressive" behaviors. In J. P. Hill (Ed.), *Minnesota Symposium on Child Psychology,* Vol. 5. Minneapolis, Minnesota: Univ. of Minnesota Press, 1971.

Patterson, G. R. & Gullion, M. E. *Living with children.* Champaign, Illinois: Research Press, 1971.

Patterson, G. R., Jones, R., Whittier, J., & Wright, M. A. A behavior modification technique for the hyperactive child. *Behaviour Research and Therapy,* 1965, **2,** 217–226.

Patterson, G. R., Ray, R., & Shaw, D. Direct Intervention in Families of Deviant Children. Paper presented at meeting of Oregon Psychological Association—Washington State Psychological Association, May 1968.

Paul, G. L. *Insight vs. desensitization in psychotherapy: An experiment in anxiety reduction.* Stanford, California: Stanford Univ. Press, 1966.

Paul, G. L. Insight vs. desensitization in psychotherapy two years after termination. *Journal of Consulting Psychology,* 1967, **31,** 333–348.

Paul, G. L. Behavior modification research: design and tactics. In C. M. Franks (Ed.), *Behavior therapy: Appraisal and status.* New York: McGraw-Hill, 1969. (a)

Paul, G. L. Outcome of systematic desensitization. I: Background and procedures, and uncontrolled reports of individual treatments. In C. M. Franks (Ed.), *Behavior therapy: Appraisal and status.* New York: McGraw-Hill, 1969. (b)

Paul, G. L. Outcome of systematic desensitization. II: Controlled investigations of individual treatment, technique variations, and current status. In C. M. Franks (Ed.), *Behavior therapy: Appraisal and status.* New York: McGraw-Hill, 1969. (c)

Paul, G. L. Physiological effects of relaxation training and hypnotic suggestion. *Journal of Abnormal Psychology,* 1969, **74,** 425–437. (d)

Paul, G. L., & Shannon, D. T. Treatment of anxiety through systematic desensitization in therapy groups. *Journal of Abnormal Psychology,* 1966, **71,** 124–135.

Paul, G. L., & Trimble, R. W. Recorded vs. "Live" relaxation training and hypnotic suggestion: Comparative effectiveness for reducing physiological arousal and inhibiting stress response. *Behavior Therapy,* 1970, **1,** 285–302.

Pavlov, I. P. *Conditioned reflexes: An investigation of the physiological activity of the cerebral cortex* (translated by G. V. Anrep). London and New York: Oxford Univ. Press, 1927.

Pavlov, I. P. *Lectures on conditioned reflexes,* Vol. 1 (translated by W. H. Gantt). London: Lawrence & Wishart, 1928.

Persely, G., & Leventhal, D. B. The effects of therapeutically oriented instructions and the pairing of anxiety imagery and relaxation in systematic desensitization. *Behavior Therapy,* 1972, **3,** 417–424.

Peters, H. N., & Jenkins, R. L., Improvement of chronic schizophrenic patients with guided problem-solving motivated by hunger. *Psychiatric Quarterly Supplement,* 1954, **28,** 84–101.

Petrik, N. The token economy. Unpublished manual. Veterans Administration Hospital, St. Cloud, Minnesota, 1971.

Pfeiffer, E. A. & Johnson, J. B. A new electrode for the application of electrical shock in aversive conditioning therapy. *Behaviour Research and Therapy,* 1968, **6,** 393–394.

Phillips, E. L. Achievement place: Token reinforcement procedures in a home-style rehabilitation setting for "predelinquent" boys. *Journal of Applied Behavior Analysis,* 1968, **1,** 213–223.

Phillips, E. L., Phillips, E. A., Fixen, D. L., & Wolf, M. M. Achievement Place: Modification of the behaviors of pre-delinquent boys within a token economy. *Journal of Applied Behavior Analysis,* 1971, **4,** 45–59.

Poindexter, A. The factor of repetition in learning to type. *Kentucky Personality Bulletin,* 1936, **17,** 3–4.

Polin, A. T. The effects of flooding and physical suppression as extinction techniques on an anxiety motivated avoidance locomotor response. *Journal of Psychology,* 1959, **47,** 235–245.

Pollitt, J. D. Natural history studies in mental illness: a discussion based on a pilot study of obsessional states. *Journal of Mental Science,* 1960, **106,** 93–113.

Poppen, R. L. Counterconditioning of conditioned suppression. Unpublished doctoral dissertation, Stanford University, 1968.

Poppen, R. L. Counterconditioning of conditioned suppression in rats. *Psychological Reports,* 1970, **27,** 659–671.

Potter, S. *One-upmanship, being some account of the activities and teachings of the Lifemanship Correspondence College of One-upness and Games life-mastery.* New York: Holt, 1952.

Powell, J., & Azrin, N. The effects of shock as a punisher for cigarette smoking. *Journal of Applied Behavior Analysis,* 1968, **1,** 63–71.

Premack, D., Toward empirical behavioral laws: I. Positive reinforcement. *Psychological Review*, 1959, **66,** 219–233.

Premack, D., Reinforcement theory. In D. Levine (Ed.), *Nebraska Symposium on Motivation: 1965.* Lincoln: Univ. of Nebraska Press, 1965.

Prince, G. S. A clinical approach to parent-child interaction. *Journal of Child Psychology and Psychiatry,* 1961, **2,** 169–184.

Quinn, J. T. & Henbest, R. Partial failure of generalization in alcoholics following aversion therapy. *Quarterly Journal of Studies on Alcoholism,* 1967, **28,** 70–75.

Rachman, S. Aversion therapy: Chemical or electrical? *Behaviour Research and Therapy,* 1965, **2,** 289–299.

Rachman, S. Studies in desensitization—II: Flooding. *Behaviour Research and Therapy,* 1966, **4,** 1–6. (a)

Rachman, S. Studies in desensitization—III: Speed of generalization. *Behaviour Research and Therapy,* 1966, **4,** 7–15. (b)

Rachman, S. The role of muscular relaxation in desensitization therapy. *Behaviour Research and Therapy,* 1968, **16,** 159–166.

Rachman, S. Treatment by prolonged exposure to high intensity stimulation. *Behaviour Research and Therapy,* 1969, **7,** 295–302.

Rachman, S. & Teasdale, J. Aversion therapy and behaviour disorders: An analysis. Coral Gables, Florida: Univ. of Miami Press, 1969.

Rathus, S. A. An experimental investigation of assertive training in a group setting. *Journal of Behavior Therapy and Experimental Psychiatry,* 1972, **3,** 81–86.

Raymond, M. J. Case of fetishism treated by aversion therapy. *British Medical Journal,* 1956, **2,** 854–857.

Raymond, M. J. & O'Keeffe, K. A case of pin-up fetishism treated by aversion conditioning. *British Journal of Psychiatry,* 1965, **111,** 579–581.

Redd, W. H., Effects of mixed reinforcement contingencies on adults' control of children's behavior. *Journal of Applied Behavior Analysis,* 1969, **2,** 249–254.

Rehm, L. P., & Marston, A. R. Reduction of social anxiety through modification of self-reinforcement: An instigation therapy technique. *Journal of Consulting Psychology,* 1968, **32,** 565–574.

Rimm, D. C. Assertive training used in treatment of chronic crying spells. *Behaviour Research and Therapy,* 1967, **5,** 373–374.

Rimm, D. C. Comments on: "Systematic desensitization: Expectancy change or counter-conditioning?" *Behaviour Research and Therapy,* 1970, **8,** 105–106.

Rimm, D. C. Thought stopping and covert assertion in the treatment of phobias. *Journal of Consulting and Clinical Psychology,* 1973.

Rimm, D. C., & Bottrell, J. Four measures of visual imagination. *Behaviour Research and Therapy,* 1969, **7,** 63–69.

Rimm, D. C., deGroot, J. C., Boord, P., Heiman, J., & Dillow, P. V. Systematic desensitization of an anger response. *Behaviour Research and Therapy,* 1971, **9,** 273–280. (a)

Rimm, D. C., Hill, G. A., Brown, N. N., & Stuart, J. E. Group assertive training in the treatment of inappropriate anger expression. *Psychological Reports,* 1974, in press.

Rimm, D. C., Kennedy, T. D., Miller, H. L. Jr., & Tchida, G. R. Experimentally manipulated drive level and avoidance behavior. *Journal of Abnormal Psychology,* 1971, **78,** 43–48. (b)

Rimm, D. C., Keyson, M., & Hunziker, J. Group assertive training in the treatment of antisocial aggression. Unpublished manuscript, Arizona State University, 1971. (c)

Rimm, D. C., & Litvak, S. B. Self-verbalization and emotional arousal. *Journal of Abnormal Psychology,* 1969, **74,** 181–187.

Rimm, D. C. & Mahoney, M. J. The application of reinforcement and participant modeling procedures in the treatment of snake-phobic behavior. *Behaviour Research and Therapy,* 1969, **7,** 369–376.

Rimm, D. C., & Madieros, D. C. The role of muscle relaxation in participant modeling. *Behaviour Research and Therapy,* 1970, **8,** 127–132.

Rimm, D. C., Saunders, W. D., & Westel, W. Thought stopping and covert assertion in the treatment of snake phobias. Unpublished manuscript, Southern Illinois University, 1973.

Risley, T. R. The effects and side effects of punishing the autistic behaviors of a deviant child. *Journal of Applied Behavior Analysis,* 1968, **1,** 21–34.

Risley, T. R. & Wolf, M. M. Establishing functional speech in echolalic children. *Behaviour Research and Therapy,* 1967, **5,** 73–88.

Ritter, B. The group treatment of children's snake phobias, using vicarious and contact desensitization procedures. *Behaviour Research and Therapy,* 1968, **6,** 1–6. (a)

Ritter, B. The effect of contact desensitization on avoidance behavior, fear ratings, and self-evaluative statements. *Proceedings of the 76th annual Convention of the American Psychological Association,* 1968, **3,** 527–528. (b)

Ritter, B. Eliminating excessive fears of the environment through contact desensitization. In J. D. Krumboltz & C. E. Thoreson (Eds.), *Behavioral Counseling: Cases and techniques.* New York: Holt, 1969. (a)

Ritter, B. Treatment of acrophobia with contact desensitization. *Behaviour Research and Therapy,* 1969, **7,** 41–45. (b)

Ritter, B. The use of contact desensitization, demonstration-plus-participation, and demonstration alone in the treatment of acrophobia. *Behaviour Research and Therapy,* 1969, **7,** 157–164. (c)

Robbins, L. C. The accuracy of parental recall of aspects of child development and of child rearing practices. *Journal of Abnormal and Social Psychology,* 1963, **66,** 261–270.

Roberts, A. H. Self-control procedures in modification of smoking behavior: Replication. *Psychological Reports,* 1969, **24,** 675.

Robinson, F. P. *Effective study.* New York: Harper, 1946.

Rocha e Silva, M. I., & Ferster, C. B. An experiment in teaching a second language. *Sonderdruck aus IRAL,* 1966, **4,** 85–113.

Rogers, C. R. *On becoming a person.* Boston: Houghton, 1961.

Romanczyk, R. G., Kent, R. N., Diament, C., & O'Leary, K. D. Measuring the reliability of observational data: a reactive process. *Journal of Applied Behavior Analysis,* 1973, in press.

Roos, P. Development of an intensive habit-training unit at Austin State School. *Mental Retardation,* 1965, **3,** 12–15.

Rosenthal, R. On the social psychology of the psychological experiment: The experimenter's hypothesis as unintended determinant of experimental results. *American Scientist,* 1963, **51,** 268–282.

Royer, F. L., Rynearson, R., Rice, W., & Upper, D. An inexpensive quickly built shock grid for use with humans. *Behavior Therapy,* 1971, **2**(2), 251–252.

Ruhl, R. A. Negative practice versus positive practice in the eliminating of typing errors. *Journal of General Psychology,* 1935, **13,** 203–211.

Russo, S., Adaptations in behavioural therapy with children. *Behaviour Research and Therapy,* 1964, **2,** 43–47.

Rutherford, B. R. The use of negative practice in speech therapy with children handicapped by cerebral palsy, athetoid type. *Journal of Speech Disorders,* 1940, **5,** 259–264.

Sachs, D. A. & Mayhall, B. Behavioral control of spasms using aversive conditioning with a cerebral palsied adult. *Journal of Nervous and Mental Disorders,* 1971, **152,** 362–363.

Sachs, L. B., Bean, H., & Morrow, J. E. Comparison of smoking treatments. *Behavior Therapy,* 1970, **1,** 465–472.

Salter, A. *Conditioned reflex therapy.* New York: Farrar, Straus, 1949.

Salter, A. The theory and practice of conditioned reflex therapy. A. Salter, J. Wolpe, & L. J. Reyna (Eds.), In *The Conditioning Therapies: The Challenge in Psychotherapy.* New York: Holt, 1964.

Sanders, B. D. Behavior rehearsal and imaginal desensitization in reducing public speaking anxiety. Unpublished doctoral dissertation, Stanford University, 1967.

Sanderson, R. E., Campbell, D., & Laverty, S. G. An investigation of a new aversive conditioning treatment for alcoholism. *Quarterly Journal of Studies on Alcoholism,* 1963, **24,** 261–275.

Sarason, I. Verbal learning, modeling, and juvenile delinquency. *American Psychologist,* 1968, **23,** 254–266.

Sarason, I. G. & Glanzer, V. J. Social influence techniques in clinical and community psychology. In C. D. Spielberger (Ed.), *Current Topics in Clinical and Community Psychology.* New York: Academic Press, 1969.

Schachter, J. Pain, fear, and anger in hypertensive and normotensives: A psychophysiological study. *Psychosomatic Medicine,* 1957, **19,** 17–29.

Schacter, S. Some extraordinary facts about obese humans and rats. *American Psychologist,* 1971, **26,** 129–144.

Schacter, S., & Singer, J. E. Cognitive, social, and physiological determinants of emotional state. *Psychological Review,* 1962, **69,** 379–399.

Schacter, S., & Wheeler, L. Epinephrine, chlorpromazine, and amusement. *Journal of Abnormal and Social Psychology,* 1962, **65,** 121–128.

Schaefer, H. H., & Martin, P. L. Behavior therapy for "apathy" of hospitalized schizophrenics. *Psychological Reports,* 1966, **19,** 1147–1158.

Schaefer, H. H. & Martin, P. L. *Behavioral therapy.* New York: McGraw-Hill, 1969.

Schmauk, F. J. Punishment, arousal, and avoidance learning in sociopaths. *Journal of Abnormal Psychology,* 1970, **76,** 325–335.

Schmidt, E., Castell, D., & Brown, P. A retrospective study of 42 cases of behaviour therapy. *Behaviour Research and Therapy,* 1965, **3,** 9–20.

Schofield, W. Changes in response to the MMPI following certain therapies. *Psychological Monographs,* 1950, **64** (Whole No. 311).

Schofield, W. A further study of the effects of therapies on MMPI responses. *Journal of Abnormal and Social Psychology,* 1953, **48,** 67–77.

Schubot, E. D. The influence of hypnotic and muscular relaxation in systematic desensitization of phobic behavior. Unpublished doctoral dissertation, Stanford University, 1966.

Schwitzgebel, R. A new approach to understanding delinquency. Federal Probation, 1960, pp. 5–9.

Schwitzgebel, R. Delinquents with tape recorders, *New Society,* January 31, 1963.

Schwitzgebel, R. Short-term operant conditioning of adolescent offenders on socially relevant variables. *Journal of Abnormal Psychology,* 1967, **72,** 134–142.

Schwitzgebel, R., & Kolb, D. A. Inducing behavior change in adolescent delinquents. *Behaviour Research and Therapy* 1964, **1,** 297–304.

Seitz, P. F. Dynamically-oriented brief psychotherapy: Psychocutaneous excoriation syndromes. *Psychosomatic Medicine,* 1953, **XV,** 200–213.

Semat, H. *Introduction to atomic and nuclear physics.* New York: Holt, 1954.

Serber, M., & Nelson, P. The ineffectiveness of systematic desensitization and assertive training in hospitalized schizophrenics. *Journal of Behavior Therapy and Experimental Psychiatry,* 1971, **2,** 107–109.

Shadel, C. A. Aversion treatment of alcohol addiction. *Quarterly Journal of Studies on Alcoholism,* 1944, **5,** 216–228.

Shaffer, L. F. The problem of psychotherapy. *American Psychologist,* 1947, **2,** 459–467.

Sherman, J. A. Use of reinforcement and imitation to reinstate verbal behavior in mute psychotic. *Journal of Abnormal Psychology,* 1965, **70,** 155–164.

Sherrington, C. S. *Integrative action of the nervous system.* New Haven, Connecticut: Yale Univ. Press, 1906.

Sidman, M. *Tactics of scientific research.* New York: Basic Books, 1960.

Siegel, G. M., Lenske, J., & Broen, P. Suppression of normal speech disfluencies through response cost. *Journal of Applied Behavior Analysis,* 1969, **2,** 265–276.

Siegeltuch, M. B. & Baum, M. Extintion of well-established avoidance responses through response prevention (flooding). *Behaviour Research and Therapy,* 1971, **9,** 103–108.

Skinner, B. F. The behavior of organisms. New York: Appleton, 1938.

Skinner, B. F. Are theories of learning necessary? *Psychological Review,* 1950, **57,** 193–216.

Skinner, B. F. *Science and human behavior.* New York: Macmillan, 1953.

Skinner, B. F. Operant Behavior. In W. K. Honig (Ed.), *Operant behavior: Areas of research and application.* New York: Appleton, 1966.

Skinner, B. F. *Contingencies of reinforcement: A theoretical analysis.* New York: Appleton, 1969.

Skinner, B. F. *Beyond freedom and dignity.* New York: Knopf, 1971.

Slack, C. W. Experimenter-subject psychotherapy: a new method of introducing intensive office treatment for unreachable cases. *Mental Hygiene,* 1960, **44,** 238–256.

Slater, S. L., & Leavy, A. The effects of inhaling a 35% carbon dioxide, 65% oxygen mixture upon anxiety level in neurotic patients. *Behaviour Research and Therapy,* 1966, **4,** 309–316.

Sloane, H. N. Jr., Johnston, M. K., & Harris, F. R. Remedial procedures for teaching verbal behavior to speech deficient or defective young children. In H. N. Sloane, Jr., & B. A. MacAulay (Eds.), *Operant procedures in remedial speech and language training.* Boston: Houghton, 1968.

Solomon, R. L. Punishment. *American Psychologist,* 1964, **19,** 239–253.

Solomon, R. L., & Brush, E. S. Experimentally derived conceptions of anxiety and aversion. In M. R. Jones (Ed.), *Nebraska symposium on motivation,* Lincoln, Nebraska: Univ. of Nebraska Press, 1956.

Solomon, R. L., Kamin, L. J., & Wynne, L. C. Traumatic avoidance learning: the outcomes of several extinction procedures with dogs. *Journal of Abnormal and Social Psychology,* 1953, **48,** 291–302.

Solyom, L. & Miller, S. B. Reciprocal inhibition by aversion relief in the treatment of phobias. *Behaviour Research and Therapy,* 1967, **5,** 313–324.

Spielberger, C. D., & De Nike, L. D. Descriptive behaviorism versus cognitive theory in verbal operant conditioning. *Psychological Review,* 1966, **73,** 306–326.

Srnec,—, & Freund, K. Treatment of male homosexuality through conditioning. *International Journal of Sexology,* 1953, **7,** 92–93.

Staats, A. W. A case in and a strategy for the extension of learning principles to problems of human behavior. In L. Krasner & L. P. Ullman (Eds.), *Research in behavior modification.* New York: Holt, 1965.

Staats, A. W. & Butterfield, W. H. Treatment of nonreading in a culturally deprived juvenile delinquent: an application of reinforcement principles. *Child Development,* 1965, **36,** 925–942.

Staats, A. W., Finley, J. R., Minke, K. A., & Wolf, M. Reinforcement variables in the control of unit reading responses. *Journal of the Experimental Analysis of Behavior,* 1964, **7,** 139–149. (a)

Staats, A. W., Minke, K. A., Finley, J. R., Wolf, M., & Brooks, L. O. A reinforcer system and experimental procedure for the laboratory study of reading acquisition. *Child Development,* 1964, **35,** 209–231. (b)

Staats, A. W., Minke, K. A., Goodwin, W., & Landeen, J. Cognitive behavior modification: Motivated learning reading treatment with subprofessional therapy-technicians. *Behaviour Research and Therapy,* 1967, **5,** 283–299.

Stampfl, T. G. Implosive therapy: a learning theory derived psychodynamic therapeutic technique. In Lebarba & Dent (Eds.), *Critical Issues in Clinical Psychology.* New York: Academic Press, 1961.

Stampfl, T. G. Implosive therapy, Part I: The theory. In S. G. Armitage (Ed.), *Behavioral modification techniques in the treatment of emotional disorders.* Battle Creek, Michigan: V.A. Publication, 1967.

Stampfl, T. G. & Levis, D. J. Essentials of implosive therapy: A learning-theory-based psychodynamic behavioral therapy. *Journal of Abnormal Psychology,* 1967, **72,** 496–503. (a)

Stampfl, T. G. & Levis, D. J. Phobic patients: Treatment with the learning theory approach of implosive therapy. *Voices: The Art and Science of Psychotherapy,* 1967, **3,** 23–27. (b)

Stampfl, T. G. & Levis, D. J. Implosive therapy—A behavioral therapy? *Behaviour Research and Therapy,* 1968, **6,** 31–36.

Staub, E. Duration of stimulus-exposure as determinant of the efficacy of flooding procedures in the elimination of fear. *Behaviour Research and Therapy,* 1968, **6,** 131–132.

Steffy, R. A., Hart, J., Craw, M., Torney, D., & Marlett, N. Operant behaviour modification techniques applied to severely regressed and aggressive patients. *Canadian Psychiatric Association Journal,* 1969, **14,** 59–67.

Stevenson, H. W., Social Reinforcement of Children's Behavior. In L. P. Lipsitt & C. C. Spiker (Eds.), *Advances in Child Development and Behavior,* Vol. 2. New York: Academic Press, 1965.

Stevenson, H. W. *Children's learning.* New York: Appleton, 1971.

Stevenson, I. Direct instigation of behavioral changes in psychotherapy. *AMA Archives of General Psychiatry,* 1959, **1,** 115–123.

Stevenson, I. & Wolpe, J. Recovery from sexual deviations through overcoming non-sexual neurotic response. *American Journal of Psychiatry,* 1960, **116,** 737–742.

Stewart, M. A. Psychotherapy by reciprocal inhibition. *American Journal of Psychiatry,* 1961, **118,** 175–177.

Storms, M. D., & Nisbett, R. E. Insomnia and the attribution process. *Journal of Personality and Social Psychology,* 1970, **16,** 319–328.

Strahley, R. F. Systematic desensitization and counterphobic treatment of an irrational fear of snakes. Unpublished doctoral dissertation, University of Tennessee, 1965.

Straughan, J. H. Treatment with child and mother in the playroom. *Behaviour Research and Therapy,* 1964, **2,** 37–41.

Straughan, J. H. The application of operant conditioning to the treatment of elective mutism. In H. N. Sloane, Jr., & B. A. MacAulay (Eds.), *Operant procedures in remedial speech and language training.* Boston: Houghton, 1968.

Strum, I. E. The behavioristic aspect of psychodrama. *Group Psychotherapy,* 1965, **18,** 50–64.

Stuart, R. B. Behavioral control over eating. *Behaviour Research and Therapy,* 1967, **5,** 357–365.

Stuart, R. B. A three-dimensional program for the treatment of obesity. *Behaviour Research and Therapy,* 1971, **9,** 177–186.

Stunkard, A. J. The management of obesity. *New York State Journal of Medicine,* 1958, **58,** 79–87.

Suinn, R. M. The desensitization of test-anxiety by group and individual treatment. *Behaviour Research and Therapy,* 1968, **6,** 385–387.

Sulzbacher, S. I. & Houser, J. E. A tactic to eliminate disruptive behaviors in the classroom: Group contingent consequences. *American Journal of Mental Deficiency,* 1968, **73,** 88–90.

Sushinsky, L., & Bootzin, R. Cognitive desensitization as a model of systematic desensitization. *Behavior Research and Therapy,* 1970, **8,** 29–34.

Szasz, T. S. *The myth of mental illness: Foundations of a theory of personal conduct.* New York: Harper, 1961.

Taylor, D. W. A comparison of group desensitization with two control procedures in the treatment of test anxiety. *Behaviour Research and Therapy,* 1971, **9,** 281–284.

Taylor, J. A. A personality scale of manifest anxiety. *Journal of Abnormal and Social Psychology,* 1953, **48,** 285–290.

Taylor, J. G. A behavioral interpretation of obsessive-compulsive neurosis. *Behaviour Research and Therapy,* 1963, **1,** 237–244.

Terrace, H. S. Stimulus control. In W. K. Honig (Ed.), *Operant behavior.* New York: Appleton, 1966.

Terrell, G. & Ware, R. Role of delay of reward in speed of size and form discrimination learning in children. *Child Development,* 1961, **32,** 409–415.

Tharp, R. G., & Wetzel, R. J. *Behavior modification in the natural environment.* New York: Academic Press, 1969.

Thoreson, C. E., & Mahoney, M. J. *Behavioral self-control.* New York: Holt, 1974.

Thorndike, E. L. Animal intelligence: an experimental study of the associative processes in animals. *Psychological Review,* 1898, Monograph Supplement **2,** No. 8.

Thorndike, E. L. *Animal intelligence.* New York: Macmillan, 1911.

Thorndike, E. L. *The psychology of learning* (Educational Psychology, II). New York: Teachers College, 1913.

Thorpe, J. G., Schmidt, E., Brown, P. T., & Castell, D. Aversion-relief therapy: A new method for general application. *Behaviour Research and Therapy,* 1964, **2,** 71–82.

Thorpe, J. G., Schmidt, E., & Castell, D. A comparison of positive and negative (aversive) conditioning in the treatment of homosexuality. *Behaviour Research and Therapy,* 1963, **1,** 357–362.

Todd, F. J. Coverant control of self-evaluative responses in the treatment of depression: A new use for an old principle. *Behavior Therapy,* 1972, **3,** 91–94.

Tolman, C. W., & Mueller, M. R. Laboratory control of toe-sucking in a young rhesus monkey by two kinds of punishment. *Journal of the Experimental Analysis of Behavior,* 1964, **7,** 323–325.

Tooley, J. T., & Pratt, S. An experimental procedure for the extinction of smoking behavior. *Psychological Record,* 1967, **17,** 209–218.

Trexler, L. D., & Karst, T. O. Rational-Emotive Therapy, placebo, and no-treatment effects on public-speaking anxiety. *Journal of Abnormal Psychology,* 1972, **79,** 60–67.

Tyler, V. O., & Straughan, J. H. Coverant control and breath holding as techniques for the treatment of obesity. *Psychological Record,* 1970, **20,** 473–478.

Ullmann, L. P., & Krasner, L. (Eds.), *Case studies in behavior modification.* New York: Holt, 1965.

Ullmann, L. P., & Krasner, L. *A psychological approach to abnormal behavior.* Englewood Cliffs, New Jersey: Prentice-Hall, 1969.

Underwood, B. J. *Psychological research.* New York: Appleton, 1957.

Upper, D. A "ticket" system for reducing ward rules violations on a token economy program. Paper presented at the Association for Advancement of Behavior Therapy. Washington, D.C., September, 1971.

Valins, S. Cognitive effects of false heart-rate feedback. *Journal of Personality and Social Psychology,* 1966, **4,** 400–408.

Valins, S., & Ray, A. Effects of cognitive desensitization on avoidance behavior. *Journal of Personality and Social Psychology,* 1967, **7,** 345–350.

Varenhorst, B. B. Helping a client speak up in class. In Krumboltz, J. E., & Thoresen, C. E. (Eds.), *Behavioral Counseling.* New York: Holt, 1969.

Velten, E. A laboratory task for induction of mood states. *Behaviour Research and Therapy,* 1968, **6,** 473–482.

Voegtlin, W. L. The treatment of alcoholism by establishing a conditioned reflex. *American Journal of Medical Science,* 1940, **199,** 802–810.

Voegtlin, W. L., Lemere, F., Broz, W. R., & O'Hallaren, P. Conditioned reflex therapy of chronic alcoholism: IV. A preliminary report on the value of reinforcement. *Quarterly Journal of Studies on Alcoholism,* 1941, **2,** 505–511.

Voegtlin, W. L., Lemere, F., Broz, W. R., & O'Hallaren, P. Conditioned reflex therapy of alcoholic addiction: VI. Follow-up report of 1042 cases. *American Journal of Medical Science,* 1942, **203,** 525–528.

Vogler, R. E., Lunde, S. E., Johnson, G. R., & Martin, P. L. Electrical aversion conditioning with chronic alcoholics. *Journal of Consulting and Clinical Psychology,* 1970, **34,** 302–307.

Vogler, R. E., Lunde, S. E., & Martin, P. L. Electrical aversion conditioning with chronic alcoholics: Follow-up and suggestions for research. *Journal of Consulting and Clinical Psychology,* 1971, **36,** 450.

Wagner, M. K. & Bragg, R. A. Comparing behavior modification approaches to habit decrement—smoking. *Journal of Consulting and Clinical Psychology*, 1970, **34,** 258–263.

Wahler, R. G. Setting generality: Some specific and general effects of child behavior therapy. *Journal of Applied Behavior Analysis*, 1969, **2,** 239–246.

Wahler, R. G., & Erickson, M. Child behavior therapy: A community program in appalachia. *Behaviour Research and Therapy*, 1969, **7,** 71–78.

Wahler, R. G., & Pollio, H. R. Behavior and insight: A case study in behavior therapy. *Journal of Experimental Research in Personality*, 1968, **3,** 45–56.

Wahler, R. G., Winkel, G. H., Peterson, R. F., & Morrison, D. C. Mothers as behavior therapists for their own children. *Behaviour Research and Therapy*, 1965, **3,** 113–124.

Wakeham, G. Query on "A revision of the fundamental law of habit formation." *Science,* 1928, **68,** 135–136.

Wakeham, G. A quantitative experiment on Dr. K. Dunlap's "Revision of the fundamental law of habit formation." *Journal of Comparative Psychology*, 1930, **10,** 235–236.

Walker, H. M. & Buckley, N. K. The use of positive reinforcement in conditioning attending behavior. *Journal of Applied Behavior Analysis*, 1968, **1,** 245–250.

Walton, D. The application of learning theory to the treatment of a case of neurodermatitis. In H. J. Eysenck (Ed.), *Behaviour Therapy and the Neuroses.* Oxford: Pergamon, 1960.

Walton, D. Experimental psychology and the treatment of a tiquer. *Journal of Child Psychology and Psychiatry*, 1961, **2,** 148–155.

Walton, D. Massed practice and simultaneous reduction in drive level: Further evidence of the efficacy of this approach to the treatment of tics. In H. J. Eysenck (Ed.), *Experiments in Behaviour Therapy.* Oxford: Pergamon, 1964.

Walton, D., & Mather, M. D. The application of learning principles to the treatment of obsessive-compulsive states in the acute and chronic phases of illness. *Behaviour Research and Therapy*, 1963, **1,** 163–174. (a)

Walton, D., & Mather, M. D. The relevance of generalization techniques to the treatment of stammering and phobic symptoms. *Behaviour Research and Therapy*, 1963, **1,** 121–125. (b)

Walton, D., & Mather, M. D. The application of learning principles to the treatment of obsessive-compulsive states in the acute and chronic phases of illness. In H. J. Eysenck, (Ed.), *Experiments in behavior therapy.* Oxford: Pergamon, 1964.

Ward, Michael H., & Baker, Bruce L. Reinforcement Therapy in the Classroom. *Journal of Applied Behavior Analysis*, 1968, **1,** 323–328.

Ware, R. & Terrell, G. Effects of delayed reinforcement on associative and incentive factors. *Child Development*, 1961, **32,** 789–793.

Watson, D. L., & Tharp, R. G. *Self-directed behavior: Self-modification for personal adjustment.* Montery, California: Brooks Cole, 1972.

Watson, J. B. The place of the conditioned reflex in psychology. *Psychological Review,* 1916, **23,** 89–116.

Watson, J. B., & Rayner, R. Conditioned emotional reactions. *Journal of Experimental Psychology,* 1920, **3,** 1–14.

Weitzman, B. Behavior therapy or psychotherapy. *Psychological Review,* 1967, **74,** 300–317.

Wetzel, R. J., Baker, J., Roney, M. & Martin, M. Outpatient treatment of autistic behavior. *Behaviour Research and Therapy,* 1966, **4,** 169–177.

White, J. G. Neurotic habit formations and the experimental analysis of learning (conditioning). Paper read to the Ulster Neuropsychiatric Society, April 1962.

Wilde, G. J. S. Behaviour therapy for addicted cigarette smokers: A preliminary investigation. *Behaviour Research and Therapy,* 1964, **2,** 107–109.

Wilkins, W. Desensitization: Social and cognitive factors underlying the effectiveness of Wolpe's procedures. *Psychological Bulletin,* 1971, **76,** 311–317.

Williams, C. D. The elimination of tantrum behavior by extinction procedures. *Journal of Abnormal and Social Psychology,* 1959, **59,** 269.

Williams, C. D. Extinction and other principles of learning in the treatment and prevention of children's disorders. Paper read at the meetings of the American Psychological Association, St. Louis, September, 1962.

Willis, R. W. A study of the comparative effectiveness of systematic desensitization and implosive therapy. Unpublished doctoral dissertation, University of Tennessee, 1968.

Willis, R. W. & Edwards, J. A. A study of the comparative effectiveness of systematic desensitization and implosive therapy. *Behaviour Research and Therapy,* 1969, **7,** 387–395.

Wilson, F. S. & Walters, R. H. Modification of speech output of near-mute schizophrenics through social-learning procedures. *Behaviour Research and Therapy,* 1966, **4,** 59–67.

Winkler, R. C. Management of chronic psychiatric patients by a token reinforcement system. *Journal of Applied Behavior Analysis,* 1970, **3,** 47–55.

Wolf, M. M., Giles, D. K., & Hall, V. R. Experiments with token reinforcement in a remedial classroom. *Behaviour Research and Therapy,* 1968, **6,** 51–64.

Wolf, M. M., Hanley, E. L., King, L. A., Lachowicz, J., & Giles, D. K. The timer-game: A variable interval contingency for the management of out-of-seat behavior. *Exceptional Children,* 1970, **37,** 113–117.

Wolf, M. M. & Risley, T. R. Analysis and modification of deviant child behavior. Paper read at the American Psychological Association meeting. Washington, D.C. September, 1967.

Wolf, M. M., Risley, T., & Mees, H. L. Application of operant conditioning procedures to the behavior problems of an autistic child. *Behaviour Research and Therapy*, 1964, **1,** 305–312.

Wolf, S., & Wolff, H. G. Evidence on the genesis of peptic ulcer in man. *Journal of the American Medical Association*, 1942, **120,** 670–675.

Wolf, S., & Wolff, H. G. *Human gastric function.* London and New York: Oxford Univ. Press, 1947.

Wollersheim, J. P. Effectiveness of group therapy based upon learning principles in the treatment of overweight women. *Journal of Abnormal Psychology*, 1970, **76,** 462–474.

Wolpe, J. Objective psychotherapy of the neuroses. *Southern African Medical Journal*, 1952, **26,** 825–829.

Wolpe, J. Reciprocal inhibition as the main basis of psychotherapeutic effects. *Archives of Neurology and Psychiatry*, 1954, **72,** 205–226.

Wolpe, J. *Psychotherapy by reciprocal inhibition.* Stanford, California: Stanford Univ. Press, 1958.

Wolpe, J. The systematic desensitization treatment of neuroses. *Journal of Nervous and Mental Disease*, 1961, **132,** 189–203.

Wolpe, J. *The practice of behavior therapy.* Oxford: Pergamon, 1969.

Wolpe, J. Dealing with resistance to thought-stopping: A transcript. *Journal of Behavior Therapy and Experimental Psychiatry*, 1971, **2,** 121–125.

Wolpe, J. & Lang, P. J. A fear survey schedule for use in behavior therapy. *Behaviour Research and Therapy*, 1964, **2,** 27–30.

Wolpe, J., & Lazarus, A. A. *Behavior therapy techniques: A guide to the treatment of neuroses.* Oxford: Pergamon, 1966.

Wolpin, M., & Pearsall, L. Rapid deconditioning of a fear of snakes. *Behaviour Research and Therapy*, 1965, **3,** 107.

Wolpin, M. & Raines, J. Visual imagery, expected roles and extinction as possible factors in reducing fear and avoidance behavior. *Behaviour Research and Therapy*, 1966, **4,** 25–37.

Woodworth, R. S. & Schlosberg, H. *Experimental psychology.* New York: Holt, 1954.

Wright, H. F. Observational Child Study. In P. H. Mussen (Ed.), *Handbook of research methods in child development.* New York: Wiley, 1960.

Wynne, L. C., & Solomon, R. L. Traumatic avoidance learning: Acquisition and extinction in dogs deprived of normal peripheral autonomic function. *Genetic Psychology Monographs*, 1955, **52,** 241–284.

Yamagami, T. The treatment of an obsession by thought stopping. *Journal of Behavior Therapy and Experimental Psychiatry,* 1971, **2,** 133–135.

Yates, A. J. Symptoms and symptom substitution. *Psychological Review,* 1958, **65,** 371–374.

Yates, A. J. *Behavior therapy.* New York: Wiley, 1970.

Young, E. R., Rimm, D. C., & Kennedy, T. D. An experimental investigation of modeling and verbal reinforcement in the modification of assertive behavior. *Behaviour Research and Therapy,* 1973, **11,** 317–319.

Yuille, J. C., & Paivio, A. Imagery and verbal mediation instructions in paired-associate learning. *Journal of Experimental Psychology,* 1968, **78,** 436–441.

Zimmerman, E. H., Zimmerman, J., & Russell, C. D. Differential effects of token reinforcement in instruction-following behavior in retarded students instructed as a group. *Journal of Applied Behavior Analysis,* 1969, **2,** 101–112.

Zytowski, D. G. The study of therapy outcomes via experimental analogues: A review. *Journal of Consulting Psychology,* 1966, **13,** 235–240.

Author Index

Numbers in italics refer to the pages on which the complete references are listed.

Subject Index